W9-AGE-742

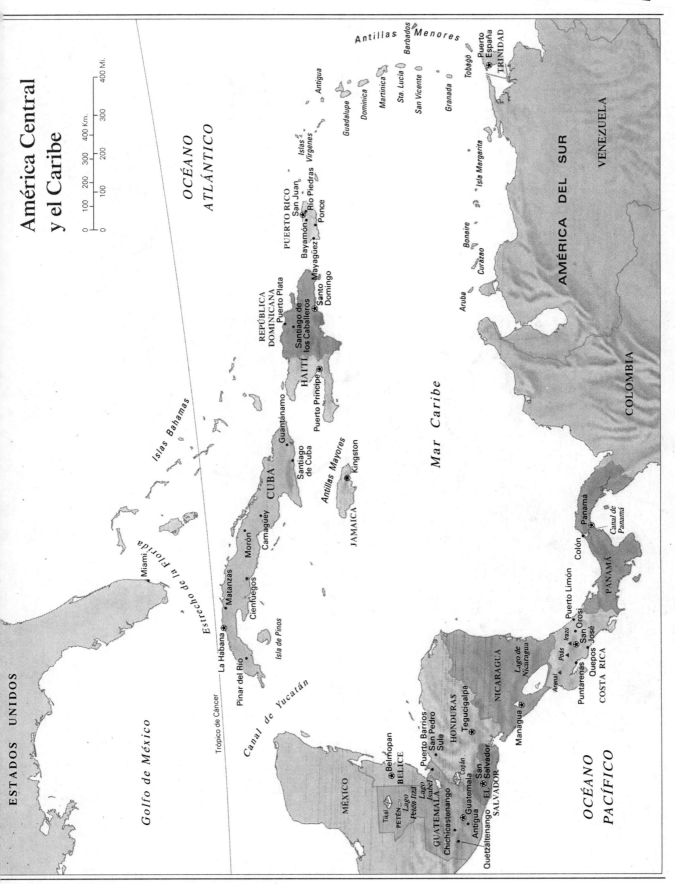

América Central y el Caribe

400 Mi.

0   100   200   300   400 Km.
0   100   200   300   400 Mi.

ESTADOS UNIDOS

OCÉANO ATLÁNTICO

Golfo de México

Miami

Estrecho de la Florida

Islas Bahamas

Trópico de Cáncer

Canal de Yucatán

CUBA

La Habana ✪
Pinar del Río
Matanzas
Cienfuegos
Isla de Pinos
Morón
Camagüey
Santiago de Cuba
Guantánamo

Antillas Mayores

JAMAICA
Kingston ✪

Mar Caribe

HAITÍ
Puerto Príncipe ✪

REPÚBLICA DOMINICANA
Puerto Plata
Santiago de los Caballeros
Santo Domingo ✪

PUERTO RICO
San Juan
Bayamón
Mayagüez
Río Piedras
Ponce

Islas Vírgenes

Guadalupe
Dominica
Martinica
Sta. Lucía
San Vicente
Barbados
Granada

Antillas Menores

Antigua

Tobago
Puerto España ✪
TRINIDAD

VENEZUELA

AMÉRICA DEL SUR

Isla Margarita
Bonaire
Curazao
Aruba

COLOMBIA

MÉXICO

BELICE
Belmopán ✪

Tikal
PETÉN
Lago Petén Itzá
Lago Isabel
Copán
Puerto Barrios
San Pedro Sula

GUATEMALA
Guatemala ✪
Antigua
Quetzaltenango
Chichicastenango

EL SALVADOR
San Salvador ✪

HONDURAS
Tegucigalpa ✪

NICARAGUA
Managua ✪
Lago de Nicaragua

Arenal
Poás
Puntarenas
COSTA RICA
Quepos
San José ✪
Irazú
San Orosi
Puerto Limón

Colón
Panamá ✪
PANAMÁ
Canal de Panamá

OCÉANO PACÍFICO

CAMINOS

with Student Activities Manual

THIRD EDITION

Joy Renjilian-Burgy
Wellesley College

Ana Beatriz Chiquito
Massachusetts Institute of Technology
University of Bergen, Norway

Susan M. Mraz
University of Massachusetts, Boston

Houghton Mifflin Company
Boston   New York

CAMINOS, THIRD EDITION
By Joy Renjilian-Burgy, Ana Beatriz Chiquito, and Susan M. Mraz
Copyright © 2008 Houghton Mifflin Company. All rights reserved.

Publisher: Rolando Hernández
Senior Sponsoring Editor: Glenn A. Wilson
Executive Marketing Director: Eileen Bernadette Moran
Development Manager: Judith Bach
Development Editor: Kim Beuttler
Senior Project Editors: Amy Johnson and Carol Newman
Art and Design Manager: Jill Haber
Senior Photo Editor: Jennifer Meyer Dare
Composition Buyer: Chuck Dutton
New Title Project Manager: James Lonergan
Marketing Assistant: Lorreen Ruth Pelletier
Editorial Assistants: Erin Beasley/Emily Meyer/Paola Moll

Text credits: Page 487

STUDENT ACTIVITIES MANUAL, THIRD EDITION
By Joy Renjilian-Burgy, Ana Beatriz Chiquito, Susan M. Mraz, Mary-Anne Vetterling
Copyright © 2008 Houghton Mifflin Company. All rights reserved.

Publisher: Rolando Hernández
Senior Sponsoring Editor: Glenn A. Wilson
Executive Marketing Director: Eileen Bernadette Moran
Development Editor: Kim Beuttler
Project Editor: Harriet C. Dishman/Michael E. Packard
New Title Project Manager: Susan Brooks-Peltier
Editorial Assistant: Erin Beasley
Marketing Assistant: Lorreen Ruth Pelletier

Custom Publishing Editor: Dan Luciano
Custom Publishing Production Manager: Christina Battista
Project Coordinator: Sara Abbott

Cover Designer: Allison Murphy
Cover Image: © Carlos Sotelo/stock.xchng

This book contains select works from existing Houghton Mifflin Company resources and was produced by Houghton Mifflin Custom Publishing for collegiate use. As such, those adopting and/or contributing to this work are responsible for editorial content, accuracy, continuity and completeness.

Compilation copyright © 2008 by Houghton Mifflin Company. All rights reserved.

No part of this work may be reproduced or transmitted in any form or by any means, electronic or mechanical, including photocopying and recording, or by any information storage or retrieval system without the prior written permission of Houghton Mifflin Company unless such copying is expressly permitted by federal copyright law. Address inquiries to College Permissions, Houghton Mifflin Company, 222 Berkeley Street, Boston, MA 02116-3764.

Printed in the United States of America.

ISBN-13: 978-0-618-96411-6
ISBN-10: 0-618-96411-8
1021922

4 5 6 7 8 9 – CCI– 09

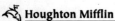 **Houghton Mifflin**
                              Custom Publishing

222 Berkeley Street • Boston, MA 02116
Address all correspondence and order information to the above address.

Welcome to **Caminos,** and congratulations for choosing to learn Spanish. Perhaps you want to travel to learn more about other cultures; or possibly you will use Spanish in your chosen profession; or maybe you just need to fulfill a language requirement at your institution. Whatever your reason for studying Spanish, one thing is certain: you will in the future most likely find yourself in a real-life situation where your knowledge of Spanish will help you to better communicate at work, at home, or in your community.

Spanish is spoken by a diverse population of almost 500 million people world-wide and is second only to Mandarin Chinese. In the United States alone, 12.5% of the population is Spanish-speaking (Bureau of the Census 2000), making Hispanics the largest minority, numbering over 39 million. It also makes the United States the third largest Spanish-speaking country in the world. Wherever you live, as you begin to learn Spanish, look for opportunities to benefit from the Spanish being spoken around you—on television, in newspapers, at the movies, or in your community.

By studying with **Caminos** not only will you learn how to speak Spanish, but you also will have the opportunity to explore the numerous cultures that make up the ethnic tapestry of the twenty-one Spanish-speaking countries of the world. Our hope is that by discovering their diversity and vitality you will make learning Spanish a passionate, life-long pursuit.

—Joy Renjilian-Burgy
Ana Beatriz Chiquito
Susan M. Mraz

5
Vacaciones en la playa

VOCABULARIO Y LENGUA

► Checking into a hotel
► Using direct object pronouns
► Talking about the beach and leisure activities
► Narrating events in the past: Preterite of verbs with spelling changes: *ir, ser, dar*

► Discussing vacations
► Using double object pronouns
► Narrating events in the past: Preterite of stem-changing *-ir* verbs
► Narrating events in the past: Preterite of irregular verbs

CAMINOS DEL JAGUAR

► Voleibol y amor en la playa
► Dos espías

LECTURA

► Vamos al Caribe hispano: Cuba, Puerto Rico y la República Dominicana

NOTAS CULTURALES

► El turismo en el Caribe hispano
► Los parques nacionales

ESTRATEGIAS

► **Reading:** How to use the dictionary
► **Writing:** Using a dictionary

168 ciento sesenta y ocho

Caminos sets the stage for learning by outlining each color-coded section of the unit so that the architecture of the unit is apparent.

Luis Germán Cajiga, *Flamboyán entre palmeras*

Preguntas del tema

► ¿Adónde te gusta ir de vacaciones?
► ¿Qué actividades te gusta hacer?
► ¿Con quién/es vas de vacaciones?
► ¿Cuál es tu hotel favorito?

Primer paso • ciento sesenta y nueve 169

Questions related to the theme of the unit prepare you for the material to come.

Each unit of *Caminos* contains two *pasos*. The *Primer paso's Vocabulario y lengua* section starts with a visual and related text to contextualize the presentation. Vocabulary sections present cognates and thematic vocabulary and expressions visually.

Más palabras y expresiones

Cognados
el (mini) bar
confirmar
la recepción

el/la recepcionista
la reservación
reservar

Sustantivos
el alojamiento
el botones
el buzón
el cajero automático
el cambio de dinero / moneda
el cheque de viajero
el/la conserje
el (dinero en) efectivo
el estacionamiento / aparcamiento
el equipaje
la habitación
la maleta
el salón (la sala) de conferencias
la tarifa
la tarjeta de crédito / débito

lodging, accommodations
bellhop
mailbox
automated teller machine (ATM)
money exchange
traveler's check
concierge
cash
parking lot
luggage
room
suitcase
conference room
rate, fare, tariff
credit / debit card

Verbos

Primer paso • ciento setenta y uno

PRIMER PASO

Vocabulario y lengua

CHECKING INTO A HOTEL

HOTEL NACIONAL, HABANA, CUBA

Inaugurado el 30 de diciembre de 1930, El Nacional es uno de los hoteles más clásicos de la Habana. Su lujo¹, elegancia, distinción y servicios de primera clase², se mantienen intactos después de seis décadas en la industria hotelera³ cubana. Rodeado⁴ por hermosos jardines, el hotel ocupa un lugar privilegiado cerca del Malecón habanero, ofreciendo una de las vistas⁵ más bellas de la ciudad. Sus huéspedes⁶ pueden disfrutar de habitaciones⁷ espléndidas y cómodas.

luxury
first class
hotel industry / surrounded

views
guests
rooms

FACILIDADES DE LAS HABITACIONES
TV satélite
Minibar
Radio despertador⁸
Teléfono

Aire acondicionado
Baño privado
Radio
Refrigerador

alarm clock

Online Study Center
For additional practice with this unit's vocabulary and grammar, visit the *Caminos* website at http://college.hmco.com/languages/spanish/renjilian/caminos/3e/student_home.html. You can also review audio flashcards, quiz yourself, and explore related Spanish-language sites.

FACILIDADES DEL HOTEL
Bar
Centro de negocios
Elevador / Ascensor
Estacionamiento
Restaurante
Sala de ejercicios
Servicios médicos

Buró de turismo
Caja de seguridad
Jardín
Piscina
Sala de conferencias
Servicio de habitación
Tenis

170 ciento setenta • Unidad 5

The vocabulary presentation is immediately reinforced with listening and comprehension activities, role-plays, and other pair and group activities.

Actividades

1 **Hotel Real de Minas.** Listen to the description of a hotel in Guanajuato, México, then determine whether the statements are **verdadero (V)** or **falso (F)**. Correct the false statements.

1. _____ Guanajuato es una ciudad bonita.
2. _____ El Hotel Real de Minas es un hotel económico.
3. _____ Hay 12 restaurantes en el hotel.
4. _____ Hay 175 habitaciones en el hotel.
5. _____ Veinte suites tienen aire acondicionado.
6. _____ No hay estacionamiento.
7. _____ Hay un bar cerca de la alberca.
8. _____ Su número de teléfono es el 63-215-80.

2 **¿Qué es?** Write the correct word that matches each definition.

1. Cuando viajas, pones mucha ropa (*clothing*) allí.
2. Es una forma de pagar el hotel si no tienes dinero en efectivo.
3. Se usa para abrir una puerta.
4. Allí descansas en el hotel.
5. Allí los turistas reciben la llave de la habitación.
6. Es un aparato para ir al piso doce.
7. Es la persona que ayuda a los huéspedes a encontrar sitios turísticos.
8. Es un lugar donde guardar el coche.

3 **Símbolos internacionales.** Match the international hotel symbols on the right with their meanings on the left.

_____ piscina (alberca)
_____ dos camas sencillas
_____ tarjetas de crédito
_____ cama sencilla
_____ cambio de moneda
_____ restaurante
_____ salón de conferencias
_____ teléfono
_____ ascensor
_____ bar
_____ estacionamiento
_____ cama doble
_____ televisión
_____ perros no
_____ minibar

4 **¿Qué necesitas?** State what hotel amenities you will need in the following situations. Follow the model.

▶ MODELO: Tienes hambre.
Necesito un restaurante.

1. No tienes dinero.
2. Debes llamar a tu madre.
3. Tus maletas son muy grandes.
4. Tu habitación está en el piso veinticuatro.
5. Tienes sed.
6. Quieres hacer ejercicio.
7. Tienes hambre a medianoche y el restaurante está cerrado (*closed*).
8. Llegas al hotel en coche.

173 ciento setenta y dos ▶ Unidad 5

---

5 **En el hotel.** Complete the following conversation between a guest and the receptionist at a hotel using the vocabulary from the word bank below.

con vista al mar	¿En qué le puedo servir?	tarjeta de crédito
reservar	¡Que disfruten de su estadía!	habitación
sencilla	¿A nombre de quién?	

—Buenas tardes.
—Buenas tardes. Quisiéramos _____ una habitación para esta noche.
—De los Señores Guzmán.
—¿Por cuántas noches?
—Por dos, por favor.
—¿Qué tipo de _____ prefiere Ud.?
—Nos gustaría una habitación _____
—¿Con cama _____ o doble?
—Con una cama doble. ¿Cuánto cuesta?
—La habitación cuesta $132 por noche.
—Muy bien. ¿Se puede pagar con _____?
—Claro que sí.

6 **Entre nosotros.** Role-play the following situation with a partner.

Turista:	Recepcionista:
You are traveling through Spain by bicycle. After a difficult day, you arrive at your hotel very tired. When you arrive, the receptionist tells you that he or she doesn't have your reservation. You have a copy of your confirmation. Do whatever you can to get a room for the night.	A young bicyclist arrives at your hotel, but you can't find his or her reservation in the computer. There's a medical conference (**congreso**) in the hotel and there are no rooms left. Do your best to solve this dilemma.

USING DIRECT OBJECT PRONOUNS

Preparando el viaje

Amanda No encuentro mi bolsa azul. **La** necesito para empacar mis cosas.
Arturo Yo **la** tengo. Aquí está la bolsa. También tengo los boletos de avión.
Amanda **Los** tienes también. ¡Qué bien! Mil gracias.

Primer paso ◆ ciento setenta y tres 173

Charts highlight key material such as verb or pronoun forms, while examples illustrate the explanations.

Amanda ¿Y el dinero?
Arturo También **lo** tengo aquí. Supongo que llamaste a la embajada norteamericana y sacaste las visas, ¿verdad?
Amanda ¿Las visas? Claro, ayer hablé con la embajada para pedir**las.**
Arturo Es importante tener**las.**
Amanda Tienes razón. Sin visas no podemos viajar.

A direct object is the person or thing that directly receives the action of the verb. In the first sentence on page 173, **mi bolsa azul** is a direct object. Once the object is stated, it is often replaced by a direct object pronoun to avoid redundancy: *La necesito para empacar mis cosas.*

In the dialog above, can you identify the direct object nouns that correspond to the direct object pronouns in boldface? Note that third person direct object pronouns agree in number and gender with the nouns that they replace.

Direct object pronouns			
me	*me*	**nos**	*us*
te	*you*	**os**	*you*
lo, la	*him, her, you, it*	**los, las**	*them, you*

The direct object **lo** is often used to express a previously-mentioned idea as in, *Sí lo sé.* (Yes, I know it.)

Direct object pronouns precede the conjugated verb.

—¿Y **los** boletos? —And the tickets?
—**Los** recogemos en Madrid. —We'll pick them up in Madrid.

When the direct object pronoun is used with a conjugated verb and an infinitive (**tengo que comprar, voy a hacer, acabo de escribir,** etc.) the pronoun can go either before the conjugated verb or attached to the end of the infinitive.

Quiero pedir **una habitación** *I want to ask for a larger room.*
más grande.
La quiero pedir. *I want to ask for it.*
Quiero pedir**la.**

Direct object pronouns are attached to the end of the infinitive when the infinitive is used with expressions such as **es importante / bueno / necesario,** etc., or in prepositional expressions such as **para recibirlas, de visitarla.**

—Me gusta tener **un buen mapa.** —I like to have a good map.
—Sí, es bueno tener**lo.** —Yes, it's good to have it.

When the direct object pronoun is used with progressive forms (**estar** + present participle), the pronoun can go either before the conjugated form of **estar** or attached to the end of the participle. When attached to the participle, you must add a written accent.

—¿Estás escribiendo **la tarjeta postal?** —Are you writing the postcard?
—Sí, **la** estoy escribiendo. —Yes, I'm writing it.
—Sí, estoy escribiéndo**la.**

Actividades

1 **Sin repeticiones.** Write sentences replacing the direct object nouns with direct object pronouns. Follow the model.

▶ MODELO: Miranda compra los pasajes. *Miranda buys the tickets.*
Miranda los compra. *Miranda buys them.*

174 ciento setenta y cuatro ▶ Unidad 5

Grammar explanations have been revised, and topics have been resequenced throughout the program to decrease the breadth of topics and increase the depth of coverage. Grammar points are introduced by language modeling texts, often in the form of a dialogue. They are then followed by grammar explanations and activities that progress from mechanical to open-ended.

Each *paso* presents an installment of the all-new **Caminos del jaguar** graphic novel, which parallels the award-winning **Caminos del jaguar** video. The graphic novel tells the story in easy-to-understand Spanish that you can read on your own or as an advance organizer for the video. The mystery-adventure story also provides a fascinating view into Mayan culture, supports further learning, and reinforces topics presented in the textbook.

As with the *Primer paso*'s *Vocabulario y lengua* section, the *Segundo paso*'s *Vocabulario y lengua* starts with a drawing and related text to contextualize the presentation.

The contextualized presentation of the vocabulary emphasizes its use in real life and reinforces learning.

To support greater understanding of the material, comprehension questions and a role-play and writing activity accompany each installment.

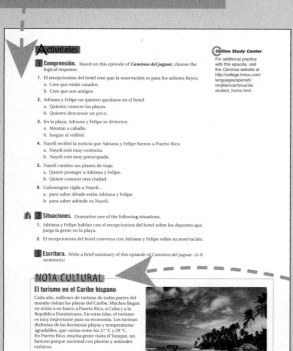

Notas culturales on the regions featured in **Caminos del jaguar** provide you with a context in which to learn about Hispanic cultures and make cross-cultural comparisons. These cultural notes include information on the traditions, pastimes, and geography throughout the Spanish-speaking world.

The *Lectura* section offers authentic works and author-generated passages thematically related to the active vocabulary and culture notes of the unit.

Reading strategies provide you with various techniques for approaching diverse texts. A variety of pre- and post-reading exercises, including comprehension checks, personalized questions, and expansion activities, supporting skill development.

Lectura

Online Study Center
For further reading practice online, visit the *Caminos* website at http://college.hmco.com/languages/spanish/renjilian/caminos/3e/student_home.html.

Reading Strategy

How to use the dictionary

When reading a text in Spanish, go through it several times, checking for words you already know as well as for cognates, which you have studied in earlier chapters. You should also try to guess the meaning of words you do not know through the context of the sentence and the text. Once you have applied this strategy, use the dictionary to confirm your guesses. The dictionary may give you several different meanings for a word. It is important to determine the grammatical form of the word because that can affect its meaning. Note the following facts about Spanish dictionaries.

► Verbs (**verbos**) appear in the infinitive form. If you are looking up a conjugated form of a verb, you will have to determine its infinitive before you start your search.
► Masculine and feminine forms of nouns (**sustantivos**) are listed and marked *m.* or *f.* The meaning of a noun may change depending on its form.
► Only the masculine singular form of an adjective (**adjetivo**) is usually listed and marked *adj.*
► Idiomatic expressions (**expresiones idiomáticas**) are listed by their most important word. Sometimes you need several attempts to determine the main word.
► The letter **ñ** is listed as a separate letter after **n**. In older dictionaries, the letter combinations **ll** (as in **llover**) and and **ch** are listed as separate letters, after **l** and **c** respectively.

Vamos al Caribe hispano: Cuba, Puerto Rico y la República Dominicana

Las tres islas caribeñas de habla española, Cuba, Puerto Rico y la República Dominicana, tienen una herencia¹ tricultural común: la indígena² de cada región, la española y la africana. Esta mezcla étnica les da gran riqueza a sus tradiciones, a su música, a su literatura y a su vida diaria, pero cada isla tiene también su identidad propia. Las islas tienen bellas playas y hermosa arquitectura colonial. Estas islas del Caribe comparten aspectos de su cultura, herencia y tradiciones con otras regiones hispanas como las costas caribeñas de Costa Rica, Panamá, Colombia y Venezuela.

¹heritage; ²indigenous; ³race

La Playa de Varadero, La Habana, Cuba

Pareja dominicana en la playa

Cuba

Cuba es la más grande de las tres islas caribeñas. Fue el segundo lugar⁴ al que llegó Cristóbal Colón⁵. Los españoles llevaron esclavos africanos para trabajar en las plantaciones de azúcar⁶. Al azúcar lo llamaban "el oro blanco" por su valor económico en esa época. Con el tiempo, se mezclaron los africanos con los españoles para producir la rica mezcla racial que hoy existe en la isla. En 1959 Fidel Castro lideró una revolución en Cuba y por más de treinta años, hasta 1990, Cuba estuvo bajo el socialismo de la Unión Soviética. Actualmente⁷ la isla está en transición económica. Tiene más de once millones de habitantes.

Puerto Rico

Puerto Rico es la más pequeña de las tres islas hispanas y es un Estado Libre Asociado⁸ de los Estados Unidos. Los puertorriqueños pueden viajar libremente entre la isla y los EE. UU.⁹ La población indígena de la isla de Puerto Rico, los taínos o arauacos, tenía¹⁰ una sociedad bastante avanzada en esta isla de 175 kilómetros de largo¹¹ y 56 kilómetros de ancho¹². La población hoy en día¹³ es de casi cuatro millones de habitantes.

La República Dominicana

La República Dominicana comparte¹⁴ la misma isla que la República de Haití. Este país fue el primer centro administrativo español en América y sus

Un arrecife de coral en el Mar Caribe

habitantes indígenas, los taínos, la llamaban "Quisqueya". La población de la isla tiene también herencia europea y africana debido a¹⁵ los esclavos que llevaron a trabajar allí. Actualmente es un gran centro turístico en la región caribeña, aunque también sufre de mucha pobreza económica y desigualdad social. Tiene casi¹⁶ ocho millones de habitantes.

⁴place; ⁵Christopher Columbus; ⁶sugar; ⁷Today; ⁸free associated state; ⁹U.S.; ¹⁰had; ¹¹in length; ¹²in width; ¹³today; ¹⁴shares; ¹⁵because of; ¹⁶almost

---

Actividades

1 ¿Verdadero o falso? Write **V** if the following ideas are **verdaderas** or **F** if they are **falsas.** Correct the false sentences.

1. _____ El azúcar fue importante para la economía de Cuba.
2. _____ Cuba es la más pequeña de las islas de habla española.
3. _____ Los taínos llamaban *(called)* "Quisqueya" a Puerto Rico.
4. _____ En las islas caribeñas de habla española hay una mezcla étnica de influencia indígena, española y africana.
5. _____ Puerto Rico es un Estado Libre Asociado de los Estados Unidos.
6. _____ Haití y Cuba comparten la misma isla.
7. _____ Puerto Rico tiene ocho millones de habitantes.

2 Cómo buscar palabras en el diccionario. Keep a list of the words that you needed to look up in the dictionary for this reading and compare them with that of a friend. Are there any that you could have guessed without looking them up? Which ones?

3 Compara y contrasta. Compare and contrast the different characteristics of Cuba, the Dominican Republic, and Puerto Rico. Which island do you find the most interesting? Why? Work with a partner.

	Cuba	Puerto Rico	La República Dominicana
Población			
Etnicidad			
Sistema político			
Productos económicos			
Otros aspectos			

4 Conversaciones cortas. Work with a partner to answer the following questions.

1. ¿Qué islas hay en tu región? ¿Cómo son? ¿Tienen playas?
2. ¿A qué isla del mundo quieres viajar? ¿Dónde está? ¿Cómo es?
3. ¿Qué influencia étnica hay en tu región o estado?
4. ¿A qué grupo étnico pertenecen los padres y los abuelos de tu compañero/a de cuarto?
5. ¿Qué idiomas hablan en tu país actualmente? ¿Y en tu familia?

Escritura

Writing Strategy

Using a dictionary

Review the reading strategy prior to reading this strategy. To use a dictionary effectively, be sure to keep the following in mind.

There are many translations for some words. Look for the definition that best suits your needs. Once you have selected a word in the English-Spanish section, cross check its meaning in the Spanish-English section of the dictionary to assure accuracy, and be sure to read any grammar notes that will tell you about irregular forms, different translations, and so on. Always review the guide to using a particular dictionary to understand important symbols and abbreviations. Below are some common abbreviations and sample dictionary entries.

Workshop

f.	femenino	*adv.*	adverbio	*adj.*	adjetivo	
m.	masculino	*s.*	sustantivo (*noun*)			

fan[1] (fan) **I.** s. (*paper*) abanico; (*electric*) ventilador *m*; AGR. aventadora **II.** tr. **fanned, fan-ning** (*to cool*) abanicar; FIG. (*to stir up*) avivar, excitar; AGR. aventar —intr. • **to f. out** abrirse en abanico

fan[2] (fan) s. FAM. (*enthusiast*) aficionado, hincha *m*.

support (se-port´) **I.** tr. (*weight*) aguantar, sostener, corroborar; (*a spouse, child*) mantener; (*a cause, theory*) sostener, respaldar; (*with money*) ayudar • **to s. oneself** (*to earn one's living*) ganarse la vida; (*to learn*) apoyarse **II.** s. (*act*) apoyo; (*maintenance*) mantenimiento; ARQ., TEC. soporte *m*.

Strategy in Action

For additional practice using a dictionary, complete the exercises below and in the *Escritura I* section of your Student Activities Manual for *Unidad 5*.

1 Usando el diccionario. Refer to the dictionary entries above to translate the italicized words. Be sure to use the appropriate form of the word or phrase. Work in groups.

1. Can I count on your *support*?
2. I can't *support* myself on this salary.
3. My psychology instructor *supports* the Freudian school of thought.
4. The house has good *support* beams.
5. I'm a sports *fan*.
6. It's hot outside and you need to *fan* yourself to keep cool.
7. Turn on the *fan*! It's hot in here.

2 Querido/a amigo/a. You are on vacation. Write a postcard to your best friend, telling about your trip. Describe the hotel, its amenities, what there is to do, and what you like and don't like about the hotel. Then narrate a sequence of events to tell your friend what you did on your first day there. Be sure to use the preterite tense to talk about the things you did.

3 Mi primer día del trabajo. Congratulations! You just landed your dream job. Your first day on the job, however, was not what you expected. By the end of the day you are very frustrated and decide to write an email to your best friend to tell him / her all about your bad day. Describe your day to your friend, and don't forget to include all the details. Remember to use the preterite.

Online Study Center
For further writing practice, visit the *Caminos* website at http://college.hmco.com/languages/spanish/renjilian/caminos/3e/student_home.html.

Segundo paso • doscientos uno **201**

The new *Artes y letras* section introduces you to the music, art, and literature of the Spanish-speaking world. Appearing after every even-numbered unit, this section includes an overview of well-known personalities as well as short pieces on art and music specific to the featured region.

Caminos also takes a process approach to writing. Each writing section includes a writing strategy to ease you into the activities that follow and culminates in the writing of some type of prose.

The end-of-unit *Resumen de vocabulario* lists include thematically and functionally grouped active vocabulary presented in the unit for easy review and reference.

Resumen de vocabulario

PRIMER PASO

CHECKING INTO A HOTEL

Sustantivos

el alojamiento	lodging, accommodations
el ascensor/elevador	elevator
el botones	porter
el buzón	mailbox
el cajero automático	automated teller machine (ATM)
el cambio de dinero/moneda	money exchange
el cheque de viajero	traveler's check
el/la conserje	concierge
el despertador	alarm clock
el (dinero en) efectivo	cash
la elegancia	elegance
el equipaje	luggage
el estacionamiento	parking lot
la habitación	room
el/la huésped	guest
el lujo	luxury
la maleta	suitcase
el (mini) bar	(mini)bar
la primera/segunda clase	first / second class
la recepción	reception
el/la recepcionista	receptionist
la reservación	reservation
el salón (la sala) de conferencias	conference room
la tarifa	rate, fare, tariff
la tarjeta de crédito	credit card
la vista	view

Verbos

alojar(se)	to stay (in a hotel)
atender (ie)	to attend to, wait on
confirmar	to confirm
hacer una llamada (de larga distancia / por cobrar)	to make a (long distance / collect) phone call
registrar	to register
reservar	to reserve

Adjetivos

cómodo/a	comfortable
doble	double
lujoso/a (de lujo)	luxurious
sencillo/a	single (room or bed)

Otras expresiones

¿A nombre de quién?	In whose name?
¿En qué le(s) puedo servir?	How can I help you?
con desayuno	with breakfast
con media pensión	with two meals
con vista al mar	with an ocean view
¿Cuánto cuesta... ?	How much does . . . cost?
¿Dónde puedo cambiar el dinero?	Where can I exchange money?
Lo siento.	I'm sorry.
por supuesto	of course
¡Que disfrute/n de su estadía/estancia!	Enjoy your stay!

TALKING ABOUT THE BEACH

Sustantivos

el balón (beach) ball	
las gafas de sol	sunglasses
la novela	novel
el picnic	picnic
la playa	beach
el protector/bronceador solar	sunscreen
el/la radio	radio
la sandalia	sandal
el sombrero	hat
la sombrilla	parasol / beach umbrella
la toalla	towel
el traje de baño	bathing suit

Verbos

broncearse	to get a tan
bucear	to go skindiving, snorkeling
buscar conchas	to look for shells

202 doscientos dos • Unidad 5

ARTES Y LETRAS

EL CARIBE

Online Study Center
To learn more about the people featured in this section, visit the *Caminos* website at http://college.hmco.com/languages/spanish/renjilian/caminos/3e/student_home.html.

PERSONALIDADES

Hay muchas personalidades importantes en las artes de las islas del Mar Caribe. Las influencias en muchas de sus creaciones de arte, música y literatura son de origen africano, indígena y europeo. Entre los artistas cubanos están Wilfredo Lam, pintor surrealista y Yamilys Brito, que incluye imágenes con palabras en algunas de sus obras artísticas. Entre los artistas importantes de Puerto Rico hay dos que crean carteles de acontecimientos en la isla: José Alicea y Lyzette Rosado. En la República Dominicana dos artistas famosos son Enriquillo Rodríguez y Clara Ledesma.

Muchos caribeños recibieron un Grammy Latino en 2005. De Puerto Rico ganaron Marc Anthony por el Mejor Álbum de Salsa; Elvis Crespo por el Mejor Álbum de Merengue y Mejor Álbum de Rock Vocal; y Obie Bermúdez, por el Mejor Vocal Pop Masculino. También el dominicano Juan Luis Guerra ganó en dos categorías: el Mejor Álbum Cristiano en español y la Mejor Canción Tropical del año. Entre los cubanos, Bebo Valdés ganó por el Mejor Álbum de Jazz Latino; Israel "Cachao" López por el Mejor Álbum Tropical Tradicional y la cantante Lila Downs, que nació en Cuba, recibió el Grammy Latino por el Mejor Álbum Folklórico de 2005.

Hay muchos escritores caribeños de importancia en las épocas recientes. La puertorriqueña Esmeralda Santiago, la dominicana Julia Álvarez y la cubana Cristina García son tres novelistas que viven en Estados Unidos y escriben sobre la condición humana de los caribeños. Visita el sitio web de *Caminos* para leer más en español sobre estas personalidades y otros caribeños influyentes.

"Crecer no tiene que ver con ser famoso, crecer está dentro de ti. Y llevar la música de mi pueblo es lo que me ha hecho crecer". —Carlos Vives (Colombia)

Comprensión
Trabajando en parejas, háganse las preguntas.
1. ¿Qué influencias hay sobre el arte, la música y la literatura del Caribe? ¿Conoces alguna obra de los artistas mencionados?
2. ¿En qué categorías ganaron los cantantes los Grammy Latinos? ¿Cuál prefieres escuchar tú? ¿Por qué?

ARTE

AIMÉE GARCÍA
Aimée García es una artista cubana que nació en 1972 en la ciudad de Matanzas. Su arte apareció en muchas exhibiciones en Cuba, México, Corea del Sur y Estados Unidos. En el año 1999 hizo *La guía*, pintura que es una combinación de óleo en lienzo, con hilo y madera.

guide

La guía

oil on canvas
string / wood

Comprensión
Trabajando en parejas, estudien esta pintura y contesten las preguntas.
1. La artista está pintando una escena con árboles. ¿Qué colores usa para pintar la escena? En tu opinión, ¿qué hora del día es?

trees

2. Describe a la artista en la pintura. ¿De qué color es su vestido? ¿Cuántos años crees que tiene ella? ¿Cuántos años tiene la artista Aimée García?
3. ¿Qué función tiene la jirafa? ¿Hay otro animal posible?

giraffe

4. ¿De qué colores es la jirafa? En tu opinión, ¿qué efecto produce en la pintura? ¿cómico? ¿absurdo? ¿interesante? ¿...? ¿Por qué?
5. ¿Qué relación hay entre la fotografía de la artista y la artista en la pintura? ¿Son dos mujeres diferentes o es la misma persona?
6. ¿Te gusta o no te gusta esta pintura? ¿Por qué?

> Poems, quotes, and literary excerpts by writers of the region help further develop reading and critical thinking skills.

"...tengo el gusto de andar por mi país, dueño de cuanto hay en él".
—Nicolás Guillén (Cuba), "Tengo"

"Estatuas"
Las estatuas mueren también, si nadie las mira.

Comprensión
En parejas, contesten las preguntas.
1. ¿Es el poema sobre las personas, los lugares o las cosas?
2. En la opinión del poeta, ¿cuándo mueren las estatuas?
3. El poeta indica que las estatuas son como personas. ¿Qué opinas tú?
4. Describe una estatua famosa de tu región: ¿De qué color es? ¿Dónde está? ¿Es grande o pequeña? ¿De quién es quién? ¿Por qué es importante? ¿Por qué (no) te gusta?

"Apuntes" para el poema

Notes

Hice apuntes
para escribir un poema a la primavera,
y de tanto leerlo escribirlo.
sólo quedó el recuerdo de las flores,
el recuerdo de su cromía,
y mi asombro ante tanto verdor.

memory
amazement / greenness

Comprensión
Trabajando en parejas, contesten las preguntas.
1. Antes de crear el poema, ¿qué escribió el poeta?
2. ¿A qué estación del año le escribió el poema?
3. ¿Qué quedó de las flores que el poeta puso en el poema?
4. Al final del poema, ¿qué color asocia el poeta con la primavera?
5. ¿De qué color es tu flor favorita? ¿Tiene un aroma delicado o fuerte?
6. ¿Te gustan más las flores de la primavera o del verano? En tu región, ¿hay flores también en el otoño o en el invierno?

MÚSICA

OLGA TAÑÓN
La artista musical, Olga Tañón, es puertorriqueña. Ganó un Grammy Latino de la Mejor Interpretación Vocal Femenina de 2003 por su álbum, "Sobrevivir". Ella canta diversos estilos música como merengue y balada pop. Tañón incluye en su nuevo álbum, "A puro fuego", sus discos más celebrados de los diez años pasados de su carrera.

Survive

PureFire

Comprensión
Trabajen en parejas para contestar las preguntas.
1. ¿De dónde es Olga Tañón?
2. Según la lectura, ¿qué tipo de música canta? ¿Qué premio ganó?
3. ¿Cómo se llaman dos de sus álbumes musicales? ¿Qué emociones despiertan los títulos?
4. ¿A qué otro/a cantante hispánico/a conoces? ¿De dónde es? ¿Qué canta?

LITERATURA

NORBERTO JAMES RAWLINGS
El autor Norberto James Rawlings nació en la República Dominicana en 1945. Este poeta dominicano es también profesor de español. Se graduó de la Universidad de La Habana y, en 1992, recibió su doctorado en lengua y literatura hispánica de Boston University. Los poemas aquí son de su nuevo libro, *La urdimbre del silencio* (*The Weaving of Silence*), que se publicó en 2000 en La República Dominicana.

> Comprehension activities reinforce linguistic practice of the themes presented through the art, music, and literature.

Student Components

STUDENT TEXTBOOK

This textbook is your primary resource for learning Spanish. It contains cultural information, vocabulary and grammar presentations and practice, and activities to help you develop listening, speaking, reading, and writing skills in Spanish.

IN-TEXT AUDIO CD

Packaged with your textbook, the audio CD contains recordings that correlate to activities in the *Vocabulario y lengua* sections of the units. There are generally two listening activities in each unit, designed to develop your listening skills.

STUDENT ACTIVITIES MANUAL (SAM)

The Student Activities Manual contains workbook, lab, and video activities that provide important additional practice of topics in your text. The Workbook section, which parallels the organization of the units in your text, includes activities to reinforce the vocabulary and grammar that you learn in class as well as practice to help develop your reading and writing skills. The Lab section contains a variety of listening activities for each unit to build your ability to comprehend spoken Spanish. The Video section of the SAM provides pre- and post-viewing activities that correspond to each episode of the *Caminos del jaguar* video.

SAM AUDIO CD PROGRAM

The SAM Audio CDs contain the recorded material that coordinates with the lab activities in the Student Activities Manual.

CAMINOS DEL JAGUAR VIDEO

Available in DVD format as well as on the *Caminos* Online Study Center, this award-winning video features an exciting, action-packed mystery that incorporates myth, folklore, and local regional culture. Filmed on location in Mexico, Spain, Costa Rica, Puerto Rico, Ecuador, and the United States, the video's twenty-four segments are divided into two 7- to 12-minute segments per unit. The graphic novel episodes in the textbook parallel and summarize each video episode to prepare you for viewing, and video activities in the SAM help focus your viewing and check your understanding of the episodes.

e-SAM POWERED BY QUIA

This online version of the Student Activities Manual contains the same content as the print version, plus the material recorded on the SAM Audio CDs, in an interactive environment that provides immediate feedback for many activities so you can monitor your progress. It also includes links to the video and to verb charts and Spanish-English and English-Spanish vocabularies from the textbook.

e-SAM

The Blackboard/Web CT Premium Access Code Card allows access to the SAM on the Blackboard or Web CT platform. These platforms also include links to verb charts and Spanish-English and English-Spanish vocabularies from the textbook.

e-BOOK + e-SAM

A completely interactive experience, the e-Book provides the entire text online, integrated with links to a wide variety of resources that are accessible with the click of a mouse. Each resource expands on the content of the text and allows you to practice and reinforce what you have learned. Each link is located at the point of relevance in the text. A synchronous voice chat feature also allows you to collaborate with other students and your instructor on pair and group activities. In addition, audio pronunciations of each chapter's active vocabulary and grammar terms are included.

ONLINE STUDY CENTER

The *Caminos* web site includes a variety of activities and resources to help you practice vocabulary and grammar, review for quizzes and exams, and explore Spanish-language web sites. The **Improve Your Grade** section includes MP3 files of the in-text audio; the video transcript; flashcards; web search activities; interactive multimedia activities (drag-and-drop, matching, multiple choice, fill-in, games, and more) that practice unit vocabulary and grammar and reinforce understanding of the *Caminos del jaguar* video through video-based activities. **Ace the Test** offers ACE practice tests designed to check your progress with unit vocabulary and grammar, as well as video comprehension. **Resources** provides web links to cultural sites (attractions, cuisine, geography, etc.), maps, and academic resources. The Online Study Center is accessible at **http://college.hmco.com/languages/ spanish/renjilian/caminos/3e/student_home.html.**

SMARTHINKING ONLINE TUTORING

Access online tutorial support using chat technology, feedback tools, and virtual whiteboards. SMARTHINKING lets you work one-on-one with trained Spanish tutors in live sessions during your usual homework hours. If a question arises outside of a tutorial session, you can submit it to a tutor any time and receive a reply within 24 hours or access around-the-clock independent study resources. You can learn more about SMARTHINKING at **http://college.hmco.com/languages/ spanish/renjilian/caminos/3e/student_home.html.**

Scope and Sequence

Acknowledgments

We would like to thank the World Languages group of Houghton Mifflin's College Division for supporting us throughout the different stages of development and production of *Caminos.* To Rolando Hernández, Glenn Wilson, Kim Beuttler, Sandy Guadano, Beth Wellington, Eileen Bernadette Moran, Amy Johnson, Carol Newman, Emily Meyer, Paola Moll, and Shirley Webster, we appreciate your helpful insights and guidance. To Mary-Anne Vetterling, we express our deepest thanks for all your contributions to this project.

My deepest gratitude to Wellesley College and the Spanish Department for your enduring love and professional support on all my *caminos;* to the Knapp Media and Technology Center, for your continued assistance; to the Education Department, for your partnership in so many educational endeavors; and to Natalie Drorbaugh, María García, Kerry Renjilian-Gough, and Hillary Hurst for your constant contributions and assistance.

—*Joy Renjilian-Burgy*

Special thanks to Senior Lecturer Douglas Morgenstern, Professor Steven Lerman, and all my colleagues at MIT for their inspiration and support.

—*Ana Beatriz Chiquito*

I would like to thank the members of the Department of Hispanic Studies, University of Massachusetts, Boston, for creating such a collegial atmosphere in which to teach and learn. A very special thanks to Reyes Coll-Tellechea, Clara Estow, Esther Torrego, and Peggy Fitzgerald for your support and encouragement. I also thank our students and language instructors for your inspiration and collaboration.

—*Susan M. Mraz*

We would like to gratefully acknowledge our reviewers, focus group participants, and special contributors:

Estíbaliz Alonso, *University of Iowa*
Francisco Álvarez, *Miracosta Community College – Oceanside Campus*
María Amores
Brenda Barceló, *University of California – Santa Cruz*
Rebeca Bataller, *University of Iowa*
Robert Baum, *Arkansas State University*
Patricia Bazán-Figueras, *Fairleigh Dickinson University*
Rosamel S. Benavides, *Humboldt State University*
Raquel Blázquez-Domingo, *University of South Carolina – Columbia*
Christine Bridges-Esser, *Lamar University*
Alan Bruflat
Obdulia Castro, *University of Colorado*
Clara Chávez Burchardt, *Rose State College*
Susan Cheuvront, *University of Iowa*
Alicia Cipria, *University of Alabama*
Guillermo "Memo" Cisco, *Oakland Community College – Auburn Hills Campus*
Felice Coles, *University of Mississippi*
Purificación Crowe, *University of South Carolina – Columbia*
José Cruz, *Fayatteville Technical Community College*
Lee Daniel, *Texas Christian University*
Mary Doerfeld, *University of Iowa*
María Dorantes, *University of Michigan*
Gene DuBois, *University of North Dakota*

Héctor Enríquez, *University of Texas – El Paso*
Toni Esposito, *University of Pennsylvania*
Ana Esther Fernández, *University of Iowa*
Ken Fleak, *University of South Carolina – Columbia*
Yolanda Flores, *University of Vermont*
Donald B. Gibbs, *Creighton University*
Mark Goldin, *George Mason University*
Juan Gómez-Canseco, *Santa Fe Community College*
Ana González, *University of North Carolina – Charlotte*
Yolanda L. González, *Valencia Community College – East Campus*
María Grana, *Houston Community College*
Lisa Hall López, *Trident Technical College*
D. Carlton Hawley
Nancy Hayes, *University of Iowa*
Ellen Haynes, *University of Colorado – Boulder*
Margarita Hodge, *Northern Virginia Community College – Alexandria Campus*
Cathy House, *Miracosta Community College – San Elijo Campus*
April Howell, *Coastal Carolina Community College*
Paloma Lapuerta, *Central Connecticut State University*
Susan Larson
Luis E. Latoja, *Columbus State Community College*
Miguel Lechuga
Roxana Levin, *St. Petersburg Jr. College – Tarpon Campus*
Margarita Lezcano
Judith Liskin Gasparro, *University of Iowa*
Rosa M. López Cañete, *The College of William and Mary*
Constance Marina, *Regis College*
William Martínez, Jr., *California Polytechnic State University*
James C. Michnowicz, *The University of Virginia's College at Wise*
Montserrat Mir, *Illinois State University*
Stephen C. Mohler, *University of Tennessee at Martin*
Holly Monheimer, *University of Pennsylvania*
Paula Moore, *North Arkansas College*
Patricia Moore-Martínez, *Temple University*
Rachelle Morea, *Norfolk State University*
Glen Morocco, *La Salle University*
Janet B. Norden, *Baylor University*
Ana Oscoz, *University of Iowa*
Federico Perez-Piñeda, *University of South Alabama*
Inmaculada Pertusa, *University of Kentucky*
Margarita Pillado-Miller, *Grinnell College*
Anne Pomerantz, *University of Pennsylvania*
Oralia Preble-Niemi, *University of Tennese – Chattanooga*
Gunther F. Puschendorf, *College of Alameda*
Celia Ramírez, *Big Bend Community College*
Herlinda Ramírez Barradas, *Purdue University Calumet*
Cheryl Reagan, *Sussex County Community College*
April Reyes, *University of South Dakota*
Victoria Robertson, *California State University - Hayward*
Karen L. Robinson, *University of Nebraska at Omaha*
Beatriz Rosado, *Virginia State University*
Benita Sampedro, *Hofstra University*
Amanda Samuelson, *University of Iowa*
Joy Saunders, *Texas Tech University*
Virginia Shen, *Chicago State University*
Wayne Steely
Suzanne Stewart, *Daytona Beach Community College*

Octavio de la Suaree, *William Paterson University*
Nancy Taylor Mínguez, *Old Dominion University*
Veronica Tempone, *Indian River Community College*
George Thatcher, *Treasure Valley Community College*
Dulce Tienda-Martagón, *University of South Carolina – Columbia*
Jacquelyn Torres, *University of Iowa*
Vicky L. Trylong, *Olivet Nazarene University*
Beverly Turner, *Truckee Meadows Community College*
John H. Turner, *Bowdoin College*
Mayela Vallejos-Ramírez
Helen Webb, *University of Pennsylvania*
Joseph Weyers, *College of Charleston*
Helen Wilson, *Towson University*

CAMINOS

Sylvia Laks
Casitas 1

- ▶ Greetings
- ▶ Introductions
- ▶ The Spanish Alphabet

- ▶ Hispanics in the United States
- ▶ Nationalities
- ▶ Myth and Mystery: Who's Who in *Caminos del jaguar*

SALUDOS (GREETINGS)

Buenos días

—Buenos días. ¿Qué tal?   *—Good morning. How's it going?*
—Muy bien, gracias, ¿y tú?   *—Very well, thank you, and you?*
—Bastante bien, gracias.   *—Quite fine, thanks.*

Buenas tardes

Paciente	Buenas tardes, doctora. ¿Qué hay de nuevo?	*Good afternoon, doctor. What's new?*
Doctora	Nada en particular. ¿Cómo está usted?	*Nothing special. How are you?*
Paciente	Muy mal, bastante mal.	*Very bad, quite bad.*
Doctora	¿Verdad? Lo siento.	*Really? I'm sorry.*

Buenas noches

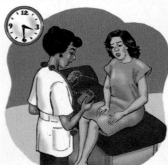

—Buenas noches.   *—Good night.*
—Buenas noches. Hasta mañana.   *—Good night. See you tomorrow.*
—Adiós. Hasta pronto.   *—Good-bye. See you soon.*
—Chao.   *—Bye.*

Note: **Buenos días** is normally used from sunrise to noon; **buenas tardes** from noon through approximately suppertime; and **buenas noches** after the evening meal.

Actividades

Online Study Center

For additional practice with this unit's vocabulary and grammar, visit the *Caminos* website at http://college.hmco.com/languages/spanish/renjilian/caminos/3e/student_home.html. You can also review audio flashcards, quiz yourself, and explore related Spanish-language sites.

1 **¿Día, tarde o noche?** Indicate whether you would say **"Buenos días,"** **"Buenas tardes,"** or **"Buenas noches"** in each of the following situations.

1. You see a friend at an afternoon matinée.
2. You run into a classmate at an after-dinner theater.
3. Your mom calls you before breakfast.
4. You have a doctor's appointment after a late lunch.
5. You talk with your roommate before going to bed.

2 **Conversación.** You run into your Spanish professor in the hallway and have a brief conversation. Number the following lines from 1–6 to put the conversation in a logical order. Then read the conversation with a partner.

  2   Buenos días. ¿Qué hay de nuevo?
  6   Chao.
  1   Buenos días.
  5   Adiós. Hasta mañana.
  3   Nada en particular. ¿Cómo está usted?
  4   Bastante bien, gracias.

3 **Saludos.** Recombine expressions from the conversations above to create a conversation around the theme of greetings. Work with a partner.

PRESENTACIONES (*INTRODUCTIONS*)

En la cafetería

Sara	Hola. ¿Cómo te llamas?	*Hello. What's your name?*
Pablo	Me llamo Pablo. ¿Y tú?	*My name is Pablo. And you?*
Sara	Me llamo Sara.	*My name is Sara.*
Pablo	Mucho gusto.	*Pleased to meet you.*
Sara	Igualmente.	*Likewise.*

En la oficina

Rafael	Hola. ¿Cómo se llama usted?	*Hello. What's your name?*
Mirta	Me llamo Mirta Pérez. ¿Y usted?	*My name is Mirta Pérez. And you?*
Rafael	Me llamo Rafael Ramírez.	*My name is Rafael Ramírez.*
Mirta	Mucho gusto.	*Pleased to meet you.*
Rafael	El gusto es mío.	*The pleasure is mine.*

En la sala de clase

—Buenos días, profesora.
—Buenos días. ¿Cómo te llamas?
—Me llamo David Romero Solar. ¿Y usted?
—Me llamo Susana Alegría Ramírez.
—Mucho gusto, profesora.
—El gusto es mío. ¡Bienvenido, David!

—*Good morning, professor.*
—*Good morning. What's your name?*
—*My name is David Romero Solar. And you?*
—*My name is Susana Alegría Ramírez.*
—*It's a pleasure, professor.*
—*The pleasure is mine. Welcome, David!*

Actividades

1 El gusto es mío. Look at the conversations above. With whom would you use the following phrases?

1. ¿Cómo te llamas? / ¿Y tú? _____
2. ¿Cómo se llama usted? / ¿Y usted? _____

2 ¿Cómo te llamas? Practice introducing yourself to three classmates. Use the conversation between Sara and Pablo as a model.

3 ¿Cómo se llama usted? Using the conversations above as models, role-play with different classmates using formal introductions as: (a) head of your school, (b) president of your country, or (c) a famous celebrity.

As your instructor pronounces the 27 letters of the Spanish alphabet with their corresponding names, repeat each one, noting some of the differences compared with the English alphabet (which has only 26 letters).

La letra	El nombre	La letra	El nombre	La letra	El nombre
a	*a*	j	*jota*	r	*ere*
b	*be, be grande*	k	*ka*	s	*ese*
c	*ce*	l	*ele*	t	*te*
d	*de*	m	*eme*	u	*u*
e	*e*	n	*ene*	v	*uve, ve chica*
f	*efe*	ñ	*eñe*	w	*doble ve, doble u*
g	*ge*	o	*o*	x	*equis*
h	*hache*	p	*pe*	y	*i griega*
i	*i*	q	*cu*	z	*zeta*

Note: In older dictionaries you will find the letters **ch** (*che*) and **ll** (*elle, doble ele*); these were removed from the Spanish alphabet in 1994. Also, **rr** (*erre*) is now considered a sound, not a letter.

Las consonantes (*Consonants*)

The letters **b** and **v** have the same pronunciation as *b* at the beginning of words. These letters have the same pronunciation as *v* between two vowels.	bien, victoria uva, sabe
The **c** of **ca, co, cu** is pronounced like the *c* in *cot*.	cama, coco, cubo
The **c** of **ce, ci** is pronounced like the *c* in *center* in Latin America, and with a *th* sound in Spain.	cerebro, cierto
The **g** of **ga, go, gu** is pronounced like *go*.	gato, gorro, guante
The **g** of **ge, gi** is pronounced like *helium*.	gente, gira
The letter **h** is always silent.	hotel, hospital
The letter **j** is pronounced like the *h* in *heavy*.	jaguar
The letters **k** and **w** are usually found in words borrowed from other languages.	kilogramo, *windsurf*
The letter combination **ll** is pronounced like the *y* in the word *you* or like the *s* in the word *measure*.	lluvia, calle
The letter combination **que** is always pronounced like *kay* in the word *okay*.	queso, quetzal
The letter combination **qui** is always pronounced like the word *key*.	Quijote, arquitecto
The letter **r** at the beginning of a word is trilled just like the *rr* sound in Spanish.	Rita, rosa
The letter **r** between two vowels is pronounced like a double *d* or *t*, as in *ladder* or *butter*.	para, cura
The letter **z** is pronounced like *s* in Latin America and like *th* in Spain.	lápiz, zona

Las vocales (*Vowels*)

Because vowels are critical in Spanish pronunciation, it is important to master their sounds. Repeat the following words after your instructor. Be sure to pay close attention to your instructor's face as you listen to the words.

La vocal	La pronunciación	El vocabulario	El inglés
a	*as in the word "palm"*	casa	*house*
		fama	*fame*
		cama	*bed*
e	*as in the word "very"*	lento	*slow*
		verde	*green*
		mes	*month*
i	*as in the word "elite"*	mitad	*half*
		primo	*cousin*
		vino	*wine*
o	*as in the word "oh"*	no	*no*
		oso	*bear*
		todo	*all*
u	*as in the word "lunar"*	luna	*moon*
		uno	*one*
		cuna	*crib*

Acentuación (*Stress*)

A few basic guidelines will help you learn which syllable to stress when pronouncing words in Spanish. By carefully studying these rules, you will listen, speak, read, and write with greater ease.

1. Spanish words ending in a vowel (**a, e, i, o, u**), **n** or **s** carry the spoken stress on the second to last syllable. No written accent is necessary.

   ofi**ci**na *office* **chi**cos *boys* **ha**blan *you / they speak*
   clase *class* pro**gra**ma *program* estudi**an**tes *students*

2. Words ending in a consonant other than **n** or **s** carry the spoken stress on the last syllable. No written accent is necessary.

   liber**tad** *liberty* pa**pel** *paper* ha**blar** *to speak*
   re**loj** *watch* escri**bir** *to write* profe**sor** *professor*

3. Words that are exceptions to the previous two rules carry written accents to indicate which syllable carries the stress.

   in**glés** *English* sim**pá**tico *nice*
   página *page* televi**sión** *television*

4. Written accents in words ending in **-ión** are not needed in the plural:

   composi**ción** composi**cio**nes lec**ción** lec**cio**nes

5. The following words, when used as *interrogatives*, always carry accents:

   ¿cómo? *how?* ¿qué? *what?*
   ¿cuándo? *when?* ¿quién/es? *who?*
   ¿dónde? *where?* ¿por qué? *why?*
   ¿cuánto/a/s? *how much?, how many?* ¿cuál/es? *which?, what?*

6. Although their pronunciation remains the same, certain words carry accents to distinguish their meaning:

el	*the*	él	*he*
como	*as, like*	¿cómo?	*how?*
tu	*your*	tú	*you*
si	*if*	sí	*yes*

Actividades

1 **Pronunciemos.** With a classmate, pronounce the following words. Then ask each other how to spell each one in Spanish. Use the letter and pronunciation charts above for reference. Note that if a word carries an accent, add the phrase **con acento** to the name of the letter. Follow the model.

▶ **MODELO:** —*¿Cómo se deletrea **lápiz** en español?*
—*ele, a con acento, pe, i, zeta*

1. amigo
2. igualmente
3. rápido
4. página
5. bien
6. gemelo
7. códice
8. televisión
9. gusto
10. español
11. sí
12. jaguar
13. lápiz
14. profesora
15. universidad
16. hola

2 **Los acentos.** Add the missing accent to each word, if needed.

1. señora
2. aguila
3. papel
4. television
5. programas
6. lapices
7. luz
8. dificil

Hispanics in the United States

Today, almost 500 million people worldwide speak Spanish! Spanish is spoken by approximately 350 million people in 21 countries (Mexico: 98 million; Spain: 39 million; United States: 39 million; Argentina: 35 million; Colombia: 36 million; Venezuela: 22 million; Peru: 20 million). Spanish is the world's third most spoken language, after Mandarin Chinese and English, and ranks second in terms of native speakers.

The U.S. Census Bureau reports that the nation's Hispanic population is expected to jump to 59.7 million by 2020. The 40 million Hispanics currently living in the United States make up 14% of the total population. This population growth has increased demand for Spanish language media: radio, television, newspapers, and magazines.

Hispanics contribute to all aspects of life in the United States; from the foods we eat, to the music we enjoy; they are political leaders, athletes, news anchors, entertainers, scientists, teachers, and students. Their ethnic diversity is also noteworthy and reflects the cultural richness of the Spanish-speaking world.

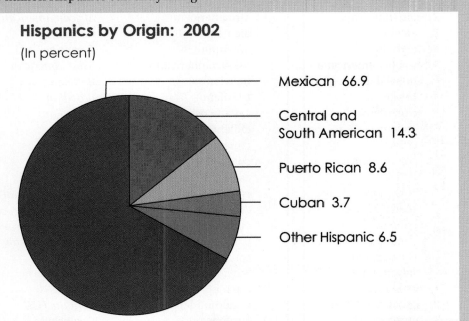

Hispanics by Origin: 2002
(In percent)

- Mexican 66.9
- Central and South American 14.3
- Puerto Rican 8.6
- Cuban 3.7
- Other Hispanic 6.5

Source: U.S. Census Bureau, Annual Demographic Supplement to the March 2002 Current Population Survey.

Discusión en grupos

1. Why are you studying Spanish? How do you think this course will be useful for you in the near or distant future?
2. Is there a large Hispanic population in your community? If so, where are they from? If not, what are the ethnic backgrounds of the people in your community?
3. Look at the map of Hispanics in the United States at the front of your textbook. Which states have the largest Hispanic population? Which states have the smallest? How does your state compare to other states on the map? Why do you think certain states have larger Hispanic populations than others?
4. Discuss which states might have a large percentage of people from these countries: México, Puerto Rico, Cuba, and Guatemala. Why do you think this is so?

NACIONALIDADES / IDENTIDADES
(NATIONALITIES / IDENTITIES)

Caela	¿De dónde eres?		Where are you from?
Aída	Soy de La Paz. Soy boliviana. ¿Y tú?		I am from La Paz. I am Bolivian. And you?
Caela	Soy hondureña. Soy de Tegucigalpa.		I'm Honduran. I am from Tegucigalpa.
Aída	Mucho gusto.		It's a pleasure.
Caela	El gusto es mío.		The pleasure is mine.

Nacionalidades / Identidades

Country / Island	For females	For males	English
África + Estados Unidos	afroamericana	afroamericano	African American
Alemania	alemana	alemán	German
Argentina	argentina	argentino	Argentine
Asia + Estados Unidos	asiáticoamericana	asiáticoamericano	Asian American
Bolivia	boliviana	boliviano	Bolivian
Brasil	brasileña	brasileño	Brazilian
Canadá	canadiense	canadiense	Canadian
Chile	chilena	chileno	Chilean
China	china	chino	Chinese
Colombia	colombiana	colombiano	Colombian
Corea	coreana	coreano	Korean
Corea + Estados Unidos	coreanoamericana	coreanoamericano	Korean American
Costa Rica	costarricense	costarricense	Costa Rican
Cuba	cubana	cubano	Cuban
Cuba + Estados Unidos	cubanoamericana	cubanoamericano	Cuban American
Ecuador	ecuatoriana	ecuatoriano	Ecuadorian
El Salvador	salvadoreña	salvadoreño	Salvadoran
España	española	español	Spanish
Estados Unidos	estadounidense	estadounidense	from the U.S.
Europa	europea	europeo	European
Francia	francesa	francés	French
Guatemala	guatemalteca	guatemalteco	Guatemalan
Haití	haitiana	haitiano	Haitian
Honduras	hondureña	hondureño	Honduran
Inglaterra	inglesa	inglés	English
Irlanda	irlandesa	irlandés	Irish
Italia	italiana	italiano	Italian
Japón	japonesa	japonés	Japanese
México	mexicana	mexicano	Mexican
México + Estados Unidos	mexicanoamericana	mexicanoamericano	Mexican American
Nicaragua	nicaragüense	nicaragüense	Nicaraguan
Panamá	panameña	panameño	Panamanian
Paraguay	paraguaya	paraguayo	Paraguayan
Perú	peruana	peruano	Peruvian
Portugal	portuguesa	portugués	Portuguese
Puerto Rico	puertorriqueña	puertorriqueño	Puerto Rican
República Dominicana	dominicana	dominicano	Dominican
Rusia	rusa	ruso	Russian
Uruguay	uruguaya	uruguayo	Uruguayan
Venezuela	venezolana	venezolano	Venezuelan

Actividades

1 Nacionalidades. Below are some of the characters you will meet in *Caminos del jaguar.* Read where they are from and, using the Nacionalidades / Identidades chart, identify their nationalities. Work in groups.

Me llamo Luis Ortiz López.

Soy de Puerto Rico.

Soy _____

Me llamo Patricia.

Soy de San Antonio, Texas.

Soy _____

Me llamo Gerardo Covarrubias.

Soy de España.

Soy _____

Me llamo Zulaya Piscomayo Curihual.

Soy de Ecuador.

Soy _____

Me llamo Esperanza.

Soy de México.

Soy _____

2 Orígenes. How many of these people do you recognize? Identify their nationalities. Refer to the nationality chart on page 8. Be sure to use the nationality that corresponds to a female or a male.

1. Penélope Cruz
2. Hideki Matsui
3. Audrey Tatou
4. Gloria Estefan
5. Luciano Pavarotti

6. Shakira
7. Vladimir Putin
8. David Ortiz
9. Prince William
10. Carlos Santana

3 ¡Hola! In pairs, role-play two of the characters from *Actividad 2.* Use the information about their names and nationalities to create a conversation in which you practice greetings, introductions, and expressions of courtesy.

Myth and Mystery

The *Popol Vuh*, the sacred book of the Mayans, reveals the story of the Mayan Hero Twins (**Los héroes gemelos**) **Yax-Balam** (YASH-BA-LAM) and **Hun-Ahau** (U-NA-HOW). They are twin figures from Mayan lore who symbolize the triumph of good over evil. The Jaguar Twins have mythical powers and are the central figures in this exciting mystery.

According to the Mayans, the universe is divided into three worlds: the sky (**el cielo**), the earth (**la tierra**), and the underworld (**Xibalbá**)—a parallel world beneath the earth, full of plants, animals, and people. In the *Popol Vuh*, the Jaguar Hero Twins overpowered the Lords of Xibalbá.

The Mayans played a ball game similar to modern-day soccer. The hero twins Yax-Balam and Hun-Ahau were the best ball players on earth, but the noise they made while playing the game infuriated the Lords of Xibalbá. The Lords invited the Jaguar Twins to play ball in Xibalbá and designed a series of challenges to make the twins fail. However, the Hero Twins won the game as well as the challenges and became gods themselves.

The story in **Caminos del jaguar** is based on this myth of the Jaguar Twins. In our video, archaeology professor Nayeli Paz Ocotlán, of the University of Puebla, has just published her book, *Los héroes gemelos de Xibalbá,* which narrates the history of Yax-Balam and Hun-Ahau.

These representations of the Jaguar Twins were created to accompany the great Mayan King Pacal to Xibalbá when he died on August 31. Centuries later, thieves stole these artifacts from the grave site and sold them for riches.

Join us and two archaeology students, Adriana and Felipe, who take a journey down an unexpected path where the forces of good and evil (**los buenos y los malos**) battle over the fate of the Jaguar Hero Twins. Will the missing Jaguar Twins find their way back to Mexico or will they fall into the wrong hands forever?

NAYELI PAZ OCOTLÁN

Born to a Mexican mother and a Spanish father, Nayeli was raised in New York City and later studied at the Universidad Autónoma de México (UNAM). She is now a well-known professor of archaeology at the Universidad de Puebla, where she is dedicated to locating Mexican artifacts and preserving them. She is an expert on the story of the Jaguar Twins and has recently published the book, *Los héroes gemelos de Xibalbá*. Hernán, her husband, died in the Mexican earthquake of 1985. Nayeli feels responsible for his death.

GAFASNEGRAS

Born and raised in Mexico City, she was one of Nayeli's first archaeology students in Puebla and has always been jealous of her. Her nickname is Gafasnegras because she wears sunglasses. (**gafas**=*glasses*, **negras**=*dark*). Her real name is Mariluz Gorrostiaga Hinojosa.

ADRIANA REYES TEPOLE

Born in San Antonio, Adriana Reyes Tepole grew up in Guayaquil, Ecuador, where her father worked on a United Nations project. When she was twelve, the family then returned to Texas, the birthplace of her father. Her mother is from Puebla, Mexico. Adriana recently studied at the Universidad de Puebla and lived with her maternal grandparents. Currently a graduate student in archaeology at the University of Texas at San Antonio, she was awarded a summer fellowship to go on an excavation with Nayeli.

FELIPE LUNA VELILLA

For many years, Felipe lived with his Venezuelan father in Caracas before returning to Miami to live with his Cuban mother and stepfather. He completed his undergraduate studies in archaeology at the University of Miami and is doing graduate work at the University of Texas at San Antonio. He also has been awarded a summer fellowship to go on a dig with Nayeli.

ARMANDO DE LANDA CHÁVEZ

Armando is a Mexican entrepreneur who helps fund Adriana and Felipe's summer travels.

LA ABUELITA (*GRANDMOTHER*)

Nayeli's grandmother lived in Puebla all her life and Nayeli was her favorite grandchild. She has passed away but visits Nayeli often in vivid dreams. Nayeli adores her grandmother.

MYSTERIOUS RING-FINGERED MAN

Friend or foe? You decide.

DOÑA CARMEN QUESADA ARAYA

Doña Carmen, an art collector, lives on a ranch outside of San José, Costa Rica. Nayeli is her godchild, and the two have been very close for years. Nayeli's mother and doña Carmen were art history majors and best friends in college. After Nayeli's mother died, doña Carmen funded Nayeli's college studies.

Resumen de vocabulario

Adiós.	Good-bye.
Bastante bien, gracias.	Pretty well, thanks.
¡Bienvenido!	Welcome!
Buenas noches.	Good evening. / Good night.
Buenas tardes.	Good afternoon.
Buenos días.	Good morning.
Chao.	Bye.
¿cómo?	how?
¿Cómo está usted? / ¿Cómo estás tú?	How are you?
¿Cómo se llama usted? / ¿Cómo te llamas?	What's your name?
¿cuál/es?	which?, what?
¿cuándo?	when?
¿cuánto/a/s?	how much?, how many?
¿dónde?	where?
El gusto es mío.	The pleasure is mine.
está / están	is, are
Hasta mañana.	See you tomorrow.
Igualmente.	Likewise.
Lo siento.	I'm sorry.
Me llamo...	My name is . . .
Mucho gusto.	Pleased to meet you.
Muy bien, gracias.	Very well, thank you.
Muy mal, bastante mal.	Very bad, quite bad.
Nada en particular.	Nothing special.
¿por qué?	why?
porque	because
¿qué?	what?
¿Qué hay de nuevo?	What's new?
¿Qué tal?	How's it going?
¿quién/es?	who?
¿Verdad?	Really?
¿Y usted? / ¿Y tú?	And you?

MÁS PALABRAS Y EXPRESIONES

Abre (tú) / Abran (ustedes) el libro a la página...	*Open your book to page...*
la actividad	*activity*
el/la alumno/a	*student*
el/la amigo/a	*friend*
el/la chico/a	*boy, girl*
la clase	*class*
¿Cómo se dice... ?	*How do you say . . . ?*
el/la compañero de clase (de cuarto)	*classmate (roommate)*
Con permiso.	*Excuse me.*
contesta (tú) / contesten (ustedes)	*answer (verb)*
De nada.	*You're welcome.*
el/la doctor/a (Dr. / Dra.)	*doctor*
don (D.)	*male title of respect, used with first name*
doña (Dña.)	*female title of respect, used with first name*
en grupos	*in groups*
en parejas	*in pairs*
escucha (tú) / escuchen (ustedes)	*listen*
el/la estudiante	*student*
habla (tú) / hablen (ustedes)	*speak*
Hasta la vista.	*Until we meet again.*
Hasta luego / mañana.	*See you later / tomorrow.*
más despacio	*more slowly*
No sé.	*I don't know.*
¡Ojo!	*Be careful!*
la página	*page*
Perdón.	*Pardon. / Excuse me.*
por favor	*please*
la pregunta	*question*
pregunta (tú) / pregunten (ustedes)	*ask*
el/la profesor/a	*professor*
¿Qué quiere decir... ?	*What does . . . mean?*
la regla	*rule*
regular	*OK*
repite (tú) / repitan (ustedes)	*repeat*
señor (Sr.)	*Mr.*
señora (Sra.)	*Mrs.*
señorita (Srta.)	*Miss*
Sí, cómo no.	*Of course.*
también	*also*
la unidad	*unit*
¡Vamos! / ¡Vámonos!	*Let's go!*

1
En la universidad

VOCABULARIO Y LENGUA

► Describing things in a room
► Using articles and nouns
► Identifying colors (Noun and adjective agreement)
► Counting from 0 to 199

► Discussing academic schedules and subjects
► Telling time
► Describing people and things using **ser**
► Using adjectives

CAMINOS DEL JAGUAR

► ¿Arqueóloga o criminal?
► El destino llama

LECTURA

► Estudiantes talentosos

NOTAS CULTURALES

► Los héroes gemelos
► Los mayas de México

ESTRATEGIAS

► **Reading:** Identifying cognates and prefixes
► **Writing:** Creating a cluster diagram

Miguel Suárez-Pierra, *Girasol*

Preguntas del tema

► ¿Cómo es la universidad? ¿enorme? ¿moderna? ¿excelente?

► ¿Son fascinantes las clases?

► ¿Cuál es una clase popular? ¿historia? ¿matemáticas? ¿biología?

► ¿Hay estudiantes interesantes en la universidad?

PRIMER PASO

Vocabulario y lengua

DESCRIBING THINGS IN A ROOM

¿Qué hay en el cuarto? (*What is in the room?*)

Cognates (**cognados**) are words that have similar spellings and meanings in both Spanish and English. How many of these cognates can you match with items in the drawing below?

un teléfono	una televisión	un calendario	una lámpara
una calculadora	un/a computador/a	un mapa	una rosa
una oficina	una universidad	un/a radio	

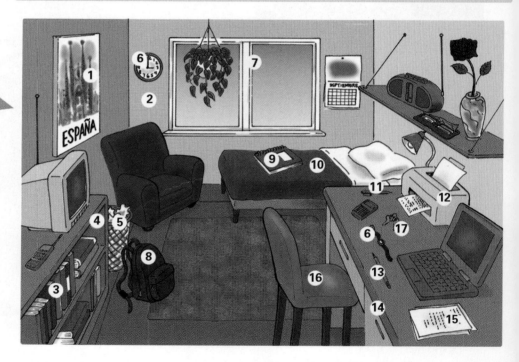

Online Study Center

For additional practice with this unit's vocabulary and grammar, visit the *Caminos* website at http://college.hmco.com/languages/spanish/renjilian/caminos/3e/student_home.html. You can also review audio flashcards, quiz yourself, and explore related Spanish-language sites.

1. un cartel
2. una pared
3. unos libros
4. un estante
5. un basurero
6. un reloj
7. una ventana
8. una mochila
9. un cuaderno
10. una cama
11. un bolígrafo / una pluma
12. una impresora
13. un lápiz
14. un escritorio
15. unos papeles
16. una silla
17. unas llaves

Más palabras y expresiones

Sustantivos

un borrador	*a blackboard eraser*	una puerta	*a door*
una carpeta	*a folder*	un pupitre	*a writing desk*
un dormitorio	*a bedroom*	una residencia	*a dormitory*
una mesa	*a table*	una sala de clase	*a classroom*
una pizarra	*a blackboard*	una tiza	*a piece of chalk*

Otras expresiones

de	*of, from*
en	*in, on, at*
(no) hay	*there is (not); there are (not)*
y	*and*

Actividades

1 ¿Qué hay en el cuarto? Listen to the description of Ernesto's room. Number the items in the order that you hear them. Not all items will be mentioned.

2 Asociaciones.
Match each word in the left-hand column with the most closely associated word in the right-hand column.

d	1. papel	a.	estante
b	2. pizarra	b.	tiza
f	3. silla	c.	bolígrafo
h	4. cartel	d.	impresora
a	5. libro	e.	residencia
g	6. cuaderno	f.	escritorio
e	7. universidad	g.	mochila
c	8. lápiz	h.	pared

3 En la sala de clase.
Work with a partner to list as many things in your classroom as you can.

▶ **MODELO:** —¿Qué hay en la sala de clase?   —*What is in the classroom?*
—Hay una pizarra.   —*There is a chalkboard.*

4 En el cuarto.
List three things in your bedroom and three things *not* in your bedroom. Play "twenty questions" with your partner to guess what is on each other's lists. Follow the model.

▶ **MODELO:** —¿Hay una computadora?   —*Is there a computer?*
—Sí, hay una computadora.   —*Yes, there is a computer.*
or   *or*
—No, no hay una computadora.   —*No, there isn't a computer.*

USING ARTICLES AND NOUNS

Indefinite articles: *a, an, some*

un alumno

unos alumnos

una alumna

unos alumnos

unas alumnas

The indefinite article has four forms.

	Masculine	Feminine
Singular	un	una
Plural	unos	unas

Definite articles: *the*

el libro

los libros

la silla

las sillas

The definite article has four forms.

	Masculine	Feminine
Singular	el	la
Plural	los	las

Masculine and feminine nouns

Nouns in Spanish are either masculine or feminine. Usually, nouns that refer to males are masculine and nouns that refer to females are feminine.

Masculine	Feminine	
el alumno	**la** alumna	*the student*
el amigo	**la** amiga	*the friend*
el chico	**la** chica	*the boy, the girl*
el compañero de clase	**la** compañera de clase	*the classmate*
el profesor	**la** profesora	*the teacher*
el señor	**la** señora	*Mr., Mrs.*

Nouns ending in **-ista** or **-e** that refer to people can be either masculine or feminine. The context or the article will indicate the gender.

Masculine	Feminine	
el art**ista**	**la** art**ista**	*artist*
el dent**ista**	**la** dent**ista**	*dentist*
el estudiant**e**	**la** estudiant**e**	*student*
el pacient**e**	**la** pacient**e**	*patient*

In some cases, the nouns for people are different for men and women.

Masculine		Feminine	
el hombre	*man*	**la** mujer	*woman*
el padre	*father*	**la** madre	*mother*

Most nouns that refer to things and end in **-o** are masculine while most feminine nouns end in **-a.**

Masculine		Feminine	
el calendari**o**	*calendar*	**la** pintur**a**	*painting*
el basurer**o**	*garbage can*	**la** calculador**a**	*calculator*
el libr**o**	*book*	**la** impresor**a**	*printer*

There are nouns whose gender is not obvious just by looking at the endings. But certain endings may give you a clue about a noun's gender.
Nouns ending in **-ión, -dad,** and **-tad** are usually feminine.

la lecc**ión**	*lesson*	**la** activi**dad**	*activity*	**la** liber**tad**	*liberty*
la composic**ión**	*composition*	**la** ciu**dad**	*city*	**la** mi**tad**	*half*

Certain nouns ending in **-ma** are masculine. These are exceptions. Here are some that are used frequently.

el cli**ma**	*climate*	**el** idio**ma**	*language*
el siste**ma**	*system*	**el** proble**ma**	*problem*
el te**ma**	*theme*	**el** progra**ma**	*program*

Nouns ending in **-e** may be masculine or feminine.

la clas**e**	*class*	**el** puent**e**	*bridge*
la gent**e**	*people*	**el** cin**e**	*movie theater*

Whenever a feminine word begins with a stressed **a** (with or without a written accent), the definite article **el** is used to avoid combining two stressed sounds.

el agua	*water*	**el** águila	*eagle*	**el** alma	*soul*

Here are three common words that are exceptions to the rules above:

el dí**a**	*day*	**la** man**o**	*hand*	**el** map**a**	*map*

When talking *about* people with titles such as **señor, señora, señorita, doctor** and **doctora,** the definite article is used. When talking *to* them directly, the definite article is not used.

El señor Medina es doctor.	*Mr. Medina is a doctor.*
Doctor Medina, ¿cómo está usted?	*Doctor Medina, how are you?*

Plural of nouns

Nouns ending in a vowel generally add **-s** to form the plural.

el alumn**o**	los alumn**os**
la chic**a**	las chic**as**
la clas**e**	las clas**es**

Nouns ending in a consonant add **–es** to form the plural.

el pape**l**	los pape**les**
el relo**j**	los relo**jes**

When pluralizing nouns ending in **–z**, the **–z** changes to **–c** before **–es.**

el lápi**z**	los lápi**ces**

Nouns typically keep their gender in both singular and plural forms. One common exception is:

el art**e** *art*	**las** art**es** *the arts*

Actividades

1 Los artículos indefinidos. Identify the correct indefinite article for these words.

1. _____ actividades
2. _____ ciudades
3. _____ carteles
4. _____ cuartos
5. _____ compañeras
6. _____ estudiantes
7. _____ impresoras
8. _____ televisiones

2 Los artículos definidos. For each noun, give the correct definite article. Then, give the plural form of the noun and article.

1. _____ cuaderno

   _____

2. _____ día

   _____

3. _____ lápiz

_____

4. _____ mano

_____

5. _____ papel

_____

6. _____ reloj

_____

7. _____ silla

_____

8. _____ teléfono

_____

3 Práctica. Work with a partner. Replace the indefinite article **un** or **una** with the definite article **el** or **la.** Then make each word plural. Follow the model.

▸ **MODELO:** Student 1: _un libro_   Student 1: _unos libros_
  Student 2: _el libro_   Student 2: _los libros_

1. un señor
2. una estudiante
3. una calculadora
4. un basurero
5. una composición
6. un tema
7. una compañera de clase
8. una mano

4 ¿Qué es? Work with a partner. Indicate whether each noun is masculine, feminine, or both, by writing the definite article **el, la,** or both articles in front of each noun. Then say the words aloud.

1. _el_ puente
2. _la_ artista
3. _la_ bolsa
4. _el_ calendario
5. _la_ dentista
6. _el_ cine
7. _la_ clase
8. _el_ día

9. _____ idioma
10. _____ impresora
11. _____ estudiante
12. _____ mapa
13. _____ oportunidad
14. _____ papel
15. _____ profesor
16. _____ señora

5 Hombres y mujeres. Work with a partner. Read aloud a word from the list and your partner will give its equivalent in the opposite gender. Be careful to use the correct definite or indefinite article.

▸ **MODELO:** Student 1: _un hombre_   Student 2: _una mujer_

1. un profesor
2. el chico
3. un señor
4. una estudiante
5. la mujer
6. una alumna
7. un amigo
8. el artista

IDENTIFYING COLORS
(NOUN AND ADJECTIVE AGREEMENT)

¿De qué color es? (*What color is it?*)

rosado negro café morado

rojo azul

blanco amarillo verde

anaranjado gris

Both Spanish and English use adjectives to describe the color of an object. In Spanish, adjectives usually modify nouns and must agree in *gender* (masculine or feminine) and *number* (singular or plural) with the nouns they modify. Adjectives that end in **-o** or **-a** have corresponding plural forms ending in **-os** and **-as.** The ending needed depends on the gender of the noun.

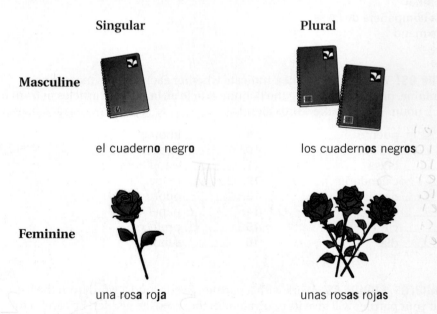

	Singular	Plural
Masculine	el cuaderno negro	los cuadernos negros
Feminine	una rosa roja	unas rosas rojas

Adjectives that end in any letter other than **-o** or **-a** have only two forms, singular and plural.

	Singular		Plural	
Masculine	el libro interesante	*the interesting book*	los libros interesantes	*the interesting books*
Feminine	la clase interesante	*the interesting class*	las clases interesantes	*the interesting classes*

To describe a noun with more than one adjective, connect the adjectives with the conjunction **y** (*and*).

el libro blanco y rojo.   *the white and red book*

Actividades

1 Los colores. Name the colors of the items in the picture on page 18. Make the color agree with the item and add the correct definite article. Work with a partner. Follow the model.

▶ **MODELO:** _____ mochila _____
        la mochila <u>roja</u>

1. __el__ basurero __verde__
2. __la__ cama __azul__
3. __los__ papeles __blancos__
4. __la__ pared __amarilla__
5. __la__ rosa __roja__
6. __el__ teléfono __azul__
7. __el__ cuaderno __verde__
8. __la__ lámpara __amarilla__

2 Adjetivos. Add the correct definite article to each noun in Column A. Ask your partner to select an adjective from Column B and make it agree with that noun. Take turns. Follow the model.

▶ **MODELO:**
    Student A   Student B
    los libros   *verdes*

A

1. libros
2. silla
3. alfombras
4. mochila
5. papel
6. lápices
7. foto
8. mapa

B

a. blanco
b. rojo
c. interesante
d. gris
e. amarillo
f. verde
g. azul
h. negro

3 Cosas y colores. Work in pairs to describe the objects and their colors in the drawing.

▶ **MODELO:**
—¿Qué hay en la oficina?
—Hay unos lápices amarillos.

—*What is in the office?*
—*There are some yellow pencils.*

Los números del 0 al 199

¿Cuál es tu número de teléfono?

Es el cinco, cincuenta y cinco; tres, doce; cuarenta y ocho, cero, nueve.

0	cero	10	diez	20	veinte	30	treinta
1	uno	11	once	21	veintiuno	40	cuarenta
2	dos	12	doce	22	veintidós	50	cincuenta
3	tres	13	trece	23	veintitrés	60	sesenta
4	cuatro	14	catorce	24	veinticuatro	70	setenta
5	cinco	15	quince	25	veinticinco	80	ochenta
6	seis	16	dieciséis	26	veintiséis	90	noventa
7	siete	17	diecisiete	27	veintisiete	100	cien
8	ocho	18	dieciocho	28	veintiocho	101	ciento uno
9	nueve	19	diecinueve	29	veintinueve	199	ciento noventa y nueve

Number notes

uno / una	**Uno** changes to **una** in front of a feminine noun: *41 computers* = cuarenta y **una** computadoras **Uno** changes to **un** in front of a masculine noun: *31 telephones* = treinta y **un** teléfonos
veinte +	**Veinte** + is usually written as one word: *23* = **veintitrés** *25* = **veinticinco**
treinta + *to* **noventa+**	The numbers from 31–39; 41–49 etc. are always written as three separate words: *37* = **treinta y siete** *98* = **noventa y ocho** Note that **"y"** appears only between the "tens" and "ones" place.
cien	**Cien** is used when the number is *exactly* 100: *100 students* = **cien alumnos** *100 books* = **cien libros**
ciento	**Ciento** is used in the numbers **101** to **199;** it doesn't change its form: *103 computers* = En la universidad hay **ciento tres** computadoras.

Actividades

1 La clase de matemáticas.
In pairs, practice these mathematical problems in Spanish. Follow the model.

▶ **MODELO:** $5 + 33 =$ <u>38</u>.
   Cinco más treinta y tres son treinta y ocho.
   $33 - 5 =$ <u>28</u>.
   Treinta y tres menos cinco son veintiocho.

1. $85 + 11 =$ _____.
2. $73 - 27 =$ _____.
3. $15 + 67 =$ _____.
4. $24 - 13 =$ _____.
5. $101 + 36 =$ _____.

6. $99 - 12 =$ _____.
7. $183 + 14 =$ _____.
8. $199 - 94 =$ _____.
9. $75 + 111 =$ _____.
10. $43 - 10 =$ _____.

2 Las páginas amarillas panameñas.
In pairs, practice saying the phone numbers taken from the Panamanian Yellow Pages. Follow the model.

▶ **MODELO:** ¿Cuál es el número de teléfono de la Universidad Interamericana de Panamá?
   Es el cinco, cero, siete; dos, sesenta y tres; setenta y siete, ochenta y siete

UNIVERSIDAD INTERAMERICANA DE PANAMA
Av Manuel Espinosa Batista, Pmá
PANAMÁ – Panamá, Panamá
Teléfono: (507) 263-7787
Fax: (507) 263-3688

LA CASA DEL MÚSICO
Vía Rdo J Alfaro, L-15
PANAMÁ – Panamá, Panamá
Teléfono: (507) 260-9715

INFOTUR
Vía España Perejil, Pmá
PANAMÁ – Panamá, Panamá
Teléfono: (507) 227-3729

UNIVERSIDAD LATINA
Vía Rdo J Alfaro
PANAMÁ – Panamá, Panamá
Teléfono: (507) 230-8600
Fax: (507) 230-8606

COLEGIO INTERNACIONAL OXFORD
Av Fdco Boyd, Pmá
PANAMÁ – Panamá, Panamá
Teléfono: (507) 265-6422
Fax: (507) 265-7446

UNIVERSIDAD AMERICANA
Cl Rdo Arias y Av 3 Sur, Area Bancaria
PANAMÁ – Panamá, Panamá
Teléfono: (507) 213-1967
(507) 213-1214

3 Números importantes.
You need to make up a class list of phone numbers for five of your classmates. Interview your classmates and complete the following chart with this information. Follow the model.

▶ **MODELO:**
—¿Cómo te llamas?
—Me llamo Marcos.
—¿Cuál es tu número de teléfono?
—Es el seis, noventa y nueve; cinco, veinticuatro; cuarenta y nueve, setenta y seis.

—*What's your name?*
—*My name is Marcos.*
—*What is your phone number?*
—*It's six, ninety-nine; five, twenty-four, forty-nine, seventy-six*

	Nombre	Teléfono
Modelo:	Marcos	699-524-4976
1.	_____	_____
2.	_____	_____
3.	_____	_____
4.	_____	_____
5.	_____	_____

¿Arqueóloga o criminal?

En la Universidad de San Antonio...

¡Hola! ¿Eres amigo de Felipe Luna?

No, no soy amigo de Felipe Luna. ...98, 99, ¡100!

Perdona, ¿eres amiga de Felipe Luna?

¿Quién es Felipe Luna?

Felipe no es muy alto y tiene el pelo castaño.

Lo siento. No soy amiga de Felipe Luna.

Eres futbolista, ¿verdad?

Pues, sí...

¡Ay, qué bueno! ¿Eres amigo de Felipe Luna?

¿Cómo es Felipe?

Pues, no es muy alto.

¿Es rubio?

No, tiene el pelo castaño.

Es gordo, ¿verdad?

No, es delgado.

¿De qué color tiene los ojos?

Cafés.

¿Es guapo?

Pues...

Sí, sí, Adriana. ¡Soy guapo!

¡Ay, Felipe, claro que eres guapo!

En la oficina de Nayeli...

Noticias, noticias, noticias: ¿Arqueóloga o criminal?

En la cancha de fútbol de la universidad.

¡Tres meses en México!

La excavación en Puebla es una oportunidad increíble.

Y Nayeli es una profesora excepcional.

¿Es largo el viaje de San Antonio a Puebla?

Sí, es muy largo. Yo hago las reservaciones en autobús.

Muy bien, Adriana, ¡qué organizada eres!

En la oficina de Nayeli.

ADRIANA Y FELIPE

Arqueóloga, ¡ja!

Actividades

Online Study Center

For additional practice with this episode, visit the *Caminos* website at http://college.hmco.com/languages/spanish/renjilian/caminos/3e/student_home.html.

1 Comprensión. Based on this episode of *Caminos del jaguar,* choose the logical response.

1. Adriana y Felipe están en...
   a. la cancha de fútbol.
   b. la cancha de béisbol.

2. Felipe es...
   a. delgado y guapo.
   b. gordo y guapo.

3. ¿Dónde es la excavación?
   a. en Puebla
   b. en San Antonio

4. La excavación es...
   a. una oportunidad terrible.
   b. una oportunidad increíble.

5. Adriana es...
   a. organizada.
   b. desorganizada.

6. El viaje a Puebla...
   a. es muy largo.
   b. no es muy largo.

2 Situaciones. Role-play one of these situations with a classmate.

1. Adriana asks three persons whether they are Felipe's friends.
2. Felipe and Adriana talk about the excavation and their trip to Puebla.

3 Escritura. Write a brief description of Felipe and Adriana (4–6 sentences).

NOTA CULTURAL

Los héroes gemelos

The story of Yax Balam and Hun-Ahau, the Jaguar Twins and heroes of the Mayan mythology is told in the sacred book of the Mayans, the **Popol Vuh.** The twins were two very clever young Mayan ball players who liked to challenge others with their unusually good skills at the ball game. This game was a difficult one and would often cost players their lives. When the gods of the Mayan underworld, Xibalbá, realized that the twins seemed to be invincible, they decided to set up a trap to kill them and invited the boys to play a ball game with them. The Mayan Jaguar Twins accepted the challenge. Once in Xibalbá, they had to overcome incredible challenges and defeated the evil gods. After their victory in Xibalbá, the Jaguar Hero Twins became two bright stars in the sky.

SEGUNDO PASO

Vocabulario y lengua

DISCUSSING ACADEMIC SCHEDULES AND SUBJECTS

Una semana típica (*A typical week*)

Online Study Center

For additional practice
with this unit's vocabulary
and grammar, visit the
Caminos website at
http://college.hmco.com/
languages/spanish/
renjilian/caminos/3e/
student_home.html.
You can also review audio
flashcards, quiz yourself,
and explore related
Spanish-language sites.

In many Spanish-speaking countries, the calendar week begins on Monday. Some countries, however, use calendars that start with Sunday, as in the United States. In Spanish, the days of the week are masculine and are not capitalized.

el lunes	(*on*) *Monday*
los lunes	(*on*) *Mondays*

To talk about the days of the week, use the following models.

¿Qué día es hoy?	*What day is today?*
Hoy es martes.	*Today is Tuesday.*
¿Qué día es mañana?	*What day is tomorrow?*
Mañana es miércoles.	*Tomorrow is Wednesday.*

To talk about what someone studies and on which day(s), use the following models.

Adela **estudia** música los jueves.	*Adela studies music on Thursdays.*
Adela **no estudia** los domingos.	*Adela doesn't study on Sundays.*

Actividades

1 ¿Qué estudia? (*What does she study?*) Answer these questions according to Adela's schedule.

1. ¿Qué estudia los lunes?
2. ¿Estudia historia? ¿Cuándo?
3. ¿Qué estudia los jueves?
4. ¿Cuándo estudia química?
5. ¿Qué estudia los viernes?
6. ¿Qué estudia los martes?
7. ¿Estudia los sábados y los domingos?

2 El horario de Luis. (*Luis's schedule.*) Work with a partner to complete Luis's schedule with the information given.

1. Estudia música los martes y jueves.
2. Estudia historia los lunes.
3. Estudia español los jueves.
4. Estudia arqueología los viernes.
5. Estudia química los lunes, miércoles y viernes.
6. No estudia los sábados.

¿Qué fecha es hoy? (*What is today's date?*)

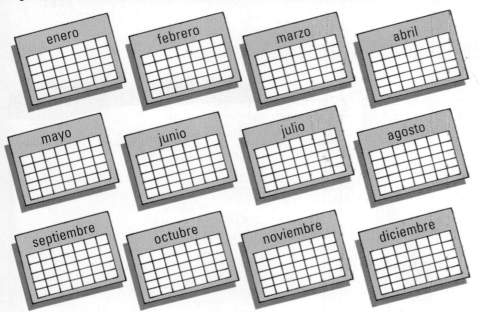

To talk about dates, use these models.

¿Qué fecha es hoy?	*What is today's date?*
¿Cuál es la fecha de hoy?	*What is today's date?*
Hoy es el veintitrés de septiembre.	*Today is September 23.*

As with the names of days, months are not capitalized in Spanish. In Latin America, the first day of the month is **el primero.**

Hoy es el **primero** de abril.	*Today is April first.*

For dates in Spanish, the day of the month always comes first: **9/12 = el nueve de diciembre.** This is different from the United States, where the the month precedes the day.

Actividades

1 ¿Qué fecha es? Say the following dates in Spanish.

1. December 9
2. October 15
3. July 4
4. April 19
5. January 1
6. March 13
7. May 31
8. February 22

2 Fechas importantes. Write the dates in Spanish for these occasions. Then practice them with a classmate.

► MODELO: Independence Day (USA)
el cuatro de julio *the fourth of July*

1. Valentine's Day
2. Thanksgiving Day this year
3. April Fool's Day
4. New Year's Eve
5. Your birthday
6. Your sister or brother's birthday
7. The first day of classes this term
8. The last day of classes this term

En la universidad (*At the university*)

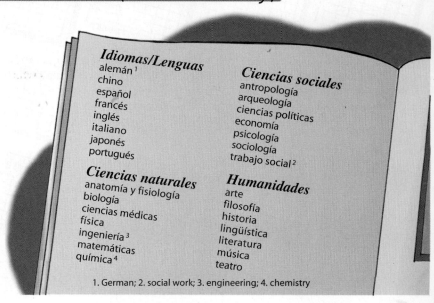

Idiomas/Lenguas
alemán [1]
chino
español
francés
inglés
italiano
japonés
portugués

Ciencias sociales
antropología
arqueología
ciencias políticas
economía
psicología
sociología
trabajo social [2]

Ciencias naturales
anatomía y fisiología
biología
ciencias médicas
física
ingeniería [3]
matemáticas
química [4]

Humanidades
arte
filosofía
historia
lingüística
literatura
música
teatro

1. German; 2. social work; 3. engineering; 4. chemistry

A false cognate (**cognado falso**), sometimes called **amigo falso,** is a word in Spanish that looks like a word in English but has a different meaning. Below are some examples you may encounter when talking about academic subjects.

▶ To ask what someone's major is, you say **¿Cuál es tu** *(your)* **especialización?** The word **mayor** means *older.*

▶ The faculty of a university is **el profesorado. La facultad** means *school,* as in **La facultad de humanidades,** *The School of Humanities.*

▶ An academic subject is **la materia. El sujeto** often refers to the grammatical subject of a sentence.

Actividades

1 Asociaciones. What subject areas do you associate with these words? Use your knowledge of cognates.

1. el átomo
2. el cadáver
3. el laboratorio
4. el oxígeno
5. la composición
6. las elecciones
7. la fórmula
8. la infección
9. los números
10. la psicosis
11. la sociedad
12. la trompeta

2 ¿Qué enseña? (*What does s/he teach?*) Work with a partner to determine in which academic department you would find the following people.

1. Sigmund Freud
2. Isaac Newton
3. Stephen King
4. Abraham Lincoln
5. Florence Nightingale
6. Jane Goodall
7. Aristotle
8. Malcolm X
9. Pablo Picasso
10. Carlos Santana

3 ¿Qué estudias? Ask three of your classmates to name a subject they are studying other than Spanish. Then, based on their answer, guess what other subject they might be studying. Write the subjects next to the **materia** categories below. Conduct your interview according to the model.

▶ MODELO: —¿Qué estudias?   —*What do you study?*
           —Estudio matemáticas.   —*I study mathematics.*
           —¿Estudias química?   —*Do you study chemistry?*
           —No, no estudio química,   —*No, I don't study chemistry,*
            estudio psicología.   *I study psychology*

	Estudiante 1	Estudiante 2	Estudiante 3
Materia 1	_____	_____	_____
Materia 2	_____	_____	_____

Subject pronouns

In Spanish, subject pronouns are used to clarify or emphasize a subject. In most cases they are optional because you can tell what the subject is by looking at the verb ending.

Subject pronouns					
	Singular		**Plural**		
1st person	**yo**	*I*	**nosotros / nosotras**	*we*	
2nd person	**tú**	*you (fam.)*	**vosotros / vosotras**	*you (Spain)*	
3rd person	**usted (Ud.)**	*you (formal)*	**ustedes (Uds.)**	*you*	
	él / ella	*he / she*	**ellos / ellas**	*they*	

Tú
Used when addressing familiar people in an informal, friendly situation. (Normally used with friends, family, and co-workers.)

Usted (Ud.)
Used when speaking in formal situations with unfamiliar people or when you need to show respect for someone (grandparents, colleagues, certain professionals).

Ustedes (Uds.)
Latin America distinguishes between formal and informal situations only in the singular form. This distinction does not exist when speaking to more than one person; therefore **ustedes** is the form used in the plural in both formal and informal situations.

Vosotros/as

Spain distinguishes between informal and formal forms in the plural. In an informal situation, **vosotros/as** is used. For formal situations, **ustedes** is used.

Nosotras, vosotras, ellas

Used only when referring to all-female groups.

The verb *ser* (*to be*)

Ser is one of the most common verbs in Spanish and has irregular conjugation forms.

ser *(to be)*						
	Singular			**Plural**		
1st person	yo	**soy**	*I am*	nosotros / nosotras	**somos**	*we are*
2nd person	tú	**eres**	*you are*	vosotros / vosotras	**sois**	*you are*
3rd person	usted él / ella	**es**	*you are* *he /she is*	ustedes ellos / ellas	**son**	*you are* *they are*

Ser has many uses. This list summarizes some of them. (Note that the first letter of each usage type spells POTIONS. This mnemonic device can help you remember the uses of the verb.)

   Ser is used to describe:

P eople	Arturo **es** inteligente.	*Arturo is intelligent.*
O ccupations	Ellos **son** estudiantes.	*They are students.*
T hings / Time*	La silla **es** negra.	*The chair is black.*
	Son las tres.	*It's three o'clock.*
I dentity	**Soy** Roberto.	*I am Roberto.*
O rigin	**Somos** de México.	*We are from Mexico.*
N ationality	Ellos **son** mexicanos.	*They are Mexican.*
S ubstance: What things are made of	El libro **es** de papel.	*The book is made of paper.*

*You will learn how to use **ser** to tell time on page 40.

When using **ser** to describe someone's occupation or nationality, the indefinite article is omitted unless an adjective follows the description.

Carmen es artista.	*Carmen is an artist.*
Carmen es cubanoamericana.	*Carmen is Cuban-American.*
Carmen es **una** artista cubanoamericana.	*Carmen is a Cuban-American artist.*
Carmen es **una** artista talentosa.	*Carmen is a talented artist.*

Remember to connect adjectives with the conjunction **y** (*and*) when describing someone or something with more than one adjective.

Enrique es alto **y** guapo.	*Enrique is tall and handsome.*

Before a word that starts with **i-** or **hi-, y** changes to **e.**

La profesora es simpática **e** inteligente.	*The professor is friendly and intelligent.*
Hay clases de inglés **e** historia.	*There are English and history classes.*

To place emphasis on an adjective, use **muy** + *adjective.*

El libro es **muy** interesante.	*The book is very interesting.*
Los estudiantes son **muy** inteligentes.	*The students are very intelligent.*

Negation

Simple negation is formed by adding **no** before the verb.

Nosotros **no** somos de México.	*We are not from Mexico.*
El libro **no** es amarillo.	*The book is not yellow.*

To answer a question negatively, start the sentence with **no,** in addition to adding **no** before the verb.

—¿La ventana es blanca?	—*Is the window white?*
—**No,** la ventana **no** es blanca.	—*No, the window is not white.*
—¿Eres de España?	—*Are you from Spain?*
—**No, no** soy de España.	—*No, I'm not from Spain.*

Actividades

1 ¿Quién eres? Work with a partner to complete the dialog with the correct forms of **ser.** Take turns answering the questions affirmatively or negatively. If answering negatively, do not forget to add **no** before the verb.

1. ¿Tú _____ estudiante de español? Sí / No, yo _____ estudiante de español.
2. ¿Tú _____ de los Estados Unidos? Sí / No, yo _____ de los Estados Unidos.
3. ¿El / La profesor/a _____ de México? Sí / No, él / ella _____ de México.
4. ¿La pared _____ azul? Sí / No, la pared _____ azul.
5. ¿Nosotros/as _____ amigos/as? Sí / No, nosotros/as _____ amigos/as.

2 Isabel. Complete Isabel's description of her classroom and life at school with the correct forms of **ser.**

Me llamo Isabel. Yo (1) __Soy__ estudiante de español. Mis compañeros de clase también (*also*) (2) __son__ estudiantes de español. La profesora (3) __es__ muy inteligente y simpática. ¡La clase de español (4) __es__ muy interesante! En la sala de clase hay mesas, sillas, computadoras y libros. Las computadoras (5) __son__ excelentes y modernas y las mesas (6) __son__ de Puerto Rico. En las mochilas de los estudiantes hay libros, calculadoras y papeles. Los libros (7) __son__ interesantes y las calculadoras (8) __son__ muy prácticas. Las actividades de deportes (*sports*) (9) __son__ muy divertidas (*fun*). Hay golf, volibol y básquetbol. Nosotros (10) __somos__ estudiantes muy afortunados.

3 ¿De dónde son? Working with a partner, state where these people are from and their nationalities. Be sure to review the vocabulary for nationalities on page 8.

▶ MODELO: Gabriela Sabatini
Gabriela Sabatini <u>es</u> de Buenos Aires. <u>Es argentina</u>.	*Gabriela Sabatini is from Buenos Aires. She's Argentinean.*

1. Juan Luis Guerra _____ de Santo Domingo. _____.
2. Cameron Díaz y su familia _____ de California. _____.

3. Arantxa Sánchez _____ de Barcelona. _____.
4. Rigoberta Menchú _____ de Chimel, Guatemala. _____.
5. Laura Esquivel _____ de México. _____.
6. Isabel Allende _____ de Santiago. _____.
7. Yo _____ de _____. _____.
8. Mi compañero/a de cuarto _____ de _____. _____.

USING ADJECTIVES

¿Cómo son? (*What are they like?*)

El diablo es malo.

Sara es trabajadora.

Pedro es amable.

El ángel es bueno.

Carlos es perezoso.

Raquel es tímida.

Rosa

David

alta   bajo

Luisa

Graciela

Daniel

rubia   moreno   pelirroja

Don Diego

Beatriz

joven   viejo, mayor

GATO   PERRO

gordo   delgado

Elvira   Antonio

fea   guapo

In some countries it is more polite to say **mayor** (*older*) or **grande** instead of **viejo/a** (*old*) to describe someone's age. Also **gordito/a** (*fat*) is used instead of **gordo/a** as a term of affection in some countries.

COSAS (THINGS)

 La computadora es nueva.

 La computadora es vieja.

 La mesa es grande.

 La mesa es pequeña.

 El coche es rápido.

 El coche es lento.

 El lápiz es largo.

 El lápiz es corto.

Más palabras y expresiones

Cognados

atractivo/a	fascinante	organizado/a	romántico/a
cómico/a	inteligente	pesimista	serio/a
excepcional	optimista	popular	tímido/a

Adjetivos

agradable	*pleasant*
amable	*friendly*
antipático/a	*unfriendly*
bueno/a	*good*
desagradable	*unpleasant*
difícil	*difficult*
envidioso/a	*envious*
fácil	*easy*
hermoso/a, bonito/a, lindo/a	*beautiful, pretty, lovely*
listo/a	*smart, clever*
malo/a	*bad*
perezoso/a, flojo/a	*lazy*
simpático/a	*nice, friendly*
trabajador/a	*hard-working*

Actividades

1 **¿Cómo son?** Working with a partner, ask and answer questions about the people or animals in the drawings on page 37. Follow the model.

▶ **MODELO:** Sara
—¿Cómo es Sara?   —*What is Sara like?*
— Sara es trabajadora.   — *Sara is hard-working.*

1. Graciela
2. el gato
3. Beatriz
4. el ángel
5. Don Diego
6. David
7. Luisa
8. Raquel
9. Elvira
10. Carlos
11. Antonio
12. el diablo
13. Rosa
14. Daniel
15. el perro

2 **Futuros arqueólogos.** Listen to the description of the main characters in *Caminos del jaguar,* and fill in the blanks with the missing words.

Adriana y Felipe son (**1**) _____ de arqueología en los Estados Unidos.
(**2**) _____ es morena. Ella es (**3**) _____, amable y atractiva. Felipe es
(**4**) _____. Es (**5**) _____, muy simpático y (**6**) _____ .

3 **La oficina.** Here is a list of items in Alberto's design office. Find the objects, state how many there are, and describe their appearance.

▶ **MODELO:** —¿Cuantos basureros   —*How many trash cans*
          hay en la oficina?   *are there in the office?*
          —Hay un basurero.   —*There is one trash can.*
          —¿Cómo es?   —*What does it look like?*
          —Es grande y anaranjado.   —*It's big and orange.*

radio
reloj
papel
ventana
basurero
teléfono
computadora
lámpara
carpeta
estante
lápiz
escritorio
cartel
silla
libro

4 **Personalidades.** Describe the following people. Include both physical and personality traits.

1. Shakira
2. Carlos Santana
3. Antonio Banderas
4. Andy García
5. Rosie Pérez
6. Christina Aguilera
7. Enrique Iglesias
8. Rafael Nadal
9. ¿...?

5 **Así es.** Write a brief description of one of your classmates on a piece of paper. Be sure to include details such as hair color, type of clothing, etc. Your instructor will collect these descriptions and hand them out at random for students to read. Try to guess each person being described.

TELLING TIME

¿Qué hora es? (*What time is it?*)

Time is expressed with the verb **ser**. Use **¿Qué hora es?** to ask what time it is. When giving the time, **es** is used only with times that begin with **una** (*one*); otherwise use **son**.

Son las once.	*It's eleven o'clock.*
Es la una.	*It's one o'clock.*

Son las dos de la tarde.

The exact time of day can be expressed by adding **de la mañana / tarde / noche.**

Son las cinco **de la mañana.**	*It's five A.M.* (*in the morning*)
Es la una **de la tarde.**	*It's one P.M.* (*in the afternoon*)
Son las ocho **de la noche.**	*It's eight P.M.* (*in the evening*)

Es la una y media de la mañana.

Son las cuatro y veinte de la tarde.

Time *after* the hour is expressed using **y** + *minutes* (or + **cuarto / media**).

Son las siete **y** veinte (de la noche).	*It's seven twenty* (*P.M.*).
Es la una **y cuarto.**	*It's quarter past one* (*one-fifteen*).
Son las seis **y media.**	*It's six-thirty.*

Son las once menos cuarto de la mañana.

Time *before* the hour is expressed using **menos** + *minutes* (or + **cuarto**).

Son las cinco **menos** veinte.	*It's twenty minutes to five.*
Es la una **menos cuarto.**	*It's a quarter to one.*

Es mediodía. **Es medianoche.**

To express noon and midnight you can say for either one

Son las doce.	*It's twelve o'clock.*

or use the expressions **mediodía** and **medianoche** as shown on the clocks.

To express "at" what time an event occurs, use **a + la/s** + *hour*.

—¿Es la clase **a las** dos de la tarde?   —*Is the class at two P.M.?*
—No, es **a la** una de la tarde.   —*No, it's at one P.M.*

General time periods are expressed using **por la mañana / tarde / noche.**

—¿Estudia Juan **por la mañana**?   —*Does Juan study in the morning?*
—No, Juan estudia **por la tarde** y   —*No, Juan studies in the afternoon and*
  por la noche.   *in the evening (at night).*

Actividades

1 **¿Qué hora es?** With a partner take turns telling the time on each clock below.

5:30

10:40

4:15

12:00

7:55

9:45

2 **La hora en el mundo.** You have friends all over the world and to keep in touch
with them, you need to know what time it is where they live. Use the clocks in
different time zones to figure out what time it is in each location for each time
indicated. Complete the chart and practice telling time with a partner.

Tokyo, Japón   Anchorage, AL   Los Ángeles, CA   Nueva York, NY   Madrid, España

1. _____   _____   _____   _____   2:30 A.M.
2. _____   3:00 P.M.   _____   _____   _____
3. _____   _____   _____   4:45 P.M.   _____
4. _____   _____   1:16 P.M.   _____   _____
5. 10:48 A.M. _____   _____   _____   _____

El destino llama

Actividades

Online Study Center

For additional practice with this episode, visit the *Caminos* website at http://college.hmco.com/languages/spanish/renjilian/caminos/3e/student_home.html.

1 Comprensión. Based on this episode of *Caminos del jaguar,* choose the logical response.

1. Adriana reserva *(reserves)* dos boletos para...
   a. San Antonio.   b. (Puebla.)

2. El viaje es...
   a. el lunes.   b. (el viernes.)

3. La arqueología es...
   a. (muy seria.)   b. muy fácil.

4. Adriana opina que Felipe es...
   a. (inteligente.)   b. desagradable.

5. Felipe opina que Adriana es...
   a. (trabajadora.)   b. cubana.

6. La familia de Felipe es...
   a. de Miami.   b. (de Cuba.)

7. Arturo opina que Felipe es...
   a. fascinante.   b. romántico.

8. Nayeli viaja *(travels)* en...
   a. (taxi.)   b. autobús.

2 Situaciones. With a classmate, dramatize one of the situations below.

1. Adriana and Felipe talk about Nayeli's book.
2. Felipe and Arturo talk about Adriana and the excavation.
3. Adriana and Patricia talk about Felipe and the excavation.

3 Escritura. Describe one of the places listed below (4–6 sentences).

1. El apartamento de Felipe
2. El apartamento de Adriana
3. La estación de autobuses

NOTA CULTURAL

Los mayas de México

The Mayan civilization is one of the great civilizations of Central America. Long before the Spaniards arrived in the region, they lived in what is today southern Mexico, Guatemala, western Honduras, El Salvador, and northern Belize. Their descendents comprise a large ethnic group that still speaks the ancient Mayan language and keeps many of the Mayan traditions alive. The Mayans had advanced knowledge of astronomy and mathematics, and developed their own hieroglyphical writing, a numerical system, and an elaborate calendar. They were also skilled architects and built pyramids and palaces in stone, many of which we can admire today in Tikal, Copán, and Palenque. As artists, they created beautiful pottery and textiles and developed important trade routes with several other ethnic groups in Central America. Their mythology is depicted in old graphic books, or **códices,** representing the beliefs of the Mayan religion and views of the world and the afterlife.

Lectura

Online Study Center

For further reading practice online, visit the *Caminos* website at http://college.hmco.com/languages/spanish/renjilian/caminos/3e/student_home.html.

PRELECTURA

In the reading that follows, you will practice recognizing *cognates*, a valuable skill that will help you learn Spanish. Cognates, or **cognados,** are words that have similar spellings and meanings in two languages. The strategies that follow will help you identify cognates in a text.

Reading Strategy

Recognizing Cognates

Knowing cognates can help you increase your Spanish vocabulary tremendously. The following is a list of adjectives that can be used to describe people, places, and things. Listen to your instructor and pronounce these words to hear how they compare to similar words in English. What are the comparable endings for these groups of words in English?

arrogante	importante	pesimista
egoísta	increíble	profesional
elegante	interesante	realista
emocional	internacional	sentimental
evidente	nacional	terrible
excelente	natural	tradicional
final	optimista	transparente
horrible	original	tropical
idealista	persistente	virtual

Actividades

1 **¿Qué quiere decir?** What do the words in the cognates list mean?

2 **Categorías.** The cognates you've learned fall into four categories according to their endings. List them in the following chart. The first one is done for you.

-nte	-ista	-al	-ible
arrogante	_____	_____	_____
_____	_____	_____	_____
_____	_____	_____	_____

Reading Strategy

Identifying Prefixes

By adding prefixes to some cognates you can expand your Spanish vocabulary even further. The prefix **in-** means "not," and is very common in both English and Spanish. Note that in Spanish **in-** is spelled **im-** before **b** and **p.**

3 Opuestos.
With a partner, take turns saying aloud the opposites of the given words.

► MODELO: conveniente   *inconveniente*
            perfecto   *imperfecto*

in-	im-
dependiente	probable
estable	personal
flexible	posible
formal	paciente
tolerante	popular

4 ¿Positivo o negativo?
From the cognates you've learned, which adjectives have positive meanings? Which are negative? Which can be both? Work in pairs and write down the adjectives that fit into each of these categories.

Positivo	Negativo	Positivo y negativo

Now, describe yourself to a classmate, using one positive and one negative characteristic. Begin with **Soy...** *(I am . . .).*

5 Persona a persona.
Working in pairs, ask each other these questions that include cognates.

1. ¿De dónde eres? ¿Y tu familia?
2. Y tu compañero/a de cuarto, ¿de dónde es?
3. ¿Es enorme tu universidad?
4. En tu opinion, ¿qué especialización es difícil? ¿Cuál es interesante?
5. ¿Qué día es tu favorito en la universidad?
6. ¿Qué materias son fáciles, en tu opinión?

6 Personalización.
Complete each sentence below with the most appropriate cognate.

personal   elegante   popular
favorita   inteligente   optimistas

1. Las relaciones internacionales es una especialización _____.
2. Soy una estudiante excelente. Soy _____.
3. Me llamo Jennifer López y soy _____.
4. Mis amigos y yo somos muy _____.
5. El problema es _____ no académico.
6. ¿Es el arte mexicano o colombiano tu materia _____?

Estudiantes talentosos

Mi nombre es Rosa Fernández y soy de la República Dominicana. Mis idiomas son el inglés y el español. Soy estudiante universitaria en la ciudad de Nueva York, con una especialización en la historia y cultura de Latinoamérica. Soy poeta bilingüe y actriz. Las telenovelas[1] son mis programas preferidos en la televisión. También soy bailarina[2] de danzas afrocaribeñas. El autobús es mi transporte público favorito. En el futuro mi plan es ser profesora de historia y cultura latinoamericanas. Soy tradicional y realista.

Me llamo Cuahtémoc Villagrán. Soy guatemalteco, de la ciudad de Chichicastenango. Soy estudiante de doctorado[3] de psicología clínica. Tengo[4] clase los lunes, miércoles y viernes. Los martes y jueves, soy investigador[5] en un laboratorio de biología. Mi intención es ser psicólogo en una clínica internacional, en la capital, para las personas con serios problemas emocionales. Soy una persona flexible y optimista. Los sábados, el fútbol es una parte importante de mi vida, que es simplemente fantástica.

¡Hola! Me llamo Elena Vera y soy una española alta y rubia. Mi apartamento en Madrid, que es una ciudad enorme con millones de personas, es espectacular y muy decorado. Mi motocicleta es una máquina rápida y conveniente para la ciudad. Soy creativa, especialmente en componer[6] música original contemporánea. Los viernes y sábados, soy guitarrista en las discotecas, con un grupo de amigos universitarios. La antropología es mi especialización en la Universidad Complutense de Madrid. En el futuro, mi idea es ser antropóloga internacional en Asia, África y las Américas. Soy una persona natural, independiente y sentimental.

[1]soap operas; [2]dancer; [3]Ph.D.; [4]I have; [5]researcher; [6]in composing.

POSTLECTURA

1 Cognados en acción. Re-read the profiles of the three talented university students. Make a list of the cognates that you recognize. In class, compare your list with a partner.

2 Estudiantes fascinantes. Answer the following questions with a classmate.

1. ¿De dónde es Rosa? ¿Cuál es su especialización? ¿En dónde?
2. ¿De dónde es Cuahtémoc? ¿En qué laboratorio es investigador?
3. ¿De dónde es Elena? ¿Qué transporte es su preferencia?
4. Es la intención de Cuahtémoc de ser psicólogo en el futuro. ¿En dónde? ¿Quiénes van a ser (will be) sus pacientes?
5. ¿Cuáles son las intenciones de Elena y Rosa en el futuro?
6. En tu opinion, ¿quién de los tres estudiantes es muy interesante? ¿Por qué?

3 Personalidades famosas. Using as many cognates as possible, write a description in Spanish of three famous people. Read your descriptions and have your classmates guess who is being described. Work in groups of four.

Escritura

When beginning to write in a new language, it is a good idea to use strategies that help you organize your thoughts. Although you might be tempted to write in English and then translate your writing into Spanish, you can become a better writer if you apply some of the suggestions provided in this textbook. At the end of each segment in your Student Activities Manual, you will also practice these strategies in a section called *Escritura*.

Online Study Center

For further writing practice online, visit the *Caminos* website at http://college.hmco.com/languages/spanish/renjilian/caminos/3e/student_home.html.

Writing Strategy

Creating a Cluster Diagram

A cluster diagram is a commonly used visual organizer. It allows you to see the connection between main topics and details and helps you find the words that you need to write in Spanish.

Workshop

1. Choose your topic and write it in the center of a piece of paper. Circle it.
2. Focus on the main ideas for your topic. Write them down, circle them, and connect them to your topic.
3. Think about these main ideas and write any related words around them until you have a diagram that looks like this one.

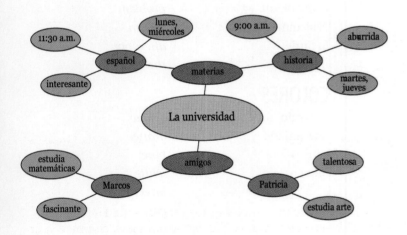

Strategy in Action

For additional practice with the strategy of creating a cluster diagram, turn to the *Escritura* section of your Student Activities Manual.

La vida universitaria. You are homesick and decide to send your best friend a letter describing your university. Include a description of your classes and new friends. Using the cluster diagram above as a guide, create your own diagram to organize your thoughts before writing the letter.

Resumen de vocabulario

PRIMER PASO

¿QUÉ HAY EN EL CUARTO?

Sustantivos (Nouns)

el basurero	garbage can
el bolígrafo	pen
el borrador	blackboard eraser
la calculadora	calculator
el calendario	calendar
la cama	bed
la carpeta	folder
el cartel	poster
el/la computador/a	computer
el cuaderno	notebook
el dormitorio	bedroom
el escritorio	desk
el estante	bookshelf
la impresora	printer
la lámpara	lamp
el lápiz	pencil
el libro	book
la llave	key
el mapa	map
la mesa	table
la mochila	backpack
la oficina	office
el papel	paper
la pared	wall
la pizarra	blackboard
la pluma	pen
la puerta	door
el pupitre	writing desk
el/la radio	radio
el reloj	watch, clock
la residencia	dormitory
la rosa	rose
la sala de clase	classroom
la silla	chair
el teléfono	telephone
la televisión	television
la tiza	a piece of chalk
la universidad	university
la ventana	window

OTRAS EXPRESIONES

de	of, from
en	in, on, at
(no) hay	there is (not); there are (not)
y	and

USING ARTICLES AND NOUNS

Sustantivos

el/la artista	artist
la composición	composition
el hombre	man
la lección	lesson
la madre	mother
la mitad	half
la mujer	woman
la noche	night
el padre	father
la pintura	painting
el problema	problem
el sistema	system
la tarde	afternoon
el tema	theme

COLORES

amarillo	yellow
anaranjado	orange
azul	blue
blanco	white
café	brown
gris	grey
morado	purple
negro	black
rojo	red
rosado	pink
verde	green

LOS NÚMEROS DEL 0 AL 199

0	cero	20	veinte
1	uno	21	veintiuno
2	dos	22	veintidós
3	tres	23	veintitrés
4	cuatro	24	veinticuatro
5	cinco	25	veinticinco
6	seis	26	veintiséis
7	siete	27	veintisiete
8	ocho	28	veintiocho
9	nueve	29	veintinueve
10	diez	30	treinta
11	once	40	cuarenta
12	doce	50	cincuenta
13	trece	60	sesenta
14	catorce	70	setenta
15	quince	80	ochenta
16	dieciséis	90	noventa
17	diecisiete	100	cien
18	dieciocho	101	ciento uno
19	diecinueve	199	ciento noventa y nueve

SEGUNDO PASO

Los días de la semana

el lunes	*Monday*
el martes	*Tuesday*
el miércoles	*Wednesday*
el jueves	*Thursday*
el viernes	*Friday*
el sábado	*Saturday*
el domingo	*Sunday*

Otras expresiones

el día	*day*
estudia	*he / she studies / you (formal) study*
la fecha	*date*
el horario	*schedule*
hoy	*today*
mañana	*tomorrow*
el primero	*first*

Los meses del año

enero	*January*
febrero	*February*
marzo	*March*
abril	*April*
mayo	*May*
junio	*June*
julio	*July*
agosto	*August*
septiembre	*September*
octubre	*October*
noviembre	*November*
diciembre	*December*

EN LA UNIVERSIDAD
Sustantivos

el alemán	*German*
la anatomía	*anatomy*
la antropología	*anthropology*
la arqueología	*archaeology*
el arte	*art*
la biología	*biology*
el chino	*Chinese*
las ciencias médicas	*medical sciences*
las ciencias naturales	*natural sciences*
las ciencias políticas	*political science*
las ciencias sociales	*social sciences*
la economía	*economics*
el español	*Spanish*
la especialización	*major*
la facultad	*school (as in School of Humanities)*
la filosofía	*philosophy*
la física	*physics*
la fisiología	*physiology*
el francés	*French*
la historia	*history*
las humanidades	*humanities*
el idioma	*language*
la ingeniería	*engineering*
el inglés	*English*
el italiano	*Italian*
el japonés	*Japanese*
la lingüística	*linguistics*
la literatura	*literature*
las matemáticas	*mathematics*
la materia	*subject (in school)*
la música	*music*
el portugués	*Portuguese*
el profesorado	*faculty*
la psicología	*psychology*
la química	*chemistry*
la sociología	*sociology*
el sujeto	*subject (part of speech)*
el teatro	*theater*
el trabajo social	*social work*

Otras expresiones

estudias	*you study*
estudio	*I study*

DESCRIBING PEOPLE AND THINGS
Adjetivos

agradable	*pleasant*
alto/a	*tall*
amable	*friendly*
antipático/a	*unfriendly*
atractivo/a	*attractive*
bajo/a	*short (height)*
bonito/a	*pretty*
bueno/a	*good*
cómico/a	*funny, comical*
corto/a	*short (length)*
delgado/a	*thin*
desagradable	*unpleasant*
difícil	*difficult*
envidioso/a	*envious*
excepcional	*exceptional*
fácil	*easy*
fascinante	*fascinating*
feo/a	*ugly*
flojo/a	*lazy*
gordo/a	*fat*
grande	*big, large*
guapo/a	*handsome, good-looking*
hermoso/a	*beautiful*
inteligente	*intelligent*
joven	*young*
largo/a	*long*
lento/a	*slow*
lindo/a	*lovely*
listo/a	*smart, clever*
malo/a	*bad*
mayor	*older*
moreno/a	*dark-haired*
nuevo/a	*new*
optimista	*optimistic*
organizado/a	*organized*
pelirrojo/a	*redhead*
pequeño/a	*small*

perezoso/a	lazy
pesimista	pessimistic
popular	popular
rápido/a	fast
romántico/a	romantic
rubio/a	blonde
serio/a	serious
simpático/a	nice, friendly
tímido/a	shy / timid
trabajador/a	hard-working
viejo/a	old

Subject pronouns

yo	I
tú	you (fam.)
usted (Ud.)	you (formal)
él / ella	he / she
nosotros / nosotras	we
vosotros / vosotras	you (Spain)
ustedes (Uds.)	you
ellos / ellas	they

Otras expresiones

| muy | very |

Verbo

| ser | to be |

LA HORA
Sustantivos

cuarto	quarter (ex: It's quarter past two.)
el mediodía	noon
media	half (thirty); (ex: It's two thirty.)
la medianoche	midnight

Otras expresiones

de la mañana / tarde / noche	in the morning / afternoon / evening (for specific time periods)
menos	minus
por la mañana / tarde / noche	in the morning / afternoon / night (for general time periods)
¿Qué hora es?	What time is it?

En la ciudad

VOCABULARIO Y LENGUA

- ► Describing an apartment
- ► Expressing possession
- ► Identifying furnishings and household chores
- ► Describing actions in the present: Regular verbs

- ► Indicating likes and dislikes
- ► Expressing location and emotion with *estar*
- ► Talking about places in a city
- ► Describing present actions in progress

CAMINOS DEL JAGUAR

- ► Malas noticias
- ► Jaguares gemelos

LECTURA

- ► Bienvenidos a Puebla: Ciudad de ángeles

NOTAS CULTURALES

- ► La universidad de las Américas
- ► Los códices mayas

ESTRATEGIAS

- ► **Reading:** Asking questions
- ► **Writing:** Brainstorming ideas

Joan Miró, *Prades, the Village*

Preguntas del tema

► ¿Es grande o pequeña tu casa? ¿Cuántos cuartos hay en la casa?

► ¿Hay restaurantes internacionales en tu ciudad?

► ¿Hay un museo famoso?

► ¿Hay un parque central?

Vocabulario y lengua

DESCRIBING AN APARTMENT

Un apartamento en la Colonia Villareal[1]

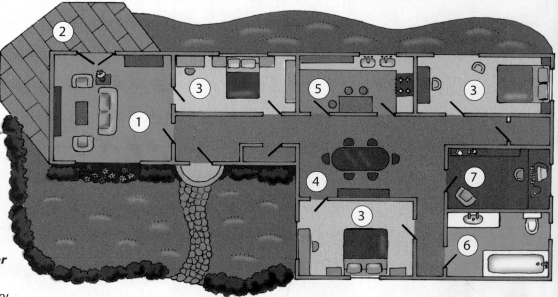

Online Study Center

For additional practice with the unit's vocabulary and grammar, visit the *Caminos* website at http://college.hmco.com/languages/spanish/renjilian/caminos/3e/student_home.html. You can also review audio flashcards, quiz yourself, and explore related Spanish-language sites.

1. la sala
2. la terraza
3. el dormitorio
4. el comedor
5. la cocina
6. el (cuarto de) baño
7. la oficina

Más palabras y expresiones

Cognados

el balcón	completo/a	moderno/a
el clóset	el garaje	privado/a

---

[1]In Mexico, a **colonia** is similar to a town district.

Sustantivos

el alquiler, la renta	*rent*
la bañera, la tina	*bathtub*
la casa	*house*
la ducha	*shower*
el/la dueño/a	*owner*
el piso	*floor; apartment (Spain)*
el/la inquilino/a	*tenant*
el jardín	*garden, yard*
la piscina, la alberca	*swimming pool*

Otras expresiones

amplio/a	*spacious*
barato/a	*inexpensive*
con	*with*
caro/a	*expensive*
pequeño/a	*small*
pero	*but*

Actividades

1 El apartamento ideal. You have found the perfect apartment. Work with a partner to discuss the floor plan. Follow the model.

▶ MODELO:
—¿Cuántos dormitorios hay?   —*How many bedrooms are there?*
—Hay dos dormitorios.   —*There are two bedrooms.*
—¿Hay una piscina?   —*Is there a swimming pool?*
—No, pero hay un jardín.   —*No, but there is a garden.*

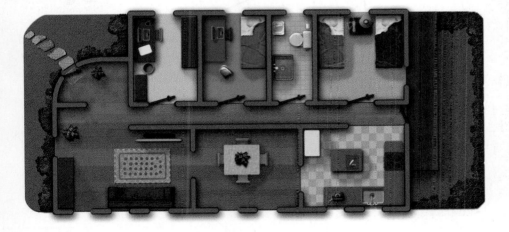

2 ¿Qué cuarto es? Think of one room in the apartment shown in *Actividad 1*. Have a partner guess which room you've chosen, then switch roles.

> MODELO: —¿Hay una computadora?
> —Sí, hay una computadora.
> —¿Es el dormitorio pequeño?
> —Sí, es el dormitorio pequeño.

3 Necesito compañero/a. You decide that it would be more economical to look for an apartment with a roommate. Write down the five most important things that you need in an apartment. Then find a classmate whose list matches yours with at least 3 of the items. Once you have found a match, present your roommate to the class and describe what you have in common.

EXPRESSING POSSESSION

¡El auto de Álvaro es grande, moderno y bonito!

Sí, pero su casa es pequeña y vieja.

La casa de María y Benito es grande, moderna y bonita, pero mi auto es fantástico.

¡Y nuestra casa es muy elegante!

¡Y tu perro es maravilloso también!

There are many ways to express possession. Look at the conversations above and find these expressions in Spanish.

Álvaro's car	María and Benito's house
his house	my car
our house	your dog

In English the words *my, your, his, her, our,* and *their* are called possessive adjectives.

Possessive Adjectives

English	Singular	Plural
my	mi	mis
your (fam., sing.)	tu	tus
your (formal, sing.), his, her, its	su	sus
our	nuestro, nuestra	nuestros, nuestras
your (fam. plural, Spain)	vuestro, vuestra	vuestros, vuestras
your (formal, plural), their	su	sus

Your (formal singular), *his*, *her*, *its*, *your* (plural), and *their* all use the same possessive adjective in the singular, **su,** and in the plural, **sus.**

1. In Spanish, a possessive adjective must agree in number (singular/plural) with the noun it modifies.

mi auto	*my car*	su perro	*(his, her, their, your) dog*
tus autos	*your cars*	sus perros	*(his, her, their, your) dogs*

2. In addition to agreeing in number, **nuestro/a** and **vuestro/a** also agree in gender.

nuestro apartamento	*our apartment*	nuestra casa	*our house*
nuestros apartamentos	*our apartments*	nuestras casas	*our houses*

3. The preposition **de** is also used to express possession before names or pronouns.

El auto **de Álvaro** es grande.   —*Álvaro's car (the car of Álvaro) is big.*

¡El perro **de él** es maravilloso también!   —*His dog is marvelous too!*

When the preposition **de** precedes the article **el,** the two words contract to form **del.** There is no contraction with the pronoun **él.**

—El perro es **del** chico, ¿verdad?   —*The dog is the boy´s, isn´t it?*
—Sí, el perro es **de él.**   —*Yes, its his.*

4. Use **de quién** to ask who owns something. (Note that the verb **ser** agrees with the item possessed, not with **quién.**) When asking about ownership of more than one thing, and you suspect that there is also more than one owner, you may use **de quiénes.**

—**¿De quién es** la casa grande?   —*Whose large house is it?*
—Es de Pablo.   —*It belongs to Pablo. (singular)*
—Es de María y Benito.   —*It belongs to María and Benito. (plural)*
—**¿De quiénes son** las plumas?   —*Whose pens are they?*
—Son de los estudiantes.   —*They belong to the students. (plural)*

Actividades

1 **Práctica.** Replace the English word in parentheses with the appropriate Spanish possessive adjective. Then create a sentence with the phrase.

► MODELO: mochila *(my)*
          Mi mochila es verde y negra.

1. computadoras *(his)*
2. auto *(our)*
3. ducha *(their)*
4. compañero/a de cuarto *(my)*
5. jardín *(our)*
6. apartamento *(her)*
7. balcón *(your, familiar)*
8. clases *(our)*
9. oficina *(their)*
10. dormitorio *(your, formal)*

2 Posesión. Create sentences using **ser** and the correct possessive adjective.

▶ MODELO: el libro / de Paco
Es su libro.

1. la clase / de nosotros
2. las llaves / de Uds.
3. la televisión / de Rosalita
4. el apartamento / de los Gómez
5. el estéreo / de ellos
6. los cuadernos / de la profesora
7. el teléfono / de papá
8. la computadora / de ella

3 Preguntas. Answer the questions. Work with a partner.

▶ MODELO: —¿De quién es la televisión? (la Sra. Pérez)
—*La televisión es de la Sra. Pérez.*

1. ¿De quién es el auto? (nosotros)
2. ¿De quién es el estéreo? (mi compañero/a de cuarto)
3. ¿De quiénes son las impresoras? (él y ella)
4. ¿De quién es el teléfono celular? (los señores Vera)
5. ¿De quién son los papeles? (la estudiante de español)
6. ¿De quiénes son las mochilas? (ellos)

4 ¿De quién es? Ask and answer who owns each of the items listed in the chart below.

▶ MODELO: —¿De quién es la televisión?
—*La televisión es de Alicia.*

Alicia	Roberto	Mis amigos	Ella	Nosotros	Ellos
televisión	auto	estéreo	impresoras	papeles	teléfonos
sillas casa	llaves	llaves	calculadora	mesita	mochilas

5 ¿Qué hay aquí? Make a list of six things in the classroom or at home. Then take turns asking a partner who owns them.

▶ MODELO: —*En la clase hay muchos cuadernos.*
—*¿De quiénes son?*
—*Son de los estudiantes.*

Los muebles y quehaceres de la casa (*Furniture and household chores*)

Los muebles

1. el espejo
2. la cómoda
3. el ropero,
   el armario
4. la alfombra
5. el sillón
6. la mesita
   de noche
7. el lavabo,
   el lavamanos
8. el/la secador/a
   de pelo
9. la escoba
10. el inodoro
11. las escaleras
12. la mesita
13. el sofá
14. la aspiradora
15. el/la refrigerador/a
16. la estufa

Los quehaceres
(*Household chores*)

17. aspirar, pasar
    la aspiradora
    (por la alfombra)
18. barrer (el piso)
19. arreglar (la cama)
20. lavar (los platos)
21. sacar (la basura)
22. sacudir (los muebles),
    sacar el polvo de
    (los muebles) (*Spain*)

Otros quehaceres

cocinar	*to cook*
limpiar / ordenar (el cuarto)	*to clean / tidy (the room)*
planchar (la ropa)	*to iron (clothes)*
secar (los platos, la ropa)	*to dry (the dishes, clothes)*

Actividades

🎧 **1** **El apartamento de Elena** Make a diagram of Elena's apartment. Begin by drawing a large rectangle; then add the following rooms, labeled in Spanish: bedroom, living room, bathroom, and kitchen and dining room. Then, as she describes the apartment, draw and label all of the items found in each room.

👥 **2** **¿Recuerdas?** Work with a partner to review the names of the rooms and furniture that appear in the drawing of the house on page 59. Take turns pointing to items and naming each one. Try to use as many vocabulary terms from *Unidad 1* as you can.

3 **Los quehaceres.** Match the drawings with the chores.

1. _____ planchar la ropa
2. _____ ordenar el cuarto
3. _____ aspirar la alfombra
4. _____ barrer el piso
5. _____ sacudir los muebles

6. _____ lavar los platos
7. _____ cocinar
8. _____ secar los platos
9. _____ hacer la cama
10. _____ sacar la basura

a.

b.

c.

d.

e.

f.

g.

h.

i.

j.

4 **El apartamento perfecto.** You are a real estate agent and have some
furnished apartments you need to rent. Which apartment would you suggest for
each the following clients? Work in groups.

Clientes	Apartamentos
1. **La familia Rodríguez:** 2 adultos, 3 hijos (*children*) muy activos, 2 autos.	**Apartamento a:** Un dormitorio amplio, cocina con comedor, balcón, sala, jardin y garaje.
2. **La familia Iglesias:** 2 adultos, 1 auto, 1 perro *(dog)*.	**Apartamento b:** Un jardín grande, un dormitorio grande y un dormitorio pequeño, cocina amplia con comedor, jardín y balcón.
3. **El Sr. Roberts:** 1 adulto muy activo, 2 perros, 1 auto.	**Apartamento c:** 3–4 dormitorios grandes, 2 baños, cocina amplia, comedor y garaje.
4. **La familia Castillo:** 1 adulto, 1 hijo pequeño.	**Apartamento d:** Un dormitorio amplio, una oficina grande, garaje, jardín y piscina.

5 **Soy creativo/a.** Draw one of the apartments above complete with furnishings
labeled in Spanish. Share your apartment design with a classmate.

DESCRIBING ACTIONS IN THE PRESENT: REGULAR VERBS

Present indicative of regular *-ar, -er,* and *-ir* verbs

Él canta.   Ellos corren.

Ella sube la escalera.

A verb is made up of two parts: the *stem* and the *ending*. The stem defines the
word's meaning. The ending indicates the subject and tense.

estudiar *(to study)*		
estudi stem	**o** ending (1st person, singular = I)	*I study*
estudi stem	**an** ending (3rd person, plural = they, you)	*they, you (plural) study*

Spanish verbs are categorized by their infinitive form (*to sing, to run, to climb,* etc.).
There are three main categories: infinitives ending in **-ar (cantar), -er (correr),** or **-ir
(subir).**

Regular verbs are conjugated by replacing the **-ar, -er,** or **-ir** infinitive ending with
an ending that reflects both tense and person. The present indicative tense of regular verbs is formed as follows.

Present Indicative Tense of Regular Verbs

		-ar verbs		-er verbs		-ir verbs	
		cantar	*to sing*	**corr**er	*to run*	**sub**ir	*to climb*
Singular							
1st	yo	cant**o**	*I sing*	corr**o**	*I run*	sub**o**	*I climb*
2nd	tú	cant**as**	*you sing*	corr**es**	*you run*	sub**es**	*you climb*
3rd	usted	cant**a**	*you sing*	corr**e**	*you run*	sub**e**	*you climb*
	él / ella		*he / she sings*		*he / she runs*		*he / she climbs*
Plural							
1st	nosotros/ nosotras	cant**amos**	*we sing*	corr**emos**	*we run*	sub**imos**	*we climb*
2nd	vosotros/ vosotras	cant**áis**	*you sing*	corr**éis**	*you run*	sub**ís**	*you climb*
3rd	ustedes ellos / ellas	cant**an**	*you sing* *they sing*	corr**en**	*you run* *they run*	sub**en**	*you climb* *they climb*

The present indicative tense describes actions that happen in the present.

Yo **estudio** arqueología.	*I study / am studying archaeology.*
Celina **habla** inglés.	*Celina speaks / is speaking English.*
Nosotros **bebemos** leche.	*We drink / are drinking milk.*

Common Regular Verbs

-*ar* verbs

acabar	*to finish*	hablar	*to speak*	pasar	*to happen; pass*
acabar de + (infinitive)	*to have just (done something)*	investigar	*to research*	practicar	*to practice*
alquilar	*to rent*	lavar	*to wash*	preguntar	*to ask*
andar	*to walk, move*	llamar	*to call*	tomar	*to take*
bailar	*to dance*	llegar	*to arrive*	trabajar	*to work*
buscar	*to look for*	llevar	*to bring*	terminar	*to finish*
caminar	*to walk*	mandar	*to send*	usar	*to use*
comprar	*to buy*	mirar	*to look at*	viajar	*to travel*
desear	*to wish for*	necesitar	*to need*	visitar	*to visit*
escuchar	*to listen*				

-*er* verbs

aprender	*to learn*
beber	*to drink*
comer	*to eat*
comprender	*to understand*
creer	*to believe*
leer	*to read*
responder	*to answer*

-*ir* verbs

abrir	*to open*
compartir	*to share*
decidir	*to decide*
describir	*to describe*
escribir	*to write*
recibir	*to receive*
vivir	*to live*

To express actions that have just happened, use **acabar de** + infinitive.

¿**Acabas de** llegar?	*Have you just arrived?*
Sí, **acabo de** llegar.	*Yes, I have just arrived.*

Actividades

1 Actividades estudiantiles.
Complete the following activities using the correct present indicative tense form of the verb in parentheses.

1. Yo _____ (comprar) una mochila.
2. Elena _____ (hablar) tres idiomas.
3. Juan y Pepe _____ (trabajar) en la oficina.
4. Isabel _____ (viajar) a México.
5. Carmen y yo _____ (estudiar) arqueología.
6. Nosotros _____ (comer) en el comedor.
7. Alicia _____ (vivir) en una casa grande.
8. Yo _____ (abrir) las ventanas.
9. Rosita _____ (alquilar) un apartamento moderno.

2 La vida en la universidad.
Paloma is on the phone telling her sister about a few of her academic activities for this week. What does she say? Imagine that you are Paloma and create sentences from the phrases below using the **yo** form (1st person singular).

1. estudiar para un examen
2. escribir una composición en inglés
3. visitar el museo de arte
4. investigar en el laboratorio de química
5. mirar un video de antropología
6. practicar el español

3 Preguntas personales.
In pairs, ask each other the following questions. Then share three interesting pieces of information that you have learned about each other with another pair.

1. ¿Estudias español?
2. ¿Escribes cartas o correo electrónico (*e-mail*)?
3. ¿Lees libros?
4. ¿Hablas mucho por teléfono?
5. ¿Necesitas dinero (*money*)?
6. ¿Usas bolígrafo? ¿lápiz?
7. ¿Miras televisión?
8. ¿Vives en una residencia, un apartamento o una casa?

4 Actividades recientes.
With a partner, pretend that you are talking with your roommate about the activities that you and your friends have just finished. Use **acabar de** + infinitive to describe the activities.

▶ MODELO: Enrique (comer) sopa.
Enrique acaba de comer sopa.

1. Patricio (escuchar) música
2. Paco y Graciela (comprar) pizza
3. Elvira (escribir) una carta
4. Las chicas (mirar) un video
5. Rodrigo y yo (lavar) el auto
6. Mario (recibir) un cheque
7. Yo (practicar) deportes

5 Querido/a amigo/a.
Write a postcard to a friend describing your dormitory, apartment or house and what you do there. Use as many different verbs as possible.

Malas noticias

Oficina de Nayeli, Universidad de las Américas.

Mmmm...

Nayeli no está en la oficina.

¡Es muy extraño!

Yo también busco a Nayeli. Soy amigo de ella. Me llamo Armando de Landa Chávez.

Mucho gusto. Me llamo Felipe Luna Velilla.

Y yo me llamo Adriana Reyes Tepole.

¿Por qué buscan a Nayeli? ¿Hay problemas?

Somos estudiantes de la profesora Nayeli.

Yo soy amigo de Nayeli y... hay malas noticias...

¡No, es un error!

¿Arqueóloga o criminal? ¡No es posible! ¡Vamos a la casa de Nayeli ahora!

Muchas gracias, Sr. de Landa. Usted es muy amable.

Mi coche está aquí. ¡Vamos!

En la casa de Nayeli.

¿Dónde está Nayeli?

Nayeli es la mujer más honesta que existe.

Esperanza, ¿dónde está Nayeli?

No sé. ¿Desean café?

Esperanza tiene información importante.

Sí, sí, pero es necesario escuchar a Esperanza.

¿Qué es?

La nota no es para usted.

¡Ay, caramba! ¡Qué mala suerte!

Nayeli empaca el jaguar auténtico en su bolsa.

Nayeli toma un avi[ón] en el aeropu[erto]. ¡Nayeli es nu[eva] criminal[?] ¿Dónde es[tá?]

Ciudad de México. Policía mexicana.

Actividades

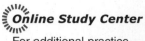

Online Study Center

For additional practice with this episode, visit the *Caminos* website at http://college.hmco.com/languages/spanish/renjilian/caminos/3e/student_home.html.

1 Comprensión. Based on this episode of *Caminos del jaguar*, choose the logical response.

1. Adriana y Felipe buscan a...
   a. Nayeli.
   b. Armando.

2. Hay una nota en...
   a. la oficina de Nayeli.
   b. la oficina de Armando.

3. Armando es amigo de...
   a. Adriana y Felipe.
   b. Nayeli.

4. La nota en la puerta es...
   a. para Armando.
   b. para Adriana y Felipe.

5. Esperanza trabaja en...
   a. la casa de Nayeli.
   b. la oficina de Nayeli.

6. La policía cree que...
   a. Nayeli es inocente.
   b. Nayeli no es inocente.

2 Situaciones. Role-play one of the following situations.

1. Armando, Felipe and Adriana introduce themselves to each other.
2. The detectives discuss what Nayeli does with the Jaguar Twin.

3 Escritura. Write a brief summary of this episode of *Caminos del jaguar* in Spanish. (4–6 sentences)

NOTA CULTURAL

La Universidad de las Américas

This university is located in San Andrés de Cholula, five kilometers outside of the city of Puebla and 120 kilometers (about one hour by car) from Mexico City, in an area where pre-Hispanic, colonial, and modern Mexico converge. On a clear day the university offers a magnificent view of four of the tallest volcanoes in Mexico: Orizaba, Popocatépetl, Iztaccíhuatl, and La Malinche.

SEGUNDO PASO

Vocabulario y lengua

INDICATING LIKES AND DISLIKES

¿Qué te gusta hacer? (*What do you like to do?*)

Online Study Center

For additional practice
with this unit's vocabulary
and grammar, visit the
Caminos website at
http://college.hmco.com/
languages/spanish/
renjilian/caminos/3e/
student_home.html.
You can also review audio
flashcards, quiz yourself,
and explore related
Spanish-language sites.

1. caminar
2. escribir cartas
3. tocar la guitarra
4. escuchar música
5. pintar
6. jugar al volibol
7. leer libros
8. hablar con amigos

Más palabras y expresiones

Verbos

alquilar videos	*to rent videos*
dar un paseo	*to take a walk*
hacer ejercicio	*to exercise*
mirar una película	*to watch a movie*
navegar por Internet (la Red / la web)	*to surf the Internet (Web)*
practicar deportes	*to play sports*
ver televisión	*to watch television*

Otras expresiones

mucho	*a lot, very much*
(un) poco	*(a) little*
también	*also, too*

Using *gustar* (*to like*)

To say that you . . .	use this structure:	
like to do one activity or a series of activities,	**me / te gusta** + *infinitive*	
	Me gusta pintar.	*I like to paint.*
	Te gusta estudiar y comer.	*You like to study and to eat.*
like one specific thing,	**me / te gusta** + *singular noun*	
	Me gusta mucho la clase de español.	*I like Spanish class a lot.*
	Te gusta el fútbol.	*You like soccer.*
like many things or a series of things,	**me / te gustan** + *plural noun*	
	Me gustan las clases de idiomas.	*I like language classes.*
	Te gustan el fútbol y el volibol.	*You like soccer and volleyball.*
do not like any of the above,	add **no** before the structure.	
	No me gusta pintar.	*I don't like to paint.*
	No te gusta el fútbol.	*You don't like soccer.*

Actividades

1 ¿Qué te gusta? With a partner, ask each other what you like to do. If you answer in the affirmative, add a second activity that you also like to do. If you answer in the negative, add an activity that you like. Follow the model.

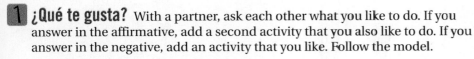

▶ MODELO:
—¿Te gusta leer libros?   —*Do you like to read books?*
—Sí, me gusta leer libros. También me gusta escribir cartas.   —*Yes, I like to read books. I also like to write letters.*

or

—No, no me gusta leer libros, pero me gusta escribir cartas.   —*No, I don't like to read books, but I do like to write letters.*

1. ¿Te gusta el arte?
2. ¿Te gustan las clases de ciencias?
3. ¿Te gusta navegar por Internet?
4. ¿Te gusta el fútbol?
5. ¿Te gustan los deportes?
6. ¿Te gusta caminar?
7. ¿Te gusta la música jazz?
8. ¿Te gusta hablar con amigos?

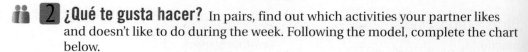

2 ¿Qué te gusta hacer?

In pairs, find out which activities your partner likes and doesn't like to do during the week. Following the model, complete the chart below.

▶ MODELO:

—¿Qué te gusta hacer los lunes?
—*What do you like to do on Mondays?*

—Me gusta estudiar y escuchar música.
—*I like to study and to listen to music.*

—¿Qué no te gusta hacer?
—*What don't you like to do?*

—No me gusta hacer ejercicio.
—*I don't like to exercise.*

	Te gusta	No te gusta
lunes	estudiar, escuchar música	hacer ejercicio
martes	_____	_____
miércoles	_____	_____
jueves	_____	_____
viernes	_____	_____
sábado	_____	_____
domingo	_____	_____

EXPRESSING LOCATION AND EMOTION WITH *ESTAR*

La señora **está** en el sofá. **Está** aburrida.

La niña **está** en la sala. **Está** triste.

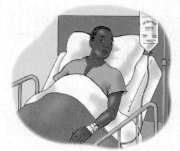

El señor **está** en el hospital. **Está** enfermo.

El chico **está** en la escuela. **Está** contento.

El chico y la chica **están** en el restaurante.
Están enamorados.

The verb **estar** is used to indicate the location of people or objects. **Estar** is also used to express emotional states at a specific moment in time or in a particular situation.

estar *(to be)*			
Singular		**Plural**	
yo	est**oy**	nosotros / nosotras	est**amos**
tú	est**ás**	vosotros / vosotras	est**áis**
Ud. / él / ella	est**á**	Uds. / ellos/ ellas	est**án**

Note that the first person singular is irregular, and that all the other forms, except for the first person plural, carry written accents.

Useful adjectives of emotion

aburrido/a	*bored*	enamorado/a	*in love*
alegre	*happy*	enfermo/a	*sick*
alterado/a	*upset*	enojado/a	*angry*
borracho/a	*drunk*	entusiasmado/a	*enthusiastic*
calmado/a	*calm*	fascinado/a	*fascinated*
cansado/a	*tired*	harto/a	*fed up, disgusted*
celoso/a	*jealous*	listo/a	*ready*
confundido/a	*confused*	nervioso/a	*nervous*
contento/a	*happy*	preocupado/a	*worried*
deprimido/a	*depressed*	seguro/a	*sure*
desilusionado/a	*disappointed*	triste	*sad*
emocionado/a	*excited*		

Actividades

1 **Memoria perfecta.** You are constantly misplacing things, but luckily you have a roommate who remembers where you put them. You call him/her to ask for help. With your partner, take turns asking each other questions.

▶ MODELO: llaves / estante
—*¿Dónde están las llaves?*
—*Están en el estante.*

1. cuadernos / cama
2. radio / cuarto de baño
3. mi libro de español / mochila
4. reloj / escritorio
5. papeles / silla
6. teléfono / mesa

2 ¿Dónde están?

Make a list of all the people and things in the house pictured below. Then, ask your partner where each one can be found. Take turns.

► MODELO: televisión
—¿Dónde está la televisión?
—La televisión está en la cocina.

3 Reacciones.

How would you feel in the following situations? Write your reactions and then share them with a classmate.

► MODELO: Your paycheck is late.
—Estoy preocupado/a.

1. You have an exam tomorrow.
2. You just found your true love.
3. You have the flu.
4. Your favorite aunt or uncle died.
5. You passed your most difficult class.
6. Your roommate stole some money.

4 Entrevista.

Interview six of your classmates to find out how they're doing today. Report your findings to the class.

► MODELO: —¿Cómo estás?   —How are you?
—Estoy muy contento/a.   —I am very happy.
—¿Por qué?   —Why?
—Porque mañana hay fiesta.   —Because there is a party
                                                        tomorrow.

5 Emociones. Complete these ideas.

1. Estoy contento/a cuando...
2. Estoy triste cuando...
3. Estoy enojado/a porque...
4. Estoy cansado/a porque...
5. Estoy desilusionado/a porque...
6. Estoy entusiasmado/a porque...

TALKING ABOUT PLACES IN A CITY

¿Qué hay en la ciudad? (*What's in the city?*)

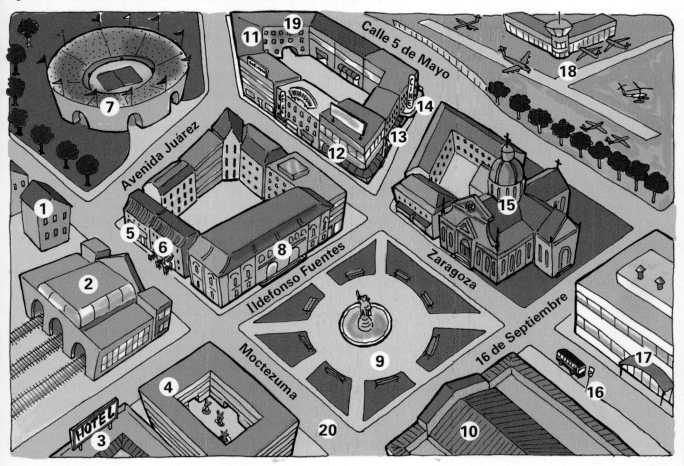

1. el edificio (*building*)
2. la estación de tren (*train station*)
3. el hotel
4. el museo
5. la librería (*bookstore*)
6. el café
7. el estadio
8. el correo (*post office*)
9. la plaza
10. la biblioteca (*library*)

11. el centro comercial (*shopping center*)
12. la tienda (*store*)
13. el restaurante
14. el cine (*movie theater*)
15. la iglesia (*church*)
16. la parada de autobús (*bus stop*)
17. el hospital
18. el aeropuerto
19. el almacén (*department store*)
20. la calle (*street*)

Actividades

1 **¿Dónde está?** Work with a partner to identify and locate the buildings in the city map above. Follow the model.

► MODELO: —¿Dónde está la tienda?   —*Where is the store?*
           —Está en la calle Zaragoza.   —*It's on Zaragoza Street.*

2 **¿Dónde están?** Teresa has received a phone message from her friend Lisa who is traveling in Mexico City. While looking at the map on page 71, listen to what Lisa says. On a sheet of paper, write down all the things she does and the places she mentions.

3 **Una ciudad ideal.** Create your own city by drawing and labeling an original city plan. Include at least seven buildings and places from the city map on page 71.

4 **Los planes.** Now work with a partner and compare your city plans. Follow the model.

▶ MODELO:　—¿Hay un restaurante en la ciudad?　—*Is there a restaurant in the city?*
　　　　　　—Sí, hay un restaurante. (No, no hay un restaurante.)　—*Yes, there is a restaurant. (No, there isn't a restaurant.)*
　　　　　　—¿Dónde está el restaurante?　—*Where is the restaurant?*
　　　　　　—Está en la calle Carolina.　—*It's on Carolina Street.*

5 **¿Qué haces?** *(What do you do?)* Now work in pairs, and state where you do the following activities. Follow the model.

▶ MODELO:　—¿Dónde lees libros?　—*Where do you read books?*
　　　　　　—Leo libros en la biblioteca.　—*I read books in the library.*

beber café	esperar el autobús	mirar una película
caminar	estudiar	pagar mucho dinero
comer	hablar con amigos	tomar el tren
comprar	mirar arte	tomar un avión

DESCRIBING PRESENT ACTIONS IN PROGRESS

Present Progressive Tense
Gente en acción (*People in action*)

Natalia y José
están hablando.

Iván
está comiendo.

La señora Cortés
está escribiendo.

To describe an action in progress, use the *present progressive* tense. It is formed with the verb **estar** and the *present participle*. The present participle of regular verbs is formed by dropping the -**ar,** -**er,** or -**ir** ending of the verb and adding -**ando** for -**ar** verbs and -**iendo** for -**er** and -**ir** verbs.

Present participle of regular verbs		
-ar	**-er**	**-ir**
hablar: habl**ando** *speak — speaking*	comer: com**iendo** *eat — eating*	escribir: escrib**iendo** *write — writing*

Present Participles with a Spelling Change

In Spanish, whenever the unaccented letter **i** appears between two vowels, it changes to **y**. Present participles of verbs such as **leer, creer,** and **construir** *(to build)* include this change (le**y**endo, cre**y**endo, constru**y**endo). Most verbs ending in **–uir** [for example, **incluir** *(to include)* and **destruir** *(to destroy)*] also have this spelling change.

Liliana **está leyendo** el menú.	*Liliana is reading the menu.*
Los señores López **están construyendo** una casa nueva.	*Mr. and Mrs. López are building a new house.*

Expressions

Since the simple present tense can often be translated as "am / is / are reading / eating, etc.," the following expressions are frequently used with the present progressive tense to show that this tense focuses on the action in progress.

ahora	*now*
en este momento	*at this moment, now*

Actividades

1 Situaciones. Create complete sentences combining the phrases below in a meaningful way. Use the present progressive tense. Follow the model.

▶ **MODELO:** Gabriel / beber café / restaurante
Gabriel está bebiendo café en el restaurante.

A	B	C
1. Anabel	subir al autobús	la tienda
2. Julia y Nicolás	practicar el fútbol	la biblioteca
3. Mi profesora	alquilar un cuarto	la computadora
4. El Sr. Rodríguez	comprar una computadora	el correo
5. Mis amigos	leer un libro	el hotel
6. Tu amiga Nubia	pagar el cartel	el centro comercial
7. Nuestro profesor	mandar una carta	el estadio
8. Su compañero de clase	comer pizza	la parada de autobús
9. Yo	navegar por Internet	el aeropuerto
10. Nosotros	tomar el avión	el restaurante

2 ¿Qué están haciendo?

Use the present progressive tense to ask your partner what Leonor and Mario are doing. Add a place in the city or in the house where you think the action is occurring. Follow the model.

► **MODELO:** —¿Qué está haciendo Mario en la librería?
—Mario está comprando un libro.

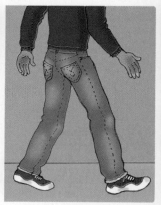

3 En este momento... With a partner, discuss what people are doing right now in the places listed.

▶ MODELO: tus amigos en la plaza

—¿Qué están haciendo tus amigos en la plaza?   —*What are your friends doing in the plaza?*

—Mis amigos están caminando.   —*My friends are walking.*

1. tus compañeros/as en la escuela
2. tu profesor/a en la clase
3. la gente en las calles
4. los / las estudiantes en la escuela
5. las personas en un restaurante
6. la gente en el cine
7. tus amigos/as en el centro comercial
8. la gente en el museo

4 En el parque. Refer to the picture on page 66 and, with a partner, discuss what the people are doing in the park.

_____

_____

_____

_____

_____

_____

_____

Jaguares gemelos

Oficina de Nayeli en su casa, en Puebla.

Este jeroglífico, ¿qué significa? ¿Pájaro...? ¡Avión! El número de un vuelo. ¡Vuelo número novecientos cuarenta y nueve! ¿Adónde? ¡Claro, Madrid! ¡Nayeli está en Madrid!

En la sala de la casa de Nayeli.

¿Qué dice la nota?

Creo que Nayeli está en Madrid.

¿Madrid? ¿Pero por qué en Madrid?

Vamos a Madrid, pero es muy caro.

Pero Adriana, ¿y la excavación?

Nuestra profesora está en peligro.

Soy amigo de Nayeli y yo pago el viaje. No es difícil: los boletos aéreos, una tarjeta de crédito, dinero y una computadora para la comunicación.

¿Qué crees, Adriana?

No sé. Estoy preocupada.

Adriana, es necesario confiar en él.

Sí, claro.... No hay muchas opciones...

Su oferta es generosa.

... y sincera.

Muchas gracias. Usted es un amigo muy bueno.

Aquí está la nota para el Sr. Guzmán.

Sí, señorita, muchas gracias.

¡Gracias!

En la oficina de Armando

Armando, ¿cómo está todo?

Señora, todo está bien. Y ¿usted, en Costa Rica?

Bien, pero ¿todo está bien?

Claro, Adriana y Felipe viajan a Madrid.

¡Perfecto!

Muy bien. ¿Hablamos todos los días?

¡Todo está bajo control!

Si los jaguares no están juntos, México va a sufrir problemas económicos.

La profesora Nayeli Paz Ocotlán es la figura principal de la investigación de la policía.

Actividades

Online Study Center

For additional practice
with this episode, visit
the *Caminos* website at
http://college.hmco.com/
languages/spanish/
renjilian/caminos/3e/
student_home.html.

1 Comprensión. Based on this episode of *Caminos del jaguar*, choose the logical response.

1. Adriana y Felipe están en...
   a. la universidad.
   b. la casa de Nayeli.

2. El jeroglífico describe...
   a. el número de un vuelo *(flight)*.
   b. el título de un libro.

3. Nayeli está en...
   a. México.
   b. Madrid.

4. Felipe está preocupado por...
   a. Adriana.
   b. la excavación.

5. ¿Quién paga el viaje de Adriana y Felipe a Madrid?
   a. Felipe
   b. Armando

6. Armando habla por teléfono con...
   a. doña Carmen.
   b. Esperanza.

2 Situaciones. Dramatize one of the following situations.

1. Adriana and Felipe discuss Armando's offer to pay for their trip to Madrid.
2. Armando's phone conversation with someone in Costa Rica.

3 Escritura. Write a brief summary of this episode of *Caminos del jaguar* in Spanish. (4–6 sentences).

NOTA CULTURAL

Los códices mayas

The Mayans employed a writing system of
hieroglyphs (similar to the Aztecs of Central
Mexico), and left engraved symbols and
pictures on animal skin, papyrus (paper
made from tree bark), or stone. The greatest
examples of Mayan writing can be found in
four documents (**códices**), located today in
Dresden (Germany), Paris, Madrid, and the
Distrito Federal (Mexico City). The códices
describe ceremonies for the new year, and
contain prophecies, astronomical data,
and agricultural records. The Madrid
codex describes daily activities such as
bee keeping and hunting. It is thought to
be a kind of manual used by Mayan priests
to counsel the public.

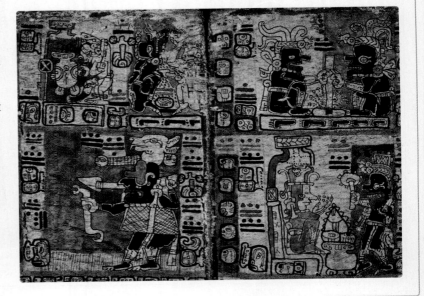

Lectura

Online Study Center

For further reading practice online, visit the *Caminos* website at http://college .hmco.com/languages/ spanish/renjilian/caminos/ 3e/student_home.html.

PRELECTURA

Reading Strategy

Asking questions

To achieve effective skills as a reader, training yourself to read in another language is one important step. Asking yourself questions *before* you read, *while* you are reading, and *after* you read facilitates your comprehension and memory.

1 Antes de leer. Before you read this article, ask yourself these questions.

1. What theme(s) or topic(s) does the title indicate?
2. Do I already know something about the topic?
3. What clues do the photos and captions reveal about the reading?
4. Before I begin reading, what else seems relevant?

2 Al leer. While you are reading, ask yourself these questions.

1. What topic(s) and theme(s) can I identify? After reading the title of the article, have I guessed correctly?
2. Which vocabulary words do I already know? Do they relate to the topic and themes? In order to understand the passage, which words are essential for me to know?
3. Can I understand the gist of the reading without looking up many words in a dictionary?
4. Which words can I skim over and still understand the reading?
5. Can I summarize each each paragraph?
6. As I read, what else can I identify as important to know?

Bienvenidos[1] a Puebla: Ciudad de ángeles

La casa de las muñecas, Puebla, México

Una leyenda mexicana indica que los ángeles llegaron[2] a Puebla y trazaron[3] las calles rectas[4] para[5] usarlas más fácilmente. Por eso, se llama Puebla de los Ángeles. Es la capital del estado de Puebla y está en el altiplano[6] central de México. Está a noventa minutos de la ciudad de México en automóvil, a tres horas de la ciudad de Oaxaca, a tres horas y media del Puerto de Veracruz y a seis horas de Acapulco. La temperatura media[7] varía entre 20 °C y 30 °C.

---

[1]Welcome; [2]arrived; [3]designed; [4]straight; [5]in order to; [6]high plain; [7]average

La Capilla de la Virgen del Rosario

La hermosa talavera de Puebla

Puebla es famosa por sus estructuras barrocas[8] de ladrillo[9] rojo, piedra[10] gris, estuco[11] blanco y por los espectaculares azulejos de Talavera. La Catedral de Puebla tiene altas torres[12] y un hermoso altar con adornos de ónice[13], mármol[14] y oro[15], diseñado[16] por Manuel Tolsá, el famoso arquitecto de origen español.

La Biblioteca Palafoxiana es un espectacular edificio de la época colonial. Tiene más de 40.000 libros, todos muy valiosos[17]. Algunos[18] especialistas consideran la Capilla[19] de la Virgen del Rosario como la octava maravilla[20] del mundo por los impresionantes adornos interiores. El Convento Colonial de Santa Rosa es hoy un museo de cerámica. El Museo Amparo, con muchos adelantos[21] tecnológicos, es uno de los más modernos de América Latina. La Universidad Benemérito de Puebla, construida en 1578, es muy importante también.

---

[8]baroque; [9]brick; [10]stone; [11]stucco; [12]towers; [13]onyx; [14]marble; [15]gold; [16]designed [17]valuable; [18]Some; [19]Chapel; [20]eighth wonder; [21]advances

POSTLECTURA

3 Después de leer. After you read the article, ask yourself these questions.

1. What are the main ideas of the reading?
2. What themes or topics does the reading reveal?
3. To help me better understand the reading, which words do I need to look up?
4. What other information is relevant?

4 Ciudad de ángeles. With a partner, ask each other these questions based on the reading.

1. ¿Dónde está Puebla de los Ángeles? ¿Por qué se llama así?
2. ¿En automóvil, a cuántas horas está Puebla de Oaxaca? ¿de la capital? ¿del Puerto de Veracruz? ¿de Acapulco?
3. ¿Cuál es la temperatura media de la ciudad?
4. Menciona tres edificios importantes de Puebla.
5. ¿De dónde es el arquitecto de la Catedral de Puebla? ¿Cómo se llama?
6. ¿De qué color son los edificios del centro de la ciudad?
7. ¿Cómo se llama el museo moderno con avances tecnológicos?
8. El artículo menciona una biblioteca y una universidad. ¿Cuáles son?

Escritura

Online Study Center

For further writing practice online, visit the *Caminos* website at http://college .hmco.com/languages/ spanish/renjilian/caminos/ 3e/student_home.html.

Writing Strategy

Brainstorming ideas

Before writing an essay or a report, it is often useful to brainstorm your ideas, especially with a partner or in a group. In order to do this effectively, write only in Spanish.

Workshop

1. Write down your ideas on paper as they occur to you. They can be single words, phrases, or questions.
2. Write quickly and in no particular order. Do not stop to evaluate which ideas are good.
3. Once the ideas are written, read the list and circle the ideas that you will use in your writing.

The following is a possible brainstorm for an essay that describes your apartment.

grande	*me gusta*
cocina fea	*azul*
comedor	*un compañero arrogante*
no hay sofá	*jardín bonito*
dos dormitorios	*hace frío*
una buena compañera	*un dormitorio pequeño*

Strategy in Action

For additional practice with the strategy of brainstorming ideas, turn to the *Escritura* section for *Unidad 2* in your Student Activities Manual.

1 Tu casa. Create a diagram of your home. Include the rooms and the furniture in each room. Then write a description to match the diagram.

2 Un fin de semana espectacular. Write a description of the activities you do during an ideal weekend. Use the expressions you've learned to indicate likes and dislikes, and verbs in the present tense.

PRIMER PASO

DESCRIBING AN APARTMENT

Sustantivos

el alquiler, la renta	rent
el balcón	balcony
la bañera, la tina	bathtub
el (cuarto de) baño	bathroom
la casa	house
el clóset	closet
la cocina	kitchen
el comedor	dining room
el dormitorio	bedroom
la ducha	shower
el/la dueño/a	owner
el garaje	garage
el/la inquilino/a	tenant
el jardín	garden, yard
la oficina	office
la piscina, la alberca	swimming pool
el piso	floor, apartment (Spain)
la sala	living room
la terraza	terrace

Otras expresiones

amplio/a	spacious
barato/a	inexpensive
caro/a	expensive
completo/a	complete
con	with
moderno/a	modern
pequeño/a	small
pero	but
privado/a	private

POSSESSIVE ADJECTIVES

mi/mis	my
tu/tus	your (fam., sing.)
su/sus	your (formal), his, her, their
nuestro/a/nuestros/as	our
vuestro/a/vuestros/as	your (fam. plural, Spain)

IDENTIFYING FURNISHINGS AND HOUSEHOLD CHORES

Los muebles

la alfombra	rug
la aspiradora	vacuum cleaner
la cómoda	dresser
las escaleras	stairs
la escoba	broom
el espejo	mirror
la estufa	stove
el inodoro	toilet
el lavabo/el lavamanos	bathroom sink
la mesita	coffee table
la mesita de noche	night stand
el/la refrigerador/a	refrigerator
el ropero/el armario	wardrobe
el/la secadora/a de pelo	blow dryer
el sillón	armchair
el sofá	sofa

Los quehaceres (Household chores)

arreglar (la cama)	to make / fix up (the bed)
aspirar, pasar la aspiradora (por la alfombra)	to vacuum (the rug)
barrer (el piso)	to sweep (the floor)
cocinar	to cook
lavar (los platos)	to wash (the dishes)
limpiar/ordenar (el cuarto)	to clean / tidy (the room)
planchar (la ropa)	to iron (clothes)
sacar (la basura)	to take out (the garbage)
sacudir (los muebles)/ sacar el polvo de (los muebles) (Spain)	to dust (the furniture)
secar (los platos, la ropa)	to dry (the dishes, clothes)

REGULAR -AR, -ER, AND -IR VERBS

-ar verbs

acabar / acabar de + (infinitive)	*to finish / to have just (done something)*
alquilar	*to rent*
andar	*to walk, move*
bailar	*to dance*
buscar	*to look for*
caminar	*to walk*
cantar	*to sing*
comprar	*to buy*
desear	*to wish for*
escuchar	*to listen*
estudiar	*to study*
hablar	*to speak*
investigar	*to research*
lavar	*to wash*
llamar	*to call*
llegar	*to arrive*
llevar	*to bring*
mandar	*to send*
mirar	*to look at*
necesitar	*to need*
pasar	*to happen, pass*
practicar	*to practice*
preguntar	*to ask*

terminar	*to finish*
tomar	*to take*
trabajar	*to work*
usar	*to use*
viajar	*to travel*
visitar	*to visit*

-er verbs

aprender	*to learn*
beber	*to drink*
comer	*to eat*
comprender	*to understand*
correr	*to run*
creer	*to believe*
leer	*to read*
responder	*to answer*

-ir verbs

abrir	*to open*
compartir	*to share*
decidir	*to decide*
describir	*to describe*
escribir	*to write*
recibir	*to receive*
subir	*to climb*
vivir	*to live*

SEGUNDO PASO

INDICATING LIKES AND DISLIKES

Verbos

alquilar videos	*to rent videos*
dar un paseo	*to take a walk*
escribir cartas	*to write letters*
gustar	*to like (be pleasing)*
hablar con amigos	*to talk with friends*
hacer ejercicio	*to exercise*
jugar al volibol	*to play volleyball*
leer libros	*to read books*
mirar una película	*to watch a movie*
navegar por Internet (la Red/la web)	*to surf the Internet (Web)*
pintar	*to paint*
practicar deportes	*to play sports*
tocar (un instrumento)	*to play (an instrument)*
ver televisión	*to watch television*

Otras expresiones

mucho	*a lot, very much*
(un) poco	*(a) little*
también	*also, too*

EXPRESSING LOCATION AND EMOTION WITH *ESTAR*

Verbos

estar	*to be*

Adjetivos

aburrido/a	*bored*
alegre	*happy*
alterado/a	*upset*
borracho/a	*drunk*
calmado/a	*calm*
cansado/a	*tired*

celoso/a	*jealous*
confundido/a	*confused*
contento/a	*happy*
deprimido/a	*depressed*
desilusionado/a	*disappointed*
emocionado/a	*excited*
enamorado/a	*in love*
enfermo/a	*sick*
enojado/a	*angry*
entusiasmado/a	*enthusiastic*
fascinado/a	*fascinated*
harto/a	*fed up, disgusted*
listo/a	*ready*
nervioso/a	*nervous*
preocupado/a	*worried*
seguro/a	*sure*
triste	*sad*

TALKING ABOUT PLACES IN A CITY

el aeropuerto	*airport*
el almacén	*department store / warehouse*
la biblioteca	*library*
el café	*café*
la calle	*street*
el centro comercial	*shopping center*
el cine	*movie theater*
la ciudad	*city*

el correo	*post office*
el edificio	*building*
la estación de tren	*train station*
el estadio	*stadium*
el hospital	*hospital*
el hotel	*hotel*
la iglesia	*church*
la librería	*bookstore*
el museo	*museum*
la parada de autobús	*bus stop*
la plaza	*plaza*
el restaurante	*restaurant*
la tienda	*store*

DESCRIBING PRESENT ACTIONS IN PROGRESS

Sustantivos

la gente	*people (singular)*

Verbos

construir	*to build*
destruir	*to destroy*
incluir	*to include*

Otras expresiones

ahora	*now*
en este momento	*at this moment, now*

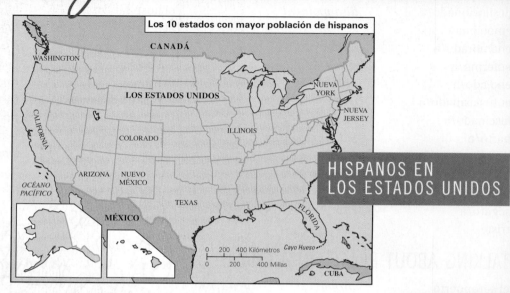

Los 10 estados con mayor población de hispanos

HISPANOS EN LOS ESTADOS UNIDOS

Online Study Center

To learn more about the people featured in this section, visit the *Caminos* website at http://college.hmco.com/languages/spanish/renjilian/caminos/3e/student_home.html.

Jorge Ramos

Jennifer López

America Ferrera

Robert Rodríguez

Arturo Moreno

Zoe Saldaña

Bill Richardson

Gustavo Santaolalla

Narciso Rodríguez

Cristina Saralegui

PERSONALIDADES

Hay aproximadamente cuarenta y dos millones de hispanos en los Estados Unidos. Son de familias de las veintiuna naciones hispanas. En su libro *La ola*[1] *latina,* el periodista[2] Jorge Ramos, nacido[3] en México, analiza las contribuciones de los hispanos a la sociedad estadounidense. Ramos ofrece la siguiente descripción de los hispanos estadounidenses cuando observa, "El latino, por definición es mezcla[4]: de culturas, de idiomas, de identidades, de posibilidades, de tiempos[5], de pasado y de futuro".

En las artes y las letras, las personalidades hispanas se destacan[6] en la literatura, el arte, la música y el cine. La revista[7] *Time* describe a los 25 hispanos más influyentes de los Estados Unidos de 2005. Incluyen también las categorías de la política y los negocios[8]. Muchas personas de habla española se identifican como "hispanos" y muchas como "latinos".

En la lista de los hispanos mencionados en *Time* están las puertorriqueñas Jennifer López (actriz y cantante) y Mari Carmen Ramírez (conservadora de arte moderno). También están los chicanos Robert Rodríguez (director de cine), Arturo Moreno (dueño[9] del equipo[10] de béisbol, los Anaheim Angels), Carmen Lomas Garza (artista) y Bill Richardson (gobernador de Nuevo México). Están adicionalmente el argentinoamericano Gustavo Santaolalla (músico y ganador[11] de un Óscar en 2006); los cubanoamericanos Narciso Rodríguez (modisto[12]), Cristina Saralegui (personalidad de televisión) y Andy García (actor).

Esta es una lista parcial de los hispanos influyentes estadounidenses. Visita el sitio web de *Caminos* para leer más en español sobre las personalidades mencionadas aquí[13] y otras[14] como Edward James Olmos, Eva Méndez, Amaury Nolasco, Jimmy Smits, Zoe Saldaña, (actores), Bárbara Bermudo (presentadora), George López (comediante), Eduardo Xol (decorador de exteriores) y Denise Quiñones (modelo y actriz).

---

[1]wave; [2]journalist; [3]born; [4]mix; [5]times; [6]stand out; [7]magazine; [8]business; [9]owner; [10]team; [11]winner; [12]fashion designer; [13]here; [14]others

Comprensión

Working in pairs, ask each other the following questions.

1. ¿Qué definición ofrece Jorge Ramos del latino? En tu familia, ¿qué idioma/s hablan? ¿Con qué cultura conectan su identidad?
2. Nombra a hispanos influyentes en cinco categorías diferentes. ¿Cuál es más impresionante, en tu opinión? ¿Por qué?

ARTE

CARMEN LOMAS GARZA

Carmen Lomas Garza es una artista chicana. Ella es de una familia mexicana que reside en los Estados Unidos en Texas. Pero ahora°, la artista vive en San Francisco, donde pinta y escribe libros sobre las tradiciones mexicanas. En la introducción de uno de sus libros de cuadros° y relatos°, *Cuadros de familia*, la autora chicana Sandra Cisneros analiza las obras artísticas de Lomas Garza, "Éstos° son cuadros de familia y no importa si tu familia es de Kingsville o el Cairo, Sarajevo o Katmandú, también son imágenes° de tu familia". Lomas Garza pinta escenas típicas como ferias, fiestas, cumpleaños° y celebraciones.

La Tamalada° es un cuadro en que° los miembros de la familia de la artista preparan tamales.

But now

portraits / stories
These

images

birthdays

Making tamales
in which

Tamalada (Making Tamales)

Comprensión

Working in pairs, ask each other the following questions.

1. ¿Qué preparan los miembros de la familia de la artista?
2. ¿Cuántos adultos hay en el cuadro? ¿Y cuántos adolescentes y niños°? ¿Cómo son? ¿Hay animales? *children*
3. En tu opinión, ¿es de día o de noche? ¿Qué hora es?
4. ¿Qué temas observas en las dos obras de arte en el cuadro?
5. Nombra los colores que la artista usa en el cuadro.
6. ¿Cómo es el cuadro—interesante, aburrido°, excelente, positivo, tradicional, feliz? *boring*
7. ¿Quién es un artista famoso/a de tu país?
8. ¿Qué te gusta comer más—los tacos, los tamales o los burritos?

Conéctate a Internet para ver el arte de Carmen Lomas Garza y para aprender sobre otros artistas hispanos estadounidenses como Daniel Desiga, Paul Botello, Abelardo Morell, Joe Bravo, Judy Baca, Celina Hinojosa, José Esquivel, Patssi Valdez y Carlos Almaraz.

MÚSICA

LUIS FONSI

El cantante° Luis Fonsi (=Luis Alfonso Rodríguez) nació° en Puerto Rico en 1978. A los cuatro años, participó° en el famoso Coro de Niños° de San Juan. A los diez años, su familia se estableció en la Florida. Sus dos primeros álbumes se llaman "Comenzaré°" y "Eterno". Es famoso por sus baladas y su voz espectacular. Su tremendo talento está en cantar y también en crear coreografía. Cantó° también duetos con las populares cantantes latinas Cristina Aguilera, Olga Tañón y Jaci Velázquez. En su álbum de 2005, "Paso a paso°", hay canciones en honor de su esposa, la talentosa actriz latina, Adamari López. Fonsi revela que "la vida está llena° de pruebas° y las pruebas son las que nos definen como seres° humanos".

singer / was born
participated /
  Children's Choru
I will begin

He sang

Step by Step
full / challenges
beings

Comprensión

Working in pairs, ask each other the following questions.

1. ¿Cuál es el nombre original de Luis Fonsi?
2. ¿De dónde es?
3. ¿Cuántos álbumes mencionan en el texto? ¿Cómo se llaman?
4. Fonsi es famoso por una categoría de música que canta. ¿Cuál es?
5. ¿Qué cantantes latinas cantan duetos con Fonsi?
6. ¿Cómo se llama la esposa de Fonsi? ¿Cuál es su profesión?
7. ¿Te gusta la balada como forma musical?
8. ¿Quién es otro/a cantante contemporáneo/a excelente?

Conéctate a Internet para escuchar la música de Fonsi, aprender más sobre él y otros cantantes hispanos estadounidenses como Cristina Aguilera, Vicki Carr, Gloria Estefan, Diego García, Jennifer López, Los Lonely Boys, Tito Puente, Carlos Santana, Selena y Jaci Velázquez.

LITERATURA

FRANCISCO X. ALARCÓN

Francisco X. Alarcón es un poeta chicano. Tiene más de siete libros de poesía y es ganador° de honores por sus creaciones literarias. También es profesor universitario.

winner

"En estos momentos de conflicto, el mundo necesita paz . . . Y nosotros podemos empezar desde el interior de nuestro ser."
—Ricky Martin (Puerto Rico / Estados Unidos)

"Espiral universal"

no hay
finales
sólo° nuevos principios° *only / beginnings*

Comprensión

Working in pairs, ask each other the following questions.

1. ¿Cómo es la forma de un espiral: rectangular, circular o triangular?
2. Según° el poeta, ¿está el espiral limitado a un punto o lugar en el espacio? *According to*
3. El poeta comenta que no hay finales, sólo nuevos principios. ¿Estás de acuerdo°? *in agreement*
4. En tu opinión, ¿es elocuente, optimista, pesimista, provocativo, sentimental o universal el poema?

MARJORIE AGOSIN

Marjorie Agosin es de una familia chilena. La poeta estadounidense es autora de más de treinta libros de poesía. Profesora de literatura latinoamericana en Wellesley College, es también activista por los derechos° humanos. La selección aquí es del poema "La noche del jaguar". *rights*

"La noche del jaguar"

Yo toda la noche pinto
y me busco entre° el claroscuro°. *between / light and dark*
Devorando° los colores, *devouring*
me llamo entre la sombra carcomida° *disappearing shadow*
en la noche del jaguar.
Soy veloz° como una honda° canción°. *swift / deep / song*

Comprensión

Working in groups, ask each other the following questions.

1. ¿Cuándo ocurre la acción en el poema?
2. ¿Qué devora el / la artista?
3. ¿Con qué animal se asocian la noche y la velocidad?
4. En tu opinión, ¿cómo es el poema —creativo, elegante, emocional, fascinante, hondo, interesante, original, realista... ?

Conéctate a Internet para aprender más sobre los poetas aquí u otros escritores hispanos estadounidenses como Isabel Allende, Sandra Cisneros, Chiqui Vicioso, Pedro Juan Soto, Francisco Jiménez, Tomás Rivera, Sandra Benítez, Rodolfo Gonzales y Norma Cantú.

3
De viaje

VOCABULARIO Y LENGUA

▶ Talking about weather and seasons

▶ Describing actions in the present: Present indicative of stem-changing verbs: **tener, ir, venir**

▶ Discussing transportation

▶ Talking about daily routines: Reflexive actions

▶ Ordering food in a restaurant

▶ Expressing actions in the present: Verbs with irregular **yo** forms: **saber** and **conocer**

▶ Using large numbers: 200 to 2,000,000

▶ Showing location of people, places, and things: Demonstratives, adverbs of location

CAMINOS DEL JAGUAR

▶ Información confidencial

▶ Las reglas son las reglas

LECTURA

▶ Sevilla, ciudad sensacional

NOTAS CULTURALES

▶ Los terremotos en México

▶ España y el uso de **vosotros**

ESTRATEGIAS

▶ **Reading:** Skimming; Scanning

▶ **Writing:** Providing supporting details

Salvador Dalí, *Muchacha en la ventana*

Preguntas del tema

- ► ¿Dónde vives?
- ► ¿Te gusta el clima de tu ciudad?
- ► ¿Hay transporte público en tu ciudad?
- ► ¿Te gusta viajar en auto o en tren?

PRIMER PASO

Vocabulario y lengua

TALKING ABOUT WEATHER AND SEASONS

¿Qué tiempo hace? (What's the weather like?)

Buenos días, con ustedes, Gloria López. Es un buen día para viajar por España. Hace mucho sol en la región central de España. Si viajan a Madrid hoy, hace sol con una temperatura máxima de 34 grados. Si viajan a Pamplona en el norte de España, hay chubascos fuertes. En Barcelona, en el este, está parcialmente nublado con una temperatura promedio de 31 grados centígrados. Si no les gusta el calor, es posible viajar a La Coruña en el noroeste porque hay una temperatura de sólo 23 grados centígrados. Por lo general, hace muy buen tiempo hoy.

Online Study Center

For additional practice with this unit's vocabulary and grammar, visit the *Caminos* website at http://college.hmco.com/languages/spanish/renjilian/caminos/3e/student_home.html. You can also review audio flashcards, quiz yourself, and explore related Spanish-language sites.

Temperatures in most Hispanic countries are expressed in degrees Celsius (°C) using the centigrade scale.

La temperatura está a 32 grados centígrados.   *The temperature is 32 °C.*

The freezing point is 0 °C, while the boiling point is 100 °C. Use the following formulas to convert from Fahrenheit to Celsius and vice versa:

$$°C = (°F - 32) \div 1.8 \qquad °F = (°C \times 1.8) + 32$$

°C	0	10	20	30	40	50	60	70	80	90	100
°F	32	50	68	86	104	122	140	158	176	194	212

¿En qué estación estamos? *(What season is it?)*

la primavera

el verano

el otoño

el invierno

Más palabras y expresiones

Cognados

la brisa   las millas (por hora)
húmedo/a   la probabilidad
el huracán   la temperatura (mínima /máxima)
los kilómetros (por hora)   el tornado
el/la meteorólogo/a

Sustantivos

el aguacero / el chubasco	*downpour*
el cielo	*sky*
el clima	*climate*
el este	*east*
los grados centígrados / Celsius / Fahrenheit	*degrees centigrade / Celsius / Fahrenheit*
la lluvia	*rain*
la nieve	*snow*
el noreste / el noroeste	*northeast / northwest*
el norte	*north*
la nube	*cloud*
el oeste	*west*
el porcentaje	*percentage*
el promedio	*average*
el pronóstico del tiempo	*weather forecast*
el sur	*south*
el sureste / el suroeste	*southeast / southwest*
la tormenta / la tronada	*storm*

Otras expresiones

¿A cuánto está la temperatura?	*What is the temperature?*
está (parcialmente) nublado	*it's (partly) cloudy*
fuerte	*strong*
hace buen / mal tiempo	*it's good / bad weather*
hace calor / frío / fresco	*it's hot / cold / cool*
hace viento	*it's windy*
llovizna	*it's drizzling*
llueve	*it's raining*
nieva	*it's snowing*
por ciento	*percent*
seco/a	*dry*

Actividades

1 **¿Qué hay?** Match the art in the left column with the vocabulary word in the right column.

1. _____

5. _____

2. _____

6. _____

3. _____

7. _____

4. _____

a. la nieve
b. la lluvia
c. el aguacero / el chubasco
d. la tormenta / la tronada
e. el cielo
f. la nube
g. la brisa

2 **El tiempo.** You are planning your next trip and need to pack accordingly. Listen to the weather reports for the various cities you are considering and indicate the order in which each city is mentioned on the lines below.

El tiempo de hoy   _de septiembre_

BUENOS AIRES	SAN JUAN	CIUDAD DE MÉXICO	MADRID	BOGOTÁ	CARACAS
9°C/48°F	24°C/75°F	17°C/63°F	20°C/68°F	14°C/57°F	29°C/84°F

___   ___   ___   ___   ___   ___

3 **¿Cuál es la estación?** With a partner, imagine that you are traveling together to the following cities and countries around the world. Determine the season for each month listed and describe the weather at that time of year. (Remember, the seasons are reversed in the northern and southern hemispheres. Refer to the maps included in your textbook if you need to.) Follow the model.

► MODELO: Nueva York, NY / julio
—Viajamos a Nueva   —We are traveling to New York
  York en julio. ¿En qué   in July. What season is it?
  estación estamos?
—Estamos en verano.   —It's summer.
—¿Qué tiempo hace?   —What's the weather like?
—Hace mucho calor.   —It's very hot.

1. Santiago, Chile / enero
2. Boston, MA / agosto
3. Buenos Aires, Argentina / junio
4. Los Ángeles, CA / abril
5. México, D.F. / noviembre
6. San Antonio, TX / mayo
7. La Habana, Cuba / septiembre
8. Burlington, VT / febrero
9. Asunción, Paraguay / diciembre
10. Miami, FL / octubre

4 **¿Qué tiempo hace?** Work with a partner to compare the weather conditions for Santander, Valencia, Zaragoza, and Sevilla in the map at the beginning of this section. Prepare a brief report for each city with general weather conditions, season, and temperature. Present your findings to the class.

5 **El noticiero.** You were just hired by a Spanish-speaking cable network to present weather forecasts for people making travel plans. Use the Internet to find the current weather report for a city in a Spanish-speaking country, and prepare a weather forecast to present to the class. **Useful keywords:** pronóstico del tiempo, meteorología.

Present indicative of stem-changing verbs: *tener, ir, venir*

Esta tarde

At last / we found	Mauro	Aquí está el Hotel Prisma. ¡Por fin° **encontramos**° nuestro hotel!
I intend	Rosalía	Sí, ¡por fin! Yo **pienso**° dormir toda la tarde.
I prefer	Mauro	Pues yo no voy a dormir. Esta tarde **prefiero**° ir a un buen restaurante.
I'm dying of hunger	Rosalía	¡Ah! Buena idea. Me **muero** de hambre°. Vamos al restaurante Plácido Domingo.
then / you won't sleep	Mauro	¿Entonces° no **duermes**° esta tarde?
I'll request / you'll get	Rosalía	No, yo **pido**° el cuarto y tú **consigues**° el taxi. ¿De acuerdo?
	Mauro	¡Sí, de acuerdo!

Stem-changing verbs use the same present tense endings as regular **–ar, –er,** and **–ir** verbs, but a vowel change also occurs in the stem of certain forms.

Notice that the **nosotros** and **vosotros** forms do not contain a stem change.

Stem-changing verbs		
e → ie: empezar *to start, begin*	**e → i:** servir *to serve*	**o → ue:** volver *to return, come back*
yo — emp**ie**zo	s**i**rvo	v**ue**lvo
tú — emp**ie**zas	s**i**rves	v**ue**lves
Ud. / él / ella — emp**ie**za	s**i**rve	v**ue**lve
nosotros/as — empezamos	servimos	volvemos
vosotros/as — empezáis	servís	volvéis
Uds. / ellos / ellas — emp**ie**zan	s**i**rven	v**ue**lven

Common stem-changing verbs					
e → ie		**e → i**		**o → ue**	
cerrar	to close	conseguir	to get, obtain	almorzar	to have lunch
comenzar	to start, begin	decir*	to say, tell	contar	to count
concernir	to concern	pedir	to ask for	costar	to cost
entender	to understand	perseguir	to follow, pursue	dormir	to sleep
mentir	to lie	repetir	to repeat	encontrar	to find
pensar	to think	seguir	to follow, continue	morir	to die
perder	to lose	servir	to serve	mostrar	to show
preferir	to prefer			poder	to be able
querer	to want			probar	to taste, try
recomendar	to recommend			recordar	to remember
				soñar	to dream
				(con)	(about)

*__Decir__ also has an irregular form in the first person singular: **yo digo.**

¡Yo siempre **digo** "*no*"!   *I always say "no"!*

Jugar (al) *(to play games, sports)* is the only verb whose stem changes from **u** to **ue.**
(j**ue**go, j**ue**gas, j**ue**ga, jugamos, jugáis, j**ue**gan)

Remember that the weather terms **nieva** *(nevar)* and **llueve** *(llover)* that you learned on page 92 are stem-changing verbs and are used only in the third person singular.

The verb **costar** *(to cost)* is usually used, as in English, in the third person singular or plural.

Las computadoras c**ue**stan mucho dinero.   *Computers cost a lot of money.*
Viajar en autobús no c**ue**sta mucho.   *Traveling by bus doesn't cost a lot.*

The verbs **empezar a** and **pensar** are often followed by an infinitive.

emp**e**zar a + *infinitive*   *to begin doing something*
Los atletas **empiezan a correr.**   *The athletes begin running.*

p**e**nsar + *infinitive*   *to plan, intend*
Los estudiantes **piensan viajar** a Sevilla.   *The students plan to travel to Sevilla.*

Present participles

Stem-changing verbs ending in **–ar** and **–er** have regular present participle forms.
Stem-changing verbs ending in **–ir** have irregular forms.

Present participle of stem-changing *-ir* verbs	
e → i	**o → u**
pedir: p**i**diendo	dormir: d**u**rmiendo
Las chicas están p**i**diendo la comida.	El bebé está d**u**rmiendo.

More verbs that follow this pattern include:

e → i	o → u
decir: diciendo preferir: prefiriendo repetir: repitiendo seguir: siguiendo servir: sirviendo	morir: muriendo

Tener *(to have)*

Tener is an irregular verb because the first person singular form **(yo)** ends in **-go** but the remaining forms follow the pattern of stem-changing verbs.

tener *(to have)*			
Singular		**Plural**	
yo	ten**go**	nosotros / nosotras	tenemos
tú	t**ie**nes	vosotros / vosotras	tenéis
Ud. / él / ella	t**ie**ne	Uds. / ellos / ellas	t**ie**nen

Many verbs that are built from **tener** are conjugated the same way: **contener** *(to contain)*, **entretener** *(to entertain)*, **mantener** *(to maintain)*, etc.

The verb **tener** is used to express possession in the same way the verb *to have* is used in English.

—¿**Tienes** buenas amigas?   —*Do you have good friends?*
—Sí, **tengo** muchas buenas amigas.   —*Yes, I have many good friends.*

Expressions with *tener*

¿Qué tienen?

Tiene frío.

Tiene calor.

Tiene hambre.

Tiene sed.

Tiene sueño.

Tiene miedo.

Tiene prisa.

Tiene cinco años.

tener cuidado	*to be careful*
tener la culpa	*to be at fault*
tener éxito	*to be successful*
tener ganas de + *infinitive*	*to want to (do something)/*
	to feel like (doing something)
tener que + *infinitive*	*to have to (do something)*
tener razón	*to be right*
tener sentido	*to make sense*

Using *ir* and *venir*

Ir *(to go)* and **venir** *(to come)* are common irregular verbs that have many uses.

	ir *(to go)*	venir *(to come)*
yo	**voy**	**vengo**
tú	**vas**	**vienes**
Ud. / él / ella	**va**	**viene**
nosotros / nosotras	**vamos**	**venimos**
vosotros / vosotras	**vais**	**venís**
Uds. / ellos / ellas	**van**	**vienen**

To talk about future actions:		
ir + **a** + *infinitive*	¿Cómo **voy a pagar** el viaje?	*How am I going to pay for the trip?*
To express destination or origin:		
ir + **a** + *location*	Uds. **van a** la universidad.	*You go to the university.*
venir + **de** + *location*	Uds. **vienen de** la universidad.	*You are coming from the university.*
To say "Let's go!":		
¡Vamos!	Yo sé dónde está la clase.	*I know where the class is.*
	¡Vamos!	*Let's go!*
To say "*Let's . . .*" + action:		
vamos a + *infinitive*	**Vamos a buscar** un buen restaurante.	*Let's look for a good restaurant.*
To go (somewhere else) to get / for something:		
ir + **por**	Ella **va por** el café.	*She goes (somewhere else) to get the coffee.*
To come (here) to get / to come for something:		
venir + **por**	Ella **viene por** el café.	*She comes (here) to get the coffee.*

Contraction: a + el = al

Just like **de** + **el** = **del**, when the preposition **a** precedes the article **el**, they contract to form **al.** There is no contraction with the pronoun **él** *(he)*.

Voy **al** museo.   *I'm going to the museum.*
Vamos **al** hotel.   *Let's go to the hotel.*

Actividades

1 Recomendaciones del portero (doorman).

Manuel is a doorman in a large downtown hotel in Madrid. Work with a partner to complete the dialog. Use the present tense.

Manuel Me llamo Manuel Gascón y soy portero en el hotel Prisma.

Tú ¿Qué restaurante _____ (**1.** recomendar) Ud. en Madrid?

Manuel _____ (**2.** poder, yo) recomendar muchos, ¿ _____ (**3.** preferir) Ud. comida española?

Tú ¡Por supuesto! Estamos en Madrid.

Manuel Entonces, _____ (**4.** recomendar, yo) el restaurante Casa de la Paella.

Tú ¿ _____ (**5.** costar) mucho dinero la comida allí?

Manuel No, no. Allí _____ (**6.** servir, ellos) platos de varios precios.

Tú _____ (**7.** querer, yo) probar la paella.

Manuel ¡Buena idea! La gente _____ (**8.** decir) que es magnífica.

Tú Pues entonces, necesito un taxi de inmediato para ir allí.

Manuel Yo _____ (**9.** pedir) el taxi para Ud. ¡Buen provecho!

2 Los planes de Vicente.

Fill in the correct forms of the verbs in the following passage. Then answer the questions that follow.

Yo _____ (**1.** pensar) viajar por España. Voy a empezar mi viaje en Madrid y después (*after*) yo _____ (**2.** querer) visitar Granada, Málaga y Jerez en la provincia de Andalucía. Yo _____ (**3.** preferir) ir en verano porque no _____ (**4.** llover) mucho. Luis Fernando, mi amigo andaluz, _____ (**5.** decir) que yo _____ (**6.** poder) dormir y comer en su casa. Es fantástico porque yo sé que su familia _____ (**7.** servir) comidas deliciosas todos los días.

Now answer the following questions about Vicente's plans.

1. ¿Dónde piensa Vicente empezar su viaje?
2. ¿Dónde puede dormir Vicente?
3. ¿Qué lugares piensa visitar?
4. ¿Llueve mucho en Andalucía en verano?
5. ¿Cuándo prefiere ir Vicente a Andalucía?

3 ¿Qué tengo?

Use the word **si** (*if*) to create complete sentences by matching a situation (Column A) with an expression with **tener** (Column B). Follow the model.

▶ MODELO: Hay poco tiempo. / tener prisa
Si hay poco tiempo, tengo prisa.

A	B
1. Veo un tigre (*tiger*).	a. tener hambre
2. Hay un examen mañana.	b. tener miedo
3. No hay agua.	c. tener que estudiar
4. Hace mucho sol.	d. tener ganas de leer
5. Es invierno.	e. tener sueño
6. Saco una A en el examen.	f. tener frío
7. Es medianoche.	g. tener calor
8. No hay comida.	h. tener éxito
9. Estoy seguro/a.	i. tener razón
10. Compro un buen libro.	j. tener sed

4 ¿Adónde van? ¿De dónde vienen? The following people are going to (**ir** + **a**) or coming from (**venir** + **de**) different places. Follow the model to indicate their destinations or origins.

▶ MODELO: las mamás y sus hijos / ir / parque
Las mamás y sus hijos van al parque.

1. Gonzalo / venir / el centro comercial
2. nosotros / ir / las clases de español
3. ellas / ir / el estadio
4. Liliana / venir / la tienda
5. Uds. / ir / el mercado
6. tú / venir / la discoteca
7. el doctor / venir / el hospital
8. los chicos / ir / el museo
9. yo / venir / la universidad
10. Mi profesora / ir / Madrid

5 ¿Qué vas a hacer? With a partner, ask each other what you will be doing (Column B) based on the circumstances in Column A. Follow the model.

▶ MODELO: hay programas interesantes / mirar televisión
—*¿Qué vas a hacer si hay programas interesantes?*
—*Voy a mirar televisión.*

A	B
1. hace buen tiempo	a. bailar en la discoteca
2. hay un tornado	b. comprar una computadora
3. los tacos son buenos	c. salir al parque
4. el examen es mañana	d. estudiar hoy
5. tu amigo está enfermo	e. llamar al teléfono de emergencias
6. es sábado	f. comer mucho
7. hoy llueve todo el día	g. no salir de casa
8. tienes dinero	h. ir a la farmacia

6 ¿Qué piensan hacer tú y tu compañero/a? With a partner, ask each other questions to find out what each of you are planning to do next weekend. Discuss whether you can do some activities together. Try your best to persuade your friend to join you in your planned activities.

▶ MODELO: —¿Qué piensas hacer (quieres hacer / vas a hacer) el viernes por la noche?
—Quiero cenar en un buen restaurante.

— *What are you planning to (going to) do on Friday night?*
— *I want to have dinner at a good restaurant.*

día	Estudiante A	Estudiante B
viernes (por la noche)	cenar en el restaurante Taco Loco	cenar en un buen restaurante
sábado (por la tarde)	jugar al básquetbol en el estadio	jugar al golf
domingo (por la tarde)	ir al centro comercial	comprar unos libros
domingo (por la noche)	ir al cine	mirar televisión

DISCUSSING TRANSPORTATION

¿Cómo te gusta viajar?

Me gusta viajar en **bicicleta**.

Me gusta viajar en **avión**.

Más palabras y expresiones

Cognados

el chofer *(L. Am.)* / chófer *(Sp.)*	el taxi
la motocicleta	el tren
la ruta	el/la turista

Sustantivos

el autobús	*bus*
el barco	*boat*
el billete / boleto / pasaje	*ticket, passage*
el camión	*truck; bus (Mex.)*
la camioneta	*pick-up truck; van*
el coche / el auto(móvil) / el carro	*car, automobile*
el crucero	*cruise ship*
la dirección	*address*
el metro	*subway*
el viaje	*trip*

Verbos

alcanzar	*to reach, catch up with*
estar cerca / lejos (de)	*to be close / far away (from)*
llegar	*to arrive*
manejar / conducir	*to drive*
quedar	*to be (located)*
viajar	*to travel*

Otras expresiones

a pie	*on foot*
en	*by (with transportation), in, on*

Actividades

1 El viaje de una tarjeta postal. Trace the route of the postcard from Claudia to Octavio. Follow the model.

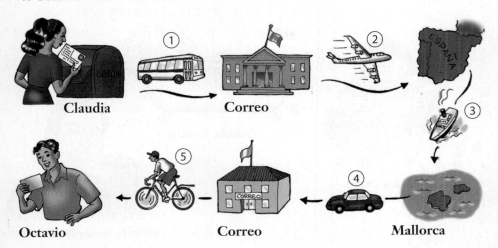

Claudia — Correo — ESPAÑA — Mallorca — Correo — Octavio

▶ **MODELO:** La tarjeta va al correo en   *The postcard goes to the post office*
autobús.   *by bus.*

1. La tarjeta va a España...
2. La tarjeta va a Mallorca...
3. La tarjeta va al correo...
4. La tarjeta va a la casa de Octavio...

2 Asociaciones. What means of transportation do you associate with these names?

1. Harley
2. Greyhound
3. Trek
4. Toyota
5. Delta
6. Amtrak
7. Checker
8. Royal Caribbean

3 ¿Cómo viajan? Working in pairs, ask each other these questions about transportation habits.

1. ¿Usas el transporte público?
2. Si vives en la universidad, ¿cómo viajas a casa en tus vacaciones?
3. Si vives en casa o en un apartamento, ¿cómo vas a la escuela?
4. ¿Te gusta viajar en motocicleta? ¿Por qué?
5. ¿Cómo vas al centro de tu ciudad?
6. Si vas a Europa, ¿vas en barco o en avión?
7. ¿Adónde vas en taxi? ¿Cuándo?
8. ¿Cómo va tu compañero/a de cuarto a la biblioteca?
9. Cuando vas al centro comercial, ¿cómo llegas a las tiendas?

4 Un viaje especial. You decide to take a trip to a Spanish-speaking country with a classmate. In pairs, discuss where you are going to go and how you are going to get there. Plan an itinerary that includes at least four different means of transportation.

▶ **MODELO:** Vamos a Puerto Rico en crucero.

Reflexive actions

Identify who performs and who receives the action of the verbs in these illustrations.

A Susana lava al perro.

B Miranda se baña.

C Roberto se cepilla los dientes.

When the subject both performs and receives the action of the verb, as in **B** and **C** above, the action is called *reflexive*. Reflexive verbs are used to discuss many daily routines in Spanish. Reflexive verbs are conjugated as shown below.

lavarse *(to wash oneself)*			
Subject Pronouns	**Reflexive Pronouns**	**Conjugated Verb**	
yo	**me**	lavo	*I wash (myself)*
tú	**te**	lavas	*you wash (yourself)*
Ud.	**se**	lava	*you wash (yourself)*
él / ella	**se**	lava	*he / she washes (himself / herself)*
nosotros/as	**nos**	lavamos	*we wash (ourselves)*
vosotros/as	**os**	laváis	*you wash (yourselves)*
Uds.	**se**	lavan	*you wash (yourselves)*
ellos / ellas	**se**	lavan	*they wash (themselves)*

To indicate that a verb is reflexive, the infinitive is usually listed with **se** attached at the end of the word. Otherwise the verb is not reflexive.

>   **levantarse** = *to get (oneself) up*
>
>   **levantar** = *to lift (something) up*

A verb is reflexive when the subject performs an action on itself. When the recipient of an action is different from the subject, the verb is not reflexive. Compare these examples.

Acuesto al niño.	*I put the child to bed.*
Me acuesto a las once.	*I go to bed at eleven o'clock.*
Despiertas a tu amigo.	*You wake up your friend.*
Tu amigo **se despierta** a las ocho.	*Your friend wakes up at eight o'clock.*

When a reflexive verb is conjugated, reflexive pronouns are always placed before the verb.

Los chicos **se** visten.	*The boys get dressed.*

When reflexive verbs are used together with an infinitive or present participle, the reflexive pronouns may either be attached to the end of these words, or precede the conjugated verb.

Los chicos van a vestir**se.**   *The boys are going to get dressed.*
Los chicos **se** van a vestir.
Los chicos **se** están vistiendo.   *The boys are getting dressed.*
Los chicos están vistiéndo**se.**

Reflexive verbs can sometimes be translated into English as *to get* or *to become* (+ action).

Yo **me** visto.   *I get dressed.*
Ella **se** levanta.   *She gets up.*

When using reflexive verbs to talk about parts of the body in Spanish, use the definite article, not the possessive adjective.

Nos lavamos **las** manos.   *We wash **our** hands.*
Tienes que cepillarte **los** dientes.   *You have to brush **your** teeth.*

Parts of the body frequently used with reflexive verbs include:

| la cara | *face* | las manos | *hands* |
| los dientes | *teeth* | el pelo | *hair* |

Common reflexive verbs

acostarse (ue)	*to go to bed; to lie down*
afeitarse	*to shave*
bañarse	*to take a bath*
cepillarse	*to brush*
despertarse (ie)	*to wake up*
divertirse (ie)	*to have a good time, enjoy oneself*
dormirse (ue)	*to fall asleep*
ducharse	*to take a shower*
irse	*to go away, leave*
levantarse	*to get up*
maquillarse	*to put on makeup*
peinarse	*to comb one's hair*
preocuparse	*to worry*
quedarse	*to stay*
quitarse (la ropa)	*to take off (one's clothes)*
secarse	*to dry off*
sentarse (ie)	*to sit down*
sentirse (ie)	*to feel*
vestirse (i)	*to get dressed*

To express the sequence in which you do things, use words such as:

primero *first*   luego *later, then, next*   por fin *finally*
entonces *then, at that time*   después *after,*
                                          afterwards

Primero me despierto a las seis de la   *First, I wake up at six in the morning,*
   mañana, **luego** me baño y **por**   *then I take a bath, and finally, I get*
   fin me visto.   *dressed.*

Actividades

1 Nuestras rutinas. You are describing the routines of several people. Follow the model to complete your descriptions. Remember to change the reflexive pronouns to agree with the subjects.

▶ **MODELO:** tú / despertarse temprano todos los días
　　　　　Tú te despiertas temprano　　*You wake up early every day.*
　　　　　todos los días.

1. yo / ducharse con agua caliente
2. Ud. / levantarse tarde
3. los chicos / quitarse el sombrero
4. el señor / afeitarse por la mañana
5. tú / vestirse con ropa moderna
6. las niñas / dormirse a las ocho y media
7. Marina / secarse el pelo

2 ¿Qué vas a hacer? Working with a partner, ask each other questions, following the model.

▶ **MODELO:** —¿Te vas a afeitar mañana?　　—*Are you going to shave tomorrow?*
　　　　　　　　　　　or
　　　　　—¿Vas a afeitarte mañana?
　　　　　—Sí, me voy a afeitar mañana. —*Yes, I am going to shave tomorrow.*
　　　　　　　　　　　or
　　　　　—Sí, voy a afeitarme mañana.

1. despertarse / a las 6:00 A.M.
2. bañarse / temprano
3. secarse el pelo / por la mañana
4. acostarse / tarde
5. quitarse los zapatos (*shoes*) / antes de dormir
6. divertirse en la discoteca / los sábados
7. cepillarse los dientes / por la mañana
8. divertirse / los fines de semana

3 En este momento. State what the people in the pictures are doing right now. Use the present progressive tense of the appropriate reflexive verb.

1. _____　　2. _____　　3. _____

4. _____　　5. _____　　6. _____

4 **Un día típico.** What does Jaime do on a typical day? Look at the pictures below and decide in which order Jaime does the following activities. Number the activities in a logical order, then write a sentence to describe each action shown in the pictures. Use reflexive verbs.

_____

_____

_____

_____

_____

_____

_____

_____

_____

Información confidencial

En el hotel de Nayeli.

Hija mía, vas a Dresden por el jaguar y llevas el jaguar a México...

¡Y después, hay un terremoto!

Sí, hija, porque llegas con el jaguar en los días mayas de la mala suerte.

¡Y Hernán muere en el terremoto!

No es tu culpa, hija mía. Tu esposo, Hernán, te ama.

¡Hernán!

En la casa de la familia Covarrubias.

Mira, mi amor, con el jaguar, vamos a ser ricos.

Tú siempre estás en problemas.

No hay problemas, ¡de verdad!

Ay Gerardo. ¡Tú y tus fantasías!

En el cuarto de hotel de Nayeli.

Señora arqueóloga: ¡con este microfonito, no te voy a perder!

En el hotel de Nayeli.

Buenas tardes.

Por favor, buscamos a Nayeli Paz Ocotlán.

Ah, sí, claro. La Sra. Paz es una huésped muy buena en nuestro hotel.

La Sra. Paz se despierta, se ducha y se viste.

Hoy, la Sra. Paz solamente va al teléfono, busca un número, escribe en un papelito...

... y hace una llamada.

Después, ella me pide la dirección de una compañía de transporte.

¿Tiene usted la dirección?

Sí, tengo la dirección. Está cerca!

¡Gracias! ¡Vamos, Adriana!

En la compañía de transportes.

¿Me puede decir cuál chofer tiene la ruta de Madrid a Sevilla.

Esa información es confidencial, señora.

¿Confidencial? ¡Soy cliente y quiero buen servicio!

¡Estos turistas! ¿Quién les entiende?

Bueno, escribo la dirección aquí: Gerardo H. Covarrubias. Callejón del Agua número 7.

Actividades

Online Study Center

For additional practice with this episode, visit the *Caminos* website at http://college.hmco.com/languages/spanish/renjilian/caminos/3e/student_home.html.

1 Comprensión. Based on this episode of *Caminos del jaguar*, choose the logical response.

1. Nayeli lleva el jaguar a...
   a. México.
   b. Dresden.

2. El jaguar llega en los días mayas...
   a. de los terremotos.
   b. de la mala suerte.

3. ¿Quién muere en el terremoto?
   a. un estudiante de Nayeli
   b. el esposo de Nayeli

4. La Sra. Covarrubias cree que el jaguar...
   a. es un buen negocio.
   b. es un problema.

5. Con el microfonito, Gafasnegras puede...
   a. escuchar a Nayeli.
   b. ver a Nayeli.

6. El portero del hotel...
   a. no tiene la dirección.
   b. tiene la dirección.

7. Nayeli busca...
   a. un número.
   b. una dirección.

8. En la compañía de transportes, Nayeli está...
   a. alterada.
   b. enamorada.

2 Situaciones. With a partner, dramatize one of the following situations.

1. The conversation between Sr. and Sra. Covarrubias.
2. Nayeli is trying to get information from the clerk at the truck company.

3 Escritura. Write a brief summary of what Nayeli does at the hotel before she leaves for the trucking company (4–6 sentences).

NOTA CULTURAL

Los terremotos *(earthquakes)* en México

At 7:17 A.M., on September 19, 1985, Mexico suffered two consecutive earthquakes that devastated the nation's capital, Mexico City. Ten thousand Mexicans died, 50,000 were injured, and 250,000 lost their homes as a result of this natural disaster. The psychological effects of these quakes still haunt many "capitalinos" to this day.

Vocabulario y lengua

ORDERING FOOD IN A RESTAURANT

¿Qué van a tomar?

Online Study Center

For additional practice with this unit's vocabulary and grammar, visit the *Caminos* website at http://college.hmco.com/languages/spanish/renjilian/caminos/3e/student_home.html.
You can also review audio flashcards, quiz yourself, and explore related Spanish-language sites.

Restaurante Dalí

Precio en euros

Entremeses			Appetizers	
	Tortilla española	2,1		Spanish omelette with potatoes and onions
	Chorizo y pan	2,7		Sausage and bread
	Queso manchego	3,0		Manchego (goat) cheese
Sopas			**Soups**	
	Gazpacho	2,4		Gazpacho (cold vegetable soup)
	Sopa de pescado	3,6		Fish soup
	Sopa del día	2,7		Soup of the day
Ensaladas			**Salads**	
	Ensalada mixta	3,6		Mixed salad
	Ensalada rusa	2,4		Potato salad
Entradas			**Entrées**	
	Especialidad de la casa:			Specialty of the house:
	Paella valenciana	8,4		Paella valenciana (rice dish usually with meat, fish and vegetables)
	Gambas al ajillo	5,4		Shrimp in garlic Sauce
	Bistec asado con patatas fritas	6,6		Steak with French fries
Postres			**Desserts**	
	Helado de chocolate, vainilla o fresa	1,8		Chocolate, vanilla, or strawberry ice cream
	Fruta del día	1,2		Fruit of the day
	Flan	1,8		Baked egg custard
Bebidas			**Drinks**	
	Sangría- 1 litro	5,4		Beverage of wine, soda, or juice, and fruit pieces
	Agua mineral con/sin gas	1,5		Mineral water (carbonated/uncarbonated)
	Té o café	1,2		Tea or coffee
	Refrescos variados	1,5		Assorted soft drinks
	Zumo/Jugo de naranja	3,0		Orange juice
	Cerveza	1,5		Beer
	Vino tinto/blanco	1,2		Red/white wine

Más palabras y expresiones

Sustantivos

el almuerzo	*lunch*
el aperitivo/el entremés	*appetizer*
el/la camarero/a, el/la mesero/a	*waiter, waitress*
la carne	*meat*
la carta, el menú	*menu*
la cena	*dinner*
la comida	*food / dinner (in some places) / lunch (in others)*
la copa	*stemmed glass, goblet*
la cuchara	*tablespoon*
la cucharita	*teaspoon*
el cuchillo	*knife*
la cuenta	*bill*
el desayuno	*breakfast*
el hambre *(f.)*	*hunger*
la legumbre	*vegetable*
el marisco	*shellfish*
el pedido	*order*
la pimienta	*(black) pepper*
el plato	*plate, dish*
la propina	*tip*
la sal	*salt*
las tapas	*small servings of food (Sp.)*
la taza	*cup*
el tenedor	*fork*
el vaso	*glass (for drinks)*

Verbos

almorzar (ue)	*to have lunch*
cenar	*to have dinner*
dejar	*to leave (something behind)*
desayunar	*to have breakfast*
disfrutar	*to enjoy*
tomar	*to drink*

Adjetivos

caliente	*hot (temperature)*
dulce	*sweet*
fuerte (una comida)	*heavy (food)*
ligero/a	*light*
picante	*hot (spicy)*
preparado/a	*prepared*
rico/a	*rich, delicious*
sabroso/a	*delicious, tasty*

Otras expresiones

¡A sus órdenes!	*At your service!*
Tengo mucha hambre.	*I am very hungry.*
¿Qué desean comer / beber / tomar?	*What would you like to eat / drink?*
¿Qué nos recomienda?	*What do you recommend?*
Estoy muerto/a de hambre.	*I'm starving / famished.*
La cuenta, por favor.	*The check, please.*
Me gustaría / Quisiera (pedir)...	*I would like (to order) . . .*

Actividades

1 Una cena importante. You are dining with a friend in a nice restaurant. With a partner, talk about the foods each of you like and dislike.

▶ **MODELO:** el bistec

—¿Te gusta el bistec?   —*Do you like steak?*
—No, no me gusta.   —*No, I don't like it.*

or

—Sí, me gusta.   —*Yes, I like it.*

1. el helado de chocolate
2. el flan
3. la ensalada rusa
4. la sopa de pescado
5. la tortilla española
6. el jugo de naranja
7. las gambas al ajillo
8. el café

2 En el café. Help your partner decide what to order. Complete the chart by asking, then recording, your partner's choice for each category on the menu from Restaurante Dalí. After deciding on what to order, calculate the total cost of each meal. Remember to add a good tip depending on the service. Follow the model.

▶ **MODELO:** —¿Qué vas a pedir de entremés?   —*What are you going to order for an appetizer?*

—Voy a pedir queso manchego.   —*I am going to order Manchego cheese.*

	El pedido	El precio
Entremés	_____	_____
Sopa	_____	_____
Ensalada	_____	_____
Entrada	_____	_____
Postre	_____	_____
Bebida	_____	_____
Propina	_____	_____
Precio total:		_____

3 Entre nosotros. Role-play the following situation with a partner.

Turista	Camarero/a
You have just spent the whole day in Sevilla sightseeing. You have been enjoying yourself so much that you haven't had time to eat. The concierge has recommended a restaurant called "Los Arcos." You are very hungry and you want to eat everything on the menu. You especially want to try **sangría, tapas, paella,** and dessert.	You work at the restaurant called "Los Arcos." Today has been a difficult day. The cook is sick and the only person who knows anything about cooking is the dishwasher. In addition, there are no desserts, shrimp, or wine. Try to make the best of the situation.

EXPRESSING ACTIONS IN THE PRESENT

Verbs with irregular *yo* forms: *saber* and *conocer*

El verano es mi estación favorita. **Hago**° muchas cosas los fines de semana. **Salgo**°
de mi casa a las seis de la mañana y **conduzco**° mi coche al parque. **Traigo**° mi guitarra
y una novela interesante. Después de leer y tocar la guitarra, **doy un paseo**° por el
parque y como en un buen restaurante que **conozco**.

I do / I leave
I drive / I bring
I take a walk

Some verbs are irregular only in the first person singular (**yo**), while the endings of
the other forms remain the same as for regular verbs. For some of these verbs, the
yo form ends in **-go** or **-zco.** The **yo** form of verbs that end in **-cer** and **-cir** tend to
have **–zco** endings.

Verbs with irregular *yo* forms		
	-go verbs **hacer** *(to make; to do)*	**-zco verbs** **conducir** *(to drive)*
yo	ha**go**	condu**zco**
tú	haces	conduces
Ud. / él / ella	hace	conduce
nosotros / nosotras	hacemos	conducimos
vosotros / vosotras	hacéis	conducís
Uds. / ellos / ellas	hacen	conducen

Common verbs that follow these patterns:

-go verbs		**-zco verbs**	
oír (o**igo**)	*to hear*	conocer (cono**zco**)	*to know, be familiar with*
poner (pon**go**)	*to put, place*	parecer (pare**zco**)	*to seem*
salir (sal**go**)	*to go out; to leave*	producir (produ**zco**)	*to produce*
traer (tra**igo**)	*to bring*	traducir (tradu**zco**)	*to translate*

In addition to being a **–go** verb, the verb **oír** has these spelling changes: **oyes, oye, oímos, oís, oyen.**

The verb **salir** *(to go out; to leave)* is useful for expressing many actions. Here are just a few.

Common expressions with *salir*:

salir a + **infinitive**	*to go out to + verb* Yo salgo a bailar los sábados.	**salir de**	*to leave from a place* Salimos de la biblioteca a las diez.
salir con	*to leave or go out with* Ramiro quiere salir con Yolanda.	**salir para**	*to leave for a place* ¿Cuándo sales para Europa?

Dar *(to give)*, **saber** *(to know)*, and **ver** *(to see)* are irregular in the **yo** form, but don't follow any particular pattern. The endings of the other forms remain the same as those for regular verbs.

	dar	saber	ver
yo	**doy**	**sé**	**veo**
tú	das	sabes	ves
Ud. / él / ella	da	sabe	ve
nosotros / nosotras	damos	sabemos	vemos
vosotros / vosotras	dais	sabéis	veis
Uds. / ellos / ellas	dan	saben	ven

Common expressions with **dar:**

dar un paseo	*to take a walk*	dar una conferencia	*to give a talk*
dar una clase	*to teach a class*	dar una fiesta	*to give a party*

Saber and *conocer*

Although the general meaning for both verbs is *to know,* each is used in Spanish to express that concept in distinct ways.

Uses of saber / conocer			
saber + *infinitive: to know how to do something*		conocer + *noun (place): to know / be familiar with (a place)*	
¿Sabes conducir?	*Do you know how to drive?*	**¿Conoces** Puerto Rico?	*Do you know Puerto Rico?*
Sabemos hablar español.	*We know how to speak Spanish.*	**Conozco** un buen restaurante.	*I know a good restaurant.*
saber + *noun (information): to know facts, such as time, dates, places, names, and pieces of information*		conocer a + noun (*person / people*): *to know someone*	
Sabemos el día y el lugar de la fiesta.	*We know the day and location of the party.*	**¿Conoces a** mi amigo Luis?	*Do you know / Have you met my friend Luis?*
No **sé** dónde están mis libros.	*I don't know where my books are.*	**Conozco a** mis compañeros de clase muy bien.	*I know my classmates very well.*

Personal *a*

A direct object is a word that receives the action of the verb. If the direct object is a person or implies a person, it must be preceded by the personal **a.** For **a** + **el,** remember to use the contraction **al.** If the direct object is a thing, then **a** is not used.

Veo la casa.	*I see **the house.** (thing)*
Veo **a** Marcos.	*I see **Marcos.** (person)*
Conozco la ciudad.	*I know **the city.** (thing)*
Conozco **a** la profesora.	*I know **the teacher.** (person)*
Conozco **al** profesor	

Actividades

1 Una invitación. Linda runs into her friend Pablo, and they talk about going to the movies. Complete their conversation with the correct form of the present tense of each verb in parentheses.

Linda ¡Hola, Pablo! ¿ _____ (saber) tú si hay películas (*movies*) buenas hoy?

Pablo Sí, hay muchas. Yo _____ (conocer) un cine muy bueno. Allí presentan películas francesas.

Linda ¿Francesas? ¡Yo no _____ (saber) francés! ¿Hay subtítulos?

Pablo No, no hay subtítulos, pero yo _____ (traducir) muy bien el francés.

Linda ¡Pablo, qué tonto eres! Es una broma (*joke*), ¿verdad?

Pablo ¡Claro que es una broma! Hay subtítulos. ¡Vamos al cine; yo _____ (conducir)!

Linda ¡Y yo pago, vamos!

2 ¡Yo también! Read what the following people do; then say whether you do these activities, too. With a classmate, take turns answering the questions.

▶ MODELO: —Nosotros salimos de casa a las siete, ¿y tú?
—*Yo también salgo de casa a las siete.*

or

—*No, no salgo de casa a las siete. Salgo a las siete y media.*

1. Ricardo sale para México, ¿y tú?
2. Nosotros conducimos autobuses grandes, ¿y tú?
3. Los estudiantes dan fiestas fantásticas, ¿y tú?
4. El profesor sale temprano, ¿y tú?
5. Ella pone la mesa antes de comer, ¿y tú?
6. El Sr. Rulfo conoce a mucha gente, ¿y tú?
7. Tu compañera traduce la tarea al inglés, ¿y tú?
8. Liliana ve televisión los domingos, ¿y tú?

3 ¿Quién sabe qué? Say what these people know or know how to do. Use **saber** or **conocer.** Follow the model and use the personal **a** if needed.

▶ MODELO: Elena / inglés
Elena sabe inglés.

1. Berta / muchos secretos
2. nosotros / Madrid
3. Verónica / no / bailar
4. ellos / el profesor Sánchez
5. Ud. / la hora
6. el chico / un buen restaurante mexicano
7. yo / planchar la ropa
8. el profesor / los nombres de los estudiantes
9. yo / no / la nueva estudiante
10. Gil y yo / cantar bien

4 Actividades. Using at least four of the verbs in the list, write a short e-mail to your best friend about things you do in a typical week. (Use the present indicative.) Then describe four things that you are going to do this weekend. (Use **ir a** + infinitive.)

hacer	conducir	ver	dar	ir
salir	poner	escribir	estudiar	traer

USING LARGE NUMBERS

¿Cómo contamos los números en español?

	Los números de 200 a 2.000.000				
200	doscientos	600	seiscientos	1.999	mil novecientos noventa y nueve
201	doscientos uno	700	setecientos	2.000	dos mil
300	trescientos	800	ochocientos	2.001	dos mil uno
400	cuatrocientos	900	novecientos	1.000.000	un millón
500	quinientos	1.000	mil	2.000.000	dos millones

Note: In most Spanish-speaking countries, numbers are punctuated with periods instead of commas.

Using numbers as adjectives

doscientos – novecientos	The numbers from 200 to 900 agree in gender with the nouns they modify. These words are always plural. *200 stores* = **doscientas** tiendas *300 rooms* = **trescientos** cuartos
mil	**Mil** remains unchanged and does not agree in gender or number with the noun it modifies. *one thousand pesos* = **mil** pesos *two thousand trains* = **dos mil** trenes. Note that **mil** means *one thousand* or *a thousand*.
millón	**Millón** (singular) is used with **un**; in all other instances use **millones** (plural). *1.005.093 pesos* = **un millón, cinco mil, noventa y tres** pesos *2.400.671 dollars* = **dos millones, cuatrocientos mil, seiscientos setenta y**[1] **un** dólares
un millón de / millones de	**Un millón de / millones de** is used only when the number is rounded out in millions. Otherwise **millones** follows the other rules above. *1.000.000 pesos* = **un millón de** pesos *5.000.000 dollars* = **cinco millones de** dólares *but* *5.100.401 girls* = **cinco millones, cien mil, cuatrocientas una** niñas

___
[1]Remember that **y** is used between the "tens" and "ones" place in numbers.

Actividades

1 **¿Cuántos jóvenes hay en Centroamérica?** You work for the United Nations and are doing research on population trends in Central America. Discuss with a partner how many young people live in the region, comparing the population figures for each country. Remember to make the numbers agree in gender with the nouns that they modify, when appropriate.

▶ MODELO: —¿Cuántas niñas hay en El Salvador?
—Hay un millón, doscientas doce mil, doscientas dieciséis niñas en El Salvador.

—How many girls are there in El Salvador?
—There are one million, two hundred twelve thousand, two hundred sixteen girls in El Salvador.

Los jóvenes de Centroamérica

País	Niños 0–14 años de edad	Niñas 0–14 años de edad
El Salvador	1.265.080	1.212.216
Costa Rica	590.261	563.196
Guatemala	2.573.359	2.479.098
Honduras	1.491.170	1.429.816
Nicaragua	1.031.897	994.633
Panamá	492.403	472.996

2 Eventos históricos.

Write out the following dates in Spanish on your own. Then work with a partner to see if you can match the events in Column A with the dates in Column B.

A		B
1. Cristóbal Colón llega a las Américas.		**a.** 1865
2. Los moros *(Moors)* llegan a España.		**b.** 1964
3. La segunda guerra mundial *(WWII)* termina (ends).		**c.** 1977
4. Un grupo de terroristas ataca Nueva York y el Pentágono.		**d.** 711
5. La disolución de la Unión Soviética ocurre.		**e.** 1492
6. Declaran la independencia de los Estados Unidos.		**f.** 2005
7. El huracán Katrina causa gran destrucción.		**g.** 1992
8. Los Beatles cantan en el *Ed Sullivan Show*.		**h.** 1776
9. La película *Saturday Night Fever* es muy popular.		**i.** 1945
10. John Wilkes Booth asesina al Presidente Abraham Lincoln.		**j.** 2001

Answers: 1. e; 2. d; 3. i; 4. j; 5. g; 6. h; 7. f; 8. b; 9. c; 10. a

3 ¿Cuántos hay?

Use the World Fact Book on the Internet (https://www.cia.gov/cia/publications/factbook/index.html) to determine the population for the following countries. Report your findings to the class in Spanish.

País	Población
España	_____
Bolivia	_____
México	_____
El Salvador	_____
Puerto Rico	_____
Argentina	_____
Perú	_____
Costa Rica	_____

SHOWING LOCATION OF PEOPLE, PLACES, AND THINGS

Demonstrative adjectives and pronouns: adverbs of location

¿Qué flores te gustan?

> Cecilia, **esas** flores rojas me gustan mucho.

> Sí, son muy bonitas, pero prefiero **aquellas** flores amarillas.

> No, **aquellas** flores no me gustan. Prefiero **éstas.**

In the drawing above, which objects are the people talking about? Which words are used to indicate where these objects are?

Demonstrative adjectives and pronouns			
Demonstrative adjectives	Demonstrative pronouns	Neuter demonstrative pronouns	
este, esta	éste, ésta	esto	*this (one)*
estos, estas	éstos, éstas		*these (ones)*
ese, esa	ése, ésa	eso	*that (one)*
esos, esas	ésos, ésas		*those (ones)*
aquel, aquella	aquél, aquélla	aquello	*that (one) (over there)*
aquellos/as	aquéllos/as		*those (ones) (over there)*

Demonstrative adjectives are used to point out people or objects. They modify a noun and are placed directly before it. They agree in gender and number with the nouns they modify.

Esta tortilla me gusta.   *I like this tortilla.*
Esa ensalada parece deliciosa.   *That salad looks delicious.*

Demonstrative pronouns are used to replace nouns. These pronouns have the same forms as the adjectives, but carry a written accent over the stressed vowel. Like demonstrative adjectives, demonstrative pronouns also agree in gender and number with the nouns they replace.

Me gusta mucho este vino,   *I like this wine very much, not **that one.***
   aquél no.
Prefiero esta sopa. **Ésa** está muy   *I prefer this soup. **That one** is very salty.*
   salada.

Neuter demonstrative pronouns are used to refer to something indefinite or abstract: an object, an event, or an idea. Note that neuter pronouns don't have written accents.

Esto representa un problema   *This represents an enormous problem.*
   enorme.
Eso no me parece bien.   *That doesn't seem OK to me.*

Adverbs of location

When using demonstrative adjectives and pronouns, the following adverbs of place are useful to describe the relative location of things: **aquí** *(here)*; **allí / ahí** *(there)*; and **allá** *(over there)*.

—Por favor, necesito **esos** libros.
—¿Cuáles libros? **¿Éstos** que están **aquí?**
—Sí, **ésos** que están **allí.**

—*Please, I need those books.*
—*Which books? These here?*
—*Yes, those that are there.*

Actividades

1 ¿Qué galletitas? Two friends are planning to buy a dessert to have after dinner. Complete their conversation with demonstrative adjectives or demonstrative pronouns, using the cues in parentheses.

Romeo   ¡Mira, Julieta, _____ (**1.** *these*) galletas María parecen muy ricas!
Julieta   No, Romeo, no me gustan, quiero _____ (**2.** *those* [*over there*]) galletitas con piña.
Romeo   De acuerdo, pero ¿ves alguna galletita de chocolate?
Julieta   Claro, mira, _____ (**3.** *these*) son de chocolate.
Romeo   ¡Qué bien! Vamos a comprar _____ (**4.** *those*) galletas de chocolate y _____ (**5.** *these*) mazapanes.
Julieta   Y yo quiero comprar también _____ (**6.** *those*) pastelitos de coco y _____ (**7.** *these*) galletas de almendra. ¿Quieres probar _____ (8. *those* [*over there*]) bollos de crema?
Romeo   Por supuesto, quiero probar de todo. ¡Nuestra cena va a ser estupenda!

2 En el restaurante. You and a friend are enjoying some wonderful restaurant meals as you travel through Spain. Compare options on the menu as you decide what to order by completing the sentences with demonstrative adjectives and pronouns.

1. _____ *(This)* ensalada es grande. _____ *(That one)* es pequeña.
2. Mira _____ *(that* [*over there*]*)* paella valenciana tiene mariscos. Prefiero _____ *(that)* bistec.
3. _____ *(That)* mesero es simpático. _____ *(That one* [*over there*]*)* es antipático.
4. _____ *(This)* gazpacho está muy frío. _____ *(That)* sopa de pollo está caliente.
5. _____ *(This)* mesa está limpia. _____ *(Those ones* [*over there*]*)* están sucias.
6. _____ *(Those)* postres son de chocolate. _____ *(These ones)* son de piña.

3 Restaurante Delicias. Describe the items in the chart using demonstrative adjectives and the vocabulary you have learned in this chapter. The adverbs above each group of foods will help you decide which demonstrative adjective you'll need. Work with a partner.

▶ MODELO: (Aquí) Esta ensalada es grande y sabrosa.

Aquí	Allí	Allá

Las reglas son las reglas

En la ciudad.

¡Ay, qué hambre! ¿Por qué no comemos algo en algún café?

Está bien, pero algo rápido.

En un café de la ciudad.

Buenas tardes, jóvenes, ¿vais a almorzar? ¿Queréis algo ligero, o algo más fuerte?

Queremos algo rápido.

Los entremeses, las sopas y las ensaladas son lo más rápido.

Perfecto.

Pero, si no sois del país, os recomiendo la especialidad de la casa.

No, no tenemos tiempo. Por favor, dos entremeses, los más populares de la casa.

Yo quiero lo mismo, gracias.

Muy bien.

Y también un gazpacho para mí.

¿Y para beber?

Un jugo de frutas.

Agua mineral con gas, por favor.

En el hotel de Nayeli.

En la compañía de transportes.

¿Conoce a esta señora?

Sí, sí, sí, ella estuvo aquí por la mañana.

¿Me puede decir… ?

¡No! ¡Esa información es confidencial!

¿Cuál información?

El nombre o la dirección del chófer de esa ruta.

¿Chofer? ¿Qué chofer? ¿Cuál ruta?

Usted está alterado. Por favor, ¡cálmese!

Yo estoy perfectamente calmado, pero usted y su amiga, la profesora, están alteradas.

Adriana, por favor, el señor sólo está haciendo su trabajo.

Esta situación es muy seria.

Señorita, ¡las reglas son las reglas!

¡Usted no comprende! ¡Qué horrible es!

¡Adriana, por favor, vámonos!

En la puerta de la compañía de transportes.

Adriana, tranquilízate. Tengo la información que necesitamos.

¿Cómo? ¿Qué dices?

Sí, el chofer se llama Gerardo H. Covarrubias. Su dirección en Sevilla es Callejón del Agua número 7.

¡Vamos al hotel de Nayeli! ¡Genial!

En el hotel de Nayeli.

¡Qué horror! Voy a llamar a la policía.

¡Dios mío!

Nayeli está en peligro. Eso está claro.

Tenemos que ver a Nayeli en Sevilla.

¡Vamos!

Actividades

Online Study Center

For additional practice with this episode, visit the *Caminos* website at http://college.hmco.com/languages/spanish/renjilian/caminos/3e/student_home.html.

1 Comprensión. Based on this episode of *Caminos del jaguar*, choose the logical response.

1. Adriana...
   - a. no tiene hambre.
   - b. tiene mucha hambre.

2. ¿Quién quiere comer algo rápido?
   - a. Adriana.
   - b. Felipe.

3. El mozo del restaurante recomienda...
   - a. la especialidad de la casa.
   - b. la especialidad española.

4. ¿Quién pide gazpacho y batido de frutas?
   - a. Adriana
   - b. Felipe

5. ¿Quién pide gazpacho y agua mineral con gas?
   - a. Adriana
   - b. Felipe.

6. El señor de la compañía de transportes no da la información...
   - a. porque él está alterado.
   - b. porque la información es confidencial.

7. ¿Adónde van Adriana y Felipe?
   - a. a Sevilla
   - b. a Madrid

8. Felipe tiene...
   - a. el nombre del chofer.
   - b. la dirección del hotel.

2 Situaciones. Dramatize one of the following situations.

1. Adriana and Felipe order a meal from the waiter at the coffee shop.
2. Adriana argues with the clerk at the trucking company.

3 Escritura. Write a brief summary (4–6 sentences) of this episode of *Caminos del jaguar.*

NOTA CULTURAL

España y el uso de *vosotros*

In Spain, the **vosotros** form is the plural of **tú** and is used to talk with friends and family. Adults often use **vosotros** to address younger people and children, who in turn will address them with **usted(es)** as a sign of respect. In Latin America, **ustedes** is the only plural form of address in all formal and informal situations. **Vosotros** is rarely used in Latin America but may occasionally be heard in very formal situations, such as religious ceremonies and political speeches.

Lectura

Online Study Center

For further writing practice online, visit the *Caminos* website at http://college .hmco.com/languages/ spanish/renjilian/caminos/ 3e/student_home.html.

PRELECTURA

1 **Nuestras ciudades favoritas.** In groups of three, take turns describing a city that each of you has visited with family or friends, or talk about the city in which you currently live. Answer the questions below.

1. ¿En qué país está la ciudad? ¿Cómo se llama? ¿Cuántos habitantes hay?
2. ¿Es una ciudad grande o pequeña? ¿Es vieja o nueva? ¿Cuántos años tiene?
3. ¿Qué edificios importantes hay? ¿Cómo son?
4. ¿Hay buenos restaurantes allí? ¿Qué tipo de comidas preparan? ¿Hay cibercafés?
5. ¿Cuáles son los principales sitios turísticos de interés?
6. ¿Qué actividades hacen ustedes de día y de noche con la familia o los amigos?
7. ¿Es famosa la ciudad por un evento, día o persona especial? Explica.

Reading Strategy

Skimming

Skimming is a reading strategy that you can apply when you want to learn information quickly from written articles. Skimming is the technique of quickly eliciting the general idea or main focus of a text or article. When reading in Spanish, skimming is very useful. First, glance quickly at any headings, titles, and obvious cognates (presented in *Unidad 1*). Second, rapidly glance at any visuals that the article or your instructor may provide. Skim the selection below and complete the activities that follow.

Sevilla, ciudad sensacional

El exquisito Parque María Luisa

La capital de la provincia de Andalucía, Sevilla, tiene cerca de[1] 700.000 habitantes. Es la cuarta[2] ciudad más grande de España. Es posible llegar a Sevilla en el AVE, el tren rápido de alta velocidad. Sevilla es conocida por sus parques muy bonitos y sus museos, iglesias, conventos, torres y palacios, que presentan una rica variedad de estilos de arquitectura.

El Parque de María Luisa

El Parque de María Luisa es extraordinario. Con sus jardines preciosos, árboles latinoamericanos y zonas sombrías[3], es un buen sitio para dar un paseo a pie o en auto.

La Catedral

La Catedral de Sevilla, de estilo gótico, es una de las catedrales más famosas del mundo. Es la tercera en tamaño[4], después de la Catedral de San Pedro en Roma y la de San Pablo en Londres[5]. Los Reyes[6] de España seleccionaron[7] la Catedral de Sevilla para la gran boda[8] de su hija Elena.

La Catedral de Sevilla, España

[1]close to; [2]fourth; [3]shady; [4]third in size; [5]London; [6]King and Queen; [7]selected; [8]wedding.

Unos jóvenes hablan y comen tapas

La Giralda

Una pareja baila flamenco

La Giralda

La Giralda es un ejemplo maravilloso del arte islámico. Una alta torre[9] rectangular de casi 117.5 metros de altura, está junto a[10] la Catedral de Sevilla. En 1184 se empezó[11] su construcción de arquitectura musulmana[12] y en 1555 el arquitecto Hernán Ruiz agregó[13] el campanario[14], como el de una iglesia cristiana, con una gran figura de bronce como veleta[15]. Desde la torre hay una magnífica vista[16] panorámica de la ciudad de Sevilla.

La música y danza flamencas

La música y danza flamencas son típicas de Sevilla, donde los bailes se llaman "sevillanas", en honor de su origen en esta ciudad. Las sevillanas están llenas de ritmos hipnóticos, pasión y drama. Es fascinante mirar esta danza y escuchar la música de Sevilla.

Las tapas al aire libre[17]

En Sevilla hay bares al aire libre donde muchas personas comen tapas. La hora más animada para disfrutar de las tapas es de la una a las cuatro de la tarde, cerca de la orilla[18] del río Guadalquivir.

---

[9]tower; [10]next to; [11]was begun; [12]Muslim; [13]added; [14]bell tower; [15]weather vane; [16]view; [17]outside; [18]shore

POSTLECTURA

2 Información general. In the selection above, skim the headings of the text for the different characteristics that make Sevilla an exciting Spanish city. In pairs, ask each other, **Menciona cinco aspectos atractivos de Sevilla.** Then, study the photos, taking turns reading the captions under each one to gather further information rapidly about the content of the selection. Ask each other, **¿Qué cognados hay y qué significan?**

Reading Strategy

Scanning

Scanning is a commonly used reading strategy, especially for reading selections that contain many new vocabulary terms. In scanning, look for specific details that support the general information you've already learned.

3 Aspectos básicos. After scanning this selection, jot down one basic characteristic of each of these attractions in Sevilla.

1. El Parque de María Luisa
2. La Catedral y La Giralda
3. La música y la danza flamencas
4. Las tapas al aire libre

Escritura

Online Study Center

For further writing practice online, visit the *Caminos* website at http://college .hmco.com/languages/ spanish/renjilian/caminos/ 3e/student_home.html.

Writing Strategy

Providing supporting details

One way of making your writing interesting for the reader is to provide details about your topic that support or explain your main idea. The result is more vivid and convincing prose. Read the Workshop below to see how providing supporting details about a character from *Caminos del jaguar* makes the sample passage much more interesting.

Workshop

Main idea	Gafasnegras es mala.
Supporting details	Ella siempre lleva gafas de sol. Piensa robar el jaguar. Ella persigue a Nayeli. Pone un microfonito en la agenda de Nayeli.
Sample passage	No sabemos quién es, pero sabemos que lleva sus famosas gafas de sol. Desde el primer episodio de la historia, ella persigue a Nayeli porque piensa robar el jaguar. Desordena la habitación de Nayeli y pone un microfonito en su agenda para saber dónde está Nayeli.

Strategy in action

For additional practice in providing supporting details, turn to the *Escritura* section of *Unidad 3* in your Student Activities Manual.

1 Nuestro viaje. You and your friend are planning on spending the summer in Spain. You each have limited resources ($750). Create an itinerary of cities and sites to visit, where to stay, and what to eat. Plan to travel to a minimum of four places and to use at least three different means of transportation. Use the map in the front of the book for reference. Write a postcard to your friend describing the itinerary you plan. Include a main idea and supporting details.

2 Mi universidad. Get a copy of your campus map or sketch one out. Plan a tour for a prospective student to show her/him where everything is. Use demonstrative adjectives and pronouns.

Resumen de vocabulario

PRIMER PASO

TALKING ABOUT WEATHER AND SEASONS

Sustantivos

el aguacero/el chubasco	*downpour*
la brisa	*breeze*
el cielo	*sky*
el clima	*climate*
el este	*east*
los grados centígrados/ Celsius/Fahrenheit	*degrees centigrade/ Celsius / Fahrenheit*
el huracán	*hurricane*
el invierno	*winter*
los kilómetros (por hora)	*kilometers (per hour)*
la lluvia	*rain*
el/la meteorólogo/a	*meteorologist*
las millas (por hora)	*miles (per hour)*
la nieve	*snow*
el noreste/el noroeste	*northeast/northwest*
el norte	*north*
la nube	*cloud*
el oeste	*west*
el otoño	*autumn, fall*
el porcentaje	*percentage*
la primavera	*spring*
la probabilidad	*probability*
el promedio	*average*
el pronóstico del tiempo	*weather forecast*
el sur	*south*
el sureste/el suroeste	*southeast/southwest*
la temperatura (mínima/máxima)	*(minimum/maximum) temperature*
la tormenta/la tronada	*storm*
el tornado	*tornado*
el verano	*summer*

Otras expresiones

¿A cuánto está la temperatura?	*What is the temperature?*
está (parcialmente) nublado	*it's (partly) cloudy*
fuerte	*strong*
hace buen/mal tiempo	*it's good/bad weather*
hace calor/frío/fresco	*it's hot/cold/cool*
hace viento	*it's windy*
húmedo/a	*humid*
llovizna	*it's drizzling*
llueve	*it's raining*
nieva	*it's snowing*

por ciento	*percent*
seco/a	*dry*

VERBS

almorzar (ue)	*to have lunch*
cerrar (ie)	*to close*
comenzar (ie)	*to start, begin*
concernir (ie)	*to concern*
conseguir (i)	*to get, obtain*
contar (ue)	*to count*
contener	*to contain*
costar (ue)	*to cost*
decir (i)	*to say, tell*
dormir (ue)	*to sleep*
empezar (ie)	*to begin*
encontrar (ue)	*to find*
entender (ie)	*to understand*
entretener	*to entertain*
ir	*to go*
jugar (ue) (al)	*to play (a sport)*
mantener	*to maintain*
mentir	*to lie*
morir (ue)	*to die*
mostrar (ue)	*to show*
pedir (i)	*to ask for*
pensar (ie)	*to think*
perder (ie)	*to lose*
perseguir (i)	*to follow, pursue*
poder (ue)	*to be able*
preferir (ie)	*to prefer*
probar (ue)	*to taste, try*
querer (ie)	*to want*
recomendar (ie)	*to recommend*
recordar (ue)	*to remember*
repetir (i)	*to repeat*
seguir (i)	*to follow, continue*
servir (i)	*to serve*
soñar (ue) (con)	*to dream (about)*
tener	*to have*
venir	*to come*
volver (ue)	*to return*

EXPRESSIONS WITH *TENER*

tener calor	*to be hot; to feel hot*
tener cuidado	*to be careful*
tener la culpa	*to be at fault*

tener éxito	to be successful
tener frío	to be cold
tener ganas de + *infinitive*	to feel like (doing something)
tener hambre	to be hungry
tener miedo	to be afraid
tener prisa	to be in a hurry
tener que + *infinitive*	to have to (do something)
tener razón	to be right
tener sed	to be thirsty
tener sentido	to make sense
tener sueño	to be sleepy, tired
tener *X* años	to be *X* years old

DISCUSSING TRANSPORTATION

Sustantivos

el autobús	bus
el avión	plane
el barco	boat
la bicicleta	bicycle
el billete/boleto/pasaje	ticket, passage
el camión	truck; bus (Mex.)
la camioneta/el camión	pick-up truck; van
el chofer (L. Am.)/ el chófer (Sp.)	driver; chauffeur
el coche/el auto (móvil)/el carro	car, automobile
el crucero	cruise ship
la dirección	address
el metro	subway
la motocicleta	motorcycle
la ruta	route
el taxi	taxi
el tren	train
el/la turista	tourist
el viaje	trip

Verbos

alcanzar	to reach, catch up with
estar cerca / lejos (de)	to be close/far away (from)
llegar	to arrive
manejar/conducir	to drive

quedar	to be (located)
viajar	to travel

Otras expresiones

a pie	on foot
después	after
en	by (with transportation), in,

TALKING ABOUT DAILY ROUTINES

Sustantivos

la cara	face
los dientes	teeth
las manos	hands
el pelo	hair

Verbos

acostarse (ue)	to go to bed; to lie down
afeitarse	to shave
bañarse	to take a bath
cepillarse	to brush
despertarse (ie)	to wake up
divertirse (ie)	to have a good time, enjoy oneself
dormirse (ue)	to fall asleep
ducharse	to take a shower
irse	to go away, leave
levantarse	to get up
maquillarse	to put on makeup
peinarse	to comb one's hair
preocuparse	to worry
quedarse	to stay
quitarse (la ropa)	to take off (one's clothes)
secarse	to dry off
sentarse (ie)	to sit down
sentirse (ie)	to feel
vestirse (i)	to get dressed

Otras expresiones

después	afterwards
entonces	then, at that time
luego	later, then, next
por fin	finally
primero	first

SEGUNDO PASO

ORDERING FOOD IN A RESTAURANT

Sustantivos

el agua (f.) (mineral)	(mineral) water
el almuerzo	lunch
el aperitivo/el entremés	appetizer

el bistec	steak
el café	coffee
el/la camarero/a, el/ la mesero/a	waiter, waitress
la carne	meat
la carta, el menú	menu

la cena	*dinner*	
la cerveza	*beer*	
el chorizo	*sausage*	
la comida	*food/dinner/lunch*	
la copa	*stemmed glass, goblet*	
la cuchara	*tablespoon*	
la cucharita	*teaspoon*	
el cuchillo	*knife*	
la cuenta	*bill*	
el desayuno	*breakfast*	
la ensalada (mixta/rusa)	*(mixed/potato) salad*	
el flan	*baked egg custard*	
la fruta	*fruit*	
la gamba	*shrimp*	
el gazpacho	*cold vegetable soup*	
el hambre *(f.)*	*hunger*	
el helado (de chocolate, vainilla, fresa)	*(chocolate, vanilla, strawberry) ice cream*	
la legumbre	*vegetable*	
el marisco	*shellfish*	
la paella (valenciana)	*rice, meat, and seafood dish (from Valencia)*	
el pan	*bread*	
la patata/papa	*potato*	
el pedido	*order*	
el pescado	*fish*	
la pimienta	*(black) pepper*	
el plato	*plate, dish*	
la propina	*tip*	
el queso	*cheese*	
el refresco	*soft drink*	
la sal	*salt*	
la sangría	*wine, fruit, soda drink*	
la sopa	*soup*	
las tapas	*small servings of food (Sp.)*	
la taza	*cup*	
el té	*tea*	
el tenedor	*fork*	
la tortilla española	*Spanish omelette*	
el vaso	*glass (for drinks)*	
el vino (tinto/blanco)	*(red/white) wine*	
el zumo/jugo	*juice*	

Verbos

almorzar (ue)	*to have lunch*
cenar	*to have dinner*
dejar	*to leave (something behind)*
desayunar	*to have breakfast*
disfrutar	*to enjoy*
tomar	*to drink*

Adjetivos

caliente
dulce
frito/a
fuerte (una
ligero/a
picante
preparado/a
rico/a
sabroso/a
variado/a

Otras expre

¡A sus órdenes	
Tengo mucha hambre.	*I am very hungry.*
¿Qué desean comer/ beber/tomar?	*What would you like to eat/drink?*
¿Qué nos recomienda?	*What do you recommend?*
Estoy muerto/a de hambre.	*I'm starving/famished.*
La cuenta, por favor.	*The check, please.*
Me gustaría/ Quisiera (pedir)...	*I would like (to order) . . .*

VERBS WITH IRREGULAR *YO* FORMS

conducir	*to drive*
conocer	*to know, be familiar with*
dar	*to give*
hacer	*to do, make*
oír	*to hear*
parecer	*to seem*
poner	*to put, place*
producir	*to produce*
saber	*to know*
salir	*to go out; to leave*
traducir	*to translate*
traer	*to bring*
ver	*to see*

DEMONSTRATIVES

aquel, aquella (aquél, aquélla); aquello	*that (one) (over there)*
aquellos/as (aquéllos/as)	*those (over there)*
ese, esa (ése/ésa); eso	*that (one)*
esos, esas (ésos/as)	*those*
este, esta(éste, ésta); esto	*this (one)*
estos, estas (éstos/as)	*these*

Adverbs

allá	*over there*
allí (ahí)	*there*
aquí	*here*

La vida diaria

aquín Sorolla y Bastida, *El Jardín*

Preguntas del tema

► ¿Qué profesión piensas tener en el futuro?
► ¿Qué profesión es interesante? ¿Cuál es aburrida?
► ¿Cómo es tu familia?
► ¿Qué te gusta hacer con la familia?

Vocabulario y lengua

DISCUSSING PROFESSIONS

Somos vecinos *(neighbors)*

[4A] Laura Guzmán piensa ser *abogada* y su compañera Lourdes Vardi es *música*.

[4B] Los *artistas* trabajan intensamente. La *escultora* trabaja con madera (*wood*), mientras que el *fotógrafo* saca fotos (*takes pictures*).

[3A] Los hijos de los señores Terranova piensan ser *médicos*.

[3B] El *plomero* arregla el baño de la *farmacéutica* Aída Sosa.

[2A] El *cocinero* le sirve la comida a la familia Lara.

[2B] Una *pintora* pinta la sala de Eduardo Calasa, un *hombre de negocios*.

[1A] Los *jardineros* trabajan en el jardín del Dr. Martín.

[1B] Pablo es *peluquero* y trabaja en la Peluquería Pablo.

Profesiones y oficios

For many professions and occupations, the masculine nouns end in –**o** and the feminine nouns end in –**a**:

el/la arqueólogo/a *archaeologist*
el/la arquitecto/a *architect*
el/la criado/a *servant, maid*

el/la psicólogo/a *psychologist*
el/la secretario/a *secretary*
el/la veterinario/a *veterinarian*

For other professions, the masculine nouns end in –**ero** and the feminine nouns end in –**era**:

el/la bombero/a *firefighter*
el/la carpintero/a *carpenter*
el/la cartero/a *mail carrier*

el/la consejero/a *counselor*
el/la enfermero/a *nurse*
el/la ingeniero/a *engineer*

Masculine nouns ending in –**or** are made feminine by adding an –**a**:

el/la contador/a *accountant*
el/la profesor/a *professor*
el/la vendedor/a *salesperson*

el/la programador/a
programmer
el/la trabajador/a *worker*

[handwritten: pintor → male painter]

Nouns for professions ending in –**ista** or in –**e** have the same form for both masculine and feminine professions.

el/la agente de viajes *travel agent*
el/ la dentista *dentist*
el/la electricista *electrician*

el/la gerente *manager*
el/la periodista *journalist*
el/la recepcionista *receptionist*

Other occupations that have only one form include: **el / la atleta** *(athlete)* and **el / la policía** *(police officer)*. Exceptions such as **el jefe** *(male boss)* and **la jefa** *(female boss)*, **el presidente** and **la presidenta**, are examples of how Spanish has adapted to reflect changes in the workforce.

Online Study Center

For additional practice with this unit's vocabulary and grammar, visit the *Caminos* website at http://college.hmco.com/languages/spanish/renjilian/caminos/3e/student_home.html. You can also review audio flashcards, quiz yourself, and explore related Spanish-language sites.

Actividades

1 Querido amiguito. Laura, the law student in Apartment 4A, is writing a letter to her friend Mauro. Refer to the drawing on page 130 and complete her letter using vocabulary from the list below.

artistas	jardineros	cocinero	música	criada	peluquero
farmacéutica	pintora	guitarra	plomero	hijos	médico

Querido Mauro:

Saludos desde Puerto Rico. Aquí me estoy divirtiendo muchísimo, aunque *(although)* estudio demasiado. Mi compañera de cuarto se llama Lourdes y es
(1) _____ . Toca la (2) _____ y escucha el jazz y la música clásica.
Es muy buena compañera. Mis vecinos, los señores Lara, son muy simpáticos.
Son muy ricos y tienen un (3) _____ que prepara la comida y una
(4) _____ que limpia la casa.
Mis vecinos están siempre muy ocupados. El Dr. Martín emplea a dos
(5) _____ para arreglar su jardín. Pablo, el (6) _____ , tiene clientes
todo el día. Esta semana, desde el lunes, una (7) _____ está pintando el
apartamento del vecino del 2B. Ya casi termina. A los dos (8) _____ de los
vecinos de abajo les gusta mucho jugar al "(9) _____ y paciente" ¡con sus
animales! La vecina del 3B es (10) _____ y, antes de salir para el trabajo,
descubre que la llave *(faucet)* del agua no funciona y ahora el (11) _____
está en su apartamento para arreglar la llave. En el apartamento de al lado *(next door)*, los (12) _____ están trabajando toda la tarde. ¡Qué ruido! *(What noise!)* y qué tarde tan terrible. Bueno, tengo mucho sueño y necesito descansar un poco. ¡Me voy a acostar! Escríbeme pronto.

Abrazos de,
Laura

2 Asociaciones. Which professions do you associate with the following words? Provide both masculine and feminine forms for each.

1. las aspirinas
2. la pintura
3. las rosas
4. la bañera
5. el cepillo
6. el piano
7. el bistec
8. la justicia
9. el teléfono
11. los animales
12. el edificio

3 Profesionales. Combining an element from each column, discuss with a partner what each person does in his/her profession. Follow the model.

► MODELO: El profesor   enseñar   español
—¿Qué hace el profesor?
—*El profesor enseña español.*

1. El arqueólogo	limpiar	edificios
2. La pintora	apagar	los muebles
3. Los criados	diseñar	los pacientes
4. La médica	hacer	la casa
5. El bombero	pintar	el dinero
6. La carpintera	construir	el fuego
7. El arquitecto	calcular	excavaciones arqueológicas
8. La contadora	examinar	las casas

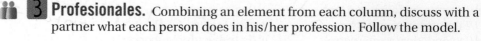

4 Una nueva civilización. NASA has discovered a new uninhabited planet (**un planeta deshabitado**) that is very similar to Earth. They have enough money to send one spaceship (**nave espacial**) to the planet to start a new civilization. The spaceship can hold only six people. Work in groups to decide who from the list below gets to go and why. Report your decisions to the class.

María Hernández (56), ingeniera	Esteban Rosas (24), enfermero
Efraín Jaramillo (48), médico	Clara Cabañas (30), programadora de computadoras
Raúl Ramírez (18), estudiante	Pablo Pérez (36), periodista y esposo de Penélope
Jaime Méndez (23), policía	Penélope Pérez (23), consejera y esposa de Pablo
Luisa Ortiz (31), carpintera	Alicia Vázquez (26), psicóloga

5 En mi barrio *(neighborhood).* Write a description of five people with different professions in your neighborhood. Describe who they are, what they do, and what they are like.

USING INDIRECT OBJECT PRONOUNS

My parents buy a stereo **for me.**   The girls sell cookies **to us.**

Indirect objects indicate *to, for,* or *from* whom an action is done. The highlighted pronouns in each example above correspond to the indirect objects of the sentences: "they buy the stereo *for me*" and "they sell cookies *to us.*"

Indirect object pronouns			
me	*(to, for, from) me*	**nos**	*(to, for, from) us*
te	*(to, for, from) you*	**os**	*(to, for, from) you*
le	*(to, for, from) you, him, her*	**les**	*(to, for, from) you, them*

Indirect object pronouns can either precede the conjugated verb or be attached to the end of the infinitive or present participle.

Te voy a comprar el pasaje.	*I am going to buy you the ticket.*
Voy a decir**te** una cosa.	*I am going to tell you something.*
La alumna **le** está haciendo preguntas.	*The student is asking him / her / you questions.*
La alumna está haciéndo**le** preguntas.	
Paco **me** quiere comprar el coche.	*Paco wants to buy the car for / from me.*
Paco quiere comprar**me** el coche.	

Common verbs used with indirect object pronouns					
agradecer	*to thank, be grateful for*	entregar	*to hand in, deliver*	pedir (i)	*to ask for, request*
comprar	*to buy*	enviar	*to send*	preguntar	*to ask a question*
contar (ue)	*to tell*	escribir	*to write*	prestar	*to lend*
contestar	*to answer*	explicar	*to explain*	regalar	*to give (gifts)*
dar	*to give*	hablar	*to speak*	servir (i)	*to serve*
deber*	*to owe*	mandar	*to send*	traer	*to bring*
decir (i)	*to tell*	ofrecer	*to offer*	vender	*to sell*
enseñar	*to teach*	pagar	*to pay*		

*__Deber__ + *infinitive* also means *should* as in: Debes contarme todo. *(You should tell me everything.)*

Prepositional pronouns

Pronouns that appear after a preposition are called *prepositional pronouns*. In Spanish, they have the same forms as the subject pronouns except for the first person (**mí**) and second person (**ti**) singular.

Prepositional pronouns							
mí	*me*	**usted**	*you*	**nosotros/as**	*us*	**ustedes**	*you (plural)*
ti	*you*	**él / ella**	*him / her*	**vosotros/as**	*you*	**ellos / ellas**	*them*

Spanish frequently uses *both* the indirect object pronoun *and* the preposition **a** + noun / prepositional pronoun to emphasize and/or clarify to whom the indirect object pronoun refers.

La profesora **le** explica la lección **a usted**.	*The teacher explains the lesson to you.*
La profesora **le** explica la lección **a Julia**.	*The teacher explains the lesson to Julia.*
Les mandan el paquete **a ellas**.	*They send the package to them.*
Les mandan el paquete **a los chicos**.	*They send the package to the boys.*
Nos escriben **a nosotros**.	*They write to us.*
Nos escriben **a Yolanda y a mí**.	*They write to Yolanda and me.*

While the prepositional phrase is optional, the indirect object pronoun must always be used.

Sus padres **le** dan un regalo.		*His / Her parents give **him / her** a gift.*
Sus padres **le** dan un regalo **a ella**.	*or*	*Her parents give a gift **to her**.*

Making requests and asking questions: *Pedir* and *preguntar*

In Spanish there are two verbs that mean *to ask:* **pedir** and **preguntar.** Both verbs are often used with indirect object pronouns. **Pedir** is used *to ask for* or *to request* something from someone. **Pedir** is also used to order food or drinks, or to place an order when you want to buy something.

El profesor les **pide** la tarea a los estudiantes.	*The teacher asks the students for their homework.*
Mi amiga me **pide** dinero.	*My friend asks me for money.*

Preguntar is used to obtain information about someone or something. **Preguntar por** means *to inquire* about someone or something.

El turista le **pregunta** la hora al guía.	*The tourist asks the guide for the time.*
Javier me **pregunta** si tengo hambre.	*Javier asks me if I'm hungry.*
Mi tía Amalia siempre **pregunta por** ti.	*My aunt Amalia always asks about you.*

Actividades

1 ¿A quién? Provide the correct form of the indirect object pronoun that corresponds to the **boldface** noun or pronoun in each sentence.

1. La arqueóloga _____ da una conferencia **a los estudiantes.**
2. Nosotros _____ pagamos los honorarios **a la ingeniera.**
3. La médica _____ escribe una receta **a ti.**
4. La vendedora _____ va a vender un estéreo **a mí.**
5. El abogado _____ va a decir la verdad **a usted.**
6. El cocinero _____ sirve la cena **a nosotros.**
7. Hoy _____ vamos a pagar **al plomero.**
8. Los pintores _____ están pintando la casa **a ustedes.**

2 Conversación privada. Ana and Laura are gossiping. You overhear their conversation and have to match the boldface pronouns they use with the people from the list below. Who are they talking about? Follow the model.

▶ **MODELO:** Ana: Oye, Laura, yo **les** dije **a ellas** que la fiesta es en tu casa…
Ana está hablando de las amigas de Laura.

el novio de Ana   las amigas de Laura   los padres de Laura
Laura   Ana   Ana y Laura

1. Laura: ¡Ay, Ana! Tengo que pedir**les** permiso a **ellos.** ¡Es su casa!
2. Ana: Laura, estoy segura de que ellos **nos** van a decir que sí.
3. Laura: Creo que sí, Ana. Puedes enviar**le** a **él** una invitación.
4. Ana: Gracias, **te** agradezco mucho.
5. Laura: ¡**Te** digo que tú eres mi mejor amiga!

3 ¿De quién hablas? Combine the words to form complete sentences. Follow the model.

▶ **MODELO:** la profesora / preguntar / a los estudiantes
La profesora les pregunta   *The professor asks the students.*
a los estudiantes.

1. ellos / contestar las preguntas / a la profesora
2. los médicos / ofrecer ayuda / a nosotros
3. ustedes / pedir el horario del tren / al empleado
4. yo / escribir correo electrónico / a mis amigos
5. el empleado siempre / desear feliz viaje / a los pasajeros
6. mi mamá / pedir un favor / a mí
7. el chico / hablar cordialmente / a la policía

4 ¿Qué haces? Based on the following situations, complete the sentences with the appropriate form of **pedir** or **preguntar (por).** Follow the model.

▶ **MODELO:** Estás en un restaurante y   *You are in a restaurant and want*
quieres el menú.   *the menu. What do you do?*
¿Qué haces?
Yo le **pido** el menú al mesero.   *I ask the waiter for the menu.*

1. Tu amigo le debe dinero al banco. ¿Qué hace el banco?
El banco le _____ el dinero a mi amigo.
2. Estoy en la playa y necesito hacer una llamada importante. ¿Qué hago?
Tú le _____ a alguien un teléfono celular.
3. Conoces a alguien muy interesante en una fiesta. ¿Qué haces?
Yo le _____ cómo se llama.
4. Estás enfermo/a y necesitas medicinas. ¿Qué haces?
Yo le _____ las medicinas al médico.

5. Quieres invitar a alguien al cine. ¿Qué haces?
Yo le _____ si quiere ir al cine conmigo.

6. No sabes cómo está tu amiga María Rosa. ¿Qué haces?
Yo _____ ella.

5 Preguntas personales. With a classmate, take turns asking and answering the following questions.

▶ **MODELO:** ¿Quién te da regalos? (mi amigo Juan)
—¿Quién te da regalos?   —*Who gives you gifts?*
—Mi amigo Juan me da regalos.   —*My friend Juan gives me gifts.*

1. ¿Quiénes te hablan por teléfono? (mis amigos)
2. ¿Quién te escribe cartas? (la familia)
3. ¿Quién nos prepara la comida? (el cocinero)
4. ¿Quién les enseña español a ellos? (la profesora)
5. ¿Quién te debe dinero? (Ramiro y Rafael)
6. ¿Quién les pide su opinión a ustedes? (el presidente)
7. ¿Quiénes te dicen la verdad? (los abogados)
8. ¿Quién te paga el alquiler de tu casa? (mis padres)

6 ¿Qué hacen? Your young nephew is asking you about what different people do for work. Make a list of six professions and write a sentence about each to tell him what they do and for whom. Include indirect object pronouns in your statements.

▶ **MODELO:** **el cartero**   El cartero les entrega cartas a los vecinos.

INDICATING LIKES AND DISLIKES: *GUSTAR* AND SIMILAR VERBS

As you have learned, the verb **gustar** is used to express likes and dislikes. In Spanish, **gustar** literally means "*is pleasing to.*" Spanish uses indirect object pronouns to show "to whom" something is pleasing. Notice how the structure works.

Indirect Object Pronoun	Verb	Subject	
Me	gustan	los deportes.	*I like sports.* *(literally: Sports are pleasing to me.)*
Te	gusta	pintar.	*You like to paint.* *(literally: Painting is pleasing to you.)*

Use **gusta** when the subject is a singular noun, an infinitive, or a series of infinitives. Use **gustan** when the subject is a plural noun or a series of nouns.

¿Te **gusta** tener una mascota?   *Do you like to have a pet?*
Sí, me **gustan** los animales.   *Yes, I like animals.*

Gustar and similar verbs are used with all of the indirect object pronouns in the same way.

Gustar			
me gusta(n)	*I like it / them*	**nos** gusta(n)	*we like it / them*
te gusta(n)	*you like it / them*	**os** gusta(n)	*you (plural) like it / them*
le gusta(n)	*you like it / them; he / she likes it / them*	**les** gusta(n)	*you (plural) they like it / them*

Verbs like gustar			
caer bien / mal	*to like / dislike (a person)*	**interesar**	*to interest, be of interest*
encantar	*to delight, like very much (love)*	**molestar**	*to bother, annoy*
faltar	*to lack, need; to be left (to do)*	**parecer**	*to seem, appear to be*
fascinar	*to fascinate*	**preocupar**	*to worry*
importar	*to matter, be important, be of concern*		

Note that many of these verbs are used in a similar way in English. We don't say "I interest reading," but rather "Reading interests me."

Me interesa leer.   *Reading interests me.*
Te molestan las personas   *Unfriendly people bother you.*
   antipáticas.

As with all indirect object pronouns, the preposition **a** + noun or prepositional pronoun can be used to emphasize or clarify the recipient of the action.

A mí me importa la comunidad.   *My community matters to me.*
Al arquitecto le interesan las casas.   *The arquitect is interested in houses.*

When verbs like **gustar** are used with reflexive verbs, the reflexive pronoun is attached to the infinitive of the reflexive verb. Remember that the reflexive pronoun must match the subject.

A Juan le fascina **vestirse** con   *Juan likes to dress in expensive clothes.*
   ropa cara.
Me molesta **levantarme** temprano.   *It annoys me to get up early.*
      (Getting up early annoys me.)

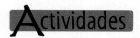 **ctividades**

1 Gustos.
Combine the words and phrases to form complete sentences. Follow the model.

► **MODELO:** a tí / preocupar / ir al dentista
A ti te preocupa ir al dentista.

1. a mí / caer bien / el profesor
2. al pintor / encantar / pintar
3. a nosotros / preocupar / los problemas en el mundo
4. a la arquitecta / interesar / construir casas
5. a la médica / parecer / importante atender a sus pacientes
6. a los cocineros / faltar / los ingredientes para la sopa
7. a las arqueólogas / fascinar / excavar
8. a los abogados / importar / la opinión del juez *(judge)*
9. al músico / gustar / las canciones de Enrique Iglesias
10. a la vendedora / caer bien / los clientes

2 ¿Te gusta?
With a partner, take turns asking each other for the following information.

► **MODELO:** gustar / las ensaladas
—¿Te gustan las ensaladas?   —*Do you like salads?*
—Sí, me gustan las ensaladas.   —*Yes, I do like salads.*
—No, no me gustan las ensaladas.   —*No, I don't like salads.*

1. encantar / las canciones románticas
2. interesar / las novelas de misterio
3. gustar / los libros para jóvenes
4. molestar / el problema del tráfico
5. preocupar / los problemas ecológicos
6. fascinar / las nuevas tecnologías
7. gustar / el cine mexicano
8. caer mal / las personas que fuman

3 ¿Te caen bien o mal?
Work in pairs. Make a list of people you know or of fictional characters from TV, film, or literature. Then ask each other whether you like or dislike the people you've listed. Follow the model.

► **MODELO:** Jennifer López
—¿Te cae bien Jennifer López?   —*Do you like Jennifer López?*
—Sí, me cae bien porque...   —*Yes, I like her because . . .*

or

—No, me cae mal porque...   —*No, I don't like her because . . .*

4 ¿Te importa?
You have to prepare a report for your sociology class. Following the model, ask four to six students questions about the survey topics below. Write their answers in the chart. Write **M** for **mucho, P** for **poco,** and **N** for **nada.** Report your findings to the class and discuss why certain things are important and others are not.

► **MODELO:** la ecología   *ecology*
—Marcela, ¿te importa la ecología?   —*Marcela, is ecology important to you?*
—Sí, me importa mucho.   —*Yes, it is important to me.*

or

—No, me importa poco.   —*No, it's not very important to me.*
—No, no me importa nada.   —*No, it's not important to me at all.*

Nombre del estudiante	La ecología	El dinero	Los amigos	Las clases
Marcela	M_____	_____	_____	_____

USING AFFIRMATIVE, NEGATIVE, AND TRANSITIONAL EXPRESSIONS

Affirmative expressions	
algo	something, anything
todo	everything
todo el mundo	everybody, everyone
alguien	someone, somebody
algún, alguno/a/os/as	some, any
siempre	always
todos los días	every day
también	also, too
(o) ... o	(either) . . . or

Negative expressions	
nada	nothing
nadie	no one, nobody
ningún, ninguno/a	none, not any
nunca, jamás	never
tampoco	neither, either
(ni)...ni	neither . . . nor

Transitional expressions	
a veces	at times
algunas veces	sometimes
casi siempre / nunca / nada	almost always / never / nothing
de vez en cuando	from time to time
muchas veces	many times

Affirmative expressions and affirmative transitional expressions can be placed before or after the verb.

Yo **siempre** hago la tarea.
Yo hago **siempre** la tarea.

I always do my homework.

Casi siempre hacemos la tarea.

We almost always do our homework.

Nadie and **nunca** are often used before the verb, while **nada** is normally placed after it.

Nunca practico deportes.	*I never play sports.*
Nadie dice la verdad.	*No one tells the truth.*
No tengo **nada.**	*I don't have anything.*

When the negative expressions **nada**, **nadie**, or **nunca** follow the verb, Spanish uses an additional **no** before the verb as in the previous example: **no** + *verb* + ***negative expression.***

Los domingos **no** voy **nunca** al cine.	*I never go to the movies on Sundays.*
No viene **nadie.**	*No one is coming.*

Nadie and **alguien** refer to people and require the personal **a** when used as direct objects.

—¿Visitas **a alguien** los fines de semana?	*—Do you visit anyone on weekends?*
—No, **no** visito **a nadie.**	*—No, I don't visit anyone.*

All forms of **alguno** and **ninguno** agree in number and gender with the noun they modify, but drop the **-o** before a masculine singular form. **Ninguno** is mostly used in the singular form.

—¿Hay aquí **algunos** estudiantes de Miami?	*—Are there any students from Miami?*
—No, no hay **ningún** estudiante de Miami.	*—No, there are no students from Miami.*
—¿Tienes **algunos** problemas?	*—Do you have any problems?*
—No, no tengo **ninguno.**	*—No, I don't have any.*

Actividades

1 **Los contrarios.** Change the following affirmative statements to make them negative. Some statements require two changes.

► MODELO:	Necesito comer algo antes de la reunión.	*I need to eat something before the meeting.*
	No necesito comer nada antes de la reunión.	*I don't need to eat anything before the meeting.*

1. Quiero conocer a alguien interesante.
2. Ellos siempre viajan en tren.
3. Algunas postales tienen la dirección correcta.
4. Tengo todo listo para el viaje en tren.
5. Elena siempre toma taxi para ir a la universidad.
6. Tengo que decirte algo.
7. Voy al cine mañana. También voy a la biblioteca.
8. Todo el mundo quiere vivir en Sevilla.

2 Sucede todos los días. You have just returned from a vacation. It was not a very good trip and you have some bad things to say about it. Follow the model and create a dialog with a partner.

▶ MODELO: —¿Hay muchos hoteles buenos?

—*Are there many good hotels?*

—No, no hay ningún hotel bueno.

—*No, there aren't any good hotels.*

1. ¿Siempre sirven buena comida en los restaurantes?
2. ¿Siempre hay actividades divertidas?
3. ¿Hay algunos viajes interesantes?
4. ¿Hay alguna discoteca buena?
5. ¿Hay algunos centros comerciales?
6. ¿Siempre encuentras transporte en la ciudad?

3 ¡Nunca hago nada! Use the timeline below to indicate the activities you do or don't do and how often. Write a sentence for each item on the timeline, then discuss them with a partner.

▶ MODELO: —Casi siempre asisto a clase, ¿y tú?
—Siempre asisto a clase.

nunca   casi nunca   a veces   casi siempre   siempre

¿Hablas por teléfono?

¿Comes en restaurantes?

¿Vas al cine con tus amigos?

CAMINOS DEL JAGUAR

Un negocio sucio

Actividades

Online Study Center

For additional practice with this episode, visit the *Caminos* website at http://college.hmco.com/languages/spanish/renjilian/caminos/3e/student_home.html.

1 Comprensión.
Based on this episode of *Caminos del jaguar,* choose the logical response.

1. Pacal es...
   a. un objeto de arte maya.
   b. un rey maya.

2. El Sr. Covarrubias tiene el jaguar porque...
   a. es un negocio bien pagado.
   b. es un objeto de arte.

3. La Sra. Covarrubias está...
   a. muy contenta con el jaguar.
   b. preocupada.

in espera going to queto ehed eta Ecuador

4. A la Sra. Covarrubias...
   a. no le interesa el dinero.
   b. le interesa el dinero.

5. El Sr. Covarrubias tiene que...
   a. guardar el jaguar en casa.
   b. enviar el jaguar a otro país.

6. Adriana y Felipe viajan en el AVE porque...
   a. deben llegar rápido.
   b. tienen poco dinero.

7. A Adriana...
   a. le cae bien Felipe.
   b. no le cae bien Felipe.

8. ¿Qué le pide Nayeli al Sr. Covarrubias?
   a. la dirección en Quito
   b. información sobre el negocio

2 Situaciones.
Dramatize one of the following situations.

1. Mrs. and Mr. Covarrubias try to hide because they are afraid of the Jaguar Twin.
2. Mrs. Covarrubias tells her husband what she thinks about his business plan.

3 Escritura.
Write a brief summary of what happens in this episode (4–6 sentences).

NOTA CULTURAL

La estación de Atocha

Atocha Station is the largest train station in Madrid. The station features beautiful, lush gardens with tropical palms and waterfalls. It was recently remodeled by Rafael Moneo, an internationally known Spanish architect. Local and long-distance trains arrive and depart from Atocha daily. The AVE (Alta Velocidad España), the high-speed train that connects Sevilla and Lérida to the capital, also uses Atocha as its terminal. On March 11, 2004, Spain suffered two deadly bomb attacks on passenger trains. One of the attacks occurred at Atocha.

SEGUNDO PASO

Vocabulario y lengua

TALKING ABOUT FAMILY MEMBERS

Online Study Center

For additional practice with this unit's vocabulary and grammar, visit the *Caminos* website at http://college.hmco.com/languages/spanish/renjilian/caminos/3e/student_home.html. You can also review audio flashcards, quiz yourself, and explore related Spanish-language sites.

Pablo Rosas González
padre / papá

Marinela Suárez de Rosas
madre / mamá

Micifús
gata

Sultán
perro

Julio Ramón Iglesias
novio

Rosaura
hermana

Maricarmen
hermana

Me llamo Velia Rosas Suárez

Roberto
hermano

Aniela Gómez de Rosas
cuñada

Conchita
tortuga

Beto
pájaro

Orejón
conejo

Leticia
sobrina

Pedro
sobrino

Spanish speakers often use **somos** and not **son** to indicate how many people are in their own family. This form includes themselves in the number of family members.

The endings **–ito/-ita** are often added to nouns and adjectives to express affection or a smaller size. There must be gender and number agreement.

Mi hij**ita** está en la primaria.	*My dear / little daughter is in elementary school.*
Mi hij**ito** tiene 3 años.	*My dear / little son is 3 years old.*
Somos cinco en mi familia.	*There are five in our family.*

Más palabras y expresiones

Sustantivos

el/la abuelo/a	*grandfather / grandmother*
el/la bebé	*baby*
el/la bisabuelo/a	*great-grandfather / great-grandmother*
el/la chico/a	*boy / girl*
el/la esposo/a	*husband / wife*
el/la hermanastro/a	*stepbrother / stepsister*
el/la hijastro/a	*stepson / stepdaughter*
el/la hijo/a	*son / daughter*
la madrastra	*stepmother*
el marido	*husband*
la mascota	*pet*
el/la nieto/a	*grandson / granddaughter*
el/la niño/a	*boy / girl / child*
la nuera	*daughter-in-law*
el padrastro	*stepfather*
el/la pariente	*family member, relative*
el/la primo/a	*cousin*
el/la suegro/a	*father-in-law / mother-in-law*
el/la tío/a	*uncle / aunt*
el yerno	*son-in-law*

Verbos

abrazar	*to hug*
casarse (con)	*to get married (to)*
enamorarse (de)	*to fall in love (with)*
estar casado/a	*to be married*
estar divorciado/a	*to be divorced*
estar enamorado/a	*to be in love*
estar separado/a	*to be separated*
nacer	*to be born*
ser mayor	*to be older*
ser menor	*to be younger*
ser soltero/a	*to be single*

Actividades

1 **La familia de Marinela.** If Marinela were telling the story about her family, the family relationships would change. Look at the family tree on page 144 and describe the relationships between the following people from Marinela's point of view.

1. Me llamo Marinela y mi _____esposo_____ se llama Pablo.
2. Tengo cuatro _____hijos_____.
3. Mi _____hermano____ se llama Roberto.
4. Su _____esposa_____ se llama Aniela.
5. Mis _____nietos_____ son Pedro y Leticia.
6. Mi _____hija_____ mayor se llama Rosaura.
7. Rosaura tiene un _____novio_____ muy guapo.

2 La familia de Velia. Listen to the story of Velia's family, and fill in the missing words.

La familia de Velia

Me llamo Velia Rosas Suárez y tengo una (1) _____ muy grande. Mi
(2) _____ se llama Pablo y mi (3) _____ se llama Marinela.
Mis (4) _____ son muy simpáticos. Somos cuatro (5) _____ . Mi
(6) _____ Roberto tiene treinta y cinco años y es alto y guapo.
Su (7) _____ se llama Aniela. Aniela es mi (8) _____ . Ellos tienen dos
(9) _____ : el (10) _____ se llama Pedro y la (11) _____ se llama
Leticia. Leticia tiene tres mascotas, un (12) _____ que se llama Orejón, un
(13) _____ que se llama Beto y una (14) _____ , Conchita. ¡Ella quiere
ser veterinaria! Quiero mucho a mis (15) _____ . ¡Soy su (16) _____
favorita!

Mi (17) _____ mayor Rosaura tiene un (18) _____ que se llama
Julio. Ellos están muy enamorados y van a casarse este verano. Mi hermana
Maricarmen es (19) _____ y es estudiante. Ella tiene una
(20) _____ que se llama Micifús.

¿Y yo? Yo estoy (21) _____ , no tengo (22) _____ y vivo con mi
(23) _____ Sultán.

3 ¿Quién es? Work with a partner to determine which family member is being described.

► MODELO: la esposa de mi hermano
—¿Quién es la esposa de mi hermano?
—*Es tu cuñada.*

1. el esposo de mi madre
2. el padre de mi madre
3. los hijos de mis hijos
4. la hija de mi tía
5. el hermano de mi prima
6. el esposo de mi hija
7. la hermana de mi padre
8. la madre de mi abuelo
9. las hijas de mi hermana
10. la única *(only)* hija de mi abuela

4 Entre nosotros. Interview a partner about his or her family. Use questions as provided in the model. Then draw a family tree that represents the family members, including their names and ages.

► MODELO: —¿Cuántos hermanos tienes?
—¿Cómo se llaman?
—¿Cuántos años tienen?

5 Mi familia. Write a paragraph about your family. Include a description of each family member, his or her name, age, relationship to you, profession, and other interesting facts.

Mini historia de amor

Son novios y están enamorados

You have already learned some basic uses of **ser** and **estar** *(to be)*. The following short story summarizes the different ways these two verbs are used.

Uses of *ser:* El noviazgo *(The courtship)*

1. **States identity.**

   La novia **es** Juliana Castro; el novio **es** Luis Orozco.

   The fiancée is Juliana Castro; the fiancé is Luis Orozco.

2. **Describes origin of things and people.**

   Luis **es** de Buenos Aires y Juliana **es** de Quito.

   Luis is from Buenos Aires and Juliana is from Quito.

3. **Indicates someone's occupation or profession.**

   Juliana **es** médica y Luis **es** arquitecto.

   Juliana is a doctor and Luis is an architect.

4. **Describes nationality.**

   Él **es** argentino y ella **es** ecuatoriana.

   He is Argentinean and she is Ecuadorian.

5. **Describes inherent characteristics of things and people.**

   Juliana **es** muy bonita y Luis **es** encantador.

   Juliana is very pretty and Luis is charming.

6. **Describes the material of which something is made.**

   El anillo de Juliana **es** de oro y tiene un diamante enorme.

   Juliana's ring is made of gold and has an enormous diamond.

7. **States where an event takes place.**

   La boda **es** en la iglesia de San Felipe.

   The wedding is in the church of San Felipe.

Uses of *estar:* La boda *(The wedding)*

8. **Describes location of places, buildings, and things.**

   La iglesia de San Felipe **está** en el centro de la ciudad, cerca del parque.

   The San Felipe Church is downtown, close to the park.

9. **Describes location of people.**

   Cuando la novia llega, algunos invitados **están** en el parque, pero Luis ya **está** en la iglesia.

   When the bride arrives, some guests are in the park, but Luis is already at the church.

10. **Describes how things look or appear at a certain moment.**

    La novia **está** muy hermosa hoy, con su vestido blanco y largo. Luis también **está** guapísimo, con su traje negro.

    The bride is (looks) very beautiful today, in her long, white dress. Luis is (looks) also very handsome, in his black suit.

11. Describes mental or emotional states.

Todos **están** contentos: la novia,
    el novio y los invitados; pero
    una amiga de Juliana, Berta,
    está muy emocionada.

*Everyone is happy: the bride,
    the groom, and the guests; but
    a friend of Juliana's, Berta,
    is very moved.*

12. Describes ongoing actions with a progressive tense.

Cerca, un hombre guapo **está**
    mirando a Berta intensamente...
    ¡Cupido **está** preparando
    un nuevo romance!

*Close by, a handsome man is gazing
    intensely at Berta . . .
    Cupid is preparing
    a new romance!*

FIN

THE END

Actividades

1 Comprensión Answer the following questions about the story.

1. ¿Quién es la novia?
2. ¿De dónde es la novia?
3. ¿De dónde es el novio?
4. ¿Cuál es la profesión de Juliana? ¿y la profesión de Luis?
5. ¿Dónde están los invitados cuando llega la novia?
6. ¿Cómo está la novia ese día? ¿y el novio?
7. ¿Cómo están todos los invitados?
8. ¿Dónde es la boda?
9. ¿Dónde está la iglesia?
10. ¿Qué está preparando Cupido?

2 ¡Adivina! Guess the subject of each riddle.

1. Es presidente de un país grande e importante. Su casa es blanca y está en la capital del país. ¿Quién es?
2. Son prácticos. Pueden ser grandes, pequeños, viejos, nuevos, bonitos y feos, buenos y malos, caros y baratos. Están generalmente en las calles contaminando el aire. Otras veces están en el garaje de la casa. ¿Qué son?
3. Son hermosas. Son de muchos colores y formas. Tienen perfume. Generalmente están en los jardines, pero a veces están adornando las casas. ¿Qué son?
4. Es clara y transparente. Está en el océano y en los ríos *(rivers)*, en el aire y en las nubes. En invierno es nieve y en verano puede ser vapor *(mist)*. ¿Qué es?

3 Ahora, ¡adivina tú! Now, create a riddle and ask a partner to guess what it is.

4 Mi historia. Now create your own story about two people who meet on your campus, demonstrating at least three uses of **ser** and three uses of **estar.** Some possible ideas:

1. amor en la cafetería
2. de compras en la tienda
3. los novios en la fiesta
4. el romance en el laboratorio de ciencia

¿Dónde está la profesora Jaramillo?

1C: Sra. Coronado
1B: Carlitos Coronado
1A: Sr. Coronado

2C: Profesora Jaramillo

3C: Paula Peña
3B: Ricardo Ríos

4B: Federica Fuentes
4A: Manuel Mendoza

La Sra. Coronado está **junto a** la ventana.

Carlitos está **entre** la Sra. y el Sr. Coronado.

La profesora Jaramillo está **delante de** la Sra. Coronado.

Ricardo está **detrás de** Federica.

Paula está **al lado de** Ricardo.

Las bolsas están **debajo de** los asientos.

Las maletas están **encima del** portaequipajes.

El Sr. Coronado está **lejos de** Federica.

La profesora Jaramillo está **cerca de** la Sra. Coronado.

Mrs. Coronado is sitting next to the window.

Carlitos is between Mr. and Mrs. Coronado.

Professor Jaramillo is in front of Mrs. Coronado.

Ricardo is behind Federica.

Paula is next to Ricardo.

The bags are beneath the seats.

The suitcases are on top of the luggage rack.

Mr. Coronado is far from Federica.

Professor Jaramillo is close to Mrs. Coronado.

Prepositions can be used to state location, position in space, direction, sequence in time, or abstract relationships between objects, events, and people.

Additional prepositions of place			
bajo	under	enfrente de	in front of, facing
dentro de	inside of	fuera de	outside of
en	in, on, at	sobre	on, on top of

Prepositions of time					
a	to, for	después de	after	para*	for, to, in order to
antes de	before	durante	during	por*	for, by means of
con	with	hacia	toward	según	according to
de	from, of	hasta	until	sin	without
desde	from, since				

_____
* You will learn more about the uses of **por** and **para** in *Unidad 6*.

Remember that the first and second person singular forms of prepositional pronouns are **mí** and **ti**. All the others retain the form of the subject pronoun (See pages **56–57**). The preposition **con** has its own forms for the first and second persons singular: **conmigo** *(with me)*, **contigo** *(with you)*.

Manuel va **conmigo** a la estación. *Manuel goes to the station with me.*
Me gusta viajar **contigo**. *I like traveling with you.*

Entre *(between, among)* is different from the other prepositions because it must always be followed by one or more subjects or subject pronouns.

¡**Entre tú y yo** no hay secretos! *There are no secrets between you and me!*
Esta información es un secreto *This information is a secret between us.*
  entre nosotros.

The preposition pairs **de/a** and **desde/hasta** are often used to express a time period or a distance covered from one place to another.

Trabajo **desde** las 3 P.M. **hasta** *I work from 3 to 4 P.M.*
  las 4 P.M.
Estudio **desde** la mañana **hasta** *I work from morning to evening.*
  la tarde.
El AVE viaja **de** Madrid **a** Sevilla. *The AVE train travels from Madrid to Sevilla.*

Actividades

1 ¿Dónde están? Refer back to the illustration of the passengers in the train on page 150. Say where the following people can be found. Follow the model.

▶ **MODELO:** Carlitos / el Sr. Coronado
Carlitos está al lado del *Carlitos is next to Mr. Coronado.*
  Sr. Coronado.

1. la Sra. Coronado / Carlitos
2. Manuel / Federica
3. la profesora Jaramillo / Paula / la Sra. Coronado
4. Ricardo / Federica
5. Manuel / Ricardo
6. Carlitos / Ricardo

La sra. coronado está al lado del carlitos y la ventana.

Manuel está al lado de la Federica.

la profesora está detrós de Paula y delante de la coronado.

2 Conversaciones.

You are in a disco and overhear the following exchanges and questions. Complete each dialog with a preposition from the list below. You can use some prepositions more than once.

| con | conmigo | contigo | de | en | para | sin |

1. —¡Estas flores son _____ ti, mi amor!
   —¿Son _____ mí las flores? ¡Qué cariñoso eres!
2. —¿Quién está _____ Mariana?
   —Francisco, su primo, está _____ ella.
3. —¿Quieres ir _____ al cine mañana?
   —No gracias, no puedo ir _____.
4. —¿Eres la hermana _____ Jorge Vázquez?
   —Sí, soy la hermana mayor _____ él.
5. —Tú sabes que no puedes vivir _____ mí, ¿verdad?
   —Sí, yo sé muy bien que no puedo vivir _____ ti.
6. —¿Dónde está mi billete de tren?
   —Está _____ tu mochila.

3 Secuencia.

Choose the sentence ending that best describes the sequence in which you do the following things.

1. Por la noche...
   a. me duermo antes de acostarme.   **b.** me acuesto antes de dormirme.

2. Por la mañana...
   a. me ducho después de levantarme.   **b.** me ducho antes de levantarme.

3. En la universidad...
   a. pienso antes de hablar.   **b.** hablo antes de pensar.

4. En casa...
   a. estudio después de ver televisión.   **b.** veo televisión después de estudiar.

5. En mi auto...
   a. conduzco después de dormir poco.   **b.** no conduzco después de dormir poco.

6. Cuando viajo...
   a. llego antes de la salida del tren.   **b.** llego después de la salida del tren.

4 ¡Colas para todo!

Working with a partner, describe where each person is standing in the line to purchase bus tickets.

▶ MODELO: —El abuelo está detrás   —*The grandfather is behind*
           de la señora alta, ¿verdad?   *the tall lady, isn't he?*
           —No, el abuelo está   —*No, the grandfather is in*
           delante de ella.   *front of her.*

5 ¿Dónde están?

Have your partner use the questions below to ask where objects are in your room. As you give their locations, your partner will make a rough sketch placing the objects according to your instructions. Switch roles, then check each other's drawings to see if they are correct.

1. ¿Dónde están tu cama, tu lámpara y tu silla?
2. ¿En qué lugar está tu computadora?
3. ¿Qué cosas hay al lado de tu computadora?
4. ¿Tienes un teléfono en tu cuarto? ¿Dónde está?
5. ¿Qué tienes en la pared?
6. ¿Dónde están la puerta y la ventana? ¿Hay balcón? ¿Dónde está el balcón?
7. ¿Qué otros objetos hay en tu cuarto? ¿Dónde están?

NARRATING EVENTS IN THE PAST: PRETERITE OF REGULAR VERBS

Spanish uses two main verb tenses, the **preterite** and the **imperfect,** to describe past events. You will study the preterite in this unit and the imperfect in *Unidad 6.* The story below, *El sábado pasado,* illustrates the main uses of the preterite. The words in **boldface** are the preterite forms of regular verbs. The endings of these forms are added to the stem to form the preterite indicative tense. Identify these endings and then find them in the verb chart that appears after the story.

El sábado pasado

▶ To indicate a completed action or the start or the end of an action or event.

El sábado pasado, mi madre **invitó** a mis abuelos a cenar.

Last Saturday my mother invited my grandparents to dinner.

▶ To state or sum up opinions, attitudes, and beliefs.

Me **pareció** una gran idea.

It seemed like a great idea.

▶ To narrate a sequence of completed past actions.

Hablé con mi hermano y **decidimos** preparar algo especial. Él **compró** las bebidas, yo **compré** los ingredientes y **preparamos** la cena.

I spoke with my brother and we decided to prepare something special. He bought the drinks, I bought the ingredients, and we prepared the dinner.

▶ To narrate actions that happened within a fixed period of time.

Cenamos entre las 7 y las 9 de la noche. Nadie **se levantó** de la mesa hasta que **terminamos.** A mis abuelos les **encantó** la cena.

We ate dinner between 7 and 9 P.M. No one left the table until we finished. My grandparents loved the dinner.

Preterite of regular verbs			
	-ar hablar	-er comer	-ir decidir
yo	habl**é**	com**í**	decid**í**
tú	habl**aste**	com**iste**	decid**iste**
Ud. / él / ella	habl**ó**	com**ió**	decid**ió**
nosotros/as	habl**amos**	com**imos**	decid**imos**
vosotros/as	habl**asteis**	com**isteis**	decid**isteis**
Uds./ ellos / ellas	habl**aron**	com**ieron**	decid**ieron**

Note that the first and the third person singular forms have a written accent. Also, verbs that end in –**er** and –**ir** use the same set of endings in the preterite.

Most stem-changing verbs that end in –**ar** and –**er** in the present tense are regular in the preterite.

Encontr**é** las llaves de mi coche.   *I found my car keys.*
El carpintero volvi**ó** tarde a su casa.   *The carpenter arrived home late.*

[handwritten: Not stem change in preterite]

Actividades

1 ¿Comprendiste? Match the *El sábado pasado* story characters listed in the left-hand column with their actions in the right-hand column.

1. Los hermanos
2. El abuelo
3. A los abuelos
4. El chico
5. La madre
6. A la chica
7. La cena
8. Nadie

a. escuchó la conversación de la abuela.
b. invitó a los abuelos a cenar.
c. terminó a las nueve de la noche.
d. les encantó la cena.
e. prepararon la cena.
f. compró las bebidas.
g. le gustó mucho la idea.
h. se levantó de la mesa durante la cena.

2 Quehaceres. With a partner, ask each other questions following the model.

▶ **MODELO:** —¿Lavaste los platos?   —*Did you wash the dishes?*
—Sí, lavé los platos.   —*Yes, I washed the dishes.*

or

—No, no lavé los platos.   —*No, I didn't wash the dishes.*

1. aspirar la alfombra de la sala   *[handwritten: ¿Aspiraste la alfrombra de la sala? Sí aspiré.]*
2. limpiar la cocina   *[handwritten: limpiaste, limpié]*
3. barrer el piso   *[handwritten: Barriste el piso → barrí]*
4. arreglar los estantes   *[handwritten: arreglaste, arreglé]*
5. guardar *(put away)* los platos   *[handwritten: guardaste, guardé,]*
6. preparar la cena   *[handwritten: preparaste, preparé]*

3 Estudio y trabajo. Rewrite each sentence using the preterite forms of the verbs in **boldface**. Follow the model.

▶ **MODELO:** (Yo) **me quito** los zapatos antes de acostarme.
Me quité los zapatos antes de acostarme.

1. No **entiendo** nada en la clase.   *[handwritten: entender entendí]*
2. Los estudiantes **celebran** toda la noche.   *[handwritten: celebraron]*
3. **Nos preocupamos** por el examen.   *[handwritten: preocupamos]*
4. ¿**Usas** tu computadora nueva en la presentación?   *[handwritten: usaste]*
5. Ustedes **conocen** la capital de España, ¿verdad?   *[handwritten: conocieron]*
6. Mi familia y yo **pasamos** un día feliz con mis abuelos.   *[handwritten: pasamos]*
7. Les **mando** los documentos por Internet.   *[handwritten: mandar mandé]*
8. ¿**Recibes** mis mensajes electrónicos?   *[handwritten: recibiste]*

4 Rutinas. Write a paragraph describing your day yesterday. Use at least five verbs from the list.

levantarse	despertarse	cepillarse	lavarse
ducharse	bañarse	volver	trabajar
acostarse	estudiar	caminar	comer

CAMINOS DEL JAGUAR

¡Susto espantoso!

En la casa del Sr. Covarrubias.

¿Podemos hablar con el Sr. Covarrubias?

Gerardo no está.

¿No sabe cuándo regresa?

Entonces, ¿no sabe usted nada?

No, no sé cuándo regresa.

No, lo siento, pero no sé nada.

Vámonos, Adriana, aquí no vamos a solucionar nada.

Gracias, Sra. Covarrubias.

Quién sabe dónde está Gerardo en su camión.

En la ciudad.

¿Y ahora qué hacemos?

Voy al Archivo de Indias para investigar. Nayeli pasa mucho tiempo allí.

Voy a leer el correo electrónico en el hotel. A ver si el Sr. de Landa tiene noticias de Nayeli.

Buena idea.

Nos vemos en el hotel más tarde.

En el hotel, habitación de Felipe.

Ah, ¡qué bien! Un mensaje del Sr. de Landa.

Queridos Adriana y Felipe: Todo está arreglado. Sus boletos están en Barajas, en la aerolínea Iberia. Tienen que volver a Madrid en dos días para tomar el avión desde allí. ¡Buena suerte!

¡Gol! ¡Ahhh, Nayeli está bien! ¡Nos vamos a encontrar con ella en la hermosa isla de Puerto Rico!

En el hotel, habitación de Felipe.

Adriana, ¡qué te pasa!

¡Qué miedo!

¿Cómo?

Al regresar del Archivo de Indias al hotel, vi a un hombre con un anillo raro.

¿Quién puede ser ese hombre del anillo?

No sé... pero no importa porque nos vamos para Puerto Rico.

¿A Puerto Rico?

¿Y los pasajes?

Sí, el Sr. de Landa dice que Nayeli está allí y está bien.

Están en Barajas. ¡Imagínate! ¡Nos vamos a la playa!

¡Nayeli está bien y nos vamos a encontrar con ella en San Juan!

En la agencia de viajes.

Un boleto a Quito, por favor, lo antes posible.

¿Mañana por la mañana?

Está bien, gracias, muy amable.

¿Quito? ¡Nos vamos a Quito!

Actividades

Online Study Center

For additional practice
with this episode, visit
the *Caminos* website at
http://college.hmco.com/
languages/spanish/
renjilian/caminos/3e/
student_home.html.

1 **Comprensión.** Based on this episode of *Caminos del jaguar*, choose the logical response.

1. El Sr. Covarrubias...
   a. va a regresar pronto a casa.
   b. no está en casa.

2. En el Archivo de Indias, Adriana...
   a. busca a Nayeli.
   b. lee el correo electrónico.

3. El Sr. de Landa les da a Adriana y Felipe...
   a. dos pasajes para Barajas.
   b. dos pasajes de ida y vuelta para Puerto Rico.

4. Nayeli va a viajar a...
   a. Quito.
   b. San Juan.

5. Adriana vio a un hombre con...
   a. un anillo raro.
   b. una cara rara.

6. En San Juan, Adriana y Felipe...
   a. van a ver a Nayeli.
   b. van a ver al Sr. de Landa.

7. Gafasnegras sabe que Nayeli...
   a. va a viajar a Quito.
   b. va a viajar a Puerto Rico.

2 **Situaciones.** Dramatize one of the following situations.

1. Armando tells Adriana and Felipe that the tickets are ready.
2. Adriana and Felipe talk to Sra. Covarrubias about her husband's whereabouts.

3 **Escritura.** Write a brief summary of this episode (4–6 sentences).

NOTA CULTURAL

El Archivo General de Indias

El Archivo General de Indias is the library in which
documents and records from three centuries of Spanish
colonial rule in the Americas (or Indies) are stored.
Among the documents contained in the archives is a
letter written in 1590 by Miguel de Cervantes, author of
the *Quijote*, requesting employment in the New World.
The Archivo is located in a beautiful colonial building
in the heart of Sevilla.

Lectura

Online Study Center

For further reading practice online, visit the *Caminos* website at http://college.hmco.com/languages/spanish/renjilian/caminos/3e/student_home.html.

PRELECTURA

1 Quiero ser turista. Describe a country that you would like to visit as a tourist. Then use the Internet or another source to learn particular characteristics that make this country popular for visitors. Read about some of the country's most attractive sites that not only beckon tourists from around the globe, but also provide many activities for local citizens. Answer the following questions as you research your chosen destination.

1. ¿Qué país quieres visitar? ¿En qué continente está el país? ¿Cuál es la población? ¿Qué idioma/s hablan allí?
2. ¿Cómo son la geografía y el clima del país?
3. ¿Cuántos turistas visitan el país en el verano? ¿Qué sitios son los más populares?
4. ¿De dónde son los nuevos inmigrantes que viven allí? ¿Qué culturas representan? ¿Qué idioma/s hablan?
5. Menciona una persona importante de allí. ¿Quién es?
6. ¿Por qué quieres visitar ese país?

Reading Strategy

Making notes in the margin

A useful reading strategy is to make notes in the margin of the text while you are reading. This technique allows you to respond actively to information and ideas presented by an author. As you read the following facts and features about Spain, jot these items in the margins:

a. The main topic of each paragraph.
b. Any questions you may have that stem logically from the information presented.
c. Your own answers or hunches about the questions you have formulated.
d. Information you can provide to supplement the reading based on written or other sources with which you are familiar.

A España le encantan los turistas

¿Sabes que cada año el número de turistas que visitan España es mayor que[1] el número de habitantes del país? ¡Pues así es! La población[2] del país suma 40.397.000, mientras que recibe a unos 65 millones de visitantes. Es un país muy popular porque ofrece no solamente mar y montañas, museos, castillos[3] y comidas ricas, sino[4] también un agradable espíritu de bienvenida[5].

_____

[1]greater than; [2]population; [3]castles; [4]but; [5]welcome

El Parque Güell de Antonio Gaudí

Estadio olímpico de Barcelona

Barcelona

Barcelona es una ciudad de mucho prestigio, sofisticada y contemporánea. Se encuentra en Cataluña y allí hablan catalán y español. Más de 21 millones de turistas extranjeros escogen Cataluña para pasar sus vacaciones. Tiene importantes museos de arte, restaurantes y la famosa catedral, del arquitecto Antonio Gaudí, llamada La Sagrada Familia. La ciudad da al[6] mar y hay una playa muy popular con muchas diversiones para turistas y residentes.

Las Ramblas

Las Ramblas es el lugar favorito de la ciudad donde se pasean[7] muchos jóvenes y familias. Hay cafés y terrazas al aire libre[8], tiendas, kioskos, pintores y artistas. ¡Hay tanto que ver, comer y escuchar!

Estadio para las Olimpiadas

El inmenso estadio fue construido[9] para los Juegos Olímpicos de 1992. También construyeron una villa para atletas. Para esa ocasión, se hicieron muchos nuevos espacios deportivos que permanecen hoy en día[10].

"Puppy"

De Barcelona, vale la pena[11] hacer una excursión a Bilbao, en el País Vasco, ciudad famosa por la construcción del nuevo Museo Guggenheim, concebido por el arquitecto Frank O. Gehry. El notable edificio de titanio, caliza[12] y vidrio[13] es enorme. También es impresionante la escultura del perrito, "Puppy", símbolo del museo, que se compone de 60.000 plantas y flores y es casi tan alto como[14] el museo.

Artistas en las Ramblas, Barcelona

"Puppy", el enorme perrito enfrente del Museo Guggenheim

[6]faces; [7]stroll; [8]outdoor; [9]was built; [10]today; [11]it's worth; [12]limestone; [13]glass; [14]as tall as.

POSTLECTURA

2 **¡Me importan los números!** With a classmate, practice reading aloud the numbers and dates from the reading.

3 **Nuestras reacciones.** In groups of four, make a chart of your group's reactions to the reading by comparing the notes you each made in the margin. Follow these steps:

1. Jot down the main topics that you identified in the reading.
2. Write your own questions in the chart.
3. Write down your ideas regarding each question.
4. Add any references to other information that you may already know from other sources.

	Preguntas	Mi idea	Otra referencia
Tema 1: Aspectos atractivos **Tema 2:**	¿ Por qué es tan popular España?	_____ _____	_____ _____
_____ **Tema 3:**	_____	_____	_____
Tema 4:	_____	_____	_____

4 **Comprensión.** Working in pairs, answer these questions based on the reading.

1. ¿Cuántos habitantes tiene España?
2. ¿Cuántos turistas visitan el país anualmente? ¿Por qué?
3. ¿En qué parte del país está Barcelona? ¿Cómo es?
4. ¿Qué actividades hay en las Ramblas?
5. ¿Desde cuándo tiene Barcelona un estadio olímpico?
6. ¿Dónde está el Museo Guggenheim? ¿Quién es "Puppy" y cómo es?

5 **Comparaciones y contrastes.** In pairs, compare and contrast tourism in your country and in Spain. Ask each other these questions.

1. ¿En qué parte del mundo está tu país? ¿Cuál es la población? ¿Qué lengua/s hablan?
2. ¿Qué te gusta hacer con familia o amigos?
3. Describe el clima y la geografía en diferentes partes del país.
4. ¿Cuántos turistas visitan tu país en el verano? ¿Qué sitios son los más populares?
5. ¿De qué países vienen los visitantes?
6. ¿Cuál es la composición cultural de tu país? ¿De dónde son los nuevos inmigrantes que viven allí? ¿Qué lengua/s hablan? ¿Qué religiones practican?
7. Describe a una persona importante de tu región. ¿Cuál es su profesión?
8. Describe un lugar o monumento representativo de la cultura de tu país o región.

6 **De viaje a dos ciudades españolas.** You and a classmate have been invited to give a brief talk to a Spanish class about traveling to two destinations in Spain. Use the Internet to research and design a brochure with appealing visuals. Title your two-paragraph presentation "*Dos ciudades fascinantes de España*."

Escritura

Online Study Center

For further writing practice online, visit the *Caminos* website at http://college.hmco.com/languages/spanish/renjilian/caminos/3e/student_home.html.

Writing Strategy

Creating a timeline

A good way to organize information visually is by use of a timeline. This strategy is useful when writing about a sequence of events, whether over a brief or lengthy period of time. A timeline helps you to see connections between earlier and subsequent events.

Workshop

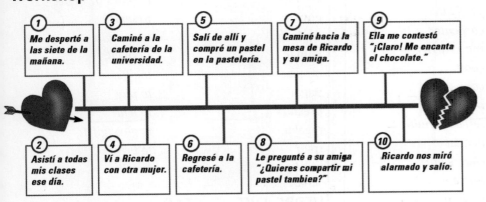

1. Me desperté a las siete de la mañana.
2. Asistí a todas mis clases ese día.
3. Caminé a la cafetería de la universidad.
4. Ví a Ricardo con otra mujer.
5. Salí de allí y compré un pastel en la pastelería.
6. Regresé a la cafetería.
7. Caminé hacia la mesa de Ricardo y su amiga.
8. Le pregunté a su amiga "¿Quieres compartir mi pastel tambien?"
9. Ella me contestó "¡Claro! Me encanta el chocolate."
10. Ricardo nos miró alarmado y salío.

Primero me desperté a las 7.00 de la mañana. Asistí a todas mis clases ese día y luego caminé a la cafetería para almorzar con mi novio, Ricardo. Entré en la cafetería media hora antes de nuestra cita y vi a Ricardo —¡besándose con otra chica! Ellos no me vieron. Compré un pastel de chocolate en la pastelería. Regresé a la cafetería y caminé a la mesa de Ricardo y su amiga. Le pregunté a su amiga: "¿Quieres compartir mi pastel también?" Ella me contestó: "¡Claro! Me encanta el chocolate". Ricardo nos miró alarmado y salió. Ahora, su amiga Laura es mi mejor amiga.

Strategy in action

For additional practice writing a timeline, turn to the *Escritura* section of *Unidad 4* in your Student Activities Manual.

1 **Mi primer día de clase.** Use a timeline to record at least five things that happened on your first day of class. Then, write a brief paragraph to describe the events of that day. Use the preterite tense.

2 **Una fiesta familiar.** Think of a special day that you spent with some members of your family (birthday, Thanksgiving, etc.) and write a story narrating the events of that day. Use the preterite tense.

PRIMER PASO

DISCUSSING PROFESSIONS

Sustantivos

el/la abogado/a	*attorney, lawyer*
el/la agente de viajes	*travel agent*
el/la arqueólogo/a	*archaeologist*
el/la arquitecto/a	*architect*
el/la artista	*artist*
el/la atleta	*athlete*
el/la bombero/a	*firefighter*
el/la carpintero/a	*carpenter*
el/la cartero/a	*mail carrier*
el/la cocinero/a	*cook*
el/la consejero/a	*counselor*
el/la contador/a	*accountant*
el/la criado/a	*servant, maid*
el/la dentista	*dentist*
el/la electricista	*electrician*
el/la enfermero/a	*nurse*
el/la escultor/a	*sculptor*
el/la fotógrafo/a	*photographer*
el/la gerente	*manager*
el hombre de negocios	*businessman*
el/la ingeniero/a	*engineer*
el/la jardinero/a	*gardener*
el/la jefe/a	*boss*
el/la médico/a	*doctor*
la mujer de negocios	*businesswoman*
el/la músico/a	*musician*
el/la peluquero/a	*hair stylist*
el/la periodista	*journalist*
el/la pintor/a	*painter*
el/la plomero/a	*plumber*
el/la policia	*police officer*
el/la presidente/a	*president*
el/la profesor/a	*professor*
el/la programador/a de computadoras	*computer programmer*
el/la psicólogo/a	*psychologist*
el/la recepcionista	*receptionist*
el/la secretario/a	*secretary*
el/la trabajador/a	*worker*
el/la vendedor/a	*salesperson*
el/la veterinario/a	*veterinarian*

COMMON VERBS USED WITH INDIRECT OBJECT PRONOUNS

agradecer	*to thank, be grateful for*
contestar	*to answer*
dar	*to give*
deber	*to owe, should*
enseñar	*to teach*
entregar	*to hand in, deliver*
enviar	*to send*
explicar	*to explain*
hablar	*to speak*
ofrecer	*to offer*
pagar	*to pay*
prestar	*to lend*
regalar	*to give (gifts)*
traer	*to bring*
vender	*to sell*

VERBS LIKE *GUSTAR*

caer bien/mal	*to like / dislike (a person)*
encantar	*to delight, like very much (love)*
faltar	*to lack, need; to be left (to do)*
fascinar	*to fascinate*
importar	*to matter, be important, be of concern*
interesar	*to interest, be of interest*
molestar	*to bother, annoy*
parecer	*to seem, appear to be*
preocupar	*to worry*

AFFIRMATIVE, NEGATIVE, AND TRANSITIONAL EXPRESSIONS

a veces	*at times*
algo	*something, anything*
alguien	*someone, somebody*
algún	*some, any*
algunas veces	*sometimes*
alguno/a/os/as	*some, any*
casi siempre/ nunca/nada	*almost always / never / nothing*

de vez en cuando	*from time to time*	(o) ... o	*(either) . . . or*
muchas veces	*many times*	siempre	*always*
nada	*nothing*	también	*also, too*
nadie	*no one, nobody*	tampoco	*neither, either*
(ni) ... ni	*(neither) . . . nor*	todo	*everything*
ningún	*none, not any*	todo el mundo	*everybody, everyone*
ninguno/a nunca, jamás	*never*	todos los días	*every day*

SEGUNDO PASO

TALKING ABOUT FAMILY MEMBERS

Sustantivos

el/la abuelo/a	*grandfather / grandmother*
el/la bebé	*baby*
el/la bisabuelo/a	*great-grandfather / great-grandmother*
el/la chico/a	*boy / girl*
el conejo	*rabbit*
el/la cuñado/a	*brother-in-law / sister-in-law*
el/la esposo/a	*husband / wife*
el/la gato/a	*cat*
el/la hermanastro/a	*stepbrother / stepsister*
el/la hermano/a	*brother, sister*
el/la hijastro/a	*stepson / stepdaughter*
el/la hijo/a	*son / daughter*
la madrastra	*stepmother*
la madre / mamá	*mother, mom*
el marido	*husband*
la mascota	*pet*
el/la nieto/a	*grandson / granddaughter*
el/la niño/a	*boy / girl / child*
el/la novio/a	*boyfriend / girlfriend*
la nuera	*daughter-in-law*
el padrastro	*stepfather*
el padre / papá	*father, dad*
el pájaro	*bird*
el/la pariente	*family member, relative*
el/la perro/a	*dog*
el/la primo/a	*cousin*
el/la sobrino/a	*nephew / niece*
el/la suegro/a	*father-in-law / mother-in-law*
el/la tío/a	*uncle / aunt*
la tortuga	*turtle*
el yerno	*son-in-law*

Verbos

abrazar	*to hug*
casarse (con)	*to get married (to)*
enamorarse (de)	*to fall in love (with)*
estar casado/a	*to be married*
estar divorciado/a	*to be divorced*
estar enamorado/a	*to be in love*
estar separado/a	*to be separated*
nacer	*to be born*
ser mayor	*to be older*
ser menor	*to be younger*
ser soltero/a	*to be single*

Preposiciones

a	*to, for*
al lado de	*next to, side by side*
antes de	*before*
bajo	*under*
cerca de	*close to*
con	*with*
de	*from, of*
debajo de	*beneath, under*
delante de	*in front of*
dentro de	*inside of*
desde	*from, since*
después de	*after*
detrás de	*behind*
durante	*during*
en	*in, on, at*
encima de	*on top of, above*
enfrente de	*in front of, facing*
entre	*between, among*
fuera de	*outside of*
hacia	*toward*
hasta	*until*
junto a	*next to*
lejos de	*far from*
para	*for, to, in order to*
por	*for, by means of*
según	*according to*
sin	*without*
sobre	*on, on top of*

ESPAÑA

Online Study Center

To learn more about the people featured in this section, visit the *Caminos* website at http://college .hmco.com/languages/ spanish/renjilian/caminos/ 3e/student_home.html.

PERSONALIDADES

Tomatito

Bebe

Julio Iglesias

Enrique Iglesias

Alejandro Sanz

Manu Chao

España es un país multicultural. Además de español, muchos habitantes hablan otras lenguas españolas: vasco[1], catalán[2] y gallego[3]. La historia española refleja la influencia de tres culturas importantes: la cristiana, la judía[4] y la islámica (también llamada musulmana[5]). Estas influencias se ven en el arte, la arquitectura, el cine, la comida, la moda, la música y la literatura de España.

Hay muchas personalidades de España distinguidas en sus profesiones: la diseñadora de joyas[6] Paloma Picasso; el modista[7] Cristobal Balenciaga, el arquitecto Antonio Gaudí; los artistas Salvador Dalí y Joan Miró; los actores Penélope Cruz y Antonio Banderas; el director de cine Pedro Almodóvar; el Príncipe de Asturias[8] y su esposa doña Letizia; los escritores Miguel de Cervantes, Federico García Lorca y Ana María Matute son también personalidades famosas de España.

---

[1]Basque; [2]Catalan; [3]Galician; [4]Jewish; [5]Muslim; [6]jewelry designer; [7]fashion designer; [8]Prince of Asturias

Comprensión

Working in pairs, ask each other the following questions.

1. ¿Es España unicultural?
2. ¿Cuántos idiomas hablan los españoles? ¿Cuáles son?
3. Nombra las diferentes culturas que han contribuido° a la civilización española.
4. ¿En qué areas se reflejan las influencias religiones en España?

have contributed

"Cuando quiero algo, lo busco con cabeza de hielo, corazón de fuego y mano de hierro".

Antonio Banderas, *Cristina La Revista* (España)

ARTE

JOSÉ MANUEL MERELLO

José Manuel Merello es un pintor expresionista. Nació° en el año 1960. Estudió° álgebra, geometría y filosofía en las universidades de España. Este artista contemporáneo ha tenido muchas exposiciones° y es ganador de varios premios / galardones por su arte. Esta obra de arte acrílica se titula *Niño soñando con°* su bicicleta.

He was born / He studied

exhibitions

dreaming about

Niño soñando con su bicicleta

Comprensión

Working in pairs, ask each other the following questions.

1. ¿Cuántos años crees que tiene este niño?
2. ¿Con qué sueña el niño, según° el título de la pintura?
3. ¿Adónde crees que quiere ir el niño?
4. ¿Qué colores usa el artista? ¿Qué temas interpretas en la obra?
5. Describe la pintura: ¿Es realista, surrealista, sentimental, original?

according to

MÚSICA

En algunas familias españolas, las tradiciones musicales son notables. Por ejemplo, "Tomatito" (José Fernández Torres) toca la guitarra flamenca, como su padre y su abuelo. En 2005, ganó un Grammy Latino por el mejor álbum flamenco, "Aguadulce°".

Sweet water

Otro guitarrista con un nombre similar es el legendario "El Tomate" (Juan Muñoz), que tiene fama como el "gurú de la guitarra". Él tuvo influencia en tres de sus cinco hijas (Lucía, Lola y Pilar) para formar su grupo musical, "Las Ketchup". Su primer disco, "Las hijas del tomate" les ganó un premio europeo.

Bebe (Verónica Sánchez) ganó un Grammy Latino como el mejor Nuevo Artista del año 2005. De padres músicos, Bebe pasó la vida rodeada de° guitarras, baterías° y pianos. Su estilo es original.

spent her life surrounded by / drums

Julio Iglesias y su hijo Enrique Iglesias son de Madrid. Julio ha vendido° más de 250.000.000 millones de discos, mientras° Enrique Iglesias ha vendido más de 40.000.000 millones de álbumes. Estos dos artistas internacionales son ganadores de los premios más prestigiosos de la música. También, Julio está en el libro de

has sold
while

Las Ketchup

any records mundiales de Guinness por vender más discos en más idiomas que cualquier° otro cantante en la historia de la música. Él vive en Miami.

Otro madrileño influenciado musicalmente por su padre es Alejandro Sanz (Alejandro Sánchez Pizarro). Cuando recibió su primer *dedicated it to* Grammy Latino, Alejandro se lo dedicó° a su padre, ya muerto. Este cantante *sounds* español de fama internacional es popular por su música de sonidos° pop, flamenco y mediterráneo.

Los padres del cantante español "Manu Chao" (José-Manuel Thomas Arthur Chao) llevaron a la familia a vivir en Francia durante la dictadura de Francisco Franco. Con sus hermanos, tocaron conciertos en Latinoamérica. Su banda de hoy, "Manu Chao", es un grupo de cantantes y músicos de diferentes países. Canta en español, francés, árabe, gallego, inglés y portugués.

Otros distinguidos cantantes y grupos españoles son Miguel Bosé, Ana Belén, "Monja enana", "La oreja de Van Gogh", "El mago de Oz", Plácido Domingo, Rocío Durcal y José Carreras. Conéctate a Internet para aprender más sobre ellos.

Comprensión

Working in pairs, ask each other the following questions.

1. ¿Cuál de los cantantes dedicó su Grammy Latino a su padre?
has sold 2. ¿Quién ha vendido° más discos en muchas lenguas?
3. ¿Cuál de los músicos canta en español, francés, árabe y portugués?
4. ¿Cuáles de los artistas musicales tienen nombres similares?
5. ¿Quién tiene su residencia en los Estados Unidos?
gave 6. ¿A quién le dieron° el Grammy Latino por el Nuevo artista del año 2005?

LITERATURA

GUSTAVO ADOLFO BÉCQUER

Gustavo Adolfo Bécquer es uno de los poetas más importantes del movimiento romántico de la literatura española. Él vivió entre 1836–1870. Su poesía se nota por su tono íntimo, sus temas sobre los placeres° y las penas del amor, lo ideal y los sueños°.

pleasures / drea
while / you gaze

"Rima XXI"

¿Qué es poesía?, dices mientras°
    clavas° en mi pupila tu pupila azul;
¿Qué es poesía? ¿Y tú me lo
    preguntas? Poesía... eres tú.

Comprensión

Working in pairs, ask each other the following questions.

1. ¿Qué pregunta el poeta? ¿De qué color es la pupila?
2. ¿Cuántas personas hay en el poema? ¿Con qué compara a la segunda persona?
3. El poeta dice, "Poesía eres tú". ¿Qué otra comparación es posible?

"Vengo a buscar lo que busco.
Mi alegría° y mi persona...."   *joy*

Federico García Lorca, "Romance de la pena negra"

4. ¿Qué descripciones evoca el poema, en tu opinión? ¿Es elocuente, realista, apasionado°, bonito, tonto, sensual, positivo, romántico, idealista, exagerado?   *de pasión*
5. Dramatiza el poema con un/a compañero/a de clase.

PALOMA PEDRERO

La española Paloma Pedrero es dramaturga°, directora / productora de cine, actriz y profesora de arte dramático. Nació en 1957. En sus obras, escribe sobre las diferentes tradiciones culturales de su país. En esta escena de su drama, *Resguardo° personal*, Pedrero nos presenta la relación conflictiva entre una pareja, Gonzalo y Marta.   *playwright*

Claim check

Resguardo personal

G: Marta, yo te quiero°. Te juro que te quiero.   *I love you*
M: Ya lo sé°. Me enseñaste algo que no conocía°...   *I already know / I didn't know*
G: Vuelve a casa. Podemos arreglar° las cosas...   *fix*
M: Me enseñaste lo insólito° del amor: la destrucción.   *flip, weird side*
G: Quiero seguir viviendo contigo. Creo que no está todo perdido°...   *lost*
M: Puede ser que la destrucción sea° parte del amor...   *is*
G: ¡No me quieres escuchar!
M: No.
G: No tienes interés en hablar conmigo.
M: Sí.
G: ¿Sí?
M: Sí, que no, que no tengo interés.
G: ¿Vas a volver a casa?
M: No.
G: Te advierto° que no te lo voy a pedir más.   *warn*
M: Te lo agradezco°. Tengo prisa.   *thank*
G: Es tu última oportunidad.

Comprensión

With a partner, dramatize the dialog. Then, answer these questions.

1. ¿Qué temas presenta la autora en esta escena dramática?
2. ¿Cuántos años tienen Gonzalo y Marta, en tu opinión?
3. ¿Cómo está Gonzalo? ¿Calmado, convincente, tolerante, decidido, flexible, desilusionado, determinado, romántico, estable, frustrado...?
4. ¿Con qué actitud reacciona Marta? ¿Calmada, convincente, tolerante, desilusionada, decidida, determinada, romántica, estable, flexible, frustrada?
5. ¿Quién tiene prisa? ¿Va a volver a casa? ¿Por qué?
6. Gonzalo le dice a Marta, "Es tu última oportunidad". En tu opinión, ¿qué le va a contestar Marta?
7. Describe el tono de este diálogo: alegre, melancólico, tenso, triste.
8. En el poema de Bécquer y el drama de Pedrero, ¿qué temas y tonos tienen en común y cuáles son diferentes?

UNIDAD

5
Vacaciones en la playa

VOCABULARIO Y LENGUA

- Checking into a hotel
- Using direct object pronouns
- Talking about the beach and leisure activities
- Narrating events in the past: Preterite of verbs with spelling changes: *ir, ser, dar*

- Discussing vacations
- Using double object pronouns
- Narrating events in the past: Preterite of stem-changing *-ir* verbs
- Narrating events in the past: Preterite of irregular verbs

CAMINOS DEL JAGUAR

- Volibol y amor en la playa
- Dos espías

LECTURA

- Vamos al Caribe hispano: Cuba, Puerto Rico y la República Dominicana

NOTAS CULTURALES

- El turismo en el Caribe hispano
- Los parques nacionales

ESTRATEGIAS

- **Reading:** How to use the dictionary
- **Writing:** Using a dictionary

is Germán Cajiga, *Flamboyán entre palmeras*

Preguntas del tema

► ¿Adónde te gusta ir de vacaciones?
► ¿Qué actividades te gusta hacer?
► ¿Con quién/es vas de vacaciones?
► ¿Cuál es tu hotel favorito?

Vocabulario y lengua

CHECKING INTO A HOTEL

HOTEL NACIONAL, HABANA, CUBA

luxury
first class
hotel industry / surrounded

Inaugurado el 30 de diciembre de 1930, El Nacional es uno de los hoteles más clásicos de la Habana. Su **lujo**°, **elegancia**, distinción y servicios de **primera clase**°, se mantienen intactos después de seis décadas en la **industria hotelera**° cubana. **Rodeado**° por hermosos jardines, el hotel ocupa un lugar privilegiado cerca del Malecón habanero, ofreciendo una de las **vistas**° más bellas de la ciudad. Sus **huéspedes**° pueden disfrutar de **habitaciones**° espléndidas y cómodas.

views
guests
rooms

FACILIDADES DE LAS HABITACIONES

TV satélite
Minibar
Radio despertador°
Teléfono

Aire acondicionado
Baño privado
Radio
Refrigerador

alarm clock

FACILIDADES DEL HOTEL

Bar
Centro de negocios
Elevador / Ascensor
Estacionamiento
Restaurante
Sala de ejercicios
Servicios médicos

Buró de turismo
Caja de seguridad
Jardín
Piscina
Sala de conferencias
Servicio de habitación
Tenis

Online Study Center

For additional practice with this unit's vocabulary and grammar, visit the *Caminos* website at http://college.hmco.com/ languages/spanish/ renjilian/caminos/3e/ student_home.html. You can also review audio flashcards, quiz yourself, and explore related Spanish-language sites.

Más palabras y expresiones

Cognados

el (mini) bar
confirmar
la recepción

el/la recepcionista
la reservación
  reservar

Sustantivos

el alojamiento	*lodging, accommodations*
el botones	*bellhop*
el buzón	*mailbox*
el cajero automático	*automated teller machine (ATM)*
el cambio de dinero / moneda	*money exchange*
el cheque de viajero	*traveler's check*
el/la conserje	*concierge*
el (dinero en) efectivo	*cash*
el estacionamiento / aparcamiento	*parking lot*
el equipaje	*luggage*
la habitación	*room*
la maleta	*suitcase*
el salón (la sala) de conferencias	*conference room*
la tarifa	*rate, fare, tariff*
la tarjeta de crédito / débito	*credit / debit card*

Verbos

alojar(se)	*to stay (in a hotel)*
atender (ie)	*to attend to, wait on*
hacer una llamada (de larga distancia/ por cobrar)	*to make a (long distance / collect) phone call*

Adjetivos

cómodo/a	*comfortable*
doble	*double*
lujoso/a (de lujo)	*luxurious*
sencillo/a	*single (room or bed)*

Otras expresiones

¿A nombre de quién?	*In whose name?*
¿En qué le(s) puedo servir?	*How can I help you?*
con desayuno	*with breakfast*
con media pensión	*with two meals*
con vista al mar	*with an ocean view*
¿Cuánto cuesta... ?	*How much does . . . cost?*
¿Dónde puedo cambiar el dinero?	*Where can I exchange money?*
Lo siento.	*I'm sorry.*
por supuesto	*of course*
¡Que disfrute/n de su estadía / estancia!	*Enjoy your stay!*

Actividades

1 Hotel Real de Minas. Listen to the description of a hotel in Guanajuato, México, then determine whether the statements are **verdadero (V)** or **falso (F).** Correct the false statements.

1. _____ Guanajuato es una ciudad bonita.
2. _____ El Hotel Real de Minas es un hotel económico.
3. _____ Hay 12 restaurantes en el hotel.
4. _____ Hay 175 habitaciones en el hotel.
5. _____ Veinte suites tienen aire acondicionado.
6. _____ No hay estacionamiento.
7. _____ Hay un bar cerca de la alberca.
8. _____ Su número de teléfono es el 63-215-80.

2 ¿Qué es? Write the correct word that matches each definition.

1. Cuando viajas, pones mucha ropa (*clothing*) allí.
2. Es una forma de pagar el hotel si no tienes dinero en efectivo.
3. Se usa para abrir una puerta.
4. Allí descansas en el hotel.
5. Allí los turistas reciben la llave de la habitación.
6. Es un aparato para ir al piso doce.
7. Es la persona que ayuda a los huéspedes a encontrar sitios turísticos.
8. Es un lugar donde guardar el coche.

3 Símbolos internacionales. Match the international hotel symbols on the right with their meanings on the left.

_____ piscina (alberca)
_____ dos camas sencillas
_____ tarjetas de crédito
_____ cama sencilla
_____ cambio de moneda
_____ restaurante
_____ salón de conferencias
_____ teléfono
_____ ascensor
_____ bar
_____ estacionamiento
_____ cama doble
_____ televisión
_____ perros no
_____ minibar

4 ¿Qué necesitas? State what hotel amenities you will need in the following situations. Follow the model.

► MODELO: Tienes hambre.
Necesito un restaurante.

1. No tienes dinero.
2. Debes llamar a tu madre.
3. Tus maletas son muy grandes.
4. Tu habitación está en el piso veinticuatro.
5. Tienes sed.
6. Quieres hacer ejercicio.
7. Tienes hambre a medianoche y el restaurante está cerrado (*closed*).
8. Llegas al hotel en coche.

5 En el hotel. Complete the following conversation between a guest and the receptionist at a hotel using the vocabulary from the word bank below.

con vista al mar	¿En qué le puedo servir?	tarjeta de crédito
reservar	¡Que disfruten de su estadía!	habitación
sencilla	¿A nombre de quién?	

—Buenas tardes. _____

—Buenas tardes. Quisiéramos _____ una habitación
  para esta noche.

—_____

—De los Señores Guzmán.

—¿Por cuántas noches?

—Por dos, por favor.

—¿Qué tipo de _____ prefiere Ud.?

—Nos gustaría una habitación _____.

—¿Con cama _____ o doble?

—Con una cama doble. ¿Cuánto cuesta?

—La habitación cuesta $132 por noche.

—Muy bien. ¿Se puede pagar con _____?

—Claro que sí. _____

6 Entre nosotros. Role-play the following situation with a partner.

Turista:	Recepcionista:
You are traveling through Spain by bicycle. After a difficult day, you arrive at your hotel very tired. When you arrive, the receptionist tells you that he or she doesn't have your reservation. You have a copy of your confirmation. Do whatever you can to get a room for the night.	A young bicyclist arrives at your hotel, but you can't find his or her reservation in the computer. There's a medical conference (**congreso**) in the hotel and there are no rooms left. Do your best to solve this dilemma.

USING DIRECT OBJECT PRONOUNS

Preparando el viaje

Amanda No encuentro mi bolsa azul. **La** necesito para empacar mis cosas.

Arturo Yo **la** tengo. Aquí está la bolsa. También tengo los boletos de avión.

Amanda **Los** tienes también. ¡Qué bien! Mil gracias.

Amanda	¿Y el dinero?
Arturo	También **lo** tengo aquí. Supongo que llamaste a la embajada norteamericana y sacaste las visas, ¿verdad?
Amanda	¿Las visas? Claro, ayer hablé con la embajada para pedir**las.**
Arturo	Es importante tener**las.**
Amanda	Tienes razón. Sin visas no podemos viajar.

A direct object is the person or thing that directly receives the action of the verb. In the first sentence on page 173, **mi bolsa azul** is a direct object. Once the object is stated, it is often replaced by a direct object pronoun to avoid redundancy: *La necesito para empacar mis cosas.*

In the dialog above, can you identify the direct object nouns that correspond to the direct object pronouns in boldface? Note that third person direct object pronouns agree in number and gender with the nouns that they replace.

Direct object pronouns			
me	*me*	**nos**	*us*
te	*you*	**os**	*you*
lo, la	*him, her, you, it*	**los, las**	*them, you*

The direct object **lo** is often used to express a previously mentioned idea as in, *Sí **lo** sé.* (Yes, I know it.)

Direct object pronouns precede the conjugated verb.

—¿Y **los boletos?**   —*And the tickets?*
—**Los** recogemos en Madrid.   —*We'll pick them up in Madrid.*

When the direct object pronoun is used with a conjugated verb and an infinitive (**tengo que comprar, voy a hacer, acabo de escribir,** etc.) the pronoun can go either before the conjugated verb or attached to the end of the infinitive.

Quiero pedir **una habitación**   *I want to ask for a larger room.*
   más grande.
La quiero pedir.   *I want to ask for it.*
Quiero pedir**la.**

Direct object pronouns are attached to the end of the infinitive when the infinitive is used with expressions such as **es importante / bueno / necesario,** etc., or in prepositional expressions such as **para recibir***las,* **de visitar***la.*

—Me gusta tener **un buen mapa.**   —*I like to have a good map.*
—Sí, es bueno tener**lo.**   —*Yes, it's good to have it.*

When the direct object pronoun is used with progressive forms (**estar** + present participle), the pronoun can go either before the conjugated form of **estar** or attached to the end of the participle. When attached to the participle, you must add a written accent.

—¿Estás escribiendo **la tarjeta postal?**   —*Are you writing the postcard?*
—Sí, **la** estoy escribiendo.   —*Yes, I'm writing it.*
—Sí, estoy escribiéndo**la.**

Actividades

1 Sin repeticiones. Write sentences replacing the direct object nouns with direct object pronouns. Follow the model.

▶ MODELO: Miranda compra los pasajes.   *Miranda buys the tickets.*
            Miranda los compra.   *Miranda buys them.*

1. Quiero mucho a Manuela.
2. Compré unas gafas.
3. Miro los balcones de Sevilla.
4. Los turistas escuchan música.
5. Acuesto al niño en su cama.
6. Desperté a mi hermano temprano.
7. Usted llamó al médico.
8. Podemos tomar el autobús.
9. Llamamos a nuestra profesora.

2 Preguntas personales.
You are making final preparations for a trip with a friend. Use direct object pronouns to answer your friend's questions. Be careful with the verb tenses in your answers. Follow the model.

▶ MODELO: ¿Llamaste al agente de viajes?
Sí, lo llamé. / No, no lo llamé.

1. ¿Depositaste dinero en el banco?
2. ¿Compraste un nuevo traje de baño?
3. ¿Tienes una maleta grande?
4. ¿Vas a empacar tus maletas?
5. ¿Terminaste todo tu trabajo?
6. ¿Tienes la reservación de hotel?
7. ¿Escogiste un hotel bonito?
8. ¿Tu familia te va a ayudar con el perro?
9. ¿Alquilaste un coche?
10. ¿Tienes todo listo?

3 Un viaje a Uruguay.
You and your friend are getting ready for a trip to Uruguay. You check with each other to see if everything is done. Follow the model and use direct object pronouns.

▶ MODELO: reservar el hotel
—¿Reservaste el hotel?
—Sí, lo reservé.

reserve the hotel
—Did you reserve the hotel?
—Yes, I reserved it.

1. recibir la visa
2. escribir las cartas
3. comprar los pasajes
4. recibir la confirmación del hotel
5. comprar las nuevas maletas
6. mandar las cuentas
7. encontrar las maletas
8. confirmar los planes para el viaje

4 Un viaje.
You and two of your friends are planning to go on vacation this weekend. Make a list of things to do using both an infinitive and a direct object noun. Then divide the tasks evenly by taking turns asking each other questions about who is going to do each item. Be sure to use direct object pronouns in your answers. Follow the model.

▶ MODELO: llevar / la radio
—¿Quién va a llevar la radio?
—Yo puedo llevarla.
   Yo la puedo llevar.

take / the radio
—Who's going to take the radio?
—I can take it.

Vamos a la playa.

1.	jugar (al) volibol	*to play volleyball*
2.	las gafas de sol	*sunglasses*
3.	la novela	*novel*
4.	tomar el sol	*to sunbathe*
5.	el traje de baño	*bathing suit*
6.	el/la radio	*radio*
7.	la toalla	*towel*
8.	el protector / bronceador solar	*sunscreen*
9.	el balón	*beach ball*
10.	buscar conchas	*to look for shells*
11.	pasearse / dar un paseo	*to take a walk / stroll*
12.	el sombrero	*hat*
13.	las sandalias	*sandals*
14.	el picnic	*picnic*
15.	la sombrilla	*beach umbrella*
16.	hacer castillos de arena	*to make sand castles*
17.	hacer esquí acuático	*to water ski*
18.	nadar	*to swim*

Más palabras y expresiones

Verbos

broncearse	*to get a tan*
bucear	*to go skindiving, snorkeling*
hacer surfing	*to go surfing*
ir de pesca (pescar)	*to go fishing (to fish)*
montar a caballo	*to go horseback riding*
montar en bicicleta	*to go bicycling*
navegar en velero	*to go sailing*
protegerse	*to protect oneself*
quemarse	*to get a sunburn*

Actividades

1 ¿Qué es? Choose the best word or expression for each definition. There may be more than one correct answer.

1. una actividad que haces en el agua
2. algo que usas para protegerte del sol
3. algo que puedes leer
4. es un buen ejercicio
5. algo que buscas en la playa para una colección
6. algo que te pones en los pies (*feet*)
7. la comida que llevas a la playa
8. algo que usas cuando quieres escuchar música

2 Me toca a mí. Now write three of your own definitions similar to those in *Actividad 1*. Read them to a classmate and have him or her guess the vocabulary words being defined.

3 Memoria. As a class, create a chain sentence that describes what you all like to do at the beach. One person starts by stating what he or she likes to do. The next person repeats the statement, then adds his or her own activity. Take turns and try to remember what each of your classmates has said before you. Follow the model.

▶ **MODELO:** Student A: *Cuando voy a la playa, juego al volibol.*
Student B: *Cuando voy a la playa, juego al volibol y monto en bicicleta.*
Student C: *Cuando voy a la playa, juego al volibol, monto en bicicleta y...*

4 Playas caribeñas. You are planning a vacation to the Caribbean next summer. Find a beach where you would like to go on vacation and prepare a three-day travel itinerary for your trip. State 3–5 activities you plan to do each day. Use your favorite online search engine to find information on beaches in the Caribbean. The following phrases will help you find information in Spanish: "playas Puerto Rico," "playas Venezuela," "playas República Dominicana," "playas Colombia," and "playas Cuba".

Actividades en la playa

Ayer **fui** a la playa con mi hermano Miguel. Yo **busqué** conchas, **jugué** al volibol y **almorcé** un sandwich y fruta. Mi hermano Miguel **leyó** las tiras cómicas, **construyó** bonitos castillos de arena, pero se **cayó** y **destruyó** todo. ¡**Fue** un día muy divertido!

There are two irregular verbs and seven verbs with spelling changes in the preterite in the selection above. Identify the infinitives for each boldfaced verb. Which infinitives have irregular forms in the preterite? What spelling changes do you notice?

Preterite of verbs with spelling changes

Verbs ending in –**car,** –**gar,** and –**zar** have regular preterite endings except for spelling changes in the first person singular **yo** form. There are no spelling changes in the other forms.

Verbs with spelling changes in the first person		
	c → qu	g → gu	z → c
	buscar *(to look for)*	**jugar** *(to play)*	**abrazar** *(to hug)*
yo	bus**qué**	ju**gué**	abra**cé**
tú	buscaste	jugaste	abrazaste
Ud., él/ella	buscó	jugó	abrazó
nosotros/as	buscamos	jugamos	abrazamos
vosotros/as	buscasteis	jugasteis	abrazasteis
Uds., ellos/as	buscaron	jugaron	abrazaron

Other verbs with spelling changes in the yo form include:

c → qu		g → gu		z → c	
explicar	**expliqué**	llegar	**llegué**	almorzar	**almorcé**
practicar	**practiqué**	pagar	**pagué**	comenzar	**comencé**
tocar	**toqué**	entregar	**entregué**	empezar	**empecé**

Te **expliqué** el itinerario del viaje.
Llegué a Costa Rica en barco.
Empecé la excursión en San Juan.

I explained the trip itinerary to you.
I arrived in Costa Rica by boat.
I started the tour in San Juan.

In the following verbs, the **i** changes to **y** in the third person singular and plural forms in the preterite.

El criminal **huyó** de la policía.
Los turistas **leyeron** las revistas.

The criminal fled from the police.
The tourists read the magazines.

creer *(to believe)*		Other verbs with *y* in the third person ending			
yo	creí	caer	*to fall*	cayó	cayeron
tú	creíste	leer	*to read*	leyó	leyeron
Ud., él, ella	creyó	construir	*to build*	construyó	construyeron
nosotros/as	creímos	huir	*to flee*	huyó	huyeron
vosotros/as	creísteis	oír	*to hear*	oyó	oyeron
Uds., ellos/as	creyeron				

Preterite indicative of *ir, ser,* and *dar*

The verbs **ir, ser,** and **dar** are irregular in the preterite. Notice that **ir** and **ser** have the same forms.

Preterite indicative of *ir, ser* and *dar*			
	ir *(to go)*	**ser** *(to be)*	**dar** *(to give)*
yo	**fui**	**fui**	**di**
tú	**fuiste**	**fuiste**	**diste**
Ud., él, ella	**fue**	**fue**	**dio**
nosotros/as	**fuimos**	**fuimos**	**dimos**
vosotros/as	**fuisteis**	**fuisteis**	**disteis**
Uds., ellos/as	**fueron**	**fueron**	**dieron**

Stating how long ago something happened

To ask and answer questions about how long *ago* you did something, use the structure below with **hace** plus the preterite.

¿Cuánto tiempo **hace que** + *verb in preterite tense?*
Hace + *period of time* + **que** + *verb in preterite tense*

¿Cuánto tiempo **hace que** Carlos visitó a sus amigos en Perú?
Hace dos años **que** los visitó.

How long ago did Carlos visit his friends in Peru?
He visited them two years ago.

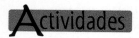

1 Mi primer día de práctica.
Mario's internship at the travel agency started yesterday, and he describes his day to his friend Lupe. Change all the verbs to the preterite to tell Mario's story in the past. Follow the model.

▶ MODELO: **Me levanto** a las siete...
Me levanté a las siete...

Me levanto (1) a las siete. **Me ducho (2), desayuno (3)** y **tomo (4)** el autobús número setenta y tres para la oficina. **Llego (5)** a la agencia a las ocho y media. **Bebo (6)** un café con leche con mi jefa y **converso (7)** con ella sobre mis responsabilidades en el trabajo. Después **llegan (8)** muchos clientes y me **preguntan (9)** por ofertas de viajes a diferentes lugares. A mediodía, **almuerzo (10)** con mi jefa y con otro de los empleados en un pequeño café cerca de la agencia. Por la tarde, **empieza (11)** a llegar la gente después de las cuatro. Algunas personas **buscan (12)** información sobre viajes, otras **confirman (13)** y **pagan (14)** sus pasajes. A las seis de la tarde, **salgo (15)** para casa, pero antes **ceno (16)** en el restaurante La Buena Mesa con Ricardo, otro de los chicos de la agencia. ¡Qué día tan interesante y productivo!

2 Un fin de semana maravilloso.
Nela describes her weekend in Boston. Use the preterite of each of the verbs in parentheses to complete her paragraph.

El fin de semana pasado _____ (**1.** ser) muy divertido. Mis amigas Rosa, Marta y yo _____ (**2.** ir) de vacaciones a Boston porque _____ (**3.** comprar) un viaje muy barato en la agencia de viajes "Viajes Boston". _____ (**4.** Salir, nosotras) de Nueva York muy tarde el viernes por la noche y_____ (**5.** llegar) a medianoche a la ciudad. El sábado, Rosa y Marta _____ (**6.** visitar) primero a su abuela que vive allí. Después, _____ (**7.** entrar, nosotras) a la famosa tienda Filene's Basement y _____ (**8.** probarse) unos zapatos y unas chaquetas. El domingo, _____ (**9.** ir, nosotras) a comer a un restaurante elegante en la calle Newbury. Marta y Rosa _____ (**10.** comer) arroz con pollo pero yo solamente _____ (**11.** beber) un jugo de frutas. Por la tarde, _____ (**12.** visitar, nosotras) el Museo de Ciencias y por la noche _____ (**13.** ir, nosotras) a una discoteca. Allí _____ (**14.** conocer, nosotras) a unos chicos muy simpáticos y con ellos, _____ (**15.** escuchar, nosotras) música y _____ (**16.** bailar) toda la noche. _____ (**17.** Salir, nosotras) de Boston el lunes a las 6.00 de la mañana. ¡Queremos regresar muy pronto a Boston!

3 Ayer.
In pairs, discuss what you did yesterday using the preterite for the following settings. Choose two verbs from each of the lists in parentheses.

▶ MODELO: En casa (despertarse tarde / limpiar la cocina / descansar)
—Ayer, me desperté tarde y limpié la cocina.

At home (wake up late / clean the kitchen / rest)
—Yesterday, I woke up late and cleaned the kitchen.

1. En casa (almorzar / despertarse / tocar música).
2. En la escuela (estudiar / leer mi libro de español / ir a la biblioteca).
3. En el gimnasio (jugar al volibol / practicar deportes / caminar rápido).
4. En el cine (mirar una película/ beber un refresco / reunirse con amigos).
5. En la tienda (comprar / buscar / pagar) muchas cosas.
6. En el parque (practicar deportes/ jugar al béisbol / correr).

4 Eventos de la vida. Complete the chart below by filling in the year in which you experienced each of the events listed in the second column. Then, in pairs, ask your partner how long ago these events occurred. Follow the model.

▶ MODELO: 1997 / llevar ropa formal
   —¿Cuánto tiempo hace que llevaste ropa formal?
   —Hace (diez) años que llevé ropa formal.

año	eventos
_____	nacer
_____	comenzar la escuela primaria
_____	abrazar a mi primer amor
_____	graduarse de la escuela secundaria
_____	asistir a una fiesta
_____	tocar un instrumento
_____	aprender a montar en bicicleta
_____	ir de vacaciones a una playa
_____	comprar un disco compacto
_____	manejar un coche

5 Actividades en la playa. Look at the illustration on page 76, and, in pairs, describe which of these activities you did or didn't do during your last trip to the beach or during a vacation. Be sure to indicate how long ago you did the activities and whether or not you liked them.

6 De vacaciones en la playa. Imagine that you are one of the people in the photograph and describe what you did on vacation last summer. Write a postcard to your best friend using the preterite tense.

Volibol y amor en la playa

Adriana y Felipe llegan a San Juan, Puerto Rico buscando a Nayeli. Van al hotel y se registran.

Buenas tardes, señor y señora Reyes. ¿Desean una habitación doble?

No. Mi reservación es para "Adriana Reyes".

Y mi reservación está bajo "Felipe Luna".

¡Aquí hay tanto que hacer! Se puede navegar en velero.

¡Y la isla es bellísima! Ay, Adriana, hay momentos perfectos, como éste.

Sí. También se puede montar a caballo o hacer surfing.

¡Vamos a jugar al volibol con esos chicos!

Mientras tanto, en México y Sevilla.

Hay malas noticias: Tus estudiantes, Adriana Reyes y Felipe Luna, están en Puerto Rico.

¡No puede ser! ¿Por qué no están todavía en Puebla? Les dejé instrucciones clarísimas.

Parece que no las recibieron.

Esto es muy peligroso. Adriana y Felipe no tienen ninguna experiencia.

Aquí hay algo extraño. Tengo que hacer algo para protegerlos. ¡Ay! ¡Adriana y Felipe!

Abuelita, la suerte me volvió la espalda. ¿Qué debo hacer?

Descubriste el jaguar y volviste a México con él. Ahora debes de estar con tu familia y con tus amigos. Los seres humanos son más importantes que las cosas.

Agencia de viajes. Buenas tardes.

Beatriz, ya no voy a viajar a Quito. Por favor, necesito un billete para San Juan, Puerto Rico.

Ah... ya sé para dónde va Nayeli.

En Sevilla, Gafasnegras habla por teléfono con otro criminal:

Nayeli va a San Juan. No la voy a perder de vista. En Puerto Rico, se acaba el juego.

Actividades

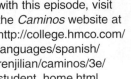

1 Comprensión. Based on this episode of *Caminos del jaguar*, choose the logical response.

1. El recepcionista del hotel cree que la reservación es para los señores Reyes.
   a. Cree que están casados.
   b. Cree que son amigos.

2. Adriana y Felipe no quieren quedarse en el hotel.
   a. Quieren conocer las playas.
   b. Quieren descansar un poco.

3. En la playa, Adriana y Felipe se divierten.
   a. Montan a caballo.
   b. Juegan al volibol.

4. Nayeli recibió la noticia que Adriana y Felipe fueron a Puerto Rico.
   a. Nayeli está muy contenta.
   b. Nayeli está muy preocupada.

5. Nayeli cambia sus planes de viaje.
   a. Quiere proteger a Adriana y Felipe.
   b. Quiere conocer otra ciudad.

6. Gafasnegras vigila a Nayeli...
   a. para saber dónde están Adriana y Felipe.
   b. para saber adónde va Nayeli.

2 Situaciones. Dramatize one of the following situations.

1. Adriana y Felipe hablan con el recepcionista del hotel sobre los deportes que juega la gente en la playa.

2. El recepcionista del hotel conversa con Adriana y Felipe sobre su reservación.

3 Escritura. Write a brief summary of this episode of *Caminos del jaguar*. (4–6 sentences)

NOTA CULTURAL

El turismo en el Caribe hispano

Cada año, millones de turistas de todas partes del mundo visitan las playas del Caribe. Muchos llegan en avión o en barco a Puerto Rico, a Cuba y a la República Dominicana. En estas islas, el turismo es muy importante para su economía. Los turistas disfrutan de las hermosas playas y temperaturas agradables, que varían entre los 27 °C y 29 °C. En Puerto Rico, mucha gente visita el Yunque, un famoso parque nacional con plantas y animales exóticos.

Vocabulario y lengua

DISCUSSING VACATIONS

Unas vacaciones maravillosas

Borinquen

on board

CRUCERO CARIBEÑO

Disfrute de una fantástica aventura en Puerto Rico, a bordo°
de los espectaculares barcos de la compañía Cruceros S.A.
Duración: 9 días y 8 noches
Precio: 925 dólares americanos
Incluye desayuno continental. Otras comidas son adicionales.

ATRACCIONES

Comida Buffet • Bar a bordo
Discoteca nocturna° • Tiendas
Clases de baile con excelentes instructores

GIMNASIO COMPLETO

Ejercicios aeróbicos en grupo
Médico especialista en medicina deportiva
Equipos de ejercicios con pesas°
Masaje terapéutico°

Online Study Center

For additional practice
with this unit's vocabulary
and grammar, visit the
Caminos website at
http://college.hmco.com/
languages/spanish/
renjilian/caminos/
3e/student_home.html.
You can also review audio
flashcards, quiz yourself,
and explore related
Spanish-language sites.

nightly

weights
therapeutic massage

Más palabras y expresiones

Cognados

la aerolínea	la limosina
el club	el transporte
la confirmación	las vacaciones
la excursión / el tour	

Sustantivos

el (des)embarque	*(un)loading*
la despedida	*farewell*
el folleto	*brochure*
el/la guía	*tour guide*
la guía	*guidebook*
la isla	*island*
el paquete	*package (tour)*
el recreo	*recreation*
el traslado	*transfer*

Verbos

averiguar	*to find out*
avisar	*to advise, to warn*
descansar	*to rest*
encontrarse (ue) (con)	*to meet (with) someone*
estar a punto de	*to be on the verge of*
estar de acuerdo	*to agree*
estar/irse de vacaciones	*to be / go on vacation*
gozar (de)	*to enjoy*
recoger	*to pick up, to get*
reunirse (con)	*to meet (with) someone*

Otras expresiones

bello/a	*beautiful*
¡Buen viaje!/¡Feliz viaje!	*Have a nice trip!*
libre	*free (independent)*
Ni idea.	*I haven't got a clue.*
¡Oye!	*Hey! ; Listen!*
¡Qué gusto!	*What a pleasure!*

Actividades

1 Vacaciones en Puerto Rico. You and your friends just came back from the cruise to Puerto Rico shown on page 184. When you return to school, a classmate asks you questions about your trip. Work with a partner to ask and answer questions about what you did on your cruise. Follow the model. **¡OJO!** Be sure to use the preterite.

> ► MODELO: ¿Adónde / ir / tú?
> —¿Adónde fuiste?
> —Fui a Puerto Rico.

1. ¿Cómo / viajar / tú?
2. ¿Por / cuántos / días y noches / durar / el crucero?
3. ¿Cuánto / costar / el crucero?
4. ¿Qué / tipo de desayuno / comer / tú?
5. ¿Dónde / bailar / tú y tus amigos?
6. ¿Enfermarse / los viajeros?
7. ¿Disfrutar / Uds. / del viaje?

2 Un viaje a Chiapas. Listen to the advertisement about a vacation in Chiapas, México, and fill in the missing words.

¿Sueña Ud. con tener una (**1**) _____, repleta de (**2**) _____, (**3**) _____ y (**4**) _____? Nosotros tenemos el (**5**) _____ que Ud. busca.

Venga a Chiapas, uno de los estados más bellos de la República (**6**) _____. Es un mosaico que combina la (**7**) _____ histórica de la región con una inmensa riqueza natural, marcando así en su gente un estilo de vida lleno de tradiciones y de admiración por su medio.

En Chiapas se mezcla el (**8**) _____ clima de la (**9**) _____ montaña con el calor de la selva (**10**) _____; es un lugar siempre (**11**) _____ con una gran diversidad de fauna.

Paseando por el río Grijalva se puede ver el impresionante Cañón del Sumidero. Se pueden admirar las (**12**) _____ de Agua Azul, unas de las más bellas de México, o (**13**) _____ las Lagunas de Montebello.

La región de Chiapas es escenario de una de las más (**14**) _____ culturas prehispánicas, los mayas, con sus misteriosas ciudades, como Palenque, Yaxchilán y Bonampak, entre otras.

Nuestras (**15**) _____ duran entre cinco y ocho días con (**16**) _____, (**17**) _____, visitas y alimentación. Todo esto cuesta solamente $5.700 hasta $6.900 pesos, dependiendo del (**18**) _____ y del tipo de alojamiento.

Hacemos (**19**) _____ todo el año con excursiones diarias.

No pierda esta (**20**) _____. Llámenos hoy para pedir más información.

3 Disfruten de un viaje. Working in groups of three, create a brochure for a vacation to a place where everyone in your group wants to go. Be sure to include the destination, price, what the package includes, and special offers.

4 En la agencia de viajes. Using the sample brochures you created in *Actividad* 3, work in pairs or groups of three to role-play a conversation between travel agent and traveler(s). Be sure your conversation includes the following:

► Greetings
► Where to go and why (likes / dislikes, etc.)
► Examination of different brochures and what each destination offers
► Discussion of prices and what they include
► Decision on a trip and purchase / sale of a package
► Thank-you's / Good-bye's

Fiesta sorpresa

Pedro	¡La fiesta sorpresa de Maricarmen va a ser fenomenal!
Marisa	¿Y ya sabes cuál es el precio de todo esto?
Pedro	No, Rosaura **nos lo** está calculando.
Marisa	¿Ya les mandaste las invitaciones a todos?
Pedro	**Se las** mandé a casi todos. Falta Rosaura. Voy a enviár**sela** mañana.
Marisa	¿Ya pediste las flores?
Pedro	Sí, la tienda **me las** va a enviar aquí. Y la torta, ¿quién **nos la** trae?
Marisa	**Nos la** trae Sofía.
Pedro	Muy bien. Creo que a Maricarmen le va a gustar la fiesta.

The indirect object pronoun always precedes the direct object pronoun when both are in the same sentence.

¿Quién **te** manda _flores?_	*Who sends you flowers?*
Mi novio **me las** manda.	*My boyfriend sends them to me.*

The indirect object pronouns **le** or **les** change to **se** when they precede the direct object pronouns **lo/s** or **la/s.**

—¿**Les** mandaste <u>las</u> <u>invitaciones</u> a los niños?	—*Did you send the invitations to the children?*
—Sí, hoy **se las** mandé.	—*Yes, I sent them to them today.*
—¿**Le** mandaste <u>la invitación</u> a Susana?	—*Did you send the invitation to Susana?*
—Sí, **se la** mandé.	—*Yes, I sent it to her.*

In verbal expressions with an infinitive or a progressive form, the two pronouns can precede the conjugated verb or be attached to the end of the infinitive or the present participle. A written accent needs to be added when two pronouns are attached to the infinitive.

—¿**Le** vas a mandar <u>los documentos</u> a Esther?	—*Are you going to send the documents to Esther?*
—Sí, voy a mandár**selos**.	—*Yes, I'm going to send them to her.*
—Sí, **se los** voy a mandar.	
—¿**Les** estás calculando <u>el precio</u>?	—*Are you calculating the price quote for them?*
—Sí, estoy calculándo**selo**.	—*Yes, I'm calculating it for them.*
—Sí, **se lo** estoy calculando.	

The pronoun **se** can refer to many people. Use a prepositional pronoun, a noun, or a proper name to clarify its meaning.

—¿Cuándo **le** mandaste las invitaciones a Rosana?	—*When did you send the invitations to Rosana?*
—**Se las** mandé **a ella** anteayer.	—*I sent them to her the day before yesterday.*

Reflexive verbs follow the same rules for the position of the pronouns. Note that the reflexive pronoun always precedes the direct object pronoun.

—¿No **te** vas a lavar <u>las manos?</u>	—*Aren't you going to wash your hands?*
—Sí, voy a lavár**melas** / **me las** voy a lavar.	—*Yes, I am going to wash them.*
—¿**Te** lavaste <u>el pelo</u>?	—*Did you wash your hair?*
—Sí, **me lo** lavé.	—*Yes, I washed it.*

Actividades

1 **Una fiesta para los padres.** Nora is planning a surprise anniversary party for her parents, and her Aunt Teresa offers to help her. Fill in the correct form of the direct and/or indirect object pronouns in the passage. Some phrases require two object pronouns.

Tía Nora, ¿es cierto que tú estás preparando la fiesta de aniversario de tus papás?

Nora Sí, tía, yo _____ (**1**) estoy preparando. Va a ser el seis de mayo.

Tía ¿Con quién _____ (**2**) estás preparando? ¿Con Emilita?

Nora Sí, Emilita _____ (**3**) está ayudando a preparar todo.

Tía ¿Quién _____ (**4**) está comprando los refrescos (a ti)?

Nora Mi hermano Jorge _____ (**5**) está comprando. Vamos a servir vino, también.

Tía Necesitan música, ¿no? Nosotros podemos ayudar_____ a Uds. (**6**) también.

Nora Sí, tía, ¿puedes comprar_____ (**7**) (a nosotros) el último CD de Shakira?

Tía Claro, _____ (**8**) voy a comprar mañana mismo.

Nora Gracias. ¡Eres la tía más maravillosa del mundo!

2 **¿Para quién es?** You bought some gifts for your family. Review your shopping list with your aunt. She's going to help you wrap and mark all the gifts. Following the model, work with a partner to create a dialog.

▶ MODELO: estas medias / a mi abuelita
  —*¿A quién le compraste estas medias?*
  —*Se las compré a mi abuelita Adela.*

1. este traje de baño / a mi sobrina Mercedes
2. este sombrero de playa / a mi madrastra René
3. esta toalla de colores / a mi hermana mayor
4. este protector solar / a mi mamá
5. estos pantalones deportivos / a mi novio/a
6. estas fotos del verano / a todos

3 **¿Qué haces si... ?** You would like to find out what your friends would do if you or another person needed help. Work with a partner and ask each other the following questions, answering with direct and indirect object pronouns.

▶ MODELO: —*Si tus amigos se casan, ¿les regalas muchas flores?*
—*Sí, se las regalo.*

1. Si tengo frío y necesito un suéter, ¿me lo prestas?
2. Si vamos a un restaurante, ¿me pides un plato delicioso?
3. Si un/a amigo/a está enfermo/a, ¿le compras las medicinas?
4. Si necesitamos una sombrilla de playa, ¿nos la traes?
5. Si tus amigos/as están de vacaciones, ¿te escriben muchas tarjetas postales?
6. Si necesitamos un protector solar, ¿nos lo traes?
7. Si la policía te pide decir la verdad, ¿se la dices?
8. Si necesito tu juego de dominó, ¿me lo prestas?

4 **¿Y tú qué haces?** Work in pairs. Discuss the following activities with your partner, asking each other which things you do and for whom. Follow the model.

▶ MODELO: escribir tarjetas de cumpleaños
—*¿Escribes tarjetas de cumpleaños? ¿A quiénes se las escribes?*
—*Se las escribo a mis amigos y a mis hermanos.*

1. preparar la cena
2. reservar las habitaciones en el hotel
3. servir buena comida
4. dar dinero para ir de compras
5. escribir muchas cartas
6. comprar regalos
7. hablar español
8. mandar una postal

NARRATING EVENTS IN THE PAST: PRETERITE OF STEM-CHANGING —*IR* VERBS

En la playa

El domingo pasado, Roberto y su esposa Ana fueron a la playa con su perro. Llevaron sombreros, gafas de sol, un radio y libros para leer. Ellos caminaron **sonriendo°** a la playa y su perrito los **siguió°** con mucha alegría. En el kiosko, Roberto **pidió°** refrescos y su esposa **se sirvió°** una porción grande de fruta.

smiling / followed
asked for / served herself

preferred / fell asleep
had fun

Ana se acostó debajo de una gran sombrilla para escuchar la radio. Roberto **prefirió°** estar en la arena leyendo su novela, pero **se durmió°** y no leyó nada. Todos **se divirtieron°** mucho.

Stem-changing **–ir** verbs in the present are also stem-changing in the preterite. In the present, these verbs have three kinds of stem changes: **e→ie, e→i,** and **o→ue.** In the preterite, there are two kinds of stem changes: **e→i** and **o→u.** These changes occur in the third person singular and plural of the preterite forms.

Note that the first and third person singular preterite forms carry the stress on the last syllable and have written accents.

–*ir* verbs: e → i		
preferir		**Other verbs with the same pattern**
yo	preferí	divertirse, sugerir *(to suggest)*
tú	preferiste	pedir, despedirse *(to say good-bye)*
Ud., él, ella	**prefirió**	repetir, vestirse
nosotros/as	preferimos	seguir, conseguir, perseguir
vosotros/as	preferisteis	sentirse
Uds., ellos/as	**prefirieron**	servir; reír *(to laugh)*, sonreír *(to smile)*, freír *(to fry)*

–*ir* verbs: o → u		
dormir		**Another verb with the same pattern**
yo	dormí	morir
tú	dormiste	
Ud., él, ella	**durmió**	
nosotros/as	dormimos	
vosotros/as	dormisteis	
Uds., ellos/as	**durmieron**	

Stem-changing **–ir** verbs have the same vowel change in the preterite as in their progressive forms.

El mesero **está sirviendo** la cena.   *The waiter is serving dinner.*
Él nos la **sirvió** ayer.   *He served it to us yesterday.*
Los huéspedes del hotel   *The hotel guests are sleeping.*
  están durmiendo.
Ellos no **durmieron** bien anoche.   *They did not sleep well last night.*

The third person preterite forms of the verbs **(son)reír** and **freír** have simplified spellings: **sonrió, rio, (son)rieron, frio, frieron.** Note that the verbs **rio** and **frio** do not need a written accent in the preterite.

Actividades

1 **¿Qué pasó?** You are telling everyone at a family reunion about your recent cruise to Cancún. Join the words to create sentences in the preterite that describe what everyone did during the vacation. Follow the model.

▶ MODELO: Ana y Tomás /preferir ir a la playa
Ana y Tomás prefirieron ir a la playa.

1. Nosotros/ despedirse / de la familia
2. Mis padres / conseguir / los vuelos a un buen precio
3. Mi hermana menor / vestirse / de blanco en la playa
4. Nadie /dormir / mucho en el crucero
5. Los niños / pedir / tacos cada noche
6. Yo /preferir / comer chiles rellenos
7. Los meseros / servirnos / mucha comida
8. Toda la familia / divertirse / en Cancún

2 **Punto de vista.** Retell the story **En la playa** on page 190 from a different point of view. Make all necessary changes. Begin the story like this:

El domingo pasado mi amigo Mario y yo...

3 **Pasatiempos de verano.** Interview a friend about his / her last vacation trip, asking questions using the phrases below. After the interview, report your findings to the class.

▶ MODELO: sentirse contento/a / en la playa
—*Sandra, ¿te sentiste contenta en la playa?*
—*Sí, me sentí contenta en la playa.*
(To the class:) *Sandra se sintió contenta en la playa.*

1. preferir / bailar en la discoteca o bucear en el mar
2. dormir bien / todas las noches
3. divertirse / en la playa
4. vestirse / elegantemente para salir por la noche
5. pedir / un pasaje de primera clase o de clase económica
6. conseguir / un buen hotel
7. reír / mucho
8. despedirse / de todos antes de salir

4 **Querido diario.** Write a journal entry of ten sentences in the preterite to describe what you did yesterday. Choose from the following verbs.

acostarse	dormir	practicar
bailar	ducharse	levantarse
buscar	empezar	llegar
caminar	estudiar	pedir
despertarse	ir	sentirse
divertirse	jugar	vestirse

Profesionales en el trabajo

La cartera **puso** la carta en el buzón.

El electricista **vino** a mi casa para instalar mi nueva estufa.

Los bomberos **condujeron** el camión al incendio.

There are three main groups of irregular verbs in the preterite. They can be categorized by the changes they share in their stems.

Group 1: Verbs with **u** in the stem.

Group 2: Verbs with **i** in the stem.

Group 3: Verbs with **j** in the stem.

Notice that these verbs have a different set of endings than those used for regular verbs. Unlike regular verbs, there are no written accents on the **yo** or **él / ella / Ud.** forms.

Group 1: Verbs with *u* in the stem			
	tener → u	Other verbs with the same pattern	
yo	tuv**e**	andar	and**uv-**
tú	tuv**iste**	estar	est**uv-**
Ud., él, ella	tuv**o**	haber	**hubo**
nosotros/as	tuv**imos**	poder	p**ud-**
vosotros/as	tuv**isteis**	poner	p**us-**
Uds., ellos/as	tuv**ieron**	saber	s**up-**

Hubo (*there was, there were*) is the preterite of **haber.** Lik**e** **hay** (*there is, there are*), there is only one form for singular and plural meanings.

No **hubo** problemas con la reservación.

There were no problems with the reservation.

Ayer **hubo** un accidente.

There was an accident yesterday.

Saber in the preterite means *to find out; to learn.*

Group 2: Verbs with *i* in the stem			
	venir → i	Other verbs with the same pattern	
yo	vin**e**	hacer	hic-
tú	vin**iste**	querer	qu**is-**
Ud., él, ella	vin**o**		
nosotros/as	vin**imos**		
vosotros/as	vin**isteis**		
Uds., ellos/as	vin**ieron**		

In the third person singular form of **hacer,** the **c** becomes **z** before the vowel **o:** **usted / él / ella hizo.** This spelling change keeps the pronunciation of all forms consistent.

Group 3: Verbs with *j* in the stem			
	decir → j	Other verbs with the same pattern	
yo	dij**e**	conducir	cond**uj-**
tú	dij**iste**	producir	prod**uj-**
Ud., él, ella	dij**o**	reducir	red**uj-**
nosotros/as	dij**imos**	traducir	trad**uj-**
vosotros/as	dij**isteis**	traer	tra**j-**
Uds., ellos/as	dij**eron**		

The endings of these verbs are the same as the endings in Groups 1 and 2, except in the third person plural where the ending is –**eron: producir** → **produjeron.**

Note the vowel change in **decir** from **e** to **i** in the verb stem.

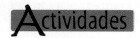

Actividades

1 Cosas. Working in pairs, create logical sentences with elements from each of the columns below. Follow the model.

> ► **MODELO:** Tú hiciste paella para la cena.
> *You made paella for dinner.*

A	B	C
Yo	decir	viajar a Cancún
Los profesores	hacer	paella para la cena
El chofer	conducir	cosas muy buenas sobre sus alumnos
El cocinero del restaurante	poner	las invitaciones en el buzón
Los programadores de computadoras	querer	las nuevas impresoras a la oficina
Tú	traer	el auto hasta el hotel

2 En la playa. Your cousin has a summer job at a beach resort. Working with a partner, take turns asking and answering questions (using the preterite) about what happened yesterday. Follow the model.

> ► **MODELO:** ustedes (traducir el menú al español)
> —¿Qué hicieron ustedes? —*What did you do?*
> —Nosotros tradujimos —*We translated the menu to Spanish.*
> el menú al español.

1. los empleados (poner revistas en las habitaciones)
2. el conserje (hacer llamadas por teléfono)
3. ustedes (tener que subir las maletas de los huéspedes)
4. los huéspedes (estar en la playa)
5. tú (no poder descansar)
6. los turistas (ponerse protector solar)
7. el recepcionista (decirnos "Buenos días".)
8. el gerente del hotel (reducir el precio de algunas habitaciones)

3 Encuesta. Interview your classmates to find out who in your class has completed the following activities. Your goal is to find someone who did and someone who did not do each of the activities. Report your findings to the class. Follow the model.

> ► **MODELO:** traer el libro a la clase
> Student A: —¿Trajiste el libro a clase? —*Did you bring your book to class?*
> Student B: —Sí, lo traje a clase. —*Yes, I brought it to class.*
> Student C: —No, no lo traje a clase. —*No, I did not bring it to class.*
> Lo dejé en mi coche. *I left it in my car.*
> (To the class) —Pablo trajo su libro a —*Pablo brought his book to class*
> clase pero Alicia no lo *but Alicia didn't bring it.*
> trajo.

1. venir a clase a tiempo
2. llegar tarde
3. conducir a la universidad
4. andar a la universidad a pie
5. decirle "Hola" al / a la profesor/a
6. hacer la tarea
7. traducir el vocabulario al inglés
8. poner la mochila en el piso

4 Una vacación familiar. Write a short paragraph (8–10 sentences) describing a memorable family vacation from the past. Use these questions to guide your writing.

¿Qué ocasión celebraron?

¿Adónde fueron de vacaciones?

¿Quiénes fueron?

¿Qué hicieron?

¿Quién hizo una comida especial?

¿Qué comieron?

¿Hubo un incidente interesante? ¿Qué pasó?

¿Quién dijo un cuento chistoso *(funny)*?

¿Se divirtieron?

5 Un día en Acapulco. Work with a partner. Imagine that you and your friends are in Acapulco and just had a busy day enjoying the attractions. Look at the drawings and number them according to the sequence in which you both prefer to have done the activities. Then, write a caption for each one using the suggested verbs and linking words in the two lists below.

bailar	comer	comprar	descansar	llegar
nadar	pasear	pedir	tomar el sol	tomar un taxi

luego	primero	finalmente / por último	cuando
todo el día	después	toda la noche	toda la tarde

Dos espías

En el Yunque...

Qué belleza, ¿no?

¡Ah, sí! La belleza del Yunque es impresionante.

¿Estás pensando en Cuba?

En Cuba, no; estoy pensando en una linda leyenda cubana sobre el primer hombre y la primera mujer. Es también sobre el principio de la humanidad.

¡Qué interesante!

Mientras los primos siguen vigilando a Adriana y Felipe...

Luis, tenemos que vigilar a Adriana y a Felipe. La Sra. Gafasnegras nos va a matar si los perdemos de vista.

Sí, pero anoche no dormí. Pensé en mis exámenes toda la noche. Los presenté esta mañana.

Ay, Luis, no estamos aquí para hablar de tus exámenes. Tienes que estar alerta.

Tú debes tranquilizarte. No pasa nada.

¿Sabes que, yo —tu primo— estoy a punto de recibir mi título de programador?

Luis, ¡no estamos aquí para hablar de tus estudios de programador!

¿Por qué no puedes compartir mi alegría?

Luis, ¿no ves que estamos en medio de algo muy serio? Tienes que concentrarte, por favor.

¡Ay! Ya se van Adriana y Felipe. ¡No sé quién te va a matar, la Sra. Gafasnegras o yo!

Perro que ladra no muerde.

Luis, ¿cómo piensas sacar fotos si tienes la lente tapada[1]?

Perdón, señor Primo "Perfecto"...

Nayeli llega a San Juan de Puerto Rico y alguien la está esperando...

Nayeli, busco el jaguar Yax-Balam, el héroe gemelo. ¿Dónde está? Tú lo sabes.

No lo sé, no lo sé. No tengo idea de dónde está. ¿Quién es usted?

Actividades

1 Comprensión. Based on this episode of *Caminos del jaguar*, choose the logical response.

1. Luis y su primo están vigilando a Adriana y Felipe.
   a. Están en Sevilla
   b. Están en el Yunque.

2. Felipe le cuenta una historia a Adriana.
   a. Es un cuento puertorriqueño.
   b. Es una leyenda cubana.

3. Luis no se puede concentrar en su trabajo.
   a. Piensa en la Sra. Gafasnegras.
   b. Quiere un futuro mejor.

4. El primo de Luis está furioso con él.
   a. El primo quiere estudiar para ingeniero.
   b. El primo no quiere perder a Adriana y Felipe.

5. Luis tiene problemas en sacar una foto de Adriana y Felipe.
   a. No funciona la cámara.
   b. Tiene la lente tapada.

6. Nayeli tiene mucho miedo en Puerto Rico.
   a. Gafasnegras la ataca en el coche.
   b. No puede encontrar a Adriana y Felipe.

2 Situaciones. Dramatize one of the following situations.

1. Nayeli y Gafasnegras hablan sobre dónde están Adriana y Felipe.
2. Luis y su primo hablan sobre los estudios de Luis.

3 Escritura. Write a brief summary of this episode of *Caminos del jaguar*. (4–6 sentences)

NOTA CULTURAL

Los parques nacionales

Los Estados Unidos estableció el primer parque nacional del mundo en 1872 para proteger el ecosistema del parque Yellowstone. Desde entonces, y con el crecimiento de las ciudades, estos parques son más y más importantes para proteger la naturaleza, la fauna (animales) y la flora (plantas, flores y árboles) y mantener el equilibrio ecológico del planeta. En los países hispanos, hay numerosos parques nacionales, muchos de ellos declarados por las Naciones Unidas como Patrimonio Cultural de la Humanidad *(World Heritage Site)*, por ejemplo el Parque de Doñana en España, el Parque de Ischigualasto en la Argentina y el Parque Nacional de Tikal en Guatemala.

Parque Nacional de Tikal

Lectura

Online Study Center

For further reading
practice online, visit the
Caminos website at
http://college.hmco.com/
languages/spanish/
renjilian/caminos/3e/
student_home.html.

Reading Strategy

How to use the dictionary

When reading a text in Spanish, go through it several times, checking for words you
already know as well as for cognates, which you have studied in earlier chapters. You
should also try to guess the meaning of words you do not know through the context
of the sentence and the text. Once you have applied this strategy, use the dictionary
to confirm your guesses. The dictionary may give you several different meanings for
a word. It is important to determine the grammatical form of the word because that
can affect its meaning. Note the following facts about Spanish dictionaries.

► Verbs (**verbos**) appear in the infinitive form. If you are looking up a conjugated
  form of a verb, you will have to determine its infinitive before you start your search.
► Masculine and feminine forms of nouns (**sustantivos**) are listed and marked *m.*
  or *f.* The meaning of a noun may change depending on its form.
► Only the masculine singular form of an adjective (**adjetivo**) is usually listed and
  marked *adj.*
► Idiomatic expressions (**expresiones idiomáticas**) are listed by their most
  important word. Sometimes you need several attempts to determine the main
  word.
► The letter **ñ** is listed as a separate letter after **n.** In older dictionaries, the letter
  combinations **ll** (as in **llover**) and and **ch** are listed as separate letters, after **l**
  and **c** respectively.

Vamos al Caribe hispano: Cuba, Puerto Rico y la República Dominicana

Las tres islas caribeñas de
habla española, Cuba,
Puerto Rico y la República
Dominicana, tienen una
herencia[1] tricultural común:
la indígena[2] de cada región,
la española y la africana. Esta
mezcla[3] étnica les da gran
riqueza a sus tradiciones, a
su música, a su literatura y a
su vida diaria, pero cada isla

tiene también su identidad propia. Las islas tienen bellas playas y hermosa arquitectura colonial. Estas islas
del Caribe comparten aspectos de su cultura, herencia y tradiciones con otras regiones hispanas como las
costas caribeñas de Costa Rica, Panamá, Colombia y Venezuela.

[1]heritage; [2]indigenous; [3]mix

La Playa de Varadero, La Habana, Cuba

Pareja dominicana en la playa

Cuba

Cuba es la más grande de las tres islas caribeñas. Fue el segundo lugar[4] al que llegó Cristóbal Colón[5]. Los españoles llevaron esclavos africanos para trabajar en las plantaciones de azúcar[6]. Al azúcar lo llamaban "el oro blanco" por su valor económico en esa época. Con el tiempo, se mezclaron los africanos con los españoles para producir la rica mezcla racial que hoy existe en la isla. En 1959 Fidel Castro lideró una revolución en Cuba y por más de treinta años, hasta 1990, Cuba estuvo bajo el socialismo de la Unión Soviética. Actualmente[7] la isla está en transición económica. Tiene más de once millones de habitantes.

Puerto Rico

Puerto Rico es la más pequeña de las tres islas hispanas y es un Estado Libre Asociado[8] de los Estados Unidos. Los puertorriqueños pueden viajar libremente entre la isla y los EE. UU.[9] La población indígena de la isla de Puerto Rico, los taínos o arauacos, tenía[10] una sociedad bastante avanzada en esta isla de 175 kilómetros de largo[11] y 56 kilómetros de ancho[12]. La población hoy en día[13] es de casi cuatro millones de habitantes.

La República Dominicana

La República Dominicana comparte[14] la misma isla que la República de Haití. Este país fue el primer centro administrativo español en América y sus habitantes indígenas, los taínos, la llamaban "Quisqueya". La población de la isla tiene también herencia europea y africana debido a[15] los esclavos que llevaron a trabajar allí. Actualmente es un gran centro turístico en la región caribeña, aunque también sufre de mucha pobreza económica y desigualdad social. Tiene casi[16] ocho millones de habitantes.

Un arrecife de coral en el Mar Caribe

---

[4]place; [5]Christopher Columbus; [6]sugar; [7]Today; [8]free associated state; [9]U.S.; [10]had; [11]in length; [12]in width; [13]today; [14]shares; [15]because of; [16]almost.

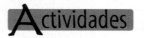

Actividades

1 **¿Verdadero o falso?** Write **V** if the following ideas are **verdaderas** or **F** if they are **falsas.** Correct the false sentences.

1. _____ El azúcar fue importante para la economía de Cuba.
2. _____ Cuba es la más pequeña de las islas de habla española.
3. _____ Los taínos llamaban *(called)* "Quisqueya" a Puerto Rico.
4. _____ En las islas caribeñas de habla española hay una mezcla étnica de influencia indígena, española y africana.
5. _____ Puerto Rico es un Estado Libre Asociado de los Estados Unidos.
6. _____ Haití y Cuba comparten la misma isla.
7. _____ Puerto Rico tiene ocho millones de habitantes.

2 **Cómo buscar palabras en el diccionario.** Keep a list of the words that you needed to look up in the dictionary for this reading and compare them with that of a friend. Are there any that you could have guessed without looking them up? Which ones?

3 **Compara y contrasta.** Compare and contrast the different characteristics of Cuba, the Dominican Republic, and Puerto Rico. Which island do you find the most interesting? Why? Work with a partner.

	Cuba	Puerto Rico	La República Dominicana
Población	_____	_____	_____
Etnicidad	_____	_____	_____
Sistema político	_____	_____	_____
Productos económicos	_____	_____	_____
Otros aspectos	_____	_____	_____

4 **Conversaciones cortas.** Work with a partner to answer the following questions.

1. ¿Qué islas hay en tu región? ¿Cómo son? ¿Tienen playas?
2. ¿A qué isla del mundo quieres viajar? ¿Dónde está? ¿Cómo es?
3. ¿Qué influencia étnica hay en tu región o estado?
4. ¿A qué grupo étnico pertenecen los padres y los abuelos de tu compañero/a de cuarto?
5. ¿Qué idiomas hablan en tu país actualmente? ¿Y en tu familia?

Escritura

Writing Strategy

Using a dictionary

Review the reading strategy prior to reading this strategy. To use a dictionary effectively, be sure to keep the following in mind.

There are many translations for some words. Look for the definition that best suits your needs. Once you have selected a word in the English–Spanish section, cross check its meaning in the Spanish–English section of the dictionary to assure accuracy, and be sure to read any grammar notes that will tell you about irregular forms, different translations, and so on. Always review the guide to using a particular dictionary to understand important symbols and abbreviations. Below are some common abbreviations and sample dictionary entries.

Workshop

f.	femenino	*adv.*	adverbio	*adj.*	adjetivo
m.	masculino	*s.*	sustantivo (*noun*)		

fan¹ (fan) **I.** s. (*paper*) abanico; (*electric*) ventilador *m;* AGR. aventadora **II.** tr. **fanned, fan-ning** (*to cool*) abanicar; FIG. (*to stir up*) avivar, excitar; AGR. aventar —intr. • **to f. out** abrirse en abanico

fan² (fan) s. FAM. (*enthusiast*) aficionado, hincha *m.*

support (se-port`) **I.** *tr.* (*weight*) aguantar, sostener, corroborar; (*a spouse, child*) mantener; (*a cause, theory*) sostener, respaldar; (*with money*) ayudar ∗ **to s. oneself** (*to earn one's living*) ganarse la vida; (*to learn*) apoyarse **II.** s. (*act*) apoyo; (*maintenance*) mantenimiento; ARQ., TEC. soporte *m.*

Strategy in Action

For additional practice using a dictionary, complete the exercises below and in the *Escritura I* section of your Student Activities Manual for *Unidad 5.*

1 Usando el diccionario. Refer to the dictionary entries above to translate the italicized words. Be sure to use the appropriate form of the word or phrase. Work in groups.

1. Can I count on your *support*?.
2. I can't *support* myself on this salary.
3. My psychology instructor *supports* the Freudian school of thought.
4. The house has good *support* beams.
5. I'm a sports *fan.*
6. It's hot outside and you need to *fan* yourself to keep cool.
7. Turn on the *fan*! It's hot in here.

2 Querido/a amigo/a. You are on vacation. Write a postcard to your best friend, telling about your trip. Describe the hotel, its amenities, what there is to do, and what you like and don't like about the hotel. Then narrate a sequence of events to tell your friend what you did on your first day there. Be sure to use the preterite tense to talk about the things you did.

3 Mi primer día del trabajo. Congratulations! You just landed your dream job. Your first day on the job, however, was not what you expected. By the end of the day you are very frustrated and decide to write an email to your best friend to tell him / her all about your bad day. Describe your day to your friend, and don't forget to include all the details. Remember to use the preterite.

Online Study Center

For further writing practice, visit the *Caminos* website at http://college.hmco.com/languages/spanish/renjilian/caminos/3e/student_home.html.

PRIMER PASO

CHECKING INTO A HOTEL

Sustantivos

el alojamiento	*lodging, accommodations*
el ascensor/elevador	*elevator*
el botones	*porter*
el buzón	*mailbox*
el cajero automático	*automated teller machine (ATM)*
el cambio de dinero/ moneda	*money exchange*
el cheque de viajero	*traveler's check*
el/la conserje	*concierge*
el despertador	*alarm clock*
el (dinero en) efectivo	*cash*
la elegancia	*elegance*
el equipaje	*luggage*
el estacionamiento	*parking lot*
la habitación	*room*
el/la huésped	*guest*
el lujo	*luxury*
la maleta	*suitcase*
el (mini) bar	*(mini)bar*
la primera/ segunda clase	*first / second class*
la recepción	*reception*
el/la recepcionista	*receptionist*
la reservación	*reservation*
el salón (la sala) de conferencias	*conference room*
la tarifa	*rate, fare, tariff*
la tarjeta de crédito	*credit card*
la vista	*view*

Verbos

alojar(se)	*to stay (in a hotel)*
atender (ie)	*to attend to, wait on*
confirmar	*to confirm*
hacer una llamada (de larga distancia/ por cobrar)	*to make a (long distance / collect) phone call*
registrar	*to register*
reservar	*to reserve*

Adjetivos

cómodo/a	*comfortable*
doble	*double*
lujoso/a (de lujo)	*luxurious*
sencillo/a	*single (room or bed)*

Otras expresiones

¿A nombre de quién?	*In whose name?*
¿En qué le(s) puedo servir?	*How can I help you?*
con desayuno	*with breakfast*
con media pensión	*with two meals*
con vista al mar	*with an ocean view*
¿Cuánto cuesta... ?	*How much does . . . cost?*
¿Dónde puedo cambiar el dinero?	*Where can I exchange money?*
Lo siento.	*I'm sorry.*
por supuesto	*of course*
¡Que disfrute/n de su estadía/estancia!	*Enjoy your stay!*

TALKING ABOUT THE BEACH

Sustantivos

el balón *(beach) ball*	
las gafas de sol	*sunglasses*
la novela	*novel*
el picnic	*picnic*
la playa	*beach*
el protector/ bronceador solar	*sunscreen*
el/la radio	*radio*
la sandalia	*sandal*
el sombrero	*hat*
la sombrilla	*parasol / beach umbrella*
la toalla *towel*	
el traje de baño	*bathing suit*

Verbos

broncearse	*to get a tan*
bucear	*to go skindiving, snorkeling*
buscar conchas	*to look for shells*

hacer castillos de arena	to make sandcastles	nadar	to swim
hacer esquí acuático	to water ski	navegar en velero	to go sailing
hacer surfing	to go surfing	pasearse/dar un paseo	to go for a walk
ir de pesca (pescar)	to go fishing (to fish)	protegerse	to protect oneself
jugar (al) volibol	to play volleyball	quemarse	to get a sunburn
montar a caballo	to go horseback riding	tomar el sol	to sunbathe
montar en bicicleta	to go bicycling		

SEGUNDO PASO

DISCUSSING VACATIONS

Sustantivos

la aerolínea	airline
el club	club (nightclub)
la confirmación	confirmation
el (des)embarque	(un)loading
la despedida	farewell
la discoteca	discotheque
la excursión / tour	excursion / tour
el folleto	brochure
el/la guía	tour guide
la guía	guidebook
la isla	island
la limosina	limousine
el paquete	package (tour)
el recreo	recreation
el transporte	transportation
el traslado	transfer
la vacación	vacation

Verbos

averiguar	to find out
avisar	to advise, warn
descansar	to rest
encontrarse (ue) (con)	to meet (with) someone
estar a punto de	to be on the verge of
estar de acuerdo	to agree
estar/irse de vacaciones	to be / go on vacation
gozar (de)	to enjoy
recoger	to pick up, get
reunirse (con)	to meet (with) someone

Otras expresiones

a bordo	on board
bello/a	beautiful
¡Buen viaje! / ¡Feliz viaje!	Have a nice trip!
libre	free (independent)
Ni idea.	I haven't got a clue.
¡Oye!	Hey! / Listen!
¡Qué gusto!	What a pleasure!

IRREGULAR AND STEM-CHANGING VERBS IN THE PRETERITE

despedirse	to say good-bye
freír	to fry
reducir	to reduce
reír	to laugh
sonreír	to smile
sugerir	to suggest

6

El tiempo libre

VOCABULARIO Y LENGUA

- Enjoying music and dance
- Describing in the past: Imperfect
- Talking about sports and exercise
- Distinguishing between **por** and **para**

- Discussing television and movies
- Giving instructions and making requests: Formal commands
- Using adverbs ending in -**mente**

CAMINOS DEL JAGUAR

- Prisioneros en peligro
- ¡Bomba!

LECTURA

- Diversos deportes del Caribe

NOTAS CULTURALES

- El Yunque
- El Centro Ceremonial Indígena de Tibes

ESTRATEGIAS

- **Reading**: Identifying main ideas
- **Writing**: Freewriting

Dania Sierra, *Guajiro verde*

Preguntas del tema

- ► ¿Qué haces en tu tiempo libre?
- ► ¿Qué música prefieres escuchar?
- ► ¿Cuáles son tus deportes favoritos?
- ► ¿Qué programas de televisión te gusta ver? ¿Por qué?

Vocabulario y lengua

ENJOYING MUSIC AND DANCE

Mosaico musical hispano

play a role

En todo el mundo hispano, la música y el baile **juegan un papel**° central en la vida diaria. A la gente le gusta escuchar o bailar algunos de estos **ritmos** tradicionales.

El flamenco

La **guitarra** y las **castañuelas** son los instrumentos principales del *flamenco.* El *cantaor* o la *cantaora* transmite con *voice* su **voz**° los sentimientos más profundos *soul* del **alma**° de Andalucía. Otros ritmos españoles son el *pasodoble*, del centro de España y la *jota*, del norte.

El mariachi

musicians

Los **músicos**° del **mariachi** llevan el hermoso traje de *charro* mexicano. Sus instrumentos principales son los **violines** y las **trompetas.** El Mariachi Vargas de Tecalitlán es el más famoso de México. La *ranchera* es el ritmo típico que **interpreta** el mariachi. Dos conocidos cantantes de música mexicana son Vicente Fernández y su hijo, Alejandro Fernández, que también canta *baladas*.

Online Study Center

For additional practice with this unit's vocabulary and grammar, visit the *Caminos* website at http://college.hmco.com/languages/spanish/renjilian/caminos/3e/student_home.html. You can also review audio flashcards, quiz yourself, and explore related Spanish-language sites.

El rock latino y la música pop

El rock latino y la música pop tienen influencias de la música internacional, especialmente de los grandes conjuntos de Norteamérica. Uno de los **grupos** hispanos que

reflects

más **refleja**° estas influencias es Maná de México, que combina la música rock con temas *singers* sociales. Otros populares **cantantes**° y compositores latinos son Shakira, Carlos Vives y Juanes de Colombia, Alejandro Sanz de España y Carlos Santana de México.

Los ritmos caribeños

Los **tambores**° marcan el ritmo bailable° del Caribe. El *merengue* es de la República Dominicana, el *son* es de Cuba y la *cumbia* es de Colombia. La *salsa* combina los ritmos caribeños con el jazz. Mark Anthony, Celia Cruz, Juan Luis Guerra, el Buena Vista Social Club y Joe Arroyo son intérpretes muy conocidos de los ritmos caribeños.

drums / danceable

El tango

El **tango** tiene su origen en los barrios populares de Buenos Aires. El instrumento tradicional que acompaña el tango es el **acordeón.** Poco a poco, esta hermosa música **se volvió**° popular en toda la Argentina y finalmente, en todo el mundo.

became

La música de los Estados Unidos

Las comunicaciones modernas facilitan la transmisión de la música de los Estados Unidos a través de **los discos compactos,** de la televisión y del Internet. Por eso, los jóvenes de los países hispanos conocen los ritmos estadounidenses por su nombre original, como: **el rock, el jazz, el hip-hop, los blues.**

Más palabras y expresiones

Cognados

la banda	la percusión
el concierto	el piano
la flauta	el saxofón

Sustantivos

los audífonos	*headphones*
el bailarín / la bailarina	*dancer*

la batería	*drum set*
la canción	*song*
el conjunto	*group, band*
la guitarra bajo	*bass guitar*
la letra	*lyrics*
el parlante	*speaker*
el reproductor MP3	*MP3 player*

Verbos

bailar	*to dance*
cantar	*to sing*
grabar	*to record, tape*
tocar (un instrumento)	*to play (an instrument)*

The ending **–ista** is often used to refer to the person who plays a particular instrument: el/la **guitarrista** *(guitarist)*, el/la **pianista** *(pianist)*.

Actividades

1 Juanes. Listen to a brief description of the life of Juanes, and complete the following statements with the correct answer.

1. Juanes nació en _____ .
   a. 1969   b. 1972   c. 1960

2. El verdadero nombre de Juanes es _____ .
   a. Juan Ernesto   b. Juan Esteban   c. Juan Sebas

3. Juanes empezó su carrera con Ekhimosis, un grupo de _____ .
   a. música hip-hop   b. música rock   c. música jazz

4. "A Dios le pido" es el título de _____ .
   a. un disco compacto   b. una canción   c. un concierto

5. Juanes ganó tres premios Grammy Latinos en _____ .
   a. 2000   b. 2002   c. 2001

6. "Mi sangre" es _____ .
   a. un disco compacto   b. una canción   c. un concierto

7. Luna y Paloma son _____ de Juanes.
   a. hermanas   b. hijas   c. amigas

2 Asociaciones. Look at the CD covers below and match each with its corresponding musical style.

a. Mariachi   b. Rock   c. Tango   d. Flamenco   e. Merengue

1. _____

2. _____

3. _____

4. _____

5. _____

3 Instrumentos. What instruments do or did the following people play? Compare your answers with a partner.

1. Elton John
2. Itzhak Perlman
3. Louis Armstrong
4. Carlos Santana
5. Kenny G.
6. Paul McCartney
7. Alicia Keyes
8. Tito Puente

4 Preguntas personales. With a partner, answer these questions.

1. ¿Qué tipo de música te gusta?
2. ¿Te gusta bailar? ¿cantar? ¿dónde? ¿cuándo?
3. ¿Cuál es tu grupo musical favorito? ¿Por qué?
4. ¿Quién es tu cantante favorito/a? ¿Por qué?
5. ¿Toca algún miembro de tu familia un instrumento? ¿Cuál?
6. ¿Tocas tú algún instrumento musical? ¿Cuál?
7. ¿Asistes a conciertos de música? ¿A cuáles?
8. ¿Tienes un reproductor MP3? ¿Cuál? ¿Dónde lo escuchas?
9. ¿Prefieres usar audífonos o usas parlantes para escuchar música? ¿Por qué?
10. ¿Compras música en disco compacto o en Internet? ¿Por qué?

5 La música del mundo hispano. Choose one of the music genres presented on page 206–207 and find information about one of its artists. You can listen to samples of music on the Internet at websites like Amazon.com or by using iTunes. Then search for additional information to present to your classmates. Include the following information in your presentation: name of the artist, country of origin, type of music, instruments played, lyrics of a song you like, most popular songs or albums, and your personal opinion of the musician.

DESCRIBING IN THE PAST: IMPERFECT

You have learned to use the preterite to talk about completed actions in the past. In addition to this form, Spanish uses a second past form called the **imperfect.** The imperfect may have several meanings in English, for example: **el perro saltaba** = *the dog was jumping, the dog used to jump, the dog would jump, the dog jumped.*

Read the following description of the drawings and note the highlighted verbs in the imperfect. Time expressions like **a veces** *(sometimes),* **unas (otras) veces** *(sometimes / other times),* **todos los días (semanas)** *(every day / week)* are generally used with the imperfect to emphasize the habitual or repetitive nature of this tense.

Las mascotas de Fernando y sus hermanos

Use the imperfect...

▶ To talk about one's age and weather in the past.

Aquí estoy yo cuando **tenía** diez años. Ese día **hacía** buen tiempo.

▶ To describe past states of mind, feelings, likes, and dislikes.

Este es mi hermano Tomás. Él **prefería** los canarios y los gatos. A mí me **gustaban** las mariposas.

▶ To describe how people, things or places seemed or looked.

Ayer, el perro de Felicia, mi hermana, **estaba** muy inquieto.

▶ To describe how things used to be.

Unas veces, las mascotas **vivían** en paz. Otras veces, **había** caos total.

▶ To describe what people normally used to do, their habits, and routines, and how often they used to do them.

Todos los veranos **pasábamos** unas semanas en el campo y **jugábamos** juntos.

Todos los días **nos acostábamos** cansados y satisfechos.

Almost all Spanish verbs are regular in the imperfect.

The imperfect			
	–ar	–er	–ir
	estar	tener	sentir (to be sorry, regret)
yo	estaba	tenía	sentía
tú	estabas	tenías	sentías
Ud. / él /ella	estaba	tenía	sentía
nosotros/as	estábamos	teníamos	sentíamos
vosotros/as	estabais	teníais	sentíais
Uds. / ellos / ellas	estaban	tenían	sentían

Note that –er and –ir verbs have the same endings. Note also that –er and –ir verbs have written accents in all forms, whereas –ar verbs have an accent only on the nosotros form.

All verbs that have stem changes in the present or the preterite are regular in the imperfect.

Había (there was, there were) is the imperfect of haber. Like hay (there is, there are), there is only one form for singular and plural meanings.

Había un gato en el parque.　　There was a cat in the park.
Había muchos insectos allí.　　There were many insects there.

There are only three irregular verbs in the imperfect.

	ser	ir	ver
yo	era	iba	veía
tú	eras	ibas	veías
Ud./ él /ella	era	iba	veía
nosotros/as	éramos	íbamos	veíamos
vosotros/as	erais	ibais	veíais
Uds./ ellos / ellas	eran	iban	veían

Actividades

1 Eventos. Match the events listed in Column A with the information in Column B.

A

1. _____ íbamos todos los años a Madrid.
2. _____ me sentía feliz.
3. Nunca hacía _____
4. _____ eran enemigos.
5. No había _____
6. ¿Tenías mascotas _____?
7. _____ siempre se levantaba temprano.
8. _____ le gustaba saltar.

B

a. Al perro
b. tú
c. Yo
d. El perro y el gato
e. buen tiempo.
f. Nosotros
g. Usted
h. muchos insectos.

2 Mi pasado.
Fill in the blanks with the imperfect form of the verbs in parentheses.

Cuando yo _____ (**1.** ser) joven, siempre _____ (**2.** comer) mucho. Yo _____ (**3.** ir) a restaurantes y _____ (**4.** pedir) hamburguesas, leche y muchos postres. En verano mis hermanos y yo _____ (**5.** ir) de vacaciones a la playa y _____ (**6.** divertirse) muchísimo. Yo siempre _____ (**7.** jugar) con mis amigos y no _____ (**8.** tener) que trabajar. También mis amigos y yo _____ (**9.** navegar) mucho por Internet cuando _____ (10. tener) tiempo por las tardes.

3 Un trabajo de verano.
You are describing a previous summer job, talking about what you used to do and how often you did it. Complete the description using the following adverbial expressions of time. Then, compare your answers with those of a partner.

con frecuencia   generalmente
todos los días   siempre
a veces   otras veces

El verano pasado trabajé como recepcionista en un canal de televisión. Cuando sucedía algo muy interesante, (**1**) _____ salían varios periodistas para ver los eventos. (**2**) _____ viajaban en auto, (**3**) _____ iban en dos autos, con los técnicos. (**4**) _____, yo atendía a muchas personas y (**5**) _____ llegaba gente muy importante para hablar por televisión. Y (**6**) _____ yo les pedía su autógrafo.

4 El vecindario *(neighborhood).*
A friend of yours visited relatives in another city. Ask your friend questions about their neighborhood. Then, present the description of the neighborhood to your class.

1. ¿Estaba el vecindario cerca del centro de la ciudad?
2. ¿Cómo era? ¿grande? ¿pequeño?
3. ¿Había discoteca?
4. ¿Tenía muchas tiendas?
5. ¿Cómo eran las tiendas?
6. ¿Estaba cerca de la playa?
7. ¿Tenía buenos supermercados?
8. ¿Era deliciosa la comida en los restaurantes?
9. ¿La gente podía jugar al tenis? ¿al golf? ¿al básquetbol?
10. ¿...?

5 Así era yo.
Tell your classmates about yourself and your life when you were a child. Answer questions such as: What did you look like? What was your family like? Who were your friends? What did you like to do? What did you usually do together? What was your favorite TV show? Who were your favorite singers or groups?

¿Qué deporte quieres practicar?

Más palabras y expresiones

Cognados

entrenar	el gimnasio
el/la espectador/a	practicar
esquiar	el uniforme

Sustantivos

el/la aficionado/a, fanático/a	*fan*
la cancha	*court, field*
el/la deportista	*athlete; sports enthusiast*
el/la entrenador/a	*trainer*
el equipo	*team; equipment*
el/la jugador/a	*player*
el partido	*game*
la pista	*ice rink; running track*

Verbos

ganar	*to win*
jugar (ue) (al)	*to play (a sport or game)*
patear	*to kick*
perder (ie)	*to lose*

Actividades

1 Soy atleta. Match the descriptions of the sports in Column A with the name of the sport in Column B.

A	B
_____ 1. En la escuela tenemos dos equipos. Ponemos la pelota en una cesta alta.	a. ciclismo
_____ 2. Este deporte es violento. Lo juegan dos personas con guantes grandes.	b. baloncesto
_____ 3. Solamente necesitamos una pelota y buenos zapatos. Somos dos equipos.	c. béisbol
_____ 4. Practico este deporte en la piscina de mi escuela.	d. fútbol
_____ 5. ¡Este deporte es también un medio de transporte! El vehículo tiene dos ruedas.	e. boxeo
_____ 6. Somos dos equipos. Golpeamos la pelota con un bate y ¡corremos mucho!	f. natación

2 ¿Qué necesitamos?
Work with a partner and talk about the equipment that you need to play or to practice the following sports. Follow the model.

► **MODELO:** —¿Qué necesitas para jugar al béisbol?
—Para jugar al béisbol, necesitamos una pelota, unos guantes y....

1.

2.

3.

4.

5.

6.

7.

8.

3 ¿Cómo son los deportes?
Work with a partner to decide which sport(s) you associate with each of these words. Explain the reasons for your choices.

violento/a	caro/a	rápido/a	barato/a
entretenido/a	aburrido/a	interesante	peligroso/a

4 Encuesta.
Ask three classmates the following questions about sports. Write down their answers and present your findings to the class.

1. ¿Cuál es tu deporte favorito? ¿Por qué?
2. ¿Cuál es tu equipo favorito? ¿Por qué?
3. ¿Quién es tu jugador/a favorito/a? ¿Por qué? ¿Qué deporte juega?

Persona	Deporte favorito	Equipo favorito	Jugador/a favorito/a

Por and **para** correspond in general to the English preposition *for,* but they are not interchangeable in Spanish. These are their main uses.

Uses of *por*	Uses of *para*

1A. To state the cause or motive of an action. (*because, on account of, for the sake of*)

Trabajo **por** mi equipo... y el equipo es famoso **por** mí.
I work for my team's sake . . . and my team is famous because of me.

1B. To state the purpose of actions, things, and tools. (*in order to, for*)

¡Jugamos **para** ganar la copa!
We play to win the cup!

2A. To describe spatial motion. (*by, around, through, along, via*)

Tomás jugó fútbol **por** todos los Estados Unidos.
Tomás played soccer all around the United States.

2B. To specify destination. (*to, headed to*)

Salí temprano **para** el estadio.
I left early for the stadium.

3A. To indicate acting in someone's place, on his/her behalf.

Ayer jugué **por** Luis.
Yesterday, I played in Luis's place.

3B. To indicate the recipient of an action or an object.

Esta copa es **para** mi novia.
This cup is for my girlfriend.

Uses of *por*	Uses of *para*

4A. To describe the period of time of an action, period of time in a day, percentages, and units of measure.

Entrené **por** tres horas sin pausa.
I trained for three hours without a break.

4B. To indicate a future deadline to meet.

Tengo que entrenar **para** el cinco de mayo.
I have to train for May fifth.

5A. To indicate the physical media used to send messages or things: radio, TV, Internet, fax, mail, and telephone. *(on, by, through)*

Tomás habla **por** televisión y las cartas de sus aficionados le llegan **por** aire, **por** tierra y **por** mar.
Tomás talks on TV. He receives his fan mail by air, land, and sea.

5B. To explain that something or someone falls short or exceeds your expectations.

Para ser tan joven, Tomás es un excelente jugador de fútbol.
For one so young, Tomás is an excellent soccer player.

Common expressions with *por*

ir **por** + *person / thing to go for; to pick up*	**por** favor *please*
	por fin *finally*
pagar **por** *to pay for*	**por** lo menos *at least*
pasar **por** *to stop by*	**por** lo tanto *therefore*
por ejemplo *for example*	**por** supuesto *of course*

Common expressions with *para*

para mí / ti / etc. *in my / your opinion ; for me / you*	**para** nada *no way, not at all*
	estar **para** + *verb to be about to + verb*
para siempre *forever*	

Actividades

1 **Usos.** Without translating the following sentences, discuss which preposition **(por / para)** would be the best to use in each situation. Work with a partner. Then, exchange your selections with another pair and evaluate their answers.

1. I am always doing things *on your behalf.*
2. Laura, here is a letter *for* you.
3. You have to be done with the project *by* tomorrow morning.
4. Will you miss me, honey? I am going to be away *for* a whole month!
5. Students are working hard *in order to* pass the exam.
6. Would you please teach this class *for* me? I can't make it tomorrow.
7. Where are you *headed for* at this hour?
8. *For* whom are all those gifts that you bought?

2 **¿Por o para?** Work with a partner and fill in the correct preposition in the following sentences.

1. Compramos el casco _____ su bajo precio.
2. Mis papás compraron unos patines _____ mí.
3. Vamos a estar en el estadio _____ una hora.
4. La discoteca me gustó mucho _____ su música moderna.
5. Voy a imprimir el programa _____ ellos.
6. Si no quieres jugar tenis, yo juego _____ ti.
7. Debes tener tu equipo listo _____ mañana.
8. Estuvimos en Madrid y ¡viajamos _____ todas partes!

3 **Música.** Create sentences for the situations depicted based on the following drawings. Use **por** and/or **para.** Use the text that applies to each drawing as a hint.

4 El palacio deportivo. Read the following ad for a sporting goods store. Then, using the same format, create your own ad for a boutique, an event, or a product. Use **por** to describe why your specific event, boutique, or product is so attractive. Use **para** to describe your target audience: who is this event, product, or boutique for?

El Palacio Deportivo
¡Para todas sus necesidades deportivas!

¡Para niños y adultos!

¡Para deportes de invierno y de verano!

¡Para todas las edades!

Somos su tienda deportiva preferida…

…por los bajos precios
…por la alta calidad
…por la gran variedad de productos

Visítenos
en el Centro Comercial
Villa Nueva

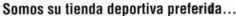

¡Prisioneros en peligro!

Hotel de Adriana y Felipe. Adriana está preocupada.

¡Felipe!

¿Qué te pasa?

Mira, ese hombre me persiguió en Sevilla.

¿Cuál hombre? Yo no vi a nadie.

El hombre del anillo raro. Estaba hablando por teléfono.

¿Estás segura, Adriana?

Estoy ciento por ciento segura.

Riiing ... riiing ... riiing

¿Bueno? ¿Nayeli?

Sí, soy yo.

Estábamos muy preocupados sin saber de ti.

Estoy bien. ¿Está Felipe contigo?

Sí, claro.

Tienes que escucharme sin preguntar por qué. Felipe y tú deben alquilar un auto y venir a buscarme.

¿Adónde?

Los espero en el Centro Ceremonial Indígena de Tibes, en Ponce.

¡Nayeli! ¿Qué pasa?

Nos vemos pronto, manejen con cuidado.

¡Nayeli, Nayeli!

¿Qué te dijo Nayeli?

Algo está mal. ¡Vámonos!

¿Adónde vamos?

Vamos a alquilar un auto y a comprar un mapa de la isla. Después, vamos a Ponce, al Centro Ceremonial Indígena de Tibes.

Todo esto está cada vez más raro.

Quito: En la oficina de correos.

Buenas tardes.

Buenas tardes.

Por favor, vengo por un paquete a mi nombre, Zulaya Piscomayo Curihual.

Sí, el paquete llegó hace dos días.

Favor de firmar su nombre aquí.

Muchas gracias.

Ya llegamos al Centro Ceremonial Indígena de Tibes.

Aquí es.

¡Adriana y Felipe son inocentes!

Cerca del Centro Ceremonial Indígena de Tibes.

¡No, amiga mía, no!

Por favor, son sólo estudiantes. No saben nada. Son inocentes.

¡Qué mujer más arrogante! No tienes ningún poder para decir nada.

Por favor.

Aquí tengo la información. Ya no te necesito ni a ti ni a nadie. Mi plan va muy bien.

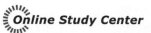
Online Study Center

For additional practice
with this episode, visit
the *Caminos* website at
http://college.hmco.com/
languages/spanish/
renjilian/caminos/3e/
student_home.html.

Actividades

1 Comprensión. Based on this episode of *Caminos del jaguar,* choose the
logical response.

1. ¿Vio Felipe al hombre que persiguió a Adriana?
   a. Sí, lo vio.
   b. No, no lo vio.

2. ¿Estaba segura Adriana que era el hombre del anillo raro?
   a. Estaba muy segura.
   b. No estaba muy segura.

3. ¿Adriana llama a Nayeli?
   a. No, Nayeli llama a Adriana.
   b Sí, Adriana llama a Nayeli.

4. Antes de hablar con Nayeli, Adriana y Felipe estaban muy...
   a. alterados.
   b. preocupados.

5. Después de la llamada, Adriana piensa que...
   a. hay algo extraño.
   b. hay algo interesante.

6. Nayeli dice que Felipe y Adriana...
   a. no son sus estudiantes.
   b. son inocentes.

7. El plan de Gafasnegras...
   a. no va muy bien.
   b. va muy bien.

2 Situaciones. Dramatize one of the following situations.

1. Gafasnegras tells Nayeli that she already has the information.
2. Adriana and Felipe discuss what they have to do.

3 Escritura. Write a summary of what Nayeli tells Adriana on the phone. (4–6
sentences)

NOTA CULTURAL

El Yunque

El Yunque es el parque nacional más importante de Puerto
Rico. Es un bosque lluvioso extraordinario. Tiene más de
240 especies de árboles y cientos de especies de animales
diferentes. Allí encontramos la boa puertorriqueña, el
papagayo *(parrot)* y el coquí. El coquí es una ranita *(small
frog)* nativa de la isla de Puerto Rico.

SEGUNDO PASO

Vocabulario y lengua

DISCUSSING TELEVISION AND MOVIES

Online Study Center

For additional practice with this episode, visit the *Caminos* website at http://college.hmco.com/languages/spanish/renjilian/caminos/3e/student_home.html.

El cine de Pedro Almodóvar

direct

wider

Pedro Almodóvar Caballero es un famoso **director** del cine español. Comenzó a **dirigir**° películas en 1980 con su primera película *Pepi, Luci, Bom y otras chicas del montón*. En 1985 con la película *Matador* se dio a conocer a un público más amplio° y al año siguiente con *La ley del deseo* inicia una nueva etapa más moderada. En 1987 con *Mujeres al borde de un ataque de nervios* consigue que su **fama** se extienda a Europa e incluso llegue a América. Consiguió ser **nominado** a los Óscar con la película *Mujeres al borde de un ataque de nervios* en la **categoría**

foreign / honor

de mejor película **extranjera**°, pero no obtuvo el **galardón**°.

Su trabajo *Todo sobre mi madre* se ha confirmado como una de sus mejores películas por su solidez y la emoción que provoca; de hecho ganó su primer Óscar en el año 2000.

genres

box-office draw

Sus películas son una miscelánea de **géneros**° que van desde la **comedia** como su película *Volver*, hasta el **drama,** como *Matador*. Almodóvar es uno de los directores más **taquilleros**° del cine español e internacional.

Sinopsis de *Volver* (2006)

Volver cuenta la historia de tres mujeres que sobreviven muchos obstáculos, que incluyen el fuego, la superstición, la locura e incluso la muerte. Las protagonistas son Raimunda,

worker / unemployed

casada con un **obrero**° **desempleado**° y una hija adolescente; Sole, su hermana, se gana la vida como peluquera; y la madre de ambas,

fire

muerta en un **incendio**°, junto a su marido.

Volver es una comedia donde los vivos y los muertos conviven

causing

provocando° situaciones cómicas o de una emoción intensa y genuina. El modo en que los muertos continúan presentes en sus vidas hace que los muertos

fearless

no mueran nunca. *Volver* muestra una España espontánea, divertida e **intrépida**°.

Más palabras y expresiones

Cognados

el actor	de acción	la escena	la nominación
la actriz	de ciencia ficción	filmar	romántico/a
cómico/a	de horror, de terror	el filme	la secuencia
criticar	de misterio	la narración	la sinopsis

Sustantivos

el acontecimiento	*event*
la actuación	*acting*
el argumento	*plot*
el billete, la entrada	*ticket*
la cartelera	*listing*
la crítica	*criticism*
el guión	*script*
el largometraje	*feature film*
la pantalla	*screen*
el papel	*role*
el personaje (principal, secundario)	*(main, secondary) character*
el/la protagonista	*main character*
la reseña	*review*
la taquilla	*box office*
la trama	*plot*

Verbos

actuar	*to act*
estrenar	*to premiere*
hacer el papel	*to play a role*
juzgar	*to judge*
presentar (pasar) una película	*to show a movie*
reseñar	*to review*
suceder	*to occur*
tratar de	*to deal with, treat*

Adjetivos

de amor	*love (adj.)*
de suspenso	*thriller (adj.)*
de vaqueros	*western (adj.)*

Actividades

1 Preguntas personales. Work with a partner and answer the following questions.

1. ¿Te gusta ir al cine? ¿Por qué?
2. ¿Qué tipo de películas te gustan? ¿de amor? ¿cómicas? ¿de horror? ¿... ?
3. ¿Quién es tu actor/actriz favorito/a? ¿Por qué? ¿Cómo es?
4. ¿Cuál es tu película favorita? Explica la trama y menciona quiénes actúan en ella.
5. ¿Vas a ver una película porque lees las reseñas, ves los anuncios o por tus amigos?

2 ¿Qué película vieron?
Work with a partner and match what people describe in Column A with the type of movie listed in Column B.

A	B
____ 1. Al principio, era aburrida, pero finalmente, nos reímos muchísimo.	a. película de terror
____ 2. Había muchos caballos *(horses)*, revólveres, sombreros y mucho ruido.	b. película de suspenso
____ 3. Era una película muy lenta, pero por fin, la policía encontró al culpable.	c. película de amor
____ 4. ¡Al final de la película se casaron y fueron muy felices!	d. película de ciencia ficción
____ 5. Todos los personajes eran robots o personas de otros planetas.	e. comedia
____ 6. Durante toda la película tuve mucho miedo.	f. película de vaqueros

3 Las películas de hoy.
Choose a movie that's showing this week in your area and write a sinopsis or review. Present it to the class.

GIVING INSTRUCTIONS AND MAKING REQUESTS: FORMAL COMMANDS

Deme dos entradas

The highlighted words in the drawings are commands, or imperative forms, which are used to request something from people whom you address formally with **usted or ustedes.**

Regular verbs

To create the formal imperative (**Ud.** and **Uds.** commands), drop the **–o** of the first person singular **yo** form in the present tense and add the opposite ending. Add **–e** or **–en** to **–ar** verbs and **–a** or **–an** to **–er** and **–ir** verbs to create the **Ud.** or **Uds.** commands respectively. To make a command negative, add **no** before the verb.

–ar verbs	–er and –ir verbs		Subject
tomar	**comer**	**escribir**	
tome	coma	escriba	usted
no tome	no coma	no escriba	
tom**en**	com**an**	escrib**an**	ustedes
no tom**en**	no com**an**	no escrib**an**	

If a verb has a stem change in the **yo** form of the present (**pienso, sirvo, duermo**), it maintains that change in the formal command forms: **piense(n), sirva(n), duerma(n).**

If a verb is irregular in the **yo** form of the present (**salgo, conduzco, veo**), it maintains that change in the formal command forms: **salga(n), conduzca(n), vea(n).**

Verbs with spelling changes

If an infinitive ends in **–car, –gar,** or **–zar,** it undergoes a spelling change in order to maintain the same sound as in the infinitive.

	infinitive	yo present indicative	usted / ustedes command
-car	buscar	busco	bus**que** / bus**quen**
-gar	pagar	pago	pa**gue** / pa**guen**
-zar	empezar	empiezo	empie**ce** / empie**cen**

Irregular verbs

	dar	estar	ir	saber	ser
usted	dé	esté	vaya	sepa	sea
ustedes	den	estén	vayan	sepan	sean

Position of pronouns with commands

Direct and indirect object pronouns and reflexive pronouns are attached to an affirmative command and precede a negative command. When a pronoun is added to an affirmative command of two or more syllables, a written accent is generally needed to maintain the original stress.

¿Quiere ver una buena película? **Alquíle***la* en nuestra tienda!	*Do you want to see a good movie?* *Rent it in our store.*
En el teatro, **no** *se* **siente** en la silla equivocada.	*Don't sit in the wrong seat at the theater.*
Envíe*nos* su pedido, pero **no** *nos* **pague** la película todavía.	*Send us your order today, but don't pay us for the movie yet.*

The subject pronoun is used infrequently with commands and is only used to emphasize the request. Subject pronouns always follow the verb in both negative and affirmative commands.

Vaya usted a la taquilla para comprar el billete.	*Go to the box office to buy the ticket.*
No hablen ustedes durante la película, por favor.	*Don't talk during the movie, please.*

Remember: When speaking about someone with a title (**señor/a, señorita, profesor/a, doctor/a,** etc.), Spanish uses the definite article: **La doctora Beatriz Pinzón trabaja en la compañía EcoModa.** The article is omitted when the person is addressed directly: **Doctora Pinzón, pase a mi oficina, por favor.**

Actividades

1 Está prohibido.
You have been asked to write rules and instructions for students in your film class. Use the list below to tell them what they are allowed and not allowed to do. Use **Uds.** commands. Work with a partner.

1. No / llegar tarde.
2. No / comer o beber en la clase.
3. Ver todas las películas asignadas.
4. Elegir las películas de la lista aprobada *(approved)*.
5. No / hacer ruido en la clase.
6. No / tocar el DVD sin permiso.
7. Tomar apuntes durante la película
8. Leer reseñas en Internet como modelos.
9. Escribir una reseña de cada película.

2 Para nuestros visitantes.
You are preparing a brochure for a hotel describing the attractions that you offer. Use the formal **Uds.** command form of the verbs below to write the brochure. Use each verb only once.

visitar	comenzar	leer	enviar	nadar
sentarse	cenar	pagar	ver	divertirse

1. _____ en nuestro restaurante Ricascosas, en la terraza.
2. _____ todas sus cuentas con cualquier tarjeta de crédito.
3. _____ en la piscina desde las ocho de la mañana hasta las nueve de la noche.
4. _____ los periódicos del día gratis *(free)* en nuestra recepción.
5. _____ en nuestras cómodas sillas y sofás a leer tranquilamente.
6. _____ las cartas en la oficina de correos del hotel.
7. _____ el día con un desayuno continental en su habitación.
8. _____ la ciudad en nuestros buses turísticos.
9. _____ en nuestra discoteca, la mejor de la ciudad.
10. _____ una selección exclusiva de películas desde su habitación.

3 El nuevo ayudante.
A movie-theater owner has a new assistant who constantly asks what to do. Role-play the situation in pairs, asking the following questions. Follow the model, using formal commands and object pronouns.

▶ MODELO: —¿Les envío el horario a los periódicos?
—*Sí, envíeselo.*
or
—*No, no se lo envíe.*

1. ¿Le pido dos cafés al bar?
2. ¿Les doy el horario de trabajo a los empleados?
3. ¿Pago las cuentas hoy?
4. ¿Les pido las películas nuevas a los distribuidores?
5. ¿Les entrego la lista a ellos mañana?
6. ¿Quito los carteles viejos de la sala de entrada?
7. ¿Pongo el dinero en la taquilla?
8. ¿Les mando los cheques a los empleados hoy?

4 Consejero.
Choose one of the situations described below and give instructions regarding what to do or what not to do in each case. Use as many verbs as you can.

1. You have rented a movie and are showing your friends how to play it on the DVD and watch on the television screen.
2. You are organizing a sports tournament. Tell various people which sports are allowed and what they have to do regarding invitations, food for the visitors, selling the tickets, transportation, and so on.
3. You are taking care of your neighbor's big, mischievous dog. You usually address the dog with the **usted** form because he looks so impressive. Tell him what to do and what not to do while you are taking care of him.
4. Explain to prospective students how to succeed at your college or university.

USING ADVERBS ENDING IN -MENTE

Adverbs of manner describe how an action is done. These adverbs are usually formed in Spanish by adding **–mente** to the singular form of the adjective. If the adjective has **–a** and **–o** endings, **–mente** is added to the feminine form. When the adjective ends in another vowel or in a consonant, no change is necessary and **–mente** is added directly to the end of the adjective. The **–mente** ending in Spanish corresponds to the *–ly* ending of many English adverbs *(easy→ easily)*. Note that written accents on the adjectives are retained when the **–mente** ending is added.

generoso/a	generosa**mente**	*generously*
impaciente	impaciente**mente**	*impatiently*
difícil	difícil**mente**	*with difficulty*

| Nosotros trabajamos **continuamente**. | *We work continuously.* |
| Soy **inmensamente** feliz. | *I am enormously happy.* |

These very commonly used adverbs may be used with or without **–mente**:
fácil / fácilmente; difícil / difícilmente; rápido / rápidamente.

Actividades

1 Cine. Complete the following sentences with the adverb form of the adjective given in parenthesis.

1. Voy al cine _____ (frecuente) con mis amigos o hermanos.
2. _____ (General) vemos películas cómicas.
3. El protagonista actuaba muy _____ (lento).
4. Los otros actores trabajaron _____ (perfecto).
5. El director contó la historia muy _____ (claro).
6. A mí me gustó _____ (especial) la actriz principal.

2 ¿De qué manera? Use adverbs to tell how the following people do these activities.

▶ MODELO: *El examen es fácil. Yo hago el examen fácilmente.*

1. La explicación de Julia es muy clara. Julia explica las cosas muy _____.
2. Nuestras conversaciones son agradables. Luis y yo conversamos _____.
3. Mi trabajo es muy duro. Yo trabajo _____.
4. Ese tren es muy rápido. Ese tren anda muy _____.
5. La ropa de Verónica es elegante. Verónica se viste _____.
6. Carlos es un escritor profesional. Carlos escribe _____.

3 Estilo personal. In pairs, ask each other the following questions about how you, your family, or friends usually do things. Then, create five new questions with different adverbs about life at the university. Ask another pair your questions.

1. ¿Caminas rápidamente? ¿lentamente?
2. ¿Llegas a clase puntualmente todos los días?
3. ¿Chateas con tus amigos frecuentemente? ¿infrecuentemente?
4. ¿Esperas a tus amigos pacientemente? ¿impacientemente?
5. ¿Tus amigos se visten elegantemente para las fiestas?
6. ¿Te duchas inmediatamente después de levantarte todos los días?

4 Invitación. Discuss with your friend which type of movies you frequently like to see, those you generally don't like to see and where you normally see them. Use adverbs ending in **–mente** in your conversation.

¡Bomba!

En un lugar desierto.

¿Para dónde nos llevan? ¿Qué van a hacer con nosotros?

Preguntas demasiado, Nayeli.

¡Ah, una computadora! Quiero ver qué tiene.

¡Calma, Luis! Éste no es el momento para mirar computadoras.

Pero esta computadora es muy moderna, tiene CD-ROM, parlantes...

No más, Luis, no más.

Doña Mariluz, ¿usted sabe que pronto voy a ser un gran programador?

¿Tiene correo electrónico?

Claro, doña Mariluz, déjeme enseñarle... pero no tengo la contraseña...

¿Cuál es la contraseña?

¡Ay señor, déjeme tranquila!

¡Ya no más!

¡Ja, ja, ja!

Olvídenlo. Nos queda poco tiempo. Sigamos con el plan.

¿Puedo quedarme con la computadora, doña Mariluz?

Tengo que pensarlo.

¡Vamos!

En una casita abandonada.

¡Adiós, amigos míos! ¿Ven ese aparato?

¡Es una bomba!

La puedo detonar con un control remoto.

¡Por favor, no les haga nada malo a Adriana y a Felipe!

Nunca vas a cambiar, Nayeli. Siempre vas a ser una mártir hasta el final.

Ya no te necesito, Nayeli, porque ya sé dónde está el jaguar. Les dejo la computadora. ¡Es un regalo para sus últimas horas!

No, doña Mariluz, la computadora es para mí. ¡No puede explotar la pobre computadora!

Ustedes acaban de perder. ¡Adiós para siempre!

Actividades

Online Study Center

For additional practice with this episode, visit the *Caminos* website at http://college.hmco.com/languages/spanish/renjilian/caminos/3e/student_home.html.

1 Comprensión. Based on this episode of *Caminos del jaguar,* choose the logical response.

1. Gafasnegras piensa que Nayeli...
   a. piensa demasiado.
   b. pregunta demasiado.

2. Nayeli no sabe...
   a. adónde van.
   b. dónde está Adriana.

3. Luis está muy interesado en...
   a. los prisioneros.
   b. la computadora.

4. El primo de Luis está...
   a. muy importante.
   b. muy impaciente.

5. Al final, Gafasnegras...
   a. le da la computadora a Luis.
   b. no le da la computadora a Luis.

6. Gafasnegras no necesita...
   a. el jaguar
   b. a Nayeli.

2 Situaciones. Dramatize one of the following situations.

1. Gafasnegras tells Nayeli, Adriana, and Felipe that she is going to detonate the bomb.
2. Nayeli tells Gafasnegras and the cousins that Adriana and Felipe are innocent and should be let free.

3 Escritura. Write a brief summary of what happens in this episode with Adriana, Felipe and Nayeli. (4–6 sentences)

NOTA CULTURAL

El Centro Ceremonial Indígena de Tibes

Éste es el sitio arqueológico más importante del Caribe. Está cerca de la ciudad de Ponce, Puerto Rico y representa más de mil años de la historia de los indios taínos en la época precolombina. La excavación empezó en 1975 y el lugar es ahora un gran parque arqueológico con un importante museo. Todos los años llegan allí más de 80.000 visitantes para ver las casas de los taínos, llamadas *bohíos* y para ver los sitios dónde practicaban su religión y jugaban deportes como el fútbol.

Lectura

☼ Online Study Center

For further reading practice online, visit the *Caminos* website at http://college.hmco.com/languages/spanish/renjilian/caminos/3e/student_home.html.

PRELECTURA

Reading Strategy

Identifying main ideas

In *Unidad 3* you learned about skimming to determine the content and main ideas of a reading. In this unit you will focus on skimming to identify the main ideas of paragraphs. A reading or passage generally contains three important elements:

1. **Topic:** The topic or theme can often be found in titles and subtitles.
2. **Topic sentence:** The topic sentence, usually the first sentence in a paragraph, states the main idea of a paragraph.
3. **Supporting details:** These can be facts about the topic or anecdotes to make the subject more interesting.

Locating the topic sentence of each paragraph gives you critical clues about the main ideas of a passage. To identify the details that support the main ideas, you must read the selection more closely.

1 Sin diccionario. Without using a dictionary, quickly read the following selection about Caribbean sports. For each paragraph, identify and write the topic and topic sentence. Do not worry about the details.

▶ **MODELO:** Topic: *el béisbol*
Topic sentence: *En los países de Cuba, Puerto Rico y la República Dominicana, el deporte nacional es el béisbol.*

Diversos deportes del Caribe

El béisbol

En los países de Cuba, Puerto Rico y la República Dominicana, el deporte nacional es el béisbol. Muchos caribeños lo practican desde la llegada de los estadounidenses a las islas. Los chicos jóvenes juegan en las calles y en los parques y los partidos despiertan[1] gran interés en la población. Muchos jugadores dominicanos, cubanoamericanos y puertorriqueños juegan en las ligas profesionales de los Estados Unidos y varios de ellos han tenido grandes éxitos[2]. Cuba es el único país que por ahora prohíbe la participación de cubanos en las ligas norteamericanas. Este deporte es popular también en las regiones caribeñas de Panamá y Colombia, donde también hay exitosos equipos femeninos.

David Ortiz, jugador dominicano de béisbol en Estados Unidos

[1]awaken; [2]have been very successful.

El futbolista cubano Mikal Galindo, ahora juega en los Estados Unidos

Niños hispanos jugando al fútbol americano

El fútbol

Los indígenas mayas de Centroamérica y México y los arauacos[3] de la zona caribeña practicaban el fútbol en los juegos ceremoniales. Jugaban con una pesada[4] pelota de caucho[5] y usaban la cintura[6] para mantener la pelota en el aire sin tocar el suelo[7]. Este juego fue un precursor del juego moderno que conocemos hoy, con millones de aficionados en todo el mundo[8].

El fútbol americano

Los caribeños no juegan mucho este deporte, pero los partidos norteamericanos tienen espectadores en todo el mundo hispano porque se transmiten por los canales hispanos de televisión desde Miami. La gente de muchos países sabe los nombres de los equipos más populares de los Estados Unidos y es común encontrar a jóvenes que usan camisetas[9] y gorras con los emblemas de equipos populares de fútbol americano.

El básquetbol

El básquetbol es otro de los deportes populares en el Caribe y en gran parte de las regiones hispanas. La televisión de los Estados Unidos tuvo mucha influencia en su introducción en las islas del Caribe.

Jugadores puertorriqueños de básquetbol

---

[3]Arawak Indians [4]heavy; [5]rubber; [6]waist; [7]ground; [8]in the whole world; [9]T-shirts.

2 Información adicional. In order to obtain additional information, read the selection again. Then, working in pairs, discuss these questions.

1. Describe la importancia en el Caribe de cada deporte mencionado en la lectura.
2. ¿Cuál es el deporte más popular en tu región? ¿Quiénes lo practican? ¿Cuál es tu equipo preferido?
3. ¿Cuál es el jugador más talentoso de este año en béisbol, fútbol o básquetbol? ¿Para qué equipo juega?
4. Compara tus preferencias deportivas con las de tus compañeros.

3 Deportes en mi vida. Write a paragraph about favorite sports in your school and your life. If you do not play sports, write about a friend or relative. Include answers to these questions.

1. ¿Qué deportes practican en tu universidad en las diferentes estaciones (en invierno, primavera, verano y otoño)? ¿Juegas tú en algún equipo de la escuela?
2. ¿Qué deportes prefieres como jugador/a o espectador/a? ¿Por qué?

4 Un partido de béisbol. You went to a baseball game during spring training and took this foto. Write a letter to a friend to describe your experience. Include the following information in your letter. Where did you go? What was the weather like? Who did you see play? What did you eat? Who won the game? What did you do after the game?

Escritura

Writing Strategy

Freewriting

One way to jump-start the writing process is to practice freewriting. This is a good way to see what ideas you may have about a subject before organizing your writing. The workshop provides some guidelines for generating ideas.

Online Study Center

For further writing practice online, visit the *Caminos* website at http://college .hmco.com/languages/ spanish/renjilian/caminos/ 3e/student_home.html.

Workshop

1. Choose a topic that you are going to write about in Spanish—one of your own or one that has been assigned. Write it at the top of the page.
2. You may either sit in front of the computer or write in longhand. Avoid the temptation you may have to correct errors while writing.
3. Write about the idea in Spanish for five to ten minutes without stopping. For now, don't correct grammar, spelling, accents, or punctuation.
4. If you do not know the conjugation of a verb, write the infinitive.
5. If you do not know the Spanish word, write the word in English so you don't lose your train of thought.
6. If you can't think of the next word, write the last word over and over again until you have an idea.
7. After you are finished, read over your writing. Underline or highlight the important ideas and organize them as part of your outline.
8. Now you can begin to write your composition using these ideas.

Strategy in Action

For additional practice with freewriting, complete the exercises below and in the *Escritura* section of your Student Activities Manual for *Unidad 6*.

1 El concierto ideal. You have been chosen to represent your school to organize a concert with two different artists or groups that represent your school population. Write a letter to the Dean of Students explaining who you want to invite and why.

2 Mi película favorita. Write a synopsis of your favorite movie of all time. Include the main characters, plot, and why you like the movie.

Resumen de vocabulario

PRIMER PASO

ENJOYING MUSIC AND DANCE

Sustantivos

el acordeón	accordion
los audífonos	headphones
el bailarín/la bailarina	dancer
la balada	ballad
la banda	band
la batería	drum set
los blues	blues
la canción	song
el/la cantante	singer
las castañuelas	castanets
el concierto	concert
el conjunto	group, band
el disco compacto, CD	compact disc, CD
el flamenco	Spanish-style music
la flauta	flute
el grupo	group
la guitarra	guitar
la guitarra bajo	bass guitar
el/la guitarrista	guitarrist
el hip-hop	hip-hop
el jazz	jazz
la letra	lyrics
el mariachi	mariachi musician
el merengue	Dominican-style music
el/la músico/a	musician
el parlante	speaker
la percusión	percussion
el/la pianista	pianist
el piano	piano
la ranchera	Mexican-style music
el ritmo	rhythm
el rock	rock
la salsa	salsa (music)
el saxofón	saxophone
el tambor	drum
el tango	tango
el reproductor MP3	MP3 player
la trompeta	trumpet
el violín	violin
la voz	voice

Verbos

bailar	to dance
cantar	to sing
grabar	to record, tape
interpretar	to interpret
jugar un papel	to play a role
tocar (un instrumento)	to play (an instrument)
volverse	to become

TALKING ABOUT SPORTS AND EXERCISE

Sustantivos

el/la aficionado/a, fanático/a	fan
los anteojos	swim goggles
el básquetbol/baloncesto	basketball
el bate	baseball bat
el béisbol	baseball
la bicicleta	bicycle
el boxeo	boxing
la caminata	walking
la cancha	court, field
el casco	helmet
la cesta	wicker basket
el ciclismo	biking
el deporte	sport
el/la deportista	athlete; sports enthusiast
el/la entrenador/a	trainer
el equipo	team; equipment
el/la espectador/a	spectator
el esquí	ski; skiing
el fútbol	soccer
el fútbol americano	football
la gimnasia	gymnastics
el gimnasio	gym
el golf	golf
el gorro de baño	swim cap
el guante	baseball glove
el hockey	hockey
el jai alai	jai alai
el/la jugador/a	player
la natación	swimming

el palo de golf	golf club	el uniforme	uniform
el palo de hockey	hockey stick	el vestido de baño	swimwear
el partido	game	los zapatos de tenis	tennis shoes, sneakers
el patinaje	skating		
los patines de ruedas	inline skates		

Verbos

los patines para hielo	ice skates
la pelota, el balón	ball
la pista	ice rink; running track
la raqueta	tennis racket
la ropa de gimnasia	gymwear
el tenis	tennis

entrenar	to train
esquiar	to ski
ganar	to win
jugar (ue) (al)	to play (a sport or game)
patear	to kick
perder (ie)	to lose
practicar	to practice

SEGUNDO PASO

DISCUSSING TELEVISION AND MOVIES

Sustantivos

el acontecimiento	event
el actor	actor
la actriz	actress
la actuación	acting
el argumento	plot
el billete, la entrada	ticket
la cartelera	listing
la categoría	category
el cine	movies; movie theater
la comedia	comedy
la crítica	criticism
el director	director
el drama	drama
la escena	scene
la fama	fame
el filme	film
el género	genre
el guión	script
el largometraje	feature film
la narración	narration
la nominación	nomination
la pantalla	screen
el papel	role
la película	movie
el personaje (principal, secundario)	(main, secondary) character
el/la protagonista	main character
la reseña	review
la secuencia	sequence
la sinopsis	synopsis

la taquilla	box office
la trama	plot

Verbos

actuar	to act
criticar	to criticize
dirigir	to direct
estrenar	to premiere
filmar	to film
hacer el papel	to play a role
juzgar	to judge
nominar	to nominate
presentar (pasar) una película	to show a movie
reseñar	to review
sentir (ie)	to be sorry, regret
suceder	to occur
tratar de	to deal with, treat

Adjetivos

ciencia ficción	science fiction
cómico/a	funny (adj.)
de acción	action (adj.)
de amor	love (adj.)
de ciencia ficción	science fiction (adj.)
de horror, de terror	horror (adj.)
de misterio	mystery (adj.)
de suspenso	thriller (adj.)
de vaqueros	western (adj.)
extranjero/a	foreign
romántico/a	romantic
taquillero/a	box office draw / hit

FLORIDA

Cayos

Islas Bahamas

La Habana

CUBA

Isla de Pinos

Guantánamo

JAMAICA

HAITÍ

La Española

Pico Duarte

Santo Domingo

REPÚBLICA DOMINICANA

San Juan

PUERTO RICO

Antillas Menores

OCÉANO ATLÁNTICO

Mar Caribe

| 0 | 150 | 300 Kilómetros |
| 0 | 150 | 300 Millas |

EL CARIBE

Online Study Center

To learn more about the people featured in this section, visit the *Caminos* website at http://college.hmco.com/languages/spanish/renjilian/caminos/3e/student_home.html.

PERSONALIDADES

Wilfredo Lam

Marc Anthony

José Alicea

Bebo Valdés

Juan Luis Guerra

Hay muchas personalidades importantes en las artes de las islas del Mar Caribe. Las influencias en muchas de sus creaciones de arte, música y literatura son de origen africano, indígena y europeo. Entre los artistas cubanos están Wilfredo Lam, pintor surrealista y Yamilys Brito, que incluye imágenes con palabras en algunas de sus obras artísticas. Entre los artistas importantes de Puerto Rico hay dos que crean carteles de acontecimientos en la isla: José Alicea y Lyzette Rosado. En la República Dominicana dos artistas famosos son Enriquillo Rodríguez y Clara Ledesma.

Muchos caribeños recibieron un Grammy Latino en 2005. De Puerto Rico ganaron Marc Anthony por el Mejor Álbum de Salsa; Elvis Crespo por el Mejor Álbum de Merengue y Mejor Álbum de Rock Vocal; y Obie Bermúdez, por el Mejor Vocal Pop Masculino. También el dominicano Juan Luis Guerra ganó en dos categorías: el Mejor Álbum Cristiano en español y la Mejor Canción Tropical del año. Entre los cubanos, Bebo Valdés ganó por el Mejor Álbum de Jazz Latino; Israel "Cachao" López por el Mejor Álbum Tropical Tradicional y la cantante Lila Downs, que nació en Cuba, recibió el Grammy Latino por el Mejor Álbum Folklórico de 2005.

Hay muchos escritores caribeños de importancia en las épocas recientes. La puertorriqueña Esmeralda Santiago, la dominicana Julia Álvarez y la cubana Cristina García son tres novelistas que viven en Estados Unidos y escriben sobre la condición humana de los caribeños. Visita el sitio web de *Caminos* para leer más en español sobre estas personalidades y otros caribeños influyentes.

Obie Bermúdez

Lila Downs

Israel "Cachao" López

Esmeralda Santiago

Elvis Crespo

Comprensión

Trabajando en parejas, háganse las preguntas.

1. ¿Qué influencias hay sobre el arte, la música y la literatura del Caribe? ¿Conoces alguna obra de los artistas mencionados?
2. ¿En qué categorías ganaron los cantantes los Grammy Latinos? ¿Cuál prefieres escuchar tú? ¿Por qué?

ARTE

AIMÉE GARCÍA

Aimée García es una artista cubana que nació en 1972 en la ciudad de Matanzas. Su arte apareció en muchas exhibiciones en Cuba, México, Corea del Sur y Estados Unidos. En el año 1999 pintó *La guía*°, pintura que es una combinación de óleo en lienzo°, con hilo° y madera°.

ide

La guía

oil on canvas
string / wood

Comprensión

Trabajando en parejas, estudien esta pintura y contesten las preguntas.

1. La artista está pintando una escena con árboles°. ¿Qué colores usa para pintar la escena? En tu opinión, ¿qué hora del día es? *trees*
2. Describe a la artista en la pintura. ¿De qué color es su vestido? ¿Cuántos años crees que tiene ella? ¿Cuántos años tiene la artista Aimée García?
3. ¿Qué función tiene la jirafa°? ¿Hay otro animal posible? *giraffe*
4. ¿De qué colores es la jirafa? En tu opinión, ¿qué efecto produce en la pintura? ¿cómico? ¿absurdo? ¿interesante? ¿...? ¿Por qué?
5. ¿Qué relación hay entre la fotografía de la artista y la artista en la pintura? ¿Son dos mujeres diferentes o es la misma persona?
6. ¿Te gusta o no te gusta esta pintura? ¿Por qué?

MÚSICA

OLGA TAÑÓN

La artista musical, Olga Tañón, es puertorriqueña. Ganó
un Grammy Latino de la Mejor Interpretación Vocal
Femenina de 2003 por su álbum, "Sobrevivir°". Ella canta
diversos estilos musicales como merengue y balada pop.
Tañón incluye en su nuevo álbum, "A puro fuego°", sus
discos más celebrados de los diez años pasados de su
carrera.

Survive

Pure Fire

Comprensión

Trabajen en parejas para contestar las preguntas.

1. ¿De dónde es Olga Tañón?
2. Según la lectura, ¿qué tipo de música canta? ¿Qué premio ganó?
3. ¿Cómo se llaman dos de sus álbumes musicales? ¿Qué emociones despiertan los títulos?
4. ¿A qué otro/a cantante hispánico/a conoces? ¿De dónde es? ¿Qué canta?

LITERATURA

NORBERTO JAMES RAWLINGS

El autor Norberto James Rawlings nació en la República Dominicana
en 1945. Este poeta dominicano es también profesor de español.
Se graduó de la Universidad de La Habana y, en 1992, recibió su
doctorado en lengua y literatura hispánica de Boston University.
Los poemas aquí son de su nuevo libro, *La urdimbre del silencio*
(*The Weaving of Silence*), que se publicó en 2000 en La República
Dominicana.

"...tengo el gusto de andar por mi país,
dueño de cuanto hay en él".

—Nicolás Guillén (Cuba), "Tengo"

"Estatuas"

Las estatuas
mueren también,
si nadie las mira.

Comprensión

En parejas, contesten las preguntas.

1. ¿Es el poema sobre las personas, los lugares o las cosas?
2. En la opinión del poeta, ¿cuándo mueren las estatuas?
3. El poeta indica que las estatuas son como personas. ¿Qué opinas tú?
4. Describe una estatua famosa de tu región: ¿De qué color es? ¿Dónde está? ¿Es grande o pequeña? ¿De qué o de quién es? ¿Por qué es importante? ¿Por qué (no) te gusta?

"Apuntes° para el poema"

Hice apuntes
para escribir un poema a la primavera,
y de tanto (re)escribirlo,
sólo quedó de las flores,
el recuerdo° de su aroma,
y mi asombro° ante tanto verdor°.

Notes

memory
amazement / greenness

Comprensión

Trabajando en parejas, contesten las preguntas.

1. Antes de crear el poema, ¿qué escribió el poeta?
2. ¿A qué estación del año le escribió el poema?
3. ¿Qué quedó de las flores que el poeta puso en el poema?
4. Al final del poema, ¿qué color asocia el poeta con la primavera?
5. ¿De qué color es tu flor favorita? ¿Tiene un aroma delicado o fuerte?
6. ¿Te gustan más las flores de la primavera o del verano? En tu región, ¿hay flores también en el otoño o en el invierno?

7

De compras

VOCABULARIO Y LENGUA

- ▶ Talking about stores and shopping
- ▶ Shopping for clothes
- ▶ Contrasting the preterite and the imperfect: Verbs with different meanings in the preterite: **Conocer, poder, querer, saber**

- ▶ Bargaining in a marketplace
- ▶ Asking for and giving directions
- ▶ Making comparisons; Superlatives; Possessive pronouns

CAMINOS DEL JAGUAR

- ▶ Ganas de vivir
- ▶ Magia en Mitad del Mundo

LECTURA

- ▶ Soy Rumiaya, el alma de la roca

NOTAS CULTURALES

- ▶ Quito, Ecuador
- ▶ El nombre del Ecuador

ESTRATEGIAS

- ▶ **Reading:** Tapping background knowledge
- ▶ **Writing:** Paraphrasing

...fael González y González, *Mercadito*

Preguntas del tema

▶ ¿Te gusta ir de compras? ¿Por qué?

▶ ¿Cuál es tu tienda favorita? ¿Qué venden?

▶ ¿Qué ropa prefieres llevar a las fiestas? ¿y a las clases?

▶ ¿Qué regalos compras para tus amigos?

Vocabulario y lengua

TALKING ABOUT STORES AND SHOPPING

En el centro comercial *(At the shopping center)*

En el almacén Márquez

Store clerk	**Dependiente**°	Buenos días señor, ¿en qué le puedo servir?
customer	Sebastián (**Cliente**°)	Es el cumpleaños de mi novia Raquel, y necesito un regalo especial para ella. ¿Tiene Ud. alguna sugerencia?
Of course!	Dependiente	**¡Claro que sí!**° Tenemos muchas cosas bonitas... joyas, perfumes, ropa.
shop window / size	Sebastián	Vi unos suéteres en el escaparate°, pero no sé su **talla**°.
	Dependiente	¿Quizás un reloj o un perfume?
	Sebastián	¿Cuánto cuestan los relojes?
[1]**nuevo sol** = currency in Perú	Dependiente	Tenemos una selección amplia desde 475 nuevos soles[1].
to spend	Sebastián	Uf, realmente no puedo **gastar**° tanto. ¿Tiene algo **a un**
at a lower price		**precio más bajo**°?
display case	Dependiente	Pues, aquí en el **mostrador**° tenemos perfumes finos desde 167 nuevos soles.
on sale	Sebastián	¿Hay alguna fragancia **en oferta**°?
	Dependiente	Bueno, en oferta tenemos la fragancia "Pasión". Si la compra,
free		Ud. recibe una bufanda **gratis**°.
deal / I'll take it!	Sebastián	¡Qué **ganga**°! **¡Me la llevo!**°
register / receipt	Dependiente	Bueno, puede pagar en la **caja**°. Aquí tiene el **recibo**° si la
to return		quiere **devolver**°.
	Sebastián	Gracias.

Many store names are formed by adding **-ería** to the type of products they sell or services they provide. Others, such as music or department stores, tend to have individual brand names. Note that the word farmacia does not have an accent on the "i". The stress falls on the syllable **"ma"**.

Online Study Center

For additional practice with this unit's vocabulary and grammar, visit the *Caminos* website at http://college.hmco.com/languages/spanish/renjilian/caminos/3e/student_home.html. You can also review audio flashcards, quiz yourself, and explore related Spanish-language sites.

Actividades

1 ¿Dónde se compra? ¿En qué tipo de tienda puedes comprar estos artículos?

1. aspirina
2. unos guantes
3. una fragancia Armani
4. maquillaje *(makeup)*
5. una novela de amor
6. un cuaderno
7. unas rosas
8. un reloj
9. una raqueta de tenis

2 Quiero devolver el perfume. Raquel decide devolver el perfume que le compró su novio, Sebastián, porque no le gustó la fragancia. Escucha su conversación con el dependiente del almacén y completa las frases.

1. Raquel habló con...
   a. Sebastián.
   b. el dependiente.
   c. Patricia.

2. Raquel no tenía el recibo porque...
   a. lo perdió.
   b. el perfume fue un regalo.
   c. compró el perfume en otra tienda.

3. El dependiente le podía ofrecer...
   a. el dinero.
   b. otra fragancia.
   c. crédito.

4. El dependiente le dijo a Raquel que...
   a. el perfume estaba en oferta.
   b. el perfume era caro.
   c. el perfume era verde y azul.

5. El perfume incluía...
   a. un pastel de cumpleaños.
   b. una bufanda verde y azul.
   c. una bufanda azul y roja.

6. La mujer en la joyería...
   a. compraba un reloj.
   b. compraba perfume.
   c. llevaba una bufanda.

7. Raquel estaba sorprendida porque...
   a. la mujer con la bufanda era su amiga.
   b. no le gustaba la bufanda.
   c. la bufanda era bonita.

3 En la tienda. Estás en una tienda comprando algo para tus vacaciones. Completa la conversación entre el/la cliente y el/la dependiente. Trabajen en parejas. parejas.

Dependiente Buenas tardes. ¿ _____ servir?
Cliente Buenas tardes. Voy de vacaciones este fin de semana y necesito _____ .
Dependiente ¿Adónde va?
Cliente _____ .
Dependiente ¡Ah, qué bien, es un lugar maravilloso y además lo que *(what)* Ud. busca está en _____ !
Cliente ¡Qué suerte! También necesito _____ porque allí hace mucho sol.

Dependiente	Pues tenemos una gran variedad. Hay en todos los colores.
Cliente	¿Dónde están?
Dependiente	Aquí en el _____.
Cliente	¿ _____?
Dependiente	Sí, lo tenemos en rojo.
Cliente	¿ _____?
Dependiente	Todo le cuesta $25. Puede Ud. pagar en la _____.
Cliente	Gracias.

4 **El triángulo amoroso.** Raquel decide hablar con Sebastián y Patricia para decirles lo que pasó cuando ella fue a la tienda para devolver el perfume. Inventa su conversación. Trabajen en grupos de tres.

SHOPPING FOR CLOTHES

Comprando ropa *(Buying clothes)*

1. la chaqueta
2. el traje
3. la camisa
4. la ropa interior
5. los pantalones
6. el abrigo
7. el impermeable
8. el saco
9. el vestido
10. la blusa
11. la falda
12. las botas
13. los zapatos
14. los calcetines
15. las medias
16. el cinturón
17. la bolsa
18. los guantes
19. el sombrero
20. la gorra
21. la bufanda
22. la corbata

de puntos

de rayas

de cuadros

La ropa del golfista
le queda floja/grande.
(fits him loosely)

de manga larga   de manga corta

de tacón alto   de tenis

La ropa de la muchacha
le queda estrecha/pequeña.
(fits her tightly)

La ropa del golfista **le queda floja / grande.**
(is loose / big)

La ropa de la muchacha **le queda estrecha / pequeña.** *(is tight / small)*

Más palabras y expresiones

Sustantivos

el algodón	*cotton*
la camiseta	*T-shirt*
la lana	*wool*
la mancha	*stain*
el par	*pair*
el paraguas	*umbrella*
la ropa interior	*underwear*
la seda	*silk*
la sudadera	*sweatsuit, sweatshirt*
el suéter	*sweater*

Verbos

(des)atar	*to (un)tie*
estar / de moda	*in style*
estar	*to be in style*
estar roto/a, sucio/a, manchado/a	*to be ripped, dirty, stained*
ir de compras	*to go shopping*
llevar	*to wear*
probarse (ue)	*to try on*
quedarle (a alguien)	*to fit (someone)*

Actividades

1 **¿Qué piensas comprar?** ¿Qué ropa piensas comprar para estas ocasiones? Haz una lista para cada ocasión y compárala con la lista de un/a compañero/a.

1. asistir a un partido de fútbol americano
2. ir a una discoteca nueva
3. ir a la fiesta de cumpleaños de tu novio/a
4. presentarte a tu primera entrevista *(interview)* de trabajo
5. ir a la playa
6. ir a esquiar
7. asistir a una boda muy elegante
8. ir a la clase de español

2 **¿Qué está de moda?** Describe lo que llevan estas personas.

3 **¿Qué lleva?** Trae una foto de un/a amigo/a o de una persona famosa a la clase y describe lo que lleva.

4 **Entre nosotros.** Trabaja con un/a compañero/a para crear un diálogo entre un/a dependiente de una tienda de ropa y un/a cliente que llega a última hora.

Cliente	Dependiente
Hoy estuviste de compras en una tienda de ropa. Cuando llegas a casa, te das cuenta de que la ropa que compraste tiene una mancha y no la puedes usar en la fiesta de esta noche. Decides regresar a la tienda para devolverla y comprar algo diferente. Estás de muy mal humor y tienes mucha prisa porque ya es bastante tarde. ¿Qué haces?	Trabajas en una tienda de ropa pequeña. Estás muy cansado/a porque hoy fue un día muy largo. Faltan quince minutos para cerrar y de repente llega un/a cliente para cambiar ropa que está manchada. Tu jefe/a se llevó las llaves de la caja y no puedes abrirla para atender al /a la cliente. Soluciona el dilema.

CONTRASTING THE PRETERITE AND THE IMPERFECT

Preterite or imperfect?

In narration, the imperfect establishes the context of the story by describing the background of what happened, the physical and mental states of the speakers or characters, what things looked like, and how they used to be. In contrast, the preterite moves the story forward in time by providing an account of what happened at a specific moment in time: what people said or did, and what events took place. Review what you have learned about these forms in *Unidades 4, 5,* and *6* before you read the following summary of their uses.

The preterite is used . . .	The imperfect is used . . .
► To indicate a completed action in the past.	► To set up a continuous background or a scenario in which events or actions occur in the past. This includes telling time, indicating age, and describing weather in the past.

Ayer **fui** a la tienda.

Yesterday I went to the store.

Eran las siete de la mañana. **Hacía** sol y no **llovía.**

It was seven o'clock A.M. It was sunny and it wasn't raining.

► To indicate a series of completed actions in the past.

► To describe mental, emotional, or physical states or conditions in the past.

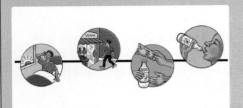

Esta mañana **me desperté, fui** a la tienda, **compré** un refresco y lo **bebí.**

This morning I woke up, went to the store, bought a soft drink and drank it.

Yo **pensaba** que mis llaves **estaban** en la mesita de noche.

I thought that my keys were on the nightstand.

► To indicate the beginning of an action or a condition.

► To describe actions and events that were in progress in the past without emphasis on when they started or ended.

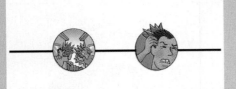

A las seis de la mañana, mis vecinos **empezaron** a gritar y me **dio** dolor de cabeza.

At 6 A.M. my neighbors started to yell and it gave me a headache.

Corría rápidamente en el parque.

I was running very fast in the park.

(continued)

► To indicate the ending of an action or condition.

La fiesta **terminó** a las *2 A.M.*
The party ended at 2 A.M.

► To describe repetitive or habitual past actions—what one used to do.

Almorzábamos juntas todos los sábados.
We used to eat lunch together every Saturday.

► To sum up a past action, condition, or opinion.

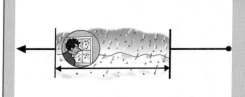

Nevó todo el día ayer. **Fue** un día horrible. No me **gustó** estar en casa.
It snowed all day yesterday. It was a horrible day. I didn't like staying at home.

► With **ir a** + *infinitive* to anticipate "what was going to (would) happen."

Iba a viajar a Teotihuacán pero tuve que trabajar.
I was going to travel to Teotihuacán but I had to work.

Using the preterite and the imperfect together

When you are talking about the past in Spanish, the imperfect and the preterite often appear together. The combination of these two tenses adds interest and suspense to the narration.

1. Background / scenario
The imperfect describes the scene or provides background information while the preterite narrates the events that happened at that moment.

Estaba lloviendo cuando **salimos** del cine.
It was raining when we left the movie theater.

2. Interrupted actions

In this case, the ongoing action doesn't continue because it is interrupted by what happens.

Lorenzo **miraba** sus telenovelas cuando el teléfono **sonó.**

Lorenzo was watching his soap operas when the phone rang.

3. Retelling: Indirect speech

Use the preterite to introduce indirect speech. The imperfect is used when retelling what someone said, thought, believed, wanted to do, or knew.

Lo siento, pero no te quiero.

Adelaida le **dijo** a Lorenzo que no lo **quería.**

Adelaida told Lorenzo that she didn't love him.

Verbs with different meanings in the preterite:
Conocer, poder, querer, saber

Some Spanish verbs have different English translations when used in the preterite. The meaning of these verbs in the imperfect remains consistent with their meaning in the present and infinitive forms. Below is a list of these verbs:

Infinitive	Preterite	Imperfect
conocer	*met a person or visited a place for the first time*	*knew, was familiar with, used to know*
poder	*managed (to do something)*	*was able to, was allowed to, could*
no poder	*was not able to do it (and didn't do it), didn't manage (to do something)*	*was not able to do it, could not do it (unknown outcome)*
querer	*intended to; wanted to but didn't do it*	*wanted to (unknown outcome)*
no querer	*refused (to do something)*	*didn't want to, wasn't feeling up to it (unknown outcome)*
saber	*found out; realized*	*used to know, knew (information)*

Conocí a Pablo en la fiesta.	*I met Pablo at the party.*
Conocimos París en la primavera.	*We visited Paris in the spring. (for the first time)*
Pude terminar la novela.	*I managed to finish the novel.*
No **pudieron** venir a la fiesta.	*They weren't able to come to the party. (and didn't)*
Quise llamarte, pero mi teléfono no funcionó.	*I intended to call you, but my phone didn't work.*
Supe la verdad ayer.	*I found out the truth yesterday.*

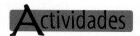

Actividades

👥 **1** **¡De perezoso a heroico! El dramático día de Diego.** Lee este cuento en voz alta *(aloud)* y haz las actividades.

1. Identifica las formas del pretérito y del imperfecto.
2. En parejas, identifiquen el uso de los verbos según la lista de arriba.
3. Inventen y contesten preguntas en el pasado sobre la historia de Diego. Pongan atención al uso del pretérito y del imperfecto.

Era muy tarde.

Perdí el tren.

El jefe no tenía ningún interés.

Vimos a dos personas que salían del almacén.

Me llamo Diego y trabajo en el Almacén Rodríguez de las cuatro de la tarde hasta las once de la noche. El jueves pasado fue un día horrible. Era muy tarde cuando me desperté, entonces salí corriendo de casa y se me olvidó el horario del tren. Por supuesto, perdí el tren de las tres y diez de la tarde y tuve que tomar el siguiente tren, una hora después. Cuando hablé con el jefe, se puso furioso porque llegué tarde. Traté de explicarle mi problema, pero él no tenía ningún interés en escuchar mis excusas. Me dijo que yo era un irresponsable; me criticó por ser perezoso y me hizo sentir muy mal.

Mi amiga Julia trabaja en el departamento de computadoras de la misma tienda, y yo soy dependiente en el departamento de música. Ese jueves por la tarde estuve muy ocupado con muchos clientes, y vendí bastantes artículos caros. Luego, a las nueve, Julia y yo salimos a cenar. Fuimos a nuestro restaurante ecuatoriano favorito. Comimos en una hora porque teníamos que regresar al trabajo.

Cuando regresamos al almacén, no había ni una estrella en el cielo. Eran las diez de la noche y todo estaba oscuro. Al acercarnos, vimos a dos personas que salían del almacén cargando máquinas pequeñas: eran una mujer alta, rubia, bien vestida y un hombre grande, de pelo oscuro y también muy elegante. A pesar de *(Despite)* las apariencias, yo estaba seguro de que eran dos ladrones *(thieves)*. De inmediato corrí hacia ellos y Julia llamó a los detectives de la tienda. Los guardias llegaron junto con la policía y se llevaron a los ladrones. ¡Fue un día muy dramático!

2 **¿Pretérito o imperfecto?** Completa las oraciones con el pretérito o imperfecto según el contexto.

1. Cuando Delmira _____ (tener) diez años, todas las noches _____ (escuchar) los cuentos *(stories)* de su abuela.

2. Los jóvenes del conjunto Maná _____ (tocar) continuamente. Ellos _____ (ir) a ser ricos y famosos algún día. Y en efecto, en los años 80 y 90 el grupo _____ (vender) millones de discos.

3. Hoy yo _____ (levantarse), _____ (hacer) la cama, _____ (lavar) la ropa y _____ (pasar) la aspiradora por la alfombra. _____ (Ser) una mañana muy productiva.

4. La noche _____ (estar) muy oscura cuando un hombre misterioso _____ (salir) a la calle.

3 Un viaje por El Caribe. Olga y Rubén hicieron un viaje por el Caribe. Completa la historia de su viaje con los verbos **conocer, querer, poder,** y **saber** en el pretérito o el imperfecto, según el contexto.

En junio Olga y Rubén hicieron un viaje por el Caribe. Fueron a la República Dominicana porque ellos _____ (**1.** querer) conocerla. En este viaje Olga y Rubén _____ (**2.** conocer) Santo Domingo y otras ciudades dominicanas. Ellos no _____ (**3.** poder) ir a Puerto Rico porque Rubén no _____ (**4.** querer = *refused*); él prefirió ir a Cuba, el país de sus antepasados (*ancestors*). Cuando llegaron a Cuba, Olga _____ (**5.** saber) que los bisabuelos de Rubén eran de Aragón, España. Esto le pareció interesantísimo y ella _____ (**6.** querer) saber más sobre la familia de Rubén. Una señora cubana que _____ (**7.** saber) mucho sobre genealogía la ayudó. De esta manera, ellos _____ (**8.** saber) que un bisabuelo de Rubén ¡era puertorriqueño! Por esta razón van a buscar sus raíces (*roots*) en la isla de Puerto Rico el año que viene.

4 Fractura. Completa el cuento del accidente de Yolanda con la forma correcta del pretérito o imperfecto.

Siempre _____ (**1.** hacer) deportes cuando _____ (**2.** ser) joven. A veces me _____ (**3.** gustar) mucho patinar en línea (*to rollerblade*). Una vez, cuando yo _____ (**4.** tener) quince años, patinaba con unos amigos, y de pronto, yo _____ (**5.** caerse). Ellos me _____ (**6.** llevar) al hospital. Mientras yo _____ (**7.** estar) en mi cama con mucho dolor, _____ (**8.** llegar) el médico y me _____ (**9.** decir): "Tú no _____ (**10.** llevar) casco cuando tú _____ (**11.** caerse), ¿verdad?" Yo le _____ (**12.** preguntar) al doctor: "¿Cómo sabe usted que yo no _____ (**13.** llevar) el casco?" Y el doctor _____ (**14.** contestar), "No es difícil saberlo. ¡Me lo _____ (**15.** decir) la fractura que tienes en la cabeza (*head*)!"

5 Yolanda. Iris y Lilia hablan de lo que le ocurrió a Yolanda. Crea su conversación usando el pretérito e imperfecto. Palabras y frases útiles: patinar *(to skate, rollerblade)*, (no) aceptar, (no) ponerse el casco, chocarse contra un poste *(to crash into a post)*, tener un accidente, terminar en el hospital *(to end up in the hospital)*.

Ganas de vivir

Actividades

Online Study Center

For additional practice with this episode, visit the *Caminos* website at http://college.hmco.com/languages/spanish/renjilian/caminos/3e/student_home.html.

1 **Comprensión.** Basándote en este episodio de *Caminos del jaguar,* elige la alternativa lógica.

1. Don Gustavo...
   a. no sabe lo que pasó en Puerto Rico.
   b. sabe lo que pasó en Puerto Rico.

2. Felipe dice que...
   a. estaban disfrutando de Puerto Rico.
   b. estaban estudiando en Puerto Rico.

3. Felipe quedó libre porque...
   a. se desató los pies.
   b. Adriana le desató los pies.

4. Felipe movió la cubeta...
   a. con las manos.
   b. con los pies.

5. ¿Quién tenía mucho miedo?
   a. Adriana y Felipe
   b. Gafasnegras

6. Para poder escapar, Adriana y Felipe...
   a. quebraron la computadora.
   b. quebraron la ventana.

7. Gafasnegras se sorprende porque...
   a. Miguel vio a Adriana y Felipe.
   b. Adriana y Felipe están vivos.

8. El jaguar Hun-Ahau está en...
   a. la casa de Nayeli.
   b. la casa de doña Carmen.

9. El paquete con el jaguar llegó a...
   a. Puerto Rico.
   b. Ecuador

2 **Situaciones.** Dramaticen una de las siguientes situaciones.

1. La conversación de don Gustavo y Adriana sobre lo que pasó en Puerto Rico.
2. La conversación entre Gafasnegras y Miguel.

3 **Escritura.** Escribe un resumen de lo que hacen Adriana y Felipe en Mitad del Mundo. (4–6 frases)

NOTA CULTURAL

Quito, Ecuador

Entre las capitales latinoamericanas, Quito —a 2.640 metros de altura— es la segunda en altura después de La Paz, Bolivia. Su población, de más de un millón de habitantes, comparte las herencias inca y española. La capital está al pie del volcán Pichincha. El centro antiguo de la ciudad conserva su arquitectura colonial: calles estrechas y empinadas (*steep*), casas blancas y hermosas iglesias con altares de oro. Al norte se encuentra el Quito moderno: anchas avenidas, parques y contemporáneos edificios y casas.

SEGUNDO PASO

Vocabulario y lengua

BARGAINING IN A MARKETPLACE

Los mercados y el arte del regateo

bargaining
handicrafts
to bargain

El **regateo°** es el arte de negociar un precio más bajo. En los mercados de **artesanías°** y en las tiendas pequeñas de España y América Latina, todavía es usual **regatear°** por el precio. En los mercados de las ciudades pequeñas, como Otavalo, al norte de Quito, los

street vendors
jewelry / weavings

vendedores ambulantes° ofrecen **joyas°**, ropa, **tejidos°** y artesanías, y los

buyers
discount

compradores° tienen la costumbre de pedir **rebaja°** en el precio.

Online Study Center

For additional practice with the unit's vocabulary and grammar, visit the *Caminos* website at http://college.hmco.com/languages/spanish/renjilian/caminos/3e/student_home.html. You can also review audio flashcards, quiz yourself, and explore related Spanish-language sites.

Cómo regatear

Para regatear en español como un experto, sigue los pasos y usa las expresiones que se detallan abajo.

1. Pide el precio: **¿Cuánto cuesta/n?, ¿En cuánto me lo(s) / la(s) deja?, ¿Qué precio tiene/n...?**
2. Reacciona: **¿20 pesos? ¿Tanto?** *(That much?)* **(¿Tan caro?)** *(That expensive?)*
3. Ofrece un precio más bajo u otra estrategia para conseguir una rebaja en el precio:

Es muy caro/a.	**¿Qué tal _____ pesos?**
Son muy caros/as.	**¿Me puede dar un descuento**
No voy a pagar tanto.	**(discount)?**
No me alcanza el dinero.	**¿Son más baratos/as si compro dos?**
Le puedo dar _____ pesos.	

4. Si el vendedor no te ofrece un precio más bajo, repite los pasos anteriores para negociar un precio promedio *(average)*.
5. Si el vendedor no quiere ofrecer una rebaja, indica que vas a buscar en otro lugar: **Bueno, voy a ver si no lo/la compro por menos en otro lado** *(somewhere else)*.
6. Si se ponen de acuerdo en *(you both agree on)* un precio, haz la compra y no te olvides de darle las gracias al vendedor: **Muchas gracias. Lo agradezco.**

Estas son algunas de las cosas que venden en los mercados.

Joyas

un anillo de esmeralda

un collar de plata con un pendiente de turquesa

una pulsera de cobre

unos aretes de piedra

un prendedor de oro

Artesanías

un tapete de lana

un plato de Talavera

un recipiente de barro

un tapiz de algodón

un juguete de madera

una máscara de jaguar

Actividades

1 Un regateo. Escucha la conversación de un regateo entre una turista y un vendedor en un mercado hispano y contesta las preguntas.

1. ¿Qué busca la turista? ¿Para quién?
2. ¿Cuánto cuestan las joyas originalmente?
3. ¿Cuánto dinero ofrece la turista después?
4. ¿Cómo contesta el vendedor?
5. ¿Qué decide hacer la turista?
6. ¿Cómo responde el vendedor?
7. ¿Cuál es el último precio que paga la turista?
8. ¿Cuánto dinero ahorra en el regateo? ¿Fue una ganga?

2 Comprando regalos. Estás de vacaciones y tienes que comprar regalos para las personas de la lista. Describe los regalos que les vas a comprar y por qué.

1. tu hermano/a
2. tu mejor amigo
3. tu mejor amiga
4. tu novio/a

5. tu madre
6. tu padre
7. una prima de quince años
8. un niño de diez años

3 El regateo. Estás en el mercado comprando regalos, pero todos los vendedores te dan precios diferentes. Crea una conversación con un/a vendedor/a. Tú regateas para obtener el mejor precio. Trabajen en parejas.

ASKING FOR AND GIVING DIRECTIONS

¿Dónde está?

Perdone la molestia, pero ¿nos puede decir dónde está el museo?

Sí, señores, sigan derecho por tres cuadras, pasen por la catedral y doblen a la izquierda. El museo está a tres cuadras a la derecha.

Más palabras y expresiones

Sustantivos

la cuadra	*street block*
la esquina	*corner*
la intersección	*intersection*
el semáforo	*traffic light*

Verbos

acelerar	*to accelerate*	parar	*to stop*
bajar (por)	*to go (down) (a street)*	pasar (por)	*to pass (by)*
cruzar	*to cross*	seguir derecho, recto	*to go straight*
dar la vuelta	*to turn around*	subir (por)	*to go up (a street)*
doblar (a)	*to turn*	tener cuidado	*to be careful*
estacionar	*to park*		

continued

Otras expresiones

a la (mano) derecha / izquierda	*on the right / left(hand) side*
¿Cómo se llega a...?	*How does one get to . . . ?*
despacio	*slowly*
hasta	*until*
¿Me puede decir dónde está/n...?	*Can you tell me where . . . is / are?*
medio/a *(adj.)*	*half*

Note: Be sure to review formal commands in *Unidad 6,* pages 224–225, so that you can use the appropriate forms for giving directions.

Actividades

1 ¿Dónde están ustedes? Tú y tu amigo están de vacaciones y piden instrucciones de cómo se llega de un lugar al otro. Mientras escuchas las instrucciones, sigue el mapa para determinar hasta dónde llegan Uds.

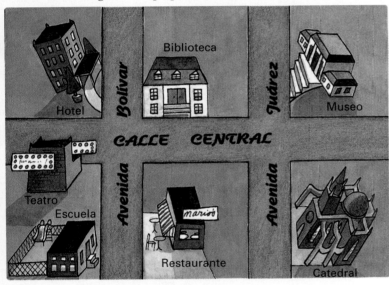

¿Dónde están Uds.?

1. _____   3. _____

2. _____   4. _____

2 ¿Cómo se llega a...?

En parejas, practiquen las instrucciones sobre cómo llegar a los lugares ilustrados en el mapa de la actividad anterior. Mientras una persona da instrucciones, la otra las sigue en el mapa. Usen mandatos formales (**Ud.**).

¿Cómo se llega...

1. del museo al teatro?
2. del hotel al restaurante?
3. de la catedral al hotel?

4. de la escuela a la catedral?
5. de la biblioteca al museo?

3 ¿Dónde está?

Una persona importante visita tu universidad y necesita saber cómo llegar a estos lugares desde la clase de español. Trabajen en parejas y usen mandatos formales (**Ud.**).

1. la cafetería
2. el edificio de la administración
3. el gimnasio
4. la biblioteca
5. la librería
6. la Facultad de Ciencias Naturales
7. la Facultad de Artes
8. la cancha de fútbol americano
9. el centro estudiantil

MAKING COMPARISONS

Making unequal comparisons

Spanish uses the following structures to compare adjectives *(age, size, appearance, and other characteristics of people and things)*, adverbs *(how people do things)*, and nouns *(people and things themselves)* that are different, and verbs *(things that people do)*.

Comparing adjectives

más *(more)* / **menos** *(less)* +
(adjective) + **que** *(than)*

El edificio es **más** alto **que** la casa.
The building is taller than the house.
La casa es **menos** alta **que** el edificio.
The house is less tall than the building.

Comparing adverbs

más (*more*) / **menos** (*less*) +
(adverb) + **que** (*than*)

El auto rojo va **más** rápido **que** el auto azul.
The red car goes faster than the blue car.
El auto azul va **menos** rápido **que** el auto rojo.
The blue car goes slower than the red car.

Comparing nouns

más (*more*) / **menos** (*less*) +
(noun) + **que** (*than*)

El muchacho tiene **más** dinero **que** la muchacha.
The boy has more money than the girl.
La muchacha tiene **menos** dinero **que** el muchacho.
The girl has less money than the boy.

Comparing verbs

verb + **más** / **menos** + **que**

Yo trabajo **más que** mi compañera.
I work more than my roommate.
Mi compañera trabaja **menos que** yo.
My roommate works less than I do.

When comparing people using pronouns, use the subject pronouns.

Tú sabes muchas **más**
   cosas **que yo.**
Ellos tienen **menos** dinero
   que nosotros.

You know a lot more
   things than I do.
They have less money than
   we do.

When a number is mentioned in the comparison, the equivalent of *than* is **de:**
más / menos + de + *number.*

Hay **más de tres** kilómetros
   hasta el centro.
La cena me costó **menos de**
   diez dólares.

It's more than three
   kilometers to downtown.
Dinner cost me less than ten
   dollars.

Some comparisons have an irregular form:

Adjective		Irregular comparative form	
bueno/a buenos/as	*good*	mejor/es	*better*
malo/a malos/as	*bad*	peor/es	*worse*
joven / jóvenes	*young*	menor/es	*younger*
viejo/a viejos/as	*old*	mayor/es	*older*

Adverb		Irregular comparative form	
bien	*well*	mejor	*better*
mal	*bad, ill*	peor	*worse*
mucho	*a lot*	más	*more*
poco	*a little*	menos	*less*

Superlatives

To form the superlative, English adds *-est* to the adjective *(the cleanest, the newest)* or uses expressions such as *the most* or *the least* with the adjective *(the most convenient, the least expensive)*. In Spanish, superlatives are formed as follows:

Superlatives

el / la / los / las (+ noun) + **más /menos** + adjective (+ **de**...)

el / la / los / las + **mejor(es) / peor(es)** (+ noun) (+ **de**...)

el / la / los / las (+ noun) + **mayor(es) / menor(es)** (+ **de**...)

Antonio Banderas es **el actor más famoso de** España.	*Antonio Banderas is the most famous actor of Spain.*
Ellas son **las más elegantes del** grupo.	*They are the most elegant of the group.*
¿Cuál es **la mejor película de** este año?	*Which is the best movie of the year?*
Ésta es **la peor hora del** día.	*This is the worst time of the day.*
Yo soy **la hermana mayor de** todos.	*I am the oldest sister of all the siblings.*

The superlative uses the preposition **de** to express *in* or *of.* Note that the irregular forms **mejor/es** and **peor/es** usually appear before the noun while **mayor/es** and **menor/es** usually appear after the noun.

Comparisons of equality

Spanish uses the following structures to compare adjectives *(age, size, appearance, and other characteristics of people and things)*, adverbs *(how people do things)*, nouns *(people and things themselves)*, and verbs *(actions)* that are the same.

Comparing adjectives and adverbs

tan + adjective / adverb + **como** = *as* + adjective / adverb + *as*

El muchacho es **tan alto como** la muchacha.
The boy is as tall as the girl.
La muchacha es **tan alta como** el muchacho.
The girl is as tall as the boy.

Comparing nouns

tanto/a/os/as + noun + **como** = *as much / many* + noun + *as*

La niña tiene **tantos juguetes como** el niño.
The girl has as many toys as the boy.
El niño tiene **tantos juguetes como** la niña.
The boy has as many toys as the girl.

Comparing verbs

verb + **tanto como** = *as much as*

La alumna canta **tanto como** el alumno.
The (female) student sings as much as the (male) student.
El alumno canta **tanto como** la alumna.
The (male) student sings as much as the (female) student.

Possessive pronouns

When making comparisons, it is common to avoid redundancy by using possessive pronouns.

el/la	mío/a	*mine*
los/las	míos/as	
el/la	tuyo/a	*yours*
los/las	tuyos/as	
el/la	suyo/a	*yours, his, hers*
los/las	suyos/as	
el/la	nuestro/a	*ours*
los/las	nuestros/as	
el/la	vuestro/a	*yours*
los/las	vuestros/as	
el/la	suyo/a	*yours, theirs*
los/las	suyos/as	

These possessive pronouns agree in gender and number with the noun they refer to.

Mi carro es más económico que **tu carro.**	*My car is more economical than* **your car.**
Mi carro es más económico que **el tuyo.**	*My car is more economical than* **yours.**
Nuestra universidad es mejor que **su universidad.**	*Our university is better than* **their university.**
Nuestra universidad es mejor que **la suya.**	*Our university is better than* **theirs.**

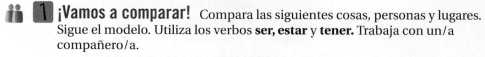

Actividades

1 **¡Vamos a comparar!** Compara las siguientes cosas, personas y lugares. Sigue el modelo. Utiliza los verbos **ser, estar** y **tener.** Trabaja con un/a compañero/a.

> ► MODELO: Nueva York / Boston (grande)
> *Nueva York es más grande que Boston.*

1. Guatemala / Argentina (pequeña)
2. metro / autobús (rápido)
3. la computadora / el teléfono celular (eficiente)
4. mi casa / tu casa (lejos de la universidad)
5. una pequeña tienda de ropa / un almacén (atención personal)
6. una rosa roja / una rosa amarilla (bonita)
7. yo / tú (alto/a)
8. los estadounidenses / los europeos (vacaciones)

2 **¿Más comparaciones?** Reescribe las oraciones haciendo comparaciones **de igualdad o desigualdad.** Sigue el modelo.

> ► MODELO: El perfume *Amor* cuesta sesenta dólares. El perfume *Flor* cuesta ochenta dólares.
> *El perfume* Flor *cuesta más que el perfume* Amor.
> Nancy es muy inteligente. Su hermano Federico también es muy inteligente.
> *Federico es tan inteligente como Nancy.*

1. En la universidad, Sonia tiene seis cursos. Abraham tiene ocho.
2. El coche *Divino* cuesta sesenta mil dólares. El coche *Elegante* cuesta setenta mil.
3. La casa de Antonio tiene siete cuartos. La casa de Guadalupe también tiene siete cuartos.
4. La casa de Eduardo tiene tres dormitorios. La casa de Pilar tiene cinco.
5. El museo de la ciudad es nuevo. El parque central también es nuevo.
6. Jorge maneja rápidamente. Alicia también maneja rápidamente.
7. En la familia de Anita hay nueve personas. En la familia de Carlos hay siete.
8. La tortuga avanza lentamente. La liebre *(hare)* avanza rápidamente.
9. La Librería Cervantes tiene muchos libros. La Librería Cortázar también tiene muchos libros.
10. A Mercedes y a Luis les gusta dar paseos por la ciudad. A nosotros también.

3 **¿Cuál es mejor?** Completa el texto con el superlativo. Usa **mayor, más** o **menos + de.** Usa artículo si es necesario. Sigue el modelo.

▶ MODELO: Mi clase era la _____ grande _____ colegio.
Mi clase era la *más* grande *del* colegio.

1. Hace poco, estuvimos en una de las ciudades _____ grandes _____ mundo: La Ciudad de México.
2. Mis dos hermanos son menores que yo. Yo soy la _____ _____ familia.
3. La selva del Amazonas es la _____ importante _____ tierra.
4. La Librería Paz es magnífica, es la librería _____ completa _____ ciudad.
5. ¿Es el inglés el idioma _____ popular _____ países occidentales?
6. Las cataratas del Niágara son las _____ grandes _____ mundo, pero no son las _____ altas. El Salto Ángel, en Venezuela, es el _____ alto.

4 **Más comparaciones.** Describe a las personas en la tabla. Luego haz comparaciones de estas personas con las de un/a compañero/a. Sigue el modelo.

▶ MODELO: Estudiante A: Mi primo, Carlos, tiene 23 años. | *My cousin Carlos is 23 years old.*
Estudiante B: Mi primo, Renato, tiene 16 años. | *My cousin Renato is 16 years old.*
Estudiante A: Entonces mi primo es mayor que el tuyo. | *Therefore my cousin is older than yours.*
Estudiante B: Mi primo es menor que el tuyo. | *My cousin is younger than yours.*

	Nombre	Edad	Personalidad	Posesiones
primo favorito	_____	_____	_____	_____
una amiga	_____	_____	_____	_____
tío preferido	_____	_____	_____	_____

5 **¿Qué piensan Uds.?** Lean las oraciones siguientes y digan si están de acuerdo o no. Si no están de acuerdo, modifiquen la oración. Comparen sus opiniones con las de sus compañeros/as.

1. El dinero es menos importante que el amor.
2. Hoy en día los hombres tienen tanta ropa elegante como las mujeres.
3. Los estudiantes universitarios trabajan más que los profesores de la universidad.
4. En los Estados Unidos, el béisbol es tan importante como el fútbol americano.
5. La comida tailandesa es mejor que la comida italiana.
6. El mejor coche de los Estados Unidos es el Ford.
7. Es más fácil hablar con los amigos que con los padres.
8. Jugar al baloncesto es menos difícil que jugar al volibol.
9. El béisbol es el deporte más popular de los Estados Unidos.
10. En California hay universidades tan buenas como en Massachusetts.

Magia en Mitad del Mundo

En el restaurante La Choza.

Don Gustavo, ¿qué plato nos recomienda?

El locro es muy delicioso. Es una sopa de papa con queso y aguacate.

Eso me parece bien.

Don Gustavo está preocupado por Adriana y Felipe.

Tienen que tener cuidado. Ustedes tienen cara de turistas... inocentes.

No somos tan inocentes como parecemos.

¡Si ven algo sospechoso en Otavalo, me llaman inmediatamente!

Bueno, quiero saber más sobre los Jaguares Gemelos.

Los jaguares estaban en la tumba de Pacal, el gran rey maya.

La historia del continente de las Américas empieza muchos siglos antes del viaje de Colón en 1492.

Pero, ¿por qué no están los Jaguares Gemelos en la tumba de Pacal... o en un museo mexicano?

Se los robaron los ladrones de sitios arqueológicos precolombinos.

Mientras don Gustavo, Adriana y Felipe cenan, Gafasnegras los vigila.

¿Y cómo y cuándo desaparece Nayeli de la historia de los jaguares? ¡En Costa Rica!

De acuerdo.

Pero primero tengo que encontrar el jaguar perdido. ¡Yax-Balam, eres mío, mío, mío, solamente mío!

Nayeli aparece en la historia de los jaguares en Dresden cuando fue a Alemania para estudiar el códice.

¿Y eso en qué año sucedió?

Fue en 1985. Las autoridades devolvieron a Yax-Balam a México e inmediatamente empezaron los desastres.

Ah, como el terremoto de 1985.

Sí, y Nayeli entró a México con Yax-Balam durante Uayeb, los cinco días de la mala suerte en el calendario maya.

¿Y el otro jaguar?

Nayeli descubrió a Hun-Ahau en París, en 1990. En este momento, Hun-Ahau está en Costa Rica, en la hacienda de doña Carmen. Yax-Balam está perdido.

Para evitar desastre, los jaguares tienen que estar en México el 31 de agosto.

¿Y por qué el treinta y uno de agosto?

Es el día en que murió Pacal.

Al norte de Quito, en la Mitad del Mundo...

¡Se pinchó la llanta justo en la Mitad del Mundo!

¡Qué suerte!

Para mí no es buena suerte. Vayan a dar un paseo mientras yo cambio la llanta.

Podemos tocarnos los dedos a través de los dos hemisferios.

Mira, puedo estar en un hemisferio en un momento y en el otro, segundos después.

Siento algo extraordinario.

¿Qué sientes?

Siento que estamos a punto de recuperar el jaguar. La Mitad del Mundo, el cielo, la tierra, Xibalbá, los tres mundos de los mayas.

Estamos a media hora de Otavalo.

Actividades

Online Study Center

For additional practice with this episode, visit the *Caminos* website at http://college.hmco.com/languages/spanish/renjilian/caminos/3e/student_home.html.

1 Comprensión. Basándote en este episodio de *Caminos del jaguar,* elige la alternativa lógica.

1. En el restaurante, Adriana pide...
   a. locro.
   b. llapingachos con fritada.

2. Don Gustavo piensa que Adriana y Felipe parecen...
   a. unos turistas sospechosos.
   b. unos turistas inocentes.

3. Originalmente, ¿dónde estaban los jaguares?
   a. En un museo
   b. En la tumba de un rey maya

4. La historia del continente de las Américas empieza...
   a. antes de 1492.
   b. después de 1492.

5. ¿Cuál es el plan de Gafasnegras?
   a. Eliminar a Nayeli
   b. Eliminar a Yax-Balam

6. Los desastres sucedieron porque el jaguar Yax-Balam llegó...
   a. solo.
   b. durante *Uayeb.*

7. La fecha para reunir los jaguares es el día que...
   a. murió Pacal.
   b. nació Pacal.

8. En la Mitad del Mundo, Adriana y Felipe...
   a. están en un hemisferio.
   b. están en dos hemisferios.

2 Situaciones. Dramaticen una de estas situaciones.

1. La conversación de Gafasnegras y Miguel.
2. La conversación de Adriana y Felipe en la Mitad del Mundo.

3 Escritura. Escribe un corto resumen sobre este episodio. (3–4 oraciones)

NOTA CULTURAL

El nombre del Ecuador

En el siglo dieciocho, un grupo de científicos franceses midieron la circunferencia de la tierra cerca de Quito, en el meridiano cero. Las medidas demostraron que la tierra no es una esfera perfecta porque es más ancha en el Ecuador que entre el Polo Sur y el Polo Norte. Los especialistas usaron en su informe "las tierras del Ecuador" para referirse al sitio de la medida. Desde entonces, el nombre del **Ecuador** se volvió popular y posteriormente se adoptó como nombre oficial del país.

Lectura

Online Study Center

For further reading practice online, visit the *Caminos* website at http://college .hmco.com/languages/ spanish/renjilian/caminos/ 3e/student_home.html.

PRELECTURA

A legend is a story that people pass down from generation to generation. Legends are often based on historical events, although these may not be verifiable. In addition, legends may combine magical or fantastic elements with factual components. Through this Ecuadorean legend, you will learn the story of a shepherd boy who tends llamas and whose soul becomes entrapped in a rock. Known as Rumiaya, the rock watches over a small lake in the Limpiopungo plains at the foot of Cotopaxi, a majestic snow-covered volcano in Ecuador. The God of the Cotopaxi allows Rumiaya to change back into a human and tell his story whenever travelers show interest in the isolated stone.

In **quechua,** the Inca language spoken in Bolivia, Ecuador, and Perú, **rumi** means *stone* or *rock*. **Aya** means *spirit* or *soul*. **Limpiopungo** is the combination of the Spanish adjective **limpio** *(clean)* and the quechua noun **pungo** *(plains)*.

Reading Strategy

Tapping background knowledge

Previous knowledge of the reading topic, plus your own experience, influence your interpretation and understanding of a text. The activities here will help activate background knowledge you have about legends.

 1 Asociaciones. Antes de leer, trabajen en grupos para repasar sus conocimientos sobre los siguientes temas.

1. Cuenta una leyenda popular de tu región. ¿Es misteriosa o melancólica, heroica, triste? ¿Se combinan elementos verdaderos con elementos fantásticos o mágicos en esa leyenda? Explica.
2. ¿Qué famosos elementos naturales hay en tu país: océanos, ríos, bosques, montañas, cañones, lagos, valles? ¿Cuál te impresiona más?
3. ¿Qué elemento natural figura en una leyenda nacional o regional de tu país?
4. Los pastores cuidan ovejas *(watch over sheep)* que pastan *(graze)* en los campos. ¿Dónde hay pastores en el mundo de hoy? ¿Cómo es su vida?

Soy Rumiaya, el alma de la roca

El gran volcán Cotopaxi, cubierto de nieve

Limpiopungo es una planicie[1] junto al Cotopaxi, el gran volcán nevado[2] del Ecuador. En este valle hay un hermoso lago de aguas limpias y cristalinas. Junto a este hermoso lago hay una piedra[3] que parece un vigía[4]. Las personas que van a este lugar dicen que, a veces, el alma[5] de esta piedra, Rumiaya, sale de ella para contar su historia.

Esto solamente sucede[6] cuando los viajeros[7] expresan mucho interés en la gran piedra y miran la piedra intensamente. De pronto, el alma de Rumiaya sale de la piedra. Lleva un grueso[8] poncho de lana de llama, zamarros[9] y un gorro muy abrigado[10] para protegerse del frío. Los ojos negros le brillan como cristales. Deslumbra[11] con su mirada[12] a los viajeros y empieza a hablar:

—Me llamo Rumiaya, el alma de la piedra. Vivo en la roca. Esta noche es especial y puedo contar mi historia. Hace mucho tiempo, solamente las llamas y los nativos del Cotopaxi vivíamos aquí. Yo era un pastorcito[13] de llamas y cuando amanecía[14], sacaba[15] las llamas a pastar[16] por la mañana. Me sentaba en la orilla[17] de la laguna y me ponía a mirar sus tranquilas y hermosas aguas durante muchas horas sin cansarme. Un día, cuando miraba embelesado[18] la laguna, una de las pequeñas llamas se acercó mucho y cayó al agua.

Sin dudarlo ni un momento, entré a la laguna para salvarla, pero empecé a hundirme[19]. No pude salir y me hundí hasta que todo se volvió[20] oscuro[21]. Un terrible frío me llenó el cuerpo[22]. Yo ya no era de esta vida.

De pronto, el gran dios de la montaña vino hacia mí y yo le dije:

—¡Gran dios de la montaña, creo que voy a morir! ¿Qué va a hacer mi alma sin mi amada[23] laguna? Si muero, ¡déjame junto a ella!

Con voz[24] de viento, el gran dios de la montaña me dijo:

—Voy a concederte[25] tu deseo. Vas a permanecer[26] eternamente junto al agua en forma de roca. Como quieres tanto a la laguna, tú mereces[27] que tu historia se conozca. Desde ahora[28] vas a ser Rumiaya, el alma de la piedra. Cuando alguien demuestre[29] interés por ti, puedes tomar la forma humana y contar tu historia.

Tan misteriosamente como viene, Rumiaya desaparece en la noche, dejando un aire de melancolía.

---

[1]plain; [2]snow-capped; [3]stone; [4]watchman; [5]soul; [6]occurs; [7]travelers; [8]heavy; [9]chaps covering pants; [10]warm; [11]Dazzles; [12]glance; [13]humble shepherd; [14]at dawn; [15]I took out; [16]graze; [17]edge; [18]spellbound; [19]to sink; [20]became; [21]dark; [22]body; [23]beloved; [24]voice; [25]grant you; [26]remain; [27]deserve; [28]From now on; [29]shows

POSTLECTURA

2 **La historia de Rumiaya: Eventos y personajes.** Trabajen en grupos para contestar las preguntas.

1. ¿Quiénes son los personajes de la leyenda? Describan sus personalidades.
2. ¿Quién narra la historia?
3. ¿Qué llevaba el pastorcito al salir de la piedra?
4. ¿Quién vive en la planicie? Según la ropa que lleva, ¿cómo es el clima allí?
5. ¿Por qué se cayó a la laguna una de las pequeñas llamas?
6. ¿Encontró el pastorcito la llama? ¿Qué pasó después?
7. Describe la voz del gran dios de la montaña.
8. ¿En qué convirtió el dios de la montaña al pastorcito?
9. ¿Cuándo puede contar Rumiaya su historia?
10. En tu opinión, ¿qué visión tenían de la naturaleza los nativos del Cotopaxi?

3 Suciopungo. Escribe la forma del imperfecto o del pretérito del verbo en esta breve historia.

La planicie _____ (**1.** estar) sucia y llena de basura. Los viajeros que _____ (**2.** pasar) por allí no _____ (**3.** preocuparse) ni de la ecología ni de las plantas y animales que _____ (**4.** vivir) en ella. Un día, el rey de aquel país _____ (**5.** prohibir) tirar papeles y restos de comida en la planicie porque él _____ (**6.** querer) conservarla limpia. Desde ese día, el rey _____ (**7.** empezar) a castigar personalmente a todos los infractores (*offenders*) hasta que Suciopungo _____ (**8.** convertirse) en Limpiopungo.

4 Nuestro planeta. El rey tiene muchas órdenes para los habitantes de su reino. Elige el infinitivo apropiado de la lista de abajo para completar las ideas. Se puede usar más de uno para completarlas.

aceptar   tirar   obedecer   cuidar   limpiar   tener   castigar   proteger

1. El rey quiere _____ el reino más limpio del mundo.
2. Para los habitantes es necesario _____ las órdenes del rey siempre.
3. Es importante _____ la planicie sucia y no _____ basura en ella.
4. El rey va a _____ a los infractores.
5. Todos los habitantes tienen que _____ la responsabilidad de cuidar los lagos y las lagunas.
6. Es esencial _____ la naturaleza para disfrutar de un planeta limpio.

5 Clasificaciones. Trabajen en parejas. Una persona de cada pareja hace una lista de los eventos que le parecen verdaderos en la historia de Rumiaya; la otra persona hace una lista de los eventos que le parecen de fantasía. Discutan las razones de cada uno/a para clasificar los eventos como fantasía o realidad.

6 Una leyenda original. Escribe en español una corta leyenda de dos párrafos sobre un tema de tu región, del campo o de la ciudad. Incluye elementos de la realidad y de la fantasía.

Una representación del dios Quetzalcoatl

Escritura

Online Study Center

For further writing practice online, visit the *Caminos* website at http://college .hmco.com/languages/ spanish/renjilian/caminos/ 3e/student_home.html.

Writing Strategy

Paraphrasing

One good way to check your understanding of something you have heard, seen, or read is to paraphrase, or to put information and ideas in your own words. This is a common technique for practicing new language structures and reinforcing new vocabulary without copying or quoting the source verbatim.

Workshop

The following examples show possible ways to paraphrase descriptions from the story of Rumiaya.

Original: Limpiopungo es una planicie junto al Cotopaxi, el gran volcán nevado del Ecuador.

Paraphrase: Limpiopungo es un lugar en Ecuador. Está al lado de un volcán que se llama Cotopaxi.

Original: Junto a este hermoso lago hay una piedra que parece un vigía.

Paraphrase: Una piedra grande está junto al lago. La piedra está cuidándolo.

Strategy in Action

For additional practice with paraphrasing, complete the exercises below and in the *Escritura* section of your Student Activities Manual for *Unidad 7.*

1 Limpiopungo. En tus propias palabras, escribe un resumen de dos párrafos de la leyenda de Limpiopungo.

2 Un cuento de niños. ¿Recuerdas los cuentos de tu niñez? Escribe un resumen de tu cuento favorito de cuando eras niño/a con tus propias palabras. Unos cuentos populares son: La cenicienta (*Cinderella*), El patito feo (*The Ugly Duckling*), Los tres cerditos (*The Three Little Pigs*), La Bella Durmiente (*Sleeping Beauty*) y Blancanieves (*Snow White*).

La lista de abajo contiene vocabulario útil para los cuentos de niños. Si las palabras que necesitas no se encuentran en la lista, búscalas en un buen diccionario inglés-español.

Once upon a time	*Érase una vez*	king	*el rey*	princess	*la princesa*
broom	*la escoba*	knight /	*caballero*	prison	*la cárcel*
castle	*el castillo*	gentleman		queen	*la reina*
crown	*la corona*	magic (*adj.*)	*mágico/a*	thief	*el ladrón /*
devil	*el diablo*	magic (*n.*)	*la magia*		*la ladrona*
dragon	*dragón*	magic wand	*la varita*	to have bad /	*tener mala /*
fairy tale	*cuento de hadas*		*mágica*	good luck	*buena suerte*
forest, woods	*el bosque*	magician	*el / la mago/a*	treasure	*el tesoro*
ghost	*el fantasma*	monster	*el / la monstruo/a*	witch	*el / la brujo/a*
giant	*el / la gigante*	palace	*el palacio*	wizard	*el / la mago/a*
godfather	*padrino*	pirate	*el / la pirata*	wolf	*el lobo*
godmother	*madrina*	prince	*el príncipe*		

PRIMER PASO

TALKING ABOUT STORES AND SHOPPING

el almacén	*department store*
la boutique	*boutique*
la caja	*cash register*
el la cliente	*customer*
el/la dependiente	*store clerk*
el disco	*album, record*
el escaparate	*store window*
la farmacia	*pharmacy*
la florería	*florist*
la ganga	*deal, bargain*
la joyería	*jewelry store*
la lavandería	*laundromat*
la librería	*bookstore*
el maquillaje	*makeup*
el mostrador	*display case; counter*
la papelería	*stationery store;*
	office supply store
la perfumería	*perfume store*
el recibo	*receipt*
la talla	*size*
la tintorería	*dry cleaner*
la zapatería	*shoe store*

Verbos

devolver	*to return (something)*
gastar	*to spend (money)*

Otras expresiones

a un precio más bajo	*at a lower price*
¡Claro que sí!	*Of course!*
en oferta	*on sale*
gratis	*free*

SHOPPING FOR CLOTHES
Sustantivos

el abrigo	*coat*
el algodón	*cotton*
la blusa	*blouse*
la bolsa	*purse, bag*
la bota	*boot*

la bufanda	*scarf*
el calcetín	*sock*
la camisa	*shirt*
la camiseta	*T-shirt*
la chaqueta	*jacket*
el cinturón	*belt*
la corbata	*tie*
la falda	*skirt*
el guante	*glove*
el impermeable	*raincoat*
la lana	*wool*
la mancha	*stain*
las medias	*stockings, hose*
los pantalones	*pants*
el par	*pair*
el paraguas	*umbrella*
la ropa interior	*underwear*
el saco	*jacket, blazer*
la seda	*silk*
el sombrero	*hat*
la sudadera	*sweat suit, sweatshirt*
el suéter	*sweater*
el traje	*suit*
el vestido	*dress*
el zapato	*shoe*

Verbos

(des)atar	*to (un)tie*
estar de moda	*to be in style*
ir de compras	*to go shopping*
llevar	*to wear; to take*
probarse (ue)	*to try on*
quedarle (a alguien)	*to fit (someone)*

Adjetivos

estrecho/a	*tight / small*
flojo/a	*loose / big (clothes)*
grande	*large / big (clothes)*
manchado/a	*stained*
pequeño/a	*tight, small (clothes)*
roto/a	*ripped*
sucio/a	*dirty*

SEGUNDO PASO

BARGAINING IN A MARKETPLACE

Sustantivos

el anillo	*ring*
los aretes	*earrings*
la artesanía	*craft*
el barro	*clay*
el cobre	*copper*
el collar	*necklace*
el/la comprador/a	*buyer*
el descuento	*discount*
la esmeralda	*emerald*
el jaguar	*jaguar*
la joya	*jewelry*
el juguete	*toy*
el (otro) lado	*somewhere else*
la madera	*wood*
la máscara	*mask*
el mercado	*marketplace*
el oro	*gold*
el pendiente	*pendant*
la piedra	*stone*
la plata	*silver*
el plato	*dish*
el precio	*price*
el prendedor	*pin, brooch*
la pulsera	*bracelet*
la rebaja	*discount*
el recipiente	*container*
el regateo	*bargaining*
el tapete	*rug*
el tapiz	*tapestry*
el tejido	*weaving*
la turquesa	*turquoise*
el/la vendedor/a	*seller*

Verbos

rebajar	*to lower (a price)*
regatear	*to bargain*

Otras expresiones

ambulante	*mobile*
¿En cuánto me lo(s)/ la(s) deja?	*How much will you charge me for it / them?*

ASKING FOR AND GIVING DIRECTIONS

Sustantivos

la cuadra	*street block*
la esquina	*corner*
la intersección	*intersection*
el semáforo	*traffic light*

Verbos

acelerar	*to accelerate*
bajar (por)	*to go (down) (a street)*
cruzar	*to cross*
dar la vuelta	*to turn around*
doblar (a)	*to turn*
estacionar	*to park*
parar	*to stop*
pasar (por)	*to pass (by)*
seguir derecho, recto	*to go straight*
subir (por)	*to go up (a street)*
tener cuidado	*to be careful*

Otras expresiones

a la (mano) derecha/ izquierda	*on the right/ left(hand) side*
¿Cómo se llega a...?	*How does one get to . . . ?*
despacio	*slowly*
hasta	*until*
¿Me puede decir dónde está/n...?	*Can you tell me where . . . is / are?*
medio/a *(adj.)*	*half*

POSSESSIVE PRONOUNS

el/la	mío/a	*mine*
el/la	tuyo/a	*yours*
el/la	suyo/a	*yours, his, hers, theirs*
el/la	nuestro/a	*ours*
el/la	vuestro/a	*yours*

8
Salud y bienestar

VOCABULARIO Y LENGUA

► Identifying parts of the body
► Making a doctor's appointment
► Expressing requests and emotions: Present subjunctive

► Learning about foods and nutrition
► Discussing progressive actions in the past: Past progressive
► Expressing doubt or certainty: Present subjunctive / indicative

CAMINOS DEL JAGUAR

► La curandera carismática
► Un plan secreto

LECTURA

► Salud y bienestar: Toma control de tu vida

NOTAS CULTURALES

► Curanderos
► Los tejidos

ESTRATEGIAS

► **Reading:** Comparing and contrasting
► **Writing:** Using visual organizers (Venn diagrams)

Mola de Panamá con el símbolo médico

Preguntas del tema

► Cuando estás enfermo/a ¿vas al médico?

► ¿Haces ejercicio todos los días?

► ¿Qué más haces para mantener buena salud?

► ¿Comes una dieta balanceada?

PRIMER PASO

Vocabulario y lengua

IDENTIFYING PARTS OF THE BODY (LAS PARTES DEL CUERPO)

En la clase de anatomía

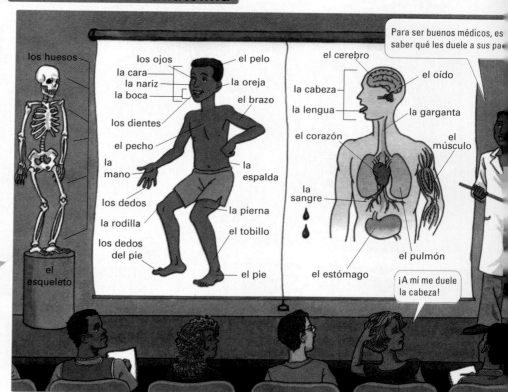

los huesos
el esqueleto
los ojos
la cara
la nariz
la boca
los dientes
el pecho
la mano
los dedos
la rodilla
los dedos del pie
el pelo
la oreja
el brazo
la espalda
la pierna
el tobillo
el pie
el cerebro
la cabeza
la lengua
el corazón
la sangre
el oído
la garganta
el músculo
el pulmón
el estómago

Para ser buenos médicos, es saber qué les duele a sus pa⋯

¡A mí me duele la cabeza!

Online Study Center

For additional practice with this unit's vocabulary and grammar, visit this *Caminos* website at http://college.hmco.com/languages/spanish/renjilian/caminos/3e/student_home.html. You can also review audio flashcards, quiz yourself, and explore related Spanish-language sites.

Actividades

1 Asociaciones. ¿Qué partes del cuerpo asocias con estas actividades?

1. jugar al volibol
2. escuchar música
3. comer
4. tocar la guitarra
5. pensar
6. nadar en la piscina
7. leer una novela
8. maquillarse
9. saludar a un/a amigo/a
10. patear

2 En el sitio correcto. Completa cada oración con la parte del cuerpo más adecuada para la acción.

1. Me pongo el sombrero en la _____.
2. Me pongo guantes porque tengo frío en las _____.
3. Uso gafas de sol para protegerme los _____.
4. Me pongo los calcetines en los _____.
5. Por la mañana me peino el _____.
6. Pruebo la comida con la _____.
7. Marco los números de teléfono con los _____.
8. Si fumo cigarrillos me duelen los _____.

3 ¿Qué les duele? Identifica las partes del cuerpo que les duelen a estas personas. Sigue el modelo.

▶ **MODELO:** A ella le duele el brazo.
Her arm hurts.

1.

2.

3.

4.

5.

6.

4 La rutina diaria. Escribe oraciones completas con las palabras de cada columna. Utiliza cada uno de los sujetos y verbos por lo menos una vez. Después, en parejas, intercambien las frases y comparen las oraciones.

A	B	C
Yo	lavarse	las manos
Tú	cepillarse	el pelo
Los niños	peinarse	los dientes
Nosotras	maquillarse	el cuerpo
Tu mejor amiga	afeitarse	la cara
Mi hermano y yo	secarse	las piernas

appointment ## Una cita° con la médica

Recepcionista	Buenos días. Oficina de la Dra. Medina.
Sr. Jaramillo	Buenos días. Habla el Sr. Jaramillo.
Recepcionista	¿En qué le puedo ayudar, Sr. Jaramillo?
twisted *Sr. Jaramillo*	Mi hija Claudia **se torció**° el tobillo y es necesario llevarla a la Dra. Medina hoy.
Recepcionista	¿Su hija puede caminar?
broken *Sr. Jaramillo*	No, no puede. Parece que tiene el tobillo **fracturado**°.
Recepcionista	Entonces es mejor llevarla a **la sala de emergencia** inmediata-mente para tomarle una **radiografía.**
Sr. Jaramillo	¿Y la Dra. Medina no puede atenderla?
Recepcionista	No, lo siento. La Dra. Medina está ahora en el hospital aten-diendo a otros **pacientes.** Al llegar al hospital, llame Ud. a la Dra. Medina. Ella puede atender a Claudia allí.
Sr. Jaramillo	Muchas gracias, señorita.
Recepcionista	No hay de qué, con mucho gusto.

Más palabras y expresiones

Cognados

el antibiótico	la inflamación
la aspirina	la inyección
curar	la medicina
el examen físico	la operación
la fractura	reducir
grave	el remedio
la infección	el síntoma

Sustantivos

el bienestar	*well-being*
el consultorio médico	*doctor's office*
el/la curandero/a	*healer*
la enfermedad	*illness*

el hielo	*ice*
el jarabe	*syrup*
la píldora, pastilla	*pill*
la presión (sanguínea)	*blood pressure*
la prueba, el análisis	*test, exam (medical)*
la receta	*prescription*
el soroche	*altitude sickness*
la vacuna	*vaccine*
la venda	*bandage*
el yeso	*cast*

Verbos

aliviarse	*to get better*
cuidarse	*to take care of oneself*
dañar	*to harm*
doler (ue)	*to hurt*
enfermarse	*to get sick*
estornudar	*to sneeze*
evitar	*to avoid*
hacer una cita	*to make an appointment*
mejorar	*to get better*
respirar	*to breathe*
romper(se) (el brazo)	*to break (one's arm)*
sangrar	*to bleed*
ser alérgico/a a..., tener alergia a...	*to be allergic to . . .*
toser	*to cough*
vendar	*to bandage*
vomitar	*to vomit*

Expresiones con *estar*

estar embarazada	*to be pregnant*
estar inflamado/a	*to be inflamed, swollen*
estar mareado/a	*to be dizzy*
estar resfriado/a	*to have a cold*

Expresiones con *tener*

tener apetito	*to have an appetite*
tener buena / mala salud	*to be in good / bad health*
tener catarro, resfrío	*to have a cold*
tener dolor	*to have pain*
tener escalofríos	*to shiver, have a chill*
tener fiebre	*to have a fever*
tener gripe	*to have the flu*
tener náuseas	*to be nauseous*
tener tos	*to have a cough*

Actividades

1 En la sala de emergencia. Escucha la conversación entre Claudia y la Dra.Medina, luego contesta las preguntas.

1. ¿Cómo sigue Claudia?
2. ¿Cuál es la buena noticia que tiene la doctora? ¿Y la mala?
3. ¿Cuándo es el próximo partido de fútbol?
4. ¿Por cuánto tiempo tiene Claudia que llevar una venda en el tobillo?
5. ¿Qué más tiene que hacer Claudia para mejorarse?
6. ¿Cuándo es el campeonato?
7. ¿Puede jugar Claudia en el campeonato?
8. ¿Qué necesita hacer Claudia para no tener problemas con el tobillo?

2 Recomendaciones médicas. ¿Qué recomienda un/a médico/a en estas circunstancias? Trabajen en parejas para inventar recomendaciones para estos síntomas. Sigan el modelo.

▶ **MODELO:** PACIENTE: Me duele la garganta.
MÉDICO/A: *Debes (Necesitas) tomar té caliente.*

1. No tengo mucho apetito.
2. Me torcí el brazo.
3. Tengo fiebre y náuseas.
4. Me duele el estómago.
5. Estoy mareado/a y tengo dolor de cabeza.
6. Tengo catarro y no puedo respirar.
7. Me duele la cabeza.
8. Fui a bailar anoche y me torcí el pie.
9. ¿...?

3 Remedios tradicionales. Haz una lista de cinco remedios caseros que conoces para curar dolores o enfermedades, por ejemplo: **sopa de pollo para un catarro.** Con una pareja comparen sus listas y hablen de los beneficios de estos remedios tradicionales en comparación con las medicinas modernas.

EXPRESSING REQUESTS AND EMOTIONS: PRESENT SUBJUNCTIVE

Es un bebé sano y fuerte. Le recomiendo que **coma** alimentos nutritivos y que **haga** ejercicio. No es bueno que usted **fume.**

No, se preocupe doctora, no fumo. Quiero que mi hijo **tenga** buena salud.

Look at the verbs in boldface. What infinitives do they come from? Notice that these verbs are identical to the formal (**Ud.**) commands that you learned in *Unidad 6*, pages 224–225. Compare the sentence structure here with the sentence structures you have learned so far. How is it different? How many subjects do you find in each sentence? These sentences are examples of the present subjunctive.

What is the present subjunctive?

The term subjunctive refers to a *mood*, not to a tense. Up to now you have primarily been using verbs in the indicative *mood*. The indicative mood expresses actions that are definite, clear, and which state factual events and outcomes. The subjunctive is a mood that expresses:

► Requests, wishes, needs, and desires
► Emotions and subjective feelings
► Doubt and uncertainty

Think of the letters **RED** to help you remember what triggers the use of the subjunctive. Not only does the subjunctive express these moods, it appears within a particular sentence structure. As you have seen in the exchange on page 278: a main clause in the indicative is linked by **que** to a dependent or subordinate clause in the subjunctive. Note also that the subject in the main clause is different from the subject in the dependent clause.

Le recomiendo	**que**	coma alimentos nutritivos.
I recommend (to you)	*that*	*you eat nutritious foods.*
No es bueno	**que**	usted fume.
It isn't good	*that*	*you smoke.*

In this unit, we will study how to form the present subjunctive and how to use it to express requests and emotions. In these cases, it is the meaning of the verb or verb phrase in the main clause that triggers the use of the subjunctive in the dependent clause.

Formation of the present subjunctive

To form the present subjunctive, follow the same rule as for formal commands.

Verb	1. Start with the present indicative yo form.	2. Drop the –o.	3. Add the opposite endings.
comprar	compro	compr-	compre
beber	bebo	beb-	beba
escribir	escribo	escrib-	escriba

Once you have the stem of the verb, add the following endings:

Present subjunctive of –ar, –er, –ir verbs			
Subject pronouns	comprar	beber	escribir
yo	compre	beba	escriba
tú	compres	bebas	escribas
Ud., él, ella	compre	beba	escriba
nosotros/as	compremos	bebamos	escribamos
vosotros/as	compréis	bebáis	escribáis
Uds., ellos, ellas	compren	beban	escriban

To form the subjunctive of the following groups of verbs, start with the present indicative **yo** form as shown in the preceding charts.

► Irregular **yo** verbs
  • salir: **salga, salgas, salga, salgamos, salgáis, salgan**
  • conducir: **conduzca, conduzcas, conduzca, conduzcamos, conduzcáis, conduzcan**
  • ver: **vea, veas, vea, veamos, veáis, vean**
► Verbs with spelling changes
  • llegar: **llegue, llegues, llegue, lleguemos, lleguéis, lleguen**
  • buscar: **busque, busques, busque, busquemos, busquéis, busquen**
  • cruzar: **cruce, cruces, cruce, crucemos, crucéis, crucen**
  • escoger: **escoja, escojas, escoja, escojamos, escojáis, escojan**
► Stem-changing -**ar** and -**er** verbs
  • pensar (e → ie): **pie**nse, **pie**nses, **pie**nse, pensemos, penséis, **pie**nsen
  • probar (o → ue): pr**ue**be, pr**ue**bes, pr**ue**be, probemos, probéis, pr**ue**ben
  • perder (e → ie): **pie**rda, **pie**rdas, **pie**rda, perdamos, perdáis, **pie**rdan
  • volver (o → ue): v**ue**lva, v**ue**lvas, v**ue**lva, volvamos, volváis, v**ue**lvan

Irregular verbs

Any verb that has an irregular stem in the formal command forms (*Unidad 6*, p. 225) has the same irregular stem in the present subjunctive.

► estar: **esté, estés, esté, estemos, estén**
► dar: **dé, des, dé, demos, den**
► ir: **vaya, vayas, vaya, vayamos, vayan**
► saber: **sepa, sepas, sepa, sepamos, sepan**
► ser: **sea, seas, sea, seamos, sean**

Like **hay** *(there is, there are)*, **haber** only has one form meaning *there is, there are* in the present subjunctive: **haya.**

Stem-changing -*ir* verbs

Verbs that end in –**ir** and have a stem change from **e → ie** or **o → ue** in the present indicative, have the same change in the present subjunctive. They have an additional change from **e → i** and **o → u** in the **nosotros** and **vosotros** forms of the present subjunctive.

mentir (e → ie)		servir (e → i)		dormir (o → ue)	
m**ie**nta	m**i**ntamos	s**i**rva	s**i**rvamos	d**ue**rma	d**u**rmamos
m**ie**ntas	m**i**ntáis	s**i**rvas	s**i**rváis	d**ue**rmas	d**u**rmáis
m**ie**nta	m**i**entan	s**i**rva	s**i**rvan	d**ue**rma	d**ue**rman

Use of the present subjunctive with verbs of request or emotion

As shown in the examples above when the meaning of the main verb or expression conveys a request or an emotion, it triggers the subjunctive in the dependent or subordinate clause. Remember that the subject in the main clause must be different from the subject in the dependent clause.

Quiero **que tú me ayudes** un poco.   *I want you to help me a little.*

When there is only one subject in both clauses, use the **infinitive** after a conjugated verb or after an impersonal expression. Impersonal expressions do not have an explicit subject (**Es necesario que..., Es importante que...**) and are often used to soften a request.

Quiero **ayudarte** un poco.   *I want to help you a little.*
Es importante no **fumar.**   *It is important not to smoke.*

When the verb in the main clause is accompanied by an indirect object pronoun, the verb in the dependent clause agrees with the person that the pronoun refers to.

<u>Les</u> sugerimos <u>a Uds</u>. que **regresen** mañana.

We suggest that you return tomorrow.

Los médicos <u>nos</u> piden que **hagamos** ejercicio todos los días.

Doctors ask us to exercise every day.

<u>Le</u> aconsejo a mi padre que se **mantenga** en forma.

I advise my father to stay in shape.

Verbs and impersonal expressions of request and emotion

The following verbs and impersonal expressions convey wishes, requests, needs, desires and emotions, or subjective feelings. When they appear in the main clause, they trigger the use of the subjunctive in the dependent or subordinate clause.

Verbs		Impersonal expressions	
aconsejar	to advise	es bueno	it's good
alegrarse (de)	to be happy	es esencial	it's essential
desear	to want	es extraño	it's strange
enojarse	to be angry	es importante	it's important
esperar	to hope	es malo	it's bad
estar contento/a de	to be happy	es mejor	it's better
gustarle	to like; to be pleasing	es necesario	it's necessary
(a alguien)	(to someone)		
lamentar	to lament, regret	es peor	it's worse
mandar	to order	es preciso	it's necessary
molestarle (a alguien)	to bother (someone)	es preferible	it's preferable
necesitar	to need	es ridículo	it's ridiculous
pedir (i)	to request, ask for	es terrible	it's terrible
preferir (ie)	to prefer	es una lástima	it's a shame
preocupar(se)	to worry	es urgente	it's urgent
querer (ie)	to want		
recomendar (ie)	to recommend		
rogar (ue)	to beg, plead		
sentir (ie)	to be sorry, regret		
sorprender	to surprise		
sugerir (ie)	to suggest		
temer	to fear, be afraid of		
tener miedo (de)	to be afraid of		

When the verb **decir** is used to give an order, it requires the subjunctive in the dependent clause. When used to inform it requires the indicative.

La médica me dice que **haga** ejercicio.

The doctor tells me to exercise.

La médica me dice que **tengo** un infección del oído.

The doctor tells me that I have an ear infection.

Ojalá

The word **ojalá** is used to express hope and is followed by the subjunctive. The origin of this word is the Arabic expression *God (Allah) willing.* Unlike the verbs and expressions in the preceding list, **ojalá** does not change form and the use of **que** is optional. **Ojalá** may also stand alone as an interjection that means "I / We / Let's hope so."

—¡Ojalá (que) te **mejores** pronto!

—I hope that you get well soon!

—¿Van a descubrir una cura para el cáncer?

—Are they going to discover a cure for cancer?

—¡Ojalá!

—Let's hope so!

Actividades

1 Consejos del médico. Completa los consejos del médico con la forma correcta del verbo. Decide si necesita el presente del subjuntivo o el infinitivo.

1. Es necesario que tú _____ tu medicina regularmente.
   a. tomes   b. tomar   c. tomas

2. El médico espera que tú _____ sus consejos.
   a. sigas   b. sigues   c. seguir

3. Si no le gusta su médico, es urgente _____ otro.
   a. buscar   b. busca   c. busque

4. Es necesario _____ muchas frutas cada día.
   a. comes   b. comas   c. comer

5. Es urgente que los jóvenes _____ de fumar.
   a. dejen   b. dejar   c. dejan

6. Quiero que tú _____ la lengua y que _____ "Aaaaaaa".
   a. sacar / decir   b. sacas / dices   c. saques / digas

7. Es mejor _____ una cita en dos semanas.
   a. pedir   b. pida   c. pide

2 ¿Qué necesitas hacer? Completa los deseos de estas personas con la forma correcta del subjuntivo. Sigue el modelo.

> ► MODELO: Mi profesora de español quiere   *My Spanish professor wants*
>   que yo haga la tarea.   *me to do the homework.*

1. Mi profesor/a de español quiere que yo...
   a. _____ (poner) atención.
   b. _____ (asistir) a clase.
   c. _____ (no llegar) tarde.
   d. _____ (estudiar) mucho.
   e. _____ (no traducir) todo al inglés.
   f. _____ (hablar) más en clase.

2. Mis padres quieren que yo...
   a. _____ (sacar) buenas notas.
   b. _____ (escoger) una buena profesión.
   c. _____ (llamarlos) cada semana.
   d. _____ (no gastar) mucho dinero en las fiestas.
   e. _____ (no conducir) mi auto muy rápido.
   f. _____ (no enfermarme).

3 Salud y bienestar. Completa estas oraciones sobre preferencias y consejos sobre la salud con el subjuntivo de los verbos entre paréntesis.

1. Doctor, quiero que usted me _____ (examinar) de inmediato.
2. Es inaceptable que tú no nos _____ (decir) la verdad.
3. Ricardo, es esencial que tú _____ (cuidarse).
4. A nadie le gusta que el doctor le _____ (poner) inyecciones.
5. Es necesario que usted nos _____ (dar) su información médica.
6. A nosotros nos preocupa que tú _____ (tener) alergias.
7. Si usted se siente mal, le sugiero que _____ (consultar) a un médico.
8. Es muy bueno que Uds. _____ (mantenerse) en forma.

4 Episodios de la vida. Varias personas expresan sus reacciones sobre estas situaciones. Pon la forma adecuada del presente del indicativo o del presente del subjuntivo del verbo entre paréntesis según el contexto. Sigue el modelo.

► MODELO: Yo _____ (esperar) que Paco _____ (comer) menos grasa.
Yo espero que Paco coma menos grasa.

1. Es bueno que la gente _____ (ser) saludable.
2. Mauro _____ (lamentar) que tú no _____ (hacer) ejercicio.
3. Ojalá que la doctora me _____ (enseñar) buena nutrición.
4. A mí me _____ (molestar) que la gente _____ (fumar).
5. Nosotros _____ (sentir) mucho que el bebé _____ (tener) fiebre.
6. Los profesores _____ (alegrarse) de que sus estudiantes _____ (saber) mucho español al final del curso.
7. Mis amigos me _____ (pedir) que no _____ (beber) y que los _____ (llevar) a casa.
8. Yo no _____ (querer) que mis amigos _____ (preocuparse) por mí.

5 Amistad. Tus buenos amigos te ayudan cuando lo necesitas. Trabajando con un/a compañero/a, conversen sobre estas situaciones posibles. Sigue el modelo.

► MODELO: Te sientes solo/a. ¿Quieres que alguien te acompañe?
Sí, quiero que alguien me acompañe. or
No, no quiero que nadie me acompañe.

1. Tienes dificultades económicas. ¿Les pides a tus amigos que te presten dinero?
2. Estás enfermo/a. ¿Quieres que yo te compre alguna medicina?
3. Te tuerces el tobillo. ¿Prefieres que el médico te ponga una venda?
4. No tienes con quién salir a pasear. ¿Quieres que yo salga contigo?
5. Te rompes el brazo y no puedes cocinar. ¿Le pides a alguien que haga tu cena?
6. Tienes un virus y no vas a la escuela. ¿Quieres que un/a amigo/a te explique la lección?
7. Tienes que estudiar para un examen difícil. ¿Quieres que tus amigos estudien contigo?
8. Es tu cumpleaños. ¿Deseas que tus padres te manden dinero o un regalo?

6 Consejos. Trabajen en parejas para darles consejos a estas personas. Usen los verbos **aconsejar, recomendar** y **sugerir**. Recuerden el uso del subjuntivo.

► MODELO: —Quiero salir a cenar en un restaurante elegante, pero no tengo mucho dinero y tengo que pagar unas cuentas. ¿Qué me aconsejas?
—*Te aconsejo que pagues las cuentas primero y que comas en McDonald's.*

1. Tengo dos invitaciones: una para asistir a un concierto con mis amigos y otra para salir a cenar con mi familia. ¿Qué me aconsejas que haga?
2. Pablo quiere romper *(to break up)* con su novia. Ella lo quiere mucho, pero Pablo está enamorado de otra muchacha. ¿Qué le sugieres a Pablo que haga?
3. Mi compañera de cuarto escucha música toda la noche y yo no puedo estudiar. ¿Qué le digo a mi compañera?
4. Había tres amigos en mi cuarto y desapareció mi reloj de oro. ¿Debo preguntarles si alguno de ellos tiene mi reloj o no debo hacerlo? ¿Qué me aconsejas que haga?
5. Toda mi ropa está sucia y mañana tengo una entrevista para un trabajo. ¿Qué me recomiendas que haga?
6. La semana que viene es el cumpleaños de mi tía, una señora mayor. ¿Qué me sugieres que le regale a ella?
7. Mi abuelo está en el hospital y quiero ir a verlo, pero tengo un examen muy importante. ¿Qué me recomiendas que haga?
8. Mi hermana debe hacer ejercicio, pero no lo hace. ¿Qué le sugiero?

La curandera carismática

Actividades

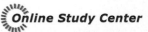
Online Study Center

For additional practice with this episode, visit the *Caminos* website at http://college.hmco.com/languages/spanish/renjilian/caminos/3e/student_home.html.

1 Comprensión. Basándote en este episodio de *Caminos del jaguar,* elige la alternativa lógica.

1. Zulaya dice que su obligación es...
   a. devolver el jaguar.
   b. guardar el jaguar.

2. La gente que quiere el jaguar...
   a. conoce a Zulaya.
   b. no conoce a Zulaya.

3. La organización de Mario confía...
   a. en el jaguar.
   b. en Zulaya.

4. Adriana se siente mal por...
   a. el viaje a Quito.
   b. el soroche.

5. El curandero quiere que vayan a la casa...
   a. del curandero.
   b. de una curandera.

6. Doña Remedios le dice a Adriana que...
   a. busque el jaguar.
   b. no busque el jaguar.

7. Gafasnegras...
   a. no busca a Zulaya.
   b. busca a Zulaya.

2 Situaciones. Dramaticen una de las siguientes situaciones.

1. La conversación de Zulaya con Mario.
2. La conversación de Adriana con doña Remedios.

3 Escritura. Describe qué sucede en el mercado cuando Adriana se siente mal. (4–6 oraciones)

NOTA CULTURAL

Curanderos

En muchas regiones de América Latina, la coexistencia de los remedios tradicionales y modernos es una práctica común. Los curanderos son tradicionalmente personas con profundos conocimientos sobre las plantas medicinales y sus usos. Muchos curanderos cultivan estas plantas o las recogen en las selvas para curar a las personas enfermas. Algunos curanderos celebran rituales para la curación, mientras que otros ya no lo hacen.

Vocabulario y lengua

LEARNING ABOUT FOODS AND NUTRITION

La pirámide de la alimentación *(The food pyramid)*

to keep ourselves / healthy

foods
to eat / quantity / upper

weight

Mantener una **dieta** balanceada es importante para **conservarnos**° **sanos**°. La pirámide de la alimentación nos muestra los productos recomendados en cada grupo de **alimentos**°. En los niveles más bajos de la pirámide están los alimentos que debemos **consumir**° en mayor **cantidad**° y en la parte superior°, están los alimentos que solamente debemos consumir en cantidades mínimas. En la base de la pirámide, vemos que controlar el **peso**° y hacer ejercicio son muy importantes para la salud.

Online Study Center

For additional practice with this units vocabulary and grammar, visit the *Caminos* website at http://college.hmco.com/ languages/spanish/ renjilian/caminos/3e/ student_home.html. You can also review audio flashcards, quiz yourself, and explore related Spanish-language sites.

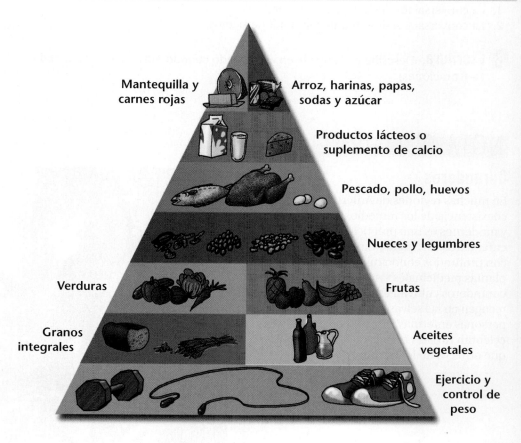

Mantequilla y carnes rojas

Arroz, harinas, papas, sodas y azúcar

Productos lácteos o suplemento de calcio

Pescado, pollo, huevos

Nueces y legumbres

Verduras

Frutas

Granos integrales

Aceites vegetales

Ejercicio y control de peso

Las porciones

El número recomendado de **porciones** depende de cuántas **calorías** necesite la persona **diariamente**. Las calorías **dependen,** a su vez, del **nivel°** de actividad que **mantenga°** la persona, de su edad, de su sexo y de sus circunstancias. Por ejemplo, una persona muy **sedentaria** necesita menos calorías que una persona **activa,** las personas jóvenes consumen, por lo general, más calorías que las personas ancianas y las mujeres embarazadas deben mantener una dieta **nutritiva°** con mucho calcio. Las personas que sufren de alergias o de alguna insuficiencia **física** pueden necesitar dietas especiales.

level
maintains

nutritious

Actividades

1 Ponlas en su grupo. Pon las comidas de la lista en el grupo de alimentos que les corresponde en la pirámide. Algunas comidas pueden pertenecer a más de un grupo. Trabajen en parejas.

verduras

jugo de naranja

yogur

taco

plátano

cereal

huevo

manzana

crema de cacahuate

mantequilla

pechuga de pollo (chicken breast)

papa (patata) al horno

queso

refrescos

frijoles (beans)

pan

2 **¿Comes una dieta balanceada?** Haz una lista de lo que comiste ayer. Después, en parejas, comparen sus listas. Hablen de lo que necesitan hacer para mantener una dieta balanceada. Presenten sus ideas a la clase.

3 **Encuesta.** Hazles una encuesta a dos compañeros sobre sus hábitos alimenticios *(eating habits)*. Después, clasifica cada uno de los alimentos nombrados en el sitio que le corresponda en la pirámide. Entonces, haz un resumen de la información que conseguiste. Dale un informe a la clase.

1. ¿Qué bebes cuando tienes sed? ¿Cuál es tu bebida favorita?
2. ¿Bebes alcohol? ¿Cuántas veces por semana? ¿Cuándo?
3. ¿Cuál es la fruta que más te gusta? ¿Cuál es la fruta que menos te gusta? ¿Por qué?
4. ¿Cuál es la verdura que más te gusta? ¿Cuál es la verdura que menos te gusta? ¿Por qué?
5. ¿Cuál es tu comida favorita? ¿Por qué?
6. ¿Cuál es la comida que menos te gusta? ¿Por qué?
7. ¿Cuántos vasos de agua tomas al día?
8. ¿Qué comes cuando tienes hambre entre las comidas?

4 **Planeando el menú.** Tienes que planear la comida de una semana para la cafetería de tu universidad. Planea un menú balanceado para todos los días.

Menú diario				
lunes	martes	miércoles	jueves	viernes
____	____	____	____	____
____	____	____	____	____
____	____	____	____	____

5 **Para todas las edades.** ¿Cómo cambiarías *(would you change)* el menú de la Actividad 4 para niños de siete a nueve años? ¿Para personas mayores? ¿Para personas con problemas cardíacos?

Menú		
Para niños	Para personas mayores	Para personas con problemas cardíacos
____	____	____
____	____	____
____	____	____

DISCUSSING PROGRESSIVE ACTIONS IN THE PAST: PAST PROGRESSIVE

¿Qué estaban haciendo esta mañana?

> Mi padre **estaba bebiendo** café.

> Mis gatos **estaban jugando** en el jardín.

> Mi hermano menor **estaba durmiendo**.

> ...s siete de ...ñana mi ...á **estaba ...parando** ...esayuno.

> Y en ese momento, mi primo Luis y yo **estábamos divirtiéndonos**.

The past progressive corresponds to the English *we were running, they were watching television, I was talking.* It describes what people were doing during a given period or at a specific moment in the past. Its use in Spanish is often accompanied by a time expression such as **en aquella época, en esos días, en ese momento.** The past progressive is formed with **estar** and a present participle. (Review the formation of the present participle in *Unidad 2*, page 63.)

Past progressive
imperfect of **estar** + present participle

Cuando me encontré con Luis, yo **estaba comprando** unas manzanas.
Estaba pensando en ti, ¡y en ese momento, tú apareciste!

When I ran into Luis, I was buying some apples.
I was thinking of you, and at that moment, you appeared!

As with the present progressive tense, direct, indirect, and reflexive object pronouns may precede **estar** or attach to the end of the present participle. In the latter case, a written accent needs to be added to show the stressed syllable.

Nos estaban llamando.
Estaban llamándo**nos.**

They were calling us.

Le estábamos escribiendo una carta.
Estábamos escribiéndo**le** una carta.

We were writing a letter to him.

Actividades

1 **Comprensión.** Selecciona la expresión más lógica para describir lo que estaban haciendo las personas en estas situaciones.

1. En la cocina, Margarita...
   a. estaba limpiando la alfombra.
   b. estaba sirviendo los refrescos.

2. En la tienda de alimentos, nosotros...
   a. estábamos escogiendo las verduras.
   b. estábamos pagando las cuentas.

3. En el hospital, tú...
   a. estabas mirando el menú.
   b. estabas buscando a un médico.

4. En la farmacia, la dependiente...
   a. estaba comprando papel.
   b. estaba vendiendo antibióticos.

5. En la cafetería, Carolina y tú...
   a. estaban cocinando.
   b. estaban tomando un café.

6. En el dormitorio, Feliciano y su hermano Toño...
   a. estaban lavando los platos.
   b. estaban recogiendo la ropa.

2 **Ayer por la tarde.** ¿Qué estaban haciendo ayer por la tarde las personas de los dibujos? Trabajen en parejas.

1. Mónica 2. Mamá 3. Papá

4. Abuela 5. El gatito 6. Guillermo

3 **¿Qué estabas haciendo...?** En parejas, conversen sobre las actividades de cada uno/a de ustedes en los días y horas descritas.

▶ MODELO: *ayer, a las tres de la tarde*
  —¿Qué estabas haciendo ayer a las tres de la tarde?
  —Estaba comiendo con amigos en la cafetería de la universidad.

1. ayer, a las once de la mañana
2. esta mañana, a las seis
3. el pasado 4 de julio por la noche
4. el sábado, a las once de la noche
5. anoche, a las siete de la noche
6. ayer, antes de la clase de español
7. el 31 de diciembre del año pasado
8. el jueves al mediodía

EXPRESSING DOUBT OR CERTAINTY: PRESENT SUBJUNCTIVE/INDICATIVE

No creo que **tenga** una fractura grave.

¿Está usted segura de que **va** a estar bien?

enso que ede llevar u perrita a casa hoy

¡Ay, dudo que **vaya** a casa hoy! Me duele mucho.

Notice in the preceding examples that when the main verb expresses doubt, uncertainty, or denial, the dependent verb is in the **subjunctive.**

Indicative			Subjunctive
Main clause expressing doubt, uncertainty, denial, disbelief	+	**que** +	dependent clause (what is doubted, denied, uncertain, not believed)

No creemos	**que**	el mercado **tenga** mangos.
We don't believe	*that*	*the market will have mangos.*
Es imposible	**que**	hoy **estén** cerradas las tiendas.
It's impossible	*that*	*the stores are closed today.*
Dudo	**que**	**podamos** llegar temprano.
I doubt	*that*	*we will arrive early.*

When the main verb expresses certainty, the **indicative** is used.

Creemos	**que**	el mercado **tiene** mangos.
We believe	*that*	*the market has mangos.*
Estoy seguro de	**que**	hoy **están** cerradas las tiendas.
I am sure	*that*	*the stores are closed today.*
No hay duda de	**que**	**podemos** llegar temprano.
There is no doubt	*that*	*we can arrive early.*

Verbs and expressions of doubt, uncertainty, denial, and disbelief			
Use the subjunctive			
dudar	*to doubt*	no es evidente	*it's not evident*
es imposible	*it's impossible*	no es seguro	*it's not sure*
es posible	*it's possible*	no es verdad	*it's not true*
es probable	*it's probable*	no está claro	*it isn't clear*
negar (ie)	*to deny*	no estar seguro/a de	*to be unsure*
no creer	*to not believe*	no pensar (ie)	*to not think*
no es cierto	*it's not certain*	puede ser	*it can be*

Common verbs and expressions of certainty			
Use the indicative			
creer	*to think; to believe*	estar seguro/a de	*to be sure*
es cierto	*it's certain, true*	no dudar	*to not doubt*
es evidente	*it's evident*	no hay duda (de)	*there's no doubt*
es obvio	*it's obvious*	no negar (ie)	*to not deny*
es seguro	*it's sure*	opinar	*to think (have an opinion)*
es verdad	*it's true*	pensar (ie)	*to think (opinion)*
está claro	*it's clear*		

In a question with **creer, opinar,** and **pensar** the indicative or the subjunctive may be used in the dependent clause. The subjunctive stresses uncertainty about the issue.

> ¿Crees que la comida **esté** mala? *Do you think that the food is spoiled?*

Quizás and **tal vez** both mean *perhaps* and are generally used with the subjunctive. Note that the word **que** is not used.

> ¿Ves mucha televisión? ¡Quizás **seas** teleadicto! *Do you watch a lot of TV? Perhaps you are a TV-addict!*

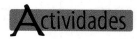

Actividades

1 Dudas y certezas. Completa las oraciones de una manera lógica.

1. Es probable que...
   a. vaya al gimnasio.
   b. va al gimnasio.

2. Dudo que...
   a. sea bueno comer mucha azúcar.
   b. es bueno comer mucha azúcar.

3. Es seguro que la ensalada...
   a. sea buena para la salud.
   b. es buena para la salud.

4. No hay duda de que...
   a. seas mi mejor amigo.
   b. eres mi mejor amigo.

5. No creo que...
   a. tienes tiempo para todo.
   b. tengas tiempo para todo.

6. Es obvio que...
   a. estés en buena forma.
   b. estás en buena forma.

2 Momentos de la vida. Completa los diálogos con el subjuntivo o el indicativo según el contexto.

Ernesto y Amanda están en un restaurante de comida rápida.

Ernesto	No creo que nosotros _____ (**1.** deber) comer un almuerzo con mucha grasa, pero dudo que tú _____ (**2.** seguir) mis consejos. Recuerda, nunca es demasiado pronto para pensar en la nutrición.
Amanda	No niego que las papas fritas _____ (**3.** ser) malas para la salud y es cierto que la ensalada _____ (**4.** contribuir) a la buena nutrición; pero, es imposible que la gente _____ (**5.** comer) solamente ensaladas y verduras. Es muy aburrido.
Ernesto	Es verdad que nosotros _____ (**6.** deber) tener una dieta balanceada. Vamos a pedir ensalada y hamburguesas, ¿de acuerdo?

Gregorio y Adelita, dos novios, se declaran su amor y amistad.

Gregorio	Adelita, es verdad que tú me _____ (**7.** querer), ¿no?
Adelita	Corazón, es cierto que te _____ (**8.** adorar) y es verdad que _____ (**9.** querer) vivir el resto de mi vida contigo.
Gregorio	Estoy seguro de que nosotros _____ (**10.** ir) a ser muy felices.
Adelita	Creo que tú y yo nos _____ (**11.** respetar) mucho.

Sami está en la oficina de la doctora Colón, una psicóloga excelente.

Sami	Es verdad que yo no _____ (**12.** sentirse) muy bien. Estoy triste.
Dra. Colón	Todos tenemos momentos bajos en la vida. Sami, no niego que _____ (**13.** estar, tú) deprimido. Es importante que _____ (**14.** hablar, tú) de tus problemas.

3 ¿Es verdad? Tú no estás de acuerdo con las opiniones de tu amigo/a. En parejas, expresen su desacuerdo usando estas expresiones: **no es verdad, niego que, dudo que, no creo que.** Sigan el modelo.

▶ MODELO: Comes muy poca fruta.
No es verdad que coma muy poca fruta.

1. La pizza es más rica que la lasaña.
2. Yo soy un/a cocinero/a excelente.
3. Mi dieta no tiene carne roja.
4. Los estudiantes prefieren comer tacos y sodas.
5. Todos los domingos hago huevos fritos.
6. En mi casa siempre hay crema de cacahuate.
7. Las manzanas y los plátanos contienen sal.
8. Los perritos comen ensalada.

4 Verdades y dudas. Escríbele un correo electrónico a tu prima, contándole las cosas que sabes y las dudas que tengas. Incluye diez ideas sobre la vida académica, social, familiar y profesional, utilizando las expresiones de duda, negación y certeza *(certainty)*.

Un plan secreto

En el mercado de Otavalo.

¡Mira, Felipe, es el amanecer!

¿Quieres entrar?

Claro.

En la tienda de Zulaya.

Buenas tardes, señorita. ¿Busca algo en especial?

¡Hola!

Me llamó la atención el tejido del amanecer. Queremos verlo.

¡Dios mío! ¡Qué coincidencia! ¿Está usted leyendo este libro?

Sí, me fascinan los objetos de arte precolombinos...

...y el misterio de las piezas perdidas, como esas dos.

¡Los héroes gemelos!

¿Qué sabe usted de ellos?

La autora es nuestra profesora de arqueología.

¿Lo dice en serio?

Sí, en este momento, Yax-Balam y Hun-Ahau son muy importantes en nuestras vidas.

¿Qué quiere decir con eso?

Pues... los gemelos están separados. Y nosotros debemos reunirlos el 31 de agosto, ni antes ni después.

Pero, ¿por qué el treinta y uno de agosto?

Ése es el día que murió Pacal, el gran rey de los mayas. Los jaguares tienen que estar con él en Xibalbá.

Pero, no entiendo. ¿Qué hacen ustedes aquí en el Ecuador?

Creemos que Yax-Balam está aquí, en Otavalo. Pero esta información es confidencial.

Adriana, tenemos que irnos.

¿Por qué? ¿Qué pasa?

¡Vámonos! ¡Vámonos!

Señorita, gracias por su compra. Deben salir por aquí.

¿Perdón?

Aquí tiene, gracias, gracias.

Señorita, la estaba esperando. Usted es la mensajera de Armando de Landa, ¿no es así?

No es el momento oportuno. Su paquete ya está listo. Aquí está.

Sí, pero ¿cómo lo sabía?

En las montañas.

¡Era Gafasnegras, la que trató de matarnos en Puerto Rico! ¿Ese es el jaguar auténtico?

Estoy segura de que es Yax-Balam. La suerte sigue con nosotros.

¡Qué mala suerte! Pero aquí no termina la historia. ¡Van a ver!

Actividades

Online Study Center

For additional practice
with this episode, visit
the *Caminos* website at
http://college.hmco.com/
languages/spanish/
renjilian/caminos/3e/
student_home.html.

1 **Comprensión.** Basándote en este episodio de *Caminos del jaguar*, elige la alternativa lógica.

1. Adriana y Felipe quieren...
   a. ver el tejido del amanecer. b. comprar el tejido del amanecer.

2. A Zulaya le interesa...
   a. el misterio del amanecer. b. el libro de Nayeli.

3. A Zulaya le fascinan...
   a. los jaguares. b. las piedras.

4. Los gemelos tienen que estar juntos en México...
   a. el 31 de agosto. b. el 31 de julio.

5. Adriana y Felipe creen que ellos...
   a. pueden confiar en Zulaya. b. no pueden confiar en Zulaya.

6. ¿Dónde está Yax-Balam?
   a. En la bolsa de Adriana. b. En la bolsa de Gafasnegras.

2 **Situaciones.** Dramaticen una de las siguientes situaciones.

1. Zulaya y Adriana hablan sobre el libro de Nayeli.
2. Zulaya le entrega una bolsa a Gafasnegras.

3 **Escritura.** Describe qué sucede cuando Gafasnegras se acerca a la tienda de Zulaya. (4–6 oraciones)

NOTA CULTURAL

Los tejidos

En muchas regiones andinas de América Latina, los tejidos son parte de la herencia cultural y el arte de hacerlos pasa de generación en generación. En Ecuador, Bolivia y Perú se usa la lana de las llamas y alpacas para tejer ropa y alfombras que después se venden en los mercados. Para teñir la lana de diferentes colores se usan tintes naturales extraídos de varios tipos de plantas. Actualmente, se usan también fibras artificiales. En el mercado de Otavalo, en Ecuador, se pueden ver las hermosas formas y colores de tejidos tradicionales.

Lectura

Online Study Center

For further reading practice online, visit the *Caminos* website at http://college.hmco.com/languages/spanish/renjilian/caminos/3e/student_home.html.

PRELECTURA

The readings that follow describe various health and wellness issues for people of different ages. They were published in several contemporary magazines in Spanish, including *GeoMundo, Cristina, Vanidades,* and *Newsweek en Español.*

Reading Strategy

Comparing and contrasting

In this reading section, there are six short articles that are different in many respects, but that also have similarities. Before reading them, do these pre-reading activities in which you will be comparing and contrasting medical conditions. This will prepare you for the reading content and will enable you to compare the ideas, solutions, or advice presented in the six articles.

1 **Cuerpos y condiciones.** En parejas, pronuncien e indiquen lo que significa cada uno de los siguientes cognados.

alcoholismo	alergia	detectar	cortisona	demencia
diabetes	infecciones	congénito	estafilococos	artritis
antibióticos	resultados	anatomía	eliminar	prevenir

2 **Opinión.** Di si cada enfermedad de la tabla te preocupa poco, algo o mucho.

Condición	Me preocupa poco	Me preocupa algo	Me preocupa mucho
la artritis			
infecciones			
la hipertensión			
el Alzheimer			
alergias			
el alcoholismo			
el cáncer			

3 **¿Más o menos?** Con un/a compañero/a, discutan cuál de las siete enfermedades es más o menos seria. Sigue el modelo.

▶ MODELO: *Yo creo que el Alzheimer es menos / más (tan) serio que (como) el cáncer. ¿Qué crees tú?*

4 **Comparaciones y contrastes.** Trabajen en parejas para comparar y contrastar los síntomas y las características de tres de las condiciones médicas de la tabla de la *Actividad 2.*

Salud y bienestar: Toma control de tu vida

Curar la artritis con piquetes de abejas[1]

La artritis a veces ataca a personas de mediana[2] edad, y los dolores que sufren son aliviados[3] mediante[4] un método tradicional. La curación consiste en obligar a una abeja a picar[5] al enfermo en el área afectada. Los pacientes que han recibido[6] el tratamiento aseguran[7] que, aunque al principio[8] el dolor del piquete es muy fuerte, con el tiempo este dolor se reduce.

Los niños y las alergias

La rinitis alérgica[9] puede afectar hasta un 42 por ciento de los niños que se encuentran en la edad escolar[10]. En un día típico, más de 10.000 niños faltan a[11] la escuela debido a problemas por las alergias estacionales[12].

Alergias en la familia es un factor muy importante para predecir[13] alergias en los niños. Por lo general, el riesgo[14] de que un niño desarrolle alergias estacionales aumenta cuando uno de los padres tiene una alergia, y es todavía más grande cuando ambos padres sufren de alergias.

¿Qué bebes — café, té o agua?

¿Te sientes cansado/a en la mañana? Es quizás porque tienes sed. Es buena idea beber un vaso de agua inmediatamente después de levantarte. De esta manera, no vas a necesitar café o té. El café y el té son populares, pero es importante que consumas ocho vasos de agua cada día.

Venciendo[15] el mal de Alzheimer

El mal de Alzheimer es una enfermedad muy seria que borra la personalidad de la persona afectada e impacta a toda la familia. No hay todavía[16] cura para esta enfermedad devastadora. Pero, la gente puede ofrecerse al Brain Endowment Bank como donante[17] para el estudio de enfermedades neurológicas.

Los científicos[18] anunciaron la semana pasada los resultados preliminares de estudios de una vacuna que podría ayudar a tratar o prevenir el mal[19] de Alzheimer. Una de las principales características del Alzheimer son los depósitos de una proteína llamada betaamiloide en el cerebro. No se sabe si estos depósitos son la causa de la pérdida[20] de memoria y demencia, pero algunos investigadores creen que eliminarlas podría reducir los síntomas.

Pequeños corazoncitos[21]

La medicina y la tecnología hacen posible milagros[22] para alargar[23] la vida, y para hacer posible la de bebés por nacer[24]. Hoy se pueden detectar enfermedades congénitas del corazón en bebés que todavía están en el vientre[25], gracias al ultrasonido[26] de frecuencia más elevada, que permite ver claramente la anatomía del pequeño corazón. Este nuevo recurso es crucial, ya que el uno por ciento de los bebés nace con problemas del corazón.

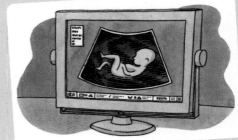

---

[1]bee stings; [2]middle; [3]relieved; [4]by means of; [5]to sting; [6]have received; [7]assure; [8]at first; [9]nasal allergy; [10]school; [11]miss; [12]seasonal; [13]predict; [14]risk; [15]Conquering; [16]yet; [17]organ donor; [18]scientists; [19]disease; [20]loss; [21]Little hearts; [22]miracles; [23]lengthen; [24]unborn; [25]womb; [26]ultrasound exam

Prevenir las infecciones

Los estafilococos[27] han causado[28] muertes[29] infantiles. Hay muchas maneras de prevenir las infecciones en general:

Lavarse es la mejor manera de combatir infecciones. Los niños deben de lavarse las manos antes de las comidas, y si es posible antes de comer cualquier cosa, y después de usar el baño.

Desinfectarse todas las heridas y cortaduras[30], pues es por donde pueden entrar los microbios al organismo.

No tocar ningún tipo de insecto, conocido o desconocido, y mucho menos escarbar[31] en la tierra buscándolos. Mantenerse alejados[32] de animales pequeños cuyos dueños[33] no sean perfectamente conocidos.

Vigilar[34] cualquier infección. Si observas que el lugar infectado empeora[35], o si no está visible, si notas que tu niño tiene una fiebre alta, llévalo inmediatamente a su médico. Si el estado del niño no mejora en 2 o 3 días, es el momento de comenzar a administrarle antibióticos.

[27]bacteria; [28]have caused; [29]deaths; [30]cuts; [31]dig; [32]far away; [33]owners; [34]Watch; [35]worsens

POSTLECTURA

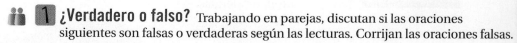

1 ¿Verdadero o falso? Trabajando en parejas, discutan si las oraciones siguientes son falsas o verdaderas según las lecturas. Corrijan las oraciones falsas.

1. El mal de Alzheimer afecta a todos en la familia.
2. El uno por ciento de los bebés nace con problemas del corazón.
3. El agua es mala para la salud.
4. Más de veinte mil estudiantes faltan a la escuela cada día a causa de las alergias.
5. Si estás cansado/a, la sed puede ser la causa.
6. Los pacientes que tienen mal de Alzheimer pierden la memoria.
7. Las alergias pueden pasar de padres a hijos.
8. La tecnología no es buena para detectar enfermedades infantiles.
9. Lavarse las manos es una buena manera de evitar infecciones.
10. Hay una nueva vacuna que reduce los síntomas del mal de Alzheimer.
11. Es mejor jugar con animales desconocidos.
12. El piquete de una abeja puede reducir los dolores de la artritis.

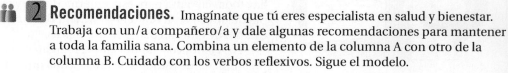

2 Recomendaciones. Imagínate que tú eres especialista en salud y bienestar. Trabaja con un/a compañero/a y dale algunas recomendaciones para mantener a toda la familia sana. Combina un elemento de la columna A con otro de la columna B. Cuidado con los verbos reflexivos. Sigue el modelo.

▶ **MODELO:** es mejor / tener un examen médico cada año
Es mejor que tengas un examen médico cada año.

A	B
(no) es importante	llevar a tu niño al médico si tiene una fiebre alta
(no) es malo	lavarse las manos antes de comer
(no) es necesario	consultar a un/a médico/a si tienes un problema serio
(no) es mejor	desinfectarse las heridas
(no) es preferible	no caminar todos los días
(no) es bueno	hacer ejercicio todos los días
(no) es urgente	no tocar los insectos para no infectarse
(no) es esencial	beber mucha agua

3 Comparaciones y contrastes. Trabaja con un/a compañero/a para comparar y contrastar los diferentes tratamientos de dos de las condiciones médicas de la lectura: las infecciones, la artritis, las alergias, el Alzheimer. ¿Qué tratamiento es mejor? ¿Por qué?

Escritura

Online Study Center

For further writing practice online, visit the *Caminos* website at http://college.hmco.com/languages/spanish/renjilian/caminos/3e/student_home.html.

Writing Strategy

Using visual organizers (Venn diagrams)

One way to organize your ideas visually when comparing or contrasting two or more items is by creating a Venn diagram. Below is a sample of a Venn diagram that has been done to compare two different popular diets **La dieta South Beach** and **La dieta Atkins.**

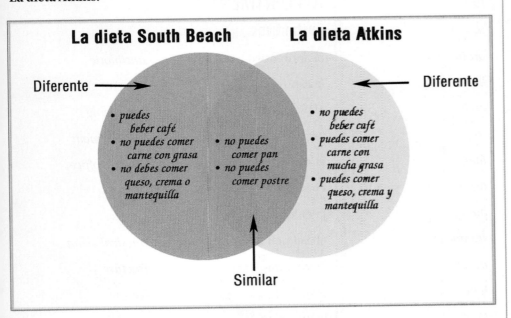

La dieta South Beach   **La dieta Atkins**

Diferente →   ← Diferente

- *puedes beber café*
- *no puedes comer carne con grasa*
- *no debes comer queso, crema o mantequilla*

- *no puedes comer pan*
- *no puedes comer postre*

- *no puedes beber café*
- *puedes comer carne con mucha grasa*
- *puedes comer queso, crema y mantequilla*

Similar

Workshop

1. Draw a Venn diagram on a piece of paper.
2. Choose a topic to compare or contrast.
3. Begin by listing the things that are unique to the items in the outer rings of each circle.
4. Then list the things that the items have in common in the center, where the circles overlap.
5. Refer to this diagram to help organize your writing.

Strategy in Action

For additional practice using visual organizers, complete the exercises below and in the *Escritura* section of your Student Activities Manual for *Unidad 8.*

1. **Dos dietas.** Compara dos diferentes dietas que son populares hoy día. Después, escribe tus recomendaciones de qué dieta sugieres y por qué.

2. **Combatir el estrés.** Compara dos diferentes métodos para combatir el estrés. Después escribe un cartel para el centro de salud de tu universidad.

Resumen de vocabulario

PRIMER PASO

IDENTIFYING PARTS OF THE BODY
Sustantivos

la boca	*mouth*
el brazo	*arm*
la cabeza	*head*
la cara	*face*
el cerebro	*brain*
el corazón	*heart*
el cuerpo	*body*
los dedos	*fingers*
los dedos del pie	*toes*
los dientes	*teeth*
la espalda	*back*
el estómago	*stomach*
la garganta	*throat*
los huesos	*bones*
la lengua	*tongue*
la mano	*hand*
el músculo	*muscle*
la nariz	*nose*
el oído	*ear (inner)*
los ojos	*eyes*
la oreja	*ear (outer)*
el pecho	*chest*
el pelo	*hair*
el pie	*foot*
la pierna	*leg*
el pulmón	*lung*
la rodilla	*knee*
la sangre	*blood*
el tobillo	*ankle*

MAKING A DOCTOR'S APPOINTMENT
Sustantivos

el antibiótico	*antibiotic*
la aspirina	*aspirin*
el bienestar	*well-being*
la cita	*appointment*
el consultorio médico	*doctor's office*
el/la curandero/a	*healer*
la enfermedad	*illness*
el examen físico	*physical exam*
la fractura	*fracture*
el hielo	*ice*
la infección	*infection*
la inflamación	*inflamation*
la inyección	*injection*
el jarabe	*syrup*
la medicina	*medicine*
la operación	*operation*
el/la paciente	*patient*
la píldora, pastilla	*pill*
la presión (sanguínea)	*blood pressure*
la prueba, el análisis	*test, exam (medical)*
la radiografía	*x-ray*
la receta	*prescription*
el remedio	*remedy*

la sala de emergencia	*emergency room*		
el síntoma	*symptom*		
el soroche	*altitude sickness*		
la vacuna	*vaccine*		
la venda	*bandage*		
el yeso	*cast*		

Verbos

aliviarse	*to get better*
cuidarse	*to take care of oneself*
curar	*to cure*
dañar	*to harm*
doler (ue)	*to hurt*
enfermarse	*to get sick*
estornudar	*to sneeze*
evitar	*to avoid*
hacer una cita	*to make an appointment*
mejorar	*to get better*
reducir	*to reduce*
respirar	*to breathe*
romper(se) (el brazo)	*to break (one's arm)*
sangrar	*to bleed*
ser alérgico/a a..., tener alergia a...	*to be allergic to . . .*
torcer(se) (el tobillo)	*to twist, sprain (one's ankle)*
toser	*to cough*
vendar	*to bandage*
vomitar	*to vomit*

Adjetivos

fracturado/a	*broken, fractured*
grave	*grave, serious*

Expresiones con *estar*

estar embarazada	*to be pregnant*
estar inflamado/a	*to be inflamed*
estar mareado/a	*to be dizzy*
estar resfriado/a	*to have a cold*

Expresiones con *tener*

tener apetito	*to have an appetite*
tener buena / mala salud	*to be in good / bad health*
tener catarro, resfrío	*to have a cold*
tener dolor	*to have pain*
tener escalofríos	*to shiver, have a chill*
tener fiebre	*to have a fever*
tener gripe	*to have the flu*
tener náuseas	*to be nauseous*
tener tos	*to have a cough*

VERBS AND EXPRESSIONS OF REQUEST AND EMOTION
Verbs

aconsejar	*to advise*
alegrarse (de)	*to be happy*
desear	*to want*
enojarse	*to be angry*

VERBS AND EXPRESSIONS OF REQUEST AND EMOTION cont.

Verbs

esperar	*to hope*
estar contento/a de	*to be happy*
gustarle (a alguien)	*to like; to be pleasing*
lamentar	*to lament, regret*
mandar	*to order*
molestarle (a alguien)	*to bother (someone)*
necesitar	*to need*
ojalá	*I / We / Let's hope so*
pedir (i)	*to request, ask for*
preferir (ie)	*to prefer*
preocupar(se)	*to worry*
querer (ie)	*to want*
recomendar (ie)	*to recommend*
rogar (ue)	*to beg, plead*
sentir (ie)	*to be sorry, regret*
sorprender	*to surprise*
sugerir (ie)	*to suggest*
temer	*to fear, be afraid of*
tener miedo (de)	*to be afraid (of)*

Impersonal expressions

es bueno	*it's good*
es esencial	*it's essential*
es extraño	*it's strange*
es importante	*it's important*
es malo	*it's bad*
es mejor	*it's better*
es necesario	*it's necessary (to someone)*
es peor	*it's worse*
es preciso	*it's necessary*
es preferible	*it's preferable*
es ridículo	*it's ridiculous*
es terrible	*it's terrible*
es urgente	*it's urgent*
es una lástima	*it's a shame*

SEGUNDO PASO

LEARNING ABOUT FOODS AND NUTRITION

Sustantivos

el alimento	*food*
la caloría	*calorie*
la cantidad	*quantity*
la dieta	*diet*
los frijoles	*beans*
el peso	*weight*
la pirámide de la alimentación	*food pyramid*
la porción	*portion*

Verbos

conservarse	*to keep*
consumir	*to consume*
depender	*to depend*

Adjetivos

activo/a	*active*
físico/a	*physical*
nutritivo/a	*nutritious*
sano/a	*healthy*
sedentario/a	*sedentary*

Adverbio

diariamente	*daily*

VERBS AND EXPRESSIONS OF DOUBT, UNCERTAINTY, DENIAL, AND DISBELIEF

dudar	*to doubt*
es imposible	*it's impossible*
es posible	*it's possible*
es probable	*it's probable*
negar (ie)	*to deny*
no creer	*to not believe*
no es cierto	*it's not certain*
no es evidente	*it's not evident*
no es seguro	*it's not sure*
no es verdad	*it's not true*
no está claro	*it isn't clear*
no estar seguro/a de	*to be unsure*
no pensar (ie)	*to not think*
puede ser	*it can be*
quizás	*maybe, perhaps*
tal vez	*maybe, perhaps*

Common verbs and expressions of certainty

creer	*to think; to believe*
es cierto	*it's certain, true*
es evidente	*it's evident*
es obvio	*it's obvious*
es seguro	*it's sure*
es verdad	*it's true*
está claro	*it's clear*
estar seguro/a de	*to be sure*
no dudar	*to not doubt*
no hay duda (de)	*there's no doubt*
no negar (ie)	*to not deny*
opinar	*to think (have an opinion)*
pensar (ie)	*to think (opinion)*

SUDAMÉRICA

Online Study Center

To learn more about the people featured in this section, visit the *Caminos* website at http://college.hmco.com/languages/spanish/renjilian/caminos/3e/student_home.html.

Michelle Bachelet

Carolina Herrera

Víctor Jara

Inca Son

Evo Morales

PERSONALIDADES

Pablo Neruda

Mercedes Sosa

Gabriel García Márquez

Los sudamericanos

Los artistas sudamericanos tratan muchos temas: el amor, la familia, el medio ambiente[1], la guerra, la política, la cultura. El tema de los derechos humanos[2] también se refleja en el arte, la música, la literatura y el cine sudamericano. En las últimas décadas del siglo[3] XX, muchos países latinoamericanos sufrieron bajo dictaduras[4] represivas. El resultado fue la desaparición[5] o muerte de miles de personas que protestaron contra los actos discriminatorios y tiránicos de sus gobiernos.

Entre[6] los chilenos, el poeta Pablo Neruda y la novelista Isabel Allende critican en sus obras la opresión sociopolítica contra los ciudadanos de su país y de otras naciones hispanoamericanas.

Los argentinos Quino, en sus tiras cómicas[7], y Mercedes Sosa, en sus canciones, cubren temas de las violaciones de derechos humanos. En el cine argentino, las películas "La historia oficial",

[1]environment; [2]human rights; [3]century; [4]dictatorships; [5]disappearance; [6]among; [7]comic strips

"En el arte, la única competencia que tengo es con lo que hice ayer."

—Shakira (Colombia)

"Tango", "Kamchatka" y otras tratan[8] de los ciudadanos desaparecidos en la Argentina durante las décadas de los setenta y ochenta.

Cien años de soledad[9] es una novela extraordinaria escrita por el colombiano Gabriel García Márquez. Varias de sus obras literarias, junto con las de Mario Vargas Llosa (Perú) y Mario Benedetti (Uruguay), que tratan de temas políticos y sociales, han sido[10] interpretadas en películas.

Visita el sitio web de *Caminos* para leer más en español sobre estas personalidades y otros sudamericanos influyentes como Michelle Bachelet, la primera mujer presidente de Chile; Evo Morales, el primer presidente indígena de Bolivia; Carolina Herrera, diseñadora venezolana; la escritora chilena Gabriela Mistral, ganadora del Premio Nobel de Literatura; los cantantes Victor Jara (Chile) y Shakira (Colombia); y los grupos Inca Son (Perú), Los Jaira (Bolivia) y Kandela y Son (Ecuador).

Mario Vargas Llosa

Shakira

Comprensión

Trabajando en parejas, háganse las preguntas.

1. ¿Cuáles son algunos de los temas de las artes y letras en Sudamérica?
2. Indiquen las profesiones de tres diferentes personalidades sudamericanas.

ARTE

FERNANDO BOTERO

El escultor° y pintor Fernando Botero nació en Colombia en 1932. Las obras de este artista prolífico aparecen en museos, plazas y avenidas famosas en las Américas, Europa y África. El volumen y la grandeza son características de su estilo artístico para pintar a personas, lugares y cosas. Es importante notar la preocupación de Botero por los derechos humanos y su crítica a la violencia que se vive en su país natal. Actualmente° tiene residencias en París, Nueva York y la Toscana.

sculptor

currently

Naturaleza muerta con helado

---

[8]deal with; [9]*One Hundred Years of Solitude* [10]have been.

Comprensión

Trabajando en parejas, háganse las preguntas sobre la obra de Botero.

1. ¿Cuáles son posibles temas de esta naturaleza muerta°? Describe el estilo del artista.
2. ¿Qué frutas hay en la pintura? ¿De qué colores son? ¿Cuál es la más jugosa°?
3. Describe los postres. ¿Cuál te apetece° más?
4. ¿De qué sabor° es el helado? ¿A cuántas personas puede servir?
5. ¿En qué cuarto puede estar la mesa? Nombra una probable ocasión para servir estos postres y frutas.
6. ¿Cómo te parece esta naturaleza muerta —deliciosa, exagerada, llamativa°, divertida, aburrida?
7. ¿Prefieres pastel de chocolate, de vainilla o de limón? ¿Por qué? ¿Cuál tiene más calorías, en tu opinión?
8. De las frutas que se ven en la pintura, ¿cuáles son buenas para la salud? ¿Cuál es tu favorita?

MÚSICA

JUANES

El cantante, guitarrista, productor y compositor, Juanes nació en Medellín, Colombia, bajo el nombre de Juan Esteban Aristizábal. A los siete años, su padre y sus tres hermanos mayores le enseñaron a tocar la guitarra. Ganador de casi dos docenas de premios prestigiosos de la música internacional (Premios Grammy Latinos, Premios MTV, Premios Lo Nuestro), incorpora muchos ritmos autóctonos° en sus canciones. Sus influencias musicales incluyen tango, ranchera, bolero, salsa, guasca y trova cubana. Sus temas son variados°: el amor, la búsqueda de la identidad, la guerra cívil en Colombia.

Comprensión

Trabajando en parejas, háganse las siguientes preguntas sobre Juanes.

1. Además de cantar, ¿qué hace Juanes en su carrera profesional?
2. ¿Dónde nació el cantante?
3. ¿Quiénes fueron los profesores de música de Juanes?
4. ¿A qué edad empezó a tocar la guitarra?
5. ¿Cómo se llaman los premios ganados por° Juanes?
6. ¿Qué ritmos incorpora Juanes en sus canciones? ¿Qué estilos de música influyen a este cantante colombiano?
7. Nombra algunos de los temas musicales de Juanes.
8. Describe a un/a cantante de tu país que canta sobre el amor, la identidad o la guerra. ¿Quién es y qué expresa en su música?

Conéctate a Internet para escuchar la música de Juanes y aprender más sobre él.

"Creo que la vida es como jugar un juego de cartas donde para ganar tienes que jugar lo mejor posible. Pero a menudo nuestra vida, como las cartas, suelen estar marcadas."

—Isabel Allende (Chile)

LITERATURA

ISABEL ALLENDE

Novelista y cuentista°, Isabel Allende nació en 1942 en Perú, de padres chilenos. En su cuento "Dos palabras", el carácter de los políticos y los efectos de la guerra° están entre los varios temas que la autora incorpora en esta narración corta. En el fragmento que sigue, una mujer llamada Belisa Crepusculario escribe discursos° para la gente. El Coronel°, soldado° y candidato para la presidencia de Chile, le pide que le escriba un discurso.

short story
writer
war

speeches
l / soldier

Dos palabras

...
—¿Eres la que vende palabras?—...
—Para servirte—...
  El Coronel se puso de pie°. La mujer vio su piel oscura y sus fieros° ojos de puma.   *stood up / fierce, wild*
—Quiero ser Presidente—dijo él.
  Estaba cansado de recorrer esa tierra maldita° en guerras inútiles y derrotas° que ningún subterfugio   *wretched / defeats*
  podía transformar en victorias.
  ...al Coronel no le interesaba convertirse en otro tirano...Su idea consistía en ser elegido°   *elected*
  por votación popular.
—Para eso necesito hablar como un candidato. ¿Puedes venderme las palabras para un discurso?—
  preguntó el coronel a Belisa Crepusculario.
—¿Cuánto te debo por tu trabajo, mujer?—...
—Un peso, Coronel.
—No es caro—dijo él abriendo la bolsa° que llevaba colgada° del cinturón...   *bag/he wore hanging*
—Además tienes derecho° a una ñapa°. Te corresponden dos palabras secretas dijo Belisa   *right/ bonus*
  Crepusculario.

Comprensión

Con un/a compañero/a, háganse las preguntas sobre la lectura.

1. Nombra las partes del cuerpo que la autora menciona en el cuento.
2. ¿Qué animal menciona?
3. ¿Qué vende Belisa Crepusculario? ¿A quién?
4. ¿De qué estaba cansado el Coronel como soldado? ¿Qué adjetivo usa el Coronel para describir las guerras? ¿Estás de acuerdo?
5. ¿Qué quiere ser el Coronel? ¿Por qué necesita él las palabras de Belisa? ¿Cómo prefiere ser elegido él?
6. ¿Cuánto tiene que pagar el Coronel a Belisa por el discurso? ¿Es caro o barato? ¿Qué más le regala Belisa al Coronel?
7. ¿Qué tipo de Presidente quiere ser el Coronel?
8. La época de política represiva de los años pasados en Chile es un tema importante de esta selección. ¿Qué es lo contrario de una dictadura? ¿Cómo son los políticos de tu región?

9
La tecnología

VOCABULARIO Y LENGUA

► Talking about technology
► Contrasting the indicative and subjunctive in adjective clauses
► Giving instructions: Familiar *tú* commands

► Discussing cars
► Contrasting the indicative and subjunctive in adverbial clauses
► Describing actions in the recent and remote past: Present and past perfect indicative

CAMINOS DEL JAGUAR

► ¿Misión cumplida?
► Intuiciones y acusaciones

LECTURA

► Coches de hoy y mañana

NOTAS CULTURALES

► El padrino / La madrina
► Los parques nacionales de Costa Rica

ESTRATEGIAS

► **Reading:** Defining audience and purpose
► **Writing:** Developing a point of view

Gilbert "Magú" Luján, *Cruising Turtle Island*

Preguntas del tema

- ► ¿Pasas mucho tiempo navegando por Internet? ¿Por qué?
- ► ¿Cuál es el aparato de tecnología que más usas?
- ► ¿Cuál es el mejor coche? ¿el peor coche?
- ► ¿Cómo es el coche ideal?

PRIMER PASO

Vocabulario y lengua

TALKING ABOUT TECHNOLOGY

Online Study Center

For additional practice with this unit's vocabulary and grammar, visit the *Caminos* website at http://college.hmco.com/languages/spanish/renjilian/caminos/3e/student_home.html. You can also review audio flashcards, quiz yourself, and explore related Spanish-language sites.

Hotel moderno con alta tecnología

Los días en los que un teléfono y un televisor eran los aparatos tecnológicos más avanzados dentro de una habitación ya son cosa del pasado. Hoy en día, la tecnología tiene un papel° muy importante en los servicios del hotel. Aquí hay algunos de los cambios.

role

La alta tecnología

Casi todas las habitaciones están equipadas con computadoras para **acceder a Internet**° con conexiones de **alta velocidad**° o de **conexión sin cables**° (WiFi).

acce(s)
Inter(net)
high
wire(less)

Los televisores están colgados o **instalados**° en la pared. Tienen **pantallas planas**° de plasma o de LCD interactivos. A través de estos televisores se puede acceder a Internet con un **teclado**° **inalámbrico**°, mantener videoconferencias y ver quién llama a la puerta. Además, hay videoconsolas con cientos de **videojuegos**° para mantener entretenidos a los niños y aparatos de **realidad virtual.**

insta(lled)
flat s(creen)
keybo(ard)
wirel(ess)
video(games)

cont. on next page

Para la comodidad

Las habitaciones tienen climatización inteligente, programas informáticos que controlan las luces, **robots** de limpieza, sensores de luz, **control remoto** universal para hacer todo desde la cama, hasta subir la persiana°.

Venetian blinds

Páginas electrónicas

En las estanterías de la habitación hay libros electrónicos con pantallas **táctiles**° y numerosos textos **almacenados**°.

Cara a cara

El teléfono tiene una pantalla en la que el huésped ve a la persona que le atiende en recepción.

Un buen despertar

Las mesitas tienen un sistema emisor de ondas° que favorece el sueño. En algunos casos integran teléfono, **fax,** televisor y computadora. Y, si uno quiere desayunar en la cama, puede hacerlo en una bandeja° equipada con una pantalla en la que se puede ver las noticias o leer el **correo electrónico**°.

soundwave machine

tray

e-mail

Más palabras y expresiones

Cognados

el aparato
la aplicación
automático/a
la batería
el botón

la cámara
copiar
digital
el directorio
el documento
en línea
entrar

la función
el icono
el módem
multimedia
el programa
el teléfono celular
la videocámara

Sustantivos

el archivo	*computer file*
la ayuda	*help*
el buscador	*search engine*
la computadora portátil	*laptop*
la contraseña	*password*
el disco duro	*hard drive*
la (alta) definición	*(high) definition*
el entretenimiento	*entertainment*
la (video) grabadora	*(video) recorder*
el mensaje	*message*
el paso	*step*
el ratón	*mouse*
la red	*network*

Verbos

apagar	*to turn off, to shut off*
apuntar	*to point, to jot down*
archivar, guardar	*to save, to file*
bajar	*to download*
cargar	*to charge*
colgar (ue)	*to hang (up)*

desempeñar	*to carry out*
imprimir	*to print*
iniciar	*to begin*
mover (ue)	*to move; to shift*
prender, encender (ie)	*to turn on*
presionar, hacer clic, pulsar, oprimir	*to click (with the mouse); to push (a button)*

Adjetivos

disponible	*available*

Actividades

1 Habitación 2020. Lee la descripción del hotel del futuro (pp. 310–311) y determina qué servicios ofrece. Pon una X al lado de cada servicio que se ofrece.

_____ computadora
_____ desayuno virtual
_____ juegos electrónicos
_____ libros electrónicos
_____ máquina fax
_____ procesador automático de comidas
_____ robot-camarero
_____ teléfono con pantalla
_____ teclado inalámbrico
_____ teléfonos táctiles
_____ minibar automático
_____ televisor interactivo

2 ¿Qué describe? Escucha las descripciones de unos nuevos aparatos tecnológicos y escribe el número de la descripción al lado del aparato que le corresponda.

a. _____

b. _____

c. _____

d. _____

e. _____

3 **¡Qué buena es la tecnología!** A veces la tecnología no funciona como debe. Acabas de recibir un correo electrónico de una amiga, pero no puedes leer todo el mensaje. Completa el mensaje con las siguientes palabras.

mensaje	computadora	ayuda	impresora
programa	teléfono	tecnología	

Tema:
Fecha:
Para:

¡Hola!

Hoy compré una nueva _*_. Traté de instalar el *$_ < para mandarte un mensaje electrónico, pero dice que hay errores. La *$* tampoco funciona y no puedo imprimir este *$<*. Yo sé que soy nueva con la *&$v**_, pero esto es ridículo. Por favor, necesito tu $*&_*. ¡Llámame, porque sé que por lo menos funciona mi *&_!_!

Tu amiga,
Leticia

4 **Combinaciones.** Trabaja con un/a compañero/a para crear siete oraciones. Combinen palabras de cada columna y agreguen más palabras para hablar de la tecnología. Sigan el modelo.

▶ **MODELO:** *Yo prendo mi computadora por la mañana para leer mi correo electrónico.*

A	B	C
Yo	prender	archivo
Tú	mandar	párrafo
Mis amigos	abrir	computadora
Los profesores	cerrar	palabras
Ud.	buscar	mensaje
Tú y yo	imprimir	programa
Mi mamá	escribir	documento

5 **Nuevos productos.** Usa el Internet para buscar un nuevo producto tecnológico. Primero, busca en una página web en español como las siguientes y trae una copia del producto a la clase. Luego, en grupos de tres, hablen de sus productos y escojan el que más les guste para presentar a la clase.

http://www.apple.com/es

http://www.microsoft.com/argentina

http://www.palm.com/mx

http://www.sony.com.co

CONTRASTING THE INDICATIVE AND SUBJUNCTIVE IN ADJECTIVE CLAUSES

Dilema

Trabajo en una oficina que **tiene** tecnología vieja e ineficiente, pero sueño con una oficina que **tenga** tecnología moderna y eficiente.

Adjective clauses: An adjective clause is a subordinate clause introduced by **que** that modifies a noun, in the same way that a simple adjective does.

Simple adjective	Adjective clause
Tengo una computadora **vieja.**	Tengo una computadora **que es vieja.**
I have an old computer.	*I have a computer that is old.*
Quiero una computadora **nueva.**	Quiero una computadora **que sea nueva.**
I want a new computer.	*I want a computer that is new.*

The indicative is used when the verb in the subordinate clause refers to a specific or existent person or thing.

Trabajo en una compañía que **está** lejos de mi casa.	*I work at a company that is far from my home.*
Tengo un secretario que **sabe** muchísimo de computadoras.	*I have a secretary who knows a lot about computers.*

The subjunctive is used when the verb in the subordinate clause refers to an indefinite, non-existent, or unknown person or thing.

Quiero una computadora que **tenga** los últimos avances tecnológicos.	*I want a computer that has the latest technological advances.*
Busco una cámara digital que **saque** buenas fotos de acción.	*I'm looking for a digital camera that takes good action pictures.*

Many double negative expressions introduce adjective clauses that require the subjunctive: **No conozco a nadie que..., No hay nada que..., No hay ningún lugar que...,** etc.

Necesitamos a alguien que **sepa** hacer páginas web.	*We need someone who knows how to do web pages.*
No hay nadie que **tenga** la computadora perfecta.	*There isn't anyone who has the perfect computer.*

Actividades

1 Gustos y preferencias. Completa las preguntas con el presente del subjuntivo de los verbos entre paréntesis. Luego, contesta las preguntas con un/a compañero/a.

1. ¿Quieres una computadora de mano que _____ (venir) con correo electrónico?
2. ¿Prefieres un televisor que _____ (tener) una pantalla de plasma o de LCD?
3. ¿Buscas videojuegos que no _____ (contener) mucha violencia?
4. ¿Necesitas una computadora portátil que _____ (ser) más pequeña?
5. ¿Buscas restaurantes que _____ (ofrecer) una conexión sin cables?
6. ¿Sólo bajas música que te _____ (gustar) del Internet?

2 Cambios necesarios. A veces hay cosas que queremos cambiar en nuestras vidas. Usa el verbo **tener** o **conocer** para explicar lo que tienes y verbos como **querer, necesitar** y **buscar** para explicar lo que necesitas. Sigue el modelo.

▶ MODELO: un/a profesora
Tengo una profesora que enseña español pero necesito una profesora que enseñe portugués.

1. una clase
2. un coche
3. una grabadora de música
4. un teléfono
5. una conexión al Internet
6. una película
7. una cámara
8. un/a presidente
9. un apartamento
10. una televisión

3 Un/a compañero/a ideal.
Necesitas buscar un/a compañero/a de cuarto. ¿Cuáles son las cualidades más importantes? ¿Cuáles son las cualidades menos importantes? Pon estas cualidades en orden de importancia. Luego, trabajen en parejas y decidan cuáles son las tres cosas más importantes y las tres cosas menos importantes. Sigue el modelo.

► MODELO: —*Busco un/a compañero/a que me trate bien.*
—*No quiero un/a compañero/a que fume.*

_____ (no) limpiar su cuarto
_____ (no) fumar
_____ (no) tocar música a todas horas
_____ ser amable
_____ pagar las cuentas a tiempo

_____ tener computadora
_____ tratarme bien
_____ (no) estudiar mucho
_____ (no) hacer mucho ruido
_____ (no) tener mascotas

4 Un trabajo ideal.
Necesitas buscar un trabajo nuevo. Decides escribir un anuncio clasificado en el periódico. Escribe un anuncio que describa tu trabajo ideal, incluyendo la tecnología que conoces. Comienza tu anuncio con esta frase: "Se busca un trabajo que…"

GIVING INSTRUCTIONS: FAMILIAR *TÚ* COMMANDS

Cómo bajar música con iTunes

Conéctate al Internet.
Abre el programa de iTunes.
Haz clic en la tienda de música.
Busca tu música favorita.
Escucha la canción para asegurar que es la que quieres.
Haz clic en "Comprar canción" o "Comprar álbum".
Escribe tu contraseña. (¡**No olvides** tu tarjeta de crédito!)
Oprime el botón "Comprar" y **baja** la música a iTunes.
Escucha la música en tu computadora y **ponla** en tu iPod.
¡**Disfrútala**!

In *Unidad 6,* you learned the formation and uses of the formal **Ud. / Uds.** commands. Look at the **tú** commands in the preceding instructions. Do you recognize some of the forms? Which forms are new? Where are the pronouns placed in the affirmative and the negative commands?

Affirmative *tú* commands

To form the *affirmative tú* command, use the third person singular of the present tense. All verbs with irregular third person singular forms have an irregular **tú** command form. Review the formation of the present tense on pages 94, 95, and 96.

Infinitive	affirmative *tú* command	Infinitive	affirmative *tú* command
cantar	canta	entender (ie)	entiende
beber	bebe	pedir (i)	pide
escribir	escribe	oír	oye
recordar (ue)	recuerda	leer	lee

The subject pronoun **tú** is sometimes used for emphasis. If used in a command, the pronoun follows the command form.

Busca tú un nuevo juego electrónico para tu primo.

Look for a new videogame for your cousin.

Irregular affirmative *tú* commands

The following verbs have irregular forms for the affirmative **tú** commands:

Infinitive	affirmative *tú* command	Infinitive	affirmative *tú* command
decir	di	salir	sal
hacer	haz	ser	sé
ir	ve	tener	ten
poner	pon	venir	ven

Negative *tú* commands

The *negative familiar* commands are the same as the present subjunctive forms for **tú,** which you learned in *Unidad 8.* Review these forms on pages 278–281.

Infinitive	negative *tú* command	Infinitive	negative *tú* command
cantar	no cantes	oír	no oigas
beber	no bebas	ir	no vayas
escribir	no escribas	ser	no seas
recordar (ue)	no recuerdes	poner	no pongas
entender (ie)	no entiendas	conducir	no conduzcas
pedir (i)	no pidas	ver	no veas

Object pronouns

Direct and indirect object pronouns and reflexive pronouns are attached to the end of affirmative commands. When pronouns are attached, a written accent is needed if the stress falls on the third or fourth syllable from the end of the word.

¡Dinos la contraseña, por favor!	*Tell us the password, please!*
¡Dínosla, por favor!	*Tell it to us, please!*
Escríbeme pronto.	*Write to me soon.*

Direct and indirect object pronouns and reflexive pronouns precede the verb in all negative commands.

No **le** saques la foto a Juan todavía.	*Don't take the photo of Juan yet.*
No **se la** saques todavía.	*Don't take it (the photo) of him yet.*
No **te** duermas.	*Don't fall asleep.*

Actividades

1 Consejos. Dale consejos a un/a compañero/a de clase de cómo tener éxito en la universidad. Sigue el modelo.

> ► **MODELO:** _____ (Despertarse) temprano.
> *Despiértate temprano.*

1. _____ (Salir) de casa a tiempo.
2. No _____ (llegar) tarde a las clases.
3. _____ (Mantenerse) alerta en clase.
4. _____ (Escuchar) a los profesores.
5. _____ (Estudiar) todos los días.
6. _____ (Ir) a la biblioteca y _____ (leer) la tarea.
7. _____ (Hacer) ejercicios en el gimnasio con un/a amigo/a.
8. Si estás enfermo/a y no puedes ir a clase, _____ (mandarle) un correo electrónico a un/a compañero/a de clase y _____ (pedirle) la tarea.
9. No _____ (acostarse) tarde.
10. _____ (Dormir) bien cada noche para reducir el estrés.

2 Instrucciones. Tu profesor/a te pide que escribas un informe (*report*) para tu clase de español y necesitas buscar la información en Internet. Le pides sugerencias al /a la profesor/a. En parejas, pongan en orden sus sugerencias. Usen mandatos informales afirmativos (**tú**).

abrir la primera página web	escribirlo en tus propias palabras
abrir tu buscador favorito	escribir palabras clave en español
apuntar la información importante	repetir los pasos hasta encontrar la información que necesitas
entregárselo al/a la profesor/a	organizar la información para el informe
hacer clic en "Búsqueda"	leerla

3 Ayuda.
Tu primo viene de visita y, como tu dormitorio está muy desorganizado, un amigo te ayuda a arreglarlo antes de la visita. Contesta sus preguntas con mandatos informales. No te olvides de usar los pronombres necesarios. Sigue el modelo.

► MODELO: ¿Dónde pongo los libros?
Ponlos en el estante.

1. ¿Dejo los CDs en la mesa?
2. ¿Te presto mi cama de aire?
3. ¿Qué hago con la ropa que está en el piso?
4. ¿Cierro la puerta del armario?
5. ¿Apago la computadora?
6. ¿Hago la cama?
7. ¿Barro el piso?
8. ¿Dónde guardo tu iPod?
9. ¿Qué hago con el dinero que encontré en el escritorio?
10. ¿Pongo los zapatos debajo de la cama?

4 De visita.
Tu primo está de visita, pero no sabe usar las cosas en tu apartamento. Mientras estás en clase, él te llama varias veces para preguntarte cómo usar las siguientes cosas. Trabajen en parejas y escriban de 2 a 4 mandatos informales para cada situación.

1. ¿Cómo funciona el televisor?
2. Tengo hambre y no sé usar tu microondas.
3. Quiero mandar un correo electrónico, pero no tengo tu contraseña.
4. Quiero escuchar música pero no sé como usar tu iPod.
5. Veo que tienes TiVO. ¿Cómo puedo grabar una película?
6. Me gustaría jugar con los videojuegos. ¿Cómo lo hago?

5 Apoyo técnico.
En parejas, escriban diez consejos para una amiga que va a empezar a trabajar para un servicio de apoyo técnico. Va a recibir muchas llamadas al día y a veces las personas que llaman van a ser poco amables. ¿Qué debe hacer ella cuando hable con los clientes? ¿Qué no debe hacer?

¿Mision cumplida?

En la finca de doña Carmen, en Costa Rica.

¡Nayeli! ¡Qué gusto verte, ahijada!

Madrina, qué bueno sentirme segura. Aquí nadie me está vigilando.

Aquí estás protegida.

Ay, madrina, tengo que contarle la historia del jaguar perdido.

Tranquila, hija, tenemos tiempo para eso.

No, madrina, no hay tiempo.

Usted conoce a Armando de Landa, ¿verdad? Fue mi compañero de estudios en México.

Sí, era un chico alto, brillante, serio.

Creo que él se robó el jaguar y me culpó a mí. Y él también mandó a Adriana y a Felipe a buscarme a mí y al jaguar.

Por favor, Nayeli, eso es ridículo, ya sabes que Armando es buena persona.

No, madrina, yo sé que Armando es malo.

No, hija, tienes que controlar tu imaginación. Duerme un poco.

Está bien, madrina, voy a mi cuarto a descansar un rato.

Armando llama por teléfono desde México.

Voy a mandar a alguien para recoger el paquete.

No. El paquete se lo entregué a una señora de gafas oscuras.

¿Por qué no esperó mis instrucciones? Ella es una ladrona y usted es su cómplice. No voy a pagarle nada.

¡Usted es el ladrón! Su dinero no me interesa.

Adriana y Felipe llegan a la casa de doña Carmen, en Costa Rica.

¡Gooool! ¡Estamos llegando al final de esta aventura!

Esto no es fútbol, Felipe.

¡Nayeli!

¡Qué gusto verlos aquí fuera de peligro!

¡Hola! ¡Adelante!

Perdonen el desorden, pero están pintando la casa.

La señora dice que tenemos que terminar para el mediodía.

No importa, madrina, vamos a estar invisibles.

Aquí lo tienes: ¡Yax-Balam!

¡Qué belleza! No recordaba la fuerza que tiene. Es sobrenatural.

¿Por qué no los reunimos?

Buena idea, Adriana.

Por fin están reunidos los dos jaguares. Misión más o menos cumplida ... pero los jaguares todavía no están en México.

Nayeli recibe una sorpresa.

¿Señora Nayeli Paz Ocotlán?

Sí, soy yo.

Esta rosa amarilla es para usted.

Qué bonita. ¿De quién puede ser?

No lo sé.

No importa. Vamos a celebrar. Estamos juntos y los jaguares también.

Actividades

Online Study Center

For additional practice with this episode, visit the *Caminos* website at http://college.hmco.com/languages/spanish/renjilian/caminos/3e/student_home.html.

1 Comprensión. Basándote en este episodio de *Caminos del jaguar,* elige la alternativa lógica.

1. Nayeli se siente segura con su madrina porque...
   a. la madrina se preocupa.
   b. se siente protegida.

2. La madrina quiere escuchar la historia...
   a. inmediatamente.
   b. después.

3. Nayeli dice que...
   a. tiene mucho tiempo.
   b. tiene poco tiempo.

4. Doña Carmen dice que...
   a. no recuerda a Armando.
   b. recuerda a Armando.

5. Nayeli dice que Armando...
   a. es brillante y serio.
   b. se robó el jaguar.

6. Armando está furioso con Zulaya porque...
   a. Zulaya no quiere su dinero.
   b. Zulaya no esperó sus instrucciones.

7. Adriana y Felipe le llevan a Nayeli el jaguar...
   a. Yax-Balam.
   b. Hun-Ahau.

8. Adriana dice que la misión está...
   a. casi cumplida.
   b. cumplida.

2 Situaciones. Dramaticen una de las siguientes situaciones.

1. Doña Carmen recibe a Nayeli en su casa.
2. Armando habla con Zulaya por teléfono.

3 Escritura. Escribe un resumen de lo que dice Adriana cuando le entrega el jaguar a Nayeli. (4–6 oraciones)

NOTA CULTURAL

El padrino / La madrina

En las culturas hispanas es un honor ser elegido/a como padrino o madrina. Se elige generalmente a algún miembro de la familia o a un amigo íntimo. Su función es tomar el lugar del padre o de la madre cuando sea necesario para asegurar el bienestar del ahijado o la ahijada. Generalmente hay una relación importante entre padrinos y ahijados. Muchas veces, la madrina o el padrino contribuye a pagar los gastos de celebraciones especiales como el bautizo y algunos cumpleaños especiales como la fiesta de quinceañera de la ahijada.

SEGUNDO PASO

Vocabulario y lengua

DISCUSSING CARS

Online Study Center

For additional practice with this unit's vocabulary and grammar, visit the *Caminos* website at http://college.hmco.com/languages/spanish/renjilian/caminos/3e/student_home.html. You can also review audio flashcards, quiz yourself, and explore related Spanish-language sites.

Necesitamos comprar un coche

—Mire mamá, el limpiaparabrisas funciona muy bien.

1. el baúl, maletero
2. el espejo retrovisor
3. el limpiaparabrisas
4. la llanta, rueda
5. las luces
6. el parabrisas
7. el pito, claxon
8. la placa
9. la puerta
10. el tanque de gasolina

Más palabras y expresiones

Cognados

el acelerador	económico/a
el auto, automóvil	la gasolina
el carro	híbrido/a
compacto/a	el motor

Sustantivos

el aire acondicionado	*air conditioning*
el asiento	*seat*
el coche	*car*
la batería, pila	*battery*
la bolsa de aire, el airbag	*airbag*

la carretera	*highway*
el choque	*crash*
el cinturón de seguridad	*seatbelt*
el/la conductor/a	*driver*
el deportivo	*sports car*
los frenos	*brakes*
la licencia de manejar/conducir	*driver's license*
la llanta pinchada	*flat tire*
la multa	*fine*
el volante	*steering wheel*

Verbos

abrocharse (el cinturón)	*to buckle up (seatbelt)*
arrancar	*to start (a car, a race)*
chocar	*to collide*
conducir, manejar	*to drive*
dañar	*to injure; to damage*
frenar	*to brake*
parar	*to stop*
pitar	*to beep the horn*

Actividades

1 ¿Qué es? Identifica la parte del coche que se describe.

1. El chofer se sienta en este lugar.
2. Son absolutamente necesarios cuando llueve.
3. Se necesita para llamar la atención, ¡no para hacer ruido!
4. El coche no puede parar sin ellos.
5. Protege a los pasajeros en los accidentes.
6. Si tu coche no lo tiene, te va a dar mucho calor en el verano.
7. Allí pones tu pie y ¡el coche anda!
8. Se vende por litros en España y en los Estados Unidos por galones.
9. Si dejas las luces encendidas muchas horas, se acaba.

2 ¡Quiero comprar un Jaguar! Contesta las siguientes preguntas sobre el tipo de coche que quieres comprar.

1. ¿Qué clase de auto te gusta? ¿deportivo? ¿compacto? ¿híbrido? ¿económico? ¿de lujo? ¿camioneta? ¿Por qué?
2. ¿Qué color prefieres? ¿Por qué?
3. ¿Cuál es tu presupuesto (*budget*)?
4. ¿Qué características son esenciales en tu coche?
5. ¿Qué características son deseables pero no esenciales?

3 ¿Qué auto compramos? Tú y tu mejor amigo/a deciden comprar un coche juntos. En parejas, comparen sus respuestas a la *Actividad 2* y decidan cuál de los coches van a comprar y por qué.

4 El coche ideal. Trae a clase una foto del coche que te piensas comprar (o dibújalo) y descríbelo a la clase.

CONTRASTING THE INDICATIVE AND SUBJUNCTIVE IN ADVERBIAL CLAUSES

Siempre estacionaba mi coche enfrente de la oficina **cuando llegaba** al trabajo por la mañana.

Pero ayer **cuando llegué,** tuve un pequeño accidente porque no vi la motocicleta que estaba allí.

La policía llegó y ¡me dio una multa de $100! Debo tener más cuidado **cuando manejo.**

Mañana, **cuando vaya** al trabajo, voy en metro.

As shown in the preceding examples, an adverbial conjunction (like **cuando**) can introduce a dependent clause. What forms are used after **cuando** in each of the examples? Why do you think the present indicative is used in the third sentence while the present subjunctive is used in the last one?

Adverbial clauses, introduced by conjunctions such as **cuando,** give information such as when, how, or under what circumstances an action may occur. When using adverbial conjunctions, choose the...

▶ **Imperfect** in the dependent clause to narrate *past habitual* actions.

▶ **Preterite** in the dependent clause to describe *specific past* actions.

- ▶ **Present indicative** in the dependent clause to report *present habitual* actions.
- ▶ **Present subjunctive** in the dependent clause to indicate a *future* action.

Adverbial conjunctions that are followed by the indicative or the subjunctive according to the preceding patterns are the following:

a pesar de que	*even though, even if*
aunque	*even when, even though, even if, although*
cuando	*when*
después (de) que	*after*
en cuanto	*as soon as*
hasta que	*until*
tan pronto como	*as soon as*

Notice that with **aunque** and **a pesar de que,** the English translation changes to indicate the difference between a concrete condition or fact (present indicative) and a condition or situation that may or may not happen (present subjunctive).

Rafael siempre va al trabajo **a pesar de que se siente** enfermo.	*Rafael always goes to work even though he feels ill.*
Rafael va al trabajo **aunque se sienta** enfermo.	*Rafael goes to work even if he feels ill.*

Notice that the sentence order is flexible with adverbial conjunctions.

Leo el correo electrónico **tan pronto como** llego al trabajo.	*I read my e-mail as soon as I get to work.*
Tan pronto como llego al trabajo, leo el correo electrónico.	*As soon as I get to work, I read my e-mail.*

Actividades

1 En camino. Determina si lo que sucede son situaciones habituales (indicativo) o futuras (subjuntivo). Selecciona la posibilidad correcta.

1. Cada jueves, Roberto sale de la casa cuando...
   a. llega su colega Jaime.
   b. llegue su colega Jaime.

2. Katie piensa comprar una motocicleta tan pronto como...
   a. ahorra el dinero.
   b. ahorre el dinero.

3. Isabel va a salir de viaje después de que el mecánico...
   a. arregla su coche.
   b. arregle su coche.

4. Con el precio tan alto de la gasolina, Pepito siempre maneja su coche hasta que...
   a. se le acabe la gasolina.
   b. se le acaba la gasolina.

5. El jefe siempre maneja su carro deportivo a pesar de que la gasolina...
   a. cuesta mucho.
   b. cueste mucho.

6. Roberto piensa comprar un coche híbrido en cuanto...
   a. le pagan.
   b. le paguen.

2 La conferencia. Lorena y Sami preparan una conferencia para sus clientes. Completa la descripción de algunas de sus actividades con el indicativo o subjuntivo de los verbos en paréntesis, según el contexto.

Lorena   Tenemos que preparar el café tan pronto como _____ (**1.** llegar) los clientes de hoy.

Sami   Sí, especialmente hay que tener todo listo cuando el jefe _____ (**2.** venir).

Lorena	Sami, ¿hiciste el registro en cuanto _____ (**3.** recibir) la lista de clientes?
Sami	Por supuesto, lo hice tan pronto como el secretario me _____ (**4.** traer) la lista.
Lorena	¿Piensas salir temprano hoy, después de que _____ (**5.** hacer, nosotros) la última presentación del día?
Sami	No, Lorena, es importante quedarme en la oficina hasta que _____ (**6.** terminar, yo) de escribir todos los informes para el archivo. ¿Y tú?
Lorena	Voy a buscar mi coche que está con el mecánico. Por eso, aunque _____ (**7.** dejar, yo) algunas cosas sin hacer, tengo que salir a las cinco.

3 Ayer y mañana. Escríbele un correo electrónico a tu amigo/a, describiéndole lo que tú ya hiciste y lo que van a hacer tú y tus compañeros de apartamento. Sigue el modelo.

► MODELO: El verano pasado, tan pronto como tuve el dinero, alquilé una cabaña en la playa con mis amigos.
El mes que viene, tan pronto como... *tenga dinero, voy a alquilar otra cabaña en la playa con mis amigos.*

1. Anoche cuando llegué a casa, me preparé una bebida de frutas en mi batidora. Mañana, cuando...
2. En cuanto recibimos nuestros salarios el mes pasado, pagamos la cuenta de teléfono, pero no pagamos la cuenta de la electricidad. Este mes, en cuanto...
3. Ayer no cenamos hasta que todos llegaron de la universidad. Hoy, tampoco vamos a cenar hasta que...
4. Yayo se duchó esta mañana tan pronto como se levantó. Mañana, Yayo también va a ducharse tan pronto como...
5. El año pasado, cuando recibí dinero de mi abuela, me compré ropa nueva. Esta semana, cuando...

DESCRIBING ACTIONS IN THE RECENT AND REMOTE PAST: PRESENT PERFECT AND PLUPERFECT (PAST PERFECT) INDICATIVE

Un día muy ocupado

Tomás	¿Qué **has hecho**° hoy, Mario?	*have you done*
Mario	**He estudiado**° mucho, **he limpiado** la casa, **he ido**° al supermercado y ahora estoy preparando la cena. Voy a preparar un plato que nunca **había preparado**° antes.	*I have studied / I have cleaned / have gone* *had prepared*
Tomás	Oye, pues yo **no he cenado**° todavía...	*I haven't had dinner*
Mario	Entonces ven a cenar conmigo.	
Tomás	Mil gracias. ¿Eres buen cocinero?	
Mario	Por supuesto. Nos vemos más tarde. Hasta luego.	

Present perfect and pluperfect (past perfect) indicative

A perfect tense has two parts: a conjugated form of the helping verb **haber** and the past participle of the main verb.

The present perfect uses the present tense of **haber.** The pluperfect (past perfect) uses the imperfect of **haber.**

The past participle of regular verbs is formed by adding **–ado** to the stem of **–ar** verbs and **–ido** to the stems of **–er** and **–ir** verbs.

> hablar: habl + -ado = **hablado**
> querer: quer + -ido = **querido**
> venir: ven + -ido = **venido**

The present perfect and pluperfect indicative *(El presente perfecto y el pluscuamperfecto del indicativo)*				
	Present perfect		Pluperfect	
yo	he		había	
tú	has	hablado	habías	hablado
Ud. / él / ella	ha	querido	había	querido
nosotros/as	hemos	venido	habíamos	venido
vosotros/as	habéis		habíais	
Uds. / ellos / ellas	han		habían	

The present perfect indicative

The present perfect tense is used to talk about a recently completed action with reference to the present. It is also used to indicate an indefinite point in the past with reference to the present.

¿Ya **has hecho** la tarea?   *Have you already done the homework?*
Nunca **he estado** en España.   *I have never been to Spain.*

The pluperfect (past perfect) indicative

Like the present perfect tense, the past perfect is used to talk about an action or event that happened before another past action or event.

Cuando yo tenía dieciséis años, ya   *When I was sixteen years old, I had*
 había comprado mi propio coche.   *already bought my own car.*

Antonio todavía no **había comido**   *Antonio hadn't eaten yet when I went by*
 cuando pasé a recogerlo.   *to pick him up.*

The perfect tenses often use the word **ya** to express *already* and the word **todavía** when answering a question negatively. It expresses *yet.*

Sentence structure

Direct and indirect object pronouns and reflexive pronouns come directly before the conjugated form of **haber.**

—¿**Has manejado** el nuevo coche híbrido?
—No, todavía no <u>lo</u> **he manejado**.

—*Have you driven the new hybrid car?*
—*No, I have driven it yet.*

—¿<u>Te</u> **habías alojado** en ese hotel antes?
—Sí, <u>me</u> **había alojado** allí.

—*Had you stayed in that hotel before?*
—*Yes, I had stayed there.*

Irregular past participles

Infinitive	Past participle	
abrir	**abierto**	*opened*
cubrir	**cubierto**	*covered*
decir	**dicho**	*said, told*
descubrir	**descubierto**	*discovered*
escribir	**escrito**	*written*
hacer	**hecho**	*made, done*
morir	**muerto**	*died*
poner	**puesto**	*put, placed*
resolver	**resuelto**	*resolved*
romper	**roto**	*broken, torn*
ver	**visto**	*seen*
volver	**vuelto**	*returned*

You must write an accent over the **i** of the **–ido** ending for those **–er** and **–ir** verbs whose stems end in -**a, -e,** or -**o.**

Infinitive	Stem	Past participle	
creer	cre-	creído	*believed*
leer	le-	leído	*read*
oír	o-	oído	*heard*
traer	tra-	traído	*brought*

Actividades

1 Hecho. Combina las palabras para crear oraciones en los tiempos perfectos. Primero, usa el **presente perfecto** y después, el **pluscuamperfecto** de los verbos. Sigue el modelo.

▶ MODELO: los científicos / descubrir / nuevas tecnologías

Los científicos han descubierto nuevas tecnologías.
The scientists have discovered new technologies.
Los científicos habían descubierto nuevas tecnologías.
The scientists had discovered new technologies.

1. las compañías de coches / producir / menos coches
2. el gobierno / limpiar / las carreteras
3. nosotros / leer / el folleto
4. yo / romper / el teclado inalámbrico
5. mi madre / no / manejar / su nuevo coche
6. ¿tú / ver / mi nuevo blog?
7. nadie / decirme / nada
8. la profesora / apagar / la computadora

2 ¿Quién lo ha hecho? Utiliza un verbo de la columna A y una expresión de la columna B para relatar qué han hecho diferentes personas. Usa el presente perfecto y un sujeto diferente para cada oración. Intenta usar las palabras **ya** y **todavía.** Sigue el modelo.

► MODELO: **A**   **B**
                    ver   la película

Mi novio y yo todavía no hemos visto la nueva película de Johnny Depp.

A	B
escribir	el coche
abrocharse	la mesa
abrir	la música
oprimir	la verdad
manejar	la composición
escuchar	el botón
poner	el cinturón
decir	la puerta

3 ¿Lo has hecho? En parejas, averigüen cuáles de las siguientes cosas ha hecho tu compañero/a durante la semana pasada.

► MODELO: manejar sin abrocharte el cinturón de seguridad
                —¿Has manejado sin abrocharte el cinturón de seguridad?
                —Sí, (No, no) he manejado sin abrocharme el cinturón de seguridad.

1. abrir la puerta para una persona del sexo opuesto
2. bajar canciones del Internet
3. ver una página web interesante
4. hacer un viaje en coche
5. leer un libro
6. ir a todas tus clases
7. hablar por teléfono mientras manejabas

4 ¿Qué había pasado antes? Francisco llegó muy tarde a la fiesta de cumpleaños de una amiga. Utiliza el pluscuamperfecto de indicativo para relatar qué había pasado antes de que llegara Francisco. Sigue el modelo.

► MODELO: La celebración (empezar) a las nueve.
                La celebración había empezado a las nueve.

1. La banda (tocar) por dos horas.
2. Algunas parejas (bailar) mucho.
3. Muchos invitados (comer) aperitivos y (beber) cerveza y vino.
4. Todos sus amigos (divertirse) muchísimo.
5. En camino a la fiesta Francisco (tener) una llanta pinchada.
6. Él no (poder) arreglarlo solo y (llamar) a un mecánico.
7. Sus amigos no (preocuparse) porque él les (decir) que iba a llegar tarde.
8. Afortunadamente no le (pasar) nada malo.

5 Las distintas épocas de mi vida. Indica cinco actividades que ya habías hecho durante diferentes épocas de tu vida: cuando tenías tres, seis, nueve, doce, quince o dieciséis años, por ejemplo. Utiliza el pluscuamperfecto del indicativo. Después, indica cinco actividades que todavía no has hecho. Sigue el modelo.

► MODELO: *Cuando yo tenía un año, ya había aprendido a caminar.*
                Todavía no he aprendido a nadar.

Intuiciones y acusaciones

Adriana y Felipe dan un paseo.

Costa Rica tiene una gran diversidad biológica.

Sí, es como un paraíso de novela.

Sí, Adriana, pero es real y lo estamos disfrutando.

Sí, ... ¡Mira la cantidad de mariposas!

Felipe, quiero comentar algo contigo.

Te estoy escuchando, Adriana, ¿de qué se trata?

Se trata de doña Carmen.

Fue muy amable con nosotros, ¿no crees?

Sí, nos trató como familia, pero me sentí muy incómoda con ella

¿Por qué te sentiste incómoda?

No lo sé. Quizás debo escuchar mi intuición y mi corazón.

Adriana, doña Carmen es la madrina de Nayeli. No puedes dudar de ella.

Lo sé, pero la personalidad que ella muestra no es la verdadera.

Adriana, hemos pasado por momentos muy difíciles. ¡Tu imaginación está trabajando horas extras!

No, Felipe, escúchame. Doña Carmen no es buena persona, estoy segura, pero no tengo pruebas.

Claro que no tienes pruebas. Dale a doña Carmen una oportunidad.

Felipe, a mí nunca me ha fallado la intuición.

Entonces, ¿qué quieres hacer?

Tengo que hablar con Nayeli, pero va a ser muy difícil. No va a comprender.

Tú sabes lo que haces. Confío en ti.

Gracias, Felipe. Eres fiel como un perro ... ¡y perdona la comparación!

¡Y tú eres astuta como un zorro!

¿Qué planean los pintores?

Esto es fácil. Mira aquí.

Sí, se apaga la electricidad y está listo.

Nayeli y Adriana dan un paseo.

Nayeli, tengo la sospecha de que doña Carmen está involucrada en el robo de Yax-Balam.

Adriana, ¡cómo puedes decir eso! Yo le debo toda mi vida a mi madrina.

Lo siento, Nayeli. Tú misma has dicho que debemos escuchar nuestras intuiciones.

Entonces no tienes pruebas, Adriana. Esta vez, tu intuición te ha engañado.

Todos cenan en la casa de doña Carmen.

¡Qué cena más sabrosa, madrina!

Es un honor tener aquí a los tres arqueólogos que salvaron a México.

¿Qué paso? Felipe, ¿dónde estás?

Aquí estoy, Adriana.

Actividades

For additional practice with this episode, visit the *Caminos* website at http://college.hmco.com/languages/spanish/renjilian/caminos/3e/student_home.html.

1 Comprensión. Basándote en este episodio de *Caminos del jaguar,* elige la alternativa lógica.

1. Costa Rica tiene...
   a. un paraíso real.
   b. mucha diversidad biológica.

2. Felipe y Adriana...
   a. disfrutan de la naturaleza.
   b. cuidan la naturaleza.

3. Felipe opina que doña Carmen es una señora...
   a. muy nerviosa.
   b. muy amable.

4. Adriana opina que la personalidad de doña Carmen...
   a. es verdadera.
   b. no es verdadera.

5. La opinión de Adriana sobre doña Carmen se basa en...
   a. pruebas.
   b. intuición.

6. Las acusaciones de Adriana...
   a. irritan a Nayeli.
   b. preocupan a Nayeli.

7. Cuando la luz se fue en la casa de doña Carmen, todos...
   a. estaban descansando.
   b. estaban cenando.

2 Situaciones. Dramaticen una de las siguientes situaciones.

1. Adriana le dice a Nayeli que no confía en su madrina.
2. Felipe y Adriana hablan sobre la madrina de Nayeli.

3 Escritura. Escribe una descripción de quiénes son los pintores que aparecen en este episodio. (4–6 oraciones)

NOTA CULTURAL

Los parques nacionales de Costa Rica

Costa Rica se conoce por la inmensa variedad biológica de su flora y de su fauna. Hay numerosas especies de pájaros, de mariposas y de otros animales, y también de flores y plantas. Este país se distingue también por los recursos económicos que dedica para preservar los grandes parques nacionales que se han establecido en el país. Entre ellos están el parque de **Braulio Carrillo, Monteverde, Pax Natura** y **Valle Escondido.**

Segundo paso ◄ trescientos treinta y uno   331

Lectura

Online Study Center

For further reading practice online, visit the *Caminos* website at http://college .hmco.com/languages/ spanish/renjilian/caminos/ 3e/student_home.html.

PRELECTURA

In this selection, we will learn some characteristics of cars advertised on the Internet. The short articles in this reading, based on different Internet sites and *Quo* magazine, include information regarding cars and technological innovations.

Reading Strategy

Defining audience and purpose

Defining the target audience and determining the intended purpose of a reading helps you read with greater focus. Ask yourself if the reading is targeted for you and your university peers, for your parents, for adolescent readers, or for readers in particular professional fields. Decide the intended purpose of the reading, as well. For example, is the purpose of the article to inform, to convince, to entertain, to react, to refute? Defining your audience and purpose also helps you think more critically and express your thoughts and feelings about what you read with clarity.

1 Coches del pasado. Antes de leer la lectura, trabajen en parejas para repasar sus conocimientos sobre los coches del pasado y del presente.

1. ¿Qué marca de coche manejaban tus abuelos? ¿y tus padres u otros parientes mayores? ¿Eran coches importados o nacionales *(domestic)*?
2. ¿Qué colores preferían? ¿Qué tipo de coche les gustaba manejar: deportivo, familiar *(station wagon)*, camioneta?
3. ¿De qué tamaño era: pequeño, grande, mediano?
4. Era automático o de cambios *(stick shift)*? ¿de dos o cuatro puertas? ¿con aire acondicionado? ¿con radio, casetes, CDs?
5. ¿Cuál es la edad legal para manejar un coche en tu estado? Algunos dicen que los jóvenes no deben sacar la licencia de manejar antes de los dieciocho años. ¿Estás de acuerdo? ¿Por qué?
6. ¿Cuál es el mejor coche si vives en la ciudad? ¿y en el campo? ¿en la playa? Explica.

2 Transporte del presente. En parejas, describan a la persona que prefiere usar cada uno de los siguientes medios de transporte.

1. una bicicleta
2. una moto
3. una camioneta
4. un "segway"
5. un coche compacto
6. un descapotable *(convertible)*
7. un coche "Zip"
8. una limosina

3 Preferencias. Escribe cinco cosas que buscas en un coche contemporáneo. Después, compara tu lista con la de un/a compañero/a. Explícale por qué.

Coches de hoy y mañana

Coches híbridos:
Toyota Prius y
Honda Civic

¿Está muerto el coche eléctrico?

Hay mucha controversia sobre el coche eléctrico. Según Piers Ward, de la revista *Top Gear,* "el auto eléctrico tiene un problema de imagen[1]". Parece que la gente necesita incentivos para comprar los coches eléctricos, como, por ejemplo, no tener que pagar impuestos[2] de coche. El futuro está incierto[3].

Combatiendo la contaminación

Para reducir la contaminación del aire causada por los coches, General Motors y otras firmas de coches invirtieron[4] cientos de millones de dólares en desarrollar[5] un coche eléctrico.

Los consumidores y las leyes

Los consumidores mostraron poco interés en el coche eléctrico. Por eso, el gobierno cambió las leyes para promover[6] autos con células[7] de combustible, autos híbridos[8] y otros que combaten la contaminación.

La compañía Ford

La compañía Ford cree que hay, quizás, un futuro para el coche eléctrico, pero ha dicho, "Estamos decepcionados[9] por el bajo nivel[10] de aceptación[11] por parte de los consumidores".

Un auto con dos motores

Según el artículo, "el presente pertenece a los autos híbridos, como el Toyota Prius y el Honda Civic Hybrid, que vienen con dos motores, uno eléctrico y otro a gasolina".

El lavacoche[12] económico del futuro

En Inglaterra un equipo de expertos diseñadores[13] de coches ha diseñado un lavacoche más económico. También es mejor para el medio ambiente durante el verano cuando no llueve tanto en muchas partes del mundo. El lavacoche funciona como un lavaplatos, usando vapores de agua. Lavar un coche con una manguera[14] usa ciento treinta y cinco litros de agua comparado con el lavacoche que usa solamente cuatro litros. Además, se puede filtrar el agua y usarla otra vez. El lavacoche es inflable[15].

Relaja y maneja

La compañía Bosch en España anuncia una innovación técnica para el automóvil: El "asiento Drive Dynamic Seat". Es un asiento que ofrece al/a la conductor/a más diversión y confort mientras[16] maneja. Además, con el sistema Bosch instalado en el coche, el / la conductor/a tiene un apoyo[17] dinámico para la columna vertebral[18] que le da masaje a la espalda durante el viaje. Es una saludable[19] innovación tecnológica, especialmente durante viajes muy largos.

El asiento Drive
Dynamic

---

[1]image; [2]taxes; [3]uncertain; [4]invested; [5]to develop; [6]promote; [7]cells; [8]hybrids; [9]disillusioned; [10]level; [11]acceptance; [12]carwash; [13]designers; [14]hose; [15]inflatable; [16]while; [17]support; [18]spine; [19]healthy

El coche BMW compacto 1

BMW Serie 1, compacto

La marca alemana BMW ofrece un coche compacto con su Serie 1. La firma lo describe como "un automóvil con carácter propio[20], con el diseño[21], la tecnología y el espíritu de un auténtico BMW". Con este modelo, BMW quiere atraer[22] a los consumidores más jóvenes.

Atascos en España

Adiós, atascos[23]

Millones de españoles están desesperados[24] a causa de los atascos de circulación[25], especialmente durante las vacaciones.

Una solución puede ser la instalación de sensores fuera[26] y dentro del coche y en diferentes partes de la carretera[27], como tienen en Italia.

La idea para los conductores es detectar peligros como congestión de tráfico, adversidades climáticas y condiciones de las calles. Los sensores avisan[28] a los conductores con mensajes sobre los peligros para evitarlos[29]. Por ejemplo, el hielo negro[30], que no se ve, es un peligro serio.

---

[20]own; [21]design; [22]to attract; [23](traffic) jams; [24]desperate; [25]traffic jams; [26]outside of; [27]highway; [28]warn; [29]avoid them; [30]black ice

POSTLECTURA

1 Conéctate. Trabajando en parejas, emparejen la información con el artículo apropiado.

La información

¿Qué artículo lees...

_____ 1. si quieres un coche con un motor eléctrico y otro a gasolina.

_____ 2. si tienes miedo del hielo negro.

_____ 3. si deseas limpiar tu coche y usar poca agua.

_____ 4. si prefieres un coche compacto con carácter propio.

_____ 5. si tienes interés en tu confort mientras manejas.

_____ 6. si deseas evitar peligros en la carretera en el futuro.

_____ 7. si buscas datos sobre los coches eléctricos.

Artículo

a. ¿Está muerto el coche eléctrico?

b. El lavacoche económico del futuro

c. Relaja y maneja

d. BMW Serie 1

e. Adiós, atascos

f. Un auto con dos motores

2 Propósitos. ¿Cuál es el propósito de cada lectura sobre los coches? Usa las letras de la actividad anterior para identificar cada artículo. (Hay tres descripciones extras.)

1. _____ Hablar del confort que provee un asiento que apoya la columna vertebral.
2. _____ Inspirarnos a comprar un coche particular.
3. _____ Convencernos de los beneficios de un lavacoche que usa poca agua.
4. _____ Entretenernos con imágenes y datos atractivos sobre los coches.
5. _____ Informarnos sobre unas innovaciones tecnológicas que ayudan a los conductores cuando manejan.
6. _____ Animarnos a construir un coche híbrido.
7. _____ Darnos opiniones sobre los coches del futuro que ayudan a proteger el medio ambiente.

3 Opiniones. En parejas, lean dos de los artículos en voz alta y discútanlos. ¿Qué datos revelan sobre los coches y para qué consumidores existen?

4 ¿Quiénes son los lectores? Determina quiénes van a ser los lectores de esta lectura y por qué. Puedes indicar más de una categoría para cada artículo:

► los jóvenes entre los 20 y 30 años
► los estudiantes universitarios
► los adultos mayores de 50 años
► modelos, hombres/mujeres de negocios
► los padres de familia
► atletas
► médicos
► actores/actrices.

5 Coche clásico contemporáneo. Trabajen en parejas para escribir un folleto sobre el coche clásico contemporáneo o para diseñar una página web. Primero, diseñen un coche que tenga características que sean atractivas para una de las siguientes personas: un/a estudiante universitario/a, un padre o una madre de familia, un/a entrenador/a (*coach*), una persona famosa. Invéntenlo (categoría, marca, símbolo o logo particular, tamaño, color, componentes, precio, consumo de gasolina, consideraciones ecológicas, placa especial). Después de diseñarlo y dibujarlo, escriban el folleto y preséntenlo a la clase.

Escritura

Online Study Center

For further writing practice online, visit the *Caminos* website at http://college.hmco.com/languages/spanish/renjilian/caminos/3e/student_home.html.

Writing Strategy

Developing a point of view

An important consideration when writing is to think about who is telling the story. You can create different ways to view your topic depending on the voice you use or the perspective taken. For example, if you are addressing children, writing from the perspective of a child may serve to reach your audience more effectively. Or, you may want to reach children by addressing their parents.

Workshop

The following technological gadgets have been created specifically for children, seniors, or both. With a partner, decide who would use each item.

Strategy in Action

For additional practice with creating a point of view, complete the following exercises and those in the *Escritura* section of your Student Activities Manual for *Unidad 9*.

1 Para niños. Escoge uno de los productos anteriores y escribe un párrafo o anuncio específicamente para niños que les anime a pedirles el aparato a sus padres. Habla del uso del aparato y de sus ventajas (*advantages*). Incluye mandatos informales (**tú**).

2 Para adultos de tercera edad. Escoge uno de los productos anteriores y escribe una descripción dirigida específicamente a personas mayores de los 60 años. Habla de los atractivos del aparato y de lo fácil que es usarlo. Incluye mandatos formales (**Ud.**).

PRIMER PASO

TALKING ABOUT TECHNOLOGY

Sustantivos

la alta velocidad	*high speed*
el aparato	*apparatus*
la aplicación	*application*
el archivo	*computer file*
la ayuda	*help*
la batería	*battery*
el botón	*button*
el buscador	*search engine*
la cámara	*camera*
la computadora portátil	*laptop*
la conexión (sin cables)	*(wireless) connection (WiFi)*
la contraseña	*password*
el control remoto	*remote control*
el correo electrónico	*e-mail*
la (alta) definición	*(high) definition*
el directorio	*directory*
el disco duro	*hard drive*
el documento	*document*
el entretenimiento	*entertainment*
el fax	*fax*
la función	*function*
el icono	*icon*
el mensaje	*message*
el módem	*modem*
la pantalla (plana)	*(flat) screen*
el paso	*step*
el plasma	*plasma*
el programa	*program*
el ratón	*mouse*
la realidad virtual	*virtual reality*
la red	*network*
el robot	*robot*
el teclado	*keyboard*
el teléfono celular	*cell phone*
la videocámara	*videocamera*
la (video) grabadora	*(video)recorder*
el videojuego	*videogame*

Verbos

acceder	*to access*
almacenar	*to store*
apagar	*to turn off, to shut off*
apuntar	*to point*
archivar, guardar	*to save; to file*
bajar	*to download*
cargar	*to charge*
colgar (ue)	*to hang (up)*
copiar	*to copy*
desempeñar	*to carry out*
entrar	*to enter*
imprimir	*to print*
iniciar	*to begin*
instalar	*to install*
mover (ue)	*to move; to shift*
prender, encender (ie)	*to turn on*
presionar, hacer clic, pulsar, oprimir	*to click (with the mouse); to push (a button)*

Adjetivos

automático/a	*automatic*
digital	*digital*
disponible	*available*
en línea	*online*
inalámbrico/a	*wireless*
multimedia	*multimedia*
táctil	*touch, tactile*

SEGUNDO PASO

Adverbial conjunctions

a pesar de que	*even though, even if*
aunque	*even when, even though, even if, although*
cuando	*when*
después (de) que	*after*
en cuanto	*as soon as*
hasta que	*until*
tan pronto como	*as soon as*

DISCUSSING CARS

Sustantivos

el acelerador	*accelerator*
el aire acondicionado	*air conditioning*
el asiento	*seat*
el auto, automóvil, carro, coche	
la batería, pila	*battery*
el baúl, maletero	*trunk*
la bolsa de aire, el airbag	*airbag*
la carretera	*highway*
el choque	*crash*
el cinturón de seguridad	*seatbelt*
el/la conductor/a	*driver*
el deportivo	*sports car*
el espejo (retrovisor)	*(rear-view) mirror*
los frenos	*brakes*
la gasolina	*gasoline*
la licencia de manejar/ conducir	*driver's license*
el limpiaparabrisas	*windshield wiper*
la llanta pinchada	*flat tire*
la llanta, rueda	*wheel, tire*
la luz	*light*
el motor	*motor*
la multa	*fine*
el parabrisas	*windshield*
el pito, claxon	*horn*
la placa	*license plate*
la puerta	*door*
el tanque de gasolina	*gas tank*
el volante	*steering wheel*

Verbos

abrocharse (el cinturón)	*to buckle up (seatbelt)*
arrancar	*to start (a car, a race)*
chocar	*to collide*
conducir, manejar	*to drive*
dañar	*to injure; to damage*
frenar	*to brake*
parar	*to stop*
pitar	*to beep the horn*

Adjetivos

compacto/a	*compact*
económico/a	*economical*
híbrido/a	*hybrid*

PRESENT AND PAST PERFECT INDICATIVE

todavía	*yet*
ya	*already*

VOCABULARIO Y LENGUA

- ► Learning about holidays and traditions
- ► Indicating subjective feelings, emotions, and attitudes in the past: Imperfect subjunctive
- ► Linking actions: Subjunctive with adverbial clauses

- ► Talking about art and artists
- ► Discussing crafts and folk art
- ► Using relative pronouns

CAMINOS DEL JAGUAR

- ► En la oscuridad
- ► ¿Traición o verdad?

LECTURA

- ► Fiestas centroamericanas: Nicaragua, Honduras, El Salvador

NOTAS CULTURALES

- ► El maíz
- ► Cuauhtémoc

ESTRATEGIAS

- ► **Reading:** Taking notes in a chart
- ► **Writing:** Summarizing

Rafael González y González, *Mercado de Palín*

Preguntas del tema

- ▶ ¿Cuál es tu día festivo favorito? ¿Por qué?
- ▶ ¿Cómo celebras tu cumpleaños? ¿con amigos? ¿con familia? ¿sólo/a?
- ▶ ¿Qué tipo de arte te gusta? ¿Por qué?
- ▶ ¿Quién es el/la artista que más admiras? Explica.

PRIMER PASO

Vocabulario y lengua

LEARNING ABOUT HOLIDAYS AND TRADITIONS

Días festivos y celebraciones

events
are celebrated / parades
fireworks

Online Study Center

For additional practice with this unit's vocabulary and grammar, visit the *Caminos* website at http://college .hmco.com/languages/ spanish/renjilian/ caminos/3e/ *resolutions* student_home.html. You can also review audio flashcards, quiz yourself, and explore related Spanish- language sites. *custom*
costumes

plaque

commemorate

Los **hechos° históricos o religiosos** y otras fechas significativas del mundo hispano **se festejan°** de muchas maneras como por ejemplo, con **desfiles°**, **festivales**, bailes, conciertos, **exhibiciones públicas, fuegos artificiales°** y **ceremonias** o **ritos** especiales. En muchos de estos eventos, la gente lleva los trajes **folclóricos** del país.

Las celebraciones familiares típicamente incluyen la preparación de comidas especiales y algunas veces, música y bailes. El fin del año se celebra con fiestas y fuegos artificiales y la gente también hace **propósitos°** para el nuevo año.

En las fiestas populares como los carnavales, a veces es **costumbre°** llevar máscaras y **disfraces°**. Cuando se celebran fechas históricas o eventos oficiales importantes, se exhiben con frecuencia **placas°** o alguna **obra de arte** como **estatuas** y **murales** para conmemorar° el hecho.

Dos fiestas importantes del mundo hispano son la Semana Santa y el Día de los Muertos.

SEMANA SANTA

Semana Santa es una celebración católica que comienza el Domingo de

Palm Sunday Ramos° y termina el Domingo *Easter Sunday* de Resurrección°. Las **tradiciones** de la Semana Santa comenzaron en el siglo XVI cuando la Iglesia Católica intentó presentar la vida de Jesucristo de una manera

Procesión de Semana Santa, Sevilla, España.

popular. En los países hispanos hay ceremonias y ritos religiosos durante esa semana. Las celebraciones más famosas tienen lugar en Sevilla, España. Las cofradías° llevan pasos°, que representan la muerte y la resurrección de Jesucristo o la Virgen María, por las calles estrechas de la ciudad. Miles de turistas visitan Sevilla durante Semana Santa para ver las impresionantes procesiones.

brotherhoods, guilds / floats

El Día de los Muertos en México

Para los mexicanos, el Día de los Muertos o Día de los Fieles Difuntos° representa algo más que la veneración a sus muertos. En México, a diferencia de otros países, la gente se pasa el día **burlándose**°, jugando y **conviviendo**° con la **muerte.** Se **celebra** con expresiones muy originales como las **calaveras**° de azúcar, el pan de muertos, calaveras de papel maché que se burlan de la muerte, y las tradicionales **ofrendas**°, las cuales se preparan con respeto por los familiares para recordar a los que se han ido. Los alimentos, flores y objetos personales del difunto son parte esencial del altar y según la creencia, los fieles difuntos regresan este día para gozar lo que más disfrutaban cuando estaban vivos. Esta fiesta se celebra entre el 31 de octubre y el 2 de noviembre.

Un grabado de "La Catrina" por el famoso artista, José Guadalupe Posada.

Dearly Departed

making fun of
living

skulls

offerings

Una ofrenda para el Día de los Muertos, que incluye pan de muertos, calaveras de azúcar, papel picado y las flores típicas, los cempasúchiles.

ENERO
1 Día de Año Nuevo
6 Día de los Reyes Magos

FEBRERO
14 Día de San Valentín
Carnaval (Semana anterior al
Miércoles de Ceniza—*Ash Wednesday*)

MARZO
Semana Santa (Fecha variable)
Domingo de Pascua (Fecha variable)

ABRIL
1 Día de los Inocentes (EE.UU., Europa)

MAYO
1 Día del Trabajo (Países hispanos)
5 Día de la Batalla de Puebla (México)

JULIO
4 Día de la Independencia (EE.UU.)

OCTUBRE
12 Día de la Raza
31 Día de las brujas

NOVIEMBRE
1 Fiesta de Todos los Santos
2 Día de los Muertos
Día de Acción de Gracias (Fecha variable)

DICIEMBRE
Hanukkah (Fecha variable)
25 Navidad
26 Kwanzaa
28 Día de los Inocentes (Países hispanos)
31 Nochevieja
Ramadán (Países islámicos/fecha variable)

Actividades

1 La Nochevieja. Escucha la presentación de cómo se celebra la Nochevieja en algunos países hispanos y contesta las preguntas.

1. ¿Cuándo celebramos la Nochevieja?
2. ¿Por qué hacemos propósitos para el año nuevo?
3. ¿Cuáles son algunos propósitos que solemos hacer?
4. ¿Qué ritual especial hay en España?
5. ¿Qué hacen para celebrar la Nochevieja en Colombia?

2 Mis celebraciones. Habla con un/a compañero/a sobre cómo celebras tú la llegada del año nuevo.

1. ¿Celebras el año nuevo? ¿Cómo lo celebras? ¿Con quién?
2. ¿Existen en tu ciudad o estado ceremonias o rituales para recibir el año nuevo?
3. ¿Es útil hacer propósitos de año nuevo? ¿Por qué?
4. ¿Cuáles son algunos propósitos que has hecho? ¿Pudiste cumplirlos?

3 Asociaciones. ¿Qué fiestas asocias con estas cosas?

1. el verano
2. un árbol verde con decoraciones y luces
3. un picnic
4. un corazón rojo
5. el otoño
6. la primavera
7. el invierno
8. un desfile
9. un regalo
10. un disfraz

4 El Día de los Inocentes. ¿Le has hecho bromas a alguien el Día de los Inocentes? ¿A quién? ¿Qué broma le hiciste y cómo reaccionó la persona? ¿Alguien te ha hecho bromas a ti? ¿Quién? Describe las bromas y cómo reaccionaste.

5 Fiestas importantes. Haz una lista de las fiestas que celebras durante el año. Incluye fiestas familiares (cumpleaños y aniversarios), fiestas universitarias (la graduación) o fiestas nacionales y regionales. Compara tu lista con la lista de un/a compañero/a y conversen sobre cómo se celebran las fiestas que han seleccionado.

6 El Día de la Independencia. Describe qué hacías para celebrar el Día de la Independencia cuando eras niño/a. Compáralo con lo que haces ahora.

Día de la Independencia

The highlighted words in the illustration are in the imperfect subjunctive. To form the imperfect subjunctive of both regular and irregular verbs, eliminate the **–ron** of the *third person plural* of the *preterite* tense and add the endings shown in the table below to the stem.

Imperfect subjunctive forms

All verbs that are irregular in the preterite are also irregular in the imperfect subjunctive. (To review the forms of the preterite, see pages 153, 178, and 189.)

Imperfect Subjunctive			
	celebrar	**poner**	**venir**
Preterite 3rd person plural	celebra~~ron~~	pusie~~ron~~	vinie~~ron~~
Stem	celebra-	pusie-	vinie-
yo	celebra**ra**	pusie**ra**	vinie**ra**
tú	celebra**ras**	pusie**ras**	vinie**ras**
Ud. / él /ella	celebra**ra**	pusie**ra**	vinie**ra**
nosotros/as	celebrá**ramos**	pusié**ramos**	vinié**ramos**
vosotros/as	celebra**rais**	pusie**rais**	vinie**rais**
Uds. / ellos / ellas	celebra**ran**	pusie**ran**	vinie**ran**

Notice that the nosotros form needs a written accent.

Hubiera (*there was, there were*) is the imperfect subjunctive of **haber**. Like **hay** (*there is, there are*), there is only one form for singular and plural meanings.

Fue excelente que **hubiera** tanta gente en la celebración del 4 de julio.	*It was excellent that there were so many people at the 4th of July celebration.*
Me encantó que **hubiera** tantos platos diferentes en la cena del Día de Acción de Gracias.	*It made me happy that there were so many different dishes for the Thanksgiving dinner.*

You may occasionally see the alternative imperfect subjunctive endings **–se, -ses, -se, -semos, -seis, -sen.**

Uses of the imperfect subjunctive

Noun clauses

When the verb in the main clause expresses a request, emotion, doubt or uncertainty in the past, the verb in the dependent clause is in the imperfect subjunctive. (Review the present subjunctive with noun clauses on pages 278–281 and 291–292.)

Request:	Yo **quería** que nosotros **celebráramos** el Carnaval.	*I wanted us to celebrate Carnival.*
Emotion:	**Fue** fantástico que **nos visitaras** el Día de Acción de Gracias.	*It was wonderful that you could visit us on Thanksgiving.*
Doubt:	La familia **dudaba** que **pudieras** venir en Semana Santa.	*The family doubted that you could come during Holy Week.*

Adjective clauses

The imperfect subjunctive is used in adjective clauses that describe people, things, or events that are uncertain, unknown or non-existent in the past. (Review the present subjunctive with adjective clauses on page 314.)

En la tienda no **había** ningún disfraz que me **gustara.**	*There wasn't a single costume that I liked in the store.*
Pedro **buscaba** un disfraz que no le **costara** mucho.	*Pedro was looking for a costume that didn't cost him a lot.*

Actividades

1 Amor, amor. Completa este párrafo sobre el Día de San Valentín usando el imperfecto de subjuntivo.

El día del amor y la amistad, el Día de San Valentín, me encantaba que mis amigos me _____ (**1.** enviar) tarjetas y regalos. Una vez, recibí una tarjeta de Héctor, en la que me pedía que _____ (**2.** salir, yo) con él. En mi respuesta, le dije que yo quería que _____ (**3.** venir, él) a mi casa y que _____ (**4.** conocer) a mis padres.

Antes de salir a cenar, mis padres nos pidieron que _____ (**5.** regresar, nosotros) temprano y así lo hicimos. Queríamos cenar en un restaurante que _____ (**6.** servir) comida italiana. Encontramos un restaurante pequeño y romántico. Desde entonces, estamos juntos y hace poco Héctor me pidió que _____ (**7.** casarse, yo) con él. Yo le sugerí que _____ (**8.** esperar, nosotros) un poco, pero creo que nos vamos a casar pronto.

2 Celebraciones. Escribe cada oración en el pasado. Sigue el modelo.

► **MODELO:** *Danilo insiste en que celebremos su cumpleaños*
en un restaurante.

Danilo insistió en que celebráramos su cumpleaños
en un restaurante.

1. Rita se alegra de que yo pueda visitarla en Navidad.
2. Luis pide un disfraz que no sea muy caro.
3. Es una sorpresa que mis amigos celebren mi cumpleaños.
4. Dudo que tú sepas mi nombre.
5. Me gusta mucho que me describas las tradiciones de tu país.
6. Anita les pide a sus padres que le compren un iPod para la Navidad.
7. Rafael quiere que vayamos al desfile.
8. Mi primo me sugiere que haga un pastel para la fiesta.

 3 Mis opiniones. Elige una frase de la columna A y complétala de una manera lógica con una frase de la columna B. Tienes que cambiar el verbo entre paréntesis en la columna B al imperfecto del subjuntivo. Después, compara tus oraciones con las de un/a compañero/a.

A	B
1. No nos gustó que	a. algunas personas no (celebrar) los días de fiesta.
2. Fue una lástima que	b. la gente no (participar) en el desfile.
3. Me pareció mal que	c. tú no (querer) regalarme nada el Día de los Reyes Magos.
4. Dudé que	d. no (haber) más gente en el Carnaval.
5. Me alegré de que	e. Pedro me (enviar) una tarjeta para el Día de San Valentín.
6. Esperábamos que	f. no (haber) disfraces el Día de las brujas.

 4 ¿Padres estrictos? Haz una lista de las cosas que tus padres te pedían que hicieras con más frecuencia cuando eras pequeño/a. Utiliza algunos de estos verbos en el pasado para comenzar tus frases. Después, pregúntale a un/a compañero/a qué le pedían sus padres.

► **MODELO:** *Mis padres me pedían que me acostara temprano.*

querer   preferir   ser importante   sugerir
pedir   insistir   decir   rogar

LINKING ACTIONS: SUBJUNCTIVE WITH ADVERBIAL CLAUSES

El altar de mi abuelito

You have already learned that some adverbial conjunctions can take the indicative or the subjunctive. (Review adverbial clauses, page 324.) Other adverbial conjunctions are *always* followed by the subjunctive regardless of the tense.

Conjunctions always followed by the subjunctive	
a fin de que	*in order that*
a menos que	*unless*
antes (de) que	*before*
con tal (de) que	*provided that*
en caso de que	*in case*
para que	*so that*
sin que	*without*

If the verb in the main clause is in the present, then the present subjunctive is used in the dependent clause. If the verb in the main clause is in the preterite or imperfect, then the imperfect subjunctive is used in the dependent clause.

No voy a la fiesta **a menos que termine** mi tarea de química.

I'm not going to the party unless I finish my chemistry homework.

Los incas adoraban al sol **para que** los **protegiera.**

The Incas worshiped the sun, so that it would protect them.

Hice un bonito altar para mi abuelo **sin que** nadie me **ayudara.**

I made a beautiful altar for my grandfather without anyone helping me.

The imperfect subjunctive is always used after the adverbial expression **como si** *(as if, as though).*

Mis amigos me hicieron bromas **como si** hoy **fuera** el Día de los Inocentes.

My friends played tricks on me as if today were April Fool's Day.

When there is no change of subject, the adverbial conjunctions above (except for **a menos que**) may be followed by an infinitive after the preposition: **antes** *de* **salir,** *para* **escuchar,** *sin* **terminar,** and so on. The sentence may begin with either clause. Note that the **que** is omitted in these cases.

Antes de ir al Carnaval, tenemos que buscar la dirección.
Before going to the Carnival, we have to look for the address.

Tenemos que buscar la dirección **antes de ir** al Carnaval.
We have to look for the address before going to the Carnival.

Actividades

1 El Carnaval. Completa las oraciones con la alternativa correcta.

1. Los vecinos organizaron una fiesta para que todos...
   a. se conozcan.
   b. se conocieran.

2. Nadie debe faltar a menos que...
   a. estuviera enfermo.
   b. esté enfermo.

3. El año pasado los chicos llevaron música sin que nadie la...
   a. pida.
   b. pidiera.

4. Mis vecinos se fueron antes de que todos...
   a. llegaran.
   b. lleguen.

5. Siempre hay bebidas sin alcohol en caso de que alguien...
   a. conduzca.
   b. condujera.

6. Generalmente el desfile termina sin que nada malo...
   a. sucediera.
   b. suceda.

 2 Así son las cosas. Elige una oración de la columna A y complétala de una manera lógica con una oración de la columna B. Compara tus oraciones con las de un/a compañero/a.

A	B
1. Te compré el estéreo	a. antes de que te envíen los libros.
2. Llegamos a tiempo	b. en caso de que el avión llegara antes de la hora.
3. Les voy a decir la verdad	c. a menos que nos ganemos la lotería.
4. Debes preguntar el precio	d. sin que tuviéramos que preguntar la dirección.
5. No podemos comprar ese auto	e. a fin de que me explicaras el problema.
6. Te llamé	f. para que tú escucharas tu música favorita.
7. Fuimos más temprano al aeropuerto	g. con tal de que Uds. no se la cuenten a nadie.

3 Nochevieja. Juan Carlos y Beatriz están haciendo una paella para la cena de Nochevieja. Completa el diálogo con la forma correcta del presente o del imperfecto del subjuntivo.

1. Mira, Juan, estos ingredientes son para que tú _____ (hacer) la paella.
2. Está bien, Beatriz, la voy a hacer con tal de que tú me _____ (ayudar).
3. Mira, te escribí la receta con letras grandes en caso de que tú no _____ (poder) leerla en el libro de cocina.
4. Todo tiene que estar listo antes de que _____ (llegar) los invitados.
5. Van a llegar temprano, a menos que _____ (ocurrir) algo inesperado.

4 Condiciones. Trabaja con un/a compañero/a para completar estas oraciones con tus propias ideas.

1. Yo siempre les ayudo a mis amigos con tal de que ellos...
2. Es bueno ahorrar dinero en caso de que...
3. Es terrible tener problemas sin que nadie te...
4. No puedo salir de vacaciones a menos que...
5. Llamé a mis padres para que ellos...
6. Ayer gasté mucho dinero, como si yo...

5 El día internacional. Tú y tus amigos/as organizaron un desfile para el día internacional del pueblo. Creen una conversación para hablar de los preparativos. Usen cuatro cláusulas adverbiales en su conversación. (antes de que, en caso de que, con tal de que, a menos que, sin que, a fin de que, para que)

▶ MODELO: Tuvimos que limpiar la calle antes de que llegara la gente.

En la oscuridad

En la finca de doña Carmen.

¿Por qué no está aquí doña Carmen?

Tranquila, Adriana.

Quizás esté investigando.

Es muy extraño que ella no esté aquí.

Adriana, las fallas eléctricas son normales aquí.

Ustedes están tranquilos, pero yo no. No me gusta que doña Carmen no esté aquí ahora.

Adriana, deja ya tus sospechas. Mi madrina está resolviendo el problema, nada más.

Madrina, ¿qué pasó?

Fui a ver qué pasaba con el generador. No entiendo por qué se fue la luz.

Quizás haya una explicación lógica.

No se preocupe, doña Carmen, su casa es maravillosa, pero en esta situación estamos muy preocupados por los jaguares.

Sí, doña Carmen, nos preocupó que nos quedáramos sin luz y pensamos en la seguridad de los jaguares.

No lo sé. Mi casa es vieja y esto sucede con frecuencia. Lo siento mucho.

Ustedes tienen razón. Vamos a verlos en la sala.

¡Qué horror! ¿Qué es eso?

¡Armando se robó los jaguares! ¿Cómo supo él que estábamos aquí?

¡No puede ser, con el trabajo que nos costó reunir a los jaguares!

No se preocupen. Tengo videocámaras, todo está vigilado. El criminal no va a escapar.

¿Y las videocámaras funcionan sin electricidad?

Ay, no había pensado en eso.

Adriana, es muy fácil sacar conclusiones erróneas.

Es verdad, tenemos que calmarnos.

Actividades

Online Study Center

For additional practice with this episode, visit the *Caminos* website at http://college.hmco.com/languages/spanish/renjilian/caminos/3e/student_home.html.

1 Comprensión.
Basándote en este episodio de *Caminos del jaguar,* elige la alternativa lógica.

1. No hay luz y Adriana pregunta si...
   a. Nayeli está tranquila.
   b. Felipe está allí.

2. Nayeli piensa que doña Carmen quizás esté...
   a. en la cocina.
   b. investigando el problema.

3. A Adriana, la situación le parece...
   a. extraordinaria.
   b. extraña.

4. Según Felipe, las fallas eléctricas son...
   a. normales.
   b. irregulares.

5. A Adriana no le gusta que doña Carmen...
   a. no esté con ellos.
   b. diga que no pasa nada.

6. Según doña Carmen, la falla ocurrió porque...
   a. la casa es muy vieja.
   b. alguien dañó el generador.

7. Doña Carmen dice que...
   a. hay videocámaras.
   b. el generador funcionó.

2 Situaciones.
Dramaticen una de las siguientes situaciones.

1. La luz se va mientras Nayeli, Adriana, Felipe y doña Carmen cenan.
2. Adriana, Felipe, Nayeli y doña Carmen se dan cuenta de que los jaguares han desaparecido.

3 Escritura.
Describe quién crees que robó el jaguar y por qué. (6–8 oraciones)

NOTA CULTURAL

El maíz

En América Latina se producen muchas variedades de maíz: blanco, amarillo, rojo y azul oscuro, casi negro. El maíz es muy importante en la alimentación de casi todos los países latinoamericanos. Es también un ingrediente esencial en muchas comidas regionales como sopas, salsas, pasteles, tamales y tortillas. En Colombia y Venezuela las arepas son tortillas similares a las mexicanas e igualmente populares.

SEGUNDO PASO

Vocabulario y lengua

Online Study Center

For additional practice with this unit's vocabulary and grammar, visit the *Caminos* website at http://college.hmco.com/languages/spanish/renjilian/caminos/3e/student_home.html. You can also review audio flashcards, quiz yourself, and explore related Spanish-language sites.

El estudio de arte *(The Art Studio)*

el pintor
el pincel
la paleta
el cuadro
el retrato
el marco

la pintura
(painting)

la madera
la escultora
el bronce
el mármol

la escultura
(sculpture)

la ceramista
la vasija
la arcilla (el barro)

la cerámica
(ceramics)

el bosquejo
el dibujante

el dibujo
(drawing)

Most artistic periods are described in English with the suffix *–ism*. The corresponding Spanish term ends in **–ismo.** For example:

modernism = **modernismo**   *impressionism* = **impresionismo**

An artist who belongs to a particular school of painting is referred to in English with the suffix *–ist*. The corresponding Spanish term ends in **–ista.** Note that the ending is the same whether the artist is male or female.

modernist = **el / la modernista**   *impressionist* = **el /la impresionista**

What do you think the Spanish terms for the following words might be: *cubism, cubist, realism, realist, surrealism, surrealist, expressionism, expressionist, romanticism, romanticist, muralism, muralist?*

Más palabras y expresiones

Cognados

el arte clásico, contemporáneo, moderno, abstracto

el/la artista

el contraste

el detalle

la figura

la forma

la ilustración

la imagen

el/la modelo

Sustantivos

la acuarela	*watercolor*
el aurorretrato	*self-portrait*
la exposición, exhibición	*art exhibit*
el lienzo	*canvas*
la luz y sombra	*light and shadow*
la naturaleza muerta	*still life*
el paisaje	*landscape, countryside*
la pintura al óleo	*oil-painting*
la vida cotidiana	*daily life*

Verbos

colgar (ue)	*to hang*
crear	*to create*
dibujar	*to draw*
ilustrar	*to illustrate*
pintar	*to paint*
significar	*to mean*

Otras expresiones

claro/a	*light*
en blanco y negro	*(in) black and white*
en color(es)	*(in) color*
oscuro/a	*dark*

Actividades

1 Museo de arte. El museo de arte de tu ciudad escribe una invitación a una exposición. Completa el texto con las palabras más adecuadas.

Lo invitamos a nuestro Museo Comunal. En el primer piso, están las vasijas de una _____ muy conocida, Rosa Flores. Al lado de esta sala están los dibujos de Arturo Mesa, un _____ de fama internacional. En el segundo piso, tenemos las _____ de cobre y madera de la escultora Marina Valle. Finalmente, queremos que usted vea los cuadros del _____ Ricardo Urrutia, nuestro artista invitado este mes.

2 Arte moderno. ¿Qué piensas de estas obras de arte? En grupos, contesten las preguntas y describan cada cuadro.

Xul Solar, *Patria B*

1. ¿Qué colores usa el artista?
2. ¿Cuáles son las formas dominantes del cuadro?
3. ¿Qué símbolos reconocen? ¿Qué relación tienen con el tema del cuadro?
4. Según su opinión, ¿tiene el artista una visión positiva del mundo? ¿Por qué?

Frida Kahlo, *Las dos Fridas* (1939)

1. ¿Es serio o divertido el cuadro? ¿Qué elementos expresan esa emoción?
2. ¿Qué diferencia hay entre las dos Fridas del cuadro?
3. ¿Qué elementos en común tienen las dos Fridas?
4. ¿Por qué creen que los corazones son visibles?
5. ¿Qué les dice este autorretrato de Frida Kahlo sobre ella?

Marisol (Marisol Escobar),
The Family (1962)

1. ¿Cómo es la familia? ¿Parece rica, pobre, feliz o infeliz? ¿Cómo lo saben?
2. Describan a cada miembro de esta familia. ¿Dónde está el padre?
3. ¿Por qué creen que la artista usa la escultura para expresar sus ideas?
4. Describan los colores.

3 Preguntas personales. Contesta las preguntas.

1. ¿Qué tipo de arte te gusta más? ¿Por qué?
2. ¿Quién es tu artista favorito/a? ¿De dónde es? ¿Qué tipo de obras crea?
3. ¿Te gusta ir a museos? ¿Por qué sí o por qué no?
4. ¿Conoces a algunos artistas hispanos? ¿Cuáles? ¿De dónde son? Describe sus obras.

4 Preséntala. En Internet, una revista o libro de arte, escoge una foto de una obra de arte de un/a artista hispano/a que te guste. Tráela a la clase y descríbesela.

Objetos artesanales

ALEBRIJES

En Oaxaca se hacen artesanías como estas figuritas de madera pintadas **a mano.** Son muy populares entre los **coleccionistas,** y además se consideran como talismanes de la buena suerte. Hay alebrijes en forma de unicornios, jaguares, jirafas, iguanas, jaguares, armadillos, etcétera.

Alebrijes en forma de jaguar, Oaxaca, México

has remained
cross
sticks / yarn

Chica mexicana con un "Ojo de Dios" en la mano

OJO DE DIOS

Muchos símbolos indígenas fueron destruidos durante la colonización española de América, pero el Ojo de Dios **ha permanecido**° desde entonces porque tiene forma de **cruz**°. Se hacen de palitos° de madera con hilos° de lana de colores brillantes. En muchas partes se usa como talismán porque se cree que trae buena suerte.

RÉPLICAS PRECOLOMBINAS

are made

En Colombia **se fabrican**° actualmente **réplicas** de objetos precolombinos de oro. Estas **piezas** se usan como joyas, como decoración en las casas o como **adornos** de bolsos o cinturones.

Una máscara precolombina, Museo del Oro, Bogotá

Artesano toledano

EL DAMASQUINADO

skillful

En la ciudad española de Toledo, **hábiles**° **artesanos** trabajan con la técnica del damasquinado, es decir, la decoración de metales preciosos. Allí se fabrican hermosos objetos como el que vemos en la foto, con adornos **dorados**° de diseños de influencia árabe.

golden

Actividades

1 Clasificación. Con un/a compañero/a, construyan una tabla para clasificar los cuatro objetos artesanales descritos *(described)* en la lectura.

	Alebrijes	Ojo de Dios	Réplicas precolombinas	Damasquinado
origen	_____	_____	_____	_____
material	_____	_____	_____	_____
uso	_____	_____	_____	_____
colores	_____	_____	_____	_____

2 Las arpilleras. En algunos países de Suramérica, las mujeres forman grupos económicos y a veces políticos para hacer unos tapices que se llaman arpilleras. Escucha el texto y escribe (**P**) si la descripción pertenece a las arpilleras del Perú y (**C**) si pertenece a las de Chile.

Una arpillera peruana

Una arpillera chilena

1. _____ expresión social
2. _____ la vida diaria
3. _____ bodas y celebraciones
4. _____ la historia del país
5. _____ dictadura militar
6. _____ historia de la artista

3 Interpretación. Compara las escenas de las dos arpilleras en la *Actividad 2*. ¿Qué o quiénes están en la escena? ¿Qué hacen?

4 Artesanías personales. Diseña un objeto artesanal que represente la historia de tus antepasados. Puede ser real o imaginario. Dibújalo y describe su historia incluyendo qué es, para qué se usa y con qué material se hace.

Exposición

Irene	Hola Elena. Te presento a Roberto.	*Elena*	Gracias, Roberto.
Roberto	Mucho gusto, Elena.	*Roberto*	¿Cuál es la técnica que usas actualmente?
Elena	Encantada. ¿Eres el periodista **con quien** hablé ayer?	*Elena*	Ahora pinto principalmente al óleo, pero **lo que** más quiero es experimentar con otras técnicas.
Roberto	Sí, soy yo. Gracias por darme esta entrevista.		
Elena	Con mucho gusto. Me dice Irene que eres el único periodista **que** sabe de arte.	*Roberto*	¿Como cuáles?
		Elena	La acuarela y la fotografía son **las que** más me interesan.
Roberto	¡Irene es **la que** más sabe! Ella dice que los cuadros **que** exhibes hoy son excelentes.	*Roberto*	Entonces me tienes que invitar a tu próxima exposición.
		Elena	¡Por supuesto!

Relative pronouns combine two sentences that have a noun or pronoun in common. The main relative pronouns in English are *that, which,* and *who/whom,* all of which are sometimes omitted. In Spanish, they must be used.

Que refers to things as well as people *(that, which, who).*

Compré un pequeño cuadro **que** quiero regalarte.	*I bought a small painting that (which) I want to give you.*
Tengo un primo **que** es escultor.	*I have a cousin who is a sculptor.*

Quien/quienes refers to people *(who / whom)* and usually follows a preposition.

Maricarmen Hernández es la médica **a quien** siempre consulto.	*Maricarmen Hernandez is the doctor whom I always consult.*
Éste es el artista **con quien** hablé de arte latinoamericano.	*This is the artist with whom I talked about Latin American art*

El/la/los/las que may refer to people or things *(the one(s) who/that, those who/that).*

Esta pintura es **la que** quiero comprar.	*This painting is the one that I want to buy.*
No quiero esa pintura, **la que** voy a comprar es aquélla.	*I don't want that painting, the one that I am going to buy is that one over there.*

Lo que refers to an idea or a previous situation (*what, that which*).

A mi papá no le gustó **lo que** le pintó   *My dad did not like what the artist*
    el artista.   *painted for him.*

Actividades

1 Referencias. Completa de una manera lógica las oraciones de la columna A con las oraciones de la columna B.

A	B
1. La casa en	a. lo que dices.
2. Queremos unas vacaciones	b. la que vivimos es nuestra.
3. El museo	c. que no sean muy caras.
4. Betty es la persona con	d. al que fui ayer me gustó mucho.
5. La exposición	e. quien debes hablar.
6. No comprendo	f. que tenemos hoy es excelente.

2 José y Josefina. José y Josefina están planeando sus actividades para el fin de semana. Completa su conversación con el pronombre relativo que corresponda. Usa **que, quien, lo que** o **el / la / los / las que.**

Josefina   ¿Qué quieres hacer hoy?
José   Me gustaría ver la exhibición de Fernando Botero (**1**) _____ se presenta en el museo de arte.
Josefina   Pues no sé. (**2**) _____ realmente quiero hacer es ir al cine. ¿Qué tal si vamos al cine hoy y al museo mañana?
José   Pero, es que ya compré las entradas para el museo.
Josefina   A ver... ¿son éstas (**3**) _____ compraste?
José   Sí, ésas son.
Josefina   Pues, la persona (**4**) _____ te las vendió se equivocó. Las entradas son para el domingo.
José   Entonces la chica con (**5**) _____ hablé se equivocó. Vamos al museo el domingo y hoy podemos ir al cine. ¿Cuál es la película (**6**) _____ quieres ver?
Josefina   (**7**) _____ quiero ver es la nueva película de Pedro Almodóvar.
José   Estupendo. Es el director español a (**8**) _____ más admiro.

3 Comprensión. Conecta lógicamente las ideas en las dos oraciones con el pronombre relativo **que.**

▶ **MODELO:**   Laura es una buena artista. Sabe mucho sobre pintura al óleo.
                 Laura es una buena artista que sabe mucho sobre pintura al óleo.

1. Diana tiene un dibujo. El dibujo es nuevo.
2. Me regalaron una escultura. La escultura es de bronce.
3. Voy al museo mañana. El museo está cerca de mi casa.
4. ¿Dónde está la arcilla? Compré la arcilla ayer.
5. Le regalé un cuadro a Yolanda. Pinté el cuadro en junio.
6. Tengo un bosquejo. El bosquejo representa una naturaleza muerta.
7. Alicia es una artista guatemalteca. Ella enseña arte a los niños.
8. Hay autorretratos de Frida Kahlo. Sus autorretratos son interesantes.

4 Lo mejor. En parejas, conversen sobre lo que más les gusta de estas situaciones.

▶ **MODELO:**   visitar un museo
                 ¿Qué es lo que más te gusta de visitar un museo?
                 Lo que más me gusta de visitar un museo es ver cuadros famosos.

1. estudiar idiomas   4. ir al cine
2. viajar a otros países   5. pintar cuadros
3. trabajar   6. ¿...?

¿Traición o verdad?

En la finca de doña Carmen.

¿Dónde están los héroes gemelos? Usted tiene que saber lo que sucedió.

Las dos piezas estaban aquí antes de la cena y ahora, no sé, ya no están. Yo estaba con ustedes.

Muy conveniente, ¿no le parece? Se va la luz y desaparecen los jaguares. Tenemos que llamar a la policía.

No, antes de llamar, voy a ver si los vecinos saben algo.

Conteste, señora, es importante que hable con usted.

Suena el teléfono...

¡Es el señor de Landa!

Sí, es él, reconozco su voz.

Hay un problema gordo.

La señorita que contraté para recuperar los héroes gemelos, Mariluz Gorrostiaga, nos robó los jaguares y va para San Antonio. La llamaré mañana, señora, cuando tenga más información.

¡La señora Gafasnegras!

Armando y mi madrina han estado trabajando juntos. No lo puedo creer. Adriana, tú tenías toda la razón. Perdóname por no haberte creído.

Tú no tienes la culpa, Nayeli. Ahora tenemos que pensar en recuperar los jaguares.

Lo sé, pero esto es un golpe muy duro. ¿Cómo pudo traicionarme mi madrina?

¡Tenemos que irnos! Adriana y yo vamos a San Antonio.

Cuídense. Su misión es muy peligrosa.

... Mariluz Gorrostiaga, nos robó los jaguares y va para San Antonio...

Ah...

Dejaste un recado muy detallado en la grabadora y creo que Nayeli, Adriana y Felipe lo oyeron. ¿Dónde están los jaguares?

Los tiene Mariluz, en San Antonio. Ella me engañó.

Y tú me ibas a engañar a mí, ¿no?

No, señora, no....

Voy a buscar a otro asistente más competente que tú.

Actividades

Online Study Center

For additional practice with this episode, visit the *Caminos* website at http://college.hmco.com/languages/spanish/renjilian/caminos/3e/student_home.html.

1 Comprensión. Basándote en este episodio de *Caminos del jaguar,* elige la alternativa lógica.

1. Adriana piensa que doña Carmen...
   a. dice la verdad.
   b. miente.

2. Doña Carmen quiere hablar primero con...
   a. la policía.
   b. los vecinos.

3. Armando dice que Mariluz Gorrostiaga se fue para...
   a. Puerto Rico.
   b. San Antonio.

4. Según Armando, Mariluz...
   a. sigue trabajando para él.
   b. ya no trabaja para él.

5. Es obvio que Armando ...
   a. tiene el jaguar.
   b. está trabajando para doña Carmen.

6. Nayeli ahora sabe que Adriana...
   a. tenía razón.
   b. no tenía razón.

7. Según doña Carmen, Armando es...
   a. incompetente.
   b. competente.

2 Situaciones. Dramaticen una de las siguientes situaciones.

1. La conversación de Armando y doña Carmen.
2. La conversación de Nayeli y Adriana después de escuchar a Armando.

3 Escritura. Describe cómo se siente Nayeli con la noticia de la traición de su madrina. (4–6 oraciones)

NOTA CULTURAL

Cuauhtémoc

Toda civilización tiene sus héroes, los cuales pueden ser míticos como los héroes gemelos o históricos como Cuauhtémoc. Cuauhtémoc fue el último emperador que gobernó el pueblo azteca, entre 1495 y 1525. Era sobrino de Moctezuma II y defendió los territorios aztecas contra los ataques de los conquistadores españoles. Por su gran valentía y determinación, Cuauhtémoc se considera un héroe nacional en México. Su imagen aparece en los billetes mexicanos de 100 pesos.

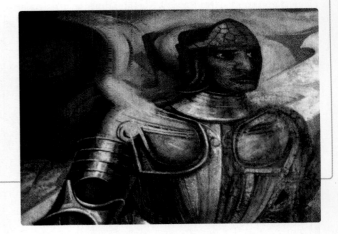

Lectura

⁜ **Online Study Center**

For further reading practice online, visit the *Caminos* website at http://college
.hmco.com/languages/
spanish/renjilian/caminos/
3e/student_home.html.

PRELECTURA

Reading Strategy

Taking notes in a chart

Often, reading passages are filled with many facts and dates. A useful strategy to apply when reading this kind of article is to keep track of the information by jotting down answers to the questions *who?*, *what?*, *when?*, *where?*, and *why?*

1 Datos básicos. Antes de leer sobre unas fiestas centroamericanas, prepara una tabla como la siguiente. Después, mientras lees, completa la tabla con la información indicada. La tabla ya contiene los nombres de los países.

País	Festival Celebración	Geografía Clima	Gobierno Economía	Población	Otros datos
Nicaragua	_____	_____	_____	_____	_____
Honduras	_____	_____	_____	_____	_____
El Salvador	_____	_____	_____	_____	_____

Fiestas centroamericanas: Nicaragua, Honduras, El Salvador

Nicaragua, Honduras y El Salvador son tres países de Centroamérica que tienen unas características en común y algunos aspectos diferentes.

Nicaragua

En área, Nicaragua es el país más grande de Centroamérica. Tiene costas tanto en el Atlántico como en el Pacífico y montañas en el centro del país. Su historia se caracteriza por muchas guerras[1] y poca paz[2]. Managua, la capital y la ciudad más grande, sufrió gran destrucción en el terremoto de 1972 y en la Revolución de 1978–1979. En agosto, hay festivales en honor al santo patrón de Nicaragua, Santo Domingo. Estos festivales se celebran con ceremonias religiosas, corridas de toros[3], carreras de caballos[4] y peleas de gallos[5].

Un desfile en el Festival de Santo Domingo, Nicaragua

---

[1]wars; [2]peace; [3]bullfights; [4]horse races; [5]cock fights

Honduras

La república de Honduras es muy montañosa; tiene una historia de inestabilidad con muchos cambios de gobierno y guerras. Económicamente, es el país más pobre de Centroamérica y también es el país de mayor población en Centroamérica. Durante dos semanas de enero, se celebra en Cedro, un pueblo al norte de Tegucigalpa, la capital hondureña, el festival del Señor del Buen Fin. Durante esta fiesta se sirven comidas tradicionales y se celebran ceremonias religiosas. Como en muchos países hispanos, el ocho de diciembre se celebra el día de la Virgen de la Concepción y las festividades se prolongan durante una semana.

El festival de la Virgen de la Concepción en Tegucigalpa, Honduras

Un festival en El Salvador

El Salvador

El Salvador es la república más pequeña y más densamente poblada de Centroamérica. Ha sufrido muchas guerras y catástrofes naturales. Es el único país de Centroamérica sin acceso al mar Caribe, pero su geografía es variada y sus numerosos volcanes producen una tierra excelente para el cultivo del café. Tiene también más de doscientas variedades de orquídeas. En El Salvador se celebran muchos festivales tanto religiosos como populares como la fiesta de El Salvador, en la que hay desfiles de carrozas[7] decorativas por las calles. El doce de diciembre es la celebración del Día del Indio, en el que hay desfiles muy coloridos en honor a la Virgen de Guadalupe.

[7]floats

POSTLECTURA

2 Comprensión. Trabajen en grupos y contesten las preguntas sobre la lectura.

1. ¿Qué desastre natural sufrió Managua?
2. ¿Cuál es el país de más población en Centroamérica?
3. ¿Cuál es la capital de Honduras?
4. ¿Cómo es Honduras geográficamente?
5. ¿Cuál es la capital salvadoreña?
6. ¿Tiene El Salvador playas en el mar Caribe?
7. ¿Qué flores hay en El Salvador? ¿Por qué se puede cultivar mucho café?
8. Menciona un festival de cada país.

3 Datos de mi tabla. En parejas, comparen la información que han puesto en la tabla de la *Actividad 1*.

4 Otros festivales centroamericanos. Trabajen en grupos para buscar información sobre algunas de las características de las otras repúblicas centroamericanas: Panamá, Costa Rica y Guatemala. Usen una tabla para escribir y comparar los datos.

5 Celebraciones cerca de mí. Trabajen en grupos de dos o tres personas. Cada estudiante describe una celebración, un festival, día de fiesta, carnaval o ceremonia religiosa especial de su estado, región o país. Incluyan detalles sobre diferentes aspectos de la celebración.

Escritura

Writing Strategy

Online Study Center

For further writing practice online, visit the *Caminos* website at http://college .hmco.com/languages/ spanish/renjilian/caminos/ 3e/student_home.html.

Summarizing

A summary is a concise version of something that you have read or seen. It contains the most important information and leaves out much of the detail. Once you have identified the main ideas and supporting details of a passage, you can connect the ideas in paragraph form. Unlike paraphrasing, the intent of a summary is to condense the material and present it in a straightforward way.

Workshop

Review the following strategies to prepare for writing a summary:

► Providing supporting details *(Unidad 3)*
► Making notes in the margin *(Unidad 4)*
► Paraphrasing *(Unidad 7)*

Strategy in Action

For additional practice with summarizing, complete the exercises below and in the *Escritura* section of the Student Activities Manual for *Unidad 10.*

1 **Resumen.** Investiga información en Internet sobre una fiesta del mundo hispano y escribe un resumen de la celebración. Compara tu composición con la de un/a compañero/a.

2 **¿Qué pasó en Costa Rica?** Escribe un resumen de los dos episodios de *Caminos del jaguar* de esta unidad. Compara tu composición con la de un/a compañero/a.

Resumen de vocabulario

PRIMER PASO

LEARNING ABOUT HOLIDAYS AND TRADITIONS

Susantivos

la calavera	skull
la ceremonia	ceremony
la costumbre	custom
el desfile	parade
el disfraz	costume
la estatua	statue
la exhibición	exhibition
el festival	festival
los fuegos artificiales	fireworks
el hecho	event
la muerte	death
el mural	mural
la obra de arte	work of art
la ofrenda	offering
el propósito	resolution, purpose, intention
el rito	rite; ritual
la tradición	tradition

Verbos

burlarse (de)	to make fun of
celebrar	to celebrate
convivir	to live with
festejarse	to celebrate

Adjetivos

folclórico/a, folklórico/a	folkloric
histórico/a	historical
público/a	public
religioso/a	religious

CONJUNCTIONS ALWAYS FOLLOWED BY THE SUBJUNCTIVE

a fin de que	in order that
a menos que	unless
antes (de) que	before
con tal (de) que	provided that
en caso de que	in case
para que	so that
sin que	without

SEGUNDO PASO

TALKING ABOUT ART AND ARTISTS

Sustantivos

la acuarela	watercolor
la arcilla / el barro	clay
el arte clásico, contemporáneo, moderno, abstracto	classic, contemporary, modern, abstract art
el/la artista	artist
el aurorretrato	self-portrait
el bosquejo	sketch
el bronce	bronze
la cerámica	ceramics
el/la ceramista	ceramist, potter
el contraste	contrast
el cuadro	painting, picture
el detalle	detail
el/la dibujante	illustrator
el dibujo	drawing
el/la escultor/a	sculptor
la escultura	sculpture
la exposición, exhibición	art exhibit
la figura	figure
la forma	form
la ilustración	illustration
la imagen	image
el lienzo	canvas
la luz y sombra	light and shadow
la madera	wood

el marco	*frame*
el mármol	*marble*
el/la modelo	*model*
la naturaleza muerta	*still life*
el paisaje	*landscape*
la paleta	*palette*
el pincel	*paintbrush*
el/la pintor/a	*painter*
la pintura	*painting*
la pintura al óleo	*oil-painting*
el retrato	*portrait*
la vasija	*vase*
la vida cotidiana	*daily life*

Verbos

colgar (ue)	*to hang*
crear	*to create*
dibujar	*to draw*
ilustrar	*to illustrate*
pintar	*to paint*
significar	*to mean*

Otras expresiones

claro/a	*light*
en blanco y negro	*(in) black and white*
en color(es)	*(in) color*
oscuro/a	*dark*

DISCUSSING CRAFTS AND FOLK ART

Sustantivos

el adorno	*decoration, adornment*
el/la artesano/a	*artisan*
el/la coleccionista	*collector*
la cruz	*cross*
la pieza	*piece*
la réplica	*replica*

Verbos

| fabricar | *to make* |
| permanecer | *to remain* |

Otras expresiones

a mano	*by hand*
dorado/a	*golden*
hábil	*skillful*

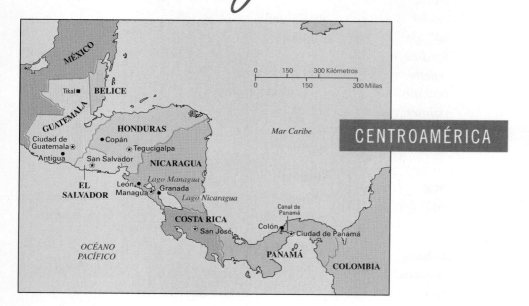

CENTROAMÉRICA

Online Study Center

To learn more about the people featured in this section, visit the *Caminos* website at http://college.hmco.com/languages/spanish/renjilian/caminos.3e/student_home.html.

PERSONALIDADES

Óscar Arias

Arzobispo Óscar Romero

Katia Cardenal

Guillermo Anderson

Claribel Alegría

Moisés Gadea

Franklin Chang-Díaz

Ricardo Arjona

Los centroamericanos

Las artes y letras de América Central incorporan una gran variedad de temas: las raíces culturales, las tradiciones indígenas del pasado y presente, las expresiones sentimentales, las distintas actitudes hacia la vida y la muerte, la juventud[1] y la vejez[2], la guerra[3] y la paz[4], lo familiar y lo desconocido[5], la religión, el amor y la identidad nacional.

Hay una larga historia de conflictos y violencia en Centroamérica. Las injusticias contra los pueblos indígenas han caracterizado[6] ciertas regiones. Miles de centroamericanos se exiliaron por razones[7] políticas para escaparse de peligros y mal tratamiento.

En sus obras, muchos escritores, músicos, artistas y otros intelectuales revelan la importancia de las culturas indígenas, afirmando las diversas raíces culturales. Dos centroamericanos ganaron el Premio Nobel de la Paz por su activismo a favor de los grupos indígenas: la escritora indígena Rigoberta Menchú de Guatemala (1992) y el ex presidente Óscar Arias de Costa Rica (1987).

El Arzobispo Óscar Romero, de El Salvador, perdió su vida por la causa de la igualdad[8] y los derechos socioeconómicos de su pueblo. El director de cine guatemalteco, Luis Argueta, examina la historia y las raíces culturales guatemaltecas en sus películas, como hace también la directora costarricense Guita Schyfter.

---

[1]youth; [2]old age; [3]war; [4]peace; [5]unknown; [6]have characterized; [7]reasons; [8]equality

"Prefiero... tener la libertad de expresar
todo lo que quiero como cantante."
—Ricardo Arjona (Guatemala)

Miguel Ángel Asturias

Otros centroamericanos han hecho contribuciones a las artes y letras con el enfoque[9] sobre las raíces culturales como fondo[10]. En la música, se destacan el hondureño Guillermo Anderson, que canta sobre la gente nativa de su región; el trío costarricense Editus, que combina jazz moderno y tradicional con auténticos sonidos latinoamericanos; el nicaragüense Moisés Gadea, que canta sobre condiciones sociales en su país.

Es importante reconocer los logros de Franklin Chang-Díaz, astronauta costarricense; y de escritores distinguidos como Claribel Alegría de El Salvador, Carmen Naranjo de Costa Rica y Miguel Ángel Asturias de Guatemala.

Visita el sitio web de *Caminos* para leer más en español sobre estas personalidades centroamericanas.

[9]focus; [10]background

Comprensión

Trabajando en parejas, háganse estas preguntas.

1. ¿Qué centroamericanos ganaron el Premio Nobel de la Paz?
2. Nombra las profesiones de las personalidades de América Central mencionadas aquí. ¿Cuál te parece más interesante?

ARTE

Ritos: Hombres del maíz, 2000

PEDRO RAFAEL GONZÁLEZ CHAVAJAY

Para muchos pueblos indígenas hispanoamericanos del pasado y del presente, el maíz* ha tenido importancia agrícola y religiosa. El maíz sirve de comida para la familia. Como elemento de las ceremonias religiosas, refleja el respeto y el amor por la tierra. Esto se puede observar también en las artes. El tema de las raíces culturales se ve en una multitud de imágenes artísticas. La obra *Ritos°: Hombres de maíz*, es del artista guatemalteco, Pedro Rafael González Chavajay.

corn

ceremonias

♊ Comprensión

Trabajando en parejas, háganse estas preguntas.

1. ¿Cómo se llama esta obra de arte? ¿De dónde es el artista?
2. ¿Cómo son las personas? ¿Qué ropa llevan?
3. ¿Cuándo ocurre este rito? ¿Qué instrumentos tocan durante la ceremonia?
4. En la cesta hay una jarra°. ¿Cómo es? ¿Para qué se usa?
5. ¿Qué ambiente° crea el uso artístico de luz y sombra?
6. ¿De qué colores es el maíz en esta obra? ¿En qué comidas populares de hoy encontramos el maíz?
7. ¿Qué producto agrícola representa tu país en el pasado y en el presente? ¿En qué comidas lo encontramos?
8. En tus propias palabras, describe esta obra.

MÚSICA

RUBÉN BLADES

Rubén Blades es una personalidad que ha hecho grandes contribuciones en los campos de la música, del cine, del derecho° y de la política.   *law*
Nació en Panamá en 1948, de padre colombiano y madre cubana. Blades dice que su abuela le enseño a cultivar el sentido° de la justicia. Al terminar sus   *sense*
estudios en la Universidad de Panamá, se hizo abogado.

    Su visión de solucionar problemas sociales y su dedicación a sus raíces caracterizan su música. Ganó su primer Grammy en 1985 y otro tres años más tarde. Canta en español y en inglés, y ha participado° con otros grupos hispanos en la fusión   *has participated*
de música irlandesa, árabe y afro-cubana, además de° salsa. Ganó también premios como actor de   *in addition to*
cine y de televisión.

    En 1994, fue candidato para la presidencia panameña, pero perdió la elección. En el año 2000, sirvió de Embajador de Buena Voluntad° para las   *Good Will Ambassador*
Naciones Unidas.

Comprensión

Trabajando en parejas, háganse estas preguntas.

1. ¿De dónde son Rubén Blades y sus padres?
2. ¿Qué le enseñó su abuela? ¿En qué campo profesional se graduó Blades en la universidad?
3. ¿Cuáles son sus otras profesiones?
4. Describe su música y sus premios. ¿En qué idioma canta?
5. ¿Qué le pasó a Blades en las elecciones presidenciales de Panamá?
6. ¿Qué hace un/a Embajador/a de Buena Voluntad? En tus propias palabras, resume el trabajo que hacen en las Naciones Unidas.

Conéctate a Internet para escuchar la música de Rubén Blades, aprender más sobre él, los cantantes ya mencionados u otros: los nicaragüenses Salvador Cardenal, "Alux Nahual", Carlos Mejía Godoy y Katia Cardenal; el guatemalteco Ricardo Arjona; el costarricense Juan Carlos Ureña y el panameño Luis Russell.

LITERATURA

ROQUE DALTON

Roque Dalton vivió entre los años 1935 y 1975. Por su activismo político fue condenado° a muerte, pero el poeta salvadoreño logró exiliarse a otras partes de Latinoamérica y Europa. Tristemente, al regresar a El Salvador, fue asesinado. Amaba la poesía y a su país; murió por sus ideales de justicia e igualdad.

condemned

"Cómo tú"

Creo que el mundo es bello,
que la poesía es como el pan,
   de todos.
Y que mis venas no terminan en mí
sino° en la sangre unánime
de los que luchan por la vida,
el amor,
las cosas,
el paisaje y el pan,
la poesía de todos.

but rather

Comprensión

Trabajando en parejas, háganse estas preguntas.

1. ¿Qué adjetivo usa el poeta para describir el mundo? ¿Es negativa o positiva su actitud?
2. ¿Con qué compara la poesía? Inventa otra comparación para la poesía.
3. ¿De quiénes es la poesía?
4. ¿Para qué luchan todos, según el poeta?
5. En tu opinión, ¿cuál es más importante: el amor o las cosas?
6. En tu opinión, ¿Cuál es el mensaje central de este poema? ¿Te gusta este mensaje o no? ¿Por qué?

RIGOBERTA MENCHÚ

Rigoberta Menchú es una indígena guatemalteca nacida en 1959. Lucha por tener un país libre de violencia contra la gente indígena. En su novela autobiográfica, *Yo, Rigoberta Menchú*, habla de la vida de su familia indígena y de las condiciones difíciles para el pueblo quiché, el grupo indígena en el norte de Guatemala del cual ella es miembro. Algunas de las memorias y actitudes que presenta en el libro siguen aquí.

ethnic groups	*Me llamo Rigoberta Menchú. Tengo veintitrés años.
includes / people	*...en Guatemala, existen veintidós etnias° indígenas...
	*Mi situación personal engloba° toda la realidad de un pueblo°....
	*...tengo mis costumbres, costumbres indígenas quichés.
paradise	*Precisamente mi tierra es un paraíso° de todo lo lindo que es la naturaleza....
in the middle	Yo casi vivo en medio° de muchas montañas.
número seis	*...yo soy la sexta° de la familia....
hardly	*Nosotros vivimos más en las montañas...que apenas° dan maíz, frijol...
	*...mis padres...han vivido una situación muy difícil y son muy pobres.

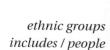

Comprensión

Trabajando en parejas, háganse estas preguntas.

1. ¿Dónde tiene sus raíces Rigoberta Menchú? ¿Cuántos años tiene en el cuento y en el año 2007?
lf 2. ¿Quiere representarse solamente a sí misma°?
3. ¿Qué costumbres practica? ¿Cuántas etnias hay en Guatemala?
4. ¿Es de una familia pequeña?
5. ¿Qué cultivaba la familia en las montañas?
6. ¿Cómo era la vida de Menchú y su familia?
7. Cuenta brevemente una autobiografía que conozcas tú.
8. ¿Hay grupos indígenas en tu región? ¿Dónde viven? Describe algo de su vida.

ERNESTO CARDENAL

Ernesto Cardenal es un poeta nicaragüense. Dedicó una gran parte de su vida a luchar contra la dictadura del general Anastasio Somoza en Nicaragua. En este poema, compara el amor por su país con el amor por una mujer.

"Epigramas"°

Yo he repartido° papeletas clandestinas°,
gritando, ¡VIVA LA LIBERTAD! en plena° calle
desafiando° a los guardias armados.
Yo participé en la rebelión de abril°:
pero palidezco° cuando paso por tu casa
y tu sola mirada me hace temblar°.

Inscriptions

I have distributed/secret messages
in the middle of
challenging
nombre de una protesta grande
I turn pale
tremble

Comprensión

Trabajando en parejas, háganse estas preguntas.

1. ¿En qué actividad política participó el narrador del poema? ¿Por qué estaba gritando?
2. ¿En qué mes ocurrió la rebelión?
3. ¿Cómo es el narrador en sus acciones políticas y amorosas: fuerte, débil, personal, popular, inestable, estable, emocional, miedoso?
4. En tu opinión, ¿por qué le hace temblar la "mirada" de la otra persona?
5. Nombra dos temas de este poema.
6. ¿Qué libertades tienes en tu país: votar, reunirse en grupos, expresar tus ideas, practicar la religión de tu preferencia, llevar armas? ¿En qué regiones no existen estas libertades?

11

Temas de la sociedad

VOCABULARIO Y LENGUA

- ► Talking about contemporary society
- ► Reacting to societal issues
- ► Using the future tense and future of probability

- ► Discussing environmental issues
- ► Expressing emotions and doubt in the past: Present and past perfect subjunctive
- ► Using the conditional tense and conditional of probability

CAMINOS DEL JAGUAR

- ► Trampa de trampas
- ► ¡Gol!

LECTURA

- ► ¡Milenios de miedos!

NOTAS CULTURALES

- ► El Instituto de Culturas Texanas
- ► El Paseo del Río en San Antonio

ESTRATEGIAS

- ► **Reading:** Distinguishing facts from opinions
- ► **Writing:** Narrowing a topic

Michael Rios, *Maya Garden*

Preguntas del tema

- ▶ ¿Qué haces para ayudar a tu comunidad?
- ▶ ¿Qué problema social te preocupa más?
- ▶ ¿Qué cosas contribuyen a la contaminación del aire? ¿del agua?
- ▶ ¿Cómo podemos reducir la cantidad de basura en el mundo?

PRIMER PASO

Vocabulario y lengua

TALKING ABOUT CONTEMPORARY SOCIETY

Jóvenes de hoy

uncertainty

worries / AIDS

increased
employment

turned into
to reach

has led to

delinquent acts
consumption
pregnancies

La juventud mexicana de hoy es una generación que está preocupada por su futuro. Para ellos, la **incertidumbre**° de la vida está siempre presente, pero la muerte no es una de sus **angustias**° principales. Sin embargo, el **SIDA**° y las drogas sí están entre sus preocupaciones. Además, estos jóvenes modernos tienen más consciencia social y por eso han **aumentado**° sus demandas de educación, **empleo**°, servicios de salud, espacios de expresión cultural y representación política.

Antes de casarse, los jóvenes del país piensan en estudiar y en **obtener** un empleo, pero en México, el trabajo se ha **convertido en**° un sueño más difícil de **alcanzar**° que el amor.

Diversos estudios indican que la crisis en la población joven ha propiciado° un aumento en el número de suicidios, **actos delictivos**°, **consumo**° de drogas y alcohol, **embarazos**° no deseados y enfermedades psicológicas.

Online Study Center

For additional practice with this unit's vocabulary and grammar, visit the *Caminos* website at http://college .hmco.com/languages/ spanish/renjilian/caminos/ 3e/student_home.html. You can also review audio flashcards, quiz yourself, and explore related Spanish-language sites.

Más palabras y expresiones

Cognados

la adicción
el/la adolescente
el beneficio
la comunidad
el crimen
la cura
la delincuencia

el/la delinquente
la depresión
la drogadicción
la justicia
la libertad
el/la policía
el programa social

la solución
el terrorismo
el/la terrorista
el tráfico de drogas
el/la voluntario/a

Sustantivos

las armas	*weapons*
el asesinato	*assassination, murder*
el/la asesino/a	*murderer*
la cárcel, prisión	*prison*
el consejo	*advice*
los desamparados	*homeless people*
el desempleo	*unemployment*
la guerra	*war*
el lío	*problem, trouble, mess*
el logro	*achievement*
el/la niñero/a	*nanny, babysitter*
la patria	*homeland*
el peligro	*danger*
la pobreza	*poverty*
el robo	*robbery*
la seguridad	*security*
el seguro médico	*health insurance*
la sociedad	*society*
la terapia	*therapy*
el/la trabajador/a social	*social worker*

Verbos

amenazar	*to threaten*
arrestar	*to arrest*
asesinar	*to assassinate, murder*
encarcelar	*to imprison*
enfrentar	*to confront, face up to*
estar desesperado/a	*to be desperate*
fracasar	*to fail*
lograr	*to achieve; to attain*
luchar	*to fight*
matar	*to kill*
tener remedio	*to have a solution*
triunfar	*to succeed, triumph*

1 **¿Verdadero o falso?** Di si estas frases son verdaderas (**V**) o falsas (**F**) según la lectura. Si son falsas, corrígelas.

1. Los jóvenes de México están preocupados por el futuro.
2. La muerte está entre sus angustias principales.
3. La educación es importante para los jóvenes mexicanos.
4. Los jóvenes piensan obtener un empleo después de casarse.
5. Es difícil encontrar empleo.
6. El consumo de drogas ha aumentado.

2 **Querida Catalina.** Una joven le escribe a Catalina, una psicóloga que da consejos en el Internet, para pedirle ayuda. Escucha lo que dice en el correo electrónico y completa la siguiente información. Después, trabajen en parejas para darle consejos a Laura.

1. Laura tiene _____ años.
   a. veinte   **b.** treinta   **c.** trece

2. Ella está _____.
   a. casada   **b.** separada   **c.** divorciada

3. Ella trabaja en una tienda de _____.
   a. zapatos   **b.** discos   **c.** ropa

4. Su trabajo _____.
   a. paga mal   **b.** tiene beneficios sociales   **c.** paga bien

5. Mientras trabaja, su _____ cuida a la hija.
   a. tía   **b.** madre   **c.** vecina

6. Laura quiere _____.
   a. quedarse en casa   **b.** cambiar de trabajo   **c.** estudiar

3 **Titulares.** Eres reportero/a para el periódico de tu pueblo. Escribe titulares para presentar los artículos sobre los siguientes temas.

▶ **MODELO:** tráfico de drogas
   Los Estados Unidos anuncian un nuevo plan para eliminar el tráfico de drogas.

1. el consumo de alcohol
2. el terrorismo
3. la pobreza
4. el SIDA
5. los actos delictivos
6. las enfermedades psicológicas
7. el desempleo
8. el asesinato

4 **Soluciones.** Trabajando en grupos, creen soluciones posibles para tres de los problemas sociales mencionados en la *Actividad 3*. La lista siguiente tiene algunas soluciones posibles.

contratar más policías   aumentar los impuestos sobre el alcohol
crear más trabajos   aumentar el sueldo mínimo

5 A escribir. Escribe una composición de dos párrafos sobre uno de los problemas sociales de la *Actividad 3* y ofrece algunas soluciones. Organiza tu composición de esta manera.

Problema
1. *Causas*
2. *Soluciones*

REACTING TO SOCIETAL ISSUES

Una encuesta nacional

En México, se les hizo una encuesta a quinientos jóvenes entre los trece y los veinticuatro años de edad sobre los problemas a los que ellos se enfrentan. Aquí hay algunas de sus respuestas.

Autoestima
¿Te sientes con capacidad para resolver todos tus problemas?

	Edad		
Frecuencia	13 a 17 años	18 a 24 años	Promedio
Siempre	22%	35%	29%
Casi siempre	47%	53%	50%
A veces	29%	12%	20%
Casi nunca	2%	—	1%

¿Te gusta tu aspecto físico?

	Sexo		Promedio
Frecuencia	Hombres	Mujeres	Hombres y mujeres
Mucho	25%	25%	25%
Algo	62%	53%	57,5%
Poco	8%	11%	9,5%
Nada	5%	11%	8%

Adicciones
¿Acostumbras tomar alcohol?

	Sexo		Promedio
Frecuencia	Hombres	Mujeres	Hombres y mujeres
Sí	55%	35%	45%
No	45%	65%	55%

¿Conoces directamente a alguien que tenga problemas con...?

	Sí	No
su forma de beber	68%	32%
el consumo de drogas	63%	37%

Actividades

1 Opiniones. Contesta las preguntas de la encuesta. Después, en grupos, recojan la información y calculen los porcentajes según las respuestas de la clase. Comparen sus opiniones con las de los jóvenes mexicanos.

2 Nuestra cápsula del tiempo. Aunque hay muchos problemas sociales en el mundo, también hay muchas cosas buenas. ¿Qué objetos representativos de nuestra época puedes poner en una cápsula del tiempo para abrir en el futuro? Con una pareja, hagan una lista de diez objetos.

Para considerar: Eventos importantes, música, comida, tecnología, ropa, cosas personales y comunicaciones.

3 En grupos. Trabajen en grupos de tres. Comparen sus listas personales de la *Actividad 2* y elijan diez objetos de sus listas. Preséntenle la nueva lista a la clase y expliquen por qué escogieron finalmente esos diez objetos.

USING THE FUTURE TENSE AND FUTURE OF PROBABILITY

Haré un buen trabajo

I will start	Sonia	Tío Efraín, el año entrante **empezaré**° mi especialización.
Will you study / will you do	Efraín	¿**Estudiarás**° para ser psicóloga o **harás**° algo diferente?
I will become / I will help	Sonia	Algo diferente, tío Efraín. **Seré**° trabajadora social y **ayudaré**° a los jóvenes que tengan problemas con las drogas y el alcohol.
you will be very successful	Efraín	Te felicito, Sonia. Estoy seguro de que **tendrás** mucho éxito°.

Most verbs in Spanish are regular in the future. The stem for most -**ar**, -**er**, and -**ir** verbs is the infinitive. All verbs share a common set of endings in the future tense.

Future tense of regular verbs				
Infinitive	Subject	Stem	Ending	Future tense
trabajar	yo	trabajar-	**é**	trabaj**aré**
creer	tú	creer-	**ás**	creer**ás**
escribir	Ud., él, ella	escribir-	**á**	escribir**á**
sentir	nosotros/as	sentir-	**emos**	sentir**emos**
dar	vosotros/as	dar-	**éis**	dar**éis**
ir	Uds., ellos, ellas	ir-	**án**	ir**án**

Notice that all endings carry written accents except the **nosotros/as** form.

There are very few verbs that are irregular in the future. The following verbs have irregular stems, but the endings are the same as for regular verbs.

Future tense of irregular verbs		
Infinitive	Stem	Future tense example
decir	dir-	yo **diré**
hacer	har-	tú **harás**
poder	podr-	Ud. **podrá**
poner	pondr-	él **pondrá**
querer	querr-	ella **querrá**
saber	sabr-	nosotros/as **sabremos**
salir	saldr-	vosotros/as **saldréis**
tener	tendr-	Uds. **tendrán**
venir	vendr-	ellos, ellas **vendrán**

Habrá *(there will be)* is the future of **haber**. Like **hay** *(there is, there are)*, **habrá** is used only in the singular where it means *there will be*.

Habrá una conferencia sobre los jóvenes en América Latina.	*There will be a talk about youth in Latin America.*
Habrá muchos participantes.	*There will be many attendees.*

The English equivalent of the future tense is *will* or *shall* plus a *verb:*

Mañana **haré** la encuesta.	*I will / shall do the survey tomorrow.*

In addition to the future tense, you have already learned two other ways of expressing the future in Spanish: **ir a** + infinitive or present indicative.

Mañana **voy a hacer** la encuesta.	*I am going to do the survey tomorrow.*
Mañana **hago** la encuesta.	*I'll do the survey tomorrow.*

The future may be used to express *probability* or *to wonder* about a present situation or action. The equivalent in English can be *probably, I / we wonder, it must be,* and so on.

Luisa	Luzmila no ha llegado. ¿Qué hora **será**?
	Luzmila hasn't arrived. I wonder what time it is.
Guillermo	No lo sé. **Serán** las tres de la tarde.
	I don't know. It's probably around three P.M.
Luisa	¿Dónde **estará** Luzmila?
	Where can Luzmila be?

Actividades

👥 **1 Nuestras preocupaciones.** Completa estas preguntas con el futuro de los verbos entre paréntesis. Después, con un/a compañero/a, discutan si estas cosas ocurrirán cuando ustedes sean mayores.

1. ¿ _____ (Haber) buena atención médica para los mayores?
2. ¿ _____ (Pagar, nosotros) mucho por nuestro seguro médico?
3. ¿ _____ (Eliminar) el gobierno la pobreza en que viven muchos ancianos?
4. ¿ _____ (Ser) posible quedarnos en nuestra casa?
5. ¿ _____ (Sufrir, nosotros) de alguna enfermedad grave?
6. ¿Nuestros hijos _____ (querer) cuidarnos cuando lo necesitemos?

👥 **2 ¿Qué será será?** Tú y tu compañero/a de estudio hablan sobre lo que harán en el futuro. Pon en futuro, en la forma de **tú,** los verbos que están entre paréntesis. Cuando termines, hazle la encuesta a tu compañero/a.

▶ **MODELO:** ¿En qué región _____ (vivir)?
¿En qué región vivirás?

1. ¿ _____ (Hacer) una maestría o un doctorado antes de empezar a trabajar?
2. ¿Qué profesión _____ (tener)? ¿ _____ (Ganar) más o menos de cien mil dólares al año?
3. ¿ _____ (Preocuparse) por los problemas sociales y económicos de los jóvenes?
4. ¿ _____ (Usar) transporte público para llegar al trabajo? ¿Qué marca de coche _____ (preferir)?
5. ¿ _____ (Alquilar) o _____ (comprar) tu apartamento o casa?
6. ¿ _____ (Fumar) o no? ¿ _____ (Consumir) alcohol o no?
7. ¿Cuántas semanas de vacaciones _____ (tomar) al año? ¿Adónde _____ (viajar) y con quién?
8. ¿ _____ (Casarse) antes de cumplir los treinta años? ¿ _____ (Querer) tener hijos? ¿Por qué sí o por qué no?

👥 **3 ¿Dónde estará?** Margarita y Enrique están esperando a su amiga Reyes, que ya está atrasada *(late)* para el almuerzo. Con un/a compañero/a, creen una conversación entre ellos sobre las posibles razones.

4 ¿Qué opinas tú? Muchas cosas pueden suceder en nuestra sociedad durante los próximos diez años. Trabajando en parejas, discutan estas afirmaciones y expliquen si están de acuerdo o no y por qué.

1. El número de suicidios entre los jóvenes aumentará.
2. Habrá menos casos de SIDA en el país.
3. Los jóvenes conseguirán trabajo muy fácilmente.
4. Todo el mundo tendrá seguro médico.
5. La pobreza y el hambre disminuirán en todo el mundo.
6. Descubrirán nuevas medicinas para curar las enfermedades mentales.
7. No habrá más ataques de terroristas en los EE.UU.
8. El gobierno permitirá la clonación de seres humanos.
9. Los jóvenes tendrán más educación.
10. El gobierno prohibirá la venta de cigarillos en todo el país.

5 Predicciones. Escribe una composición sobre la situación de uno de estos problemas sociales en el año 2020: (a) el consumo de alcohol y drogas, (b) la cura definitiva del SIDA, del cáncer o de otra enfermedad, (c) el costo de la educación universitaria, (d) la delincuencia en el país o (e) soluciones al terrorismo.

Trampa de trampas

En el apartamento de Adriana, en San Antonio.

¿Dónde estará Gafasnegras?

No sé, pero ella tiene que vender los jaguares.

Los jaguares son difíciles de vender.

Los anticuarios de San Antonio ya deben saber que son robados porque ven la televisión mexicana.

Pero, ¿cuántos anticuarios habrá en San Antonio?

Busquemos en la guía telefónica. Yo busco desde la *a* hasta la *m* y tú comienzas con la *n*.

En el anticuario, en San Antonio.

Mmm...

Bueno, ¿cuál es su conclusión?

Tengo un cliente al que le interesaría mucho. Aquí tiene la dirección y el teléfono.

Raúl, valió la pena poner el anuncio. ¡El criminal cayó en la trampa! Le di tu número.

Bien, entonces espero la llamada. Gracias, compadre.

De nada. Por la patria, haré lo que sea necesario.

Mira este anuncio de "Arte precolombino".

Queda muy cerca, iré a ver qué puedo averiguar.

Suerte, Adriana.

Señor, vi su anuncio en el periódico. ¿No ha venido una señora delgada, de pelo negro a venderle unos objetos de arte maya?

¿Y usted por qué quiere saberlo?

Estamos buscando dos objetos que pertenecen a México.

¿Puede usted darme más detalles?

Son dos objetos de barro y representan a los héroes gemelos, Yax-Balam y Hun-Ahau. Los teníamos juntos en Costa Rica y se los robaron de nuevo.

¡Usted sabe mucho y creo que dice la verdad! Debe hablar con el Sr. Guzmán.

¿Quién es él?

Es un agente mexicano, pero se hace pasar por coleccionista de arte. Aquí tiene la dirección.

Esa mujer que usted describió estuvo aquí hace poco.

¿Cómo puede ser?

No se preocupe, el Sr. Guzmán tiene todo bajo control. Ya lo verá.

Actividades

Online Study Center

For additional practice
with this episode, visit
the *Caminos* website at
http://college.hmco.com/
languages/spanish/
renjilian/caminos/3e/
student_home.html.

1 Comprensión.
Basándote en este episodio de *Caminos del jaguar,* elige la
alternativa lógica.

1. Felipe cree que Gafasnegras tiene que...
   a. esconder los jaguares.
   b. vender los jaguares.

2. Felipe y Adriana encuentran a un anticuario que sabe algo sobre...
   a. el arte precolombino.
   b. Nayeli.

3. El anticuario está contento porque Gafasnegras...
   a. va a llamar a Raúl.
   b. va a llamar a Adriana.

4. Para el anticuario, la patria es...
   a. algo indiferente.
   b. algo importante.

5. Adriana sale para averiguar la información que encontró en...
   a. el periódico.
   b. la guía telefónica.

6. El anticuario dice que Gafasnegras...
   a. ya compró los jaguares.
   b. quiere vender los jaguares.

7. El anticuario le pide a Adriana que no se preocupe porque...
   a. todo va a salir mal.
   b. el Sr. Guzmán tiene todo bajo
      control.

2 Situaciones.
Dramaticen una de las siguientes situaciones.

1. Adriana y Felipe hacen planes para buscar los jaguares.
2. El anticuario y Gafasnegras hablan sobre los jaguares.

3 Escritura.
Escribe la conversación telefónica que Adriana va a tener con el
Sr. Guzmán. (4–6 oraciones)

NOTA CULTURAL

El Instituto de Culturas Texanas

Este museo de San Antonio tiene exposiciones
que muestran la variada cultura del estado de
Texas y sus orígenes hispanos. Se exhiben
también varios objetos arqueológicos
representativos de las culturas que han formado
el estado. Hay una tienda en el museo donde
se venden libros y videos sobre las tradiciones
culturales de Texas. También se venden
reproducciones de algunas obras de arte de
su colección.

SEGUNDO PASO

Vocabulario y lengua

DISCUSSING ENVIRONMENTAL ISSUES

Consejos ecológicos

unequal

A muchos nos preocupan **el deterioro del planeta** y las **consecuencias** de nuestras desiguales° relaciones con la **naturaleza**. Pero gran parte de la gente considera que no puede hacer nada o que los problemas son tan grandes que se escapan de sus manos. Nada más falso.

It isn't about / fight
remaining species / Being aware
environment / The only thing

Existen innumerables cosas que podemos hacer día a día para ayudar a **conservar el planeta** y llevar una **existencia** más **armoniosa** con la naturaleza. **No se trata de**° una lucha° a muerte entre tecnología y naturaleza, entre el hombre y las **demás especies**°. Tomando consciencia° de nuestra **responsabilidad ecológica,** podemos aprender a coexistir adecuadamente con el medio ambiente°. Lo único° que se requiere en muchas ocasiones es una pequeña modificación en nuestro

behavior

comportamiento°. No debemos dejar de hacer o usar las cosas que nos gustan o nos son cómodas. Tan sólo debemos hacerlas de una manera más ecológica.

own

USA TU PROPIA° TAZA...

garbage

discarded
avoids

Lleva un vaso o taza a la oficina y úsalo para beber agua o café. Así no producirás **basura**° cada vez que tengas sed. Piensa en el montón de vasos **desechados**° que acumulas al año y la cantidad de basura que se evita° si tú y tus compañeros de trabajo usan su propia taza.

save (rescue)

¿QUIERES SALVAR° EL MUNDO?

save (collect)

sheet of paper / sides

Empieza por **ahorrar**° papel. El papel es producido de fibra vegetal procesada que se obtiene **explotando** los bosques del mundo. Toda hoja° tiene dos caras°. **Reusándolas** y escribiendo o imprimiendo en su reverso, reduces tu consumo de papel. Al reducir tu consumo, reduces la presión sobre los bosques y la cantidad de basura.

Online Study Center

For additional practice with this unit's vocabulary and grammar, visit the *Caminos* website at http://college.hmco.com/languages/spanish/renjilian/caminos/3e/student_home.html. You can also review audio flashcards, quiz yourself, and explore related Spanish-language sites.

¡APÁGALO!

Apaga un **bombillo°** o la computadora, impresora, televisión o cualquier otro aparato eléctrico que no estés usando. La **energía** consumida por estos equipos se produce quemando° **combustible°** caro, que **contamina** el medio ambiente o explotando nuestros **recursos°** hidroeléctricos naturales limitados y cada vez más **escasos°**.

lightbulb

burning
fuel
resources / scarce

APOYA° LAS ORGANIZACIONES QUE AYUDAN A LOS ANIMALES

Support

Hay muchas organizaciones como el WWF (World Wildlife Fund) que ayudan a proteger los animales en peligro de **extinción,** como los **elefantes, ballenas°, delfines, pingüinos, osos panda°, tigres,** tortugas y **monos°.** También hay organizaciones como el ASPCA que se dedica a prevenir la crueldad a los animales como los perros, gatos, **gallos°, caballos°** y pájaros. Puedes apoyarlas con contribuciones o puedes escribirles cartas a los políticos, ser voluntario o ¡adoptar una mascota!

whales
panda bears / monkeys

roosters / horses

Más palabras y expresiones

Cognados

la contaminación   la deforestación

Sustantivos

el calentamiento global	*global warming*
la capa de ozono	*ozone layer*
los desperdicios nucleares	*nuclear waste*
el dióxido de carbono	*carbon dioxide*
el efecto invernadero	*the greenhouse effect*
la lluvia ácida	*acid rain*

Actividades

1 **¿Verdadero o falso?** Di si las oraciones son verdaderas (**V**) o falsas (**F**). Si son falsas, corrígelas según la lectura. Trabaja con una pareja.

1. Una sola persona no puede hacer nada para resolver los problemas ecológicos.
2. Se puede vivir en armonía con la naturaleza.
3. Debemos modificar nuestras vidas modernas por completo.
4. La tecnología no puede coexistir con la naturaleza sin destruirla.
5. Debemos usar muchas tazas de plástico.
6. Debemos ahorrar papel.
7. No es necesario que apaguemos los aparatos eléctricos cuando no se usan.
8. No se puede hacer nada por los animales en peligro.
9. Los combustibles no contaminan ni el aire ni el agua.
10. Todo el mundo tiene responsabilidades ecológicas.

2 **Noticias ecológicas.** Escucha las noticias que hablan del problema de la extinción de especies y contesta las preguntas.

1. ¿Cuántas especies en peligro de extinción hay en el mundo?
2. ¿Cuáles son las causas de este problema?
3. Nombra tres especies de animales en peligro de extinción.
4. ¿Qué pasa cuando se extingue una especie?
5. ¿Por qué nos afecta a nosotros?

3 **¿Qué más podemos hacer?** Haz una lista de cinco cosas que se puede hacer para ayudar a conservar el planeta.

4 **A escribir.** ¿Cuál es el problema ecológico que más te preocupa? ¿Por qué? ¿Cómo se puede resolver?

EXPRESSING EMOTIONS AND DOUBT IN THE PAST: PRESENT AND PLUPERFECT (PAST PERFECT) SUBJUNCTIVE

Un planeta en peligro

have contaminated	Lilia	Es terrible que **hayamos contaminado**° el aire con tantos productos químicos. Ahora vivimos con el resultado.
have produced	Inés	Es verdad, pero los coches también han contribuido a esa contaminación. No me gusta para nada que las compañías de autos **hayan producido**° tantos coches grandes.
has (not) stopped	Lilia	A mí tampoco, pero también es triste que la gente no **haya dejado**° de comprarlos.
had (not) approved	Inés	Estoy de acuerdo. Los políticos no hacen mucho. A mí no me gustó que el gobierno no **hubiera aprobado**° leyes más estrictas para proteger el medio ambiente.
	Lilia	¿Y la solución?
	Inés	Tenemos que seguir luchando por la naturaleza.

You have learned that verbs expressing wishes, emotions, and similar feelings in the main clause require the use of the subjunctive in the subordinate or dependent clause.

Espero que ustedes **lean** las instrucciones.
I hope that you read the instructions.

Esperaba que ustedes **leyeran** las instrucciones.
I was hoping that you read the instructions.

When the verb in the main clause is in the present and the dependent clause refers to the recent past, the *present perfect subjunctive* is used.

Espero que **hayan leído** las instrucciones.
I hope that you have read the instructions.

When the verb in the main clause is in a past tense and the dependent clause refers to an action that occurred before the one described in the main clause, the *pluper-fect (past perfect) subjunctive* appears in the subordinate clause.

Me alegró mucho que **hubieran leído** las instrucciones.
It made me happy that you had read the instructions.

	present subjunctive	+ past participle	imperfect subjunctive	+ past participle
The present perfect and pluperfect subjunctive				
(El presente perfecto y pluscuamperfecto del subjuntivo)				
yo	**haya**		**hubiera**	
tú	**hayas**	hablado	**hubieras**	hablado
Ud. / él / ella	**haya**	querido	**hubiera**	querido
nosotros/as	**hayamos**	venido	**hubiéramos**	venido
vosotros/as	**hayáis**		**hubierais**	
Uds. / ellos / ellas	**hayan**		**hubieran**	

Remember to review how to form past participles and sentence structure with object pronouns in *Unidad 9,* pages 327–328.

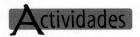

1 La contaminación. Un grupo de amigos expresan sus opiniones sobre la contaminación. Completa cada frase con la forma correcta del presente perfecto del subjuntivo. Sigue el modelo.

▶ MODELO: Es bueno que las autoridades *hayan limpiado* (limpiar) el agua contaminada en las ciudades.

1. No es verdad que todos los países _____ (solucionar) los problemas de la contaminación del medio ambiente.
2. Es una lástima que los coches _____ (ser) la causa de la contaminación del aire.
3. Temo que el número de águilas _____ (reducirse) este año.
4. Ojalá que no _____ (morirse) muchas ballenas este año en las aguas contaminadas.
5. Es bueno que el gobierno de los Estados Unidos _____ (darse cuenta) de la urgencia de proteger los animales.
6. Estoy contento de que los jóvenes _____ (utilizar) menos agua en la ducha.
7. Es bueno que los parques nacionales _____ (preservar) las flores y los bosques en peligro de extinción.
8. Me alegro de que recientemente los ecólogos _____ (preocuparse) por los animales marinos como el delfín y la ballena.

2 Las preferencias de la familia. Tú hiciste las siguientes actividades durante una visita a casa. Cuéntale a un/a compañero/a la reacción de diferentes miembros de tu familia. Sigue el modelo y emplea el pluscuamperfecto del subjuntivo.

▶ MODELO: No apagué las luces cuando salí de casa.
A mi padre no le gustó que yo no hubiera apagado las luces cuando salí de casa.

1. Le di cincuenta dólares al WWF.
2. Pasé media hora en la ducha.
3. Tiré basura en el piso.
4. Compré un coche híbrido.
5. Reciclé mis botellas de plástico.
6. Participé en una protesta contra las fábricas nucleares.

3 Emociones. Haz una lista de cinco cosas que has hecho recientemente. Luego, comparte tu lista con un/a compañero/a. Dale tu opinión a la otra persona de cada cosa en su lista. Sigue el modelo.

▶ MODELO: He comprado un nuevo coche.
Me alegro de que hayas comprado un nuevo coche.

4 Mis memorias. Imagínate que tienes noventa y cinco años y estás escribiendo tus memorias. Allí dices que te arrepientes de haber hecho cinco cosas en tu vida. Usa **ojalá** y el pluscuamperfecto del subjuntivo para describirlas. Explica también por qué te arrepientes de ellas. Sigue el modelo.

▶ MODELO: *Ojalá que yo no hubiera roto el antiguo plato de cerámica de mi mamá cuando era niño/a.*

Planes

Irene	¿**Te gustaría**° mirar esta película de amor?	*Would you like*
Carlos	No, querida. En vez de mirar la televisión, **preferiría**° navegar por Internet.	*I would prefer*
	Podríamos ver° qué oportunidades hay para ser voluntario en nuestra comunidad.	*We could see*
Irene	Buena idea. **Me encantaría**° trabajar con los jóvenes de nuestro vecindario.	*I would love*

Most verbs in Spanish are regular in the conditional. As with the future, the infinitive is the conditional stem for most **-ar, -er,** and **-ir** verbs. All verbs share a common set of endings in the conditional. Notice that these endings carry a written accent.

Conditional tense of regular verbs				
Infinitive	**Subject**	**Stem**	**Ending**	**Conditional tense**
trabajar	yo	trabajar-	**ía**	trabajar**ía**
creer	tú	creer-	**ías**	creer**ías**
escribir	Ud., él, ella	escribir-	**ía**	escribir**ía**
preferir	nosotros/as	preferir-	**íamos**	preferir**íamos**
dar	vosotros/as	dar-	**íais**	dar**íais**
ir	Uds., ellos, ellas	ir-	**ían**	ir**ían**

Irregular verbs in the conditional tense are the same verbs that have an irregular stem in the future (page 382). Conditional tense endings for irregular verbs are the same as those for regular verbs.

Conditional tense of irregular verbs		
Infinitive	**Stem**	**Conditional tense**
decir	dir-	yo **dir**ía
hacer	har-	tú **har**ías
poder	podr-	Ud. **podr**ía
poner	pondr-	él **pondr**ía
querer	querr-	ella **querr**ía
saber	sabr-	nosotros/as **sabr**íamos
salir	saldr-	vosotros/as **saldr**íais
tener	tendr-	Uds. **tendr**ían
venir	vendr-	ellos, ellas **vendr**ían

Habría *(there would be)* is the conditional form of **haber.** Like **hay** *(there is, there are)*, **habría** is used only in the singular and means *there would be.*

Pensé que **habría** soluciones para este problema.

I thought that there would be solutions for this problem.

The English equivalent of the conditional tense is *would* or *could* plus a *verb.*

—Pensé que **vendrías** hoy.
—No, te dije que no **tendría** tiempo.

—*I thought that you would come today.*
—*No, I told you that I wouldn't have time.*

The conditional can be used to show politeness or to soften a command.

—¿**Podrías** ayudarme?
—Me **gustaría,** pero no puedo hoy.

—*Could you help me?*
—*I would like to, but I can't today.*

The conditional may be used to express *probability* when there is doubt or questioning about a past situation or action. The equivalent in English can be *probably, I / we wonder* plus the past tense.

—Catalina no vino a ayudar con los niños ayer. ¿Qué le **pasaría**?

—*Catalina didn't come to help with the children yesterday. I wonder what happened to her.*

—Me imagino que **estudiaría** para su examen de cálculo.

—*I imagine that she was probably studying for her calculus exam.*

Actividades

1 Soy profesor/a. Tú sueñas con ser el / la profesor/a de la clase de español. Explica qué harías tú y qué harían tus alumnos en la clase.

1. Yo _____ (hablar) español con los alumnos siempre.
2. Mis alumnos siempre _____ (hacer) la tarea.
3. Yo _____ (ayudar) a todos los alumnos.
4. Mis alumnos _____ (sacar) buenas notas en todos los exámenes.
5. Nosotros _____ (ir) a restaurantes mexicanos, españoles y cubanos todos los meses.
6. Toda la clase _____ (llegar) a tiempo.
7. Mis alumnos _____ (escribir) composiciones excelentes.
8. Nosotros _____ (aprender) algo sobre todos los países hispanos.

2 Posibles reacciones. ¿Qué harías o dirías tú en estas situaciones? Usa diferentes verbos en el condicional para cada situación.

▶ **MODELO:** al ganar la lotería
Yo compraría una nueva casa para mis padres y viajaría por el mundo.

1. al recibir una llamada telefónica pidiendo dinero para salvar los osos polares
2. al saber que se murió la mascota de tu mejor amigo/a
3. al aceptar un trabajo en un parque nacional de Costa Rica
4. al ver a una amiga dejar basura en una mesa de la cafetería
5. al conseguir un pasaje gratis a las Galápagos
6. al ver muchos papeles en el piso de la clase
7. al ser elegido director/a de un programa de reciclaje en la universidad
8. al ir a Antártida para estudiar los pingüinos

3 ¿Qué le pasaría? Roberta llega a la oficina tarde y parece muy cansada. Luz y Rafael conversan sobre qué le pasaría a Roberta anoche. Con un/a compañero/a, creen una conversación en la que ellos discuten las posibilidades.

4 Soy reportero/a. Haz una lista de cuatro preguntas para entrevistar a dos compañeros/as de tu clase sobre el medio ambiente. Usa el condicional de algunos de los verbos de la lista. Después haz la entrevista a tus compañeros/as.

▶ **MODELO:** *¿Dejarías de usar tazas de papel?*
¿Qué harías para ayudar al medio ambiente de nuestro vecindario?

apoyar	comprar	dejar	hacer	dirigir
preocuparse	usar	reusar	tener	ayudar
ser	ahorrar	apagar	evitar	participar

¡Gol!

Actividades

Online Study Center

For additional practice with this episode, visit the *Caminos* website at http://college.hmco.com/languages/spanish/renjilian/caminos/3e/student_home.html.

1 Comprensión. Basándote en este episodio de *Caminos del jaguar,* elige la alternativa lógica.

1. Adriana le agradece al Sr. Guzmán porque...
   a. llegó muy temprano.
   b. aceptó verla.

2. Raúl es el responsable de encontrar...
   a. los jaguares robados.
   b. a Adriana y a Felipe.

3. Raúl no le había explicado nada a Adriana porque nunca pudo...
   a. verla.
   b. alcanzarla.

4. Raúl dice que en su trabajo, el anonimato...
   a. es esencial.
   b. no es esencial.

5. ¿Dónde había visto Adriana la nota que tiene Raúl?
   a. En México.
   b. En San Antonio.

6. ¿Qué golpea a Gafasnegras en la cabeza?
   a. La bolsa con los jaguares.
   b. Una pelota de fútbol.

7. ¿Qué palabra es ILEYAN al revés?
   a. Yelani.
   b. Nayeli.

2 Situaciones. Dramaticen una de las siguientes situaciones.

1. Adriana y el Sr. Guzmán se presentan en el restaurante.
2. Gafasnegras cae en la trampa del Sr. Guzmán.

3 Escritura. Escribe un resumen de la reacción de Adriana cuando se da cuenta de que Raúl es el hombre del anillo raro. (4–6 oraciones)

NOTA CULTURAL

El Paseo del Río en San Antonio

El Paseo del Río de San Antonio es uno de los lugares más atractivos de la ciudad y lo visitan miles de turistas cada año. En este sitio ocurren unos eventos muy importantes de los últimos episodios de *Caminos del jaguar.* El Paseo del Río tiene una variedad inmensa de restaurantes, hoteles, tiendas de ropa y galerías de arte. Los habitantes de San Antonio y los turistas suelen pasear por el área en barcos especiales o pasear por las anchas aceras a las orillas del río.

Lectura

Online Study Center

For further reading practice online, visit the *Caminos* website at http://college.hmco.com/languages/spanish/renjilian/caminos/3e/student_home.html.

PRELECTURA

Throughout the ages, people have been frightened by many different events and things, as the author of this reading details. He believes that fright itself is probably the most human—and animal—of feelings. He compares the fears of people in the Middle Ages, a thousand years ago, to the different worries people have in the 21st century.

Reading Strategy

Distinguishing facts from opinions

Informational texts contain descriptions of facts, situations, or events. News and historical descriptions are informational texts. These texts are not necessarily impartial and the writer may seek to influence readers in a certain way by using strategies such as giving examples that support his or her ideas, using quotes, introducing doubt, or making strong assertions. In order to distinguish facts from opinions when reading this type of text, try to become familiar with the devices used by writers to influence their readers.

1 Los miedos de mis abuelos. Escoge de la lista de abajo, según tu opinión, cinco cosas que les daban miedo a tus abuelos. Cuando termines, con un/a compañero/a, discutan qué cosas les dan miedo a las personas de su generación. Pongan sus ideas en orden de importancia y compárenlas. Pueden usar las palabras de la lista o añadir otras ideas.

la violencia	la soledad
la contaminación	los problemas económicos
los terremotos	el terrorismo
la falta de trabajo	la guerra
el robo de identidad	los desastres naturales
la falta de petróleo	la desaparición de los bosques
la falta de vivienda	el deterioro del planeta
las drogas	las enfermedades
la discriminación	el hambre

2 Mis preocupaciones y miedos. Trabaja con un/a compañero/a para identificar los problemas sociales que aparecen en el dibujo. Luego, discutan las tres cosas que más debe temer su comunidad o su país en los próximos diez años.

¡Milenios de miedos!

Si no le temes a Dios, ¡témele a la peste[1]! Si no le tienes miedo a la bomba atómica, ¡témele al SIDA! Los miedos de ayer y de hoy son una muestra[2] de que esas sensaciones también tienen historia y están sometidas[3] a procesos culturales, religiosos y políticos.

Ahora, en este milenio, podemos preguntarnos cuáles son los miedos más característicos del hombre contemporáneo. Y ayudados, por ejemplo, por el historiador francés Georges Duby, comparemos algunas de las angustias[4] del año dos mil con las del año mil.

Tal vez lo más humano (y también lo más animal) es el miedo. El más antiguo de los miedos es, quizás, el miedo a lo desconocido[5] y de él nacen múltiples terrores. Sin embargo, ha habido otras cosas peores aguardando[6] al hombre.

El hombre de hoy está lleno de inquietudes[7] y preguntas y, la mayoría de las veces, sus miedos difieren de los de hace mil años, aunque se pueden encontrar similitudes[8] entre unos y otros, como el miedo a la miseria[9], a las catástrofes naturales y a las enfermedades. A pesar de los avances tecnológicos y los descubrimientos científicos, el hombre contemporáneo está sometido[10] a nuevos desamparos[11].

Tal vez los miedos de hoy son más agudos[12] que los del medioevo, como el miedo a la desaparición de la raza humana, a la destrucción de la naturaleza, a una catástrofe nuclear, a una nueva guerra mundial.

Con todo, el miedo puede ser una especie de estimulador de búsquedas espirituales y de vuelos imaginativos. Por lo demás, a la persona que tiene miedo, todavía no se le ha acabado el mundo.

---

[1]plague; [2]sample; [3]bound; [4]anxieties; [5]the unknown; [6]awaiting; [7]worries; [8]similarities; [9]poverty; [10]is subjected to; [11]troubles; [12]acute

POSTLECTURA

3 Miedos de los milenios. Trabajen en grupos para contestar las preguntas sobre la lectura.

1. ¿Qué épocas compara el autor del texto?
2. ¿Cuál es el miedo más humano de todos?
3. ¿Qué miedos tenía la gente a partir del año mil?
4. Según el autor, ¿de qué condiciones tiene miedo el hombre moderno?
5. Cuando el autor dice que los miedos de hoy son más agudos que los del pasado, ¿qué ejemplos da?
6. ¿Qué significa el título del artículo?

4 Estrategias. Trabaja con un/a compañero/a. Busquen frases del texto para ilustrar estas estrategias que usa el autor.

a. mencionar a expertos
b. dar ejemplos
c. comparar épocas

5 ¿Estás de acuerdo? Trabaja con un/a compañero/a. Analicen esta frase del autor y discutan por qué contiene un pensamiento positivo sobre el miedo.

"A la persona que tiene miedo, todavía no se le ha acabado el mundo".

6 Mi punto de vista. Con tus propias palabras, resume los temas de la lectura. Expone brevemente cuáles son las ideas principales del autor del texto.

Escritura

Writing Strategy

Online Study Center

For further writing practice online, visit the *Caminos* website at http://college .hmco.com/languages/ spanish/renjilian/caminos/ 3e/student_home.html.

Narrowing a topic

The secret of writing a compelling paragraph is to choose a topic that is focused. If the topic is very broad, there is too much information to cover adequately. It may be necessary to narrow your topic several times before it is focused enough for a clear, concise paragraph.

Workshop

Here is an example of a topic that has been narrowed down several times.

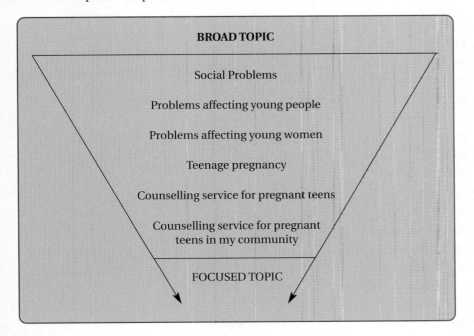

BROAD TOPIC

Social Problems

Problems affecting young people

Problems affecting young women

Teenage pregnancy

Counselling service for pregnant teens

Counselling service for pregnant teens in my community

FOCUSED TOPIC

Strategy in Action

For additional practice with narrowing a topic, complete the exercises below and in the *Escritura* section of your Student Activities Manual for *Unidad 11*.

1 Problemas del futuro. Si no resolvemos los problemas sociales de hoy, habrá muchos problemas en el futuro. Escoge un problema social y escribe tus predicciones de lo que pasará.

2 El mundo del futuro. Si no cuidamos el medio ambiente, habrá muchos problemas ecológicos en el futuro. Escoge un problema ecológico y escribe tus predicciones de lo que pasará.

PRIMER PASO

TALKING ABOUT CONTEMPORARY SOCIETY

Sustantivos

el acto delictivo	*delinquent act*
la adicción	*addiction*
el/la adolescente	*adolescent*
la angustia	*worry*
las armas	*weapons*
el asesinato	*assassination, murder*
el/la asesino/a	*murderer*
el beneficio	*benefit*
la cárcel, prisión	*prison*
la comunidad	*community*
el consejo	*advice*
el consumo	*consumption*
el crimen	*crime*
la cura	*cure*
la delincuencia	*delinquency*
el/la delincuente	*delinquent*
la depresión	*depression*
los desamparados	*homeless people*
el desempleo	*unemployment*
la drogadicción	*drug addiction*
el embarazo	*pregnancy*
el empleo	*employment*
la guerra	*war*
la incertidumbre	*uncertainty*
la justicia	*justice*
la libertad	*freedom*
el lío	*problem, trouble, mess*
el logro	*achievement*
el/la niñero/a	*nanny, babysitter*
la patria	*homeland*
el peligro	*danger*

la pobreza	*poverty*
el/la policía	*police; police officer*
el programa social	*social program*
el robo	*robbery*
la seguridad	*security*
el seguro médico	*health insurance*
el SIDA	*AIDS*
la sociedad	*society*
la solución	*solution*
la terapia	*therapy*
el terrorismo	*terrorism*
el/la terrorista	*terrorist*
el/la trabajador/a social	*social worker*
el tráfico de drogas	*drug trafficking*
el/la voluntario/a	*volunteer*

Verbos

alcanzar	*to reach*
amenazar	*to threaten*
arrestar	*to arrest*
asesinar	*to assassinate, murder*
aumentar	*to increase*
convertir	*to change, convert*
encarcelar	*to imprison*
enfrentar	*to confront, face up to*
estar desesperado/a	*to be desperate*
fracasar	*to fail*
lograr	*to achieve; to attain*
luchar	*to fight*
matar	*to kill*
obtener	*to obtain*
tener remedio	*to have a solution*
triunfar	*to succeed, triumph*

SEGUNDO PASO

DISCUSSING ENVIRONMENTAL ISSUES

Sustantivos

la ballena	*whale*
la basura	*garbage*
el bombillo	*lightbulb*
el caballo	*horse*
el calentamiento global	*global warming*
la capa de ozono	*ozone layer*
el combustible	*fuel*
el comportamiento	*behavior*
la consecuencia	*consequence*
la contaminación	*pollution, contamination*
la deforestación	*deforestation*
el delfín	*dolphin*
los desperdicios nucleares	*nuclear waste*
el deterioro	*deterioration*
el dióxido de carbono	*carbon dioxide*
el efecto invernadero	*the greenhouse effect*
el elefante	*elephant*
la energía	*energy*
la especie	*species*
la existencia	*existence*
la extinción	*extinction*
el gallo	*rooster*
la lluvia ácida	*acid rain*

la mascota	*pet*
el mono	*monkey*
la naturaleza	*nature*
el oso (panda)	*(panda) bear*
el pingüino	*penguin*
el planeta	*planet*
el recurso	*resource*
la responsabilidad	*responsibility*
el tigre	*tiger*

Verbos

ahorrar	*to save (collect)*
apoyar	*to support*
conservar	*to conserve, preserve*
contaminar	*to pollute, contaminate*
desechar	*to dispose, discard*
explotar	*to exploit*
reusar	*to reuse*
salvar	*to save (rescue)*
tratarse de	*to deal with; to be about*

Adjetivos

armonioso/a	*harmonious*
desechado/a	*discarded, disposed*
ecológico/a	*ecological*
escaso/a	*scarce*

VOCABULARIO Y LENGUA

- ► Comparing the Aztecs, Mayans, and Incas
- ► Using **si** clauses in the present
- ► Expressing hypothetical actions: **Si** clauses

- ► Discussing Hispanic contributions in the United States
- ► Contrasting **pero, sino,** and **sino que**
- ► Using passive forms

CAMINOS DEL JAGUAR

- ► ¿Chocolate o cárcel?
- ► Amor y paz

LECTURA

- ► Ecos del pasado: Héroes mayas

NOTAS CULTURALES

- ► El Zócalo
- ► El Museo Nacional de Antropología

ESTRATEGIAS

- ► **Reading**: Using a genealogical chart with notes
- ► **Writing**: Editing one's own work

Benigno Gómez, *6 Birds*

Preguntas del tema

► ¿Has visitado algún sitio arqueológico de una cultura antigua? Explica.
► ¿Qué quieres estudiar sobre la historia de las civilizaciones antiguas?
► ¿A qué hispanos famosos conoces?
► ¿Cuáles son algunas contribuciones de los hispanos en los Estados Unidos?

PRIMER PASO

Vocabulario y lengua

COMPARING THE AZTECS, MAYANS, AND INCAS

Tres grandes civilizaciones: Los aztecas, los mayas y los incas

developed

Tres civilizaciones muy **desarrolladas**° antes de la **exploración** y la **conquista** españolas, fueron la azteca, la maya y la inca.

LOS AZTECAS

Online Study Center

For additional practice with this unit's vocabulary and grammar, visit the *Caminos* website at http://college.hmco.com/languages/spanish/renjilian/caminos/3e/student_home.html. You can also review audio flashcards, quiz yourself, and explore related Spanish-language sites.

La cultura azteca se componía de varios grupos del valle central de México, los que llegaron a formar el gran **imperio** azteca desde el siglo XIV hasta la llegada de Hernán Cortés en 1519 y la muerte de su emperador, Moctezuma. Los aztecas pertenecían al grupo **étnico** y **lingüístico** de los *nahuas* y tenían una organización social y política compleja, necesaria para gobernar un gran imperio. Sus prácticas religiosas se basaban en un calendario de ceremonias y sacrificios celebrados por los sacerdotes. Los aztecas fundaron la capital de su imperio, Tenochtitlán en medio del lago Texcoco que llegó a tener entre ocho y más de trece kilómetros cuadrados de área. Aunque no se

Para los aztecas, el dios Quetzalcóatl era el creador de la humanidad y su protector.

sabe por seguro, dicen que había entre doscientos y trescientos cincuenta mil habitantes a principios del siglo XV. Cortés **venció**° a Moctezuma, el emperador azteca, y en las **ruinas** de Tenochtitlán, **fundó**° la Ciudad de México.

defeated
founded

Conocemos la historia azteca a través de las investigaciones arqueológicas y de las crónicas españolas, escritas por misioneros españoles y por cronistas aztecas en español o en náhuatl, usando el alfabeto latino. Los libros sagrados o códices se guardaban en los templos y la mayoría fue destruida durante la colonia española. Sin embargo, algunos de ellos sobrevivieron, como el Códice Borbónico que describe los días del calendario y sus ceremonias, lo mismo que el Códice Borgia.

in addition to
weavers

Los **descendientes** de los nahuas, **además de**° desempeñar oficios y profesiones modernas, cultivan la tierra y son hábiles **tejedores**° de lana y algodón.

LOS MAYAS

La gran civilización maya es una de las más importantes culturas prehispánicas del continente americano. Tuvo su **apogeo**° entre los años 200 y 900 después de Cristo, cuando construyeron grandes ciudades como Chichén Itzá, Uxmal, Itzamal y Mayapán, además de **imponentes**° **templos** y **pirámides,** muchos de los cuales podemos apreciar hoy en día. A partir del siglo X y hasta que llegaron los españoles a la región, en el siglo XVI, la cultura maya fue **decayendo**° poco a poco.

height

imposing

declining

El universo maya tiene tres niveles cósmicos: el cielo, *Caan*; la tierra, *Cab*; y el inframundo, *Xibalbá*.

Durante su época de esplendor, los mayas extendieron su imperio por lo que hoy conocemos como Centroamérica y parte de Yucatán y Mérida, en México. La cultura de este pueblo **se destacó**° por la creación y el uso de la **escritura**° **jeroglífica,** la que nos ha llegado en los hermosos libros o **códices** que se conservan en las bibliotecas de Dresden, París, Madrid y la Ciudad de México. Además de tener profundos conocimientos de astronomía, los mayas fueron también matemáticos, usaban el cero y un sistema numérico basado en múltiplos de veinte.

stood out / writing

LOS INCAS

En el sur, el imperio de los incas **se distinguió**° por su admirable organización, arquitectura, **orfebrería**° y textiles. Los incas construyeron imponentes ciudades de piedra y tenían una red de más de veinte mil kilómetros de caminos que comunicaban a los 12 millones de habitantes del imperio. Entre las ciudades de piedra están Cuzco, la antigua capital del imperio incaico, y Machu Picchu, las ruinas de una ciudad que permaneció **perdida**° por muchos **siglos**°. Cuzco fue fundada en el año 1100 y es la ciudad que lleva más tiempo **habitada**° en Suramérica.

was distinguished
gold or silver work

lost / centuries

inhabited

La majestuosa ciudad de Machu Picchu

El imperio inca duró hasta 1527, cuando el explorador y conquistador español Francisco Pizarro venció a Atahualpa, el emperador, en la batalla de Cajamarca. **Sin embargo**°, hubo muchas rebeliones y el último emperador, Túpac Amaru, fue **ejecutado**° en 1572.

Nevertheless
executed

Los descendientes de los incas siguen hablando su idioma nativo, el quechua, y participan activamente en las sociedades a las que **pertenecen**° en Bolivia, el Ecuador, el Perú, al sur de Colombia y al norte de Chile y de la Argentina.

belong

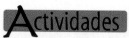

Actividades

1 Identificación. Trabajen en parejas y, según los textos anteriores, determinen si las cosas de esta lista están relacionadas con los aztecas, los mayas, los incas o con más de una de estas culturas.

1. caminos
2. ciudades de piedra
3. Chichén Itzá
4. la astronomía
5. códices
6. Tenochtitlán
7. el uso de la escritura
8. Xibalbá
9. pirámides
10. matemáticas

2 Comprensión. Contesta las preguntas según el texto sobre los aztecas, mayas e incas.

1. ¿Quiénes fueron Hernán Cortés? ¿Moctezuma? ¿Francisco Pizarro? ¿Atahualpa? ¿Túpac Amaru?
2. ¿Cuándo venció Cortés a los aztecas? ¿Qué hizo después?
3. ¿Cuáles son algunos lugares importantes del mundo maya?
4. ¿Cuándo comenzó a decaer el mundo maya?
5. ¿Cuándo venció Pizarro a los incas? ¿Dónde?
6. Menciona algunos de los logros de los aztecas, los mayas y los incas.
7. ¿Para qué construyeron caminos los incas?
8. ¿Cuántas personas vivían en el imperio inca?
9. ¿Por qué es importante la ciudad de Cuzco?
10. ¿Qué idioma hablan los descendientes de los incas?

3 Las artesanías del mundo maya. Escucha la descripción de las artesanías y escribe tres frases que describan cada uno de estos artículos.

1. _____
2. _____
3. _____
4. _____
5. _____
6. _____

USING *SI* CLAUSES IN THE PRESENT

Elena, **si miras** bien la foto de tu bisabuela, **vas a ver** que tú te pareces mucho a ella.

Es cierto, abuelita, y **si no te importa**, ¿**puedo** sacar una copia?

Tengo varias copias y **si quieres** una, te la **doy** hoy mismo.

Si me das una foto de mi bisabuela, **será** fantástico, abuelita.

In Spanish **si** (if) introduces a condition that must be fulfilled for something to happen. When **si** is followed by a verb in the present, the condition is likely to be fulfilled. In this case, the verb in the main clause may be in the present indicative or future, or it can be a command. The verb that immediately follows **si** can never be in the present subjunctive.

Si quieres una foto, te **doy / daré** una.	*If you want a photo, I'll give you one.*
Si tienes varias fotos, ¡**dame** una, por favor!	*If you have several photos, give me one, please!*

Sentences can begin with either the main clause or the **si** clause.

Te **sentirás** bien **si ayudas** a otras personas.	*You will feel good if you help other people.*
Si ayudas a otras personas, te **sentirás** bien.	*If you help other people, you will feel good.*

Actividades

1 Condiciones. Combina las frases de una manera lógica.

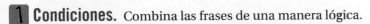

A	B
1. Si queremos aprender sobre los incas	a. es posible encontrar objetos antiguos.
2. Si haces excavaciones arqueológicas	b. aprenderás sobre el calendario azteca.
3. Si lees el Códice Borbónico	c. entenderás a 400 millones de personas.
4. Si vamos a Chichén Itzá	d. debes visitar también Machu Picchu.
5. Si aprendes español	e. conoceremos imponentes monumentos.
6. Si se dañan los códices	f. verás un hermoso paisaje desde allí.
7. Si te subes a una pirámide	g. perderemos un tesoro histórico.
8. Si viajas a la ciudad de Cuzco	h. debemos estudiar su historia.

2 Excavación arqueológica. Lee el texto siguiente y completa las oraciones con el presente, el futuro o una orden o consejo (mandato), según sea necesario.

Si _____ (**1.** querer / tú) ser arqueólogo, _____ (**2.** deber) estudiar esta carrera en la universidad. Luego, si _____ (**3.** participar) en una excavación, _____ (**4.** poner) mucha atención a las instrucciones que te den. Si _____ (**5.** estar) excavando y _____ (**6.** encontrar) un objeto de valor arqueológico, _____ (**7.** deber) siempre avisarle al jefe de la excavación. Si tú no _____ (**8.** saber) extraer el objeto o si no _____ (**9.** poder) porque es difícil, _____ (**10.** ser) necesario buscar ayuda. Si _____ (**11.** hacer) un buen trabajo, tu jefe te _____ (**12.** aumentar) el sueldo. Si _____ (**13.** tener) un poco más de dinero, _____ (**14.** vivir) mejor también. Si no _____ (**15.** cumplir) con tus deberes, _____ (**16.** perder) tu trabajo.

3 Si esto sucede... Explícale a un/a compañero/a qué haces o qué vas a hacer en estas situaciones.

1. Si alguien necesita mi ayuda...
2. Si no he estudiado la lección....
3. Si no puedo pagar mi educación...
4. Si ocurre un accidente en la calle...
5. Si estoy deprimido/a...
6. Si mi mejor amigo/a se enoja...
7. Si mi novio/a no me quiere...
8. Si alguien me insulta...

EXPRESSING HYPOTHETICAL ACTIONS: *SI* CLAUSES

¿Qué pasaría si...?

As you have learned, a **si** clause expresses a condition and the main clause in a sentence describes the expected result if the condition is fulfilled. When talking about hypothetical or contrary-to-fact situations, as shown in the drawing, the **si** clause is in the *imperfect* subjunctive and the verb in the main clause is in the *conditional* tense. Note that sentences expressing hypothetical or contrary-to-fact situations can begin with either the main clause or the **si** clause.

Actividades

1 Imaginación. Completa las oraciones siguientes de una manera lógica.

1. Leería sobre Hernán Cortés si _____ mi libro de historia.
   a. encontrara
   b. encontraría

2. Sabríamos mucho más sobre la historia maya si _____ más investigación.
   a. hubiera
   b. habría

3. Si yo _____ quechua, podría hablar con los descendientes de los incas.
   a. sabría
   b. supiera

4. Seríamos buenos tejedores de lana si _____ descendientes de los nahuas.
   a. seríamos
   b. fuéramos

5. Si _____ más códices, sabríamos mucho más sobre la cultura maya.
   a. tuviéramos
   b. tendríamos

6. Aprenderías mucha historia si _____ leer la escritura jeroglífica maya.
   a. podrías
   b. pudieras

2 Suposiciones. Basándote en las siguientes oraciones, crea suposiciones usando el imperfecto del subjuntivo y el condicional. Sigue el modelo.

▶ MODELO: Si mis padres *visitan* el Perú, *conocerán* Machu Picchu.
   Si mis padres **visitaran** el Perú, **conocerían** Machu Picchu.

1. Si nosotros tenemos dinero, iremos a Chichén Iztá.
2. Si subimos a las pirámides, veremos un paisaje hermoso.
3. Si viajas al Perú, podrás conocer unas iglesias muy hermosas.
4. Si mi hermana va a Cuzco, conocerá la antigua capital inca.
5. Si quieres saber más sobre los aztecas, debes estudiar historia.
6. Si me convierto en un dios maya, viviré en Xibalbá.

3 ¿Qué harías? Con un/a compañero/a, contesten las preguntas creando oraciones hipotéticas. Después, preséntenle las respuestas a la clase.

1. ¿Qué harías si tuvieras un accidente en el coche de tus padres?
2. ¿Cómo reaccionarías si te ofrecieran un trabajo en una planta nuclear?
3. Si conocieras al presidente de los Estados Unidos, ¿qué le dirías?
4. ¿Qué harías si no estudiaras en la universidad?
5. ¿Adónde viajarías si tuvieras un año libre y el dinero no fuera un obstáculo?
6. ¿Qué harías si fueras profesor/a de historia?
7. ¿En qué país te gustaría trabajar si fueras arqueólogo/a?

4 Si esto sucediera... Trabaja con un/a compañero/a para explicar qué harías en estas situaciones.

1. Si fuera un perro...
2. Si tuviera 100 años...
3. Si tuviera 6 años...
4. Si fuera descendiente de los incas...
5. Si supiera pintar...
6. Si viviera en el Perú...
7. Si pudiera cambiar algo en mi vida...
8. Si mis padres me dieran 5 mil dólares...

¿Chocolate o cárcel?

San Antonio, Texas.

Todo tiene un fin, la vida, la muerte, el bien, el mal...

No importa, todavía puedo hacer muchas cosas ...

¡No tendrás ninguna oportunidad!

San Juan, Puerto Rico.

¡Ay, Dios mío! ¿Qué va a decir mi esposa?

Mi carrera de programador, todo en la basura. Es tu culpa.

¡Mira, cállate! Reconozco que fue mi error.

¿Habrá computadoras en la cárcel?

Quito, Ecuador.

¡No, señor, esto es un error!

Ciudad de México, México.

¿Cómo fue usted capaz de hacer esto, Sr. de Landa?

No es como usted cree... además, el dinero lo arregla todo, ¿no?

No, no todo se puede comprar.

San José, Costa Rica.

Doña Carmen, no lo puedo creer

Le aseguro que no soy culpable.

Estoy seguro de eso. Usted es una persona muy respetable.

No se preocupe, todo se aclarará.

Lo sé, pero tengo que llevarla a la comisaría.

Tengo el mejor abogado del país.

¿Y nosotros qué? ¡Ella tiene abogado, pero nosotros no!

San Antonio, Texas.

¡Felicitaciones, Adriana! Has logrado resolverlo todo.

Nunca lo hubiera podido hacer sin ti, Felipe. ¡Fuiste el compañero perfecto, Hun-Ahau!

¡Yax-Balam! Los dos en la eterna lucha entre el bien y el mal.

¡Toma! Es algo simbólico.

Gracias, pero ¿por qué?

El cacao era muy valioso para los mayas...

¡Ah, chocolates! El chocolate es dulce, pero no tan dulce como tú...

Felipe, ¡por favor!

Actividades

Online Study Center

For additional practice
with this episode, visit
the *Caminos* website at
http://college.hmco.com/
languages/spanish/
renjilian/caminos/3e/
student_home.html.

1 Comprensión. Basándote en este episodio de *Caminos del jaguar,* elige la
alternativa lógica.

1. Gafasnegras cree que todavía puede...
   a. quedarse con los jaguares. b. hacer muchas cosas.

2. El primo de Luis se preocupa por la opinión de...
   a. su esposa. b. sus amigos.

3. Luis se preocupa porque ha perdido...
   a. su trabajo con Gafasnegras. b. su futura carrera.

4. El primo de Luis reconoce que el culpable es...
   a. él mismo. b. Luis.

5. Armando le ofrece al policía...
   a. una confesión. b. dinero.

6. Doña Carmen está segura de que no...
   a. irá a la prisión. b. tendrá otro abogado.

7. Felipe se siente muy orgulloso de Adriana porque...
   a. ella le regaló chocolates. b. ella lo resolvió todo.

8. Según Felipe, el chocolate es...
   a. tan dulce como Adriana. b. algo simbólico.

2 Situaciones. Dramaticen una de las siguientes situaciones.

1. Adriana le regala una caja de chocolates a Felipe.
2. Doña Carmen habla con el policía.

3 Escritura. Describe a cuántas personas arrestó la policía y dónde. ¿Cómo
reaccionaron estas personas? (5–6 oraciones)

NOTA CULTURAL

El Zócalo

El nombre oficial del Zócalo es "Plaza de la
Constitución" y es la segunda plaza más grande
del mundo, solamente sobrepasada por la
Plaza Roja de Moscú. Para los mexicanos, el
Zócalo representa no sólo el corazón del
Distrito Federal sino también el corazón de
todo México. En su centro hay una enorme
bandera mexicana. El Zócalo es un lugar de
reunión, y allí se celebran los actos públicos del
día de la Independencia, el 16 de septiembre.
La gente se pasea por el Zócalo y frecuenta los
restaurantes que hay alrededor, las tiendas y los
vendedores ambulantes. Cerca del Zócalo está
el Templo Mayor, uno de los monumentos más
importantes de la cultura mexicana.

Vocabulario y lengua

DISCUSSING HISPANIC CONTRIBUTIONS IN THE UNITED STATES

Online Study Center

For additional practice with this unit's vocabulary and grammar, visit the *Caminos* website at http://college.hmco.com/languages/spanish/renjilian/caminos/3e/student_home.html. You can also review audio flashcards, quiz yourself, and explore related Spanish-language sites.

population

growth

figure

Spanish-speaking

La población hispana actual

DATOS ESTADÍSTICOS

Según la Oficina del Censo de los Estados Unidos (*U.S. Census Bureau*), los hispanos constituyen la minoría más grande de los Estados Unidos. En el año 2005, la **población°** hispana era de 42,7 millones de habitantes, lo cual representa un **crecimiento°** del 90% desde 1990 cuando había solamente 22,4 millones de hispanos en el país. Esta **cifra°** constituye aproximadamente el 14% de la población del país y no incluye a los habitantes de Puerto Rico. Esta población hispana convierte a los Estados Unidos en el quinto país **de habla española°** del mundo, después de México, Colombia, Argentina y España.

Censo 2000: Los 10 estados con mayor porcentaje de población hispana
En miles de habitantes

	Porcentaje
California	31,1
Texas	18,9
New York	8,1
Florida	7,6
Illinois	4,3
Arizona	3,7
New Jersey	3,2
New Mexico	2,2
Colorado	2,1
Washington	1,3

porcentaje de población hispana

US CENSUS BUREAU

Más del 60% de los hispanos nacieron en los Estados Unidos y la mayoría son de origen mexicano. Se **pronostica**° que para el año 2050 los hispanos llegarán a ser más de 100 millones, es decir, casi la cuarta parte de la población de los Estados Unidos.

predict

Estas cifras resaltan° la importancia económica de la población hispana del país. Se calcula que el **poder adquisitivo**° de este grupo llegó a los 700 mil millones de dólares en 2006 y crecerá el 30% para llegar a 1.000.000 de millones en el año 2010.

highlight
purchasing power

Los estados con mayor población hispana son California con 12,4 millones y Texas con 7,8 millones, pero también hay una población hispana grande en los estados de Nueva York y la Florida.

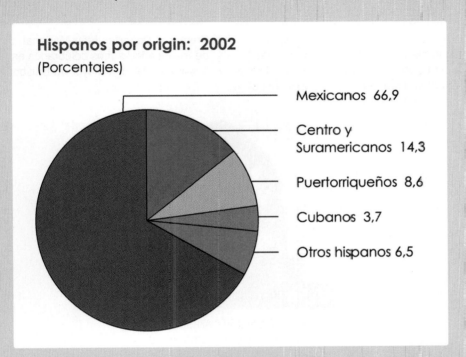

Hispanos por origin: 2002
(Porcentajes)

Mexicanos 66,9

Centro y Suramericanos 14,3

Puertorriqueños 8,6

Cubanos 3,7

Otros hispanos 6,5

GANADORES DE LOS PREMIOS° HISPANIC HERITAGE 2006

Awards

Premio de Arte: Antonio Banderas, actor de cine conocido internacionalmente.

Premio a la Educación: Dra. Juliet Villarreal García, primera latina presidente de una universidad, en la Universidad de Texas en Brownsville.

Premio al Liderazgo (*Leadership*): Teniente Coronel (retirada) Consuelo Castillo Kickbusch, la latina con el rango más alto en el 'Combat Support Field' del ejército estadounidense.

Premio al Deporte: Juan Marichal, uno de los jugadores más celebrados en la historia de la Liga Mayor de Béisbol.

Premio de Trayectoria Artística: José Feliciano, reconocido como uno de los primeros artistas latinos que entró exitosamente al mercado de música en inglés.

Actividades

 1 Comprensión. En grupos de tres, estudien la información estadística sobre los hispanos en los Estados Unidos y contesten las siguientes preguntas.

1. ¿Cuántos hispanos viven en el país?
2. ¿Cuánto aumentó la población hispana desde 1990?
3. ¿En qué estados vive la mayoría de los hispanos? ¿Por qué creen que es así?
4. ¿Cuáles son los cinco países con mayor número de personas de habla española?
5. ¿De dónde son los hispanos que viven en el país?
6. ¿Qué porcentaje de la población serán los hispanos en el año 2050?
7. ¿Cuánto es el poder adquisitivo de los hispanos? ¿Cuánto será en 2010?

 2 Los Premios Hispanic Heritage. Trabajando en parejas, lean la información sobre las personas que recibieron premios de honor en 2006 y discutan estas preguntas.

1. ¿Conoces a alguno de los ganadores de los premios?
2. ¿Qué premio te parece más importante? ¿Por qué?
3. ¿Te gustaría crear otro premio? ¿Cuál sería? ¿Por qué?

3 Los premios Emmy latinos. Escucha el pasaje sobre los premios Emmy latinos de 2006 y haz las siguientes actividades.

Seis estrellas latinas. En la tabla que sigue, empareja la persona con la descripción de su actividad artística.

Arista	Descripción
1. Fernando Arau	a. Reconocido presentador deportivo de Telemundo.
2. Saúl Lisazo	b. Presentadora de un popular *talk show* de Univisión.
3. Jessi Losada	c. Estrella de telenovelas en Televisa.
4. Lucero	d. Veterano actor de telenovelas.
5. María Elena Salinas	e. Popular presentador de un programa de la mañanas en Univisión.
6. Cristina Saralegui	f. Presentadora de noticias.

Comprensión. Di si las siguientes afirmaciones son verdaderas o falsas.

1. Las mayores compañías de medios de comunicación están en Los Ángeles.
2. Nueva York es el tercer mercado de televisión en español del país.
3. San Francisco es la ciudad con la población latina más diversa del mundo.
4. Nueva York es el centro de la industria del espectáculo y de los medios latinos.
5. La National Academy of Television piensa que la televisión en español no es importante.

4 La influencia hispana. Trabajen en grupos para completar el cuadro con los conocimientos que tienen sobre los hispanos de los Estados Unidos. Escriban qué influencia han tenido los grupos hispanos, según su país de origen, en la lengua, la comida y la música de este país. Añadan otras categorías a su gusto.

Grupo	Lengua	Comida	Música	Deportes
_____	_____	_____	_____	_____
_____	_____	_____	_____	_____
_____	_____	_____	_____	_____
_____	_____	_____	_____	_____

Planes

José   Sueño con un negocio propio, **pero** no sé si podré tenerlo.
Pedro   No solamente es una ilusión **sino** también una posibilidad.
José   ¿Por qué lo dices?
Pedro   No sólo debes soñar, **sino que** ¡debes pedir un préstamo en el banco!

In Spanish, **pero** and **sino** mean *but;* however, they are used differently. Use **sino** or **sino que** when the first element in a sentence is negative and the second element contradicts it. **Sino** connects nouns or phrases whereas **sino que** connects verb clauses. In most other cases **pero** is used to express *but.*

En el país no hay una sola minoría,   *There is not one single minority in*
  sino muchas.   *the country, but many.*
Los hispanos eran la segunda minoría   *Hispanics were the second*
  antes, **pero** ahora son la primera.   *minority, but now they are the first.*

Actividades

1 Los hispanos. Completa estas oraciones sobre lo que hacen algunas personas con **pero, sino** o **sino que** según el caso.

1. El actor Eduardo Verástegui es mexicano _____ tiene una casa en Miami.
2. Los hispanos no solamente hablan español, _____ también hablan inglés.
3. El deporte hispano más popular es el fútbol, _____ hay muchos jugadores hispanos de béisbol en los Estados Unidos.
4. Los premios Emmy latinos de 2006 no fueron en Dallas, _____ en Nueva York.
5. La población hispana no está disminuyendo, _____ sigue creciendo.
6. Penélope Cruz empezó su carrera en España _____ hace películas en Hollywood.
7. La mayoría de los hispanos vive en California, _____ también hay muchos hispanos en otros estados.
8. La población hispanohablante en el país no es pequeña _____ grande.

2 No estoy de acuerdo. Con un/a compañero/a, conversen sobre estas preferencias personales contestando la pregunta con **pero** o **sino,** según el modelo.

▶ MODELO: ¿Quieres aprender sobre historia? / no tengo tiempo / literatura
     Sí, quiero aprender sobre historia, pero no tengo tiempo.
     No, no quiero aprender sobre historia sino sobre literatura.

1. ¿Quieres votar por un candidato hispano? / no conozco a ninguno / candidato asiático
2. ¿Quieres aprender a bailar salsa? / no puedo / merengue
3. ¿Quieres colaborar en el desfile? / solamente un poco / la venta de comida
4. ¿Quieres ver los Premios Oscar en la televisión? / es muy tarde / los premios Emmy latinos

USING PASSIVE FORMS

Speech bubbles:
- Este formulario del censo **se llena** muy fácilmente.
- Sí, es cierto.
- ¡Eso no **se juega** así!
- ¡**Se me dañó** el juego!

Los formularios del censo **fueron enviados** a todos los hogares del país.

Passive structures point out actions and their consequences without focusing on who performs them. The focus is on the action itself. In Spanish, passive structures can be expressed with **se** and the passive voice.

Passive *se*

To express an action without regard to who or what performs it, Spanish uses **se +** verb preceded or followed by a subject in the third-person singular or plural.

Se presentará el *programa* mañana.	*The program will be presented tomorrow.*
Se darán los *premios* a seis personas.	*The awards will be given to six persons.*
Se prohíbe *fumar* en sitios públicos.	*Smoking is prohibited in public places.*

Passive **se** is often used in signs or advertisements.

Se vende	*For sale*
Se habla español	*Spanish is spoken*
Se prohíbe estacionar	*No parking*

Impersonal *se*

If no subject is expressed, **se** + the third-person singular of the verb is used. The impersonal **se** may be expressed in English by *one, you, they* + verb.

Se vive bien en San Diego.	*One lives well in San Diego.*
Se dice que Salma Hayek va a ganar un premio este año.	*They say that Salma Hayek will win an award this year.*

Note that **la gente dice que** or the third person plural form of the verb also introduce impersonal expressions with no particular subject, similar to impersonal **se**.

La gente dice que hay más ciudades como Machu Picchu.	*People say that there are more cities like Machu Picchu.*
Dicen que nunca vamos a encontrar esas ciudades.	*It is said that we will never find those cities.*

Passive voice

In Spanish, the passive voice is formed with **ser** + past participle. The verb agrees in number with the preceding noun (the subject) and the past participle agrees with the subject in number and in gender.

Los premios Emmy latinos **son celebrados** en Nueva York.	*The Latin Emmy Awards are celebrated in New York.*
El censo **fue realizado** en el año 2000.	*The census was done in 2000.*

Information about who performs the action may be added with the preposition **por** followed by a pronoun or a noun.

El artículo sobre los hispanos fue escrito **por ti.**	*The article about the Hispanics was written by you.*

When the person performing the action is known, a regular active sentence structure is often preferred.

Tú escribiste el artículo sobre los actores hispanos.	*You wrote the article about Hispanic actors.*

Se with unintentional actions

English expressions such as *it slipped my mind, it got late, it took on a life of its own,* and so on, refer to unintentional or unplanned occurrences. To express unintentional actions in Spanish, use **se** + indirect object pronoun + verb in the third person + subject. In addition to the verbs in the examples, other verbs that are typically used with this construction include **acabar, dañar, descomponer, quedar,** and **romper**.

Se me cayeron los platos y se quebraron.	*I dropped the plates and they broke.*
Se nos perdió tu informe.	*We lost your report (by mistake).*
¿**Se te olvidó** ir a clase?	*Did you forget to go to class?*
¿Cómo **se te ocurrió** eso?	*How did that occur to you?*

Actividades

 1 ¿Dónde? Trabajando en parejas, conversen sobre dónde o cómo se hacen las siguientes actividades. Sigan el modelo.

> ► **MODELO:** hablar español / Colombia
> —¿Dónde se habla español?   —*Where do they speak Spanish?*
> —Se habla español en Colombia.   —*Spanish is spoken in Colombia.*

1. celebrar el 4 de julio / en los Estados Unidos.
2. presentar telenovelas / en la televisión
3. encontrar mucha información / en Internet
4. ver los partidos de fútbol / en el estadio
5. oír noticias en español / en los medios hispanos
6. hablar inglés / en muchas partes
7. conseguir información sobre la población / en las estadísticas del censo
8. pronosticar el crecimiento del país / en los informes del censo

2 Los Estados Unidos. Crea oraciones pasivas con el verbo **ser.** Sigue el modelo.

> ► **MODELO:** Las familias *celebran* el Día de Acción de Gracias.
> *El Día de Acción de Gracias es celebrado por las familias.*

1. Los estadounidenses *celebran* el 4 de julio.
2. Los californianos *cultivan* las mejores frutas.
3. Las fábricas de los Estados Unidos *exportan* muchos productos.

4. Muchos inmigrantes mexicanos *recogen* las cosechas.

5. Los especialistas *calculan* las estadísticas del censo.

6. Las leyes del país *protegen* a los grupos minoritarios.

3 **Historia.** Paquita está estudiando en el Perú y le escribe a su familia sobre algunas características de las culturas precolombinas. Reconstruye lo que ella escribió siguiendo el modelo.

> ► **MODELO:** Los nazcas *fabricaron* hermosos tejidos.
> *Hermosos tejidos fueron fabricados por los nazcas.*

1. Los aztecas *usaron* el chocolate como bebida sagrada.

2. Los aztecas *realizaron* sacrificios humanos.

3. Diferentes grupos indígenas *practicaron* el juego de pelota.

4. Los artesanos *usaron* el oro y otros metales en objetos decorativos y religiosos.

5. Los mayas *estudiaron* la astronomía.

6. Los aztecas *conquistaron* grandes territorios.

4 **¿Un buen plan?** Completa las oraciones de la columna A con las de la columna B en forma lógica. Sigue el modelo.

> ► **MODELO:** **A:** *Josefa no pudo comprar nada en la tienda porque...*
> **B:** *se le olvidó el dinero en casa.*

A	B
1. Decidió ir a México porque...	**a.** se le olvidó el horario.
2. No tomó el tren a tiempo para el aeropuerto porque...	**b.** se le perdió el pasaporte.
3. Tenía los ojos muy rojos porque...	**c.** se le ocurrió la idea de conocer la tierra de los mayas.
4. No pudo subir al avión para ir a México porque...	**d.** se le perdieron las llaves de la casa.
5. No pudo entrar a su casa porque...	**e.** se le rompieron las gafas de sol.

5 **¿Qué le pasó a Mario?** Trabajando con un/a compañero/a, miren los dibujos y describan lo que le sucedió a Mario un día de mala suerte. Sigan el modelo. Después, cuenten algunas experiencias similares que tuvieron ustedes.

> ► **MODELO:** A Mario **se le cayó** el papelito con la dirección.

1. olvidar / ponerle gasolina al auto

2. acabar / la gasolina al auto

3. quedar / las llaves en el auto

4. dañar / la visita a su amiga Irma

CAMINOS DEL JAGUAR

Amor y paz

Actividades

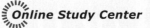

Online Study Center

For additional practice with this episode, visit the *Caminos* website at http://college.hmco.com/languages/spanish/renjilian/caminos/3e/student_home.html.

1 **Comprensión.** Basándote en este episodio de *Caminos del jaguar,* elige la alternativa lógica.

1. Sin la ayuda de Nayeli, Adriana y Felipe, los héroes gemelos...
   - a. estarían en México.
   - b. no estarían en México.

2. Nayeli dice que para ella es un honor...
   - a. estar en México.
   - b. que los héroes estén en México.

3. Adriana dice que Nayeli es demasiado...
   - a. honesta.
   - b. modesta.

4. Armando robó los jaguares cuando iban...
   - a. de Sevilla a México.
   - b. de México a Sevilla.

5. Armando culpó a Nayeli del robo de Yax-Balam porque...
   - a. ella lo encontró.
   - b. ella fue la última que lo vio.

6. Nayeli encontró a los jaguares en...
   - a. España y México.
   - b. España y Alemania.

7. Según la periodista, Nayeli y Adriana creen en...
   - a. la voz del corazón.
   - b. la voz de la razón.

2 **Situaciones.** Dramaticen una de las siguientes situaciones.

1. Nayeli y Raúl hablan sobre el significado de las rosas y su trabajo futuro.
2. Adriana y Felipe hablan de un mundo ideal.

3 **Escritura.** Al final de esta historia, Adriana y Felipe han resuelto un caso difícil. ¿Qué crees que sucederá ahora en las vidas de Adriana y Felipe? (6–7 oraciones)

NOTA CULTURAL

El Museo Nacional de Antropología

En el Museo Nacional de Antropología de la Ciudad de México, hay muchos objetos arqueológicos de gran valor. En 1964, cuando el museo fue inaugurado, el presidente de México expresó lo siguiente sobre la importancia de la institución:

   "La gente mexicana levanta este monumento para honrar las culturas admirables que florecieron durante la época precolombina en las regiones que ahora son territorios de la República. Ante los testigos de esas culturas, el México contemporáneo da un homenaje a nuestra cultura indígena en cuyo ejemplo reconocemos las características de nuestros orígenes nacionales".

Lectura

Online Study Center

For further reading practice online, visit the *Caminos* website at http://college.hmco.com/languages/spanish/renjilian/caminos/3e/student_home.html.

PRELECTURA

The *Popol Vuh was* the sacred book of the Mayans. The second part narrates how the Mayan Hero Twins overpowered the frightening Lords of the Mayan underworld, Xibalbá, a parallel world beneath ours, full of plants, animals, and people. The version of the *Popol Vuh* that we know today is a Spanish version of an old Quiché Maya book translated by the Jesuit Francisco Jiménez. The translator included, side-by-side with the Spanish text, a transcript of the original Maya Quiché language, which probably was an interpretation of a lost Mayan codex. The classical Mayan names of the Hero Twins, Hun-Ahau and Yax-Balam, are transcribed as Hunahpú and Ixbalamqué in the *Popol Vuh*.

Reading Strategy

Using a genealogical chart with notes

When you read a narration that describes many different family members, it is useful to develop a family genealogy to keep track of the people mentioned. You can also jot down a trait of each character while you create a family tree to help remember who's who. You will have an opportunity to practice this technique when you read the passage that follows.

  1 Un árbol genealógico. Antes de leer sobre los héroes gemelos, haz un árbol genealógico de tres generaciones de tu familia o de otra familia que conoces bien. Al lado de cada miembro familiar, escribe una característica o acción especial de esa persona entre paréntesis. Luego, usando el árbol genealógico y tus apuntes, descríbele esa familia a un/a compañero/a.

Ecos del pasado: Héroes mayas

El Popol Vuh, el libro sagrado de los mayas, cuenta la historia de Hunahpú[1] y de Ixbalamqué[2], los grandes Héroes Gemelos que vencieron[3] a los malvados Señores[4] de Xibalbá: Hun-Camé[5] y Vucub-Camé[6].

El padre de Hunahpú e Ixbalamqué era otro famoso gemelo maya: Hun-Hunahpú. Éste y su hermano Vucub-Hunahpú eran los mejores jugadores de pelota de la tierra y los Señores de Xibalbá los invitaron para jugar con ellos en Xibalbá. Cuando llegaron allí, los Señores de Xibalbá los mataron porque los gemelos no pudieron cumplir con las pruebas imposibles que les habían puesto. Los Señores de Xibalbá enterraron[7] a Vucub-Hunahpú en la plaza de juego de pelota y colgaron[8] la cabeza de Hun-Hunahpú en un árbol de calabazas[9].

---

[1]Lord One; [2]Little Jaguar; [3]defeated; [4]evil lords, gods; [5]Death One; [6]Death Seven; [7]buried; [8]hung; [9]pumpkin tree

Un día, Ixquic, una princesa de Xibalbá, se acercó al árbol para coger[10] una calabaza. En ese momento, la cabeza de Hun-Hunahpú le escupió[11] en la palma de la mano y ella quedó embarazada con los Héroes Gemelos. Al poco tiempo, Ixquic tuvo que escapar de Xibalbá porque los Señores iban a matarla y se refugió en casa de Ixmucané, la madre de Hun-Hunahpú y Vucub-Hunahpú. Allí nacieron los Héroes Gemelos. Cuando crecieron, llegaron a ser los mejores jugadores de pelota, tal como lo habían sido su padre y su tío.

Los Señores de Xibalbá, Hun-Camé y Vucub-Camé, se dieron cuenta de que los Héroes Gemelos jugaban tan bien como su padre y su tío y, enfurecidos, decidieron invitarlos a Xibalbá con la intención de matarlos a ellos también.

Al llegar a Xibalbá, Hunahpú e Ixbalamqué descubrieron los trucos[12] de los Señores de Xibalbá con la ayuda de varios animales. De esa manera tuvieron éxito en todas las pruebas en las que su padre y su tío habían fracasado[13]: se fumaron un cigarro sin fuego, quemaron una antorcha[14] sin gastarla[15]; sobrevivieron en la casa de la oscuridad[16], en la casa del frío, en la casa de las navajas[17], y en la casa de los murciélagos[18]. Por último, pudieron vencer[19] la misma muerte, destruyeron a los Señores de Xibalbá y se convirtieron en dioses auténticos. Desde entonces, brillan como astros en el firmamento[20].

---

[10]to pick; [11]spit; [12]tricks; [13]failed; [14]torch; [15]using it up [16]darkness; [17]knives; [18]bats; [19]defeat; [20]sky

POSTLECTURA

2 **Los Héroes Gemelos: Su genealogía.** Con un/a compañero/a, hagan un árbol genealógico de la familia de los Héroes Gemelos. Escriban entre paréntesis una o dos características o acciones de ellos y su familia.

3 **Personajes y personalidades.** Usa tus apuntes y la lectura para contestar las preguntas.

1. ¿Qué lugar era Xibalbá y quién vivía allí?
2. ¿Quiénes eran Hun-Hunahpú y Vucub-Hunahpú? ¿Y Hun-Camé y Vucub-Camé?
3. ¿Qué significan las palabras "Hun" y "Vucub", según la lectura?
4. ¿Por qué se enojaron los Señores de Xibalbá con los Héroes Gemelos?
5. ¿Cómo se llamaba la abuela de los Héroes Gemelos? ¿A quién recibió ella en su casa?
6. ¿Quién era Ixquic y por qué tuvo que huir de Xibalbá?
7. ¿Qué les gustaba hacer a los Héroes Gemelos?
8. ¿Qué cosas imposibles pudieron hacer con éxito los Héroes Gemelos?
9. ¿En qué se convirtieron los Héroes Gemelos después de vencer a los dioses de Xibalbá?

4 **¡Adelante con aventuras!** Ahora que las figuras de los gemelos están juntas en el museo en México, pueden tener más aventuras. Inventa otro mito de los Héroes Gemelos en el tiempo contemporáneo.

Escritura

Online Study Center

For further writing practice online, visit the *Caminos* website at http://college .hmco.com/languages/ spanish/renjilian/caminos/ 3e/student_home.html.

Writing Strategy

Editing one's own work

An important, yet often overlooked, step in writing is to edit your own work. It is important to focus on content and organization as well as on form. Use this self-editing checklist as a guide to editing your own writing. You can also use it as a guideline for peer editing.

Workshop

A. Focus on content. Ask yourself these questions:
   ► Is the topic interesting?
   ► Is the main idea clearly expressed?
   ► Does the supporting detail enhance the main idea?
   ► Is the order of sentences and ideas logical and easy to follow?
   ► Does the conclusion summarize my ideas?

B. Focus on form. Check the following:
   ► gender of nouns
   ► subject / verb agreement
   ► noun /adjective agreement
   ► word order within the entire sentence
   ► word order within each phrase
   ► new vocabulary
   ► influences of English idioms on Spanish
   ► spelling and capitalization
   ► punctuation
   ► use of accents

After editing your work, remember to focus on appearance. If the composition is handwritten, be sure that it is legible and that you write on every other line. If it is computer-generated, be sure to print it out double-spaced and include all necessary accents and other punctuation.

Strategy in Action

For additional practice with editing your own work, complete the exercises below and in the *Escritura* section of your Student Activities Manual for *Unidad 12*.

1 ¿A quiénes invitarías? Si pudieras invitar a tres hispanos famosos a tu casa para una cena, ¿a quiénes invitarías y por qué?

2 La siguiente misión de I.L.E.Y.A.N. Al final de *Caminos del jaguar,* Raúl habla con Nayeli de otra misión para recuperar objetos arqueológicos perdidos. Inventa su siguiente aventura y escribe lo que pasará con Nayeli y Raúl.

Resumen de vocabulario

PRIMER PASO

COMPARING THE AZTECS, MAYANS, AND INCAS

Sustantivos

apogeo	*height*
códice	*codex*
conquista	*conquest*
la descendiente	*descendent*
escritura	*writing*
exploración	*exploration*
imperio	*empire*
pirámide	*pyramid*
ruinas	*ruins*
siglo	*century*
la tejedor/a	*weaver*
templo	*temple*

Verbos

caer	*to decline*
destacar(se)	*to stand out*
distinguir(se)	*to distinguish*
fundar	*to found*
pertenecer	*to belong*
vencer	*to defeat*

Adjetivos

desarollado/a	*developed*
étnico/a	*ethnic*
habitado/a	*inhabited*
imponente	*imposing*
jeroglífico/a	*hieroglyphic*
lingüístico/a	*linguistic*
perdido/a	*lost*

Otras expresiones

además de	*in addition to*
sin embargo	*nevertheless*

SEGUNDO PASO

DISCUSSING HISPANIC CONTRIBUTIONS IN THE UNITED STATES

Sustantivos

cifra	*figure, number*
crecimiento	*growth*
población	*population*
poder adquisitivo	*purchasing power*
premio	*award, prize*

Verbos

pronosticar	*to predict*

Otras expresiones

de habla española	*Spanish-speaking*
pero	*but*
sino, sino que	*but (rather)*

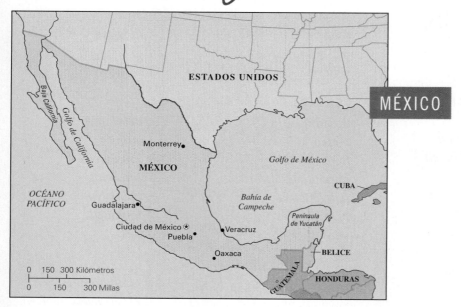

Online Study Center

To learn more about the people featured in this section, visit the *Caminos* website at http://college .hmco.com/languages/ spanish/renjilian/caminos/ 3e/student_home.html.

PERSONALIDADES

Los mexicanos

Rufino Tamayo

Octavio Paz

María Félix

Eduardo Verástegui

Jaime Camil

Gael García Bernal

Salma Hayek

Carlos Santana

El tema de la identidad cultural se refleja en el arte, la música, la literatura y el cine de México. Los artistas de pintura mural — Diego Rivera (1886–1957), David Alfaro Siqueiros (1898–1974), José Clemente Orozco (1883–1949) y Rufino Tamayo (1899–1991)— interpretan las dificultades socioeconómicas y políticas del pueblo mexicano, mezcla[1] de raíces[2] indígenas, españolas y africanas. Los muralistas describen además[3], los sueños[4] y esperanzas de la gente de clase trabajadora[5]. Retratan la grandeza e importancia de las civilizaciones azteca y maya del pasado mientras expresan asimismo la realidad mexicana de una vida dura del siglo XX. La Revolución Mexicana de 1910 les había prometido a los campesinos tierras fértiles, pan y escuelas; pero la pobreza[6] continuaba marcando sus vidas.

Las obras de los escritores mexicanos reflejan diversas perspectivas sobre el pueblo mexicano. En su libro *El laberinto de la soledad*[7], Octavio Paz, quien ganó el Premio Nobel de Literatura, define para el mundo internacional la identidad mexicana. La cultura es también el tema de los escritores y periodistas[8] José Emilio Pacheco y Elena Poniatowska. El prolífico escritor Carlos Fuentes sirvió a su país como diplomático. Laura Esquivel es tanto novelista como guionista[9].

---

[1]mixture; [2]roots; [3]in addition; [4]dreams; [5]working class; [6]poverty; [7]*The Labyrinth of Solitude*; [8]journalists; [9]screenwriter

> "Quiero utilizar la música como instrumento divino para plantar semillas[c] de esperanza".
>
> —Carlos Santana (México)

seeds

Diego Rivera

David Alfaro Siqueiros

Kate del Castillo

Jose Emilio Pacheco

Los artistas de la actualidad[10] siguen afirmando la identidad mexicana. En el cine mexicano, las películas *Ángeles negros*, *Como agua para chocolate*, *Novia que te vea*[11] y otras similares tratan diferentes cuestiones relacionadas con la identidad étnica, racial, política y cultural.

La legendaria actriz María Félix apareció en muchas películas con otros ídolos del cine mexicano del siglo veinte como Jorge Negrete y Pedro Infante. Los jóvenes actores mexicanos también son muy versátiles. Entre ellos están los actores Eduardo Verástegui y Jaime Camil, quienes empezaron su carrera como músicos.

Otro actor multitalentoso, Gael García Bernal ha recibido mucha buena crítica por su interpretación de Ernesto "Che" Guevara. La actriz y directora Salma Hayek también ha ganado mucha fama por sus películas y especialmente por su interpretación de la artista mexicana Frida Kahlo. Kate del Castillo manifiesta sus talentos dramáticos en dos dimensiones: las películas y la televisión.

Los mexicanos se destacan[12] en el mundo internacional de la música. Carlos Santana es un artista que ha tenido una larga carrera como compositor y cantante, representando a México y al mundo latino. Salvador López, el director del famoso Ballet Folklórico de México, es nieto de su fundadora, Amalia Hernández. Las danzas de la compañía, que baila en todas partes del mundo, combinan rituales indígenas y elementos modernos para representar la diversa identidad mexicana.

Visita el sitio web de *Caminos* para leer más en español sobre estas personalidades y otros mexicanos influyentes como Vicente Fox, el ex-presidente de México; María Elena Salinas, periodista y presentadora estrella de noticias[13]; Alejandro González Iñárritu, Arturo Ripstein, Marcela Fernández Violante, Alfonso Cuarón, directores de cine; Lorena Rojas, Valentino Lanús, Yolanda Andrade, José Ángel Llamas, Camila Sodi, actores; Carlos Monsiváis, Rosario Castellanos, escritores; Jacqueline Bracamontes, modelo; y Oswaldo Sánchez, jugador de fútbol.

Elena Poniatowska

Carlos Fuentes

Laura Esquivel

Alejandro González Iñárritu

---

[10]nowadays; [11]*May I see you a bride*; [12]stand out; [13]news anchor

Comprensión

Trabajando en parejas, háganse las siguientes preguntas.

1. ¿Cuáles son algunos de los temas de las artes y letras en México?
2. Describe a tres personalidades fascinantes de esta lectura.

ARTE

Frida y Diego, 1931

FRIDA KAHLO

Frida Kahlo nació en 1907 en México de padre judío europeo y madre mexicana con raíces indígenas. Tuvo una vida llena de prolífica producción artística, sufrimiento físico, activismo sociopolítico y dos matrimonios con el mismo hombre.

En sus pinturas Frida expresa la búsqueda de la identidad social y personal. De sus 143 pinturas, 55 son autorretratos. La pintora explora también la tempestuosa relación con su esposo, Diego Rivera, el gran artista mexicano. Cuando era joven, Frida sufrió un accidente que le causó dolores muy fuertes durante toda la vida. A ella la atormentaba la imposibilidad de tener hijos y su arte comunica también esta pena.

Sus obras se caracterizan por su estilo surrealista, sus colores vivos y los componentes culturales. Frida murió en 1954.

👥 Comprensión

Trabajando en parejas, háganse estas preguntas sobre el cuadro de Frida.

1. ¿Quiénes son estas dos personas?
stature, height 2. Compara a los dos en estatura°. ¿Cómo son?
3. ¿Qué ropa llevan ellos? ¿De qué colores? ¿Cuál es el más prominente?
4. El objeto que tiene Diego en la mano es una paleta con pinceles. ¿Qué profesión representa?
banner 5. Hay una cinta° con palabras sobre la cabeza de Frida. ¿Qué crees que dice el mensaje? ¿Quién lleva la cinta? Describe a la persona.
6. ¿Cómo te parece la pareja: contenta, descontenta, divertida, aburrida, serena, furiosa, resignada?
7. ¿Dónde estará la pareja: en su casa, en un baile, en una fiesta, en un museo, en un hotel?
8. ¿Qué piensas de este cuadro? ¿Te gusta? ¿Por qué? ¿Cuál es tu artista favorito/a?

MÚSICA

LUIS MIGUEL

Luis Miguel, un ídolo del pop, es hijo de un guitarrista español y de una cantante italiana. Grabó° su primer álbum a los doce años, con el título de "Enamorados°". Aunque nació en Puerto Rico en 1970, se crió° en México y el presidente de México le otorgó° la nacionalidad mexicana. Su música refleja su espíritu mexicano y su dedicación a celebrar las tradiciones musicales de su país de adopción.

Este superestrella de la música latinoamericana ha cantado en más de cien conciertos alrededor° del° mundo, ha vendido más de cincuenta y dos millones de discos y ha ganado nueve Grammys, además de° docenas de otros premios y reconocimientos°. Tiene su propia estrella en el Paseo de la Fama de Hollywood. En 2006 celebró veinticinco años de carrera musical a la edad de treinta y seis años, algo extraordinario. Sus apodos° son "Sol de México", "Luismi" y "Micky".

Las canciones más populares de Luis Miguel son de tipo bolero° o canciones románticas. Algunos de sus discos famosos son los siguientes: "Decídete" (1983), "Fiebre de amor" (1985), "Soy como quiero ser" (1987), "América y en vivo" (1992), "Segundo romance" (1994), "Amarte es un placer" (1999), "Vivo" (2000), "México en la piel" (2004), "Grandes éxitos" (2005).

He recorded
In love
was raised
bestowed on him

around

besides
recognition

nicknames
(a type of music that
originated in Spain)

Comprensión

Con un/a compañero/a, háganse estas preguntas sobre Luis Miguel.

1. ¿Dónde nació Luis Miguel? ¿Y sus padres?
2. ¿A qué edad grabó su primer álbum?
3. ¿Cómo consiguió el cantante la nacionalidad mexicana?
4. ¿Cuántos discos ha vendido? ¿Cuántos Grammys ha ganado?
5. ¿Dónde ha cantado en conciertos? ¿Cuándo celebró los veinticinco años de carrera?
6. ¿Qué tipo de música caracteriza al cantante?
7. ¿Qué significan en inglés los títulos de sus discos?
8. Describe a un/a cantante de tu país que cante música romántica o que exprese tradiciones musicales importantes. Nombra en español algunos títulos. ¿Qué ideas revelan sus canciones?

Conéctate a Internet para escuchar la música de Luis Miguel y aprender más sobre él y otros cantantes y músicos como Alicia Villareal, Alejandro Fernández, Ana Gabriel, Julieta Venegas (también compositora) y Alicia Machado (también actriz).

LITERATURA

ÁNGELES MASTRETTA

Ángeles Mastretta es periodista y escritora mexicana de novelas y cuentos. Con muchos detalles culturales, ella describe la vida diaria y muchas tradiciones mexicanas. Ha ganado premios literarios y sus obras han sido traducidas° a muchos idiomas. Nació en Puebla, México.

have been translated

En esta selección de su libro *Mujeres de ojos grandes*, la narradora nos cuenta la historia del noviazgo° inesperado° de su tía Cristina con el señor Arqueros, un español. Aquí vemos la reacción de la tía Cristina al recibir su anillo°.

engagement / unexpected

engagement ring

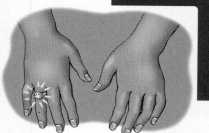

"Una sorpresa para Tía Cristina" (de *Mujeres de ojos grandes*)

anxiety
neighborhood
city square / Mexican dish / corn pancakes
stews / grated
aroma
pastures

Cuando salió de la angustia° propia de las sorpresas, la tía Cristina miró su anillo y empezó a llorar por sus hermanas, por su madre, por sus amigas, por su barrio°, por la catedral, por el zócalo°, por los volcanes, por el cielo, por el mole°, por las chalupas°, por el himno nacional, por la carretera a México, por Cholula, por Coetzálan, ...por las cazuelas°, por los chocolates rasposos°, por la música, por el olor° de las tortillas, por el río San Francisco, por el rancho de su amiga Elena y los potreros° de su tío Abelardo, por la luna de octubre y la de marzo, por el sol de febrero....

news / sparkling
priest
=amigo de su esposo /
good-byes / As if her fiancé were

Al día siguiente salió a la calle con la noticia° y su anillo brillándole°. Seis meses después se casó con el señor Arqueros frente a un cura°, un notario y los ojos de Suárez°. Hubo misa, banquete, baile y despedidas°. Todo con el mismo entusiasmo que si el novio estuviera° de este lado del mar. Dicen que no se vio novia más radiante en mucho tiempo.

👥 Comprensión

Trabajando en parejas, háganse las preguntas sobre el pasaje.

1. Cuando la tía Cristina recibió el anillo, lloró mucho. ¿Qué personas nombra ella?
2. ¿Qué comidas menciona ella?
3. ¿Cuáles son los meses del año a que se refiere?
4. ¿Qué referencias hay a la naturaleza?
5. Después de recibir el anillo, ¿a los cuántos meses se casaron la tía Cristina y el señor Arqueros? ¿De dónde es él?
6. Cuando se casó la tía Cristina, ¿quiénes estaban presentes? ¿Cómo celebraron después de la ceremonia en la iglesia?
7. ¿Quién, crees tú, está narrándonos la historia?
8. En tu opinión, ¿cómo estaba la novia el día en que se casó: deprimida, animada, radiante, pálida, alegre, triste, sentimental?

JUAN RULFO

El escritor mexicano Juan Rulfo vivió de 1918 hasta 1986. Era huérfano° y pasó una niñez difícil por la pobreza que sufría mucha gente en México en esa época. Además de su producción literaria, Rulfo ha dejado una extensa obra fotográfica. En sus obras literarias, se dedicó a describir el sufrimiento socioeconómico de su gente. Este texto es de su cuento "Es que somos muy pobres". Aquí sabemos lo que le pasa a la querida vaca° de Tacha, una joven muchacha.

orphan

beloved cow

"La vaca de Tacha" (de "Es que somos pobres")

Aquí todo va de mal en peor°. La semana pasada se murió mi tía Jacinta, y el sábado cuando ya la habíamos enterrado° y comenzaba a bajársenos la tristeza°, comenzó a llover como nunca. A mi papá eso le dio coraje°, porque toda la cosecha° de cebada° estaba asoleándose en el solar. Y el aguacero llegó de repente°, en grandes olas de agua, sin darnos tiempo ni siquiera a esconder aunque fuera un manojo°; lo único que pudimos hacer, todos los de mi casa, fue estarnos arrimados° debajo del tejabán°, viendo cómo el agua fría que caía del cielo quemaba aquella cebada amarilla tan recién cortada.

Y apenas ayer, cuando mi hermana Tacha acababa de cumplir doce años, supimos que la vaca que mi papá le regaló para el día de su santo° se la había llevado el río°.

from bad to worse
we had buried
sadness started to leave us
anger / harvest / barley
suddenly
handful
to take cover / roof

Saint's day / the river had swept it away

Comprensión

Trabajando en parejas, contesten las preguntas sobre la lectura.

1. ¿Cuándo se murió la tía Jacinta?
2. ¿Llovió mucho o poco? ¿Por qué le dio coraje al papá?
3. ¿Cómo llegó el aguacero, rápido o despacio? ¿Dónde se quedaron arrimados los de la familia?
4. ¿Cómo estaba el agua, caliente o fría?
5. ¿Cuántos años tenía Tacha?
6. ¿Quién le regaló la vaca a Tacha? ¿Qué le pasó a la vaca?
7. ¿Qué relación tiene Tacha con la persona que narra la historia?
8. ¿Cómo te hace sentir esta selección: triste, alegre, furioso/a, optimista, pesimista, furioso/a, curioso/a?

Reference Materials

Appendix A: Verb Charts

Regular verbs

Simple tenses

Infinitive	Past participle / Present participle	Indicative: Present	Imperfect	Preterite	Future	Conditional	Subjunctive: Present	Imperfect*
cantar *to sing*	cantado / cantando	canto cantas canta cantamos cantáis cantan	cantaba cantabas cantaba cantábamos cantábais cantaban	canté cantaste cantó cantamos cantasteis cantaron	cantaré cantarás cantará cantaremos cantaréis cantarán	cantaría cantarías cantaría cantaríamos cantaríais cantarían	cante cantes cante cantemos cantéis canten	cantara cantaras cantara cantáramos cantarais cantaran
correr *to run*	corrido / corriendo	corro corres corre corremos corréis corren	corría corrías corría corríamos corríais corrían	corrí corriste corrió corrimos corristeis corrieron	correré correrás correrá correremos correréis correrán	correría correrías correría correríamos correríais correrían	corra corras corra corramos corráis corran	corriera corrieras corriera corriéramos corrierais corrieran
subir *to go up, to climb up*	subido / subiendo	subo subes sube subimos subís suben	subía subías subía subíamos subíais subían	subí subiste subió subimos subisteis subieron	subiré subirás subirá subiremos subiréis subirán	subiría subirías subiría subiríamos subiríais subirían	suba subas suba subamos subáis suban	subiera subieras subiera subiéramos subierais subieran

*In addition to this form, another one is less frequently used for all regular and irregular verbs: **cantase, cantases, cantase, cantásemos, cantaseis, cantasen; corriese, corrieses, corriese, corriésemos, corrieseis, corriesen; viviese, vivieses, viviese, viviésemos, vivieseis, viviesen.**

Commands

Person	Affirmative	Negative	Affirmative	Negative	Affirmative	Negative
tú	canta	no cantes	corre	no corras	sube	no subas
usted	cante	no cante	corra	no corra	suba	no suba
ustedes	canten	no canten	corran	no corran	suban	no suban
nosotros	cantemos	no cantemos	corramos	no corramos	subamos	no subamos
vosotros	cantad	no cantéis	corred	no corráis	subid	no subáis

Stem-changing verbs: -ar and -er groups

Type of change in the verb stem	Subject	Indicative Present	Subjunctive Present	Commands Affirmative	Commands Negative	Other -ar and -er stem-changing verbs
-ar verbs **e > ie** pensar *to think*	yo	**pienso**	**piense**	—	—	atravesar *to go through, to cross;* cerrar *to close;* despertarse *to wake up;* empezar *to start;* negar *to deny;* sentarse *to sit down.*
	tú	**piensas**	**pienses**	**piensa**	no **pienses**	
	él/ella, Ud.	**piensa**	**piense**	**piense**	no **piense**	nevar *to snow* is only conjugated in the third person singular *nieva.*
	nosotros/as	pensamos	pensemos	pensemos	no pensemos	
	vosotros/as	pensáis	penséis	pensad	no penséis	
	ellos/as, Uds.	**piensan**	**piensen**	**piensen**	no **piensen**	
-ar verbs **o > ue** contar *to count, to tell*	yo	**cuento**	**cuente**	—	—	acordarse *to remember;* acostar(se) *to go to bed;* almorzar *to have lunch;* colgar *to hang;* costar *to cost;* demostrar *to demonstrate, to show;* encontrar *to find;* mostrar *to show;* probar *to prove, to taste;* recordar *to remember.*
	tú	**cuentas**	**cuentes**	**cuenta**	no **cuentes**	
	él/ella, Ud.	**cuenta**	**cuente**	**cuente**	no **cuente**	
	nosotros/as	contamos	contemos	contemos	no contemos	
	vosotros/as	contáis	contéis	contad	no contéis	
	ellos/as, Uds.	**cuentan**	**cuenten**	**cuenten**	no **cuenten**	
-er verbs **e > ie** entender *to understand*	yo	**entiendo**	**entienda**	—	—	encender *to light, to turn on;* extender *to stretch;* perder *to lose.*
	tú	**entiendes**	**entiendas**	**entiende**	no **entiendas**	
	él/ella, Ud.	**entiende**	**entienda**	**entienda**	no **entienda**	
	nosotros/as	entendemos	entendamos	entendamos	no entendamos	
	vosotros/as	entendéis	entendáis	entended	no entendáis	
	ellos/as, Uds.	**entienden**	**entiendan**	**entiendan**	no **entiendan**	
-er verbs **o > ue** volver *to return*	yo	**vuelvo**	**vuelva**	—	—	mover *to move;* torcer *to twist.*
	tú	**vuelves**	**vuelvas**	**vuelve**	no **vuelvas**	
	él/ella, Ud.	**vuelve**	**vuelva**	**vuelva**	no **vuelva**	llover *to rain* is only conjugated in the third person singular *llueve.*
	nosotros/as	volvemos	volvamos	volvamos	no volvamos	
	vosotros/as	volvéis	volváis	volved	no volváis	
	ellos/as, Uds.	**vuelven**	**vuelvan**	**vuelvan**	no **vuelvan**	

Stem-changing verbs: -ir verbs

Group I

Type of change in the verb stem	Subject	Indicative		Subjunctive		Commands	
		Present	Preterite	Present	Imperfect	Affirmative	Negative
-ir verbs e > ie or i Infinitive: sentir *to feel* Present participle: sintiendo	yo	siento	sentí	sienta	sintiera	—	—
	tú	sientes	sentiste	sientas	sintieras	siente	no sientas
	él/ella, Ud.	siente	sintió	sienta	sintiera	sienta	no sienta
	nosotros/as	sentimos	sentimos	sintamos	sintiéramos	sintamos	no sintamos
	vosotros/as	sentís	sentisteis	sintáis	sintierais	sentid	no sintáis
	ellos/as, Uds.	sienten	sintieron	sientan	sintieran	sientan	no sientan
-ir verbs o > ue or u Infinitive: dormir *to sleep* Present participle: durmiendo	yo	duermo	dormí	duerma	durmiera	—	—
	tú	duermes	dormiste	duermas	durmieras	duerme	no duermas
	él/ella, Ud.	duerme	durmió	duerma	durmiera	duerma	no duerma
	nosotros/as	dormimos	dormimos	durmamos	durmiéramos	durmamos	no durmamos
	vosotros/as	dormís	dormisteis	durmáis	durmierais	dormid	no durmáis
	ellos/as, Uds.	duermen	durmieron	duerman	durmieran	duerman	no duerman

Other similar verbs: advertir *to warn;* arrepentirse *to repent;* consentir *to consent, to pamper;* convertir(se) *to turn into;* divertir(se) *to amuse (oneself);* herir *to hurt, to wound;* mentir *to lie;* morir *to die;* preferir *to prefer;* referir *to refer;* sugerir *to suggest.*

Group II

Type of change in the verb stem	Subject	Indicative		Subjunctive		Commands	
		Present	Preterite	Present	Imperfect	Affirmative	Negative
-ir verbs e > i Infinitive: pedir *to ask for, to request* Present participle: pidiendo	yo	pido	pedí	pida	pidiera	—	—
	tú	pides	pediste	pidas	pidieras	pide	no pidas
	él/ella, Ud.	pide	pidió	pida	pidiera	pida	no pida
	nosotros/as	pedimos	pedimos	pidamos	pidiéramos	pidamos	no pidamos
	vosotros/as	pedís	pedisteis	pidáis	pedierais	pedid	no pidáis
	ellos/as, Uds.	piden	pidieron	pidan	pidieran	pidan	no pidan

Other similar verbs: competir *to compete;* despedir(se) *to say good-bye;* elegir *to choose;* impedir *to prevent;* perseguir *to chase;* repetir *to repeat;* seguir *to follow;* servir *to serve;* vestir(se) *to dress, to get dressed.*

Verbs with spelling changes

	Verb type	Ending	Change	Verbs with similar spelling changes
1	buscar *to look for*	-car	• Preterite: yo busqué • Present subjunctive: busque, busques, busque, busquemos, busquéis, busquen	comunicar, explicar, indicar, sacar, pescar
2	conocer *to know*	-cer or -cir	• Present indicative: conozco, conoces, conoce, and so on • Present subjunctive: conozca, conozcas, conozca, conozcamos, conozcáis, conozcan	nacer, obedecer, ofrecer, parecer, pertenecer, reconocer, conducir, traducir
3	vencer *to win*	-cer or -cir	• Present indicative: venzo, vences, vence, and so on • Present subjunctive: venza, venzas, venza, venzamos, venzáis, venzan	convencer, torcer *to twist*
4	leer *to read*	-eer	• Preterite: leyó, leyeron • Imperfect subjunctive: leyera, leyeras, leyera, leyéramos, leyerais, leyeran • Present participle: leyendo	creer, poseer *to own*
5	llegar *to arrive*	-gar	• Preterite: llegué • Present subjunctive: llegue, llegues, llegue, lleguemos, lleguéis, lleguen	colgar, navegar, negar, pagar, rogar, jugar
6	coger *to take*	-ger or -gir	• Present indicative: cojo • Present subjunctive: coja, cojas, coja, cojamos, cojáis, cojan	escoger, proteger, recoger, corregir, dirigir, elegir, exigir
7	seguir *to follow*	-guir	• Present indicative: sigo • Present subjunctive: siga, sigas, siga, sigamos, sigáis, sigan	conseguir, distinguir, perseguir
8	huir *to flee*	-uir	• Present indicative: huyo, huyes, huye, huimos, huís, huyen • Preterite: huí, huiste, huyó, huimos, huisteis, huyeron • Present subjunctive: huya, huyas, huya, huyamos, huyáis, huyan • Imperfect subjunctive: huyera, huyeras, huyera, huyéramos, huyerais, huyeran • Present participle: huyendo • Commands: huye tú, huya usted, huyan ustedes, huid vosotros, huyamos nosotros; no huyas tú, no huya usted, no huyan ustedes, no huyamos nosotros, no huyáis vosotros	concluir, contribuir, construir, destruir, disminuir, distribuir, excluir, influir, instruir, restituir, substituir
9	abrazar *to embrace to hug*	-zar	• Preterite: abracé, abrazaste, abrazó, and so on • Present subjunctive: abrace, abraces, abrace, abracemos, abracéis, abracen	alcanzar, almorzar, comenzar, empezar, gozar, rezar

Verbs that need a written accent

Verb type	Ending	Change	Verbs with similar spelling changes
1 sonreír *to smile*	-eír	See p. 450 for a complete conjugation of these verbs.	freír, reír
2 enviar *to send*	-iar	• Present indicative: envío, envías, envía, enviamos, enviáis, envían • Present subjunctive: envíe, envíes, envíe, enviemos, enviéis, envíen	ampliar, criar, desviar, enfriar, guiar, variar
3 continuar *to continue*	-uar	• Present indicative: continúo, continúas, continúa, continuamos, continuáis, continúan • Present subjunctive: continúe, continúes, continúe, continuemos, continuéis, continúen	acentuar, efectuar, exceptuar, graduar, habituar, insinuar, situar

Compound tenses

Indicative					Subjunctive	
Present perfect	Past perfect	Preterite perfect	Future perfect	Conditional perfect	Present perfect	Past perfect
he	había	hube	habré	habría	haya	hubiera
has	habías	hubiste	habrás	habrías	hayas	hubieras
ha cantado	había cantado	hubo cantado	habrá cantado	habría cantado	haya cantado	hubiera cantado
hemos corrido	habíamos corrido	hubimos corrido	habremos corrido	habríamos corrido	hayamos corrido	hubiéramos corrido
habéis vivido	habíais vivido	hubisteis vivido	habréis vivido	habríais vivido	hayáis vivido	hubierais vivido
han	habían	hubieron	habrán	habrían	hayan	hubieran

Irregular verbs: Compound tenses

All irregular verbs follow the same formation pattern as the regular verbs with **haber,** in all tenses. The only thing that changes is the form of the past participle of each verb. See the chart below and the individual charts of irregular verbs for these forms. In Spanish, no word can come between **haber** and the past participle.

Common irregular past participles

Infinitive	Past participle		Infinitive	Past participle	
abrir	**abierto**	*opened*	morir	**muerto**	*died*
caer	caído	*fallen*	oír	oído	*heard*
creer	creído	*believed*	poner	**puesto**	*put, placed*
cubrir	**cubierto**	*covered*	resolver	**resuelto**	*resolved*
decir	**dicho**	*said, told*	romper	**roto**	*broken, torn*
descubrir	**descubierto**	*discovered*	(son)reír	(son)reído	*(smiled) laughed*
escribir	**escrito**	*written*	traer	traído	*brought*
hacer	**hecho**	*made, done*	ver	**visto**	*seen*
leer					

Regular and irregular reflexive verbs: Position of the reflexive pronouns in the simple tenses

Example 1: *lavarse*

Infinitive	Present participle	Reflexive pronouns	Indicative					Subjunctive	
			Present	Imperfect	Preterite	Future	Conditional	Present	Imperfect
lavarse *to wash oneself*	lavándome	me	lavo	lavaba	lavé	lavaré	lavaría	lave	lavara
	lavándote	te	lavas	lavabas	lavaste	lavarás	lavarías	laves	lavaras
	lavándose	se	lava	lavaba	lavó	lavará	lavaría	lave	lavara
	lavándonos	nos	lavamos	lavábamos	lavamos	lavaremos	lavaríamos	lavemos	laváramos
	lavándoos	os	laváis	lavabais	lavasteis	lavaréis	lavaríais	lavéis	lavarais
	lavándose	se	lavan	lavaban	lavaron	lavarán	lavarían	laven	lavaran

Example 2: *ponerse*

Infinitive	Present participle	Reflexive pronouns	Indicative					Subjunctive	
			Present	Imperfect	Preterite	Future	Conditional	Present	Imperfect
ponerse *to put on, to get (sad, happy, etc.)*	poniéndome	me	pongo	ponía	puse	pondré	pondría	ponga	pusiera
	poniéndote	te	pones	ponías	pusiste	pondrás	pondrías	pongas	pusieras
	poniéndose	se	pone	ponía	puso	pondrá	pondría	ponga	pusiera
	poniéndonos	nos	ponemos	poníamos	pusimos	pondremos	pondríamos	pongamos	pusiéramos
	poniéndoos	os	ponéis	poníais	pusisteis	pondréis	pondríais	pongáis	pusierais
	poniéndose	se	ponen	ponían	pusieron	pondrán	pondrían	pongan	pusieran

Example 3: *vestirse*

Infinitive	Present participle	Reflexive pronouns	Indicative					Subjunctive	
			Present	Imperfect	Preterite	Future	Conditional	Present	Imperfect
vestirse *to get dressed*	vistiéndome	me	visto	vestía	vestí	vestiré	vestiría	vista	vistiera
	vistiéndote	te	vistes	vestías	vestiste	vestirás	vestirías	vistas	vistieras
	vistiéndose	se	viste	vestía	vistió	vestirá	vestiría	vista	vistiera
	vistiéndonos	nos	vestimos	vestíamos	vestimos	vestiremos	vestiríamos	vistamos	vistiéramos
	vistiéndoos	os	vestís	vestíais	vestisteis	vestiréis	vestiríais	vistáis	vistierais
	vistiéndose	se	visten	vestían	vistieron	vestirán	vestirían	vistan	vistieran

Regular and irregular reflexive verbs: Position of the reflexive pronouns with commands

Person	Affirmative	Negative	Affirmative	Negative	Affirmative	Negative
tú	lávate	no te laves	ponte	no te pongas	vístete	no te vistas
usted	lávese	no se lave	póngase	no se ponga	vístase	no se vista
ustedes	lávense	no se laven	pónganse	no se pongan	vístanse	no se vistan
nosotros	lavémonos	no nos lavemos	pongámonos	no nos pongamos	vistámonos	no nos vistamos
vosotros	lavaos	no os lavéis	poneos	no os pongáis	vestíos	no os vistáis

Regular and irregular reflexive verbs: Position of the reflexive pronouns in compound tenses*

	Indicative					Subjunctive	
Reflexive Pronoun	Present Perfect	Past Perfect	Preterite Perfect	Future Perfect	Conditional Perfect	Present Perfect	Past Perfect
me	he	había	hube	habré	habría	haya	hubiera
te	has	habías	hubiste	habrás	habrías	hayas	hubieras
se	ha	había	hubo	habrá	habría	haya	hubiera
nos	hemos	habíamos	hubimos	habremos	habríamos	hayamos	hubiéramos
os	habéis	habíais	hubisteis	habréis	habríais	hayáis	hubiérais
se	han	habían	hubieron	habrán	habrían	hayan	hubieran

(participles for each tense: lavado, puesto, vestido)

*The sequence of these three elements—the reflexive pronoun, the auxiliary verb **haber,** and the present perfect form—is invariable and no other words can come in between.

Regular and irregular reflexive verbs: Position of the reflexive pronouns with conjugated verb + infinitive**

	Indicative					Subjunctive	
Reflexive Pronoun	Present	Imperfect	Preterite	Future	Conditional	Present	Imperfect
me	voy a	iba a	fui a	iré a	iría a	vaya a	fuera a
te	vas a	ibas a	fuiste a	irás a	irías a	vayas a	fueras a
se	va a	iba a	fue a	irá a	iría a	vaya a	fuera a
nos	vamos a	íbamos a	fuimos a	iremos a	iríamos a	vayamos a	fuéramos a
os	vais a	ibais a	fuisteis a	iréis a	iríais a	vayáis a	fuerais a
se	van a	iban a	fueron a	irán a	irían a	vayan a	fueran a

(infinitives for each tense: lavar, poner, vestir)

The reflexive pronoun can also be placed after the infinitive: voy a lavarme,** voy a poner**me,** voy a vestir**me,** and so on.
Use the same structure for the present and the past progressive: **me** estoy lavando / estoy lavándo**me; me** estaba lavando / estaba lavándo**me.**

Irregular verbs

Andar, caber, caer

Infinitive	Past participle Present participle	Indicative						Subjunctive	
		Present	Imperfect	Preterite	Future	Conditional		Present	Imperfect
andar *to walk; to go*	andado andando	ando andas anda andamos andáis andan	andaba andabas andaba andábamos andabais andaban	**anduve** **anduviste** **anduvo** **anduvimos** **anduvisteis** **anduvieron**	andaré andarás andará andaremos andaréis andarán	andaría andarías andaría andaríamos andaríais andarían		ande andes ande andemos andéis anden	**anduviera** **anduvieras** **anduviera** **anduviéramos** **anduvierais** **anduvieran**
caber *to fit; to have enough space*	cabido cabiendo	**quepo** cabes cabe cabemos cabéis caben	cabía cabías cabía cabíamos cabíais cabían	**cupe** **cupiste** **cupo** **cupimos** **cupisteis** **cupieron**	**cabré** **cabrás** **cabrá** **cabremos** **cabréis** **cabrán**	**cabría** **cabrías** **cabría** **cabríamos** **cabríais** **cabrían**		**quepa** **quepas** **quepa** **quepamos** **quepáis** **quepan**	**cupiera** **cupieras** **cupiera** **cupiéramos** **cupierais** **cupieran**
caer *to fall*	caído cayendo	**caigo** caes cae caemos caéis caen	caía caías caía caíamos caíais caían	caí caíste **cayó** caímos caísteis **cayeron**	caeré caerás caerá caeremos caeréis caerán	caería caerías caería caeríamos caeríais caerían		**caiga** **caigas** **caiga** **caigamos** **caigáis** **caigan**	cayera cayeras cayera cayéramos cayerais cayeran

Commands

Person	andar		caber		caer	
	Affirmative	Negative	Affirmative	Negative	Affirmative	Negative
tú	anda	no andes	cabe	no **quepas**	cae	no **caigas**
usted	ande	no ande	**quepa**	no **quepa**	**caiga**	no **caiga**
ustedes	anden	no anden	**quepan**	no **quepan**	**caigan**	no **caigan**
nosotros	andemos	no andemos	**quepamos**	no **quepamos**	**caigamos**	no **caigamos**
vosotros	andad	no andéis	cabed	no **quepáis**	caed	no **caigáis**

Dar, decir, estar

Infinitive	Past participle / Present participle	Indicative Present	Imperfect	Preterite	Future	Conditional	Subjunctive Present	Imperfect
dar *to give*	dado dando	**doy** das da damos dais dan	daba dabas daba dábamos dabais daban	**di diste dio dimos disteis dieron**	daré darás dará daremos daréis darán	daría darías daría daríamos daríais darían	**dé des dé demos deis den**	**diera dieras diera diéramos dierais dieran**
decir *to say, tell*	dicho diciendo	**digo dices dice** decimos decís **dicen**	decía decías decía decíamos decíais decían	**dije dijiste dijo dijimos dijisteis dijeron**	**diré dirás dirá diremos diréis dirán**	**diría dirías diría diríamos diríais dirían**	**diga digas diga digamos digáis digan**	**dijera dijeras dijera dijéramos dijerais dijeran**
estar *to be*	estado estando	**estoy estás está** estamos estáis **están**	estaba estabas estaba estábamos estabais estaban	**estuve estuviste estuvo estuvimos estuvisteis estuvieron**	estaré estarás estará estaremos estaréis estarán	estaría estarías estaría estaríamos estaríais estarían	**esté estés esté estemos estéis estén**	**estuviera estuvieras estuviera estuviéramos estuvierais estuvieran**

Commands

Person	dar Affirmative	dar Negative	decir Affirmative	decir Negative	estar Affirmative	estar Negative
tú	da	no des	**di**	no digas	**está**	no estés
usted	**dé**	no dé	**diga**	no diga	**esté**	no esté
ustedes	**den**	no den	**digan**	no digan	**estén**	no estén
nosotros	**demos**	no demos	**digamos**	no digamos	**estemos**	no estemos
vosotros	dad	no deis	decid	no digáis	estad	no estéis

Haber*, hacer, ir

Infinitive	Past participle Present participle	Indicative					Subjunctive	
		Present	Imperfect	Preterite	Future	Conditional	Present	Imperfect
haber* to have	habido habiendo	**he** **has** **ha** **hemos** habéis **han**	había habías había habíamos habíais habían	**hube** **hubiste** **hubo** **hubimos** **hubisteis** **hubieron**	**habré** **habrás** **habrá** **habremos** **habréis** **habrán**	**habría** **habrías** **habría** **habríamos** **habríais** **habrían**	**haya** **hayas** **haya** **hayamos** **hayáis** **hayan**	**hubiera** **hubieras** **hubiera** **hubiéramos** **hubierais** **hubieran**
hacer to do	**hecho** haciendo	**hago** haces hace hacemos hacéis hacen	hacía hacías hacía hacíamos hacíais hacían	**hice** **hiciste** **hizo** **hicimos** **hicisteis** **hicieron**	**haré** **harás** **hará** **haremos** **haréis** **harán**	**haría** **harías** **haría** **haríamos** **haríais** **harían**	**haga** **hagas** **haga** **hagamos** **hagáis** **hagan**	**hiciera** **hicieras** **hiciera** **hiciéramos** **hicierais** **hicieran**
ir to go	**ido** **yendo**	**voy** **vas** **va** **vamos** **vais** **van**	**iba** **ibas** **iba** **íbamos** **ibais** **iban**	**fui** **fuiste** **fue** **fuimos** **fuisteis** **fueron**	iré irás irá iremos iréis irán	iría irías iría iríamos iríais irían	**vaya** **vayas** **vaya** **vayamos** **vayáis** **vayan**	**fuera** **fueras** **fuera** **fuéramos** **fuerais** **fueran**

Commands

Person	hacer		ir	
	Affirmative	Negative	Affirmative	Negative
tú	**haz**	no **hagas**	**ve**	no **vayas**
usted	**haga**	no **haga**	**vaya**	no **vaya**
ustedes	**hagan**	no **hagan**	**vayan**	no **vayan**
nosotros	**hagamos**	no **hagamos**	**vamos**	no **vayamos**
vosotros	haced	no **hagáis**	**id**	no **vayáis**

Note: The imperative of **haber** is not used.

*Haber also has an impersonal form **hay.** This form is used to express "There is, There are."

Jugar, oír, oler

Infinitive	Past participle / Present participle	Indicative					Subjunctive	
		Present	Imperfect	Preterite	Future	Conditional	Present	Imperfect
jugar *to play*	jugado / jugando	juego / juegas / juega / jugamos / jugáis / juegan	jugaba / jugabas / jugaba / jugábamos / jugabais / jugaban	jugué / jugaste / jugó / jugamos / jugasteis / jugaron	jugaré / jugarás / jugará / jugaremos / jugaréis / jugarán	jugaría / jugarías / jugaría / jugaríamos / jugaríais / jugarían	juegue / juegues / juegue / juguemos / juguéis / jueguen	jugara / jugaras / jugara / jugáramos / jugarais / jugaran
oír *to hear, to listen*	oído / oyendo	oigo / oyes / oye / oímos / oís / oyen	oía / oías / oía / oíamos / oíais / oían	oí / oíste / oyó / oímos / oísteis / oyeron	oiré / oirás / oirá / oiremos / oiréis / oirán	oiría / oirías / oiría / oiríamos / oiríais / oirían	oiga / oigas / oiga / oigamos / oigáis / oigan	oyera / oyeras / oyera / oyéramos / oyerais / oyeran
oler *to smell*	olido / oliendo	huelo / hueles / huele / olemos / oléis / huelen	olía / olías / olía / olíamos / olíais / olían	olí / oliste / olió / olimos / olisteis / olieron	oleré / olerás / olerá / oleremos / oleréis / olerán	olería / olerías / olería / oleríamos / oleríais / olerían	huela / huelas / huela / olamos / oláis / huelan	oliera / olieras / oliera / oliéramos / olierais / olieran

Commands

Person	jugar		oír		oler	
	Affirmative	Negative	Affirmative	Negative	Affirmative	Negative
tú	juega	no juegues	oye	no oigas	huele	no huelas
usted	juegue	no juegue	oiga	no oiga	huela	no huela
ustedes	jueguen	no jueguen	oigan	no oigan	huelan	no huelan
nosotros	juguemos	no juguemos	oigamos	no oigamos	olamos	no olamos
vosotros	jugad	no juguéis	oíd	no oigáis	oled	no oláis

Poder, poner, querer

Infinitive	Past participle / Present participle	Indicative					Subjunctive	
		Present	Imperfect	Preterite	Future	Conditional	Present	Imperfect
poder *to be able to, can*	podido pudiendo	puedo puedes puede podemos podéis pueden	podía podías podía podíamos podíais podían	pude pudiste pudo pudimos pudisteis pudieron	podré podrás podrá podremos podréis podrán	podría podrías podría podríamos podríais podrían	pueda puedas pueda podamos podáis puedan	pudiera pudieras pudiera pudiéramos pudierais pudieran
poner* *to put*	puesto poniendo	pongo pones pone ponemos ponéis ponen	ponía ponías ponía poníamos poníais ponían	puse pusiste puso pusimos pusisteis pusieron	pondré pondrás pondrá pondremos pondréis pondrán	pondría pondrías pondría pondríamos pondríais pondrían	ponga pongas ponga pongamos pongáis pongan	pusiera pusieras pusiera pusiéramos pusierais pusieran
querer *to want, wish; to love*	querido queriendo	quiero quieres quiere queremos queréis quieren	quería querías quería queríamos queríais querían	quise quisiste quiso quisimos quisisteis quisieron	querré querrás querrá querremos querréis querrán	querría querrías querría querríamos querríais querrían	quiera quieras quiera queramos queráis quieran	quisiera quisieras quisiera quisiéramos quisierais quisieran

Commands

Person	poner		querer	
	Affirmative	Negative	Affirmative	Negative
tú	pon	no pongas	quiere	no quieras
usted	ponga	no ponga	quiera	no quiera
ustedes	pongan	no pongan	quieran	no quieran
nosotros	pongamos	no pongamos	queramos	no queramos
vosotros	poned	no pongáis	quered	no queráis

*Similar verbs to **poner: imponer, suponer, componer, descomponer.**
Note: The imperative of **poder** is used very infrequently.

Saber, salir, ser

Infinitive	Past participle / Present participle	Indicative Present	Imperfect	Preterite	Future	Conditional	Subjunctive Present	Imperfect
saber *to know*	sabido sabiendo	**sé** sabes sabe sabemos sabéis saben	sabía sabías sabía sabíamos sabíais sabían	**supe** **supiste** **supo** **supimos** **supisteis** **supieron**	**sabré** **sabrás** **sabrá** **sabremos** **sabréis** **sabrán**	**sabría** **sabrías** **sabría** **sabríamos** **sabríais** **sabrían**	**sepa** **sepas** **sepa** **sepamos** **sepáis** **sepan**	**supiera** **supieras** **supiera** **supiéramos** **supierais** **supieran**
salir *to go out, to leave*	salido saliendo	**salgo** sales sale salimos salís salen	salía salías salía salíamos salíais salían	salí saliste salió salimos salisteis salieron	**saldré** **saldrás** **saldrá** **saldremos** **saldréis** **saldrán**	**saldría** **saldrías** **saldría** **saldríamos** **saldríais** **saldrían**	**salga** **salgas** **salga** **salgamos** **salgáis** **salgan**	**saliera** **salieras** **saliera** **saliéramos** **salierais** **salieran**
ser *to be*	sido siendo	**soy** **eres** **es** **somos** **sois** **son**	**era** **eras** **era** **éramos** **erais** **eran**	**fui** **fuiste** **fue** **fuimos** **fuisteis** **fueron**	seré serás será seremos seréis serán	sería serías sería seríamos seríais serían	**sea** **seas** **sea** **seamos** **seáis** **sean**	**fuera** **fueras** **fuera** **fuéramos** **fuerais** **fueran**

Commands

saber

Person	Affirmative	Negative
tú	sabe	no **sepas**
usted	**sepa**	no **sepa**
ustedes	**sepan**	no **sepan**
nosotros	**sepamos**	no **sepamos**
vosotros	sabed	no **sepáis**

salir

Person	Affirmative	Negative
tú	**sal**	no salgas
usted	**salga**	no salga
ustedes	**salgan**	no salgan
nosotros	**salgamos**	no salgamos
vosotros	salid	no salgáis

ser

Person	Affirmative	Negative
tú	**sé**	no seas
usted	sea	no sea
ustedes	sean	no sean
nosotros	seamos	no seamos
vosotros	sed	no seáis

Sonreír, tener*, traer

Infinitive	Past participle / Present participle	Indicative Present	Indicative Imperfect	Indicative Preterite	Indicative Future	Indicative Conditional	Subjunctive Present	Subjunctive Imperfect
sonreír *to smile*	sonreído sonriendo	sonrío sonríes sonríe sonreímos sonreís sonríen	sonreía sonreías sonreía sonreíamos sonreíais sonreían	sonreí sonreíste sonrió sonreímos sonreísteis sonrieron	sonreiré sonreirás sonreirá sonreiremos sonreiréis sonreirán	sonreiría sonreirías sonreiría sonreiríamos sonreiríais sonreirían	sonría sonrías sonría sonriamos sonriáis sonrían	sonriera sonrieras sonriera sonriéramos sonrierais sonrieran
tener* *to have*	tenido teniendo	tengo tienes tiene tenemos tenéis tienen	tenía tenías tenía teníamos teníais tenían	tuve tuviste tuvo tuvimos tuvisteis tuvieron	tendré tendrás tendrá tendremos tendréis tendrán	tendría tendrías tendría tendríamos tendríais tendrían	tenga tengas tenga tengamos tengáis tengan	tuviera tuvieras tuviera tuviéramos tuvierais tuvieran
traer *to bring*	traído trayendo	traigo traes trae traemos traéis traen	traía traías traía traíamos traíais traían	traje trajiste trajo trajimos trajisteis trajeron	traeré traerás traerá traeremos traeréis traerán	traería traerías traería traeríamos traeríais traerían	traiga traigas traiga traigamos traigáis traigan	trajera trajeras trajera trajéramos trajerais trajeran

Commands

Person	sonreír Affirmative	sonreír Negative	tener Affirmative	tener Negative	traer Affirmative	traer Negative
tú	sonríe	no sonrías	ten	no tengas	trae	no traigas
usted	sonría	no sonría	tenga	no tenga	traiga	no traiga
ustedes	sonrían	no sonrían	tengan	no tengan	traigan	no traigan
nosotros	sonriamos	no sonriamos	tengamos	no tengamos	traigamos	no traigamos
vosotros	sonreíd	no sonriáis	tened	no tengáis	traed	no traigáis

*Many verbs ending in -tener are conjugated like this verb: **contener, detener, entretener(se), mantener, obtener, retener.**

Valer, venir*, ver

Infinitive	Past participle / Present participle	Indicative					Subjunctive	
		Present	Imperfect	Preterite	Future	Conditional	Present	Imperfect
valer *to be worth*	valido valiendo	**valgo** vales vale valemos valéis valen	valía valías valía valíamos valíais valían	valí valiste valió valimos valisteis valieron	**valdré** **valdrás** **valdrá** **valdremos** **valdréis** **valdrán**	**valdría** **valdrías** **valdría** **valdríamos** **valdríais** **valdrían**	**valga** **valgas** **valga** **valgamos** **valgáis** **valgan**	valiera valieras valiera valiéramos valierais valieran
venir* *to come*	venido viniendo	**vengo** **vienes** **viene** venimos venís **vienen**	venía venías venía veníamos veníais venían	**vine** **viniste** **vino** **vinimos** **vinisteis** **vinieron**	**vendré** **vendrás** **vendrá** **vendremos** **vendréis** **vendrán**	**vendría** **vendrías** **vendría** **vendríamos** **vendríais** **vendrían**	**venga** **vengas** **venga** **vengamos** **vengáis** **vengan**	**viniera** **vinieras** **viniera** **viniéramos** **vinierais** **vinieran**
ver *to see*	**visto** viendo	**veo** **ves** **ve** **vemos** **veis** **ven**	**veía** **veías** **veía** **veíamos** **veíais** **veían**	vi viste vio vimos visteis vieron	veré verás verá veremos veréis verán	vería verías vería veríamos veríais verían	**vea** **veas** **vea** **veamos** **veáis** **vean**	viera vieras viera viéramos vierais vieran

Commands

Person	valer		venir		ver	
	Affirmative	Negative	Affirmative	Negative	Affirmative	Negative
tú	vale	no **valgas**	**ven**	no **vengas**	**ve**	no **veas**
usted	**valga**	no **valga**	**venga**	no **venga**	**vea**	no **vea**
ustedes	**valgan**	no **valgan**	**vengan**	no **vengan**	**vean**	no **vean**
nosotros	**valgamos**	no **valgamos**	**vengamos**	no **vengamos**	**veamos**	no **veamos**
vosotros	valed	no **valgáis**	venid	no **vengáis**	**ved**	no **veáis**

*Similar verb to **venir: prevenir**

Appendix B: Prefixes and Suffixes

Prefixes

Prefix	Meaning and use	Example	English
ante-	before	antenoche, antepasado	last night, ancestor
des-	lack of a quality	desatento/a, desafortunado/a	inattentive, unfortunate
en-/em-	used to form verbs	envejecer, emparejar	to get old, to pair/to match
ex-	previous; used with professions or roles	el expresidente, el exmarido	ex-president, ex-husband
in-/im-	lack of	inconveniente, imperfecto/a	inconvenient, imperfect
infra-	below a standard	infrahumano/a	subhuman
mega-	large, 1,000	el megáfono, el megavatio	megaphone, megawatt
micro-	small, 1/100	el microondas, el microgramo	microwave, microgram
multi-	many	multicolor, multimedia	multicolor, multimedia
post-/pos-	after	posponer, postoperatorio, el postgrado	postpone, postoperative, postgraduate
pre-	before	predecir, el precontrato	to predict, pre-contract
super-	high degree of a quality	superbuen/a, el superhombre	extra good, superman
ultra-	beyond, more than	ultramoderno/a	ultramodern
vice-	second	el vicepresidente	vice president

Suffixes

Sufffix	Meaning and use	Example	English
-able	able to; used in adjectives	adorable, criticable, pasable	adorable, criticizable, passable
-ado, -ido	past participle endings	he hablado, he comido	I have spoken, I have eaten
-ado/a -ido/a	ending of the past participle used as adjective	está cansado/a, está vencido/a	he/she is tired; he/she is defeated
-ancia	feminine noun ending	la ambulancia, la importancia	ambulance, importance
-ano/a	most common ending of adjectives of nationality	cubano/a, colombiano/a, venezolano/a	Cuban, Colombian, Venezuelan
-ante	ending of adjectives formed from verbs	abundante, fascinante, interesante	abundant, fascinating, interesting
-ario	collection	el diario, el cuestionario, el diccionario, el horario, el vocabulario	diary, questionnaire, dictionary, schedule, vocabulary
-ción	feminine noun ending	la canción, la estación, la opción, la situación	song, station, option, situation
-dad	feminine noun ending	la ciudad, la vanidad	city, vanity

(continued)

Sufffix	Meaning and use	Example	English
-eño/a	ending of some adjectives of nationality	madrileño/a, panameño/a	from Madrid, from Panama
-ense	ending of some adjectives of nationality	costarricense, estadounidense	from Costa Rica, from the United States
-ería	shop, store	la cafetería, la lechería, la joyería, la panadería	cafeteria, milk store, jewelry store, bakery
-ísimo/a	extremely; used with adjectives	buenísimo/a, riquísimo/a	extremely/very, very good/delicious
-ista	feminine or masculine ending; describes profession, skill or a specific quality	el/la capitalista, el/la lingüista, el/la optimista, el/la dentista	capitalist, linguist, optimist, dentist
-ito/a	diminutive ending	Pedrito, Juanita, la casita, amarillito	little Pedro, little Juana, little house, yellowish (a little yellow)
-mente	ending of some adverbs	actualmente, claramente	presently, clearly
-or/a	person or thing that does something; used with professions, machines and so on	el/la autor/a, el/la editor/a, el/la computador/a, el detector	author, publisher, computer, detector
-s, -es	plural ending of nouns and adjectives	los secretarios, las secretarias, fáciles	secretaries, easy
-tad	feminine noun ending	la libertad, la voluntad	freedom, will

Appendix C: Classroom Expressions

Mandatos plurales (ustedes)	Mandatos singulares (usted)	Mandatos singulares (tú)	Commands
Abran el libro.	Abra el libro.	Abre el libro.	*Open your book(s).*
Aprendan el vocabulario.	Aprenda el vocabulario.	Aprende el vocabulario.	*Learn the vocabulary.*
Cierren el libro.	Cierre el libro.	Cierra el libro.	*Close your book(s).*
Escriban la tarea.	Escriba la tarea.	Escribe la tarea.	*Write the homework.*
Escuchen.	Escuche.	Escucha.	*Listen.*
Estudien la lección.	Estudie la lección.	Estudia la lección.	*Study the lesson.*
Hagan el ejercicio.	Haga el ejercicio.	Haz el ejercicio.	*Do the exercise.*
Lean la lectura.	Lea la lectura.	Lee la lectura.	*Read the passage.*
Levanten la mano.	Levante la mano.	Levanta la mano.	*Raise your hand(s).*
Repasen la gramática.	Repase la gramática.	Repasa la gramática.	*Review the grammar.*
Repitan.	Repita.	Repite.	*Repeat.*
Siéntense.	Siéntese.	Siéntate.	*Sit down.*
Sigan.	Siga.	Sigue.	*Continue.*
Tomen asiento.	Tome asiento.	Toma asiento.	*Have a seat.*
Vayan a la pizarra.	Vaya a la pizarra.	Ve a la pizarra.	*Go to the board.*

Appendix D: *Caminos del jaguar* Video Expressions

A veces se gana y a veces se pierde.   You win some and lose some., 6
A ver si...   Let's see if . . ., 5
¡Adelante!   Come in!, 4
Algo no me suena bien.   Something is not right., 6
¡Anda pronto!   Hurry up!, 4
¡Ánimo!   Cheer up! (Come on!), 11
Antes de que desapareciera...   Before it disappeared . . ., 12
¡Ay, caramba!   Good grief!, 2
¡Cálmese!   Calm down!, 3
Cayó en la trampa.   She fell into the trap., 11
Con permiso.   Excuse me., 2
Con tan corto plazo...   On such short notice . . ., 11
Creyeron que nos habían dejado en la tumba.   They thought they had left us
   for dead., 7
Cueste lo que cueste.   No matter what it costs., 2
¿De qué se trata?   What is it about?, 1
¡Deja en paz ese aparato!   Leave that machine alone!, 6
Di que sí.   Say yes., 1
El fin sí justifica los medios.   The end justifies the means., 11
¡El que ríe último, ríe mejor!   He who laughs last, laughs best!, 8
Ella tuvo que rendirse.   She had to give up., 7
Empecemos desde el principio.   Let's start from the beginning., 7
¿En qué puedo servirles? How may I help you?, 3
¡Eres astuta como un zorro!   You are as clever as a fox!, 9
Es bueno que escuches tu corazón.   It's good that you listen to your heart., 8
Es cuestión de vida o muerte.   It's a matter of life or death., 7
Es más bravo que un león.   He is more courageous than a lion., 7
Eso no importa.   That doesn't matter., 4
Espero que todo salga bien.   I hope all goes well., 8
Está por encima de toda sospecha.   She's above suspicion., 9
Está un poco mareada.   She is a bit dizzy., 8
Esto es una despedida, mis amigos.   This is good-bye, my friends., 6
Estoy a punto de...   I'm about to . . ., 5
Estoy de acuerdo.   I agree., 2
Estoy muerto de hambre.   I'm starving., 3
Fuera de serie.   Out of this world., 12
¡Genial!   Great!, 3
Hace el papel de...   He/She plays the role of . . ., 3
Hágame el favor...   Do me the favor . . ., 6
¡Hay tanto que hacer!   There is so much to do!, 5
¡Imagínate!   Imagine!, 1
Las apariencias engañan.   Things are not always what they seem., 12
Le quita a uno el habla.   It takes your breath away., 5
¿Lo dice en serio?   Are you serious?, 8
Lo siento.   I'm sorry., 1
Me da igual.   It's all the same to me., 3
Me imagino que sí...   I imagine so . . ., 5
Me llamó la atención.   It caught my attention., 8
Me vendría bien...   I wouldn't mind . . ., 4
¡Ni locos!   No way!, 4
No corro el riesgo de ser descubierta.   I won't risk being discovered., 10

No empieces con tus indirectas.   Don't start with your little digs., 10
No es culpa tuya.   It is not your fault., 3
No es para tanto.   There's no need to make such a fuss., 10
No hay de qué preocuparse.   There's nothing to worry about., 9
No hay duda.   There's no doubt., 2
No hay por qué alarmarse.   There's no reason to be alarmed., 8
No le quiero alargar la historia...   To make a long story short . . ., 10
No les haga daño.   Don't harm them., 6
No me cae nada mal.   I don't dislike him at all., 4
No me queda otro recurso...   I have no other choice . . ., 12
No pasa nada.   Nothing is wrong., 5
No puedes perderte de vista.   You won't be out of sight., 3
No puedo quedarme con los brazos cruzados.   I can't just sit around and wait., 5
No queda más remedio.   We have no choice., 7
¿No sabe usted nada de...?   Don't you know anything about . . . ?, 12
No se me había ocurrido.   I hadn't thought of that., 10
No seas tan modesta.   Don't be so modest., 12
No te preocupes.   Don't worry., 4
No tenemos la contraseña.   We don't have the password., 6
No tengo ni la menor idea.   I don't have the slightest idea., 9
No tiene caso pensar en...   There is no point in thinking about . . ., 12
No vale la pena.   It's not worth it., 4
Nos falta lo más difícil.   The hardest part is yet to come., 11
Nunca me ha fallado.   It has never failed me., 9
Nunca se sabe.   One never knows., 10
Ojalá nunca te hubiera hecho caso.   I wish I had never listened to you., 12
Ojalá tengas razón.   I hope you are right., 8
Olvídalo.   Forget it., 1
¿Por qué le he de creer?   Why should I believe you?, 11
Pueden contar conmigo.   You can count on me., 7
Pues no sé.   I really don't know., 1
¡Qué alivio!   What a relief!, 4
¡Qué bueno!   Great!, 1
¡Qué bueno que ya te sientas mejor!   I'm glad you feel better!, 8
¡Qué envidia!   I'm so jealous!, 1
¡Qué exagerado eres!   You are so dramatic!, 1
¡Qué gusto oír tu voz!   It's so nice to hear from you!, 6
¿Qué haría sin ti?   What would I do without you?, 12
¡Qué horror!   How awful!, 3
¡Qué raro!   How strange!, 2
¡Qué sé yo!   What do I know!, 2
Quedé en verla...   We arranged to meet . . ., 11
Quizás ella pueda curarte.   She might be able to cure you., 8
Quizás hayan visto algo.   Perhaps they have seen something., 10
Quizás no lo sepas todo.   Maybe you don't know everything., 9
Se está haciendo pasar...   He is pretending to be . . ., 11
Se fueron sin dejar rastro.   They left without a trace., 10
Se le está acabando el tiempo.   She is running out of time., 11
Se nos fue la luz.   We had a power outage., 10
Se pinchó la llanta.   We have a flat tire., 7
Según sus cuentas...   According to her calculations . . ., 7
Será un placer.   It would be a pleasure., 12
Si no es molestia...   If you don't mind . . ., 2
Si no tiene ningún inconveniente...   If you don't mind . . ., 11
Siempre te metes en líos.   You're always getting in trouble., 3
Sin darse cuenta...   Without realizing it . . ., 7
Sin ti...   Without you . . ., 10
Sobre gustos, no hay nada escrito.   There is no accounting for taste., 9
¡Tenga piedad!   Have pity!, 6
Tengo fondos.   I have means (resources)., 2

Tengo un mal presentimiento.   I have a bad feeling., 2
¿Tienen reservación?   Do you have a reservation?, 5
Todo está arreglado.   Everything is taken care of., 4
Todo está saliendo muy bien.   Everything is turning out really well., 9
¡Vamos!   Let's go!, 1
Ve al grano.   Get to the point., 9
¿Y qué pasó después?   And, what happened afterward?, 5
Ya veremos...   We'll see . . . , 5
Yo cumplí con mi obligación.   I fulfilled my obligation., 9
Yo hago lo que me dé la gana.   I do as I please., 6

Spanish-English Vocabulary

This vocabulary includes most of the active vocabulary presented in the chapters. (Some exceptions are many numbers, some names of cities and countries, and some obvious cognates.) The list also includes many receptive words found throughout the chapters. The definitions are limited to the context in which the words are used in this book. Stem changes are shown for all stem-changing verbs; for example, **cerrar (ie); -ir** verbs that have both a present tense and preterite stem change are shown as **preferir (ie, i), dormir (ue, u)**. Active words are followed by a number that indicates the chapter in which the word appears as an active item; the abbreviation **P** refers to the **Capítulo preliminar.**

The following abbreviations are used:

adj.	adjective	*m.*	masculine
adv.	adverb	*Mex.*	Mexican
f.	feminine	*pl.*	plural
inf.	infinitive	*pron.*	pronoun
Lat. Am.	Latin American	*s.*	singular

A

a to, for, 4; **a bordo** on board, 5; **a fin de que** in order that, 10; **a la (mano) derecha/izquierda** on the right/left(hand side), 7; **a mano** by hand, 10; **a menos que** unless, 10; **a pesar de que** even though, even if, 9; **a pie** on foot, 3; **¡A sus órdenes!** At your service!, 3; **a un precio más bajo** at a lower price, 7; **a veces** at times, 4

abeja (*f.*) bee

abogado/a (*m., f.*) attorney, lawyer, 4

abrazar to hug, embrace, 4

abrigo (*m.*) coat, 7

abril (*m.*) April, 1

abrir to open, 2

abrocharse (el cinturón) to buckle up (seatbelt), 9

abuelo/a (*m., f.*) grandfather/grandmother, 4

aburrido/a bored, 2

acabar to finish; **acabar de** + (*inf.*) to finish; to have just (done something), 2

acceder to access, 9

acción: de acción action (*adj.*), 6

acelerador (*m.*) accelerator, 9

acelerar to accelerate, 7

acercarse to approach

aconsejar to advise, 8

acontecimiento (*m.*) event, 6

acordión (*f.*) accordion, 6

acostarse (ue) to go to bed; to lie down, 3

actitud (*f.*) attitude

actividad (*f.*) activity, P

activo/a active, 8

acto delictivo (*m.*) delinquent act, 11

actor (*m.*) actor, 6

actriz (*f.*) actress, 6

actuación (*f.*) acting, 6

actualidad: de la actualidad at the present time

actuar to act, 6

acuarela (*f.*) watercolor, 10

acuerdo: estar de acuerdo to agree, 5

adelanto (*m.*) advance

además de in addition to, 12

adicción (*f.*) addiction, 11

adiós good-bye, P

adivinar to guess

adjetivo (*m.*) adjective

adolescente (*m., f.*) adolescent, 11

¿adónde? where (to)?

adorno (*m.*) decoration, adornment, 10

advertir (ie, i) to warn

aerolínea (*f.*) airline, 5

aeropuerto (*m.*) airport, 2

afeitarse to shave, 3

aficionado/a (*m., f.*) fan, 6

agente (*m., f.*) agent, 5; **agente de viajes** travel agent, 4

agosto (*m.*) August, 1

agradable pleasant, 1

agradecer (zc) to thank, 4

agregar to add

agua (el) (*f.*) water; **agua mineral** mineral water, 3

aguacero (*m.*) downpour, 3

agudo/a acute

ahí there, 3

ahijado/a (*m., f.*) godson/goddaughter

ahora now, 2

ahorrar to save, 11

airbag (*m.*) airbag, 9

aire (*m.*) air; **aire acondicionado** air conditioner, 9; **al aire libre** outdoors

al (a + el) to the, 3; **al lado de** next to, side by side, 4

alargar to lengthen

alberca (*f.*) swimming pool, 2

alcanzar to reach, catch up with, 3, 11

alcoba (*f.*) bedroom

alegrarse (de) to be happy, 8

alegre happy, 2

alemán (*m.*) German language, 1

alemán/alemana German

alergia (*f.*) allergy; **tener alergia a...** to be allergic to . . . , 8

alérgico: ser alérgico/a a... to be allergic to . . . , 8

alfombra (*f.*) rug, 2

algo something, anything, 4

algodón (*m.*) cotton, 7

alguien someone, somebody, 4

algún, alguno/a some, any, 4; **algunas veces** sometimes, 4

alimentación (*f.*) food; nutrition, 8

alimento (*m.*) food, 8

aliviarse to get better, 8

allá there, over there, 3

allí there, over there, 3

alma (el) (*f.*) soul

almacén (*m.*) department store; warehouse, 2, 7

almacenar to store, 9

almendra (*f.*) almond

almorzar (ue) to have lunch, 3

almuerzo (*m.*) lunch, 3

alojamiento (*m.*) lodging, accommodations, 5

alojar(se) to stay (in a hotel), 5

alquilar to rent, 2; **alquilar videos** to rent videos, 2

alquiler (*m.*) rent, 2

alrededor del around, about

alterado/a upset, 2

alto/a tall, 1; **alta velocidad** (*f.*) high speed, 9

alumno/a (*m., f.*) student, P

amable friendly, 1

amado/a loved

amanecer (zc) to dawn

amar to love

amarillo/a yellow, 1

ambiente (*m.*) atmosphere

ambulante mobile, 7

amenazar to threaten, 11

amigo/a (*m., f.*) friend, P

amistad (*f.*) friendship

amor (*m.*) love; **de amor** (*adj.*), 6

amplio/a spacious, 2

análisis (*m.*) test, exam, 8

anaranjado/a orange, 1

anatomía (*f.*) anatomy, 1

ancho (*m.*) width

andar to walk; to move, 2

ángel (*m.*) angel

angustia (*f.*) worry, 11

anillo (*m.*) ring, 7

anteojos (*m.*) swim goggles, 6

antes (de) before, 4; **antes (de) que** before, 10

antibiótico (*m.*) antibiotic, 8

antipático/a unfriendly, 1

antropología (*f.*) anthropology, 1

anuncio (*m.*) announcement

año (*m.*) year; **tener X años** to be X years old, 3

apagar to turn off, shut off, 9

aparato (*m.*) apparatus, 9

aparecer (zc) to appear

apenas hardly

aperitivo (*m.*) appetizer, 3

apetito (*m.*) appetite; **tener apetito** to have an appetite, 8

aplicación (*f.*) application (tech.), 9

apodo (*m.*) nickname

apogeo (*m.*) height, 12

apoyar to support, 11

apoyo (*m.*) support

aprender to learn, 2

apuntar to point; to make a note of, 9

apuntes (*m. pl.*) notes

aquel/aquella (*adj.*) that (over there), 3

aquél/aquélla (*pron.*) that one (over there), 3

aquellos/as (*adj.*) those (over there), 3

aquéllos/as (*pron.*) those ones (over there), 3

aquí here, 3

árbol (*m.*) tree

archivar to save; to file, 9

archivo (*m.*) computer file, 9

arcilla (*f.*) clay, 10

arena (*f.*) sand; **hacer castillos de arena** to make sandcastles, 5

arete (*m.*) earring, 7

argumento (*m.*) plot, 6

arma (*f.*) weapon, 11

armario (*m.*) wardrobe, 2

armonía (*f.*) harmony

armonioso/a harmonious, 11

arqueología (*f.*) archaeology, 1

arqueólogo/a (*m., f.*) archaeologist, 4

arquitecto/a (*m., f.*) architect, 4

arrancar to start (a car, a race), 9

arreglar (la cama) to make, fix up (the bed), 2

arrestar to arrest, 11

arte (*m.*) (**las artes**) (*f. pl.*) art (the arts), 1; **arte abstracto** abstract art, 10; **arte clásico** classic art, 10; **arte contemporáneo** contemporary art, 10; **arte moderno** modern art, 10

artesanía (*f.*) craft, 7

artesano/a (*m., f.*) artisan, 10

artículo (*m.*) article

artista (*m., f.*) artist, 1, 4, 10

ascensor (*m.*) elevator, 5

asesinar to assassinate, murder, 11

asesinato (*m.*) assassination, murder, 11

asesino/a (*m., f.*) murderer, 11

asiento (*m.*) seat, 9

aspiradora (*f.*) vacuum cleaner, 2

aspirar (la alfombra) to vacuum the rug, 2

aspirina (*f.*) aspirin, 8

atender (ie) to attend to, wait on, 5

atleta (*m., f.*) athlete, 4

atractivo/a attractive, 1

audífonos (*m. pl.*) headphones, 6

aumentar to increase, 11

aunque even when, though, even if, although, 9

aurorretrato (*m.*) self-portrait, 10

auto (*m.*) car, 9

autobús (*m.*) bus, 3

autóctono/a indigenous

automático/a automatic, 9

automóvil (*m.*) car, automobile, 3, 9

averiguar to find out, 5

avión (*m.*) plane, 3

avisar to advise; to warn, 5

ayer yesterday

ayuda (*f.*) help, 9

azúcar (*m., f.*) sugar

azul blue, 1

azulejo (*m.*) tile

B

bailar to dance, 2, 6

bailarín/bailarina (*m., f.*) dancer, 6

bajar to download, 9; **bajar (por) (la calle)** to go (down) (a street), 7

bajo under, 4

bajo/a short (in height), 1

balada (*f.*) ballad, 6

balcón (*m.*) balcony, 2

ballena (*f.*) whale, 11

balón (*m.*) (beach) ball, 5, 6

baloncesto (*m.*) basketball, 6

banda (*f.*) band, 6

bañarse to take a bath, 3

bañera (*f.*) bathtub, 2

baño (cuarto de) (*m.*) bathroom, 2

bar (mini) (*m.*) (mini)bar, 5

barato/a inexpensive, 2

barco (*m.*) boat, 3

barrer (el piso) to sweep (the floor), 2

barrio (*m.*) neighborhood

barro (*m.*) clay, 7, 10

básquetbol (*m.*) basketball, 6

bastante enough; **Bastante bien, gracias.** Pretty well, thanks., P

basura (*f.*) garbage

basurero (*m.*) garbage can, 1

bate (*m.*) baseball bat, 6

batería (*f.*) drum set, 6; battery, 9

baúl (*m.*) trunk, 9

bebé (*m., f.*) baby, 4

beber to drink, 2; **¿Qué desean beber?** What would you like to drink?, 3

béisbol (*m.*) baseball, 6

belleza (*f.*) beauty

bello/a beautiful, 5

beneficio (*m.*) benefit, 11

biblioteca (*f.*) library, 2

bicicleta (*f.*) bicycle, 3, 6

bien well; **Muy bien, gracias.** Very well, thank you., P

bienestar (*m.*) well-being, 8
¡Bienvenido! Welcome!, P
billete (*m.*) ticket, 6
biología (*f.*) biology, 1
bisabuelo/a (*m., f.*) great grandfather/great grandmother, 4
bistec (*m.*) steak, 3
blanco/a white, 1
blues (*m. pl.*) blues, 6
blusa (*f.*) blouse, 7
boca (*f.*) mouth, 8
boda (*f.*) wedding
bolígrafo (*m.*) pen, 1
bolsa (*f.*) purse, bag, 7; **bolsa de aire** airbag, 9
bombero/a (*m., f.*) firefighter, 4
bombillo (*m.*) lightbulb, 11
bonito/a pretty, 1
borracho/a drunk, 2
borrador (*m.*) chalkboard eraser, 1
bosque (*m.*) forest
bosquejo (*m.*) sketch, 10
bota (*f.*) boot, 7
botón (*m.*) button, 9
botones (*m.*) porter, 5
boutique (*m.*) boutique, 7
boxeo (*m.*) boxing, 6
brazo (*m.*) arm, 8
brillar to shine, sparkle
brisa (*f.*) breeze, 3
bronce (*m.*) bronze, 10
bronceador solar (*m.*) sunscreen, 5
broncearse to get a tan, 5
bucear to go skindiving, snorkeling, 5
bueno/a good, 1; **¡Buen viaje!** Have a nice trip!, 5; **Buenas noches.** Good evening./Good night., P; **Buenas tardes.** Good afternoon., P; **Buenos días.** Good morning., P; **es bueno** it's good , 8
bufanda (*f.*) scarf, 7
burlarse de to make fun of, 10
buscador (*m.*) search engine, 9
buscar to look for, 2; **buscar conchas** to look for shells, 5
búsqueda (*f.*) search
buzón (*m.*) mailbox, 5

C

caballo (*m.*) horse, 11
cabeza (*f.*) head, 8
caer to fall, 4; **caer bien/mal** to like/dislike (a person), 4
café (*m.*) (color) brown, 1; café, 2; coffee, 3
caja (*f.*) cash register, 7; box

cajero automático (*m.*) automated teller machine (ATM), 5
calavera (*f.*) skull, 10
calcetín (*m.*) sock, 7
calculadora (*f.*) calculator, 1
calendario (*m.*) calendar, 1
calentamiento global (*m.*) global warming
caliente hot (temperature), 3
calle (*f.*) street, 2
calmado/a calm, 2
calor: hace calor it's hot, 3; **tener calor** to be hot, feel hot, 3
caloría (*f.*) calorie, 8
cama (*f.*) bed, 1
cámara (*f.*) camera, 9
camarero/a, (*m., f.*) waiter/waitress, 3
cambiar to exchange; **¿Dónde puedo cambiar el dinero?** Where can I exchange money?, 5
cambio de dinero/moneda (*m.*) money exchange, 5
caminar to walk, 2
caminata (*f.*) walking, 6
camión (*m.*) truck, bus (*Mex.*), 3
camioneta (*f.*) minivan; pickup truck, 3
camisa (*f.*) shirt, 7
camiseta (*f.*) T-shirt, 7
cancha (*f.*) court, field, 6
canción (*f.*) song, 6
cansado/a tired, 2
cantante (*m., f.*) singer, 6
cantar to sing, 2, 6
cantidad (*f.*) quantity, 8
capa de ozono (*f.*) ozone layer, 11
cara (*f.*) face, 3, 8
cárcel (*f.*) prison, 11
cargar to charge, 9
caribeño/a Caribbean
carne (*f.*) meat, 3
caro/a expensive, 2
carpeta (*f.*) folder, 1
carpintero/a (*m., f.*) carpenter, 4
carretera (*f.*) highway, 9
carro (*m.*) car, automobile, 3, 9
carta (*f.*) menu, 3
cartel (*m.*) poster, 1
cartelera (*f.*) listing, billboard, 6
cartero/a (*m., f.*) mail carrier, 4
casa (*f.*) house, 2
casado: estar casado/a to be married, 4
casarse (con) to get married (to), 4
cascada (*f.*) waterfall
casco (*m.*) helmet, 6
casi almost; **casi siempre/nunca/nada** almost always/never/nothing, 4

caso: en caso de que in case, 10
castañuela (*f.*) castanet, 6
castillo (*m.*) castle; **hacer castillos de arena** to make sandcastles, 5
categoría (*f.*) category, 6
catarro (*m.*) cold; **tener catarro** to have a cold, 8
catorce fourteen, 1
CD (*m.*) compact disc, CD, 6
celebrar to celebrate, 10
celoso/a jealous, 2
cena (*f.*) dinner, 3
cenar to have dinner, 3
centro comercial (*m.*) shopping center, 2
cepillarse to brush, 3; **cepillarse los dientes** to brush one's teeth
cerámica (*f.*) ceramics, 10
ceramista (*m., f.*) ceramist, potter, 10
cerca de close to, 4; **estar cerca (de)** to be close (to), 3
cerebro (*m.*) brain, 8
ceremonia (*f.*) ceremony, 10
cereza (*f.*) cherry
cero zero, 1
cerrar (ie) to close, 3
certeza (*f.*) certainty
cerveza (*f.*) beer, 3
cesta (*f.*) wicker basket, 6
chaqueta (*f.*) jacket, 7
Chao. Bye., P
cheque de viajero (*m.*) traveler's check, 5
chico/a (*m., f.*) boy, girl, P, 4
chino (*m.*) Chinese language, 1
chino/a Chinese, 1
chistoso/a funny
chocar to collide, 9
chofer (*Lat. Am.*) / **chófer** (*Spain*) (*m.*) chauffeur, 3
choque (*m.*) crash, 9
chorizo (*m.*) sausage, 3
chubasco (*m.*) downpour, 3
ciclismo (*m.*) biking, 6
cielo (*m.*) sky, 3
cien one hundred, 1
ciencia ficción science fiction, 6; **de ciencia ficción** (*adj.*), 6
ciencias (médicas, naturales, políticas, sociales) (*f. pl.*) (medical, natural, political, social) sciences, 1
científico/a scientific
ciento noventa y nueve one hundred ninety-nine, 1
ciento uno one hundred one, 1
cierto/a certain, true; **(no) es cierto** it's (not) certain, true, 8
cifra (*f.*) figure, 12

cinco   five, 1
cincuenta   fifty, 1
cine (*m.*)   movies; movie theater, 2, 6
cinturón (*m.*)   belt, 7; **abrocharse el cinturón**   to buckle up seatbelt, 9; **cinturón de seguridad**   seatbelt, 9
cita (*f.*)   appointment, 8; **hacer una cita**   to make an appointment, 8
ciudad (*f.*)   city, 2
claro/a   light, 10; **¡Claro que sí!**   Of course!, 7; **(no) está claro**   it's (not) clear, 8
clase (*f.*)   class, P
claxon (*m.*)   horn, 9
cliente (*m., f.*)   customer, 7
clima (*m.*)   climate, 3
clóset (*m.*)   closet, 2
club (*m.*)   club (nightclub), 5
cobre (*m.*)   copper, 7
coche (*m.*)   car, automobile, 3, 9
cocina (*f.*)   kitchen, 2
cocinar   to cook, 2
cocinero/a (*m., f.*)   cook, 4
códice (*m.*)   codex, 12
cola (*f.*)   tail; **hacer cola**   to stand in line
coleccionista (*m., f.*)   collector, 10
colgar (ue)   to hang (up), 9, 10
collar (*m.*)   necklace, 7
colocar   to place, put
color: en color(es)   in color, 10
combustible (*m.*)   fuel, 11
comedia (*f.*)   comedy, 6
comedor (*m.*)   dining room, 2
comenzar (ie)   to start, begin, 3
comer   to eat, 2; **¿Qué desean comer?**   What would you like to eat?, 3
cómico/a   funny, 1, 6
comida (*f.*)   food; dinner/lunch, 3
¿cómo?   how?, P; **¿Cómo está usted?/¿Cómo estás tú?**   How are you?, P; **¿Cómo se dice...?**   How do you say . . . ?, P; **¿Cómo se llama usted?/¿Cómo te llamas?**   What's your name?, P; **¿Cómo se llega a...?**   How does one get to . . . ?, 7
cómoda (*f.*) dresser, 2
cómodo/a   comfortable, 5
compacto/a   compact, 9
compañero/a (de clase/de cuarto) (*m., f.*)   classmate, roommate, P
compartir   to share, 2
competencia (*f.*)   competition
completo/a   complete, 2
componer   to compose
comportamiento (*m.*)   behavior, 11

composición (*f.*)   composition, 1
comprador/a (*m., f.*)   buyer, 7
comprar   to buy, 2
compras: ir de compras   to go shopping, 7
comprender   to understand, 2
computador/a (*m., f.*)   computer, 1; **computadora portátil** (*f.*)   laptop, 9
comunidad (*f.*)   community, 11
con   with, 2, 4; **con desayuno**   with breakfast, 5; **con media pensión**   with two meals, 5; **Con permiso.**   Excuse me., P; **con tal (de) que**   provided that, 10; **con vista al mar**   with an ocean view, 5
concernir (ie)   to concern, 3
concierto (*m.*)   concert, 6
condenar   to condemn
conducir (zc)   to drive, 3, 9
conductor/a (*m., f.*)   driver, 9
conejo (*m.*)   rabbit, 4
conexión (sin cables) (*f.*)   (wireless) connection (WiFi), 9
confirmación (*f.*)   confirmation, 5
confirmar   to confirm, 5
confundido/a   confused, 2
conjunto (*m.*)   group, band, 6
conocer (zc)   to know, be familiar with, 3
conquista (*f.*)   conquest, 12
consecuencia (*f.*)   consequence, 11
conseguir (i, i)   to get, obtain, 3
consejero/a (*m., f.*)   counselor, 4
consejo (*m.*)   advice, 11
conserje (*m., f.*)   concierge, 5
conservar   to conserve, preserve, 11
conservarse (sano/a)   to keep oneself (healthy), 8
construir   to construct, build, 2
consultorio médico (*m.*)   doctor's office, 8
consumir   to consume, 8
consumo (*m.*)   consumption, 11
contador/a (*m., f.*)   accountant, 4
contaminación (*f.*)   pollution, contamination, 11
contaminar   to pollute, contaminate, 11
contar (ue)   to count, 3; to tell
contener   to contain, 3
contento/a   happy, 2; **estar contento/a de**   to be happy, 8
contestar   to answer, 4
contraseña (*f.*)   password, 9
contraste (*m.*)   contrast, 10
contribuir   to contribute
control remoto (*m.*)   remote control, 9
convertir (ie, i)   to change, convert, 11

convivir   to live with, 10
copa (*f.*)   stemmed glass, goblet, 3
copiar   to copy, 9
coraje (*m.*)   anger
corazón (*m.*)   heart, 8
corbata (*f.*)   tie, 7
correo (*m.*)   post office, 2; **correo electrónico**   e-mail, 9
correr   to run, 2
corrida de toros (*f.*)   bullfight
corto/a   short (length), 1
cosecha (*f.*)   harvest
costar (ue)   to cost, 3; **¿Cuánto cuesta... ?**   How much does . . . cost?, 5
costumbre (*f.*)   custom, 10
crear   to create, 10
creatividad (*f.*)   creativity
creativo/a   creative
crecimiento (*m.*)   growth, 12
creer   to think, believe, 2, 8; **no creer**   to not believe, 8
criado/a (*m., f.*)   servant, maid, 4
crimen (*m.*)   crime, 11
crítica (*f.*)   criticism, 6
criticar   to criticize, 6
crucero (*m.*)   cruise ship, 3
cruz (*f.*)   cross, 10
cruzar   to cross, 7
cuaderno (*m.*)   notebook, 1
cuadra (*f.*)   street block, 7
cuadro (*m.*)   painting, picture, 10
¿cuál?   which?, what?, P
cualquier (*adj.*)   any
cuando   when, 9
¿cuándo?   when?, P
cuanto: en cuanto   as soon as, 9
¿cuánto/a/s?   how much?, how many?, P; **¿A cuánto está la temperatura?**   What is the temperature?, 3; **¿Cuánto cuesta... ?**   How much does . . . cost?, 5; **¿En cuánto me lo(s)/la(s) deja?**   How much will you charge me for it/them?, 7
cuarenta   forty, 1
cuarto/a   fourth
cuarto (*m.*)   quarter (of an hour), 1
cuarto de baño (*m.*)   bathroom, 2
cuatro   four, 1
cuchara (*f.*)   tablespoon, 3
cucharadita (*f.*)   teaspoon, 3
cuchillo (*m.*)   knife, 3
cuenta (*f.*)   bill, 3; **La cuenta, por favor.**   The check, please., 3
cuerpo (*m.*)   body, 8
cuidado: tener cuidado   to be careful, 3, 7
cuidarse   to take care of oneself, 8
culebra (*f.*)   snake

culpable (*m., f.*) guilty one
cumpleaños (*m.*) birthday
cuñado/a (*m., f.*) brother-in-law/
  sister-in-law, 4
cura (*f.*) cure, 11; (*m.*) priest
curandero/a (*m., f.*) healer, 8
curar to cure, 8

D

dañar to harm, 8; to injure; to
  damage, 9
dar to give, 3, 4; **dar la vuelta** to
  turn around, 7; **dar un paseo** to
  take a walk, 2
de of, from, 1, 4; **de acción**
  action (*adj.*), 6; **de amor** love
  (*adj.*), 6; **de ciencia ficción**
  science fiction (*adj.*), 6; **de habla
  española** Spanish-speaking, 12;
  de horror, de terror horror
  (*adj.*), 6; **de la mañana/tarde/
  noche** in the morning/after-
  noon/evening (for specific time
  periods), 1; **de misterio** mystery
  (*adj.*), 6; **De nada.** You're welcome., P; **de suspenso** thriller
  (*adj.*), 6; **de vaqueros** western
  (*adj.*), 6; **de vez en cuando** from
  time to time, 4
debajo de beneath, under, 4
deber to owe, 4; should, 4
debido a because of
decaer to decline, 12
decidir to decide, 2
decir (i) to say, tell, 3; **¿Cómo se
  dice... ?** How do you say . . . ?,
  P; **¿Qué quiere decir... ?** What
  does . . . mean?, P
dedo (*m.*) finger, 8; **dedo del pie**
  toe, 8
definición (*f.*) definition; **alta
  definición** high definition, 9
deforestación (*f.*) deforestation, 11
dejar to leave (something
  behind), 3
del (de + el) of the, 2
delante de in front of, 4
delectivo: acto delectivo (*m.*)
  delinquent act, 11
delfín (*m.*) dolphin, 11
delgado/a thin, 1
delincuencia (*f.*) delinquency, 11
delincuente (*m., f.*) delinquent, 11
dentista (*m., f.*) dentist, 4
dentro de inside of, 4
depender to depend, 8
dependiente (*m., f.*) store clerk, 7
deporte (*m.*) sport, 6

deportista (*m., f.*) athlete; sports
  enthusiast, 6
deportivo (*m.*) sports car, 9
depresión (*f.*) depression, 11
deprimido/a depressed, 2
derecha: a la (mano) derecha on
  the right(hand side), 7
derecho (*m.*) law, right; **seguir
  derecho** to go straight, 7
desafiar to challenge
desagradable unpleasant, 1
desamparados (*m. pl.*) homeless
  people, 11
desamparo (*m.*) trouble,
  helplessness
desaparición (*f.*) disappearance
desarrollado/a developed, 12
desarrollar to develop
desastre (*m.*) disaster
desayunar to have breakfast, 3
desayuno (*m.*) breakfast, 3; **con
  desayuno** with breakfast, 5
descansar to rest, 5
descendiente (*m., f.*) descendant, 12
desconocido/a unknown
describir to describe, 2
desde from, since, 4; **desde ahora**
  from now on
desear to wish for, 2; to want, 8;
  ¿Qué desean comer/beber?
  What would you like to eat/
  drink?, 3
desechado/a discarded,
  disposed, 11
desechar to dispose, discard, 11
desembarque (*m.*) unloading, 5
desempeñar to carry out, 9
desempleo (*m.*) unemployment, 11
desesperado: estar desesperado/a
  to be desperate, 11
desfile (*m.*) parade, 10
desilusionado/a disappointed, 2
despacio slowly, 7; **más despacio**
  more slowly, P
despedida (*f.*) farewell, 5
despedir (i, i) to fire (from a job)
despedirse (i, i) to say good-bye, 5
desperdicios nucleares (*m. pl.*)
  nuclear waste, 11
despertador (*m.*) alarm clock, 5
despertarse (ie) to wake up, 3
después after, afterwards, 3;
  después de after, 4; **después (de)
  que** after, 9
destacar(se) to stand out, 12
destruir to destroy, 2
detalle (*m.*) detail, 10
deterioro (*m.*) deterioration, 11
detrás de behind, 4

devolver (ue) to return (something), 7
día (*m.*) day, 1
diariamente daily, 8
dibujante (*m., f.*) illustrator, 10
dibujar to draw, 10
dibujo (*m.*) drawing, 10
diciembre (*m.*) December, 1
dictador (*m.*) dictator
dictadura (*f.*) dictatorship
diente (*m.*) tooth, 3, 8
dieta (*f.*) diet, 8
diez ten, 1
difícil difficult, 1
digital digital, 9
dinero money; **cambio de dinero**
  (*m.*) money exchange, 5; **(dinero
  en) efectivo** (*m.*) cash, 5; **¿Dónde
  puedo cambiar el dinero?** Where
  can I exchange money?, 5
dióxido de carbono (*m.*) carbon
  dioxide, 11
dirección (*f.*) address, 3, 7
director (*m.*) director, 6
directorio (*m.*) directory, 9
dirigir to direct, 6
disco (*m.*) record, album, 7; **disco
  compacto, CD** compact disc,
  CD, 6; **disco duro** hard drive, 9
discoteca (*f.*) discotheque, 5
discurso (*m.*) speech
diseñador/a (*m., f.*) designer
diseñar to design
diseño (*m.*) design
disfraz (*m.*) costume, 10
disfrutar to enjoy, 3; **¡Qué
  disfrute/n de su estadía!** Enjoy
  your stay!, 5
disponible available, 9
distinguir(se) to distinguish, 12
distinguido/a distinguished
divertirse (ie, i) to have a good
  time, enjoy oneself, 3
divorciado: estar divorciado/a to
  be divorced, 4
doblar (a) to fold, to bend,
  to turn, 7
doble double, 5
doce twelve, 1
doctor/a (*m., f.*) doctor, P
documento (*m.*) document, 9
doler (ue) to hurt, 8
dolor (*m.*) pain; **tener dolor** to
  have pain, 8
domingo (*m.*) Sunday, 1
don (D.) (*m.*) title of respect with
  first name, P
¿dónde? where?, P; **¿Dónde puedo
  cambiar el dinero?** Where can I
  exchange money?, 5; **¿Me puede**

decir dónde está/n... ? Can you tell me where . . . is/are?, 7

doña (Dña.) (*f.*) title of respect with first name, P

dorado/a golden, 10

dormir (ue, u) to sleep, 3; **dormirse (ue, u)** to fall asleep, 3

dormitorio (*m.*) bedroom, 1, 2

dos two, 1

drama (*m.*) drama, 6

dramaturgo/a (*m., f.*) playwright

drogadicción (*f.*) drug addiction, 11

ducha (*f.*) shower, 2

ducharse to take a shower, 3

duda doubt; **no hay duda (de)** there's no doubt, 8

dudar to doubt, 8; **no dudar** to not doubt, 8

dueño/a (*m., f.*) owner, 2

dulce sweet, 3

durante during, 4

E

ecológico/a ecological, 11

economía (*f.*) economics, 1

económico/a economical, 9

edificio (*m.*) building, 2

efectivo: (dinero en) efectivo (*m.*) cash, 5

efecto invernadero (*m.*) greenhouse effect, 11

ejemplo (*m.*) example

ejercicio: hacer ejercicio to exercise, 2

el (*m.*) the, 1

él (*m.*) he, him, 1, 4

electricista (*m., f.*) electrician, 4

elefante (*m.*) elephant, 11

elegancia (*f.*) elegance, 5

elegir (i, i) to choose

elevador (*m.*) elevator, 5

ella (*f.*) she, her, 1, 4

ellos/as (*m., f.*) they, them, 1, 4

embarazada: estar embarazada to be pregnant, 8

embarazo (*m.*) pregnancy, 11

embarque (*m.*) loading, 5

emocionado/a excited, 2

empeorar to worsen

empezar (ie) to begin, 3

empleo (*m.*) employment, 11

en in, on, at, 1; by (with transportation), in, on, at, 3, 4; **en blanco y negro** (in) black and white, 10; **en caso de que** in case, 10; **en color(es)** in color, 10; **en cuanto** as soon as, 9; **en este momento** at this moment,

now, 2; **en grupos** in groups, P; **en línea** online, 9; **en oferta** on sale, 7; **en parejas** in pairs, P

enamorado/a in love, 2; **estar enamorado/a** to be in love, 4

enamorarse (de) to fall in love (with), 4

encantar to delight, like very much (love), 4

encarcelar to imprison, 11

encender (ie) to turn on, 9

encima de on top of, above, 4

encontrar (ue) to find, 3; **encontrarse (con)** to meet (with) someone, 5

encuesta (*f.*) survey

energía (*f.*) energy, 11

enero (*m.*) January, 1

enfermarse to get sick, 8

enfermedad (*f.*) illness, 8

enfermero/a (*m., f.*) nurse, 4

enfermo/a sick, 2

enfoque (*m.*) focus

enfrentar to confront, face up to, 11

enfrente de in front of, facing, 4

enojado/a angry, 2

enojarse to be angry, 8

enorme enormous, huge

ensalada (mixta/rusa) (*f.*) (mixed/potato) salad, 3

ensayo (*m.*) essay

enseñar to teach, 4

entender (ie) to understand, 3

enterrar (ie) to bury

entonces then, at that time, 3

entrada (*f.*) ticket, 6

entrar to enter, 9

entre between, among, 4

entregar to hand in, deliver, 4

entremés (*m.*) appetizer, 3

entrenador/a (*m., f.*) trainer, 6

entrenar to train, 6

entretener to entertain, 3

entretenimiento (*m.*) entertainment, 9

entusiasmado/a enthusiastic, 2

enviar to send, 4

envidioso/a envious, 1

equilibrio (*m.*) balance

equipaje (*m.*) luggage, 5

equipo (*m.*) team; equipment, 6

escaleras (*f. pl.*) stairs, 2

escalofríos: tener escalofríos to shiver, have a chill, 8

escapar to escape

escaparate (*m.*) store window, 7

escaso/a scarce, 11

escena (*f.*) scene, 6

escoba (*f.*) broom, 2

escolar scholastic

esconder to hide

escribir to write, 2; **escribir cartas** to write letters, 2

escritor/a (*m., f.*) writer

escritorio (*m.*) desk, 1

escritura (*f.*) writing, 12

escuchar to listen, 2

escuela (*f.*) school, 1

escultor/a (*m., f.*) sculptor, 4, 10

escultura (*f.*) sculpture, 10

ese/a (*adj.*) that, 3

ése/a, eso (*pron.*) that (one), 3

esencial: es esencial it's essential, 8

esmeralda (*f.*) emerald, 7

esos/as (*adj.*) those, 3

ésos/as (*pron.*) those (ones), 3

espalda (*f.*) back, 8

español (*m.*) Spanish language, 1

español/a Spanish, 1

especialización (*f.*) major, 1

especie (*f.*) species, 11

espectador/a (*m., f.*) spectator, 6

espejo (*m.*) mirror, 2; **espejo retrovisor** rear-view mirror, 9

esperanza (*f.*) hope

esperar to hope, 8

espíritu (*m.*) spirit

esposo/a (*m., f.*) husband/wife, 4

esquí (*m.*) ski; skiing, 6; **hacer esquí acuático** to water ski, 5

esquiar to ski, 6

esquina (*f.*) corner, 7

estable stable, firm

estación de tren (*f.*) train station, 2

estacionamiento (*m.*) parking lot, 5

estacionar to park, 7

estadía (*f.*) stay; **¡Qué disfrute/n de su estadía!** Enjoy your stay!, 5

estadio (*m.*) stadium, 2

estancia (*f.*) stay, 5

estante (*m.*) bookshelf, 1

estar to be, 2; **estar a punto de** to be on the verge of, 5; **estar cerca/lejos (de)** to be close/far away (from), 3; **estar de acuerdo** to agree, 5; **estar de moda** to be in style, 7; **estar muerto/a de hambre** to be starving, famished, 3; **estar resfriado/a** to have a cold, 8; **estar de vacaciones** to be on vacation, 5

estatua (*f.*) statue, 10

estatura (*f.*) stature

este (*m.*) east, 3

este/a (*adj.*) this, 3

éste/a, esto (*pron.*) this (one), 3

estilo (*m.*) style

estómago (*m.*) stomach, 8

estornudar to sneeze, 8

estos/as (*adj.*)   these, 3
éstos/as (*pron.*)   these (ones), 3
estrecho/a   tight, 7
estrenar   to premiere, 6
estuco (*m.*)   stucco
estudiante (*m., f.*)   student, P
estudiar   to study, 2
estufa (*f.*)   stove, 2
etnia (*f.*) ethnic group
étnico/a   ethnic, 12
europeo/a   European
evidente: (no) es evidente   it's (not) evident, 8
evitar   to avoid, 8
examen físico (*m.*)   physical exam, 8
excepcional   exceptional, 1
excursión (*f.*)   excursion, tour, 5
exhibición (*f.*)   exhibition, art exhibit, performance, 10
existencia (*f.*)   existence, 11
éxito: tener éxito   to be successful, 3
exitoso/a   successful
explicar   to explain, 4
exploración (*f.*)   exploration, 12
explotar   to exploit, 11
exposición (*f.*)   art exhibit, 10
extinción (*f.*)   extinction, 11
extranjero/a   foreign, 6
extraño/a   strange, 8

F

fabricar   to make, 10
fácil easy, 1
facultad (*f.*)   School (as in School of Humanities), 1
falda (*f.*)   skirt, 7
faltar   to lack, need; to be left (to do), 4
fama (*f.*)   fame, 6
fanático/a (*m., f.*)   fan, 6
farmacia (*f.*)   pharmacy, 7
fascinado/a   fascinated, 2
fascinante   fascinating, 1
fascinar   to fascinate, 4
fauna (*f.*)   animal life
fax (*m.*)   fax, 9
febrero (*m.*)   February, 1
fecha (*f.*)   date, 1
feliz   happy; **¡Feliz viaje!**   Have a nice trip!, 5
feo/a   ugly, 1
festejarse   to celebrate, 10
festival (*m.*)   festival, 10
fiebre: tener fiebre   to have a fever, 8
figura (*f.*)   figure, 10
fijarse   to notice, pay attention

filmar   to film, 6
filme (*m.*)   film, 6
filosofía (*f.*)   philosophy, 1
finca (*f.*)   property; farm
física (*f.*)   physics, 1
físico/a   physical, 8
fisiología (*f.*)   physiology, 1
flamenco (*m.*)   Spanish-style music, 6
flan (*m.*)   baked egg custard, 3
flauta (*f.*)   flute, 6
flojo/a   lazy, 1; loose, 7
flor (*f.*)   flower
flora (*f.*)   flora
florería (*f.*)   florist, 7
folclórico/a, folklórico/a   folkloric, 10
folleto (*m.*)   brochure, 5
forma (*f.*)   form, 10
fotógrafo/a (*m., f.*)   photographer, 4
fracasar   to fail, 11
fractura (*f.*)   fracture, 8
fracturado/a   broken, fractured, 8
francés (*m.*)   French language, 1
francés/francesa   French, 1
freír (i, i)   to fry, 5
frenar   to brake, 9
frenos (*m.*)   brakes, 9
fresco: hace fresco   it's cool, 3
frijoles (*m.*)   beans
frío: hace frío   it's cold, 3; **tener frío**   to be cold, 3
frito/a   fried, 3
fruta (*f.*)   fruit, 3
fuegos artificiales (*m. pl.*)   fireworks, 10
fuera de   outside of, 4
fuerte   strong, 3; **una comida fuerte**   heavy food, 3
función (*f.*)   function, 9
fundar   to found, 12
fútbol (*m.*)   soccer, 6; **fútbol americano**   football, 6

G

gabinete (*m.*)   closet
gafas de sol (*f. pl.*)   sunglasses, 5
galleta (*f.*)   cookie
gallo (*m.*)   rooster, 11
gamba (*f.*)   shrimp, 3
ganador/a (*m., f.*)   winner; earner
ganar   to win, 6
ganas: tener ganas de + inf.   to want to (do something); to feel like (doing something), 3
ganga (*f.*)   deal, bargain, 7
garaje (*m.*)   garage, 2
garganta (*f.*)   throat, 8
gasolina (*f.*)   gasoline, 9

gastar   to spend (money), 7
gato/a (*m., f.*)   cat, 4
gazpacho (*m.*)   cold vegetable soup, 3
gemelo/a (*m., f.*)   twin
género (*m.*)   genre, 6
gente (*f., s.*)   people, 2
gerente (*m., f.*)   manager, 4
gimnasia (*f.*)   gymnastics, 6
gimnasio (*m.*)   gym, 6
golf (*m.*)   golf, 6
gordo/a   fat, 1
gorra (*f.*)   cap, 7
gorro de baño (*m.*)   swim cap, 6
gozar (de)   to enjoy, 5
grabadora (*f.*)   recorder, 9
grabar   to tape, 6
grados centígrados/Fahrenheit (*m.*)   degrees centigrade/Fahrenheit, 3
grande   big, large, 1; loose (clothes), 7
gratis   free, 7
grave   grave, serious, 8
gripe: tener gripe   to have the flu, 8
gris   gray, 1
gritar   to shout
grupo (*m.*)   group, 6; **en grupos**   in groups, P
guante (*m.*)   glove, baseball glove, 6, 7
guapo/a   handsome, good-looking, 1
guardar   to save; to file, 9
guerra (*f.*)   war, 11
guía (*m., f.*)   tour guide, 5; (*f.*)   guidebook, 5
guión (*m.*)   script, 6
guionista (*m., f.*)   script writer
guitarra (*f.*)   guitar, 6; **guitarra bajo**   bass guitar, 6
guitarrista (*m., f.*)   guitarrist, 6
gustar   to like (be pleasing), 2, 8; **Me gustaría (pedir)...**   I would like (to order) . . ., 3
gusto (*m.*)   pleasure; **El gusto es mío.**   The pleasure is mine., P; **¡Qué gusto!**   What a pleasure!, 5

H

haber (*auxiliary verb*)   to have, 9
hábil   skillful, 10
habitación (*f.*)   room, 5
habitado/a   inhabited, 12
habla: de habla española   Spanish-speaking, 12
hablar   to speak, 2, 4; **hablar con amigos**   to talk with friends, 2

hace: hace buen/mal tiempo it's good/bad weather, 3; **hace calor/frío/fresco** it's hot/cold/cool, 3; **hace viento** it's windy, 3

hacer to do; to make, 3; **hacer castillos de arena** to make sandcastles, 5; **hacer clic** to click (with the mouse); to push a button, 9; **hacer ejercicio** to exercise, 2; **hacer el papel** to play a role, 6; **hacer esquí acuático** to water ski, 5; **hacer surfing** to go surfing, 5; **hacer una cita** to make an appointment, 8; **hacer una llamada (de larga distancia/por cobrar)** to make a (long distance/collect) phone call, 5

hacia toward, 4

hallazgo (*m.*) finding, discovery

hambre (el) (*f.*) hunger, 3; **estar muerto/a de hambre** to be starving, famished, 3; **tener hambre** to be hungry, 3; **¡Tengo mucha hambre!** I am very hungry!, 3

harto/a fed up, disgusted, 2

hasta until, 4, 7; **Hasta la vista.** Until we meet again., P; **Hasta luego.** See you later., P; **Hasta mañana.** See you tomorrow., P; **hasta que** until, 9

hay there is, there are, 1; **no hay** there isn't; there aren't, 1; **no hay duda (de)** there's no doubt, 8

hecho (*m.*) event, 10

helado (de chocolate, vainilla, fresa) (*m.*) (chocolate, vanilla, strawberry) ice cream, 3

herencia (*f.*) heritage

hermanastro/a (*m., f.*) stepbrother/stepsister, 4

hermano/a (*m., f.*) brother/sister, 4

hermoso/a beautiful, 1

heroico/a heroic

híbrido/a hybrid, 9

hijastro/a (*m., f.*) stepson/stepdaughter, 4

hijo/a (*m., f.*) son/daughter, 4

hip-hop (*m.*) hip-hop, 6

historia (*f.*) history, 1

histórico/a historical, 10

hockey (*m.*) hockey, 6

hombre (*m.*) man, 1; **hombre de negocios** businessman, 4

hora (*f.*) hour; **¿Qué hora es?** What time is it?, 1

horario (*m.*) schedule, 1

horror: de horror horror (*adj.*), 6

hospital (*m.*) hospital, 2

hotel (*m.*) hotel, 2

hoy today, 1; **hoy en día** today; nowadays

huérfano/a (*m., f.*) orphan

hueso (*m.*) bone, 8

huésped (*m., f.*) guest, 5

huir to escape, 4

humanidades (*f. pl.*) humanities, 1

húmedo/a humid, 3

hundirse to drown

huracán (*m.*) hurricane, 3

I

icono (*m.*) icon, 9

idioma (*m.*) language, 1

igualdad (*f.*) equality

iglesia (*f.*) church, 2

Igualmente. Likewise., P

ilustración (*f.*) illustration, 10

ilustrar to illustrate, 10

imagen (*f.*) image, 10

imperio (*m.*) empire, 12

impermeable (*m.*) raincoat, 7

imponente imposing, 12

importante: es importante it's important, 8

importar to matter, be important, be of concern, 4

imposible: es imposible it's impossible, 8

impresora (*f.*) printer, 1

imprimir to print, 9

impuesto (*m.*) tax

inagotable inexhaustible

inalámbrico/a wireless, 9

incendio (*m.*) fire

incertidumbre (*f.*) uncertainty, 11

incierto/a uncertain

incluir to include, 2

indefinido/a indefinite

indígena indigenous

inesperado/a unexpected

infección (*f.*) infection, 8

inflamación (*f.*) inflammation, 8

inflamado/a: estar inflamado/a to be inflamed, 8

informe (*m.*) report

ingeniería (*f.*) engineering, 1

ingeniero/a (*m., f.*) engineer, 4

inglés (*m.*) English language, 1

inglés/inglesa English, 1

iniciar to begin, 9

inmenso/a immense, enormous

inodoro (*m.*) toilet, 2

inquietud (*f.*) worry

inquilino/a (*m., f.*) tenant, 2

instalar to install, 9

inteligente intelligent, 1

interesar to interest, be of interest, 4

interpretar to interpret, 6

intersección (*f.*) corner, 7

intrépido/a daring, fearless

invertir (ie, i) to invest

investigador/a (*m., f.*) researcher

investigar to research, 2

invierno (*m.*) winter, 3

inyección (*f.*) injection, 8

ir to go, 3; **ir de compras** to go shopping, 7; **ir de pesca** to go fishing, 5; **ir por** + person/thing to go for; to pick up, 6; **irse** to go away, leave, 3; **irse de vacaciones** to go on vacation, 5

isla (*f.*) island, 5

italiano (*m.*) Italian language, 1

italiano/a Italian, 1

izquierda: a la (mano) izquierda on the left(hand side), 7

J

jaguar (*m.*) jaguar, 7

jai alai (*m.*) jai alai, 6

jamás never, 4

japonés (*m.*) Japanese language, 1

japonés/japonesa Japanese, 1

jarabe (*m.*) syrup, 8

jardín (*m.*) garden, yard, 2

jardinero/a (*m., f.*) gardener, 4

jazz (*m.*) jazz, 6

jefe/a (*m., f.*) boss, 4

jeroglífico/a hieroglyphic, 12

joven young, 1

joya (*f.*) jewelry, 7

joyería (*f.*) jewelry store, 7

judío/a Jewish

jueves (*m.*) Thursday, 1

jugador/a (*m., f.*) player, 6

jugar (ue) (al) to play (a sport or game), 3, 6; **jugar (al) volibol** to play volleyball, 2, 5; **jugar un papel** to play a role, 6

jugo (*m.*) juice, 3

jugoso/a juicy

juguete (*m.*) toy, 7

julio (*m.*) July, 1

junio (*m.*) June, 1

junto a next to, 4

justicia (*f.*) justice, 11

juventud (*f.*) youth

juzgar to judge, 6

K

kilómetros (por hora) (*m.*) kilometers (per hour), 3

L

la (*f.*)   the
lado (*m.*)   side; **al lado de**   next to, side by side, 4; **(otro) lado**   somewhere else, 7
ladrillo (*m.*)   brick
ladrón/ladrona (*m., f.*)   thief
lago (*m.*)   lake
lamentar   to lament, regret, 8
lámpara (*f.*)   lamp, 1
lana (*f.*)   wool, 7
lápiz (*m.*)   pencil, 1
largo (*m.*)   length
largo/a   long, 1
largometraje (*m.*)   feature film, 6
lástima (*f.*)   shame; **es una lástima**   it's a shame, 8
lavabo (*m.*)   bathroom sink, 2
lavacoche (*m.*)   carwash
lavamanos (*m.*)   bathroom sink, 2
lavandería (*f.*)   laundromat, 7
lavar (los platos)   to wash (the dishes), 2
lección (*f.*)   lesson, 1
leer (libros)   to read (books), 2
legumbre (*f.*)   vegetable, 3
lejos (de)   far from, 4; **estar lejos (de)**   to be far away (from), 3
lengua (*f.*)   tongue, 8
lente (*m.*)   lens
lento/a   slow, 1
letra (*f.*)   lyrics, 6
levantarse   to get up, 3
libertad (*f.*)   liberty, 11
libre   free (independent), 5
librería (*f.*)   bookstore, 2, 7
libro (*m.*)   book, 1
licencia de manejar/conducir (*f.*)   driver's license, 9
lienzo (*m.*)   canvas, 10
ligero/a   light, 3
limón (*m.*)   lemon
limosina (*f.*)   limousine, 5
limpiaparabrisas (*m.*)   windshield wiper, 9
limpiar (el cuarto)   to clean, tidy (the room), 2
lindo/a   lovely, 1
línea: en línea   online, 9
lingüística (*f.*)   linguistics, 1
lingüístico/a   linguistic, 12
lío (*m.*)   problem, 11
listo/a   smart, clever, 1; **estar listo/a**   to be ready, 2
literatura (*f.*)   literature, 1
llamada: hacer una llamada (de larga distancia/por cobrar)   to make a (long distance/collect) phone call, 5

llamar   to call, 2; **¿Cómo se llama usted ?/¿Cómo te llamas?**   What's your name?, P; **Me llamo...**   My name is . . ., P
llamarse   to be named; to be called, P
llanta (*f.*)   tire, 9; **llanta pinchada**   flat tire, 9
llave (*f.*)   key, 1
llegar   to arrive, 2, 3; **¿Cómo se llega a... ?**   How does one get to . . . ?, 7
lleno/a   full
llevar   to bring, 2; to wear; to take, 7
llover (ue)   to rain
lloviznar   to drizzle *(weather)*, 3
lluvia (*f.*)   rain, 3; **lluvia ácida**   acid rain, 11
lograr   to achieve; to obtain, 11
logro (*m.*)   achievement, 11
luchar   to fight, 11
luego   later, then, next, 3; **Hasta luego.**   See you later., P
lugar (*m.*)   place
lujo (*m.*)   luxury, 5
lujoso/a (de lujo)   luxurious, 5
lunes (*m.*)   Monday, 1
luz (*f.*)   light, 9; **luz y sombra**   light and shadow, 10

M

madera (*f.*)   wood, 7, 10
madrastra (*f.*)   stepmother, 4
madre (*f.*)   mother, 1, 4
madrina (*f.*)   godmother
maíz (*m.*)   corn
mal (*m.*)   disease; **estar mal**   to feel ill, P
maleta (*f.*)   suitcase, 5
maletero (*m.*)   trunk, 9
malo/a   bad, 1; **es malo**   it's bad, 8; **Muy mal, bastante mal.**   Very bad, quite bad., P
mamá (*f.*)   mom, 4
mancha (*f.*)   stain, 7
manchado/a   stained, 7
mandar   to send, 2; to order, 8
mandato (*m.*)   order
manejar   to drive, 3, 9
manguera (*f.*)   hose
mano (*f.*)   hand, 3, 8; **a mano**   by hand, 10
mantener   to maintain, 3
manzana (*f.*)   street block, 7
mañana   tomorrow, 1; **de/por la mañana**   in the morning, 1; **Hasta mañana.**   See you tomorrow., P
mapa (*m.*)   map, 1

maquillaje (*m.*)   makeup, 7
maquillarse   to put on makeup, 3
maravilla (*f.*)   wonder
marco (*m.*)   frame, 10
mareado: estar mareado/a   to be dizzy, 8
mariachi (*m.*)   mariachi musician, 6
marisco (*m.*)   shellfish, 3
mármol (*m.*)   marble, 10
martes (*m.*)   Tuesday, 1
marzo (*m.*)   March, 1
más   more; **más despacio**   more slowly, P
máscara (*f.*)   mask, 7
mascota (*f.*)   pet, 4
matar   to kill, 11
matemáticas (*f.*)   mathematics, 1
materia (*f.*)   subject matter, 1
mayo (*m.*)   May, 1
mayor   older, 1; **ser mayor**   to be older, 4
media (*f.*)   half (hour), 1; sock, stocking, 7
medianoche (*f.*)   midnight, 1
mediante   by means of
medicina (*f.*)   medicine, 8
médico/a (*m., f.*)   doctor, 4
medio/a (*adj.*)   half, 7; average; **en medio de**   in the middle of
mediodía (*m.*)   noon, 1
mejor: es mejor   it's better, 8
mejorar   to get better, 8
menor   younger; **ser menor**   to be younger, 4
menos   minus, 1
mensaje (*m.*)   message, 9
mentir (ie, i)   to lie, 3
menú (*m.*)   menu, 3
mercado (*m.*)   marketplace, 7
merecer (zc)   to deserve
merengue (*m.*)   Dominican-style music, 6
mesa (*f.*)   table, 1
mesero/a (*m., f.*)   waiter, waitress, 3
mesita (*f.*)   coffee table, 2; **mesita de noche**   night stand, 2
meteorólogo/a (*m., f.*)   meteorologist, 3
metro (*m.*)   subway, 3
mezcla (*f.*)   mix
mí   me (*direct object*), 4
mi(s)   my, 2
miedo   fear; **tener miedo (de)**   to be afraid (of), 3, 8
miedoso/a   fearful
miembro (*m.*)   member
mientras   while
miércoles (*m.*)   Wednesday, 1
milagro (*m.*)   miracle

millas (por hora) (*f.*)   miles (per hour), 3

minibar (*m.*)   mini bar, 5

mío/a(s) (*m., f.*)   mine, 7

mirada (*f.*)   glance

mirar   to look at, 2; **mirar una película**   to watch a movie, 2

miseria (*f.*)   poverty

misterio: de misterio   mystery (*adj.*), 6

mitad (*f.*)   half, 1

mochila (*f.*)   backpack, 1

moda: estar de moda   to be in style, 7

modelo (*m., f.*)   model, 10

módem (*m.*)   modem, 9

moderno/a   modern, 2

molestar   to bother, annoy, 4; **molestarle (a alguien)**   to bother (someone), 8

momento: en este momento   at this moment, now, 2

moneda: cambio de moneda (*m.*)   money exchange, 5

modista (*m., f.*)   designer

mono (*m.*)   monkey, 11

montaña (*f.*)   mountain

montar   to go, ride; **montar a caballo**   to go horseback riding, 5; **montar en bicicleta**   to go bicycling, 5

morado/a   purple, 1

moreno/a   dark-haired, 1

morir (ue, u)   to die, 3

mostrador (*m.*)   counter, 7

mostrar (ue)   to show, 3

motocicleta (*f.*)   motorcycle, 3

motor (*m.*)   motor, 9

mover (ue)   to move, shift, 9

movimiento (*m.*)   movement

mucho (*adv.*)   a lot, very much, 2; **mucho/a** (*adj.*)   a lot of, 2; **Mucho gusto.**   Pleased to meet you., P

muebles (*m. pl.*)   furniture; **sacudir los muebles**   to dust the furniture, 2

muerte (*f.*)   death, 10

muerto/a   dead; **estar muerto/a de hambre**   to be starving, famished, 3

mujer (*f.*)   woman, 1; **mujer de negocios**   businesswoman, 4

multa (*f.*)   fine, 9

multimedia   multimedia, 9

mural (*m.*)   mural, 10

murciélago (*m.*)   bat

músculo (*m.*)   muscle, 8

museo (*m.*)   museum, 2

música (*f.*)   music, 1

músico/a (*m., f.*)   musician, 4, 6

muy   very, 1; **Muy bien, gracias.**   Very well, thank you., P; **Muy mal, bastante mal.**   Very bad, quite bad., P

N

nacer (zc)   to be born, 4

nada   nothing, 4; **casi nada**   nothing, 4; **Nada en particular.**   Nothing special., P

nadar   to swim, 5

nadie   no one, nobody, 4

nariz (*f.*)   nose, 8

naranja (*f.*)   orange

narración (*f.*)   narration, 6

natación (*f.*)   swimming, 6

naturaleza muerta (*f.*)   still life, 10

náuseas: tener náuseas   to be nauseous, 8

navegar   to travel by boat; **navegar en velero**   to go sailing, 5; **navegar por Internet (la Red/la web)**   to surf the Internet (Web), 2

necesario: es necesario   it's necessary, 8

necesitar   to need, 2, 8

negar (ie)   to deny, 8

negocio (*m.*)   business

negro/a   black, 1

nervioso/a   nervous, 2

nevado/a   snow-capped

nevar   to snow, 3

(ni)... ni   (neither) . . . nor, 4; **Ni idea.**   I haven't got a clue., 5; **ni siquiera**   not even

nieto/a (*m., f.*)   grandson/granddaughter, 4

nieve (*f.*)   snow, 3

ningún, ninguno/a   none, not any, 4

niñero/a (*m., f.*)   nanny, babysitter, 11

niñez (*f.*)   childhood

niño/a (*m., f.*)   little boy/girl (child), 4

nivel (*m.*)   level

noche (*f.*)   night, 1; **de/por la noche**   in the evening, 1

nombre   name; **¿A nombre de quién?**   In whose name?, 5

nominación (*f.*)   nomination, 6

nominar   to nominate, 6

noreste (*m.*)   northeast, 3

noroeste (*m.*)   northwest, 3

norte (*m.*)   north, 3

nosotros/as   we, us, 1, 4

noticia (*f.*)   news item

noticiero (*m.*)   news program

novela (*f.*)   novel, 5

noventa   ninety, 1

noviazgo (*m.*)   courtship

noviembre (*m.*)   November, 1

novio/a (*m., f.*)   boyfriend/girlfriend, 4

nube (*f.*)   cloud, 3

nublado/a   cloudy; **está (parcialmente) nublado**   it's (partly) cloudy, 3

nuera (*f.*)   daughter-in-law, 4

nuestro/a(s) (*m., f.*)   our, 2, 7

nueve   nine, 1

nuevo/a   new, 1; **¿Qué hay de nuevo?**   What's new?, P

nunca   never, 4; **casi nunca**   almost never, 4

nutritivo/a   nutritious, 8

O

(o)... o   (either) . . . or, 4

obra de arte (*f.*)   work of art, 10

obrero/a (*m., f.*)   worker

obtener   to obtain, 11

obvio: es obvio   it's obvious, 8

ochenta   eighty, 1

ocho   eight, 1

octubre (*m.*)   October, 1

oeste (*m.*)   west, 3

oferta: en oferta   on sale, 7

oficina (*f.*)   office, 1, 2

ofrecer (zc)   to offer, 4

ofrenda (*f.*)   offering, 10

oído (*m.*)   ear (inner), 8

oír   to hear, 3

ojalá   I/we/let's hope so, 8

ojo (*m.*)   eye, 8; **¡Ojo!**   Be careful!, P

olor (*m.*)   odor

once   eleven, 1

operación (*f.*)   operation, 8

opinar   to think (have an opinion), 8

oprimir   to click (with the mouse); to push a button, 9

optimista   optimistic, 1

opuesto/a   opposite

oración (*f.*)   sentence

ordenar (el cuarto)   to clean, tidy (the room), 2

órdenes: ¡A sus órdenes!   At your service!, 3

oreja (*f.*)   ear (outer), 8

organizado/a   organized, 1

orilla (*f.*)   edge; shore

oro (*m.*)   gold, 7

oscuro/a   dark, 10

oso (panda) (*m.*)   (panda) bear, 11

otoño (*m.*)   autumn, fall, 3

otorgar to grant, give
otro lado (*m.*) somewhere else, 7
¡Oye! Hey!; Listen!, 5

P

paciente (*m., f.*) patient, 8
padrastro (*m.*) stepfather, 4
padre (*m.*) father, 1, 4
padrino (*m.*) godfather
paella (valenciana) (*f.*) rice, meat, and seafood dish (from Valencia), 3
pagar (por) to pay for, 4
paisaje (*m.*) landscape, country-side, 10
pájaro (*m.*) bird, 4
página (*f.*) page, P
país (*m.*) country
palabra (*f.*) word
paleta (*f.*) palette, 10
palidecer (zc) to turn pale
pálido/a pale
palo (*m.*) club; **palo de golf** golf club, 6; **palo de hockey** hockey stick, 6
pan (*m.*) bread, 3
pantalla (*f.*) screen, 6; **pantalla plana** flat screen, 9; **pantalla de plasma** plasma screen, 9
pantalones (*m. pl.*) pants, 7
papa (*f.*) potato, 3
papá (*m.*) dad, 4
papel (*m.*) paper, 1; role, 6; **hacer el papel** to play a role, 6
papelería (*f.*) stationery store; office supply store, 7
paquete (*m.*) package (*tour*), 5
par (*m.*) pair, 7
para for, to, in order to, 4; **estar para** + verb to be about to + verb, 6; **para nada** no way, not at all, 6; **para mí/ti** in my/your opinion; for me/you, 6; **para que** so that, 10; **para siempre** forever, 6
parabrisas (*m.*) windshield, 9
parada de autobús (*f.*) bus stop, 2
paraguas (*m.*) umbrella, 7
parar to stop, 7, 9
parecer (zc) to seem, appear to be, 3, 4
pared (*f.*) wall, 1
pareja (*f.*) pair, couple; **en parejas** in pairs, P
pariente (*m., f.*) family member, relative, 4
parlante (*m., f.*) speaker, 6
paro: en paro on strike
párrafo (*m.*) paragraph

partido (*m.*) game, 6
pasar to happen; to pass, 2; **pasar (por)** to pass (by), 6, 7; **pasar la aspiradora (por la alfombra)** to vacuum the rug, 2; **pasar una película** to show a movie, 6
pasearse to go for a walk, 5
pastilla (*f.*) pill, 8
patata (*f.*) potato, 3
patear to kick, 6
patinaje (*m.*) skating, 6
patín (*m.*) skate; **patines en línea** inline skates, 6; **patines para hielo** ice skates, 6
paz (*f.*) peace
pecho (*m.*) chest, 8
pedido (*m.*) order, 3
pedir (i, i) to ask for, request, 3, 8
peinarse to comb one's hair, 3
pelea de gallos (*f.*) cockfight
película (*f.*) movie, 6
peligro (*m.*) danger, 11
pelirrojo/a red-head, 1
pelo (*m.*) hair, 3, 8
pelota (*f.*) ball, 6
peluquero/a (*m., f.*) hair stylist, 4
pena (*f.*) sorrow; pain
pendiente (*m.*) pendant, 7; earring
pensar (ie) to think, 3; to think (opinion), 8
pensión: con media pensión with two meals, 5
peor: es peor it's worse, 8
pequeño/a small, 1; tight (clothes), 7
pera (*f.*) pear
percusión (*f.*) percussion, 6
perder (ie) to lose, 3, 6
pérdida (*f.*) loss
perdido/a lost, 12
Perdón. Pardon./Excuse me., P
perezoso/a lazy, 1
perfumería (*f.*) perfume store, 7
periodista (*m., f.*) journalist, 4
permanecer (zc) to remain, 10
permiso: Con permiso. Excuse me., P
pero but, 2
perro/a (*m., f.*) dog, 4
perseguir (i, i) to follow, pursue, 3
personaje (principal, secundario) (*m.*) (main, secondary) character, 6
pertenecer (zc) to belong, 12
pesar: a pesar de despite
pescado (*m.*) fish (*caught*), 3
pescar to fish; **ir de pesca** to go fishing, 5
pesimista pessimistic, 1
peso (*m.*) weight, 8

pianista (*m., f.*) pianist, 6
piano (*m.*) piano, 6
picante hot (spicy), 3
picnic (*m.*) picnic, 5
pie (*m.*) foot, 8; **a pie** on foot, 3
piedra (*f.*) stone, 7
piel (*f.*) skin
pierna (*f.*) leg, 8
pieza (*f.*) piece, 10
pila (*f.*) battery, 9
píldora (*f.*) pill, 8
pimienta (*f.*) (black) pepper, 3
pincel (*m.*) paintbrush, 10
pinchar la llanta to puncture the tire
pingüino (*m.*) penguin, 11
pintar to paint, 2, 10
pintor/a (*m., f.*) painter, 4, 10
pintura (*f.*) painting, 1, 10; **pintura al óleo** oil-painting, 10
piña (*f.*) pineapple
pirámide (*f.*) pyramid, 12
piscina (*f.*) swimming pool, 2
piso (*m.*) floor, apartment (*Spain*), 2; **barrer el piso** to sweep the floor, 2
pista (*f.*) ice rink; running track, 6
pitar to beep the horn, 9
pito (*m.*) horn, 9
pizarra (*f.*) chalkboard, 1
placa (*f.*) plate, 9
placer (*m.*) pleasure
planchar (la ropa) to iron (clothes), 2
planeta (*m.*) planet, 11
plata (*f.*) silver, 7
plato (*m.*) plate, dish, 3, 7
playa (*f.*) beach, 5
plaza (*f.*) plaza, 2
plena: en plena in the middle of
plomero/a (*m., f.*) plumber, 4
pluma (*f.*) pen, 1
población (*f.*) population, 12
pobreza (*f.*) poverty, 11
poco (*m.*) little, small amount; **un poco** a little, 2
poder (ue) to be able, 3
poder adquisitivo (*m.*) purchasing power, 12
poema (*m.*) poem
poesía (*f.*) poetry
poeta (*m., f.*) poet
policía (*m., f.*) police, 4, 11
poner to put, place, 3; **ponerse de pie** to stand up
popular popular, 1
popularidad (*f.*) popularity
por for, by means of, 4; **por ciento** percent, 3; **por ejemplo** for example, 6; **por favor** please, P, 6;

por fin finally, 3, 6; **por la mañana/tarde/noche** in the morning/afternoon/night (for general time periods), 1; **por lo menos** at least, 6; **por lo tanto** therefore, 6; **por supuesto** of course, 5, 6

porcentaje (*m.*) percentage, 3

porción (*f.*) portion, 8

porque because, P

¿por qué? why, P

portero (*m.*) doorman

portugués (*m.*) Portuguese language, 1

portugués/portuguesa Portuguese, 1

posible: es posible it's possible, 8

postre (*m.*) dessert

practicar to practice, 2, 6; **practicar deportes** to play sports, 2

precio (*m.*) price, 7; **a un precio más bajo** at a lower price, 7

preciso: es preciso it's necessary, 8

predecir to predict

preferible: es preferible it's preferable, 8

preferir (ie, i) to prefer, 3, 8

pregunta (*f.*) question, P

preguntar to ask, 2

premio (*m.*) prize, 12

prendedor (*m.*) pin, brooch, 7

prender to turn on, 9

preocupado/a worried, 2

preocupar(se) to worry, 3, 4, 8

preparado/a prepared, 3

presentar una película to show a movie, 6

presidente/a (*m., f.*) president, 4

presión (sanguínea) (*f.*) blood pressure, 8

presionar to click (with the mouse); to push a button, 9

prestar to lend, 4

primavera (*f.*) spring, 3

primer/o/a (*m.*) first, 1, 3; **primera clase** (*f.*) first class, 5

primo/a (*m., f.*) cousin, 4

principio (*m.*) beginning

prisa: tener prisa to be in a hurry, 3

prisión (*f.*) prison, 11

privado/a private, 2

probabilidad (*f.*) probability, 3

probable: es probable it's probable, 8

probar (ue) to try, taste, 3; **probarse (ue)** to try on, 7

problema (*m.*) problem, 1

producir (zc) to produce, 3

profesor/a (*m., f.*) professor, P, 4

profesorado (*m.*) faculty, 1

programa (*m.*) program, 9; **programa social** (*m.*) social program, 11

programador/a de computadoras (*m., f.*) computer programmer, 4

prohibir to prohibit

promedio (*m.*) average, 3

pronosticar to predict, 12

pronóstico del tiempo (*m.*) weather forecast, 3

propina (*f.*) tip, 3

propio/a own

propósito (*m.*) resolution, purpose, intention, 10

protagonista (*m., f.*) main character, 6

protector solar (*m.*) sunscreen, 5

protegerse to protect oneself, 5

provocar to cause

prueba (*f.*) test, exam, 8

psicología (*f.*) psychology, 1

psicólogo/a (*m., f.*) psychologist, 4

público/a public, 10

pueblo (*m.*) town, people

puede ser it can be, 8

puerta (*f.*) door, 1, 9

pulmón (*m.*) lung, 8

pulsar to click (with the mouse); to push a button, 9

pulsera (*f.*) bracelet, 7

pupitre (*m.*) writing desk, 1

Q

¿qué? what?, P; **¿Qué quiere decir... ?** What does . . . mean?, P; **¿Qué tal?** How's it going?, P

quedar to be (located), 3; **quedarle (a alguien)** to fit (someone), 7; **quedarse** to stay, 3

quehacer (*m.*) chore

quemar to burn; **quemarse** to get a sunburn, 5

querer (ie) to want, 3, 8; **¿Qué quiere decir... ?** What does . . . mean?, P; **Quisiera (pedir)...** I would like (to order) . . . , 3

queso (*m.*) cheese, 3

¿quién? who?, P; **¿A nombre de quién?** In whose name?, 5

química (*f.*) chemistry, 1

quince fifteen, 1

quitarse (la ropa) to take off (one's clothes), 3

quizás maybe, perhaps, 8

R

radio (*m., f.*) radio, 1, 5

radiografía (*f.*) X-ray, 8

raíz (*f.*) root

ranchera (*f.*) Mexican-style music, 6

rápido/a fast, 1

raqueta (*f.*) tennis racket, 6

ratón (*m.*) mouse, 9

razón (*f.*) reason; **tener razón** to be right, 3

realidad (virtual) (*f.*) (virtual) reality, 9

realista realistic

rebaja (*f.*) discount, 7

rebajar to lower (a price), 7

recámara (*f.*) bedroom

recepción (*f.*) reception, 5

recepcionista (*m., f.*) receptionist, 4, 5

receta (*f.*) prescription, 8

recibir to receive, 2

recibo (*m.*) receipt, 7

recipiente (*m.*) container, 7

recoger to pick up; to get, 5

recomendar (ie) to recommend, 3, 8; **¿Qué nos recomienda?** What do you recommend?, 3

recordar (ue) to remember, 3

recreo (*m.*) recreation, 5

recto/a straight; **seguir recto** to go straight, 7

recuerdo (*m.*) memory

recurso (*m.*) resource, 11

red (*f.*) network, 9

reducir (zc) to reduce, 5, 8

reflejar to reflect

refresco (*m.*) soft drink, 3

refrigerador/a (*m., f.*) refrigerator, 2

regalar to give (gifts), 4

regatear to bargain, 7

regateo (*m.*) bargaining, 7

registrar to register, 5

regla (*f.*) rule, P

regresar to return

regular OK, P

reír (i, i) to laugh, 5

religioso/a religious, 10

reloj (*m.*) watch, clock, 1

remedio (*m.*) remedy, 8; **remedio casero** home remedy; **tener remedio** to have a solution, 11

renta (*f.*) rent, 2

repente: de repente suddenly

repetir (i, i) to repeat, P, 3

réplica (*f.*) replica, 10

reproductor MP3 (*m.*) MP3 player, 6

reseña (*f.*) review, 6

reseñar to review, 6

reservación (*f.*) reservation, 5

reservar to reserve, 5

resfriado: estar resfriado/a to have a cold, 8

resfrío: tener resfrío to have a cold, 8
residencia (*f.*) dormitory, 1
respirar to breathe, 8
responder to answer, 2
responsabilidad (*f.*) responsibility, 11
restaurante (*m.*) restaurant, 2
resumen (*m.*) summary
retrato (*m.*) portrait, 10
reunirse (con) to meet (with) someone, 5
reusar to reuse, 11
revista (*f.*) magazine
rey (*m.*) king
rico/a rich, delicious, 3
ridículo: es ridículo it's ridiculous, 8
riesgo (*m.*) risk
río (*m.*) river
riqueza (*f.*) wealth
ritmo (*m.*) rhythm, 6
rito (*m.*) rite; ritual, 10
robo (*m.*) robbery, 11
robot (*m.*) robot, 9
rock (*m.*) rock, 6
rodeado/a de surrounded by
rodilla (*f.*) knee, 8
rogar (ue) to beg, plead, 8
rojo/a red, 1
romántico/a romantic, 1, 6
romper(se) (el brazo) to break (one's arm), 8
ropa (*f., s.*) clothes, clothing; **ropa de gimnasia** (*f.*) gymwear, 6; **ropa interior** (*f.*) underwear, 7
ropero (*m.*) wardrobe, 2
rosa (*f.*) rose, 1
rosado/a pink, 1
roto/a ripped, broken 7
rubio/a blond(e), 1
rueda (*f.*) wheel, 9
ruina (*f.*) ruin, 12
ruta (*f.*) route, 3

S

sábado (*m.*) Saturday, 1
saber to know, 3; **No sé.** I don't know., P; **saber a** to taste like
sabor (*m.*) taste; flavor
sabroso/a delicious, tasty, 3
sacar to take (away), to take out; **sacar la basura** to take out the garbage, 2; **sacar el polvo de (los muebles)** (*Spain*) to dust (the furniture), 2
saco (*m.*) jacket, blazer, 7
sacudir (los muebles) to dust (the furniture), 2

sal (*f.*) salt, 3
sala (*f.*) living room, 2; **sala de clase** classroom, 1; **sala de conferencias** conference room, 5; **sala de emergencia** emergency room, 8
salir to go out, leave, 3
salón (*m.*) living room; **salón de conferencias** conference room, 5
salsa (*f.*) salsa (music), 6
salud (*f.*) health; **tener buena/ mala salud** to be in good/bad health, 8
salvar to save (rescue), 11
sandalia (*f.*) sandal, 5
sandía (*f.*) watermelon
sangrar to bleed, 8
sangre (*f.*) blood, 8
sangría (*f.*) wine. fruit, and soda drink, 3
sano/a healthy, 8
saxofón (*m.*) saxphone, 6
secador/a de pelo (*m., f.*) hair dryer, 2
secar (los platos, la ropa) to dry (the dishes, clothes), 2; **secarse** to dry off, 3
seco/a dry, 3
secretario/a (*m., f.*) secretary, 4
secuencia (*f.*) sequence, 6
secuestrar to kidnap
secuestro (*m.*) kidnapping
sed (*f.*) thirst; **tener sed** to be thirsty, 3
seda (*f.*) silk, 7
sedentario/a sedentary, 8
seguir (i, i) to follow, continue, 3; **seguir derecho/recto** to go straight, 7
según according to, 4
segundo/a second; **segunda clase** (*f.*) second class, 5
seguro/a sure, 2; **no es seguro** it's not sure, 8; **(no) estar seguro/a de** to be (un)sure, 8
seguro médico (*m.*) health insurance, 11
seis six, 1
semáforo (*m.*) stoplight, 7
semilla (*f.*) seed
sencillo/a single (room or bed), 5
sentarse (ie) to sit down, 3
sentido (*m.*) sense; **tener sentido** to make sense, 3
sentir (ie, i) to be sorry, regret, 8; **sentirse (ie, i)** to feel, 3
señor (Sr.) (*m.*) Mr., P
señora (Sra.) (*f.*) Mrs., P
señorita (Srta.) (*f.*) Miss, P

separado/a: estar separado/a to be separated, 4
septiembre (*m.*) September, 1
ser to be, 1; **ser alérgico/a a...** to be allergic to . . ., 8; **ser mayor** to be older, 4; **ser menor** to be younger, 4; **ser soltero/a** to be single, 4
ser humano (*m.*) human being
serio/a serious, 1
servir (i, i) to serve, 3; **¿En qué le(s) puedo servir?** How can I help you?, 5
sesenta sixty, 1
setenta seventy, 1
sí yes; **Sí, cómo no.** Of course., P
SIDA (*m.*) AIDS, 11
siempre always, 4; **casi siempre** almost always, 4
siento: Lo siento. I'm sorry., P, 5
siete seven, 1
siglo (*m.*) century, 12
significar to mean, 10
silla (*f.*) chair, 1
sillón (*m.*) armchair, 2
simbolizar to simbolize
simpático/a nice, friendly, 1
sin without, 4; **sin embargo** nevertheless, 12; **sin que** without, 10
sino, sino que but (rather), 12
sinopsis (*f.*) synopsis, 6
síntoma (*m.*) symptom, 8
sistema (*m.*) system, 1
sobre on, on top of, 4; about, over, on top of
sobrepasar to exceed
sobrino/a (*m., f.*) nephew/niece, 4
sociología (*f.*) sociology, 1
sofá (*m.*) sofa, 2
sol (*m.*) sun
soldado/a (*m., f.*) soldier
solo/a alone
sólo only
soltero: ser soltero/a to be single, 4
solución (*f.*) solution, 11
solucionar to solve
sombra: luz y sombra (*f.*) light and shadow, 10
sombrero (*m.*) hat, 5, 7
sombrilla (*f.*) parasol, beach umbrella, 5
someter to subdue
sonido (*m.*) sound
sonreír (i, i) to smile, 5
soñar (ue) (con) to dream (about), 3
sopa (*f.*) soup, 3; **sopa de pollo** chicken soup
soroche (*m.*) altitude sickness, 8
sorprender to surprise, 8

su(s) your (*formal*), his, her, their, 2
subir to climb, 2; **subir (por)** to go up (a street), 7
suceder to occur, 6
sucio/a dirty, 7
sudadera (*f.*) sweatsuit, sweatshirt, 7
sudamericano/a South American
suegro/a (*m., f.*) father-in-law/ mother-in-law, 4
suelo (*m.*) ground
sueño (*m.*) dream; **tener sueño** to be sleepy, tired, 3
suéter (*m.*) sweater, 7
sufrimiento (*m.*) suffering
sugerir (ie, i) to suggest, 5, 8
sujeto (*m.*) subject, 1
sur (*m.*) south, 3
sureste (*m.*) southeast, 3
suroeste (*m.*) southwest, 3
surfing: hacer surfing to go surfing, 5
suspenso: de suspenso thriller (*adj.*), 6
sustantivo (*m.*) noun
suyo/a (*m., f.*) yours, his, hers, theirs, 7

T

táctil pertaining to touch, tactile, 9
tal vez maybe, perhaps, 8
talla (*f.*) size, 7
tamaño (*m.*) size
también also, too, P, 4
tambor (*m.*) drum, 6
tampoco neither, either, 4
tan... como as . . . as, 7; **tan pronto como** as soon as, 9
tango (*m.*) tango, 6
tanque de gasolina (*m.*) gas tank, 9
tapa (*f.*) small serving of food (*Spain*), 3
tapado/a covered
tapete (*m.*) rug, 7
tapiz (*m.*) tapestry, 7
taquilla (*f.*) box office, 6
taquillero/a box office draw/hit, 6
tarde (*f.*) afternoon, 1; **de/por la tarde** in the afternoon/evening, 1
tarifa (*f.*) rate, fare, tariff, 5
tarjeta de crédito (*f.*) credit card, 5; **tarjeta postal** (*f.*) postcard
taxi (*m.*) taxi, 3
taza (*f.*) cup, 3
té (*m.*) tea, 3
teatro (*m.*) theater, 1
teclado (*m.*) keyboard, 9
tejedor/a (*m., f.*) weaver, 12
tejido (*m.*) weaving, 7

teléfono (*m.*) telephone, 1; **teléfono celular** cell phone, 9
telenovela (*f.*) soap opera
televisión (*f.*) television, 1
tema (*m.*) theme, 1
temblar (ie) to tremble
temer to fear, be afraid of, 8
temperatura (mínima/máxima) (*f.*) (minimum/maximum) temperature, 3; **¿A cuánto está la temperatura?** What is the temperature?, 3
templo (*m.*) temple, 12
tenedor (*m.*) fork, 3
tener to have, 3; **tener apetito** to have an appetite, 8; **tener buena/mala salud** to be in good/bad health, 8; **tener calor** to be hot, feel hot, 3; **tener catarro, resfrío** to have a cold, 8; **tener cuidado** to be careful, 3, 7; **tener dolor** to have pain, 8; **tener escalofríos** to shiver, have a chill, 8; **tener éxito** to be successful, 3; **tener fiebre** to have a fever, 8; **tener frío** to be cold, 3; **tener ganas de + *inf.*** to want to (do something), to feel like (doing something), 3; **tener gripe** to have the flu, 8; **tener hambre** to be hungry, 3; **tener miedo (de)** to be afraid (of), 3, 8; **tener náuseas** to be nauseous, 8; **tener prisa** to be in a hurry, 3; **tener que + *inf.*** to have to (do something), 3; **tener razón** to be right, 3; **tener remedio** to have a solution, 11; **tener sed** to be thirsty, 3; **tener sentido** to make sense, 3; **tener sueño** to be sleepy, tired, 3; **tener tos** to have a cough, 8; **tener X años** to be (X) years old, 3
tenis (*m.*) tennis, 6
teñir (i, i) to dye
terapia (*f.*) therapy, 11
terminar to finish, 2
terraza (*f.*) terrace, 2
terremoto (*m.*) earthquake
terrible: es terrible it's terrible, 8
terror: de terror horror (*adj.*), 6
terrorismo (*m.*) terrorism, 11
terrorista (*m., f.*) terrorist, 11
ti you (*direct object*), 4
tiempo (*m.*) time; **hace buen/mal tiempo** it's good/bad weather, 3; **tiempo libre** free time, 5
tienda (*f.*) store, 2
tierra (*f.*) Earth; land
tigre (*m.*) tiger, 11
tímido/a shy, timid, 1
tina (*f.*) bathtub, 2

tintorería (*f.*) dry cleaner, 7
tío/a (*m., f.*) uncle/aunt, 4
tira cómica (*f.*) comic strip
tiza (*f.*) chalk, 1
toalla (*f.*) towel, 5
tobillo (*m.*) ankle, 8
tocar to play (an instrument), 2, 6
todavía yet, 9
todo everything, 4; **todo el mundo** everybody, everyone, 4; **todos los días** every day, 4
tomar to take; to drink, 2, 3; **tomar el sol** to sunbathe, 5
torcer(se) (el tobillo) to twist, sprain (one's ankle), 8
tormenta (*f.*) storm, 3
tornado (*m.*) tornado, 3
toronja (*f.*) grapefruit
torre (*f.*) tower
tortilla española (*f.*) omelette with potatoes and onions (*Spain*), 3
tortuga (*f.*) turtle, 4
tos: tener tos to have a cough, 8
toser to cough, 8
tour (*m.*) excursion, tour, 5
trabajador/a hard-working, 1
trabajador/a (*m., f.*) worker, 4; **trabajador/a social** social worker, 11
trabajar to work, 2
trabajo social (*m.*) social work, 1
tradición (*f.*) tradition, 10
traducir (zc) to translate, 3
traer to bring, 3, 4
tráfico de drogas (*m.*) drug trafficking, 11
traje (*m.*) suit, 7; **traje de baño** bathing suit, 5
trama (*f.*) plot, 6
transporte (*m.*) transportation, 5
traslado (*m.*) transfer, 5
tratamiento (*m.*) treatment
tratar de to deal with, treat, 6; **tratarse de** to deal with; to be about, 11
trazar to design
trece thirteen, 1
treinta thirty, 1
tren (*m.*) train, 3
tres three, 1
triste sad, 2
tristeza (*f.*) sadness
triunfar to succeed, 11
trompeta (*f.*) trumpet, 6
tronada (*f.*) storm, 3
truco (*m.*) trick
tu(s) your, 2
tú you, 1; **¿y tú?** and you?, P
turista (*m., f.*) tourist, 3
turquesa (*f.*) turquoise, 7
tuyo/a (*m., f.*) yours, 7

unidad (*f.*)   unit, P
uniforme (*m.*)   uniform, 6
universidad (*f.*)   university, 1
uno   one, 1
urgente: es urgente   it's urgent, 8
usar   to use, 2
usted(es)   you, 1, 4; **¿y usted?**   and
   you?, P
uva (*f.*)   grape

V

vaca (*f.*)   cow
vacación (*f.*)   vacation, 5; **estar/irse
   de vacaciones**   to be/go on vacation, 5
vacuna (*f.*)   vaccine, 8
valer la pena   to be worth it
valioso/a   valuable
¡Vamos! /¡Vámonos!   Let's go!, P
vapor (*m.*)   mist
vaquero: de vaqueros   western
   (*adj.*), 6
variado/a   assorted, 3
variedad (*f.*)   variety
vasija (*f.*)   vase, 10
vaso (*m.*)   glass (for drinks), 3
vecindario (*m.*)   neighborhood
veinte   twenty, 1
vejez (*f.*)   old age
velocidad: alta velocidad (*f.*)   high
   speed, 9
vencer   to defeat, 12

venda (*f.*)   bandage, 8
vendar   to bandage, 8
vendedor/a (*m., f.*)   salesperson, 4;
   seller, 7; **vendedor/a ambulante**
   street vendor
vender   to sell, 4
venir   to come, 3
ventana (*f.*)   window, 1
ver   to see, 3; **ver televisión**   to
   watch television, 2
verano (*m.*)   summer, 3
verdad   true; **(no) es verdad**   it's
   (not) true, 8; **¿Verdad?**   Really?, P
verdadero/a   true
verde   green, 1
vestido (*m.*)   dress, 7; **vestido de
   baño** (*m.*)   swimwear, 6
vestirse (i, i)   to get dressed, 3
veterinario/a (*m., f.*)   veterinarian, 4
vez: algunas veces   sometimes, 4;
   de vez en cuando   from time to
   time, 4; **muchas veces**   many
   times, 4
viajar   to travel, 2, 3
viaje (*m.*)   trip, 3; **agente de viajes**
   (*m., f.*)   travel agent, 4; **¡Buen
   viaje!/¡Feliz viaje!**   Have a nice
   trip!, 5
viajero/a (*m., f.*)   traveler
videocámara (*f.*)   videocamera, 9
videograbadora (*f.*)   video
   recorder, 9
videojuego (*m.*)   video game, 9
viejo/a   old, 1
viento: hace viento   it's windy, 3
viernes (*m.*)   Friday, 1

vigilar   to watch
vino (tinto/blanco) (*m.*)
   (red/white) wine, 3
violín (*m.*)   violin, 6
visitar   to visit, 2
vista (*f.*)   view, 5; **Hasta la vista.**
   Until we meet again., P
vivir   to live, 2
volcán (*m.*)   volcano
volante (*m.*)   steering wheel, 9
voluntario/a (*m., f.*)   volunteer, 11
volver (ue)   to return, 3; **volverse**
   to become, 6; **volverse la espalda**
   to turn one's back
vomitar   to vomit, 8
vosotros/as (*m., f. pl.*)   you
   (*Spain*), 1, 4
voz (*f.*)   voice, 6
vuestro/a (*m., f.*)   your (*Spain*), 2, 7

y   and, 1
ya   already, 9
yerno (*m.*)   son-in-law, 4
yeso (*m.*)   cast, 8
yo   I, 1

zapatería (*f.*)   shoe store, 7
zapato (*m.*)   shoe, 7; **zapatos de tenis**
   (*m.*)   sneakers, tennis shoes, 6
zumo (*m.*)   juice, 3

English-Spanish Vocabulary

A

above encima de, sobre, 4
accelerate acelerar, 7
accelerator acelerador (*m.*), 9
access acceder, 9
accommodations alojamiento (*m.*), 5
according to según, 4
accordion acordión (*f.*), 6
accountant contador/a (*m., f.*), 4
achieve lograr, 11
achievement logro (*m.*), 11
acid rain lluvia ácida (*f.*), 11
act actuar, 6
acting actuación (*f.*), 6
action de acción (*adj.*), 6
active activo/a, 8
activity actividad (*f.*), P
actor actor (*m.*), 6
actress actriz (*f.*), 6
add agregar, añadir
addiction adicción (*f.*), 11
address dirección (*f.*), 3, 7
adjective adjetivo (*m.*)
adolescent adolescente (*m., f.*), 11
adornment adorno (*m.*), 10
advance adelanto (*m.*)
advice consejo (*m.*), 11
advise avisar, 5; aconsejar, 8
after después (de), 4; después (de) que, 9
afternoon tarde (*f.*), 1; **Good afternoon** Buenas tardes., P
afterwards después, 3
agent agente (*m., f.*), 5; **travel agent** agente de viajes, 4
agree estar de acuerdo, 5
AIDS SIDA (*m.*), 11
air aire (m.); **air conditioner** aire acondicionado (*m.*), 9
airbag bolsa de aire (*f.*), airbag (*m.*), 9
airline aerolínea (*f.*), 5
airport aeropuerto (*m.*), 2
alarm clock despertador (*m.*), 5
album disco (*m.*), 7
almond almendra (*f.*)
almost always/never/nothing casi siempre/nunca/nada, 4
alone solo/a
already ya, 9
also también, P, 4
although aunque, 9
altitude sickness soroche (*m.*), 8
always siempre, 4
among entre, 4

anatomy anatomía (*f.*), 1
and y, 1
angel ángel (*m.*)
anger coraje (*m.*); enojo (*m.*)
angry enojado/a, 2
ankle tobillo (*m.*), 8
announcement anuncio (*m.*)
annoy molestar, 4
answer contestar, P, 4; responder, 2
anthropology antropología (*f.*), 1
antibiotic antibiótico (*m.*), 8
any algún, alguno/a/os/as, 4
anything algo, 4
apartment apartamento (*m.*), 2; piso (*m.*) (*Spain*), 2
apparatus aparato (*m.*), 9
appear to be parecer (zc), 4; aparecer (zc)
appetizer aperitivo (*m.*), entremés (*m.*), 3
application aplicación (*f.*), 9
appointment cita (*f.*), 8
approach acercarse
April abril (*m.*), 1
archaeologist arqueólogo/a (*m., f.*), 4
archaeology arqueología (*f.*), 1
architect arquitecto/a (*m., f.*), 4
arm brazo (*m.*), 8
armchair sillón (*m.*), 2
around alrededor
arrest arrestar, 11
arrive llegar, 2, 3
art (arts) arte (*m.*) (las artes) (*f. pl.*), 1; **classic, contemporary, modern, abstract art** arte clásico, contemporáneo, moderno, abstracto (*m.*), 10; **art exhibit** exposición (*f.*), exhibición (*f.*), 10
article artículo (*m.*)
artisan artesano/a (*m., f.*), 10
artist artista (*m., f.*), 1, 4, 10
as soon as en cuanto, tan pronto como, 9
ask preguntar, P, 2; **ask for** pedir (i, i), 3, 8
aspirin aspirina (*f.*), 8
assassinate asesinar, 11
assassination asesinato (*m.*), 11
assorted variado/a, 3
at en; **at a lower price** a un precio más bajo, 7; **at that time** entonces, 3; **at this moment** en este momento, 2; **at times** a veces, 4; **At your service!** ¡A sus órdenes!, 3
athlete atleta (*m., f.*), 4; deportista (*m., f.*), 6

atmosphere ambiente (*f.*)
attend to atender (ie), 5
attitude actitud (*f.*)
attorney abogado (*m., f.*), 4
attractive atractivo/a, 1
August agosto (*m.*), 1
aunt tía (*f.*), 4
automated teller machine (ATM) cajero automático (*m.*), 5
automatic automático/a, 9
automobile coche (*m.*), auto(móvil) (*m.*), carro (*m.*), 3, 9
autumn otoño (*m.*), 3
available disponible, 9
average promedio (*m.*), 3
avoid evitar, 8

B

baby bebé (*m., f.*), 4
baby-sitter niñero/a (*m., f.*), 11
back espalda (*f.*), 8
backpack mochila (*f.*), 1
bad malo/a, 1; **it's bad** es malo, 8; **Very bad, quite bad.** Muy mal, bastante mal., P
bag bolsa (*f.*), 7
balcony balcón (*m.*), 2
ball pelota (*f.*), balón (*m.*), 6; **beach ball** balón (*m.*), 5
ballad balada (*f.*), 6
band banda (*f.*), conjunto (*m.*), 6
bandage venda (*f.*), 8; vendar, 8
bar: (mini) bar minibar (*m.*), 5
bargain ganga (*f.*), 7; regatear, 7
bargaining regateo (*m.*), 7
baseball béisbol (*m.*), 6
baseball bat bate (*m.*), 6
basket, wicker basket cesta (*f.*), 6
basketball básquetbol (*m.*), baloncesto (*m.*), 6
bass guitar guitarra bajo (*f.*), 6
bathing suit traje de baño (*m.*), 5
bathroom (cuarto de) baño (*m.*), 2
bathtub bañera (*f.*), tina (*f.*), 2
battery batería (*f.*), pila (*f.*), 9
be ser, 1; estar, 2; **be able** poder (ue), 3; **be about** tratarse de, 11; **be afraid (of)** tener miedo (de), 3, 8; temer, 8; **be allergic to ...** ser alérgico/a a..., tener alergia a..., 8; **be angry** enojarse, 8; **be born** nacer (zc), 4; **be careful** tener cuidado, 7; **be close/far away (from)** estar cerca/lejos (de), 3; **be desperate** estar

desesperado/a, 11; **be divorced** estar divorciado/a, 4; **be dizzy** estar mareado/a, 8; **be familiar with** conocer (zc), 3; **be hungry** tener hambre, 3; **be important/ of concern** importar, 4; **be in a hurry** tener prisa, 3; **be in good/bad health** tener buena/mala salud, 8; **be in style** estar de moda, 7; **be inflamed** estar inflamado/a, 8; **be located** quedar, 3; **be nauseous** tener náuseas, 8; **be on the verge of** estar a punto de, 5; **be pregnant** estar embarazada, 8; **be right** tener razón, 3; **be separated** estar separado/a, 4; **be sorry** sentir (ie, i), 8; **be successful** tener éxito, 3; **be sure** estar seguro/a de, 8; **be unsure** no estar seguro/a de, 8; **be X years old** tener X años, 3

beach playa (f.), 5; **beach umbrella** sombrilla (f.), 5

beans frijoles (m.)

beautiful hermoso/a, 1; bello/a, 5

beauty belleza (f.)

become volverse (ue), 6

bed cama (f.), 1

bedroom dormitorio (m.), 1, 2; alcoba (f.)

bee abeja (f.)

beep the horn pitar, 9

beer cerveza (f.), 3

before antes (de) (que), 4, 10

beg rogar (ue), 8

begin comenzar (ie), empezar (ie), 3; iniciar, 9

behavior comportamiento (m.), 11

behind detrás de, 4

believe creer, 2, 8

belong pertenecer (zc), 12

belt cinturón (m.), 7

beneath debajo de, 4

benefit beneficio (m.), 11

better: it's better es mejor, 8

between entre, 4

bicycle bicicleta (f.), 3, 6

big grande, 1

biking ciclismo (m.), 6

bill cuenta (f.), 3

biology biología (f.), 1

bird pájaro (m.), 4

birthday cumpleaños (m.)

black negro/a, 1; **black and white** en blanco y negro, 10

blazer saco (m.), 7

bleed sangrar, 8

blond(e) rubio/a, 1

blood sangre (f.), 8; **blood pressure** presión sanguínea (f.), 8

blouse blusa (f.), 7

blue azul, 1

blues blues (music) (m. pl.), 6

boat barco (m.), 3

body cuerpo (m.), 8

bone hueso (m.), 8

book libro (m.), 1

bookshelf estante (m.), 1

bookstore librería (f.), 2, 7

boot bota (f.), 7

bored aburrido/a, 2

boss jefe/a (m., f.), 4

bother (someone) molestar (a alguien), 8

boutique boutique (m.), 7

box office taquilla (f.), 6; **box office draw/hit** taquillero/a, 6

boxing boxeo (m.), 6

boy chico (m.), P, 4; niño (m.), 4

boyfriend novio (m.), 4

bracelet pulsera (f.), 7

brain cerebro (m.), 8

brake frenar, 9; freno (m.), 9

bread pan (m.), 3

break (one's arm) romper(se) (el brazo), 8

breakfast desayuno (m.), 3

breathe respirar, 8

breeze brisa (f.), 3

bring llevar, 2; traer, 3, 4

brochure folleto (m.), 5

broken fracturado/a, 8

bronze bronce (m.), 10

brooch prendedor (m.), 7

broom escoba (f.), 2

brother hermano (m.), 4

brother-in-law cuñado (m.), 4

brown café, 1; marrón, castaño (hair)

brush cepillarse, 3

buckle up (seatbelt) abrocharse (el cinturón), 9

build construir, 2

building edificio (m.), 2

bullfight corrida de toros (f.)

bus autobús (m.), 3; camión (m.) (Mex.), 3

bus stop parada de autobús (f.), 2

businessman hombre de negocios (m.), 4

businesswoman mujer de negocios (f.), 4

but pero, 2; (*rather*) sino, sino que, 12

button botón (m.), 9

buy comprar, 2

buyer comprador/a (m., f.), 7

by (*with transportation*) en, 3; **by hand** a mano, 10; **by means of** por, 4

Bye. Chao., P

C

café café (m.), 2

calculator calculadora (f.), 1

calendar calendario (m.), 1

call llamar, 2; **to be called** llamarse, P

calm calmado/a, 2

calorie caloría (f.), 8

camera cámara (f.), 9

canvas lienzo (m.), 10

cap gorra (f.), 7

car auto (m.), automóvil (m.), carro (m.), coche (m.), 3, 9

carbon dioxide dióxido de carbono (m.), 11

careful: Be careful! ¡Ojo!, P

Caribbean caribeño/a; Caribe (m.)

carpenter carpintero/a (m., f.), 4

carry out desempeñar, 9

cash (dinero en) efectivo (m.), 5

cash register caja (f.), 7

castanet castañuela (f.), 6

cast yeso (m.), 8

cat gato/a (m., f.), 4

catch agarrar

catch up with alcanzar, 3

category categoría (f.), 6

celebrate celebrar, festejar, 10

cell phone teléfono celular (m.), 9

century siglo (m.), 12

ceramic cerámica (f.), 10

ceramist ceramista (m., f.), 10

ceremony ceremonia (f.), 10

certain: it's (not) certain (no) es cierto, 8

certainty certeza (f.)

chair silla (f.), 1

chalk tiza (f.), 1

chalkboard pizarra (f.), 1

challenge desafiar

change convertir, 11

character (main, secondary) personaje (principal, secundario) (m.), 6; **main character** protagonista (m., f.), 6

charge cargar, 9

chauffeur chofer (m.) (Lat. Am.), chófer (m.) (Spain), 3

check revisar: The check, please. La cuenta, por favor., 3

cheese queso (m.), 3

chemistry química (f.), 1

chest pecho (m.), 8

Chinese chino/a, 1; (*language*) chino (*m.*), 1
church iglesia (*f.*), 2
city ciudad (*f.*), 2
class clase (*f.*), P
classmate compañero/a de clase (*m., f.*), P
classroom sala de clase (*f.*), 1
clay arcilla (*f.*), barro (*m.*), 7, 10
clean (the room) limpiar/ordenar (el cuarto), 2
clear: it's (not) clear (no) está claro, 8
clerk (store) dependiente (*m., f.*), 7
clever listo/a, 1
click (with the mouse) presionar, hacer clic, pulsar, oprimir, 9
climate clima (*m.*), 3
climb subir, 2
clock reloj (*m.*), 1
close cerrar (ie), 3
close (to) cerca (de), 4
closet clóset (*m.*), 2; ropero (*m.*), 2
cloud nube (*f.*), 3
cloudy: it's (partly) cloudy está (parcialmente) nublado, 3
club (nightclub) club (*m.*), 5
coat abrigo (*m.*), 7
codex códice (*m.*), 12
coffee café (*m.*), 3
cold frío/a; **be cold** tener frío, 3; **it's cold** hace frío, 3
collector coleccionista (*m., f.*), 10
collide chocar, 9
color en color(es) (*adj.*), 10
comb (one's hair) peinar(se) (el pelo), 3
come venir, 3
comedy comedia (*f.*), 6
comfortable cómodo/a, 5
community comunidad (*f.*), 11
compact compacto/a, 9
compact disc, CD disco compacto, CD (*m.*), 6
competition competencia (*f.*)
complete completo/a, 2
composition composición (*f.*), 1
computer computador/a (*m., f.*), 1
computer file archivo (*m.*), 9
computer programmer progra-mador/a de computadoras (*m., f.*), 4
concern concernir (ie), 3
concert concierto (*m.*), 6
concierge conserje (*m., f.*), 5
condemn condenar
conference room salón/sala de conferencias (*m., f.*), 5
confirm confirmar, 5

confirmation confirmación (*f.*), 5
confront enfrentar, 11
confused confundido/a, 2
conquest conquista (*f.*), 12
consequence consecuencia (*f.*), 11
conserve conservar, 11
construct construir, 2
consume consumir, 8
consumption consumo (*m.*), 11
contain contener, 3
container recipiente (*m.*), 7
contaminate contaminar, 11
contamination contaminación (*f.*), 11
continue seguir (i, i), 3
contrast contraste (*m.*), 10
contribute contribuir
convert convertir (ie, i), 11
cook cocinar, 2
cook cocinero/a (*m., f.*), 4
cool: it's cool hace fresco, 3
copper cobre (*m.*), 7
copy copiar, 9
corner esquina (*f.*), intersección (*f.*), 7
cost costar (ue), 3
costume disfraz (*m.*), 10
cotton algodón (*m.*), 7
cough toser, 8; tos (*f.*), 8
counselor consejero/a (*m., f.*), 4
count contar (ue), 3
counter mostrador (*m.*), 7
court cancha (*f.*), 6
cousin primo/a (*m., f.*), 4
craft artesanía (*f.*), 7,
crash choque (*m.*), 9
create crear, 10
creative creativo/a
creativity creatividad (*f.*)
credit card tarjeta de crédito (*f.*), 5
crime crimen (*m.*), 11
criticism crítica (*f.*), 6
criticize criticar, 6
cross cruz (*f.*), 10
cross cruzar, 7
cruise ship crucero (*m.*), 3
cup taza (*f.*), 3
cure cura (*f.*), 11; curar, 8
custard: baked egg custard flan (*m.*), 3
custom costumbre (*f.*), 10
customer cliente (*m., f.*), 7

D

dad papá (*m.*), 4
daily diariamente, 8
damage dañar, 9
dance bailar, 2, 6

dancer bailarín/ina (*m., f.*), 6; bailador/a (*m., f.*)
danger peligro (*m.*), 11
dark oscuro/a, 10
dark-haired moreno/a, 1
date fecha (*f.*), 1
daughter hija (*f.*), 4
daughter-in-law nuera (*f.*), 4
day día (*m.*), 1
deal ganga (*f.*), 7
deal with tratarse de, 11
death muerte (*f.*), 10
December diciembre (*m.*), 1
decide decidir, 2
decline decaer, 12
decoration adorno (*m.*), 10
defeat vencer, 12
definition definición (*f.*); **high definition** alta definición, 9
deforestation deforestación (*f.*), 11
degrees centigrade/Fahrenheit grados centígrados/Fahrenheit (*m.*), 3
delicious sabroso/a, rico/a, 3
delight encantar, 4
delinquency delincuencia (*f.*), 11
delinquent delincuente (*m., f.*), 11
delinquent act acto delectivo (*m.*), 11
deliver entregar, 4
dentist dentista (*m., f.*), 4
deny negar (ie), 8
department store almacén (*m.*), 2, 7
depend depender, 8
depressed deprimido/a, 2
depression depresión (*f.*), 11
descendent descendiente (*m., f.*), 12
describe describir, 2
design diseñar; diseño (*m.*);
designer diseñador/a (*m., f.*)
desk escritorio (*m.*), pupitre (*m.*), 1
destroy destruir, 2
detail detalle (*m.*), 10
deterioration deterioro (*m.*), 11
develop desarrollar
developed desarrollado/a, 12
dictator dictador (*m.*); **dictator-ship** dictadura (*f.*)
die morir (ue, u), 3
diet dieta (*f.*), 8
difficult difícil, 1
digital digital, 9
dining room comedor (*m.*), 2
dinner cena (*f.*), 3; (*in some places*) comida (*f.*), 3
direct dirigir, 6
director/a director (*m., f.*), 6
directory directorio (*m.*), 9
dirty sucio/a, 7
disappointed desilusionado/a, 2

disaster desastre (*m.*)
discard desechar, 11
discarded desechado/a, 11
discotheque discoteca (*f.*), 5
discount rebaja (*f.*), 7
disgusted harto/a, 2
dish plato (*m.*), 3, 7
dislike (*a person*) caer mal, 4
dispose desechar, 11
disposed desechado/a, 11
distinguish distinguir(se), 12;
  distinguished distinguido/a
do hacer, 3
doctor médico/a, doctor/a
  (*m., f.*), 4
doctor's office consultorio médico
  (*m.*), 8
document documento (*m.*), 9
dog perro/a (*m., f.*), 4
dolphin delfín (*m.*), 11
Dominican-style music merengue
  (*m.*), 6
door puerta (*f.*), 1, 9
dormitory residencia (*f.*), 1
double doble, 5
doubt dudar, 8; **there's no doubt**
  no hay duda (de), 8
download bajar, 9
downpour aguacero (*m.*), chubasco
  (*m.*), 3
drama drama (*m.*), 6
draw dibujar, 10
drawing dibujo (*m.*), 10
dream (about) soñar (ue) (con), 3
dress vestido (*m.*), 7
dresser cómoda (*f.*), 2
drink beber, 2; **soft drink** refresco
  (*m.*), 3
drive conducir (zc), manejar, 3, 9
driver conductor/a (*m., f.*), 9
driver's license licencia de
  manejar/conducir (*f.*), 9
drizzle (*weather*) lloviznar, 3
drug addiction drogadicción
  (*f.*), 11
drug trafficking tráfico de drogas
  (*m.*), 11
drum tambor (*m.*), 6; **drum set**
  batería (*f.*), 6
drunk borracho/a, 2
dry seco/a, 3
dry (the dishes, clothes) secar (los
  platos, la ropa), 2; **dry off**
  secarse, 3
dry cleaner tintorería (*f.*), 7
during durante, 4
dust (the furniture) sacudir (los
  muebles), sacar el polvo de (los
  muebles) (*Spain*), 2
dye teñir (i, i)

E

ear (*outer*) oreja (*f.*), 8; (*inner*)
  oído (*m.*), 8
earring arete (*m.*), 7
earth tierra (*f.*)
earthquake terremoto (m.)
east este (*m.*), 3
eat comer, 2
ecological ecológico/a, 11
economical económico/a, 9
economics economía (*f.*), 1
eight ocho, 1
eighty ochenta, 1
either tampoco, 4; **either . . . or**
  o... o, 4
electrician electricista (*m., f.*), 4
elegance elegancia (*f.*), 5
elephant elefante (*m.*), 11
elevator ascensor (*m.*), elevador
  (*m.*), 5
eleven once, 1
e-mail correo electrónico (*m.*), 9
embrace abrazar, 4
emerald esmeralda (*f.*), 7
emergency room sala de emergencia (*f.*), 8
empire imperio (*m.*), 12
employment empleo (*m.*), 11
energy energía (*f.*), 11
engineer ingeniero/a (*m., f.*), 4
engineering ingeniería (*f.*), 1
English inglés/inglesa; (*language*)
  inglés (*m.*), 1
enjoy disfrutar, 3; gozar (de), 5;
  enjoy oneself divertirse (ie, i), 3;
  Enjoy your stay! ¡Qué disfrute/n
  de su estadía!, 5
enter entrar, 9
entertain entretener, 3
entertainment entretenimiento
  (*m.*), 9
enthusiastic entusiasmado/a, 2
envious envidioso/a, 1
equipment equipo (*m.*), 6
eraser: chalkboard eraser
  borrador (*m.*), 1
escape huir, 4
essential: it's essential es esencial, 8
ethnic étnico/a, 12
even though, even if a pesar de
  que, 9; **even when, even though,**
  even if aunque, 9
evening noche, (*f.*), P; **Good**
  evening./Good night. Buenas
  noches., P
event acontecimiento (*m.*), 6;
  hecho (*m.*), 10
every day todos los días, 4

everybody, everyone todo el
  mundo, 4
everything todo, 4
evident: it's (not) evident (no) es
  evidente, 8
exam prueba (*f.*), análisis (*m.*), 8;
  physical exam examen físico
  (*m.*), 8
example ejemplo (*m.*)
exceptional excepcional, 1
excited emocionado/a, 2
excursion excursión (*f.*), tour (*f.*), 5
Excuse me. Con permiso.,
  Perdón., P
exercise hacer ejercicio, 2
exhibition exhibición (*f.*), 10
existence existencia (*f.*), 11
expensive caro/a, 2
explain explicar, 4
exploit explotar, 11
exploration exploración (*f.*), 12
extinction extinción (*f.*), 11
eye ojo (*m.*), 8

F

face cara (*f.*), 3, 8
face up to enfrentar, 11
faculty profesorado (*m.*), 1
fail fracasar, 11
fall caer, 4; **fall asleep** dormirse
  (ue, u), 3; **fall in love (with)**
  enamorarse (de), 4
fall otoño (*m.*), 3
fame fama (*f.*), 6
family member pariente (*m., f.*), 4
fan aficionado/a (*m., f.*), fanático/a
  (*m., f.*), 6
far (from) lejos (de), 4
fare tarifa (*f.*), 5
farewell despedida (*f.*), 5
fascinate fascinar, 4
fascinated fascinado/a, 2
fascinating fascinante, 1
fast rápido/a, 1
fat gordo/a, 1
father padre (*m.*), 1, 4
father-in-law suegro (*m.*), 4
fax fax (*m.*), 9
fear temer, 8
February febrero (*m.*), 1
fed up harto/a, 2
feel sentirse (ie, i), 3; **feel like**
  (*doing something*) tener ganas
  de + (*inf.*), 3
festival festival (*m.*), 10
field cancha (*f.*), 6
fifteen quince, 1
fifty cincuenta, 1

figure figura (*f.*), 10; cifra (*f.*), 12
file archivar, guardar, 9
film filmar, 6; filme (*m.*), 6; **feature film** largometraje (*m.*), 6
finally por fin, 3
find encontrar (ue), 3; **find out** averiguar, 5
fine multa (*f.*), 9
finger dedo (*m.*), 8
finish terminar, acabar, 2
fire (from a job) despedir (i, i)
firefighter bombero/a (*m., f.*), 4
fireworks fuegos artificiales (*m. pl.*), 10
first primero (*m.*), 1; primero/a (*adj.*), 3; **first class** primera clase (*f.*), 5
fish pescar, 5; (*caught*) pescado (*m.*), 3
fit (someone) quedar(le) (a alguien), 7
five cinco, 1
fix up (the bed) arreglar (la cama), 2
flat tire llanta pinchada (*f.*), 9
floor piso (*m.*), 2
florist florería (*f.*), 7
flute flauta (*f.*), 6
folder carpeta (*f.*), 1
folkloric folclórico/a, folklórico/a, 10
follow perseguir (i, i), seguir (i, i), 3
food alimento (*m.*), 8; comida (*f.*), 3; alimentación
foot pie (*m.*), 8
football fútbol americano (*m.*), 6
for a, para, por, 4
foreign extranjero/a, 6
forest bosque (*m.*)
fork tenedor (*m.*), 3
form forma (*f.*), 10
forty cuarenta, 1
found fundar, 12
four cuatro, 1
fourteen catorce, 1
fracture fractura (*f.*), 8
fractured fracturado/a, 8
frame marco (*m.*), 10
free gratis, 7; (*independent*) libre, 5; **free time** tiempo libre (*m.*), 5
freedom libertad (*f.*), 11
French francés/francesa; (*language*) francés (*m.*), 1
Friday viernes (*m.*), 1
fried frito/a, 3
friend amigo/a (*m., f.*), P
friendly amable, simpático/a, 1
friendship amistad (*f.*)
from de, desde, 1, 4; **from time to time** de vez en cuando, 4; **from now on** desde ahora
fruit fruta (*f.*), 3

fry freír (i, i), 5
fuel combustible (*m.*), 11
function función (*f.*), 9
funny cómico/a, 1, 6; chistoso/a

G

game partido (*m.*), 6; juego (*m.*)
garage garaje (*m.*), 2
garbage basura (*f.*); **garbage can** basurero (*m.*), 1
garden jardín (*m.*), 2
gardener jardinero/a (*m., f.*), 4
gas tank tanque de gasolina (*m.*), 9
gasoline gasolina (*f.*), 9
genre género (*m.*), 6
German alemán/alemana; (*language*) alemán (*m.*), 1
get conseguir (i, i), 3; recoger, 5; **get a sunburn** quemarse, 5; **get a tan** broncearse, 5; **get better** aliviarse, 8; mejorar, 8; **get dressed** vestirse (i, i), 3; **get married (to)** casarse (con), 4; **get sick** enfermarse, 8; **get up** levantarse, 3
girl chica (*f.*), P, 4; niña (*f.*), 4
girlfriend novia (*f.*), 4
give dar, 3, 4; (*gifts*) regalar, 4
glass (*drinking*) vaso (*m.*), 3
global warming calentamiento global (*m.*), 11
glove guante (*m.*), 7; **baseball glove** guante (*m.*), 6
go ir, 3; **go (down)** (*a street*) bajar (por), 7; **go away** irse, 3; **go bicycling** montar en bicicleta, 5; **go fishing** ir de pesca, 5; **go horseback riding** montar a caballo, 5; **go on vacation** estar/irse de vacaciones, 5; **go out** salir, 3; **go shopping** ir de compras, 7; **go skindiving, snorkeling** bucear, 5; **go straight** seguir (i, i) derecho, recto, 7; **go surfing** hacer surfing, 5; **go to bed** acostarse (ue), 3; **go up** (*a street*) subir (por), 7; **Let's go!** ¡Vamos!, P
goblet copa (*f.*), 3
godfather padrino (*m.*)
godmother madrina (*f.*)
godson/goddaughter ahijado/a (*m., f.*)
gold oro (*m.*), 7
golden dorado/a, 10
golf golf (*m.*), 6
golf club palo de golf (*m.*), 6
good bueno/a, 1; **it's good** es bueno, 8

Good-bye Adiós., P; **Until we meet again** Hasta la vista., P
good-looking guapo/a, 1
granddaughter nieta (*f.*), 4
grandfather abuelo (*m.*), 4
grandmother abuela (*f.*), 4
grandson nieto (*m.*), 4
grave grave, 8
gray gris, 1
great grandfather bisabuelo (*m.*), 4
great grandmother bisabuela (*f.*), 4
green verde, 1
greenhouse effect efecto invernadero (*m.*), 11
group conjunto (*m.*), grupo (*m.*), 6
growth crecimiento (*m.*), 12
guess adivinar
guest huésped (*m., f.*), 5
guidebook guía (*f.*), 5
guilty culpable
guitar guitarra (*f.*), 6
guitarrist guitarrista (*m., f.*), 6
gym gimnasio (*m.*), 6
gymnastics gimnasia (*f.*), 6
gymwear ropa de gimnasia (*f.*), 6

H

hair pelo (*m.*), 3, 8; **hair dryer** secador/a de pelo (*m., f.*), 2; **hair stylist** peluquero/a (*m., f.*), 4
half medio/a (*adj.*), 7; (*hour*) y media (*f.*), 1
hand mano (*f.*), 3, 8
hand in entregar, 4
handsome guapo/a, 1
hang (up) colgar (ue), 9, 10
happen pasar, 2
happy alegre, contento/a 2; **be happy** alegrarse (de), estar contento/a de, 8;
hard drive disco duro (*m.*), 9
hard-working trabajador/a, 1
hardly apenas
harm dañar, 8
harmonious armonioso/a, 11
harmony armonía (*f.*)
harvest cosecha (*f.*)
hat sombrero (*m.*), 5, 7
have tener, 3; **have a chill** tener escalofríos, 8; **have a cold** estar resfriado/a, tener catarro/resfrío, 8; **have a cough** tener tos, 8; **have a fever** tener fiebre, 8; **have a good time** divertirse (ie, i), 3; **have a solution** tener remedio, 11; **have an appetite** tener apetito, 8; **have breakfast** desayunar, 3; **have dinner** cenar, 3; **have just**

(**done something**)   acabar de + (*inf.*), 2; **have lunch**   almorzar (ue), 3; **have pain**   tener dolor, 8; **have the flu**   tener gripe, 8; **have to** (*do something*)   tener que + (*inf.*), 3

he   él, 1
head   cabeza (*f.*), 8
headphones   audífonos (*m. pl.*), 6
healer   curandero/a (*m., f.*), 8
health insurance   seguro médico (*m.*), 11
healthy   sano/a, 8
hear   oír, 3
heart   corazón (*m.*), 8
heavy (*food*)   (una comida) fuerte, 3; pesado/a
height   apogeo (*m.*), 12
helmet   casco (*m.*), 6
help   ayuda (*f.*), 9
her   ella, 4
here   aquí, 3
Hey!   ¡Oye!, 5
hieroglyphic   jeroglífico/a, 12
high speed   alta velocidad (*f.*), 9
highway   carretera (*f.*), 9
him   él, 4
hip-hop   hip-hop (*m.*), 6
historical   histórico/a, 10
history   historia (*f.*), 1
hockey   hockey (*m.*), 6; **hockey stick**   palo de hockey (*m.*), 6
homeless people   desamparados (*m.*), 11
hope   esperar, 8; **I/We/Let's hope so.**   Ojalá., 8
horn   pito (*m.*), claxon (*m.*), 9
horror   de horror, de terror (*adj.*), 6
horse   caballo (*m.*), 11
hospital   hospital (*m.*), 2
hot (*spicy*)   picante, 3; (*temperature*)   caliente, 3; **it's hot** hace calor, 3; **be hot/feel hot**   tener calor, 3
hotel   hotel (*m.*), 2
house   casa (*f.*), 2
how?   ¿cómo?, P; **How are you?** ¿Cómo está usted?/¿Cómo estás tú?, P; **How can I help you?** ¿En qué le(s) puedo servir?, 5; **How do you say . . . ?** ¿Cómo se dice... ?, P; **How does one get to . . . ?** ¿Cómo se llega a... ?, 7; **How much does . . . cost?** ¿Cuánto cuesta... ?, 5; **How much will you charge me for it/them?** ¿En cuánto me lo(s)/la(s) deja?, 7; **How's it going?** ¿Qué tal?, P
hug   abrazar, 4
human being   ser humano (*m.*)

humanities   humanidades (*f. pl.*), 1
humid   húmedo/a, 3
hunger   hambre (el) (*f.*), 3; **I am very hungry!** ¡Tengo mucha hambre!, 3; **I'm starving/famished** Estoy muerto/a de hambre., 3
hurricane   huracán (*m.*), 3
hurt   doler (ue), 8
husband   esposo (*m.*), 4
hybrid   híbrido/a, 9

I

I   yo, 1
ice cream (chocolate, vanilla, strawberry)   helado (de chocolate, vainilla, fresa) (*m.*), 3
ice   hielo (*m.*); **ice rink**   pista de hielo (*f.*), 6; **ice skates**   patines para hielo (*m.*), 6
icon   icono (*m.*), 9
idea: I haven't got a clue   Ni idea., 5
ill, to feel   estar mal, P
illness   enfermedad (*f.*), 8
illustrate   ilustrar, 10
illustration   ilustración (*f.*), 10
illustrator   dibujante (*m., f.*), 10
image   imagen (*f.*), 10
important: it's important   es importante, 8
imposing   imponente, 12
impossible: it's impossible   es imposible, 8
imprison   encarcelar, 11
in, on, at   en, 1, 3, 4; **in addition to** además de, 12; **in case**   en caso de que, 10; **in front of**   delante de, 4; **in front of, facing**   enfrente de, 4; **in groups**   en grupos, P; **in love** enamorado/a, 2; **in order that**   a fin de que, 10; **in order to**   para, 4; **in pairs**   en parejas, P; **in the morning/afternoon/evening** por/de la mañana/tarde/noche, 1; **In whose name?** ¿A nombre de quién?, 5
include   incluir, 2
increase   aumentar, 11
indigenous   autóctono/a, indígena
inexpensive   barato/a, 2
infection   infección (*f.*), 8
inflammation   inflamación (*f.*), 8
inhabited   habitado/a, 12
injection   inyección (*f.*), 8
injure   dañar, 9
inside of   dentro de, 4
install   instalar, 9
intelligent   inteligente, 1
intention   propósito (*m.*), 10

interest, be of interest   interesar, 4
interpret   interpretar, 6
invest   invertir (ie, i)
iron (clothes)   planchar (la ropa), 2
island   isla (*f.*), 5
Italian   italiano/a; (*language*) italiano (*m.*), 1

J

jacket   saco (*m.*); chaqueta (*f.*), 7
jaguar   jaguar (*m.*), 7
jai alai   jai alai (*m.*), 6
January   enero (*m.*), 1
Japanese   japonés/japonesa; (*language*)   japonés (*m.*), 1
jazz   jazz (*m.*), 6
jealous   celoso/a, 2
jewelry   joya (*f.*), 7; **jewelry store** joyería (*f.*), 7
journalist   periodista (*m., f.*), 4
judge   juzgar, 6
juice   zumo (*m.*), jugo (*m.*), 3
July   julio (*m.*), 1
June   junio (*m.*), 1
justice   justicia (*f.*), 11

K

keep oneself (healthy)   conservarse (sano/a), 8
key   llave (*f.*), 1
keyboard   teclado (*m.*), 9
kick   patear, 6
kill   matar, 11
kilometers (per hour)   kilómetros (por hora) (*m.*), 3
kitchen   cocina (*f.*), 2
knee   rodilla (*f.*), 8
knife   cuchillo (*m.*), 3
know   saber, conocer (zc), 3; **I don't know**   No sé., P

L

lack   faltar, 4
lake   lago (*m.*)
lament   lamentar, 8
lamp   lámpara (*f.*), 1
language   idioma (*m.*), 1
land   tierra (*f.*); aterrizar
laptop   computadora portátil (*f.*), 9
large   grande, 1
later   luego, 3
laugh   reír (i, i), 5
laundromat   lavandería (*f.*), 7
law   derecho (*m.*)

lawyer abogado (*m., f.*), 4
lazy flojo/a, perezoso/a, 1
learn aprender, 2
leave salir, irse, 3; **leave (something behind)** dejar, 3
leg pierna (*f.*), 8
lend prestar, 4
lesson lección (*f.*), 1
library biblioteca (*f.*), 2
lie down acostarse (ue), 3
light ligero/a, 3; claro/a, 10; luz (*f.*), 9; **light and shadow** luz y sombra (*f.*), 10
lightbulb bombillo (*m.*), 11
like (be pleasing) gustar, 2, 8; **I would like (to order) . . .** Me gustaría/Quisiera (pedir)..., 3; **like (*a person*)** caer bien, 4; **like very much (love)** encantar, 4
Likewise Igualmente., P
limousine limosina (*f.*), 5
line: to stand in line hacer cola
linguistic lingüístico/a, 12
linguistics lingüística (*f.*), 1
listen escuchar, P, 2; **Listen!** ¡Oye!, 5
listing cartelera (*f.*), 6
literature literatura (*f.*), 1
little poco (*m.*); **a little** un poco, 2
live vivir, 2; **live with** convivir, 10
living room sala (*f.*), 2
loading embarque (*m.*), 5
lodging alojamiento (*m.*), 5
long largo/a, 1
look at mirar, 2; **look for** buscar, 2; **look for shells** buscar conchas, 5
loose (*fitting*) flojo/a, 7; grande, 7
lose perder (ie), 3, 6
lost perdido/a, 12
lot: a lot mucho (*adv.*), 2
lot: a lot of mucho/a (*adj.*), 2
love de amor (*adj.*), 6; **be in love** estar enamorado/a, 4; amar, querer (ie)
lovely lindo/a, 1
lower (*a price*) rebajar, 7
luggage equipaje (*m.*), 5
lunch almuerzo (*m.*), 3; **(*in some places*)** comida (*f.*), 3
lung pulmón (*m.*), 8
luxurious lujoso/a (de lujo), 5
luxury lujo (*m.*), 5
lyrics letra (*f.*), 6

M

maid criada (*f.*), 4
mailbox buzón (*m.*), 5
mail carrier cartero/a (*m., f.*), 4

maintain mantener, 3
major especialización (*f.*), 1
make arreglar (la cama), 2; hacer, 3; fabricar, 10; **make a (long distance/collect) phone call** hacer una llamada (de larga distancia/por cobrar), 5; **make an appointment** hacer una cita, 8; **make fun of** burlarse (de), 10; **make sandcastles** hacer castillos de arena, 5; **make sense** tener sentido, 3
makeup maquillaje (*m.*), 7
man hombre (*m.*), 1
manager gerente (*m., f.*), 4
map mapa (*m.*), 1
marble mármol (*m.*), 10
March marzo (*m.*), 1
mariachi musician mariachi (*m.*), 6
married: be married estar casado/a, 4
mask máscara (*f.*), 7
mathematics matemáticas (*f. pl.*), 1
matter importar, 4
May mayo (*m.*), 1
maybe quizás, tal vez, 8
me mí, 4
mean significar, 10
meat carne (*f.*), 3
medical sciences ciencias médicas (*f. s.*), 1
medicine medicina (*f.*), 8
meet (with) (*someone*) encontrarse (ue) (con), reunirse (con), 5
menu carta (*m.*), menú (*m.*), 3
message mensaje (*m.*), 9
meteorologist meteorólogo/a (*m., f.*), 3
midnight medianoche (*f.*), 1
miles (per hour) millas (por hora) (*f.*), 3
mine mío/a(s) (*m., f.*), 7
minivan camioneta (*f.*), 3
minus menos, 1
mirror espejo (*m.*), 2; **rear-view mirror** espejo retrovisor (*m.*), 9
Miss señorita (Srta.) (*f.*), P
mobile ambulante, 7
model modelo (*m., f.*), 10
modem módem (*m.*), 9
modern moderno/a, 2
mom mamá (*f.*), 4
Monday lunes (*m.*), 1
money exchange cambio de dinero/moneda (*m.*), 5
monkey mono (*m.*), 11
morning mañana (*f.*); **Good morning.** Buenos días., P
mother madre (*f.*), 1, 4
mother-in-law suegra (*f.*), 4

motor motor (*m.*), 9
motorcycle motocicleta (*f.*), 3
mouse ratón (*m.*), 9
mouth boca (*f.*), 8
move andar, 2; mover (ue), 9; mudarse (relocate)
movie película (*f.*), 6; **movie theater** cine (*m.*), 2, 6
MP3 player reproductor MP3 (*m.*), 6
Mr. señor (Sr.) (*m.*), P
Mrs. señora (Sra.) (*f.*), P
much, very much mucho (*adv.*), 2
multimedia multimedia (*f.*), 9
mural mural (*m.*), 10
murder asesinar, 11; asesinato (*m.*), 11
murderer asesino/a (*m., f.*), 11
muscle músculo (*m.*), 8
museum museo (*m.*), 2
music música (*f.*), 1; **Mexican-style music** ranchera (*f.*), 6
musician músico/a (*m., f.*), 4, 6
my mi(s), 2
mystery de misterio (*adj.*), 6

N

name nombre (*m.*)
named, to be llamarse, P; **My name is . . .** Me llamo..., P
nanny niñero/a (*m., f.*), 11
narration narración (*f.*), 6
natural sciences ciencias naturales (*f. s.*), 1
necessary: it's necessary es necesario/preciso, 8
necklace collar (*m.*), 7
need faltar, 4; necesitar, 2, 8
neighborhood barrio (*m.*), vecindario (m.)
neither tampoco, 4; **neither . . . nor** ni... ni, 4
nephew sobrino (*m.*), 4
nervous nervioso/a, 2
network red (*f.*), 9
never nunca, jamás, 4
nevertheless sin embargo, 12
new nuevo/a, 1
next luego, 3; **next to** al lado de, junto a, 4
nice simpático/a, 1
nickname apodo (*m.*)
niece sobrina (*f.*), 4
night noche (*f.*), 1; **Good evening/ Good night** Buenas noches., P; **night stand** mesita de noche (*f.*), 2
nine nueve, 1
ninety noventa, 1
no one, nobody nadie, 4

nominate nominar, 6
nomination nominación (*f.*), 6
none, not any ningún, ninguno/a, 4
noon mediodía (*m.*), 1
north norte (*m.*), 3
northeast/west noreste/oeste (*m.*), 3
nose nariz (*f.*), 8
notes apuntes (*m. pl.*)
notebook cuaderno (*m.*), 1
nothing nada, 4; **Nothing special.** Nada en particular., P
noun sustantivo (*m.*)
novel novela (*f.*), 5
November noviembre (*m.*), 1
now ahora, en este momento, 2
nuclear waste desperdicios nucleares (*m.*), 11
nurse enfermero/a (*m., f.*), 4
nutritious nutritivo/a, 8

O

obtain conseguir (i, i), 3; lograr, obtener, 11
obvious: it's obvious es obvio, 8
occur suceder, 6
October octubre (*m.*), 1
of de, 1, 4; **of the** del, 2; **Of course.** Sí, cómo no., P; por supuesto, 5; ¡Claro que sí!, 7
offer ofrecer (zc), 4
offering ofrenda (*f.*), 10
office oficina (*f.*), 1, 2; **office supply store** papelería (*f.*), 7
OK regular, P
old viejo/a, 1
older mayor, 1; **be older** ser mayor, 4
omelette with potatoes and onions tortilla española (*f.*) (*Spain*), 3
on, on top of en, 3; sobre, encima de, 4; **on board** a bordo, 5; **on foot** a pie, 3; **online** en línea, 9; **on sale** en oferta, 7; **on the right/left(hand side)** a la (mano) derecha/izquierda, 7
one uno, 1
one hundred cien, 1
one hundred ninety-nine ciento noventa y nueve, 1
one hundred one ciento uno, 1
only sólo
open abrir, 2
operation operación (*f.*), 8
optimistic optimista, 1
orange anaranjado/a (*adj.*), 1; naranja

order mandar, 8; pedido (*m.*), 3
organized organizado/a, 1
our nuestro/a(s), 2
ours nuestro/a(s) (*m., f.*), 7
outdoors al aire libre
outside of fuera de, 4
owe deber, 4
owner dueño/a (*m., f.*), 2
ozone layer capa de ozono (*f.*), 11

P

package (tour) paquete (*m.*), 5
paint pintar, 2, 10
paintbrush pincel (*m.*), 10
painter pintor/a (*m., f.*), 4, 10
painting pintura (*f.*), 1, 10; cuadro (*m.*), 10; **oil painting** pintura al óleo (*f.*), 10
pair par (*m.*), 7
palette paleta (*f.*), 10
panda bear oso panda (*m.*), 11
pants pantalones (*m.*), 7
paper papel (*m.*), 1; composición (*f.*)
parade desfile (*m.*), 10
paragraph párrafo (*m.*)
parasol sombrilla (*f.*), 5
Pardon Perdón., P
park estacionar, 7
parking lot estacionamiento (*m.*), 5
pass pasar, 2; **pass by** pasar por, 7
password contraseña (*f.*), 9
patient paciente (*m., f.*), 8
pay pagar, 4
pen bolígrafo (*m.*), pluma (*f.*), 1
pencil lápiz (*m.*), 1
pendant pendiente (*m.*), 7
penguin pingüino (*m.*), 11
people gente (*f. s.*), 2
pepper (*black*) pimienta (*f.*), 3
percent por ciento, 3
percentage porcentaje (*m.*), 3
percussion percusión (*f.*), 6
perfume store perfumería (*f.*), 7
perhaps quizás, tal vez, 8
pessimistic pesimista, 1
pet mascota (*f.*), 4
pharmacy farmacia (*f.*), 7
philosophy filosofía (*f.*), 1
photographer fotógrafo/a (*m., f.*), 4
physical físico/a, 8
physics física (*f.*), 1
physiology fisiología (*f.*), 1
pianist pianista (*m., f.*), 6
piano piano (*m.*), 6
pick up recoger, 5
pickup truck camioneta (*f.*), 3
picnic picnic (*m.*), 5
picture cuadro (*m.*), 10

piece pieza (*f.*), 10
pill píldora (*f.*), pastilla (*f.*), 8
pin prendedor (*m.*), 7
pink rosado/a, 1
place poner, 3
plane avión (*m.*), 3
planet planeta (*m.*), 11
plate plato (*m.*), 3, 7; placa (*f.*), 9
play (*a sport or game*) jugar (ue) (al), 3, 6; **(an instrument)** tocar (un instrumento), 2, 6; **play a role** hacer el papel, 6; **play sports** practicar deportes, 2; **play volleyball** jugar (al) volibol, 2, 5
player jugador/a (*m., f.*), 6
playwright dramaturgo/a (*m., f.*)
plaza plaza (*f.*), 2
plead rogar (ue), 8
pleasant agradable, 1
please por favor, P
Pleased to meet you Mucho gusto., P
pleasure placer (*m.*); **The pleasure is mine.** El gusto/placer es mío., P; **What a pleasure!** ¡Qué gusto!, 5
plot trama (*f.*), argumento (*m.*), 6
plumber plomero/a (*m., f.*), 4
point apuntar, 9
police policía (*m., f.*), 4, 11
political science ciencias políticas (*f. s.*), 1
pollute contaminar, 11
pollution contaminación (*f.*), 11
popular popular, 1
population población (*f.*), 12
porter botones (*m.*), 5
portion porción (*f.*), 8
portrait retrato (*m.*), 10
Portuguese portugués/portuguesa; (*language*) portugués (*m.*), 1
possible: it's possible es posible, 8
post office correo (*m.*), 2
postcard tarjeta postal (*f.*)
poster cartel (*m.*), 1
potato patata (*f.*), papa (*f.*), 3
potter ceramista (*m., f.*), 10
poverty pobreza (*f.*), 11
practice practicar, 2, 6
predict pronosticar, 12
prefer preferir (ie, i), 3, 8
preferable: it's preferable es preferible, 8
pregnancy embarazo (*m.*), 11
premiere estrenar, 6
prepare preparar
prepared preparado/a, 3
prescription receta (*f.*), 8
preserve conservar, 11
president presidente/a (*m., f.*), 4
pretty bonito/a, 1

price precio (*m.*), 7
priest cura, sacerdote *(m.)*
print imprimir, 9
printer impresora (*f.*), 1
prison cárcel (*m.*), prisión (*f.*), 11
private privado/a, 2
prize premio (*m.*), 12
probability probabilidad (*f.*), 3
probable: it's probable es probable, 8
problem lío (*m.*), 11
produce producir (zc), 3
professor profesor/a (*m., f.*), P, 4
program programa (*m.*), 9
protect oneself protegerse, 5
provided that con tal (de) que, 10
psychologist psicólogo/a (*m., f.*), 4
psychology psicología (*f.*), 1
public público/a, 10
purchasing power poder adquisitivo (*m.*), 12
purple morado/a, 1
purpose propósito (*m.*), 10
purse bolsa (*f.*), 7
pursue perseguir (i, i), 3
push a button presionar, hacer clic, pulsar, oprimir, 9
put poner, 3; **put on makeup** maquillarse, 3
pyramid pirámide (*f.*), 12

Q

quantity cantidad (*f.*), 8
quarter (*hour*) cuarto (*m.*), 1

R

rabbit conejo (*m.*), 4
radio radio (*m., f.*), 1, 5
rain lluvia (*f.*), 3; llover, 3
raincoat impermeable (*m.*), 7
rate tarifa (*f.*), 5
reach alcanzar, 3, 11
read leer, 2; **read books** leer libros, 2
ready listo/a, 2
Really? ¿Verdad?, P
receipt recibo (*m.*), 7
receive recibir, 2
reception recepción (*f.*), 5
receptionist recepcionista (*m., f.*), 4, 5
recommend recomendar (ie), 3, 8
record grabar; disco *(m.)*
recreation recreo (*m.*), 5
red rojo/a, 1

red-head pelirrojo/a, 1
reduce reducir (zc), 5, 8
refrigerator refrigerador/a (*m., f.*), 2
register registrar, 5; registro (*m.*)
regret lamentar, sentir (ie, i), 8
relative pariente (*m., f.*), 4
religious religioso/a, 10
remain permanecer (zc), 10
remedy remedio (*m.*), 8
remember recordar (ue), 3
remote control control remoto (*m.*), 9
rent alquilar, 2; **rent videos** alquilar videos, 2; **rent** alquiler (*m.*), renta (*f.*), 2
repeat repetir (i, i), P, 3
replica réplica (*f.*), 10
request pedir (i, i), 3, 8
research investigar, 2
reservation reservación (*f.*), 5
reserve reservar, 5
resolution propósito (*m.*), 10
resource recurso (*m.*), 11
responsibility responsabilidad (*f.*), 11
rest descansar, 5
restaurant restaurante (*m.*), 2
return volver (ue), 3; **(*something*)** devolver (ue), 7
reuse reusar, 11
review reseña (*f.*), 6; reseñar, 6
rhythm ritmo (*m.*), 6
rice, meat, and seafood dish (from Valencia) paella (valenciana) (*f.*), 3
rich rico/a, 3
ridiculous: it's ridiculous es ridículo, 8
ring anillo (*m.*), 7
ripped roto/a, 7
rite/ritual rito (*m.*), 10
river río (*m.*)
robbery robo (*m.*), 11
robot robot (*m.*), 9
rock rock (music)(*m.*), 6; roca (*f.*)
role papel (*m.*), 6
romantic romántico/a, 1, 6
room habitación (*f.*), 5
roommate compañero/a de cuarto (*m., f.*), P
rooster gallo (*m.*), 11
rose rosa (*f.*), 1
route ruta (*f.*), 3
rug alfombra (*f.*), 2; tapete (*m.*), 7
ruin ruina (*f.*) 12
rule regla (*f.*), P
run correr, 2
running track pista (*f.*), 6

S

sad triste, 2
sail, go sailing navegar en velero, 5
salad (mixed/potato) ensalada (mixta/rusa) (*f.*), 3
salesperson vendedor/a (*m., f.*), 4
salsa (music) salsa (*f.*), 6
salt sal (*f.*), 3
sandal sandalia (*f.*), 5
Saturday sábado (*m.*), 1
sausage chorizo (*m.*), 3
save ahorrar, 11
save archivar, guardar, 9; **(rescue)** salvar, 11
saxophone saxofón (*m.*), 6
say decir (i), 3; **say good-bye** despedirse (i, i), 5
scarce escaso/a, 11
scarf bufanda (*f.*), 7
scene escena (*f.*), 6
schedule horario (*m.*), 1
school escuela (*f.*), 1
School (*as in School of Humanities*) facultad (*f.*), 1
science fiction ciencia ficción, 6; de ciencia ficción (*adj.*), 6
scientific científico/a
screen pantalla (*f.*), 6; **flat screen** pantalla plana (*f.*), 9, **plasma screen** pantalla de plasma (*f.*), 9
script guión (*m.*), 6
sculptor escultor/a (*m., f.*), 4, 10
sculpture escultura (*f.*), 10
search búsqueda (*f.*); **search engine** buscador (*m.*), 9
seat asiento (*m.*), 9
seatbelt cinturón de seguridad (*m.*), 9
second segundo/a; **second class** segunda clase (*f.*), 5
secretary secretario/a (*m., f.*), 4
sedentary sedentario/a, 8
see ver, 3; **See you later.** Hasta luego., P; **See you tomorrow.** Hasta mañana., P
seem parecer (zc), 4
self-portrait aurorretrato (*m.*), 10
sell vender, 4
seller vendedor/a (*m., f.*), 7
send mandar, 2; enviar, 4
sense sentido (*m.*), **to make sense** tener sentido
September septiembre (*m.*), 1
sequence secuencia (*f.*), 6
serious serio/a, 1; grave, 8
servant criado/a (*m., f.*), 4
serve servir (i, i), 3
seven siete, 1

seventy setenta, 1

shadow: light and shadow luz y sombra (f.), 10

shame: it's a shame es una lástima, 8

share compartir, 2

shave (i, i) afeitarse, 3

she ella, 1

shellfish marisco (m.), 3

shift mover (ue), 9

shine, sparkle brillar

shirt camisa (f.), 7

shiver tener escalofríos, 8

shoe zapato (m.), 7; **shoe store** zapatería (f.), 7

shopping center centro comercial (m.), 2

short (height) bajo/a, 1; **(length)** corto/a, 1

should deber, 4

show mostrar (ue), 3; **show a movie** presentar (pasar) una película, 6

shower ducha (f.), 2

shrimp gamba (f.), 3

shut off apagar, 9

shy tímido/a, 1

sick enfermo/a, 2

sickness: altitude sickness soroche (m.), 8

side by side al lado de, 4

silk seda (f.), 7

silver plata (f.), 7

since desde, 4

sing cantar, 2, 6

singer cantante (m., f.), 6

single (room or bed) sencillo/a, 5; **be single** ser soltero/a, 4

sink: bathroom sink lavabo (m.), lavamanos (m.), 2

sister hermana (f.), 4

sister-in-law cuñada (f.), 4

sit down sentarse (ie), 3

six seis, 1

sixty sesenta, 1

size (clothing) talla (f.), 7; tamaño (m.)

skate patín (m.); **inline skates** patines en línea, 6

skating patinaje (m.), 6

sketch bosquejo (m.), 10

ski esquí (m.), 6; esquiar, 6

skiing esquí (m.), 6

skilled, skillful hábil, 10, 12

skirt falda (f.), 7

skull calavera (f.), 10

sky cielo (m.), 3

sleep dormir (ue, u), 3

sleepy: be sleepy/tired tener sueño, 3

slow lento/a, 1

slowly despacio, 7; **more slowly** más despacio, P

small pequeño/a, 1; **small serving of food** tapa (f.) (Spain), 3

smart listo/a, 1

smile sonreír (i, i), 5

snake culebra, serpiente, víbora (f.)

sneaker zapato tenis (m.), 6

sneeze estornudar, 8

snow nieve (f.), 3; nevar, 3

so that para que, 10

soap jabón (m.); **soap opera** telenovela (f.)

soccer fútbol (m.), 6

social program programa social (m.), 11

social sciences ciencias sociales (f. pl.), 1

social work trabajo social (m.), 1

social worker trabajador/a social (m., f.), 11

sociology sociología (f.), 1

sock calcetín (m.), media (f.), 7

sofa sofá (m.), 2

soldier soldado/a (m., f.)

solution solución (f.), 11

solve solucionar

some algún, alguno/a/os/as, 4

somebody, someone alguien, 4

something algo, 4

sometimes algunas veces, 4

somewhere else (otro) lado (m.), 7

son hijo (m.), 4

song canción (f.), 6

son-in-law yerno (m.), 4

sorry: I'm sorry Lo siento., P, 5

soul alma (el) (f.)

sound sonido (m.)

soup sopa (f.), 3; **cold vegetable soup** gazpacho (m.), 3

south sur (m.), 3

South American sudamericano/a

southeast/west sureste/oeste (m.), 3

spacious amplio/a, 2

Spanish español/a; **(language)** español (m.), 1; **Spanish-style music** flamenco (m.), 6

Spanish-speaking de habla española, 12

speech discurso (m.)

speak hablar, 2, 4

speaker parlante (music) (m., f.), 6

species especie (f.), 11

spectator espectador/a (m., f.), 6

spend (money) gastar (dinero), 7

sport deporte (m.), 6

sports car coche deportivo (m.), 9

sports enthusiast deportista (m., f.), 6

sprain (one's ankle) torcer(se) (el tobillo), 8

spring primavera (f.), 3

stadium estadio (m.), 2

stain mancha (f.), 7

stained manchado/a, 7

stairs escaleras (f. pl.), 2

stand out destacar(se), 12

start comenzar (ie), 3; **(a car, a race)** arrancar, 9

stationery store papelería (f.), 7

statue estatua (f.), 10

stay quedarse, 3; **(in a hotel)** alojar(se), 5

steak bistec (m.), 3

steering wheel volante (m.), 9

stemmed glass copa (f.), 3

stepbrother hermanastro (m.), 4

stepdaughter hijastra (f.), 4

stepfather padrastro (m.), 4

stepmother madrastra (f.), 4

stepsister hermanastra (f.), 4

stepson hijastro (m.), 4

still life naturaleza muerta (f.), 10

stocking media (f.), 7

stomach estómago (m.), 8

stone piedra (f.), 7

stop parar, 7, 9

stoplight semáforo (m.), 7

store almacenar, 9; tienda (f.), 2; **store window** escaparate (m.), 7

storm tormenta (f.), tronada (f.), 3

stove estufa (f.), 2

strange: it's strange es extraño, 8

street calle (f.), 2; **street block** cuadra (f.), manzana (f.), 7

strong fuerte, 3

student alumno/a (m., f.), estudiante (m., f.), P

study estudiar, 1, 2

subject sujeto (m.), 1; **subject matter** materia (f.), 1

subway metro (m.), 3

succeed triunfar, 11

sugar azúcar (m.)

suggest sugerir (ie, i), 5, 8

suit traje (m.), 7

suitcase maleta (f.), 5

summer verano (m.), 3

sun sol (m.)

sunbathe tomar el sol, 5

Sunday domingo (m.), 1

sunglasses gafas de sol (f. pl.), 5

sunscreen protector/bronceador solar (m.), 5

support apoyar, 11; apoyo (m.)

sure seguro/a, 2; **it's (not) sure** (no) es seguro, 8

surf the Internet (Web) navegar por Internet (la Red/la web), 2

surprise sorprender, 8

sweatsuit, sweatshirt sudadera (f.), 7

sweater suéter (*m.*), 7
sweep (the floor) barrer (el piso), 2
sweet dulce, 3
swim nadar, 5; **swim cap** gorro de baño (*m.*), 6; **swim goggles** anteojos (*m. pl.*), 6
swimming natación (*f.*), 6; **swimming pool** piscina (*f.*), alberca (*f.*), 2
swimwear vestido de baño (*m.*), 6
symbolize simbolizar
symptom síntoma (*m.*), 8
synopsis sinopsis (*f.*), 6
syrup jarabe (*m.*), 8
system sistema (*m.*), 1

T

table mesa (*f.*), 1; **coffee table** mesita (*f.*), 2
tablespoon cuchara (*f.*), 3
tactile, pertaining to touch táctil, 9
tail cola (*f.*)
take tomar, 2; llevar, 7; **take a bath** bañarse, 3; **take a shower** ducharse, 3; **take a walk** dar un paseo, 2; **take care of oneself** cuidarse, 8; **take off (one's clothes)** quitarse (la ropa), 3; **take out (the garbage)** sacar (la basura), 2
talk hablar; **talk with friends** hablar con amigos, 2
tall alto/a, 1
tango tango (*m.*), 6
tape grabar, 6
tapestry tapiz (*m.*), 7
tariff tarifa (*f.*), 5
taste probar (ue), 3; **taste like** saber a
tasty sabroso/a, 3
taxi taxi (*m.*), 3
tea té (*m.*), 3
teach enseñar, 4
team equipo (*m.*), 6
teaspoon cucharadita (*f.*), 3
telephone teléfono (*m.*), 1
television televisión (*f.*), 1
tell decir (i), 3; contar (ue)
temperature (minimum/maximum) temperatura (mínima/máxima) (*f.*), 3
temple templo (*m.*), 12
ten diez, 1
tenant inquilino/a (*m., f.*), 2
tennis tenis (*m.*), 6; **tennis racket** raqueta (de tenis) (*f.*), 6; **tennis shoes** zapatos de tenis (*m.*), 6

terrace terraza (*f.*), 2
terrible: it's terrible es terrible, 8
terrorism terrorismo (*m.*), 11
terrorist terrorista (*m., f.*), 11
test prueba (*f.*), análisis (*m.*), 8
thank agradecer (zc), 4
that (one) ese, esa, eso (éso/a), 3; (*over there*) aquel, aquella (aquél, aquélla), 3
the el, la, los, las 1
theater teatro (*m.*), 1
them ellos/as, 4
theme tema (*m.*), 1
then entonces, luego, 3
therapy terapia (*f.*), 11
there allí, ahí, 3
there, over there allá, 3
there is (not), there are (not) (no) hay, 1
these (ones) estos, estas (éstos/as), 3
they ellos, ellas, 1
thin delgado/a, 1
think creer, pensar (ie), 3, 8; **(have an opinion)** opinar, 8
thirteen trece, 1
thirty treinta, 1
thirsty: be thirsty tener sed, 3
this (one) este, esta, esto (éste, ésta), 3
those (ones) esos, esas (ésos/as), 3; (*over there*) aquellos/as (aquéllos/as), 3
threaten amenazar, 11
three tres, 1
thriller de suspenso (*adj.*), 6
throat garganta (*f.*), 8
Thursday jueves (*m.*), 1
ticket billete (*m.*), entrada (*f.*), 6
tidy (the room) limpiar/ordenar (el cuarto), 2
tie corbata (*f.*), 7
tiger tigre (*m.*), 11
tight estrecho/a, 7; (*clothes*) pequeño/a, 7
tile azulejo (*m.*)
time vez (*f.*); **many times** muchas veces, 4; **at the present time** de la actualidad; **to have a good time** divertirse (ie, i), 3
timid tímido/a, 1
tip propina (*f.*), 3
tire llanta (*f.*), 9
tired cansado/a, 2
title of respect with first name don (D.) (*m.*), doña (Dña.) (*f.*), P
to a, para, 4
today hoy, 1
toe dedo del pie (*m.*), 8
toilet inodoro (*m.*), 2

tomorrow mañana, 1
tongue lengua (*f.*), 8
too también, 4
tooth diente (*m.*), 3, 8
tornado tornado (*m.*), 3
tour excursión (*f.*), tour (*f.*), 5; **tour guide** guía (*m., f.*), 5
tourist turista (*m., f.*), 3
toward hacia, 4
towel toalla (*f.*), 5
toy juguete (*m.*), 7
tradition tradición (*f.*)
train entrenar, 6; tren (*m.*), 3; **train station** estación de tren (*f.*), 2
trainer entrenador/a (*m., f.*), 6
transfer traslado (*m.*), 5
translate traducir (zc), 3
transportation transporte (*m.*), 5
travel viajar, 2, 3; **travel agent** agente de viajes (*m., f.*), 4
traveler viajero/a (*m., f.*)
traveler's check cheque de viajero (*m.*), 5
treat, deal with tratar de, 6
tree árbol (*m.*)
tremble temblar (ie)
trip viaje (*m.*), 3; **Have a nice trip!** ¡Buen viaje!/¡Feliz viaje!, 5
truck camioneta (*f.*), 3; camión (*m.*), 3
true cierto/a; **it's true** es cierto, 8; es verdad, 8; verdadero/a
trumpet trompeta (*f.*), 6
trunk baúl (*m.*), maletero (*m.*), 9
try probar (ue), 3; **try on** probarse, 7
T-shirt camiseta (*f.*), 7
Tuesday martes (*m.*), 1
turn doblar (a), 7; **turn around** dar la vuelta, 7; **turn off** apagar, 9; **turn on** prender, encender (ie), 9
turquoise turquesa (*f.*), 7
turtle tortuga (*f.*), 4
twelve doce, 1
twenty veinte, 1
twist (one's ankle) torcer(se) (el tobillo), 8
two dos, 1

U

ugly feo/a, 1
umbrella paraguas (*m.*), 7
uncertainty incertidumbre (*f.*), 11
uncle tío (*m.*), 4
under bajo, debajo de, 4
understand comprender, 2; entender (ie), 3

underwear ropa interior (*f.*), 7
unemployment desempleo (*m.*), 11
unfriendly antipático/a, 1
uniform uniforme (*m.*), 6
unit unidad (*f.*), P
university universidad (*f.*), 1
unknown desconocido/a
unless a menos que, 10
unloading desembarque (*m.*), 5
unpleasant desagradable, 1
until hasta, 4, 7; hasta que, 9
upset alterado/a, 2
urgent: it's urgent es urgente, 8
us nosotros/as, 4
use usar, 2

V

vacation vacación (*f.*), 5; **be on vacation** estar/irse de vacaciones, 5
vaccine vacuna (*f.*), 8
vacuum cleaner aspiradora (*f.*), 2; **vacuum the rug** aspirar, pasar la aspiradora (por la alfombra), 2
variety variedad (*f.*)
vase vasija (*f.*), 10
vegetable legumbre (*f.*), 3
veterinarian veterinario/a (*m., f.*), 4
videocamera videocámara (*f.*), 9
video game videojuego (*m.*), 9
video recorder videograbadora (*f.*), 9
view vista (*f.*), 5
violin violín (*m.*), 6
virtual reality realidad virtual (*f.*), 9
visit visitar, 2
voice voz (*f.*), 6
volcano volcán (*m.*)
volunteer voluntario/a (*m., f.*), 11
vomit vomitar, 8

W

wait on atender (ie), 5
waiter camarero (*m.*), mesero (*m.*), 3
waitress camarera (*f.*), mesera (*f.*), 3
wake up despertarse (ie), 3
walk caminar, andar, 2; **go for a walk** pasearse/dar un paseo, 5
walking caminata (*f.*), 6
wall pared (*f.*), 1
want querer (ie), 3, 8; desear, 8; **want to (*do something*)** tener ganas de + (*inf.*), 3
war guerra (*f.*), 11

wardrobe ropero (*m.*), armario (*m.*), 2
warehouse almacén (*m.*), 2
warn avisar, 5; advertir (ie, i)
wash lavar, 2; **wash the dishes** lavar los platos, 2
watch reloj (*m.*), 1; **watch a movie** mirar una película, 2; **watch television** ver televisión, 2
water agua (el) (*f.*); **mineral water** agua mineral, 3; **water ski** hacer esquí acuático, 5
watercolor acuarela (*f.*), 10
we nosotros, nosotras, 1
weapon arma (*f.*), 11
wear llevar, 7
weather tiempo (*m.*); **it's good/bad weather** hace buen/mal tiempo, 3; **weather forecast** pronóstico del tiempo (*m.*), 3
weaver tejedor/a (*m., f.*), 12
weaving tejido (*m.*), 7
wedding boda (*f.*)
Wednesday miércoles (*m.*), 1
weight peso (*m.*), 8
Welcome! ¡Bienvenido!, P; **You're welcome.** De nada., P
well bien; **Pretty well, thanks.** Bastante bien, gracias., P; **Very well, thank you** Muy bien, gracias., P
well-being bienestar (*m.*), 8
west oeste (*m.*), 3
western de vaqueros (*adj.*), 6
whale ballena (*f.*), 11
what? ¿qué?, ¿cuál?, P; **What do you recommend?** ¿Qué nos recomienda?, 3; **What does . . . mean?** ¿Qué quiere decir... ?, P; **What is the temperature?** ¿A cuánto está la temperatura?, 3; **What time is it?** ¿Qué hora es?, 1; **What would you like to eat/drink?** ¿Qué desean comer/beber?, 3; **What's new?** ¿Qué hay de nuevo?, P; **What's your name?** ¿Cómo se llama usted?/¿Cómo te llamas?, P
wheel rueda (*f.*), 9
when cuando, 9
when? ¿cuándo?
where? ¿dónde?, P; **Can you tell me where . . . is/are?** ¿Me puede decir dónde está/n... ?, 7; **Where can I exchange money?** ¿Dónde puedo cambiar el dinero?, 5; **where (to)?** ¿adónde?
which ¿cuál?, P
white blanco/a, 1
width ancho (*m.*)

wife esposa (*f.*), 4
win ganar, 6
window ventana (*f.*), 1
windshield parabrisas (*m.*), 9; **windshield wiper** limpiaparabrisas (*m.*), 9
windy: it's windy hace viento, 3
wine (red/white) vino (tinto/blanco) (*m.*), 3
wine, fruit, and soda drink sangría (*f.*), 3
winter invierno (*m.*), 3
wireless inalámbrico/a, 9; **wireless connection (WiFi)** conexión (sin cables) (*f.*), 9
wish for desear, 2
with con, 2, 4; **with an ocean view** con vista al mar, 5; **with breakfast** con desayuno, 5; **with two meals** con media pensión, 5
without sin, 4; sin que, 10
woman mujer (*f.*), 1
wood madera (*f.*), 7, 10
wool lana (*f.*), 7
work trabajar, 2
work of art obra de arte (*f.*), 10
worker trabajador/a (*m., f.*), 4
worried preocupado/a, 2
worry angustia (*f.*), 11; preocuparse, 3, 4, 8
worse: it's worse es peor, 8
write escribir, 2; **write letters** escribir cartas, 2
writing escritura (*f.*), 12

X

X-ray radiografía (*f.*), 8

Y

yard jardín (*m.*), 2
yellow amarillo/a, 1
yesterday ayer
yet todavía, 9
you tú, usted(es), vosotros/as, P, 1
young joven, 1
younger: be younger ser menor, 4
your su(s), tu(s), vuestro/a(s) (*Spain*), 2
yours suyo(s), tuyo/a(s), vuestro/a(s) (*Spain*), 7

Z

zero cero, 1

Index

Text Credits

Artes y Letras : Page 87: Reprinted with permission of the publisher, Children's Book Press, San Francisco, CA, www.childrensbookpress.org Poem from Laughing Tomatoes/Jitomates Risuenos. Poem copyright © 1997 by Francisco Alarcon; page 87: Reprinted with permission of the publisher, Children's Book Press, San Francisco, CA, www.childrensbookpress.org Poem from Laughing Tomatoes/Jitomates Risuenos. Poem copyright © 1997 by Francisco Alarcon; page 87: From Noche Estrellada by Marjorie Agosin. Reprinted by permission of the author.

Artes y Letras : Page 167: Resguardo Personal, by Paloma Pedrero. Reprinted by permission of the author.

Unit 5: Page 201: Copyright © 2001 by Houghton Mifflin Company. Adapted and reproduced by permission from The American Heritage Spanish Dictionary, Second Edition.

Artes y Letras: Page 239: From "Tengo," by Nicolas Guillen, as appeared in Los Dispositivos en la flor, Cuba: Literatura desde la Revolucion, ed. Edmundo Desnoes with Willi Luis, © 1981. Reprinted by permission of Ediciones del Norte; page 239: From La Urdimbre del Silencio, by Norberto James. (c) Norberto James Rawlings, 2005. Reprinted by permission of the author.

Unit 8: Page 297: Reprinted by permission of Editorial América, S.A. from "Contra La Artritis, Piquetes de Abejas," as appeared in GeoMundo, Año 16, Núm. 9, pg. 228; page 297: From Newsweek En Español, July 26, 2000. Copyright © 2000 Newsweek, Inc. All rights reserved. Reprinted by permission; page 298: From Vanidades, Ano 40, no. 5. Copyright © by Editorial Televisa.

Artes y Letras : Page 307: Dos Palabras from *Cuentos de Eva Luna* by Isabel Allende. © Isabel Allende. Reprinted by permission of Agencia Literaria Carmen Balcells, S. A.

Unit 9: Page 310: Reprinted with permission from Quo: El Saber Actual, No. 58, julio 2000, pp. 186-187.

Artes y Letras : Page 373: Como Tu, by Roque Dalton, from Clandestine Poems (Curbstone Press, 1990), reprinted with permission of Curbstone Press. Distributed by Perseus; page 375: By Ernesto Cardenal, fas appeared in Antologia de la poesia amorosa espanola e hispanoamericana, Ed. Victor de Lama. Copyright © 1993.

Unit 11: Page 388: Grupo Interconect © 1998; page 399: From El colombiano, July 7, 1997. Adapted by permission of the author.

Unit 12: Page 408: Reprinted with permission from Mundo Maya Magazine.

Photo Credits

Page. 1: Sylvia Laks; p. 17: Miguel Suárez Pierra; p. 43: Jose Fuste Raga/Corbis; p. 46: (t) Dex Images/Corbis, (m) Alamy/Royalty Free, (b) Alamy/Royalty Free; p. 53: Joan Miró, (*Prades, the Village (prades, el poble)*, Summer 1917, (oil on canvas, 65x72.6 cm), Solomon R. Guggenheim Museum, New York; p. 65: University of the Americas; p. 77: Archivo Iconagrafico/Corbis; p. 78: PCL/Alamy; p. 79: (r) Robert Fried, (l) Nick Wheeler/Corbis; p. 84: Deborah Feingold/Corbis (Ramos), Peter Foley/epa/Corbis (Lopez), Mario Anzuoni/Reuters/Corbis (Ferrera), Rune Helestad/Corbis (Rodríguez), Reuters/Corbis (Moreno), Rufus F Folkks/Corbis (Saldaña), Reuters/Corbis (Richardson), Gary Hershorn/Reuters/Corbis (Santoalalla), Nancy Kaszerman/Zuma/Corbis (Rodríguez), Justin Lane/epa/Corbis (Saralegui); p. 85: Carmen Lomas Garza; p. 86: (t) Gary I. Rothstein/epa/Corbis, (b) Francisco Alárcon; p. 87: Marjorie Agosin; p. 89: Archivo Inconografico, S. A./Corbis, (c) Salvador Dali, Gala-Salvador Dali Foundation/Artis Rights Society (ARS), New York; p. 107: Owen Franken/Corbis; p. 121: Nick Dolding/Taxi/Getty Images; p. 122: (t) Alamy/Royalty Free, (b) Craig Lovell/Corbis, p. 123: (m) Peter Wilson/Corbis, (r) K. H. Benser/Zefa/Corbis, (l) Getty Images; p. 129: Giraudon/Art Resource, NY; p. 143: Royalty Free/Corbis; p. 157: Masimo Listri/Corbis; p. 159: (tl) David G. Houser/Corbis, (bl) Travelstock 44/Alamy, (tr) Temp-Sport/Corbis, (br) PictureNet/Corbis; p. 164: Rafael Roa/Corbis (Tomatito), Mike Blake/Corbis (Bebe), Reuters/Corbis (J. Iglesias), Claudio Ornatle/epa/Corbis (E. Iglesias), Peter Foley/epa/Corbis (Sanz), Guadenti Sergio/Sygma/Corbis (Chao); p. 165: José Manuel Merello; p. 166: (t) Stephanie Cardinale/People Avenue/Corbis. (b) public domain, p. 167: Paloma Pedrero; p. 169 Luis Germán Cajiga; p. 170: Bob Krist/Corbis; P. 181: author; p. 183: Nell Rabinowitz/Corbis; p. 197: M. L. Sinibaldi/Corbis; p. 199: (tl) Ulrike Welsch, (tr) Larry Luxner, (b) Robert Frerck/Odyssey; p. 205: "Guajiro Verde" Oils Dania Sierra (c) 2007; p. 206: (t) Hulton-Deutsch Collection/Corbis, (m) AP/Wide World Photos, (b) Mike Segar/Reuters/Corbis; p. 207: (t) Jack Vartoogian, (b) James Sparshatt/Corbis; p. 208: Mark Serota/Reuters/Corbis; p. 221: Wolfgang Kaehler/Alamy; p. 222: (t) Warren Toda/epa/Corbis, (b) AP/Wide World Photos; p. 229: David G. Houser/Corbis; p. 230: Steven Georges/Corbis; p. 231: (tl) AP/Wide World Photos, (tr) Tony Freeman/Photo Edit, (br) Mark Serota/Reuters/Corbis; p. 236: Martine Franck/Magnum Photos (Lam), Stephanie Maze/Corbis (Alicea), Victor Fralle/Reuters/ Corbis (Anthony), Juan Herra/epa/Corbis (Valdez), Reuters/Corbis (Guerra), Getty AFP (Crespo), Chris Pizzello/Reuters/Corbis (Bermudez), Diego Gomez/epa/Corbis (Downs), Fred Prouser/Reuters/Corbis (Lopez), authors (Santiago); p. 237: Aimée García, p. 238: (t) Mike Blake Reuters/Corbis, (b) author; p. 241: Arte Maya/ Rafael González y González; p. 246: (tl) AP/Wide World Photos, (tr) Jose Luis Pelaez/Corbis, (bl) Mark Gamba/Corbis, (br) Simon Plant/Zefa/Corbis; p. 253: Pablo Corral/ Corbis; p. 254: Robert Fried; P. 265: Danny Lehman/Corbis; p. 267: Hermine Dreyfuss; p. 273: Susan Mraz; p. 285: AP/Wide World Photos; p. 295: Danny Lehman/Corbis; p.304: Luis Lemus/Corbis (Neruda), AP/Wide World Photos (Sosa), AP/Wide World Photos (Neruda), Nancy Coste/Corbis (Bachelet), Mario Anzuoni/Reuters/Corbis (Herrera),

Victor Jara (Jara), Inca Son (Son); p.305: Martin Alipaz/ EFE/Corbis (Morales), Richard Smith/Sygma/Corbis (Llosa), Peter Foley/epa/Corbis (Shakira) (br) Raul Benegas/Corbis (bl) (c) Fernando Botero, courtesy, Marlborough Gallery, New York; p. 306: Toru Hanal/Reuters/Corbis; p. 307: Ed Kash/Corbis; p. 309: Gilbert "Magu" Lujan; p. 310: Royalty Free/Alamy; p. 312: a. Sony Corporation, b. Courtesy of Apple, c. Voltiac, d. Digiwal, e. Palm; p. 321: Barry Lewis/Corbis; p. 331: Atlantide Phototravel/Corbis; p. 333: (t) John Hillary/ Reuters/Corbis, (m) Car Culture/Corbis, (b) Bosch; p. 334: BMW Motors; p.336: (t) LG Migo, (m) Susan Mraz, (b) Tek Partner; p. 341: Arte Maya/Rafael González y González; p.342: Robert Frerck/Odyssey/Chicago; p. 343: (t) The Granger Collection, (b) Robert Frerck/Odyssey/Chicago; p.353: Steve Terrill/Corbis; p.356: Christies Images, N.Y.; p. 357(t) Schalksijk/Art Resource, N.Y., (b) Museum of Modern Art, New York; p. 358; (tr) Suzanne Murphy-Larronde/DDB Stock, (mr) Suzanne Murphy-Larronde/DDB Stock; (br) Robert Frerck/ Odyssey/Chicago, (bl) Robert Frerck/Odyssey/Chicago; p. 359: (l) photo Charlotte Miller, (r) From the Marjorie Agosin Collection/photo Charlotte Miller; p. 363: Danny Lehmann/Corbis;p. 364: Betty Press/Oanos Pictures; p. 370: Marcos Delgado/Corbis (Arais), Lelf Skoogbors/ Corbis (Romero), Katia Cardenal, Guillermo Anderson, Claribel Alegria, M oises Gadea, Corbis/Sygma (Diaz), Rueters/Corbis (Arjona), Bettman/Corbis (Asturias); p. 371: Arte Maya/Pedro González Chavajay; p. 372: Neal Preston/Corbis; p. 374: Reuters/Corbis; p.375 Bernard Bisson/Corbis-Sygma; p. 377: Morton Beebe/Corbis; p.378: Robert Fried/Alamy; p. 387: Texas Institute of Cultures; . 389: Kaaren Parma Fine Art; p. 397: Sandy Felsenthal/Corbis; p. 405: Benigno Gomez; p. 407: Robert Fried/DDB Stock; p. 408: (l) David G. Hauser/Corbis, (r) D. Donne Bryant/DDB Stock; p. 413: Tibor Bognar/Corbis; p. 415: (l) Jesus Dominguez/epa/Corbis, (r) Dr. Juliet Villareal García; p. 416: Consuelo Castillo Kickbusch, Bettmann/Corbis (Marichal, Scott Gries/Getty Images (Feliciano); p. 423: Beryl Goldberg; p. 428: Bettmann/Corbis (Tamayo), Bettmann/Corbis (Paz), Getty Images (Felix), Rufus Folkks/Corbis (Verástegui), Getty Images(Camil), Cesare Zuko/Corbis (Bernal), Reuters/Corbis (Hayek), David Mercado/Reuters/Corbis (Castillo), Katy Winn/Corbi (Santana); p. 429: Bettmann/ Corbis (Rivera), Getty Images/Time Life Pictures (Siquieros), Getty Images (Pacheco), Reuters/Corbis (Poniatowske), AP/Wide World (Fuentes), James Leynse/Corbis (Esquivel); Peter Andrews/Corbis (Iñárritu) p. 430: (r)Bettmann/Corbis; (l) Frida (Frieda) Kahlo/Frieda and Diego Rivera, 1931, oil on canvas, 39 3/8 inc. x 31 in., Albert M. Bender Collection, Gift of Albert M. Bender. Banco de México; p. 431: Henry Romero/Reuters/Corbis